D0915922

USING THE
FINANCIAL AND
BUSINESS LITERATURE

BOOKS IN LIBRARY AND INFORMATION SCIENCE

A Series of Monographs and Textbooks

FOUNDING EDITOR

Allen Kent

School of Library and Information Science
University of Pittsburgh
Pittsburgh, Pennsylvania

1. Classified Library of Congress Subject Headings: Volume 1, Classified List, *edited by James G. Williams, Martha L. Manheimer, and Jay E. Daily*
2. Classified Library of Congress Subject Headings: Volume 2, Alphabetic List, *edited by James G. Williams, Martha L. Manheimer, and Jay E. Daily*
3. Organizing Nonprint Materials, *Jay E. Daily*
4. Computer-Based Chemical Information, *edited by Edward McC. Arnett and Allen Kent*
5. Style Manual: A Guide for the Preparation of Reports and Dissertations, *Martha L. Manheimer*
6. The Anatomy of Censorship, *Jay E. Daily*
7. Information Science: Search for Identity, *edited by Anthony Debons*
8. Resource Sharing in Libraries: Why · How · When · Next Action Steps, *edited by Allen Kent*
9. Reading the Russian Language: A Guide for Librarians and Other Professionals, *Rosalind Kent*
10. Statewide Computing Systems: Coordinating Academic Computer Planning, *edited by Charles Mosmann*
11. Using the Chemical Literature: A Practical Guide, *Henry M. Woodburn*
12. Cataloging and Classification: A Workbook, *Martha L. Manheimer*
13. Multi-media Indexes, Lists, and Review Sources: A Bibliographic Guide, *Thomas L. Hart, Mary Alice Hunt, and Blanche Woolls*
14. Document Retrieval Systems: Factors Affecting Search Time, *K. Leon Montgomery*
15. Library Automation Systems, *Stephen R. Salmon*
16. Black Literature Resources: Analysis and Organization, *Doris H. Clack*
17. Copyright–Information Technology–Public Policy: Part I–Copyright–Public Policies; Part II–Public Policies–Information Technology, *Nicholas Henry*
18. Crisis in Copyright, *William Z. Nasri*

ADDITIONAL VOLUMES IN PREPARATION

USING THE FINANCIAL AND BUSINESS LITERATURE

THOMAS P. SLAVENS
University of Michigan
Ann Arbor, Michigan, U.S.A.

MARCEL DEKKER, INC.   NEW YORK • BASEL

Library of Congress Cataloging-in-Publication Data
A catalog record for this book is available from the Library of Congress.

ISBN: 0-8247-5318-6

This book is printed on acid-free paper.

Headquarters
Marcel Dekker, Inc., 270 Madison Avenue, New York, NY 10016, U.S.A.
tel: 212-696-9000; fax: 212-685-4540

Distribution and Customer Service
Marcel Dekker, Inc., Cimarron Road, Monticello, New York 12701, U.S.A.
tel: 800-228-1160; fax: 845-796-1772

Eastern Hemisphere Distribution
Marcel Dekker AG, Hutgasse 4, Postfach 812, CH-4001 Basel, Switzerland
tel: 41-61-260-6300; fax: 41-61-260-6333

World Wide Web
http://www.dekker.com

The publisher offers discounts on this book when ordered in bulk quantities. For more information, write to Special Sales/Professional Marketing at the headquarters address above.

Current printing (last digit):

10 9 8 7 6 5 4 3 2 1

PRINTED IN THE UNITED STATES OF AMERICA

To Molly

Preface

This work is designed to assist in the retrieval of information in finance, commerce, industry, production, communications, transportation, and agriculture through the use of online databases, compact discs, and printed resources. These tools were selected on the basis of their authority, up-to-dateness, arrangement, style, balance, and scope, with their usefulness to investors, businesspeople, students, and librarians being paramount. Each of the entries have annotations with materials on the scope, treatment, and special features.

Appreciation is expressed to the School of Business Administration at the University of Michigan enabling the author to visit the National Library of Russia to discover materials appropriate for this book.

Contributors are listed on the following pages.

Thomas P. Slavens

Contributors

So-Yun Ahn
Sara Aichele
Michael Akea
Louise E. Alcom
Shannon Allen
Jeanine M. Amilowski
Mona Ammon
Porntip Anaprayot
Andrew F. Anderson
Stacey Anderson
Denise Anthony
Christine A. Arato
Joe Argandona
Alison Atkins
James Augur
Susan Avery
William Aylesworth
David Bachman
Timothy H. Baland
Kimberly S. Barber
Arpita J. Bathani
Brianna Baylis
Sara Bellrichard
Karen Bielski
Elizabeth L. Blakely
Timothy J. Block
Steve Bonario

Lise M. Brackbill
Rachelle H. Bradfite
Cory Brandt
Joel Brandt
Tamar Breslauer
Lynn Breyer
Liz Brozyna
Gillian Bryant
Susan Bullock
Laura Burns
Kathleen M. Cadwallader
Juan Calzoni III
Jane Campbell
Sharon L. Campbell
Charles J. Carlton
Robert B. Carowitz
Carol J. Carrara
Brian Carson
Kate Carter
Robert Cerowitz
Andrea Chambers
Dawn Chan
Linh Chang
Fang-Hwa Chen
Yu-Wen Chen
Kathryn Chmiel
Yi-Chih Chou

Mark Christel
Jean Chung
John Cicada
Terri Ciszewski
James B. Clarke
Emily E. Classon
Wendell F. Claver
Lin-Fung Co
Oi-Fung Co
William Coday
Vicki Coleman
Elisa Cortez
Dragomir Cosanri
Triza Marsh Crittle
Kimberly Crowley
Alicia Crumpton
Heather L. Cummings
David Dalquist
Sonja Daniels
Eva M. Davis
Amber Dawkins
Joan Deas
Ann Deblecourt
Beth Dierauer
Kenneth V. Downs
Craig Duden
Dorielda R. Durant

Margaret Dykens
Jeffrey M. Easter
Brent Eckert
Jonathan Edmunds
Ellen Elliot
Laventra L. Ellis
Leslie Pugh Emmons
Carol Enns
Joanne Evanoff
Craig S. Falkner
Christopher R. Farnum
Tim Fatchett
Michelle Feller
David A. Fenton
Edna Flores
Jennifer Foley
Barbara Fowler
Marcela Franco
Lori Franz
Dorie L. Freebury
Yan Fu
Yolanda Fullerton
Josz Fung
Paul C. Gahn
Renoir Gaither
James Galow
Kirsten Garlock
Veronica Gernick
Michelle Giagnon
Paula M. Gibbons
Teresa Ginal
Daphne Gioba
Brian Godlseky
Gillion Goldsmith
Bin Gong
Nat Goon
Sandra Goulef
Judith Goundji
Jon Green
June Green
V. Robin Grice
Michael Griffin
Rahul Gupta
Drin Gyuk
Leslie M. Haack

Marissa Hagen
Stefanie A. Halliday
Bridget Hamilton
James Hannigan
Daniel Hardaway
Pauline Harris
Amy Hartman
Eric Hartman
Mary T. Hartson
Lisa Hastings
Sharon Hay
Linda Heise
Sharon Herninger
Felipe E. Herrera
Suzy Herring
Diana J. Hiles
Susan Hinton
Erika Hodge
Jeff Holden
Mark Holman
Terry Hoover
Bonnie Houser
Anne Houston
Dennis Hoyner
Lisa B. Hu
Karen Jean Hunt
Laura Hunt
Christine Hysell
Trina Ihle
Lois Carolyn Imig
Laurie Isenberg
Mildred L. Jackson
Amy I. James
Tracy Myers Janevic
Shamik P. Jani
Karen L. Jania
Karen Jarrod
Yi-Lun S. Jen
Jennifer J. Jones
Angela Jones
Suzann Jude
Joanne Juhnke
Dana Juriew
Cynthia Rose Kahn
Lynn Karaszkiewicz

Laura Karnes
Beth Katz
Steven Ingram Kaye
Nika Kayne
Susan A. Kennedy
Dallas Kenny
Tammy Kilber
Gary Kilburn
Jennifer King
John E. Kiplinger
Mark Knox
Sarah A. Kolda
Vicki Kondelik
Rina Kor
Sandra L. Kortesoja
Neha Kothari
Rachael Drenovsky
  Kozal
Gretchen Krug
Catherine Kummer
Kara Kvasnicka
Joyce Kwon
Bill Landis
Amy Marie Lang
Thomas A. LaPorte
Elizabeth Larson
Dianne Lawther
Julie Lea
Hovey Lee
Ming-Ling Lee
Sandra L. Lee
Soyoung Lee
Dorothy J. Lee
Paul Lefrak
Amy Leigh
Jennifer Lentz
Celia Leung
Rachel C. Lewellen
Yu-Fan Li
Gregory Light
Doug Lind
Kathleen S. Linn
Cara List
Justin B. Louver
Gregory Lutz

Sarah Mack
Kevin Mackson
Jane Malayang
Lori A. Mardis
Markouske
Kate McBride
Lisa A. McClure
Leslie McKnight
Erin McNitt
William J. Meltzer
Joseph Mencigar
Rani Meron
Mary A. Metiva
Dori Mickelson
Andrea Monne-Foster
Perter Morville
Goodwell Motsi
Bert Nahmad
Alex Neifert
Sarah Neises
Nancy Nelson
Sarah Nesbitt
Pamela Szu Min Ng
Meegan Niemira
Karen Van Nortwick
Janine L. Odlevak
Shiloh Ogea
Maria Ogg
Philip C. Ollila
Nicholas R. Olson
Cristina M. Oproiu
Nana Osei
Reba O'Shesky
Mary Panek
Michelle Partridge
Chris Pasco-Pranger
Pamela Pavilscak
Barbara Perles
Jolee Perrine
Deborah Perry
Michelle Christine Pfaff
Julie Pierce
Sharolyn Pioritek
Thomas L. Plawman
Chris Poterala

Lydia Porthoff
Christina K. Powell
John Powell
Robin Rank
Philip Ray
Laura S. Reamy
Cindy B. Reardson
Cyndi Reeve
Patrick Rich
Frank Richardson
Linda M. Ritz
William Robby
Eric Roberts
Andrea Rogers
Laura Rooney
Leslye Rosenbaum
Jamar A. Rush
Edward Rutowski
Lisa Lee Rycenga
Latanya E. Safford
Richelle Sargent
Nicholas Scalera
Melinda L. Schafer
Paul Schaffner
Nancy Scherer
Maria E. Schieda
Ruth Schofield
Amy Schroer
Alaina Scopp
Deborah D. Sears
Caroline Serfass
Elizabeth Shaw
Robert Sherrane
William Shipley
Eric Roberts
Andrea Rogers
Laura Rooney
Leslye Rosenbaum
Jamar A. Rush
Edward Rutkowski
Lisa Lee Rycenga
Latanya E. Safford
Richelle Sargent
Nicholas Scalera
Melinda L. Schafer

Paul Schaffner
Nancy Scherer
Maria E. Schieda
Ruth Schofield
Amy Schroer
Alaina Scopp
Deborah D. Sears
Carolime Serfass
Elizabeth Shaw
Robert Sherrane
William Shipley
Elizabeth Anne Sholl
Thomas Silva
Claudia Silverman
Sarah Skilton
Lori Skolnick
Earnolyn C. Smith
Ted Smith
Mia J. Sohn
Sandeep N. Solanki
Krishna Soma
Virginia Sotirova
Caroline Stacey
Caryn Stein
Nicolyn Steinoff
Laura Stemle
Karen S. Stewart
Lisa M. Stillwell
Paul G. Streby
Karen Wallace
Struckman
Marjorie Styf
Jane L. Sumey
Natalia Sunary
Laurie Sutch
Susan Swasta
Sandra Swisher
Tiffani N. Tate
Rena Taubman
Bradley Taylor
Bill Teichert
Cynthia Terwilligan
Jennifer Thom
Devon Thomas
Michelle Thomas

Anne Tobian
Sanjay Tolia
Andrea Topolski
Jessica Tropman
Gundega Trumkalne
Kim Tsang
Christopher Turner
Debera Turner
Thomas Turner
Ken Varnum
Amanda Villareal
Martha Vander Volk
Charles Von Geik

Kathy Walcott
Holly Ward
Ruth Ward
Cynthia Webster
Amy Wei Mei
Stefanie Weigmann
Jennifer Weintraub
Heidi Weise
Bradley J. Weltman
Jean Wenger
Deborah Westmoreland
Susan Wickhorst
Mark Williams

Paul Willis
Lisa R. Wood
Sze Ying Chloe Woug
Jackie Wrosch
Yannina Yang
J. Jennifer Yang
Yeong Sam Yi
Sonia Yoffe
Mark Yoffe
Keiko Yokota-Carter
Shannon Zachary
Eunice Zhou

Contents

Contents xiii

Using the
Financial and
Business Literature

Section I

Electronic Sources

ACCOUNTING

American Institute of Certified Public Accountants (www.aicpa.org)

Users can research the American Institute of Certified Public Accountants (AICPA) web page to find information on its mission statement, operations, and member benefits such as on-line library access, invitations to class conferences, and seminars and FAQs on current accounting terms. There is a highlighted section specifically for educators and students, and one for getting helpful hints on recommended AICPA software designed to improve firm productivity such as Accountants Trial Balance (ATB), Write-Up and Lite, Depreciation, and Audit Program Generator (APG), with additional data on how and why to enroll to get this type of support from AICPA. More specifically, the "Center for Excellence in Financial Management" icon is a collection of AICPA offerings to promote membership awareness. Provided also is a link to state-by-state accessible data on regional bases of Board of Accountancy rules. Users can also find facts on assurance services beginning with a report of the Special Committee on Assurance Services, through data on defining the services, about the committee and its studies, customer focuses, and how it affects industries and firms.

CPA Exam Accounting Institute Seminars
(www.ais-cpa.com)

This site is a free service, which provides useful information for persons interested in taking CPA exams in the United States. The topic sections listed on the home pate include Changes in the CPA Exam, CPA Exam Structure and Dates, Applying to Take the CPA Exam, Citizen of Another Country, Glossary of CPA Exam Terms, and CPA Exam Answers. Within each section, additional information is provided, such as future test dates and locations, state licensing contacts, and accounting and education information resources on the Internet.

Each section contains many links. Most lead to third-party vendors whose services, such as airlines, trains, and hotels, are required when a CPA candidate travels to take the exams. A weather link is included in order to determine travel conditions on the day of the exam. For questions that a noncitizen might have, there is a link to resources about U.S. immigration law. Finally, if a state licensing board has a web site, it is linked.

ADVERTISING

Advertising Age (www.adage.com)

Advertising Age is an on-line daily publication on marketing, advertising, media news, information, and analysis. It contains news of the Internet, interactive articles, and a job search database.

Advertising Demographics
(www.demographics.com/Publications/AD/index.htm)

The American Demographics Magazine is a publication of Dow Jones and Company, Inc. The site contains a table of contents of issues from 1995 to date. A search engine is provided to find the desired articles and publications from January 1993 to the current issue.

Advertising Law Internet Site
(www.yahoo.com/Government/Law/Consumer)

The Advertising Law Internet Site discusses fundamental advertising principles and gives links to other consumer, marketing, advertising Internet sites such as the Federal Trade Commission and the Council of Better Business Bureaus, Inc. In addition, this web page allows the discussion of issues with advertising and marketing laws and the opportunity to gather information on guidelines, trade regulation rules, expert speeches, and enforcement policies. Another option this site offers is the chance to see the Federal Trade Commissions consumer brochures and business compliance manuals dealing with credit fraud and investments.

MediaFinder (www.mediafinder.com)

MediaFinder is a service center that gives the opportunity to request subscriptions, advertising, and list rental rates for an incredible amount of catalogs, newsletters, magazines, and newspapers along with other items.

PX (Sommerville, NJ: People's X-Change)

This on-line database source provides electronic advertisements in full screen format. PX enables users to buy, sell, or find an item or service through organized, user-friendly menu searches. Searches may be conducted by product, service, size, location, color, price, or keyword. Help screens are available.

The database covers the following categories: real estate, business opportunities, professional business services, employment, cars and trucks, boats, aircraft, leisure places and services, equipment, computer software, guns, art and antiques, collectibles, close outs, miscellaneous merchandise, personals, animal breeding, lost pets, electronic mail (e-mail), amusements, and other services.

Advertisements placed remain active and available for 30 days and e-mails may be anonymous.

PTS Marketing and Advertising Reference Service (Foster City: Information Access Company) [DIALOG]

The PTS Marketing and Advertising Reference Service (PTS MARS) database is composed of full-text advertisements of consumer products. It is useful to companies for identifying markets, products, services, and marketing intelligence.

AFRICAN–AMERICANS IN BUSINESS

African–American Business Alliance (www.yahoo.com/Business_and_Economy/Organizations)

The African–American Business Alliance is a web site dedicated to improving the financial structure of the African–American business community. The web site includes a database of African–American-owned operations. Direct links are available to the web site mission statement, information on computer literacy, and a link in which to enter further listings. An e-mail address is provided also for those with questions.

National Black MBA Association
(www.yahoo.com/Business_and_Economy/Organizations)

The National Black MBA Association is a web site devoted to creating economic and intellectual wealth for the Black community. Direct links are available to programs and events, committees, employment opportunities, and corporate partners. Additional links are available to information about the National Black MBA Association, how to join, business links, and the New York chapter. An e-mail address is provided for further information.

AGRICULTURE

AGRICOLA (Washington, DC: U.S. Department of Agriculture)

A product of the National Agricultural Library in the U.S. Department of Agriculture, this source is distributed on SilverPlatter 3.1 CD-ROM with quarterly updates. It is available on-line through DIALOG and BRS Information Technologies. The print equivalent is the Bibliography of Agriculture. The coverage is worldwide, offering citations to published literature in virtually every area of agriculture.

Alternate database options incorporated into AGRICOLA are CRIS and ICAR. The section on "Current Research Information Systems" provides abstracts of research in progress on agricultural and forestry research projects and nutrition. The section on "Inventory of Canadian Agri-Food Research" contains abstracts of research projects from Canadian industries and universities. These are updated annually.

Searching on AGRICOLA is by SilverPlatter software standards, with key words and Boolean operators. The onscreen help is extensive, with several option menus. Citations and abstracts may be printed or downloaded to diskettes.

The companion guide to AGRICOLA is AGRICOLearn: An Interactive Training Program. It consists of loose leaf manuals, a CD video recording, and several computer diskettes containing computer-assisted instruction. These tools may be used to achieve the desired level of expertise.

ASSOCIATIONS

Bureau of National Affairs Databases (Washington, DC: Bureau of National Affairs)

A variety of databases are produced by the Bureau of National Affairs (BNA). The databases contain information on various topics from all branches of the government and are available on Nexis.

The Antitrust and Trade Regulation Report provides information regarding legislative, judicial, and regulatory developments that affect trade practice law. It also provides information on state legislatures, Congress, state courts, federal courts, the Federal Trade Commission (FTC), and the antitrust division of the justice department. It is updated weekly, provides information on international trade, and provides full or partial text notes.

BNA Banking Daily is an electronic awareness service that provides current information on court decisions, regulatory actions, and legislative decisions that directly affect financial institutions. It also provides access to the results of recent congressional actions and the actions of regulatory agencies.

BNA Banking Report provides weekly coverage of legal, regulatory, and congressional developments. It assists in comprehending and adhering to federal and state banking regulations and laws. It is a system that monitors federal as well as international banking and financial developments. It provides weekly coverage of agencies such as the FHFB, Federal Reserve Bank (FRB), Officers' Training School (OTS), Federal Deposit Insurance Corporation (FDIC), RTC, and the Treasury Department. It also offers legal briefs, economic briefs, and briefs of legislative action.

BNA International Business Daily provides information on acquisitions, mergers, tax treaties, labor developments, property issues, international tax laws, and various topics of business and development. It pays special attention to issues of business development in the European community. It covers actions of agencies such as the Internal Revenue Service (IRS), Investment Tax Credit (ITC), Department of State, Patent and Trademark Office, MMC, and reports from the various levels of the judicial system.

BNA International Environmental Daily covers judiciary actions and legislation pertaining to environmental issues throughout the world. It provides coverage of federal and international actions on issues of air pollution, hazardous waste, solid waste management, natural resources utilization, oil pollution, world climate change, and environmental policy trends.

BNA International Finance Daily covers issues affecting the international finance community. It covers materials in the areas of investments, banking, securities, international investments, practices, monetary policy, subsidies, debt reduction, and international banking. It provides reports on agencies such as the OPIC, ECD, International Monetary Fund (IMF), the World Bank, and the OEC.

BNA International Trade Daily covers actions affecting U.S. imports and exports. It provides coverage of the actions of congressional committees, foreign investments, import relief, adjustment assistance, licensing, and financing. It provides reports from agencies such as the Department of State, the ITC, federal and state courts, the Commerce Department, and the Treasury Department.

BNA Pensions and Benefits Daily provides coverage of pension and benefits legislation and court decisions from various other BNA databases. Each update contains approximately four to six stories.

BNA Pension Reporter is a weekly report covering issues pertaining to pension and benefit plans. It covers legal developments and activities of ERISA. It provides coverage of IRS revenue rulings related to pension activities, technical advice, summaries of congressional hearings, state and local government developments, and congressional committee and bill actions.

BNA Washington Insider is an electronically based awareness service. It provides reviews on the actions of Congress, the Supreme Court, and various federal regulatory agencies. It also provides coverage of congressional hearings and actions on the floor, significant opinions of Supreme Court justices, and information from the Federal Register. This database is equipped with an index of in-demand documents and judicial opinions to provide a constant flow of information to those who need to stay current on activities in Washington.

Daily Labor Report provides coverage of nationwide labor activities. It covers decisions by state and federal courts, Congress, and the National Labor Relations Board.

Daily Report for Executives is a daily report covering areas such as legislative and judicial developments, business planning, tax policy, federal grants, contracts, international finance, product liability, agriculture, and antitrust and trade regulations. It also provides coverage of court decisions, appropriations actions, and policy developments.

Federal Contract Report is a weekly report of decisions arising from the relationship between the government and various local government agency grantees, their contractors, government contractors, and subcontractors.

Government Employee Relations Report is a weekly report of actions affecting government employees. It provides coverage of court decisions and legislation pertaining to the subject. It also provides coverage of union activities, grievance settlements, agency rulings, and legislative actions that affect public salaries.

International Trade Reporter is a weekly report on the international and foreign commerce communities. It provides coverage of foreign and domestic trade policies, regulations, U.S. legislative activities and judicial actions.

BNA Labor Relations Reporter Arbitrators' Biographies provide biographies of practicing labor arbitrators. The biographies give detailed information such as names, addresses, professional affiliations, past experiences, and issues and industries arbitrated.

Securities Regulation and Law Report is a weekly report pertaining to the regulation of securities and commodities. It covers actions of Congress, the Securities and Exchange Commission (SEC), the Financial Accounting

Standards Board, the Commodities Futures Trading Commission, and various professional associations.

The United States Law Week provides extended coverage of Supreme Court decisions, denial of reviews, grants, and summaries of all cases on the Supreme Court docket. It provides digests of precedent-setting cases and includes annual and midyear reports of the American Bar Association.

Some BNA databases are also available on Lexis such as BNA Banking Daily, BNA Banking Report, BNA International Trade Daily, International Trade Reporter, Securities Regulation and Law Report, International Environment Reporter, Antitrust and Trade Regulation Report, BNA Washington Insider, Daily Report for Executives, Securities Regulation and Law Report, and United States Law Week. Other BNA databases on Lexis are the following.

BNA Antitrust and Trade Regulation Daily is an electronic report of developments on restrictive trade practice law. It serves as a rapid notification tool of developments by various agencies, Congress, the FTC, and private industries. There is no print equivalent.

BNA Bankruptcy Law Daily reviews developments of the judicial and legislative branches of the government. It covers material pertaining to bankruptcy law and provides early notification of federal, state, and bankruptcy court decisions.

BNA Federal Contracts Daily provides coverage of developments in federal contracting agencies, Congress, and the courts. It also covers legislation pertaining to government funding, federal regulation policies, and decisions by the General Accounting Office.

BNA Securities Law Daily reports on judicial, regulatory, and congressional developments pertaining to accounting and securities.

BNA Tax Updates is an electronic news service specializing in information on taxes. It reports on tax news from the IRS, the courts, Congress, and various aspects of the private sector.

Daily Tax Reports covers developments in areas affecting accounting, taxation, and policies on budgeting and pensions. It provides in-depth coverage of legislation on taxes, congressional hearings, regulatory proposals and rulings, ruling of the courts, summaries of the courts, decisions on both the federal and state levels, IRS summaries manuals, and development reports on state and federal budgets.

BNA Environment Daily provides reports on federal, state, and private developments pertaining to pollution and the environment. It includes case summaries and is updated daily.

BNA Occupational Safety and Health Daily provides information on legislation, right-to-know laws, regulatory developments, and federal judicial developments involving safety and health.

BNA Product Liability Daily reports on the legislative, judicial, and industrial developments on product safety. It also provides coverage of court decisions and the activities of the Consumer Product Safety Commission.

BNA Toxics Law Daily provides coverage of personal injury, property damage, and toxic exposure cases. It covers the litigation process and how the cases are affected by various protection laws.

Chemical Regulation Reporter is a weekly report of information pertaining to the use and production of pesticides and chemicals. It covers issues such as the control of chemical pollution in the workplace, air, and water. It provides information on the latest pesticides, hazardous materials, and toxic substances. This database provides complete text coverage of procedures, announcements, and guidelines of the EPA.

Environment Reporter is a weekly report of legislation pertaining to pollution control, solid waste management, hazardous waste, oil pollution, mining, and natural resources utilization. It covers actions of Congress, federal courts, state legislatures, state courts, and regulatory agencies.

International Environment Reporter is a biweekly report that is designed to monitor pollution control activities. It focuses on social issues, political issues, multinational and bilateral agreements and treaties, environmental protection programs, pollution prevention measures, actions of the United Nations, and key meetings.

Occupational Safety and Health Reporter covers legislation involving the safety and health of workers at the state and federal levels. It also provides information about right-to-know laws, court decisions, congressional hearings, and investigations.

Toxics Law Reporter is a weekly report containing hazardous waste cases, news and related insurance information, litigation due to toxic exposure, and litigation for property damage. It also contains developments of the Comprehensive Environmental Response, the Resource Conservation and Recovery Act, and the Compensation and Liability Act.

The BNA Patent, Trademark, and Copyright Journal provides coverage of legislative, legal, and regulatory developments pertaining to trademark, patent, and competition law. It provides various court decisions, coverage of international developments, opinions of the Supreme Court, and rulings of the Patent and Trademark Office.

The BNA Patent, Trademark, and Copyright Law Daily covers regulatory, legal, and legislative decisions pertaining to trademark, copyright, and unfair competition law.

Tax Management Portfolios are a series of handbooks provided by reputable tax attorneys and accountants. Topics covered range from tax-related problems to foreign income. Each report contains discussions on a selected tax problem, forms, worksheets, checklists, and a bibliography of official and unofficial sources.

Tax Management Compensation Planning Journal is a monthly report of new developments, new analyses, potential problems, and current issues. It includes articles by professionals, reviews of benefit plans, unofficial information pertaining to congressional matters, planning suggestions, and information on recent Senate and House bills.

Tax Management Estates, Gifts, and Trusts Journal provides analytical articles, updates of IRS actions, reviews of current literature, and recent developments of the judicial, regulatory, and legislative systems. This journal is essentially designed to aid a tax practitioner.

Tax Management Real Estate Journal includes articles by noted tax practitioners, practitioner comments on various legislative, economic, and tax issues and information on the actions of the government.

Tax Management Weekly Report covers official actions pertaining to tax policy and tax reform. It is constantly updated with the latest trends, changes, and new developments in the area. It provides summaries of cases, IRS memoranda, and information about significant developments in legislative and judicial committees. Another function of this database is a calendar that provides a schedule of activities pertaining to tax laws and legislation and reports of actions by the Treasury Department.

Tax Management Memorandum provides reviews of new information pertaining to tax planning. It provides information that is useful to tax practitioners and is designed to curtail potential problems or areas of ambiguity.

Some BNA databases are also available on Westlaw such as Antitrust and Trade Regulation Report; BNA Antitrust and Trade Regulation Daily; BNA Bankruptcy Law Daily; BNA Environment Daily; BNA Federal Contracts Daily; BNA Patent, Trademark, and Copyright Law Daily; BNA Product Liability Daily; BNA Securities Law Daily; BNA Tax Updates; BNA Toxics Law Daily; BNA Washington Insider; Chemical Regulation Reporter; Daily Report for Executives; Daily Tax Reports; Environment Reports; Securities Regulation and Law Report; and United States Law Week. Other BNA databases on Westlaw are as follows.

The BNA Patent, Trademark, and Copyright Journal is a weekly report of developments affecting patenting, copyrighting, and trademarks. It provides full and partial texts of committee reports, Supreme Court opinions, international developments, and legislation affecting patents and trademarks.

Federal Contracts Report is a weekly report of decisions arising from the relationship between the government and various local government agency grantees, their contractors, government contractors, and subcontractors.

U.S. Law Week, Daily Edition is a daily report of the information provided in the United States Law Week.

Global Fund for Women On-Line
(www.ai.mit.edu/people/ellens/gfw.html)

The Global Fund for Women (GFW) is an international grant-making organization, which supports groups that are committed to women's well-being and full participation in society.

From the GFW homepage, one can request printed information about the GFW. The homepage states the mission of the fund and the fund's philosophy (called the "Rationale").

The homepage provides links to the following text documents.

The Programs describes the types of work for which the fund provides assistance.

Applying for a Grant provides information about who may apply for a grant (the fund prefers groups over individuals), and how to go about applying.

Board of Directors lists the members of the Board of Directors and a paragraph of biographical information about each.

Supporters provides links to lists of foundations and corporations who support the GFW. It also provides a link to the World Bank homepage (this is the only outside link available through GFW On-Line).

Advisory Council lists the names of the members of the Advisory Council as well as the cities in which they live.

Frequently Asked Questions about the Global Fund for Women is similar to most other FAQs. It answers such questions as "Who governs the Global Fund?" (the answer provides a link to the Board of Directors) and "How do you decide which groups to support?"

Assisting the GFW provides information on how to make a donation.

From the homepage, one can access the GFW Network News, which is a newsletter that comes out periodically, but does not seem to be on any regular schedule.

AUTOMOBILE INDUSTRY AND TRADE

Auto.com (www.auto.com)

Auto.com is a web site comprised of daily automotive news and reviews. Users can traverse the web site for auto news, breaking news, industry news, stock update product line reviews, auto shows, and racing information. Direct links are available to safety, affordability, driving, and test drive sites. Further links are available to a search engine and related web sites.

BANKS AND BANKING

Bankrate.com (www.bankrate.com)

This site is a listing of finance news and rates. The main focus is the presentation of average bank interest rates. It also offers the option to search for an attractive interest rate on a bank loan.

Central Banking Resource Center (patriot.net/~bernkopf)

The website provides a complete directory to the Internet sites of central banks, and of ministries of finance, economy, and treasury around the world.

Office of the Comptroller of the Currency (www.occ.treas.gov)

The Office of the Comptroller of the Currency (OCC), an independent bureau of the Treasury Department, is the oldest federal financial regulatory body and oversees the nation's federally chartered banks. Providing information about the workings of the agency and the history of banking, OCC's web page includes information for individuals heavily involved with national banks and novices interested in a cursory overview of the subject. With a few pictures and graphics, the site provides a straightforward table of contents with numerous links to additional information. The resources cover everything from the history of the OCC, its regulatory duties, legal interpretations, and publications, to consumer information. Special emphasis is made on OCC's duties under the Community Reinvestment Act. Finally, the page includes a subject index and is keyword-searchable.

Resources for Economists on the Internet (econwpa.wustl.edu/EconFAQ/EconFAQ.html)

This web site is a guide containing a variety of resources on the Internet of interest to economists. It contains a table of contents outlining the major links and areas contained within. The links include federal reserve banks of America, regional economic information systems, Bureau of Labor Statistics, U.S. Department of Commerce, working papers, information on upcoming economic conferences, on-line journals, electronic newsletters, and economic societies and associations, to name a few.

Wells Fargo (www.wellsfargo.com)

Wells Fargo and Co. is the eighth largest bank holding company in the United States based on assets with the completion of the merger with First Interstate. Stocks of Wells Fargo and Co. are traded on the New York, Pacific, London, and Frankfurt stock exchanges. Common shares outstanding after the merger total approximately 98 million shares. This site of banking information contains information on economic reports and commentary, on-line banking, personal finance, small business banking, commercial banking, international trade, an ATM express search, and historic information about Wells Fargo, to including a museum. This site is hosted by Wells Fargo and Co.

BONDS

Standard and Poor's Bond Guide (www.standardandpoors.com)

This work provides descriptions of statistics for and ratings of thousands of bonds.

BRAND CHOICES

Brands and their Companies (Detroit: Gale) [DIALOG]

Brands and Their Companies contains information on brand names and their owners, manufacturers, and distributors or importers.

Buyers Zone (www.buyerszone.com)

Buyers Zone (BZ) provides products and services for small-size and middle-size offices. Moreover, through Buyers Zone, subscribers can trade information with fellow buyers and vendors. BZ links include Goody Bag, Survey Says, Helping Hand, and Hot Sites. The Goody Bag site provides information on items before buying them, in the interest of saving the consumer money. Moreover, the Survey Says link is a guide indicator to shopping practices. The Hot Sites link suggests other informative business links.

BUSINESS ENTERPRISES

ABI/INFORM Ondisc (Louisville, KY: University Microfilms)

This source is the CD-ROM version of the on-line product by the same name. It contains references with abstracts to articles in some 800 business and management journals, covering a wide range of business-related topics. Each CD-ROM covers a 5-year period, with complete coverage going back to 1971 and the most current being about 3 months old. Access points include word or phrase, subject heading, company name, and title.

General BusinessFile (Foster City, CA: Information Access)

Business information is provided on three discs with this CD-ROM source that uses the Info Trac system. Analyst reports from Investext, major article indexing from Business Index, and company directory listings from Company ProFile are offered as one comprehensive product. In addition, news releases from listed companies are drawn from PR Newswire, another information access on-line database.

Information can be found on companies, industries, and products, as well as management, academic theories, and economic outlooks. Full-text reports on more than 8000 U.S. companies and industries are available. Reports on European, Asian, and Australian companies are included. Citations cover more than 800 journals and newspapers and over 3000 other publications with business-related information. Company information includes financial data, company analyses, and news items. Directory listings for more than 100,000 companies provide company names, addresses, descriptions, founding dates, Standard Industrial Classification (SIC) codes, and numbers of employees. Analyst reports, outlines, company outlooks, and company rankings are also available. News releases provide the full text whereas only citations are provided for journal articles.

Searches can be conducted in six ways: by subject, company, location, industry, SIC code, or product. This product is intended for use on the Info Trac system, but a subscription can be obtained without it.

The GLIS interface leads the user along, presenting a series of choices for the user to make. The GLIS also provides the user with a list of specific keywords, which is helpful in searching for specific data sets.

Although a new user can access the system as a "guest," complete functionality can only be gained by becoming a "registered" user. To register, the user need only select "help" from the main menu and the interface will lead the way through the registration process.

GLIS provides 40 on-line guides, ranging from *Matthews Global Vegetation Set* to *NASA Aerial Photography*, to aid the user in searches for relevant data sets. Also available on-line are sample images, including *Advanced Very High Resolution Radiometer* images and Landsat images.

Internet Tradeline, Inc. (www.tradeline.net)

Internet Tradeline, Inc. (ITI) offers a wide range of business solutions world-wide. The user can access a demonstration and see how their affordable Internet business sites can help improve the user's business processes. One can also locate companies and source products on the World Trade Exchange, a global business-to-business destination site. Success stories can be read as to how ITI helped their company in reducing costs, managing existing customer relationships, and attracting new customers. The latest press releases and articles featuring ITI are available.

Universal Business Service (www.worldweb.com/UBS)

Universal Business Service is a web site consisting of information regarding investing, seeking capital to establish new business, reviewing business/investment opportunities, and so on. Users who are interested in investments can gather information from this web page. There is also a search engine provided to search for other information that could not be found in the web site. For further information, users can contact Universal Business Service by the address provided in the web site.

BUSINESS NAMES

Australian Business Compendium (Alexandria, Australia: Read Only Memory)

Australian Business Compendium (ABC) is a single CD-ROM that contains vital information on 7600 companies in Australia. ABC is indexed with Dataware, an Australian search and retrieval system. ABC information can be extracted as a file, a report, or a label.

ABC requires either an IBM-compatible computer or an Apple Macintosh with SOFT PC software and a CD-ROM drive. ABC has 19 searchable fields capable of being searched individually or in combinations. The fields are: company names, addresses, suburbs, post codes, telephone numbers, facsimile numbers, executive names, numbers of employees, imports, gross sales, relationships, banks, branches, SIC codes, SIC categories, SIC names, ASIC codes, job titles, and persons. An example search would be to look for all companies with gross sales in the range of "US$20–50 M" in the category of "finance."

ABC is available with three different licenses. The site license allows the user to export or print as much information as one wishes and to use it as long as no ABC information is sold or given away. The network license has the same retrieval restrictions as a site license and requires an additional license for each work station in the network accessing ABC. Finally, the unlimited license has no restrictions on its use, except for those restrictions associated with the Dataware retrieval software.

ABC comes in one of nine export file formats. Those formats are: formatted text, Wordstar, ASCII, comma delimited, semicolon delimited, dBase III +, Lotus, DIF, and fixed field.

BizWeb (www.bizweb.com)

BizWeb provides information on companies and products for the convenience of users. The way this web site works is that companies are divided up by categories that represent the services and goods they provide. To obtain access to any business information, users may type in keywords next to the keyword search for their desired information. If they are not sure what to type, they may click onto the myriad of categories already provided by the web site. Such categories include Antique, Aviation, Computers, Electronics, Finance, Food, Marketplace, Medical, Publishing, and Travel. Once they click onto or type in the keywords, they are provided with the desired information.

BizWeb is a conglomeration of resources for product, business, and consumer information. There is a site for company data, which is grouped according to the goods and services they provide. Examples within the service category include business management, opportunity, imports, exports, law, and employment. There are additional categories such as computers, consulting, and finance, and over 100 everyday consumer products.

The second site involves connection to the top 5% of all web sites by Lycos homepage. Access to this site gives top news, city guides, a people finder, an Internet version of yellow pages, and much more.

Thirdly, there is a link to the Inc. Online web site provided for new and upcoming companies with access to new business information, resources, tools, and technology, and a network with other entrepreneurs.

Brands and Their Companies (Detroit: Gale Research Company) [DIALOG]

Brands and Their Companies contains information on brand names and their owners, manufacturers, and distributors or importers.

CD-ROM Directory (Brussels; Paris: BUREAU van DIJK)

CD-ROM databases made available by the management firm, BUREAU van DIJK, are profiled in this source. The databases fall into four categories: financial, marketing, statistical, and reference. The financial databases cover the accounts of more than 600,000 Western European companies and over 7000 banks, both U.S. and Western European. The marketing databases offer marketing data for more than 2,000,0000 Western European companies. The statistical databases cover topics such as European Economic Community trade, the European agricultural community, and international trade. The reference databases include a French language reference text, a chess encyclopedia, and French legal and regulatory information.

GTE SuperPages (superpages.gte.net)

GTE SuperPages web site is an interactive yellow page featuring comprehensive and accurate business information derived from over 5000 yellow pages directories across the United States. Users access information through a keyword search of business "FactFiles." GTE SuperPages provides full color maps and driving directions to all listed businesses. The "Consumer Guide Interactive" section features product information, ratings, reviews, and recommendations for over 100 consumer product categories. The business web site directory features categorized links to over 60,000 web sites owned and operated by businesses around the world. The "Classified Ads" section offers nationwide classified advertising, and it is free to place ads, search ads, and set up a notification. The site provides links to selected sites that allow the user to purchase goods and services on-line. There is a direct link to the Lycos City Guide, which features information, local web links, and interactive yellow pages to over 450 cities.

BUSINESS PLANNING

American Business Directory (Omaha, NE: American Business Information) [DIALOG]

The directory is a source for mailing, business, population, and marketing information, obtained from yellow pages of telephone directories and company annual reports. The data are also collected by annual telephone interviews.

American Business 20 Plus Companies (Omaha, NE: American Business Information) [DIALOG]

American Business 20 Plus Companies is a subsidiary of the American Business Directory. It has records on American enterprises with at least 20 employees. The database provides mailing, business, population, marketing, and corporate intelligence information.

American Dream Business Network (www.adbn.com)

American Dream Business Network offers business news, interviews, articles, and marketplace designed for the business consumer. The site has four sections: Features, Links, Lifestyle, and Shopping. The "Features" section covers interviews and articles aimed at improving business performance.

Links have been divided into groups to make it easier for users to find the business information for which they are searching. The on-line marketplace helps users find and order business-related products.

Best Businesses to Start (www.be-your-own-boss.com)

The Best Businesses To Start web site provides users with information and resources helpful to starting a business. The site provides business startup reports, for a small fee, that cover vital information, helping users make decisions in choosing suitable businesses to start. The "Home Employment Directory" section offers home-based income and business opportunities for over 100 U.S. companies. The directory gives a description of each opportunity and how to contact the company offering it. The site provides a mail order advertising directory, which lists publications that accept classified ads, focus on the mail order field, and have proven to be successful for many small mail order companies. The "Import–Export Resource Center" allows users to buy over 1 million products from over 30,000 companies to help start a home-based import–export business.

Business Resource Center (www.morebusiness.com)

Business Resource Center is available for people who are interested in starting and running a business. Other important information associated with the field of business is also available. Examples of items that can be found on the page are: products, reviews, financing and marketing advice, worksheets, templates, and present day news.

The Conference Board
(www.yahoo.com/Business_and_Economy/Organizations)

The Conference Board is the web site of the business membership and research organization, devoted to assisting senior executives meet business challenges. The Conference Board produces the Consumer Confidence Index and Leading Economic Indicator, provides networking opportunities through its worldwide conferences, and improves decision making through a wide range of reports on best business practices. Users can traverse the web site for information on the company expertise and products and services. Direct links are available to corporate citizenship, corporate governance, environment, health and safety, human resources and organizational effectiveness, economic research and analysis, and quality management. Product and service-related links are available to conferences, councils, economic publications and services, management research, and information services.

Further links are available to information concerning the nonprofit organization. A search engine and site map are also provided.

The Entrepreneur's Mind (www.benlore.com)

The Entrepreneur's Mind (EM) is a web resource. It contains advice and actual life stories from industry experts and successful entrepreneurs on the various aspects of emerging business and entrepreneurship. Every article of the EM informs others with lengthy profiles of entrepreneurs, how they expanded their companies, and interviews with industry professionals discussing a facet of starting and developing a new business.

Inc. (www.inc.com)

This site is dedicated to providing emerging firms with relevant and useful business advice. The on-line entrepreneur link contains a variety of resources, from finding a web site designer to avoiding legal headaches. The Inc. 500 is a service providing Inc. Magazine's annual list of America's fastest-growing private companies. Other resources include consulting information, demographics database (locate up-to-date demographic data such as income reports and population information), and a list of upcoming business conferences.

Institute of Business Forecasting (www.ibforecast.com)

The Institute of Business Forecasting is an organization devoted to helping business executives in forecasting and planning. The institute conducts seminars/conferences and publishes periodicals and books concerning business. This site presents the periodical Journal of Business Forecasting (JBF), jobs in forecasting, consulting services, conferences/seminars, forecasting books, and forecasting links. However, to get all these services, one needs to become a member. Membership can be obtained at a small fee, but obtaining membership offers many benefits such as discounts on books, seminars, and job information.

Oppnet.com (www.oppnet.com)

Oppnet.com is produced by the Opportunity Network based in Massachusetts. The objective of the site is to provide resources for the independent businessperson. Included are data on opportunities for business, services, alliances, networking, positions, and education. Within each category is a listing of titles, descriptions, and contacts. It is possible to find information on businesses that are for sale or that are looking for employees or partners, companies that offer financial or technological support, and educational experiences for entrepreneurs. Oppnet.com charges a fee for submissions.

Sitenet (www.conway.com)

Sitenet is the steadily expanding electronic edition of Site Magazine. Its international and local agency link and help business executives to decide where to open new facilities.

The American Business Disc

The American Business Disc is a CD-ROM from American Business Information that runs on IBM-PC-compatible computers. The product is intended for people who need data on companies and organizations that operate in the United States.

The 10 million businesses on the CD-ROM are accessed through a variety of search options. Choices include searches by geographical area and by Standard Industrial Classification code. Each company profile provides data such as company address, estimated sales volume, and stock exchange information. The files can be downloaded and printed. In addition, the American Business Disc is updated two times each year.

The Annual Reports Library (www.zpub.com/sf/arl)

This site is the homepage for the Annual Reports Library located in San Francisco. Although the establishment maintains a collection of annual reports and proxies, it does not allow users to browse the entire collection on-line. Rather, it provides access to the homepages of companies that post their records on the Internet, as well as connections to various search engines and tips for searching. This page is mostly dedicated to advice and articles. The main part is divided into sections for investors, authors of annual reports, administrators of nonprofit organizations, as well as students and educators. Each area provides articles on topics, such as how to read an annual report, design an effective document, or teach students to use and evaluate these reports. Information on organizations, such as the National Association of Investors and the National Investor Relations Institute, is also included. Although a membership fee is required to use the physical resources, use of the web address is free. A membership form, which the user can fill out and mail to the main office, is provided. In addition to its own articles and services, this location provides links to outside sources, such as the Wall Street Net and Business Connections at the New York Times.

21st Century Strategic Solutions (members.tripod.com/~century/index.html)

This site offers data on project management planning and scheduling. The firm, 21st Century Strategic Solutions, specializes in an array of areas including architecture, contraction, development, aircraft, electronics, and information systems. Another service is their Password Recovery and File Decryption group, which assists businesses in recovering passwords from encrypted files. Their Consulting Support group offers project risk analyses and expert witness testimony. Services are delivered electronically or on-site.

U.S. Business Advisor (www.business.gov)

U.S. Business Advisor is a web site containing information regarding the federal government's business transaction and services. This web page is dedicated to users who intend to improve their knowledge on this topic to improve their business. Interested users can browse through the given links to search other related information and articles. There is also a search engine provided in this web page. For further information, users can contact the U.S. Business Advisor by the e-mail address given in this web site.

Working Solo (www.workingsolo.com)

Working Solo contains information, articles, tapes, resources, related sites, and other outputs that one needs for starting a business or progressing to the following level. They link and assist solo entrepreneurs in all kinds of business, from around the world, and at all levels of experience. For members of the media, Working Solo has resources that can answer questions, give a sense of recent issues vital to small business owners, provide an interview, offer leads and contracts of other interesting entrepreneurs to interview, and evaluate story ideas to make sure they are on target.

CAPITAL MARKETS

Dynasty Capital Services (www.dynastycap.com)

Dynasty Capital Services is a company that is designed to help companies and entrepreneurs gain capital through investors and partnerships. This web site contains much general information about this company. Through this site, the prospective client can ask questions to the CEO and other staff members. The user is also able to find out about the other services the Dynasty Capital Services has available. There is a link to companies that Dynasty Capital Services has worked with.

CHEMICAL INDUSTRY

Chemical Business NewsBase (Cambridge, UK: The Royal Society of Chemistry) [DIALOG]

Chemical Business NewsBase is a business database on chemical and related industries particularly in Europe. The data are composed of abstracts of journals, books, press releases, company reports, and advertisements.

Chemical Industry Notes (Columbus, OH: Chemical Abstracts Service) [DIALOG]

Chemical Industry Notes provides indexes of journals, newspapers, and books that are business-related and have information on developments in the chemical industry. Areas covered by the database are government and society, marketing, products, and prices.

Chemplant Plus (East Greenstead, UK: Reed Information Services) [DIALOG]

Chemplant Plus has information on chemical manufacturing plants. It consists of two subfiles, namely, Chemical Plant Reports and Chemical Age Project File. The first subfile contains information on chemical manufacturing, whereas the second deals with the establishment of production plants around the world.

Chemstats (East Grinstead, UK: Reed Information Services) [DIALOG]

Chemstats has annual statistical information on trade chemicals and production chemicals. Some of these chemicals include petrochemicals, fertilizers, and polymers.

COMMERCE

Asia-Pacific (Seattle, WA: Aristarchus Knowledge Industries) [DIALOG]

The Asia-Pacific database contains commercial and industrial information about East Asia, Southeast Asia, the Indian Subcontinent, the Middle East, Australia, and the Pacific Island nations. The database has two types of information. The first is composed of abstracts from journals as well as documents from public organizations and private companies. The second has a Corporate Thesaurus subfile with information on business leaders and companies traded on stock exchanges in the region.

Commerce Alley (www.calley.co.jp)

Commerce Alley is a project in cooperation with the Okude Laboratory of Keio University at the Shoman Fujisan campus. The aim of the project is to study the commercial potentiality of the Internet. More than 40 middle-class corporations, from retailing, entertainment, café fine art, to any service are involved in this project. Currently, over 40 middle-class corporations make and manage their own servers, and prepare and renew their own home pages in this "alley." Most of the information is written in Japanese; however, individual companies provide English translation.

Commerce Net (www.commerce.net)

This site is designed for companies and individuals interested in conducting commercial transactions on the web. It is the product of an industry consortium that services over 500 members, including software and tele-communications companies, banks, and on-line service providers. This partnership hopes to build business opportunities and trust in Internet commerce. There are four categories of information offered here. The link "Creating Synergy" provides details about members, conferences, mailing lists, and international outreach. "Capitalizing on Opportunities" features examples of framework for electronic commerce. The "Knowledge" section offers the latest press releases, Nielson studies, events, and procedures for becoming a member. Finally, the "Making the Vision Real" heading groups together topics such as VIP awards, new innovator awards, advocacy campaigns, and company portfolios. This resource is searchable by keyword and contains a help page. Users should be aware that some articles and membership lists are for members only.

Data Interchange Standards Association (www.disa.org)

This web site, sponsored by the Data Interchange Standards Association (DISA), is a nonprofit organization that supports the development and use of electronic data interchange (EDI) standards in electronic commerce. From the home page, one can access meeting dates, meeting minutes, and membership information pertaining to national and international standards development activities. "News @ DISA" provides news about educational seminars, conferences, press releases, as well as related informational services. "EDI Reference Desk" contains a glossary of terms and acronyms related to the industry. One can search for a specific acronym, browse the full glossary, or select additional glossaries such as BABEL. The latter can be used over the Internet or downloaded as a stand-alone database to search for computer-oriented abbreviations and acronyms.

Electronic Commerce (techunix.technion.ac.il/~orena/ec)

Developed as part of a course project by students at the Israel Institute of Technology, Electronic Commerce provides a critical examination of the World Wide Web as a distribution channel and as a medium for marketing communication. Topics highlighted in the general overview include an introduction to electronic commerce, its application in the world of business, requirements for use, and its benefits and advantages as well as disadvantages.

Electronic Commerce Information Resource (www.year-x.co.uk)

Year-X has experience in forming web sites with database and publishing systems. They also focus on providing and publishing solutions for business associations that require access to the web.

International Chamber of Commerce (www.iccwbo.org)

Off to the side of the page, one can access reports on the latest stories in commerce. The electronic magazine of the ICC Business World is also available. One link explains what exactly is the ICC. It is described as a world business organization that promotes international trade, investment, and the economic market system throughout the world. They also make rules governing the conduct of business across borders. Another category one can search is the commissions in the ICC. Offered as a choice to the user, one can search in areas from advertising and marketing to transport. Information on conferences and seminars is also accessible. The site has contact information for the national committees of the ICC, which are the Americas, Europe, Africa, Middle East, and Asia Pacific. Included in the site is a list of ICC company members. These companies shape rules and policies that stimulate international trade and investment. Some companies listed are AT&T, Canon, and Dow Chemical. Other categories available are information on ICC membership and ICC public documents.

The Internet.com Guide to Electronic Commerce (e-comm.internet.com)

This site claims to be the most comprehensive tool for commerce on the Internet. The section titled "Background" contains general articles dealing with electronic business, such as "The Executive Guide to Marketing on the New Internet." This part also includes a list of materials covering advertising on the World Wide Web. The next division, "Electronic Commerce Examples," provides access to various sample pages created by industry groups, companies, consortia, and service agencies. "Visibility" is made up of tips and lessons for individuals promoting their own enterprises on the Internet as well as information on blacklisting. "Information" incorporates indexes of resources such as reading lists, conferences, newsgroups, and research groups that users may find helpful. The final portion, "Related Areas," consists of documents dealing with regulations affecting digital marketing as well as the technology that supports it. In addition to these items, people can also connect to other Internet.com locations dealing with current news and upcoming Internet events.

COMMERCIAL PRODUCTS

Computer Select (New York, NY: Ziff Desktop Information)

Computer Select is a database source covering the computer industry and its products. In CD-ROM format, it is updated monthly and is produced by Desktop Information's Computer Library Division. It provides access to approximately 200,000 full text and abstracted articles from over 175 computer and business periodicals. Product specifications, company profiles, and definitions of terms are some of the data included. It aids the user in identifying, evaluating, purchasing, and using hardware, software, and data communications products.

The search software, ZD Scan, searches by keywords, publication type, and product or company name. Boolean searching is available, including wild cards and proximity operators. The database comes in a variety of system formats. Versions in Windows, Macintosh, DOS, and UNIX are all available. The database is also available on-line through Ziff Desktop Information, Ziffnet, and Compuserve Information Services.

COMPUTERS

Amazon Online Bookstore (www.amazon.com)

Books can be ordered on-line through this site. Information on the New York Times Book Review, new books, and selected titles are given. Recommendations of books, interviews of authors, and review postings can also be done electronically at this site.

Datapro Reports and Analysis (Delran, NJ, USA: Datapro Information Services Group) [DIALOG]

Datapro Reports and Analysis provides information on developments and products in computer, communications, and office technology industries.

Data include technology trends, market overviews, company profiles, product reports, new product announcements, user satisfaction ratings, and outlooks.

Datapro Software Directory (Delran, NJ, USA: Datapro Information Services Group) [DIALOG]

This directory contains descriptions of business software for various types of computers. The information is useful to sellers and buyers of business software.

CONSULTANTS

Global Business Network (www.gbn.org)

Global Business Network (GBN) is a web site of a consulting firm, the Global Business Network, for users interested in planning corporate management strategies. The network was created to offer members consulting, scenario developments for business strategies, and learning opportunities on current issues that influence business management. It provides users a network of companies and individuals from sciences, the arts, business, and academia. The members are linked electronically and share ideas through on-line conferences. This web site gives users summaries of the company's services: consulting, scenario reports, news, a book club, and bibliographies by their staff.

Money Hunter (www.moneyhunter.com)

Money Hunter (MH) is a multimedia enterprise, which advises beginning entrepreneurs. Money Hunt provides various links to financial resources that offer strategies that increase capital ventures. In Money Hunt's web site the following resources are available: business plan templates, advice from business experts, and relevant networking possibilities. Direct links are available to various financial programs.

Quicken Financial Network (www.quicken.com)

The makers of the financial program "Quicken" sponsor the Quicken Financial Network. This site contains advice for using their software and managing money and investments. Access to stock prices is included along with ratings and advice for investors.

Select Consulting (www.selectinc.com/index.htm)

This site offers information and solutions in business groups that are systems integration, groupware, network, and Intranet/Internet. Select Consulting, an Official Microsoft Solutions Provider, focuses on understanding business goals in conjunction with a technological direction. Serving a wide array of industries, using a variety of technologies since 1994, it manages projects from the planning phase to the production support phase. This site posts project information to clients and receives performance on individual consultant or team performance 24 hr a day, 7 days a week. It provides information about the CheapDNS, one of the quality deliverables which allow multiple workstations to easily connect over the Internet. The site includes its qualifications and the latest news and information. Also available are the experience section about the solutions in practice, the site mapper to jump page to page independently of the navigation controls, and the employment section for job inquiry.

Total Quality Engineering (www.tqe.com)

Total Quality Engineering consulting company offers Hoshin Planning, Quality Improvement Tools, Quality Information Services, and Case Study Challenges to improve business competitiveness. The Hoshin is a system of forms and rules that encourage employees to analyze situations, create plans for improvement, conduct performance checks, and take appropriate actions. It was developed in Japan to communicate company policy to people in the organization. The Quality Improvement Tools educate people about the tools required to do their jobs. The company offers on-site training and self-study guides to help individuals to understand how to manage processes, resolve "out-of-control" conditions, and take steps toward constant improvement. The Quality Support Services is a total quality engineering (TQE) program that conducts both customer and supplier satisfaction surveys. Then TQE analyzes and helps one to understand the key issues that impact one's customers' satisfaction. The Quality Case Study is a program by which an individual improves decision-making skills. Total quality engineering also offers User Surveys for comments for improvement and Quality Links for fast access to related web sites.

WEFA Group Europe (www.wefa.de)

The WEFA staff is composed of economists who have language and cultural skills that keep contact of the world's economies from different states in the United States and in other countries. WEFA provides clients with independent and objective consultation where the world's economies are, where they are likely to be, and the appropriate courses of action for the businesses.

Organizational Performance Dimensions (www.opd.net)

The Organizational Performance Dimensions (OPD) web site offers human resources consulting. Although OPD services various aspects of consulting it specializes in employee selection, career management, management training, and organizational development. OPD offers assessment products and software in management development, career counseling, and employee assistance programs. OPD also offers the ability for companies to add assessment products to their assessment centers, educational resource centers, and employee assistance programs. Direct links are available to OPD services.

CONSUMERS

Bizweb (www.bizweb.com)

Bizweb is a conglomeration of resources for product, business, and consumer information. There is a site for company data which are grouped according to the goods and services which they provide. Examples within the service category include business management, opportunity, import export, law, and employment. There are additional categories such as computers, consulting, and finance, and over 100 other everyday consumer products.

The second site involves connection to the top 5% of all web sites by Lycos homepage. Access to this site gives top news, city guides, a people finder, an internet version of yellow pages, and much more.

Thirdly, there is a link to the Inc. On-line web site provided for new and upcoming companies with access to new business information, resources, tools and technology, and a network with other entrepreneurs.

Cybercop (www.ucan.org)

The Cybercop Precinct House is provided by the Utility Consumers' Action Network (UCAN) to monitor on-line consumer scams and abuses on the internet. This organization investigates reports of activities such as fraud, deceptive advertising, pyramid schemes, defamation, and service and pricing abuses. The page states that the Utility Consumers' Action Network has no authority to enforce laws, but they can direct people with complaints to the appropriate government or law enforcement agency. A form is provided along with an address and telephone number for reporting complaints. Users can provide their names or remain anonymous when submitting these letters. The section titled "Holding Cell" provides a list of sites for which complaints have been received as well as a description of the accusation and what action has been taken. Another section called "Arraignment Court" includes updates on court cases, legislation, or political action concerning the Internet, such as the *Cyber Promotions v. America Online* decision. Users can find tips and advice for avoiding on-line scams in the section labeled "Neighborhood Watch." "Community Affairs" contains a list of connections to various government and consumer agencies, such as the Internet Advocacy Center and the Privacy Rights Clearinghouse. Another section titled "Complaint Archives and Success Stories" provides a record of the complaints received by the organization, the action taken, and the outcome of the situation. In addition, it includes descriptions of some of the most unusual accusations received through Cybercop.

Product ReviewNet (www.yahoo.com/ Business_and_Economy/Consumer_Economy)

Product ReviewNet is a web site composed of thousands of product review abstracts. A search engine is provided for information of the product specified. An additional search engine is provided for comparisons of products specified. Further links are available for advertisements, a press release, and a "frequently asked questions" list. Information is provided for those interested in writing reviews for the web site. Direct links are available to other product information resources, including System Optimization.

CORPORATIONS

Corporate Affiliations (New Providence, NJ, U.S.A.: National Register Publishing Company) [DIALOG]

Corporate affiliations provide company business profiles as well as corporate linkages. They include addresses, business descriptions, executive names, staff, sales, production, net worth, total assets, and liabilities.

Corporate VAT Management (www.corporatevat.com)

At this site one can learn about the VAT, a corporate European value-added tax. A comparison between business and tourist VAT refunds is available to the user. A list of frequently asked questions complete with answers about VAT is included. The user can also obtain a description of Auto VAT, a software system that manages VAT expenses and the application process for VAT refunds. A section aimed at travel agents is at this page, claiming that they can increase their revenue by promoting VAT refund services to corporate clients. Another section of this page the user can explore is one on VAT refunds to businesses.

CREDIT

Standard and Poor's Credit Week (www.standardandpoors.com)

This site provides news and stock analyses for people interested in commercial paper, preferred stock, and bonds. Credit Week provides credit tables, calendars, and updated ratings.

DEBTS

The Public Debt (www.publicdebt.treas.gov/opd/opd.htm)

The web site is provided by the Department of Treasury, Bureau of the Public Debt. For each calendar day, this on-line resource reports the debt of the United States. Because of frequent updates, users can observe the dynamics of the growing liability. In addition to daily reports, the site offers monthly and yearly accounts of the subject. Pages of summaries are available for downloading the data in several formats. The site also presents historical information concerning the public debt and a list of frequently asked questions. A link to The Monthly Treasury Statement (MTS) of Receipts and Outlays of the U.S. Government provides information about the government's budget and financial operations.

DEMOGRAPHICS

Advertising Demographics (www.demographics.com/Publications/AD/index.htm)

The *American Demographics Magazine* is a publication of Dow Jones & Company, Inc. The site contains table of contents of issues from 1995 to date. A search engine is provided to find the desired articles and publications from January 1993 to the current issue.

D&B—Donnelley Demographics (Stanford, CT, U.S.A.: Donnelley Marketing Services) [DIALOG]

Dun and Bradstreet Demographics enables access to information from U.S. Census and projections by Donnelley Marketing Services. The data are composed of census information for all U.S. states, counties, towns or cities, and zip code areas. Projection data cover age, sex, race, industry, occupation, marital status, families, households, education, housing, and income.

DIRECTORIES

Galaxy's EINET Reference (www.einet.net/galaxy.html)

This site provides a web search, a directory for professionals, and a directory for links, including many areas such as business and finance and government.

DIVIDENDS

Standard and Poor's Dividend Record (www.standardandpoors.com)

Dividend Record covers thousands of stocks and bonds. It also carries announcements of dates with lists of redemptions and tenders, split actions, and rights.

ECONOMIC ASSISTANCE

Classic Art, Business Volume 1.0 (G&G Designs/ Communications, Multimedia Graphic Network)

Classic Art contains a library of business-related images that can be reproduced without limit. Each image contains three file formats: 8-bit grayscale TIFF, 24-bit color PICT, and 24-bit color TIFF. Designs can be customized by altering the elements, backgrounds, and styles. A try-out version of Adobe Photoshop is included.

Economic Bulletin Board

The Economic Bulletin Board (EBB) is an on-line database produced by the U.S. Department of Commerce. It includes data not only from the Bureau of Labor Statistics, and the Census Bureau, but also from the Federal Reserve Board, and a variety of other federal agencies as well.

Free on-line access to the EBB is very restricted. Callers are limited to 20 minutes at a time, and they may access only news bulletins and a limited selection of files. Guests are also limited in the types of files they may download over the Internet. For full access to the EBB from the Commerce Department, a yearly fee is required.

However, the University of Michigan has downloaded a variety of files from the EBB and has made these available on the ULibrary gopher.

The ULibrary EBB files can be accessed by making the following choices from the top level of the ULibrary gopher:

\Social Science Resources
\Economics
\Economic Bulletin Board (UMICH)

Some of the larger files are also available to users with DOS machines for anonymous ftp.

The Economic Bulletin Board information on the ULibrary gopher includes files organized into 32 different gopher menu items. The menu items are subjects or topics, and they are arranged alphabetically. Each menu item has at least one submenu, which is also arranged alphabetically.

Some of the subjects covered include economic indicators, U.S. Treasury auction results, employment statistics, prices, foreign trade statistics, and leads for foreign trade. In fact, material is included in this database that one would have to go to several reference books and periodicals to find.

For example, the *U.S. Industrial Handbook* is included in its entirety. Not only is it arranged by chapter, but it is searchable, using Veronica, by keyword. U.S. Treasury auction results are available on-line, without going to the *Federal Reserve Bulletin*.

A listing of the data files, arranged alphabetically according to the federal agency supplying the data, is provided in a document entitled "Types of Information on the Bulletin Board." That document, produced by the Commerce Department, not the University of Michigan, can be found under the first item on the ULibrary EBB gopher menu, which is called "IMPOR-TANT!! READ ME FIRST!!" It was impossible to determine whether every file listed in this document had been downloaded by the University of Michigan. However, this document was the closest thing to an index that could be found on the Gopher.

Some of the material is very current. The database is updated daily, if possible. At 2:00 P.M., the daily foreign exchange rates for 10 A.M. that morning had already been posted. The Commerce Department's weekly trade leads for the two previous weeks were also on-line.

Anyone looking for a free, fast, mostly current source of government business and economic statistics would be wise to look first at the University of Michigan Economic Bulletin Board.

I.   Economic Conversion Information Exchange Gopher

    A.   Search the Economic Conversion Information Exchange—
        The entire contents of the gopher can be searched using a free text search engine.

    B.   General Information and Background

    1.   *Bibliography*—This is an extensive list of publications and information resources related to military conversion. Included are:

        a. Articles and books published by the Economic Development Administration

        b. Journal articles and books about economic conversion

        c. Lists of organizations interested in economic conversion

        d. A list of articles on economic conversion for reasons of military cutbacks

        e. The bibliography for the NLC report (this acronym is not explained)

    2.   *Bulletins and Calendar of Events*

        a. Bulletins

        b. Calendar of Upcoming Events—This menu lists conferences dedicated to military base closings, upcoming events, recent base closings, and announcements of upcoming conferences with information on how to register for them.

    3.   *Press Releases, Speeches, and Testimony*

        a. Press Releases—Press statements by the Department of Defense related to base closings. These include standard press release information such as contact names, addresses, phone numbers, along with the text of the press release.

        b. Speeches—Statements and speeches by U.S. government officials on subjects related to military base closings and their effects.

        c. Testimony

C. Cooperative Programs for Reinvestment—Links to another gopher server, this one at the Department of Defense. Contains, among other items, information on locating resources to aid in conversion of military bases.

D. Adjustment Programs and Laws

    1.   *Federal and Other Public Programs*—Contains lists of grants available to military personnel and private citizens to help with defense conversion as well as other grants for various purposes (including Perkins Loans and Work Study).

2. *Laws and Policies*—The full text of federal laws and policies (including the Clean Air Act, Superfund Legislation, and the Defense Base Closure & Realignment Act of 1990) effecting military base closings.
3. *Major Federal Conversion Programs in Detail*—A list of government-sponsored and -managed conversion programs of the Departments of Commerce, Defense and Labor, and the Small Business Administration.
4. *Nongovernmental Programs*
5. *State and Local Programs*—A lengthy list of state and local programs.

E. Economic and Defense Data

1. *Defense Impact Data*—This menu is a catch-all for information from the Department of Defense budget to grant offerings from various state agencies.
2. *Economic Data*, which in turn leads to *Regional Data*— This is broken down by region except for Alaska and Hawaii, which are listed separately. Data given are general economic information—personal income by state, employment by industry, etc.

F. Information Sources

1. *Defense Assets*—A few information resources about the purchase and use of Department of Defense property by civilian groups.
2. *Experiences*—Case studies and histories of base closings
3. *Tools*—Text files describing experiences and means of obtaining defense department assets after base closings.

G. Who to Contact—A list of names and offices to contact regarding base closings in general and for specific bases.

II. Reis—This leads to a word-processing file that the gopher cannot open but which must be downloaded, decompressed, and then read with the appropriate word processor.

Economic Literature Index (American Economic Association) [DIALOG]

This CD-ROM contains references and abstracts from economic journals, monographs, and annuals, covering such fields as trade, microeconomics, developmental economics, labor economics, markets, business, and production.

ECONOMIC FORECASTING

Electronic Commerce (techunix.technion.ac.il/~orena/ec)

Developed in 1996 as part of a course project by students at the Israel Institute of Technology, Electronic Commerce provides a critical examination of the World Wide Web as a distribution channel and a medium for marketing communication. Topics highlighted in the general overview include an introduction to electronic commerce, its application in the world of business, requirements for use, and its benefits and advantages as well as disadvantages.

ECONOMIC INDICATORS

Economic Conversion Information Exchange Gopher

The Economic Conversion Information Exchange Gopher (URL gopher:// ecix.doc.gov/) is a compendium of information related to the closing of U.S. military bases. The information provided through this gopher is targeted at both individual entrepreneurs looking for business opportunities and municipalities faced with the shutdown of military installations in their area.

The contents of the gopher are quite informative and helpful overall. Two areas stand out as being better than the rest. First is the bibliographic section of the gopher, within the General Information and Background menu, which lists articles, books, and organizations dealing with the closing of military installations. The list of journal articles and books (more than 725 citations) is particularly useful. The second area is the list of laws and policies effecting both communities and the military within the context of a base closing. This list, located under the Adjustment Programs and Laws menu, includes complete copies of the Environmental Protection Agency's Superfund legislation, the Clean Air Act, and the Defense Base Closure and Realignment Act of 1990 (the Act of Congress which allowed these bases to be closed and transferred to private hands).

Although it is likely that the contents of the gopher will change with time, the following summation of contents should provide the reader with an overview of what is available.

Business Cycle Database (The Foundation for International Business Cycle Research or FIBCR)

This source uses leading economic indicators to monitor industrial economies in the United States and 10 other countries and is designed to assist in investment and spending decisions. Fifty-two proprietary leading indexes, 15 for the U.S. and 37 for other industrial countries, are utilized. The indexes, which are composed of over 500 economic series, are designed to signal major changes in inflation, the economy, and financial markets. Coverage begins in 1948 for the United States and in the 1950s for other countries. The database is updated monthly and is available on diskette in ASCII or Lotus Format.

EconLit on Disc

EconLit on Disc is published by the American Economic Association. The CD-ROM has an international scope and is mainly for people interested in economics. The world's literature regarding the field of economics is indexed and abstracted on the EconLit CD-ROM. Information in the form of journal abstracts, article citations, and dissertation titles is found on the disc. Abstracts date from 1987 and citations from 1969 through the present are provided. In addition, data regarding economic work in progress are available on EconLit via the Cambridge University Press Abstracts of Working Papers in Economics.

Economic Indicators (Ann Arbor: Documents Librarian, University of Michigan Graduate Library)

The Economic Indicators (EI) on-line database is accessible on the Internet (URL: gopher://una.hh.lib.umich.edu/11/ebb/indicators). It consists of a subset of information found on the Economic Bulletin Board (EBB) of the U.S. Department of Commerce, selected, downloaded, and made available under the auspices of the Documents Librarian of the University of Michigan Graduate Library (UM Library). Its domain is U.S. economic conditions.

EI contains news releases, government reports, and information on how to purchase data, methodological notes, and like products from the Department of Commerce's Bureau of Economic Analysis (BEA). Data from the Bureau of the Census and the Bureau of Labor Statistics supplement that of the BEA.

The database provides over 80 documents or files in an alphanumerical list. EI also includes three folders or directories: BCI (Business Cycle Indicators) Current Data, BCI Historical Data, and Census Construction Review Tables. A few files are notes provided by the UM Library regarding the downloading of EI files (e.g., about DOS compressed files), BEA memos of data revision or notes on the generation of the data, or notices of services offered by BEA. The majority present economic indicators ranging from Advance Retail Sales, to Frozen Fish Products, to Personal Income and Outlay. A Summary Test File for Economic Indicators is also available. Most documents feature a summary statement followed by statistical tables. These tables present current data and often compare them to the previous month and/or the same month in the previous year (e.g., Advance Retail Sales); some are also arranged by geographic region or other pertinent dimensions (e.g., Housing Starts and Building Permits). Files may be downloaded using anonymous ftp or browsed on screen.

EI does not provide an overall index, although the titles of its documents are generally indicative of their contents. There are indexes to the BCI data organized by number and by topic (e.g., "Listing all BCI series, by number," and "...by topic") that refer the user to BEA diskettes and the pages of the Survey of Current Business.

Materials in EI are updated soon after the Department of Commerce releases it onto the EBB; this ranges from daily to annually, depending on the data set. Most data in EI can be found in a depository library on paper copy or purchased from the BEA in diskette format.

White House Economic Statistics Briefing Room (www.whitehouse.gov/fsbr/esbr.html)

The White House Economic Statistics Briefing Room (ESBR) summarizes the percentage of change for the last two quarters for the economic indicators: gross domestic product, fixed investments, residential investments, personal savings rate, corporate profits, personal consumption expenditures, total U.S. expenditures for research and development, and federal obligations for research and development. The purpose of this site is to provide access to current federal economic indicators. It provides links to information produced by a number of federal agencies. The information included in the Economic Statistics Briefing Room is maintained and updated by the statistical unit of those agencies, which include, but are not limited, to the Federal Reserve Board, the Bureau of Transportation Statistics, the U.S. Bureau of Economic Analysis, and the U.S. Bureau of Census.

The eight hot linked buttons on each page of the site provide information on employment and unemployment, income, international statistics, money, prices, production, and transportation. Information is also cross-referenced in the front page table of contents by output, income, and earnings, business activity, credit, and securities markets. A comparative overview of the incomes of various sectors from personal income, per capita income, farm income, poverty, household wealth can be obtained by selecting "Income." Users who need sector information on the airline industry, for example, will find detailed information on revenue passenger miles, domestic available seat miles, operating revenue, and income for the quarter just completed. The "Money" section provides selected interest rates on 1-, 3-, and 6-month Certificates of Deposit. "International" provides several charts which reveal expenditures over the past two years up to the last quarter on the balance of trade, research and development expenditures of selected countries, and net oil imports. Sources of information are cited directly beneath each chart.

ECONOMIC POLICY

National Economic, Social, and Environmental Database (www.stat-usa.gov)

The Department of Commerce is the federal agency responsible for encouraging the growth and development of commercial ventures in the United States. The agency produces the National Economic, Social, and Environmental Data Bank (NESE) to disseminate information on key domestic topics, such as major economic indicators, education, public health, and natural resources. The NESE web site was a free, public-access resource until 1995, when it was discontinued as a separate site. NESE is currently found on STAT-USA, the Department of Commerce's fee-based information service.

The NESE Data Bank is a compilation of full-text documents, spreadsheets, tables, diagrams, and time series issued by government agencies. Examples of the information available include the following: the economic report of the President, fiscal budget of the United States, crime statistics, highway and transportation statistics, and the digest of education statistics. The Data Bank is searchable: one may browse available files by subject, program name, word in the title, issuing agency, or item number. The site is also searchable by keyword and Boolean operators may be used to narrow or broaden searches as desired.

The STAT-USA main page contains descriptive information about its capabilities, including links that allow one to "test drive" a subset of the available databases and to become a subscriber. Links to the Department of Commerce and specific agencies within the department are included. The general contact address for this web site is stat-usa@doc.gov.

ECONOMICS

The American Economic Associations Information Bibliography of Economic Literature (www.econlit.org)

The American Economic Association (AEA) Bibliography of Economic Literature offers information on economics. AEA's Economic Literature and Bibliography information can be accessed through their electronic database. This bibliographic database includes journal articles, books, dissertations, and book reviews. EconLit's economic topics include the following: Public Finance, Economic History, Regional Economics, Econometrics, Financial Institution, Labor Economics, Economic Development, Land and Economics, and various other economic topics. Direct links are available to all of this literature. AEA's Economic Literature and Bibliography can be obtained via the Internet or CD-ROM.

Bargain Finder Agent (www.yahoo.com/ Business_and_Economy/Electronic_Commerce/ or bf.cstar.ac.com/bf)

Bargain Finder Agent is a research project of Andersen Consulting's Center for Strategic Technology Research. Begun in 1995, Bargain Finder Agent looks for the nine lowest priced CD/albums from contributing stores on the web of the user's choice. Users enter the artist and title of the musical work they are seeking and the Bargain Finder Agent goes to work, listing the places where they have checked, and for those stores where the CD is contained, list the prices as well. Another option on the Bargain Finder Agent's home page is for an additional Andersen Consulting research experiment, the Lifestyle-Finder Intelligent Agent featuring "Waldo the Web Wizard" who creates a list of web pages in which users would be interested based on questions they answer surrounding their choice in music, neighborhood, and type of vehicle.

BioCommerce Abstracts and Directory (Slough, UK: BioCommerce Data) [DIALOG]

BioCommerce Abstracts and Directory contains indexes and abstracts of the business features of biotechnology and the possible commercial use of biological sciences. The database provides current abstracts and information on organizations by using them as indexing terms. Profiles of the companies in the database are provided as well.

Bloomberg Personal (www.bloomberg.com)

Bloomberg distributes information services, including financial news, market data, and analyses for financial markets and businesses. The company has built a worldwide customer base of issuers, financial intermediaries, and institutional investors.

The Bloomberg Online web site provides individual investors with news, data, and analyses. It also provides additional information on the subjects covered by the Bloomberg Personal television program, designed for knowledgeable investors.

The web site provides free access to information about world markets including the most active U.S. stocks, top U.S. mutual funds, U.S. and world equity indices, U.S. Treasury and international yield curves, municipal bond yields, active futures contracts, and foreign exchange rates. Bloomberg supports financial analyses with links to major corporations and banks, international business sites, major stock exchanges, currency exchanges, money, and credit markets. Access is provided to Hoover's Company Directory, a database which provides extensive financial information about the larger public and private companies in the United States. International financial news summaries, energy-related news, and publications are available. The site also supports such items as a college-cost calculator, a mortgage calculator, and the Web Investor Dictionary. Additional services, including proprietary Bloomberg data, are available by subscription.

Dr. Edward Yardeni's Economic Network (www.yardeni.com)

Dr. Yardeni's web page offers economic information from all over the world. Dr. Yardeni offers information through the use of financial literature. Some of the charts that he offers are the Commercial Bank, Fiscal Policy, Flow of Funds, and Money Supply. Other books range from topical studies to Federalist Papers from Publius. Some of his other services are as follows: On-line Chat Rooms Economic Indicators, Weekly Economic Analysis, and Weekly Economic Briefing. Instant information can be obtained on weekly and daily markets from the United States, industrial, and emerging countries. Within the Markets link, there is a series of services which include Stocks, Interest Rates, Foreign Exchange Rates, and Commodities. Direct links are available to all of Yardeni's services, The Federal Reserve, and Central Banks.

EconLit on OCLC

EconLit provides extensive coverage of economic research throughout the world. This database is available in OCLC and is primarily intended for people interested in economics.

Literature regarding the field of economics is indexed and abstracted in EconLit. Information in the form of journal abstracts, article citations, and dissertation titles is found in the database. Abstracts date from 1987 forward, and citations from 1969 through the present are provided. In addition, data regarding economic work in progress are available on EconLit via the Cambridge University Press Abstracts of Working Papers in Economics.

Economics Laboratory Software Archive (emlab.berkeley.edu/eml)

EML is a unit of the Institute of Business and Economic Research provided by the Department of Economics, at the University of California, Berkeley. The Laboratory emphasizes new developments in the field of computationally intensive econometrics. It is dedicated to graduate students and faculty teaching and research in the Department of Economics at the university.

The Economics/Markets/Investments Index (www.mlinet.com/mle/searchl.htm)

The Economics/Markets and Investment Index provides an index of services of interest to financial researchers, investors, and other members of the financial community. Services are offered from Market Investment and Economic Topics. Direct links are available to any of these topics. Under the Market/Investment link there is a list of topics of interest which include Bonds, Stocks, Commodities, Mutual Fund, and Currencies. The Economic Topic offers general information on Industry, Agriculture, Government, Business, and Consumer. Economic Indicators on Economic topics offer the service of monitoring investments.

Economist Intelligence Unit: Business International (New York: The Economist Intelligence Unit) [DIALOG]

Economist Intelligence Unit (EIU) Business International contains business information on various countries. The subjects covered include economic conditions, market analyses, corporate strategies, foreign exchange regulations, trade regulations, sources of revenue, and equity markets. The database also covers international business with emphasis on Euromarkets, aid finance, acquisitions and alliances, and foreign subsidiaries.

Far Eastern Economic Review (www.feer.com)

The web site contains key stories from the monthly publication *Far Eastern Economic Review*. Live market information from Dow Jones Telerate is shown. On-line search and archive facilities are provided. Access to the above information and data is free.

Internet Newsgroup: sci.econ.research

The Internet Newsgroup sci.econ.research is a newsgroup for discussion of economic issues. General topics include economic theory, mathematical modeling of economic processes, software of interest to economists, meeting and conference announcements, academic job postings, and questions about reference sources. Topics of recent discussion have included the economic impacts of drug legalization, the economic impact of crime, catastrophic insurance futures, the economic influence of Sunday shopping laws, and admission standards (grade point average and Graduate Record Exam scores) of Ph.D. programs in economics. This group is moderated and discussion tends to be intellectual and scholarly.

National Economic, Social, and Environmental Database (www.stat-usa.gov)

The Department of Commerce is the federal agency responsible for encouraging the growth and development of commercial ventures in the United States. The agency produces the National Economic, Social, and Environmental Data Bank (NESE) to disseminate information on key domestic topics, such as major economic indicators, education, public health, and natural resources. The NESE web site was a free, public-access resource until 1995, when it was discontinued as a separate site. NESE is currently found on STAT-USA, the Department of Commerce's fee-based information service.

The NESE Data Bank is a compilation of over 65,000 full-text documents, spreadsheets, tables, diagrams, and time series issued by 19 government agencies. Examples of the information available include the following: the economic report of the President, fiscal budget of the United States, crime statistics, highway and transportation statistics, and the digest of education statistics. The Data Bank is searchable: one may browse available files by subject, program name, word in the title, issuing agency, or item number. The site is also searchable by keyword and Boolean operators may be used to narrow or broaden searches as desired.

The STAT-USA main page contains descriptive information about its capabilities, including links that allow one to "test drive" a subset of the available databases and to become a subscriber. Links to the Department of Commerce and specific agencies within the department are included. The general contact address for this web site is stat-usa@doc.gov.

National Trade Data Base (Washington, DC: United States Department of Commerce)

This CD-ROM source of the National Trade Data Base (NTDB) covers international trade statistics between the United States and other countries. The database contains government-sponsored market research by country and product. It also includes exchange rates, international interest rates, names and addresses of importers in foreign countries, stock price indexes, export regulations, and other related data. Years covered vary. Trade data cover 1983 to the present and exchange rates cover 1960 to the present. Most statistics are updated annually, although some figures are updated monthly.

National Bureau of Economic Research (www.nber.org)

The National Bureau of Economic Research (NBER) is a private, nonprofit, nonpartisan research organization dedicated to promoting understanding of how the economy works. In keeping with its mission, the organization maintains a free, public-access, English-language web site for the dissemination of its economic information.

Among the resources available at the NBER site are searchable databases of NBER Working Papers, NBER books, and the organization's membership. Search is by keyword, with the ability to narrow results by month, year, and number of matches. Search results may be displayed by relevance or by reverse chronology.

In addition to the searchable databases, the NBER site contains economic data of interest to economic professionals, broken down into four categories: macro, industry, individual, and other data. Files are accessed by selecting highlighted links. Examples of the data available are "Imports and Exports by SIC Category 1958–1992" and "Consumer Expenditure Survey Extracts."

Descriptive links are also available on the NBER web site. One can access informational pages regarding the history/mission of the bureau, major programs and projects, funding, publications, and staff.

PTS U.S. Time Series (Foster City, CA: Information Access Company) [DIALOG]

PTS U.S. Time series is a source of statistical data on population, GNP, per capita income, employment, construction, production, materials, and prices. The information is collected from various publications which report on industries and products.

STAT-USA (www.stat-usa.gov)

STAT-USA is an on-line information service provided by the U.S. Department of Commerce. It was established by the Economics and Statistics Administration with the enactment of the Departments of Commerce, Justice, and State, the Judiciary, and Related Agencies Appropriations Act of 1995. STAT-USA is mandated to be self-supporting through the sale of documents using electronic technologies.

STAT-USA is a source for government-sponsored business, economic, and trade information databases. STAT-USA databases comprise the National Trade Data Bank (NTDB), Economic Bulletin Board (EBB), Global Business Procurement Opportunities (GLOBUS), and the Bureau of Economic Analysis Economic Information (BEA).

Content provided on the NTDB includes International Market Research, Export Opportunities; Indices of foreign and domestic companies; How-to market guides; Reports on demographic, political, and socioeconomic conditions for hundreds of companies. The EBB provides government-sponsored economic releases and business leads minutes after they are released, plus in-depth analyses of markets, products, and economic trends. GLOBUS provides a wide range of procurement opportunities for U.S. business from all over the world. The BEA provides new releases and detailed data files from their national, regional, and international economic accounts including income and product accounts. Information is posted 30 min from the receipt from the originating agency, and subscription orders and technical assistance are provided within four business hours.

EMPLOYEE BENEFITS

Employee Benefits Infosource (Brookfield, WI: International Foundation of Employee Benefit Plans) [DIALOG]

Employee Benefits Infosource has information on employee benefit plans in the United States and Canada The subjects covered are benefits, stock options plans, stock ownership plans, insurance, investment of benefit assets, labor relations, pension plans, profit sharing plans, retirement benefits, and social security.

The National Center for Employee Ownership (www.nceo.org)

The National Center for Employee Ownership web site contains information on employee stock ownership plans, employee stock options, and other forms of employee ownership. The site contains an overview and examples of ownership of businesses by its employees. One section contains excerpts from publications of the topic, and the library section contains large amounts of information on stocks and employee ownership. The "Columns" section contains news and opinions on employee ownership. Information on workshops, events, and training sessions is available. The site includes an on-line forum for discussion and links to useful Internet resources.

EMPLOYMENT

America's Employers (www.americasemployers.com)

America's Employers was developed by professional career consultants and was formed after the outplacement and job-finding assistance programs in which they have supplied to many *Fortune 500* companies. Their resources can be used to expand, organize, and improve one's job search whether they are considering another career or unemployed.

Candidates are Human Beings by Glen Mendelkern (www.careermag.com) David Fenton

The work offers insight on three vital views of the hiring process for prosperous professionals. Parts one, two, and three of the essay provide discussions of the communication, intimidation, and rejection involved when job searching. There has been shown to be communication avoidance and relationship barrier between employer and employee that is discussed. Also, an exploration of intimidation throughout the workplaces is elaborated upon. Lastly, rejection is touched upon, as there is advice on how to deal with and likewise deliver the "bad news." As an extra incentive there are also many tips and advice with helpful tactful suggestions, meant to further an employee's success.

Career City (www.careercity.com)

Career City has many posted job opportunities offered by different companies in various fields. It also includes a résumé database and other information for prospective job seekers. In addition to the career opportunities available through this Internet web site, there is an advice section which offers helpful advice for job seekers. Finally, Career City includes a links page with links to a virtual job interview, a job bank, and a job quiz. The job quiz offers an idea if seeking another job is right for the particular person.

Career Builder (www.careerbuilder.com)

Career Builder is for people looking for jobs. A database of prospective employers can be accessed through the Job Search option. The "Personal Search Agent" helps in the search for suitable employment by narrowing the list according to the preferences of the user. Résumés can be sent through the Internet by using the Instant Résumé feature.

Career Internetworking (www.careerkey.com)

Career Internetworking's web site is an on-line resource for users seeking employment opportunities and information in Canada. The "What's New" section provides new job postings within the last 2 weeks. Users can find information such as company profiles, positions available, salary range, and duties and responsibilities. The site contains a search engine of their database, and users may browse for jobs by position, category, location, or by company. On-line assistance is available for résumé writing and relocation resources. The site provides links to groups and support services important to career growth and success. The site also provides job search tips and articles.

Career Magazine (www.careermag.com)

Career Magazine is the on-line version of the employment publication by the same name. Included within is a database of prospective employers and an on-line résumé function for sending résumés to companies over the Internet. This site also contains many tips about how to look for jobs and how to conduct an interview. A question-and-answer section provides solutions to many problems faced by people looking for employment.

CareerMart (www.careermart.com)

At this site one can look through job listings; perform a job search by choice of company, location, job listings, and region; learn about employers; and view company home pages. CareerMart allows résumés to be posted so employees can view and find qualified applicants. A search can be done for information pertaining to colleges: campus interviews, job fairs, college events and college publications, and companies of interest. CareerMart offers ADvice, which contains information about conventions, market research, and recruitment specials. Virtual Conference Center allows seekers to participate in on-line interviews, a job fair, or talk with industry professionals and industry employers.

CareerMart's web site allows users to browse job listings, learn about employers, view company homepages, and perform job searches. Users may post résumés in the "Résumé Tent" to be viewed by employers seeking to hire. The "Newsstand" provides magazines and article covering various topics, all searchable by category. Users may browse the "College Info Center" to do a search of colleges and find details about campus interviews, job fairs, and events. CareerMart provides on-line advice for job information, recruitment, conventions, and market research. Users looking for information on employers may browse the "Companies" section for specific details.

Career Networking Group (www.careerevents.com)

Career Networking Group's web site provides users with information and resources for locating career opportunities. The site provides information on upcoming job fairs and helpful tips on finding and meeting employers. Companies interested in participating in job fairs may fill out a form on the site. Career Networking Group provides a career center with information on job hunting, résumé writing, and tips on how to make a job fair a successful opportunity to attract employers.

Career Resources Homepage (www.rpi.edu/dept/cdc/homepage.html)

Career Resources Homepage is a web site containing career-related resources. The site contains many portions covering career opportunities and information. The job search provides various commercial job databases on the Internet. The "Employer's Direct" section is composed of job databases and information servers maintained by various employers. Databases of various professional organizations, research institutions, and governmental agencies are provided. The "Career Services at Various Universities" section provides career placement and educational services offered by universities around the world. Links are provided to job resource indexes and Usenet newsgroups related to job information.

Careers (careers.wsj.com)

At this web page, articles on how to be unique, how to "sell" yourself, the importance of internships, and how to look for a job are available. A directory, to aid in the process of finding a job, is accessible. Just pick a company, industry, job function, and location, and a list of job openings will appear. Another feature of this page is by entering your name and e-mail address, you will receive notification of new employers and features on careers directly to you. A question-and-answer section about the process of looking for a job and on managing a career can be found by the user. One can find out the average salary your prospective job will pay. A list of salaries and profiles is available. Also at this site is a section for college graduates where they can get advice and counseling about their career.

CareerPath.com Job Listings (careerpath.com)

Accessible for job seekers and employers, CareerPath.com is a career-management site on the World Wide Web. They inform job seekers with information on current jobs available. They provide the opportunity to save a job search in which CareerPath.com will store the information. Help Wanted Ads and web sites are the two sources from which their listings come. Their listings do not remain in their database beyond 2 weeks. Also, one can create a résumé on-line that joins extensive database job seekers. The database is searched by employers. CareerPath.com also contains Employer Profiles, which is a full-page description of leading companies with connection to their corporate home pages and all the employer's job listings that are currently listed in the newspaper advertising database. Other information about important employment trends and getting a job is also available.

CareerSource Magazine (www.netusa.com/Empinfo/main.html)

CareerSource Magazine is an on-line publication covering employment opportunities and career training. The site is composed of four sections: Professional Careers, General Employment, Career Advice, and Career Training and Services. Information is provided on different companies looking to hire, which includes an overview, positions available, and where to send a résumé. The "Career Advice" section provides articles and links to solutions to common problems and situations.

CareerWEB (careerweb.com)

CareerWEB is an extensive web site composed of resources and information for employees to find jobs and employers to hire applicants. The site offers a keyword search to help locate several jobs in many fields of interest, such as accounting, education, engineering, law, and retail. Users may search for jobs by state or by city. Users may research all the employers on the site from the "Employer's Page" section. Employers may search all the posted résumés and advertise their companies on the site. Employees may file their résumés on the site for employers to search or be notified of opportunities that match their résumés in the "Job Match" section. The site offers a bookstore full of information on career employment, and helpful articles are available in the "Career Doctor" section. Links to other career resources are offered such as books, videos, and software. The "Career Inventory" section allows users to fill out a survey, have it evaluated, and receive feedback and suggestions on the job search process.

CJA-The Alder Group (www.cja-careers.com)

CJA-The Alder Group web site offers advice and information to help both employers and employees make decisions in filling jobs. The site offers suggestions for employees to help find careers. The "Hot Jobs" section provides information and job opportunities in some of the most successful fields today. Users may post, edit, or search résumés in the "Job Center" section. Employers can order hiring toolkits and software for training on the site. The site contains hiring and interviewing tips as well as other hints and information on the hiring process.

E-Span (www.espan.com)

E-Span is an on-line nationwide employment resource for employers and job seekers. It provides job announcements.

Employment Opportunities and Résumé Postings (galaxy.einet.net/GJ/employment.html)

Employment Opportunities and Résumé Postings is a service on the Internet accessible via Mosaic using the URL address listed above. The service's main menu provides access to different databases, each listing academic positions posted by various universities in the United States, or general positions posted by various corporations, universities, federal programs, and job-search services.

Each database affords its own menu, further separating searches by type of position desired, type of work involved, or various fields of interest. Some of the headings afford résumé postings of job seekers and include the Internet address where to forward a résumé for posting. Advertisements for both national and international job openings are prevalent and include Internet addresses and the names of contact persons to whom applicants should send résumés. The predominant listings are for academic institutions and cover administrative, faculty, executive, and research positions. Most of the postings are updated weekly.

Other services accessible through the index include Federal literature on the Job Market, and Events and Assistance, such as workshops, offered through those Career Centers on-line.

Employment Opportunities is also searchable by keyword. Using Boolean connectors, the user can search the databases for any references to the terms entered. Any postings currently on-line that correspond to the search will be listed.

1st Steps in the Hunt (www.interbiznet.com/hunt)

This site contains a database of potential employers for people looking for jobs. Many companies are listed within this database and the on-line résumé system allows the user to contact potential employers using the Internet. Another feature this site provides is Employment Search Engines that allow the users to search for companies that fit their preferences. Links to other job-seeking sites are also provided.

Head Hunter.Net (www.headhunter.net/index.htm)

Head Hunter.Net is an on-line recruiting site on the Internet. They represent listings that are original content added by their users. They constantly clean their database. Therefore, résumés are never more than 90 days old and jobs are never more than 40 days old.

Job Web (www.jobweb.com)

Job Web is a publication for the National Association of Colleges and Employees. It leads an enormous number of students and alumni through their job searches and into career positions at the nation's companies. The Job Web series provides job search guidance, high-quality career planning, and detailed information on career opportunities, which includes employees who are seeking college graduates as well.

Jobs Online (www.ceweekly.wa.com)

Jobs Online is a component of Contract Employment Weekly magazine involving an hourly updated job database. The resource is available for non-subscribers, but subscribers have access to much more, such as a job search tutorial and connection to other related information.

National Business Employment (www.nbew.com)

From the publishers of the Wall Street Journal, The National Business Employment Weekly provides job searches and career advice (for example, how to supervise a business, how to locate and begin a occupation, and information about advertising).

Occupational Outlook Handbook (www.stats.bls.gov/ocohome.htm)

This site is the on-line version of the Occupational Outlook Handbook. This site features articles about the employment market and how to find employment. Labor statistics and projections are provided from the Employment Projections Home Page along with Research Papers dealing with the economy.

Rensselaer Career Resources (www.rpi.edu/dept/cdc)

The mission of the Rensselaer Polytechnic Institute Career Development Center is to be a unit that assists students to take directions and manage their career developments. The Career Development Center promotes self-awareness, skill development, and job search by delivering services for employers, faculty, and students.

Resumania (lycos.com/topics/Careers_overall.html)

As an "interactive workbook," Resumania is attempting to help job applicants in their search for a career. Resumania will not and does not complete the process of writing a résumé for the applicant. It teaches the applicant how to write a résumé. By providing examples and models of résumés, the applicant can get a visual idea of what to do. This process gives the applicant the knowledge of résumé writing, instead of just making it less work for him or her. Resumania is teaching the skills of basic high school knowledge and refining them to make the result look professional and elegant. This is accomplished by completing six steps answering the most frequently asked about résumé writing from interested applicants. Anyone looking to learn the art of résumé writing should take advantage of this site.

Riley Guide (www.dbm.com/jobguide)

The Riley Guide involves information about internships, employment, jobs, and career advice. All materials from The Riley Guide are accessible through the Internet.

Snelling Search (www.snellingsearch.com)

SNELLING SEARCH is a search compartment of SNELLING PERSONNEL SERVICES. They concentrate on the recruitment and positioning of Information Systems. In addition, SNELLING SEARCH donates private support in linking employers and job candidates.

Technical Connections (www.technicalconnections.com)

Technical Connections links professionals to positions. They revise their materials weekly.

The Monster Board (www.monster.com)

The Monster Board is a site that has job listings for those seeking new positions. A job search can be done in the United States or internationally. Other services such as Résumé Builders, Seminars and Products, and Services are available to strengthen the skills of people who are seeking employment.

Walden Personnel Testing and Training Inc. (www.waldentesting.com)

Walden Personnel Testing and Training (WPTT) offers skills testing services. These skills testing materials can serve in hiring practices. It can also serve as an index of who you would prefer working for you. These employee-centered tests can be especially helpful in issues of promotions or restructuring information. The WPTT tests are available in a several languages. Links are available to other WPTT services.

World.Hire (world.hire.com)

World.Hire creations and services are developed by people exceptionally skilled in developing, progressing, and using technology to locate suitable employees and keep them. By providing global access through the World Wide Web and corporate intranets, World.Hide is devoted to inventing tools and services for both companies and candidates. They believe that active and cost-effective tools, which serve to automate recruiting and safekeeping, are integral and necessary for growth and success.

ENERGY

American Petroleum Institute Energy Business News Index (New York: Central Abstracting and Information Services) [DIALOG]

The American Petroleum Institute Energy Business News (APIBIZ) indexes information about the energy industry found in journals, magazines, and newsletters.

APILIT (New York: American Petroleum Institute) [DIALOG]

APILIT includes data on international non-patent publications, petroleum, and related industries. The information is gleaned from journals, government reports, proceedings from meetings, and materials from the American Petroleum Institute. The monographs and journal articles are subject indexed, using topics about the petroleum industry. Since 1981, the database has included information on chemicals connected to the petroleum industry.

APITAT (New York: American Petroleum Institute) [DIALOG]

APITAT is useful in locating patent information about the petroleum industry. Most of the indexing in the database is done using the Central Abstracting and Indexing Service Thesaurus.

ENTERPRISES

Enterprise Reengineering (www.reengineering.com)

This web site is basically a monthly on-line magazine. Enterprise Reengineering focuses its links towards news, trends, trading, and technological breakthroughs. This web site gives information about new technologies in the workplace that are up and coming. There is an option for an advertising and resource center that contributes hot links and information dealing with business.

Foundation for Enterprise Development (www.yahoo.com/Business_and_Economy/Organizations)

Foundation for Enterprise Development (FED) is a web site that helps create enterprises through equity compensation, employee ownership and involvement, and other business strategies. Direct links are available to leading companies, an electronic magazine for high-performance companies; equity solutions, reasons why America's leading companies use stock compensation; a resource library, an index of articles, case studies, and research. A further link is available for job opportunities at the foundation.

Let's Talk Business Network (www.ltbn.com)

Let's Talk Business Network, Inc. (LTBN) is a community of entrepreneurs that are interactive and supports other entrepreneurs. The community was developed so entrepreneurs could earn their desired success and receive various levels of support. LTBN provides motivational training (guidance), technology information, and resources. Let's Talk Business Radio airs audio clips and programs that provide knowledge and advice. The talk show also concentrates on franchising and small businesses.

ETHICS

Institute for Business and Professional Ethics (www.yahoo.com/Business_and_Economy/Organizations)

Institute for Business and Professional Ethics is a web site devoted to the promotion of ethical behavior through various programs and conferences. Direct links are available to information about the Institute, a site directory, a newsletter, a calendar, professional resources, and an on-line journal of ethics. Information is available for those who wish to become a member of the Institute. Further links are available to a "What's Hot" section and to related ethics links. An address and search engine is also provided.

EXCHANGE RATES

Daily Currency Exchange Rates (www.dna.lth.se/cgi-bin/kurt/rates)

This site provides daily currency exchange rates for more than 45 countries. One can select a particular currency as the base currency from the list of available countries. Then another currency can be selected with which to compare the updated values. The base currency can be compared individually among countries or simultaneously among all nations to compare its worth in the world market.

EXPORT/IMPORT

DIALOG Ondisc Directory of U.S. Importers and Exporters (New York: The Journal of Commerce/PIERS) [DIALOG]

The Directory provides semiannual trade information for U.S. companies that export and import goods. The data in each entry include annual trade statistics, products, and the importing or exporting nation.

EXPORTS

PC Financial Network

This service, available on America Online and Prodigy, permits trading on-line with money-management software.

Trade Port: Roles of the Freight Forwarder (www.yahoo.com/Business_and_Economy/Trade)

This web site deals with the role of the Freight Forwarder in exporting goods to other countries. The Forwarder helps set price quotas and looks for good deals. The Forwarder also assists in making sure that the transportation is taken care of correctly. The Forwarder helps ensure that the exporter does not waste valuable money and time in the shipping process. An additional role of the Freight Forwarder is to ensure that overseas trading regulations are met. Lastly, the shipper makes sure that documentation is filled out properly and that the payment is handled.

FINANCE

Americans for Financial Security (www.yahoo.com/Business_and_Economy/Organizations)

Americans for Financial Security (AFS) is a web site designed to display information about today's financial world. AFS keeps its members informed about current events related to their current financial security, such as state and federal taxation and tax return issues, retirement plans, personal investment strategies and money management, and access to a large number of money-saving products and services. Direct links are available to a consumer's guide, advocacy, benefits of AFS, information in the news, newsletters,

Congressional E-mail addresses, and feedback. A search engine is also provided.

CNN Financial News (cnnfn.com)

This web site provides relevant financial news and information for business. Its links include hot stories (a list of current headlines and articles pertaining to business, politics, and the economy), markets (a summary of the day's trading of stocks, bonds, and currencies), your money (a tool providing current news relating to the mutual fund market), and fn to go (an application that will track top news headlines and stock market developments reported by CNNfn while browsing other sites). The site also contains an electronic forum in which users can ask business-related questions.

D&B-Dun's Financial Records Plus (Parsippany, NJ: Dun and Bradstreet Information Services) [DIALOG]

Dun and Bradstreet-Dun's Financial Records Plus contains financial statements for companies. The data include balance sheets, income statements, and business ratios for measuring solvency, efficiency, and profitability. Company identification details found in the database are company name, address, primary and secondary SIC codes, D-U-N-S number, and number of employees.

Disclosure/Worldscope Global (Bridgeport, CT: Worldscope/Disclosure Partners)

General and detailed financial information on more than 9000 international corporations are provided by this CD-ROM database. Available through annual subscription with monthly updates, the database is operated with software that offers numerous search capabilities as well as the option of saving regularly used search patterns. Retrieved data can be displayed, printed, or transferred to disks for use in various software programs, such as spreadsheets.

The 9000 companies represent 24 industries and 40 countries, including those with the largest capital markets worldwide. The data provided for each company includes general information such as name, address, telephone number, description of business, number of employees, and detailed financial data and analysis comprising more than 500 subject areas.

Dun's Analytical Services (Murray Hill, NJ: Dun & Bradstreet)

Dun's Analytical Services is a system designed to help business people access financial information about companies. It builds on Dun & Bradstreet's core database of financial information on more than 1,000,000 companies as well as basic information on more than 9,000,000 and uses D & B's own financial analysts to interpret the information. Four services are offered: Dun's Account Consulting, which offers individualized assistance in deciding what information is needed; Dun's Statistical Reports, which compare an individual firm's performance to the rest of its industry; Dun's Narrative Reports, which summarize a company's past performance, current condition, and future prospects; and Dun's V.I.P. Service, which is an extensive, made-to-order analysis of any financial aspect of a company. Information relating to the performance of over 800 industries can also be ordered. The financial database is updated continuously and the industry norm statistics are updated quarterly.

Finance and Commerce (finance-commerce.com)

Finance and Commerce publishes information for the business and legal matters of Minnesota. The site offers News & Data of Finance and Commerce Daily Newspaper, Minnesota Court Opinions, and Public Notice of City of Minneapolis, Hennepin County. The News & Data provides Construction News, the bids and new briefs; Credit Data presents Bankruptcies, Real Estate Sales, and Court Judgment. The Court Opinions offer the past cases in Minnesota Opinion, the F & C. Advertising Rate, list of Minnesota Lawyers, and information on Legal Market Place. The Public Notice offers Minneapolis City Council Proceedings, Hennepin County Board Minutes, and St. Paul City Council Minutes.

Financial Accounting Standards Board (www.yahoo.com/Business_and_Economy/Organizations)

Financial Accounting Standards Board (FASB) is a web site designed to establish and improve standards of financial accounting and reporting for the guidance and education of the public, including issuers, auditors, and users of financial information. Users can traverse the web site for recently posted FASB documents, the mission and structure of FASB, announcements of board actions and forthcoming meetings, quarterly plans for FASB projects, international activities, press releases, summaries and status of FASB statements, exposure drafts, FASB casebook, the world according to GAAP, membership information, and publications. An E-mail link is also provided.

Financial Information Services (nmg.com/wew)

The Financial Information Services (FIS) web page provides economic information from the United States, Germany, and Japan. There is a series of information from each country that includes Consumer Survey, Foreign Exchange, Labor Market, and Inflation and Prices. The consumer survey page offers a series of graphs and charts that illustrate economic growth. The Foreign Exchange pages provide a series of rate-exchange information distributed monthly or weekly. The Labor Market page assists with unemployment by providing a Help Wanted Index. Lastly, the Inflation and Price pages offer consumer and producer indices on inflation and prices.

FRED (www.stls.frb.org/fred)

FRED is a web site that provides economic and financial information to consumers, economists, and financial institutions. Users have access to historical U.S. economic and financial data, including daily U.S. interest rates, monetary and business indicators, and exchange rates. Links to other publications on-line including statistical publications from U.S. Financial Data and National Economic Trends are also available.

IPO Central (www.ipocentral.com)

This site is produced by financial consultants at the Texas-based Hoover's Inc. IPO Central is geared toward people with money in the stock market. Users can check on stock quotations throughout the day and can create a portfolio that allows them to select the stock quotations to be viewed. Many articles are included along with links to other stock-related web sites.

Institute of Business and Economic Reports (IBER) (uclink.berkeley.edu: 160511)

This site contains a brochure (with general information relating to IBER), publications (a series of working papers related to finance, economics, and real estate economics), a bulletin (containing the most recent newsletters and information on IBER), economic history (announcements and lists of papers from recent group conferences), tax policy/public finance (announcements from the Robert D. Burch Center for Tax Policy and Public Finance at UC Berkeley, and current news and tools for economists. This site can be searched using keywords or subjects.

Interquote (www.interquote.com)

Interquote is a site advertising an on-line, real-time quote service that is continuously updated. Users can download the software from the site, but the access is fee based. Clients register for one of five membership packages offering different levels of service. Links to other financial sites are available, including Financial Chat, Investment Analysis & News, Magazines, and Internet Provider Service Links.

Knight-Ridder Financial News (www.aisa-inc.com/ knight.index.html; www.cnnfn.com/markets/bridge)

Knight-Ridder Financial, Inc., provides "real-time" news and data about world financial-market activity in Europe, the Americas, Asia, and Australia, particularly information about money markets, government and other debt, foreign exchange, and the commodity and futures markets. In July 1996, Knight-Ridder Financial, Inc. was purchased by Global Financial Information Corp., which has apparently combined the KRI resources with those of Bridge Information Systems, another subsidiary. BRIDGE News is a source of market information used by other on-line financial news publishers, such as Asia, Inc., and by subscribers with passwords—"institutional investors, brokers/dealers, exchanges, corporations, and state and local governments." It considers its information to be "principally for the international trading community."*

The BRIDGE/KRF reports are accessible by Internet users and provide primarily daily market news and information. In its present form, the BRIDGE Financial Summary and Stock Reviews page has links to a financial summary for Asia, Europe, and North and South America. The U.S. links give the day's Dow Jones Industrials Average, bond rate movements, and the effect of currency trading on the dollar. For South American countries and Mexico, the day's stock and other index movements and perhaps a lead story or commentary on market conditions in general are provided. Similar information on stock and credit markets is given for France, Germany, Australia, India, Japan, Korea, Malaysia, Singapore, and Thailand. When the user moves from the BRIDGE summary page to the individual pages for each country, the pages are accessed by way of the Cable News Network (CNNFN). The articles are written in the style of a news broadcast. The World 7-day Financial Calendar gives the dates on which significant financial reports in the various countries are scheduled to be released in the next week.

What is made available from BRIDGE to Web users would be of interest to investors geographically distant from the market; it would be a good source of daily information and would be altered to changing market conditions. A sophisticated active trader would probably need to subscribe to the in-depth coverage.

MasterCard (www.mastercard.com)

MasterCard is a worldwide payment systems company of 22,000 financial institutions that is rapidly expanding the world of Electronic Commerce. This

---

* www.aisa-inc.com/knight.about.html, p. 1. Note the "knight" in this URL.

site features its products on the Net, how to reach MasterCard International, MasterCard International products and services, protecting one's card and credit, where to use and an ATM locator, MasterCard Press Office, Employment Opportunities, and FAQs. Special features of this site include a pointer of the day or a famous witty quote, a daily listing of Foreign Currency Exchange for over 54 countries, and a TicketMaster ConcertSearch where one can purchase tickets and locate where one's favorite artist is in concert.

FINANCIAL PLANNING

African-American Business Alliance (www.yahoo.com/Business_and_Economy/Organizations)

African-American Business Alliance is a web site dedicated to improving the financial structure of the African-American business community. The web site includes a database of African-American-owned operations. Direct links are available to the web site mission statement, information on computer literacy, and a link in which to enter further listings. An E-mail address is provided also for those with questions.

FINANCIAL SERVICES

Extel International Financial Cards (London: Extel Financial Limited) [DIALOG]

Extel International Financial Cards is a source of background and financial information for quoted, unquoted, and international companies. The data provided include financial elements, pre-tax profits, premium incomes, dividend information, capital employed, share capital, assets, borrowing, and market capitalization.

Financial Industry Information Service (Washington, DC: American Bankers Association) [DIALOG]

Financial Industry Information Service (FINIS) contains information on financial service industry, products, and services. Aspects covered by the database include banks, brokers, credit unions, insurance companies, investment houses, real estate firms, thrift institutions, and similar government agencies.

FORECASTING

PTS International Forecasts (Foster City, CA: Information Access Company) [DIALOG]

PTS International Forecasts is a source of information about development potential for many countries except the United States. The subjects covered are economics, industries, products, and end-use data. The information on each country is gathered from annual reports of corporations, trade associations, the United Nations, newspapers, business journals, and bank letters.

FOREIGN STATISTICS

Asia-Pacific (Seattle, WA: Aristarchus Knowledge Industries) [DIALOG]

Asia-Pacific database contains commercial and industrial information about East Asia, Southeast Asia, the Indian Subcontinent, the Middle East, Australia, and the Pacific Island nations. The database has two types of information. The first is composed of abstracts from journals as well as documents from public organizations and private companies. The second has a Corporate Thesaurus subfile with information on business leaders and companies traded on stock exchanges in the region.

The Australian Business Index, Business Intelligence Australia

The Australian Business Index is a reference guide to the Australian and New Zealand finance and industry press. It began publishing in 1981 and has continued to grow since its establishment. This indexing service provides short citations covering many areas related to finance and industry, such as business, company, finance, trade, industry, and investment news.

The subject areas of the index include general economics, food processing, engineering, accounting, law, overseas trade, packaging, plastics, clothing, travel and tourism, telecommunications, insurance, manufacturing, pharmaceuticals, retailing, electronics, marketing, hospitality, printing, hardware, building and construction, industrial relations, management, mining, agriculture, and advertising news.

The paper index is printed in 11 monthly issues with annual cumulations in December. The microfiche format is published in 12 monthly issues and cumulates monthly. The on-line database on AUSINET is updated weekly; its database identifier is ABIX. A CD-ROM index came out in 1993. The index is printed in "British English."

Australian Business Compendium (Alexandria, Australia: Read-Only Memory)

Australian Business Compendium (ABC) is a CD-ROM that contains information on the top companies in Australia. ABC is indexed with Dataware, an Australian search and retrieval system. ABC information can be extracted as a file, a report, or a label.

ABC requires either an IBM-compatible computer or an Apple Macintosh with SOFT PC software and a CD-ROM drive. ABC has 19 searchable fields capable of being searched individually or in combinations. The fields are company names, addresses, suburbs, post codes, telephone numbers, facsimile numbers, executive names, numbers of employees, imports, gross sales, relationships, banks, branches, SIC codes, SIC categories, SIC names, ASIC codes, job titles, and persons. A sample search would be to look for all companies with gross sales in the range of "2050 million" in the category of "finance."

ABC is available with three different licenses. The site license allows users to export or print as much information as they wish and to use it as long as no ABC information is sold or given away. The network license has the same retrieval restrictions as a site license and requires an additional license for each workstation in the network accessing ABC. Finally, the unlimited license has no restrictions on its use except for those restrictions associated with the Dataware retrieval software.

ABC comes in one of nine export file formats. Those formats are formatted text, Wordstar, ASCII, comma delimited, semicolon delimited, dBase III +, Lotus, DIF, and fixed field.

Canadian Business and Current Affairs (Toronto: Micromedia) [DIALOG]

Canadian Business and Current Affairs indexes Canadian business journals and newspapers. Since 1986, corporate filings found in the Ontario Securities Commission have been indexed as well.

CanCorp Canadian Financials (Toronto: Micromedia) [DIALOG]

CanCorp Canadian Financials contains information on Canadian corporations. The data are composed of résumé, financial, textual, marketing, and filings data.

Chinese Patent Abstracts in English (Vienna: European Patent Offices) [DIALOG]

Chinese Patent Abstracts in English is a product of Patent Documentation Service Center of China. The purpose of the database is to provide English-language titles, abstracts, and patent numbers for similar patents produced outside China.

D&B-European Dun's Market Identifiers (Parsippany, NJ: Dun and Bradstreet Information Services) [DIALOG]

Dun and Bradstreet-European Dun's market identifiers provide information on European businesses. The data include name, address, SIC codes,

D-U-N-S number, sales volume, marketing data, and references to parent companies.

D&B-International Dun's Market Identifiers (Parsippany, NJ: Dun and Bradstreet Information Services) [DIALOG]

Dun and Bradstreet-International Dun's market identifiers provide business data on companies in Asia, Africa, Europe, India and outside the United States. The information on each company includes name, address, SIC codes, annual sales, number of employees, type of company, D-U-N-S number, parent company, and marketing data.

D&B-Asia-Pacific Dun's Market Identifiers (Parsippany, NJ: Dun and Bradstreet Information Services) [DIALOG]

Dun and Bradstreet Asia-Pacific Dun's market identifiers have directory listings of businesses in Asia, the Pacific Rim, Australia, and New Zealand. Information in the listings is collected from credit organizations.

Delphes European Business (Paris: Chamber of Commerce and Industry of Paris and the French Assembly of the Chambers of Commerce and Industry) [DIALOG]

Delphes European business is a French database that has information on international companies, markets, products, and industries. The data are collected from journals, newspapers, and business periodicals by the Chamber of Commerce and Industry of Paris and the French Assembly of the Chambers of Commerce and Industry.

European Taxation (Amsterdam, The Netherlands: IBFD Publications)

This CD-ROM product covers the tax systems of European countries, including information from IBFD's Guides to European Taxation. The source is composed of several databases that may be searched together or individually. Information provided includes descriptions and analyses of individual and corporate income tax systems and the VAT systems used by the European Community. Text of major European tax laws in the original language and sometimes in English translation, text of EC Directives relating to VAT and corporate income tax, and articles from European Taxation are also accessible. The system offers an index, outlines, cross-referencing, and a standardized layout that is helpful for comparisons. Updated CD-ROMs are available biannually.

European Patents Fulltext (Vienna: European Patent Office) [DIALOG]

European Benefits Fulltext is a source of patents published (updated weekly) in Europe. Details about them include claims, citations, and references.

Europages (www.europages.com)

This web site contains a directory for European businesses, available in five languages. The directory can be searched in a variety of ways including type of product or service and/or location of the corporation. Searches can be performed by way of business sectors such as agriculture, energy and raw materials, electrical and electronic equipment, etc. There are other links that provide current news and business information resources from around the world.

Far Eastern Economic Review (www.feer.com)

This web site is an interactive version of The Review, with information on Asian current affairs, business, economics, and investment. The site highlights the magazine's key stories and provides live market updates from the major stock exchanges. Links include current news (by country), business news, this week's current issue, products and services, and a search utility. No fee is required for usage, but users must complete a brief registration form.

JAPIO (Tokyo: Japanese Patent Information Organization) [DIALOG]

Japanese Patent Information Organization (JAPIO) is an on-line version of the Patent Abstracts of Japan and has information on Japanese patent applications about technology.

Japan Economic Newswire Plus (New York: Kyodod News International) [DIALOG]

Japan Economic Newswire Plus provides full-text English news produced in Japan. It covers local and international business information about Japan. Some of the sources of information are International Monetary Fund, GATT, and OECD.

Kompass Africa/Middle East (Zurich: Kompass International Management Corp.) [DIALOG]

Kompass Africa/Middle East has business information on Africa and the Middle East about manufacturing and industry. The data collected on each company are name and address, names of executives, type of industry, and products.

Kompass Asia/Pacific (Zurich: Kompass International Management Corp.) [DIALOG]

Kompass Asia/Pacific contains business information on companies in the Asia/Pacific region. The data provided are company name and address, trade name, parent company, names of executives, type of industry, and products.

Kompass Canada (Toronto: Micromedia) [DIALOG]

Kompass Canada has business information on Canadian companies. Data available include company name and address, names of executives, type of industry, products, trade, and import/export. The information is available in English, German, French, Spanish, and Italian.

Kompass Eastern Europe (Zurich: Kompass International Management Corp.) [DIALOG]

Kompass Eastern Europe has business information on Eastern European countries. Each entry includes company name and address, names of executives, type of industry, and products.

Kompass Europe (Stockholm: Affarsdata) [DIALOG]

Kompass Europe has business information on European companies. Each entry includes company name and address, description of business, size of labor force, top four executives, foreign trade status, and products. Product names are written in English, Germany, French, Spanish, and Italian.

Kompass Latin America (Zurich: Kompass International Management Corp.) [DIALOG]

Kompass Latin America is a source of business information for companies in Latin America. Each directory entry provides company name and address, names of executives, type of industry, and products.

Kompass Online/UK Kompass CD (West Sussex, U.K.: Reed International)

This source is available both on-line and in CD-ROM format. It provides company information on over 155,000 U.K. establishments in the business-to-business sector with an emphasis on manufacturing and associated service industries. All companies included in the database are listed free of charge. This database corresponds to the following print directories: U.K. Kompass Register, Kelly's Directories, Directory of Directors, Dial, British Exports, and U.K. Trade Names.

Data on products and services, directors, managers, ownership, trade names, finances, overseas agents, and registration details are provided in each entry. A detailed and comprehensive industry/product/service classification system with a multilevel structure similar to the Standard Industrial Classification (SIC) contains 45,000 searchable items. Over 340,000 named individuals with job titles are included.

Companies can be accessed directly by name or may be selected by product, postcode, turnover, or number of employees. Over 35 additional selection criteria are available. Online data may be displayed on the screen or printed as a listing or mailing labels. The fee is based on the number of companies selected and the detail of the information desired.

The data for the database are collected annually through on-site visits to companies, telephone interviews, and mailed questionnaires. Companies that do not respond to any of these methods in 2 years are removed from the database. Information on other European companies is also available from the publisher.

Korea.com (www.korea.com)

Korea.com is a web site that provides information pertaining to the Korean businesses, news, and resources. The home page provides a newsletter that gives top headlines in the Korean community. Also on the home page are the following links that give further information for users: About Korea, Calendar, Yellowpage, Newsletter, FAQ, E. Commerce, Chat, and Other Links. Under FAQ, users may ask any question they have with this web site. Some Korean is written here for users who do not have English as their first language.

NewsPage (www.newspage.com)

NewsPage is a daily news service that provides articles selected from more than 600 sources. These sources include well-known general news services, newspapers, magazines, government sources, specialized newsletters and reports. Articles are selected by the System for the Manipulation and Retrieval of Text (SMART) agent filtering technology and sorted into 2500 topics. The reader may browse the Breaking News and Front Page Business News sections or search by keywords. Another service allows the reader to design an individualized issue that is updated daily. In order to read full-text stories, it is necessary to register with the service. Several levels of free and paid subscriptions are available.

Reader's Guide Abstracts (New York, NY: H.W. Wilson)

Reader's Guide Abstracts (RGA) is a database published by the H.W. Wilson Company, a publisher of indexes such as Humanities Index, Social Science Index, and Science Index as well as other reference books like World Authors, Nobel Prize Winners, and Current Biography. The audience intended for this source is general.

RGA is identical to the Readers' Guide to Periodical Literature except that this work contains abstracts in addition to bibliographic citations and it does not include book reviews and works of creative literature. Over 240 general-interest English-language periodicals from the United States and Canada are indexed and abstracted. There is retrospective index coverage from January 1983 and retrospective abstract coverage from September 1984. The database includes more than 440,000 citations and 60,000 are added each year. Subjects include popular areas such as current events, business, art, sports, hobbies, politics, health, history, science, religion, home improvement, foreign affairs, cooking, computers, and photography.

The bibliographic citation includes author, title, journal title, volume and issue number, page number, date of publication, subject covered, illustrations and notes. The average abstract is 125 words. The indexing is standardized. There are extensive cross-references. Searchers can use Boolean operators in both keyword and subject searches. Searches can be limited by journal title, date, author's name, subject or article title.

RGA is available in CD-ROM format, on-line through WILSON-LINE, on magnetic tape as WILSONTAPE, on microfiche, and in print. A demonstration copy is available for review.

Research Libraries Information Network
(Mountain View, CA: Research Library Group)

The Research Libraries Information Network (RLIN) is an on-line bibliographic utility that provides technical support to member libraries for shared cataloging, acquisitions, and reference. Members include the Library of Congress, Conser, the National Library of Canada, the British Library, the U.S. General Printing Office (GPO), the National Library of Medicine, and the National Union Catalog. It also includes original cataloging from member research libraries. The database contains many formats and has an international scope. It is updated on a regular basis. Access is by author, title, keyword, and subject heading. Member libraries may also use the utility for interlibrary loan. Subscription to RLIN is required for use of the utility.

FOREIGN TRADE

Eastern Europe Trade Leads (University of Michigan GOpherBLUE Service)

This source of information contains files downloaded from the U.S. Department of Commerce's Economic Bulletin Board. These files are mainly for business people interested in investing in Eastern European, Baltic, and former Soviet Union enterprises.

The first type of file is Eastern Europe Trade Leads, created and compiled by the Eastern Europe Business Information Center (EEBIC), a part of the Department of Commerce, which does not endorse any of the trade leads listed. Eastern Europe Trade Leads is divided into years, and the annual compilations have to do with agriculture, housing, construction, consumer goods, high technology, manufacturing, energy, and the environment. Each country is listed alphabetically, with profiles of companies in the region that are looking for partners. Company profiles may include information such as the name of the company, what it produces, the number of employees, annual turnover, for whom it produces, names of contacts, sources of the information, and the date the information was received. Data come from Eastern European and American sources and are time-sensitive. For parties interested in pursuing any of the leads, EEBIC provides advice and assistance. Names, addresses, and telephone and facsimile numbers of additional contacts also are given.

The second type of file is Business Information Service for the Newly Independent States (BISNIS), which provides information in two forms. One is almost identical to Eastern Europe Trade Leads, except that it covers only the states of the former Soviet Union. Some of the featured industries are agribusiness, transport, construction, telecommunications/computers/electronics, medical/health care, consumer goods, and manufacturing/machinery.

BISNIS also provides listings of commercial opportunities on a monthly basis. The Department of Commerce receives information on export and joint venture opportunities from the United States and Foreign Commercial Service, the European Bank for Reconstruction and Development, the World Bank, and other institutions. These lists of business opportunities give the project titles, explain which Newly Independent States received the loan, who provided the loans, the purpose of the loans, how to obtain tender documents and whom to contact, the lot numbers, and the closing dates. This information is time sensitive, and interested parties are advised to act quickly.

Updates to Eastern Europe Trade Leads and BISNIS can be found on the World Wide Web. Simple, non-Boolean searches can also be performed at both World Wide Web sites.

The University of Michigan GOpherBLUE Service also provides other foreign-trade-related information downloaded from the U.S. Department of

Commerce's Economic Bulletin Board. These files are mainly for people interested in knowing the status of trade between the United States and the rest of the world.

Most of the files are produced by the Bureau of the Census and the Bureau of Economic Analysis. Statistics on exports, imports, and trade balances are given for Goods and Services Trade and for Merchandise Trade; revisions also are provided. Information is supplied in both textual and tabular form. The textual portion is usually a summary and analysis of the data found in the tables. Statistics are given in a year-by-year, then month-by-month, format. Tables often divide the data by areas of the world or by commodities/industries. Source data, such as the report number, which institution or agency provided the material, and contacts for further information, are also provided.

Some of the files are news releases, providing textual and tabular information. The person and department responsible for the content are named. Most of the releases can be found in other locations, such as the Department of Commerce's Economic Bulletin Board, the Internet, facsimiles, and recorded messages. Directions on how to receive the news releases via these other channels are given. Also, because the Bureau of Economic Analysis publishes the journal, Survey of Current Business, much of the data found in the Foreign Trade files can be located there as well.

Other files include a weekly exchange rate table, the net international investment position of the United States, textile and apparel-related data, a listing of American exports by state, and descriptions of footnotes found in the files.

FUND RAISING

Sherwood Forest Farms (www.cosmix.com/sherwood/farminfo.html)

Sherwood Forest Farms is a web site containing information about fundraising by selling evergreen home decoration products. This web page is dedicated for users who are raising funds for nonprofit purposes in a relatively short time, and they can contact the Sherwood Forest Farms through the given address or e-mail address. For further information, users can browse through other links provided in the web site.

FURNITURE INDUSTRY

Computer Aided Planning (Grand Rapids, MI: Sweet's Electronic Publishing)

Features of eight software applications for the office furniture industry are presented in this promotional package from Computer Aided Planning

(CAP): CAP•Spex, CAPacad, CAP•Spacetek, CAP Business Partner, CAP Salestrak, CAPcd-rom, CAP•Comparasys, and CAP•FM. A sample computer screen from each of the programs is illustrated. Features include the possible applications of each program and the reports available.

CAP software is designed to streamline the process of designing, selecting, ordering, and managing systems and office furniture through integrated software packages. A CD-ROM Fact Sheet and Microsoft Windows Fact Sheet are included to give background information about the technology discussed.

Additional data sheets included are Company & Product Overview, Hardware, Contract Furniture Manufacturers, CAPcd-rom, CAP 3D, Microsoft Windows, and two issues of Capsules, the customer newsletter. Capsules provide technology updates, schedules, and other facts for CAP users.

GOVERNMENT

American Statistics Index (Washington, DC: Congressional Information Services)

The American Statistics Index (ASI) on-line database is provided by the Congressional Information Service (CIS). This source provides publications from the judicial, legislative, and executive branches of the government. It indexes reports of statistical agencies and congressional committees, as well as offices of the judicial branch and special commissions of the President and of Congress. It provides information from newspapers, biennial and annual publications, surveys, census data, publications of an analytical nature, and most other federal publications.

The ASI provides abstracts for all its materials. Each abstract is intended to allow for evaluation prior to obtaining the document. The database provides two types of abstracts: a main abstract that covers the entire publication and an analytic abstract that covers information pertaining to bibliographic data.

This database provides many different indexes:

The Index of Subject allows access to information by way of names, subjects, names of places, agencies of the government, programs and proposals of the government, data, personal or company names, and surveys.

The Index by Category allows access to information through demographic, geographic, and economic categories. It has a multitude of subject headings, ranging from agriculture to veteran affairs. It also allows users to use a group name as a subject heading. The Demographic Category, for example, provides a second breakdown of index terms: it groups people by topics such as Blacks, age, divorced persons, women, and the poor.

The Index by Title provides a list of periodicals, reports, and conference papers. These items are arranged in alphabetical order by title.

The Listing by Agency Report Numbers provides a numerical system of locating information from either one document or a whole series of documents. The numbers in this index are grouped by name of agency, issuing department, and congressional body.

The ASI database can be searched by both CRT terminal display or printout terminal. It is updated monthly and annually. Most information obtained through the database can be found in a depository library on microfiche or paper copy.

Defense Conversion Subcommittee Info (University of Michigan GOpherBLUE Service)

Defense Conversion Subcommittee (DCS) Info is downloaded from the U.S. Department of Commerce's Economic Bulletin Board. The files are primarily intended for business people interested in investing in defense-related enterprises of the former Soviet Union.

Most of these files give background material on a bureau, institute, or plant of the former Soviet Union. The information provided includes the name of the enterprise, alternate names, address, phone, and facsimile numbers, an overview of the enterprise, primary business, former ministry subordination, approximate employment, principal officers, ownership, year established, military product lines, civil product lines, key technologies/equipment employed, conversion projects, and human resources support. The Department of Commerce is the compiler and disseminator of the data; it does not endorse the enterprises listed.

Some of the files are directories of investment opportunities for four of the former Soviet territories: Russia, Belarus, Ukraine, and Kazakhstan. A description of the Defense Conversion Subcommittee program is given, with a background of the regions, and profiles of enterprises looking for investors.

The files on Russia and Ukraine provide a directory to the aerospace industry. Subject and title indexes for aerospace concerns are provided, as well as profiles for the entities. A user's guide is also included, with explanations of titles, address and phone number formats, and names of key government contacts.

One file describes the Defense Conversion Subcommittee; it furnishes an overview of the program, goals, members, activities, and names of contacts. Other files provide a listing and some data on consultants, universities, think tanks, associations, and institutes involved in the Defense Conversion Subcommittee.

In addition, one file provides Defense Conversion Subcommittee "Weekly Update" notes. It tells what happened in certain meetings, what day the meetings were held, and names of contacts.

Economic Report of the President (www.access.gpo.gov/eop)

The document on this web site is sponsored by the U.S. Government Printing Office web site. It can search up to 200 records, from the 1997 Economic Report of the President, for the terms entered.

Federal Statistics Briefing Room (www.whitehouse.gov/fsbr/esbr.html)

This web site contains economic and social statistics information that is released currently. It also provides links to information maintained by a number of Federal agencies on employment, income, international economic statistics, money, output, prices, production, transportation, and the Social Statistics Briefing Room.

GOVDOC-L

To subscribe, send a message to LISTSERV@psuvm.psu.edu with "Subscribe GOVDOC-L yourfirstname yourlastname."

This listserv covers a variety of subjects related to collections of government documents in libraries. It is intended as a forum for librarians, although subscription to and participation in it is not restricted. A majority of the messages relate to the Federal Depository Library Program, although queries about foreign documents also appear.

GOVDOC-L lists questions that are often expanded in their responses to provide information of general interest. It also has job vacancy as well as seminar and conference announcements. Excerpts from Administrative Notes, a publication of the Government Printing Office which is sent to depository libraries, are also supplied by the GPO and highlight discontinued items in the depository program, new services offered by the GPO, and advances in technology related to the dissemination of government documents. GOVDOC-L is also a source for information on the availability and location of government information in many formats.

The Government Contractor Resource Center (govcon.com)

The Government Contractor Resource Center contains information to assist one in receiving and reserving U.S. Federal Government contracts.

Government Printing Office Access

An on-line service, the Government Printing Office (GPO) Access, provides access to Congressional bills, the Congressional Record, and many other government documents. This connection allows users to view government documents the day they are published. Over 24 databases are full-text and provide graphics.

These government publications are updated by 6 A.M. daily; the Congressional Record is available by 11 A.M. This database includes Federal Register, Congressional Bills, General Accounting Office (GAO) Reports and Public Laws. The homepage offers services to help locate and access these resources.

Small Business Administration Online (www.sbaonline.sba.gov)

This web site provides help for starting businesses, financing businesses, and expanding businesses. It provides information that is useful to businesses such as Property For Sale Disaster Assistance and Business Cards, SBAs, gopher, the FTP server, information download area, and links to business-related sites.

US Business Advisor (www.business.gov)

The US Business Advisor supplies business with one-stop access to federal government information, services, and transactions. Their goal is to make the relationship between business and government more valuable and profitable.

Government Agencies, Departments, and Information; U.S. House of Representatives (www.house.gov)

This web site provides information for visitors about Capitol Hill and the Washington, D.C. area, legislative issues that the House is going to consider, events that happened on the House floor, and committee meetings. There are also links to member pages, committee pages, leadership pages, commission pages, an Annual Schedule, and a House directory.

U.S. Securities and Exchange Commission (www.sec.gov)

This site pertains to the Securities and Exchange Commission (SEC). U.S. Securities and Exchange Commission contains such items as press releases from recent years to news on the latest activities of the commission. Users can access reports and investigations as well as read SEC rules and regulations.

Government Agencies, Departments, and Information; US Senate (www.senate.gov)

This web site provides information on legislative activities, senators and senate leadership, senate history and procedures, committee information, keyword search, and links to other resources such as FAQ and statistics.

Government Agencies, Departments, and Information; U.S. State Department (www.state.gov)

This web site, which is an official U.S. Government source, provides information about the current Secretary of State, topics such as press information and Holocaust Assets, State data such as telephone directory and biographies, support for U.S. business, international policy, travel information, and U.S. consular affairs.

PhoneDisc QuickRef+ (Digital Directory Assistance)

This CD-ROM source provides access to over 100,000 of the most frequently called organizations and businesses in the United States. Each listing contains the formal name, full address, and telephone number. Types of listings include law firms, industrial manufacturers, federal government agencies, foreign corporations, colleges and universities, libraries, and associations. Reverse indexes permit searching by name, business type, standard industrial classification code, address, zip code, and telephone number. A limit feature can be used to broaden or narrow the search. Features include tabulation of the number of listings fitting the search parameters, downloading or printing of listings, and automatically dialing a selected entry.

GRANTS

Seliger & Associates (www.seliger.com)

Seliger & Associates is a web page containing information regarding grant writing and grant source research services in the United States. This web site is dedicated for users who are searching for funds from the government to set up their own ventures. Users can also subscribe, for a fee, to a newsletter regarding current available grant opportunities. For further information, users can contact them directly through the address provided in the web site.

INDUSTRIAL RELATIONS

Labor Law II (Washington, DC: Bureau of National Affairs) [DIALOG]

The purpose of Labor Law II is to index and abstract documents about U.S. federal and state labor regulations. Full information about the decisions is found in the Labor Relations Reference manual, Labor Arbitration Reports, Fair Employment Practice Cases, Mine Safety and Health Cases, and Individual Employment Rights Cases. A single record represents one court case or an administration decision and provides the following details: case name, Bureau of National Affairs (BNA) case number, tribunal, date of decision, BNA citation, tribunal code, parallel citations, case history, docket number, circuit for each federal circuit court, and state laws in existence.

INDUSTRIAL SURVEYS

Aluminum Ingot and Mill Products (Gopher, M33D)

This document surveys companies producing aluminum ingot and mill products in the United States and imported aluminum products. It includes yearly summaries and monthly reports. These monthly reports contain statistical tables indicating net shipments and inventories of aluminum and mill products in thousands of pounds, shipments and receipts of those products by producer, inventories of aluminum ingots, mill products, and scrap by type of producer, gross shipments of products of aluminum mills by types of producers, and shipments and receipts of aluminum mill products. Types of products include sheet, plate, foil, drawing stock, wire, and cable, rod and bare wire, cable and insulated wire, rod, bar, pipe, tube, as well as shapes. Statistical data are collected by the U.S. Bureau of the Census.

Aluminum Industry Abstracts (Materials Park: Materials Information) [DIALOG]

Abstracts about aluminum are published 12 times each year. Most of the information is obtained from periodicals, patents, government documents, conference proceedings, dissertations, and books.

Industry Trends and Analysis (Waltham, MA: Decision Resources) [DIALOG]

Industry Trends and Analysis gathers information on industry forecasts, technology assessments, market, and public opinion surveys. The industries covered are chemical, health care, food processing, telecommunication, computers, and services.

Industrial Workers of the World (www.iww.org)

The Industrial Workers of the World (IWW) home page provides substantial information about the IWW union. The site is peppered with pictures and facts about the IWW and is fairly easy to browse. The IWW preamble and frequently asked questions are two features that jump out at the reader.

Societe Generale de Surveillance (www.sgsgroup.com)

Societe Generale de Surveillance (SGS Group) claims to be a world leader in inspection, testing, and certification. One part of the homepage allows the user to access specific business sectors such as Minerals Services, Environmental Services, Logistics, and Manpower. Users can also check out import regulations if they plan on exporting to one of the 29 countries that SGS services. A section on the top stories about SGS is available. One can look at financial updates on the group.

INFORMATION SERVICES

1040.Com (www.1040.com)

1040.com is an on-line service provided by Drake Software. It contains information on filing of taxes and other resources on tax forms and instructions. It provides links to state and federal tax sources.

AC Nielsen (www.excite.com/xdr/Business/Marketing)

The AC Nielsen web site gives a few links to office information, news release, Industries covered, services offered, and published reports. There is also a pull-down menu where one can select from a group of countries the AC Nielsen provides services for; links to the company past, present, and future are also provided.

Accounting and Tax Database (Louisville, KY: UMI) [DIALOG]

This database is a source of information on accounting and taxes. The data include indexes, abstracts, and full-text articles from periodicals.

@dver@ctive Multimedia Design (www.excite.com/xdr/Business/Marketing)

The @dver@active web site provides information on what each on exactly the services that the company gives. The web site includes a link to the home page of @dver@ctive. There is also a link to the where one can take a look at the recent work that @dver@ctive has performed for some of its clients. There is also a link to where the user can contact the company.

Agence France Presse International French Wire (Paris: Agence France Presse) [DIALOG]

Agence France Presse International French Wire is a source for full-text information in the French language and provides national and international news in many fields such as business and economics. The distribution of the news is targeted at French-speaking countries.

Agence France Presse English Wire (Washington, DC: Agence France Presse) [DIALOG]

Agence France Presse English Wire is a source of full-text documents dealing with national and international issues including business.

All-Internet Business-to-Business Directory (www.all-internet.com)

This directory gives access to hundreds of top shopping sites, malls, and stores. Included in their directory index are: Arts and Entertainment (art, books, videos, movies), Lifestyle (sporting goods, clothes, flowers), Malls and Such (malls, department stores and catalogs), Computing, Hobbies, Home and Garden (kitchen and cooking, home furnishings, pets), Services (travel, education, real estate), and Business-to-Business (business opportunities). Just by clicking on the desired category, a list of stores will become available. There is also an area for the user to advertise in the directory.

Alpine Technology (www.alpineventures.com)

The information that this site offers is investment criteria, portfolio companies, and how to contact Alpine. They also ask the users to leave their e-mail address to inform them when more information has been added to the page.

alt.politics.economics

This newsgroup has unsolicited, and often heated, commentary from a variety of political opinions on current topics. For a user seeking opinions on late-breaking major economic news, ape can be used as a supplement to more traditional sources. Keyword searching within posted threads or articles allows the retrieval of relevant information. Many of the postings in ape consist of commentary on congressional budget bills, tax policies, trade polices, labor issues, with concomitant ideological back-and-forth, uncensored opinions, and insults.

American City Business Journals (www.amcity.com)

The American City Business Journals offers New Publication, Career Site, Business Card Exchange, and The Book Store. The New Publication presents Biz, The Journal of Small Business that tackles the hottest issues in business. This journal offers success ideas from a variety of business owners. One can create business cards in Business Card Exchange without charge. The Career Site presents job opportunities and company profiles, and The Book Store will allow the user to buy business-related books at competitive prices. A search engine is available for the user to look for information in the current week or back issues.

Associated Press News (New York: Associated Press)
[DIALOG]

Associated Press (AP) News has full-text information on national, international, commercial, and business issues. Information from the database is obtainable 24 hours after it has been brought into the DataStream Service. It is also a source of general interest news from international media.

American Petroleum Institute Energy Business News Index
(New York: Central Abstracting and Information Services)
[DIALOG]

The American Petroleum Institute Energy Business News Index (APIBIZ) indexes information about the energy industry found in journals, magazines, and newsletters.

Barrons (www.barrons.com)

Barrons Online is a web site for investors that provides market review, commentary, and forecasts. It provides comprehensive information on the stock market and other related news and information.

The Benchmarking Exchange (www.benchnet.com)

The Benchmarking Exchange is a comprehensive electronic information system designed for individuals and organizations involved in benchmarking and process improvement. The site contains a number of resources for members including the posting board (to broadcast personal process improvement innovations to other members), a discussion area (an on-line chat group with other TBE members), company profiles, a member directory, and literature resource links.

Berkeley Libraries Location (www.lib.berkeley.edu)

This is the web site of a major research library system and as such, provides access both to its book catalogs and to newly developed digital materials. The home page is designed to accommodate both the first time and experienced users. A table of contents includes Help/Search, CyberSemester, Your Comments, About the Libraries, Collections and Resources, Library Catalogs, Map of the Libraries, UC Berkeley, and Digital Library SunSITE. The experienced user has the option to use a keyword query for direct access to digital materials.

Each table of contents item is specific to the on-line world. Cyber-Semester is a list of technology activities and courses on campus. Collections and Resources lists Internet sources for reference use. Library catalogs accesses not only Berkeley's library catalogs, but also other research catalogs in the United States and the world. The Digital SunSITE links to Berkeley and other digital library developments and includes image collections and software tools.

At the bottom of each page are graphical buttons to facilitate return to the home page or entry to the library catalog. Links are designed as part of the line text, so that as one reads an item of interest, one can click to it directly.

BioBusiness (Philadelphia: BIOSIS) [DIALOG]

BioBusiness supplies information for commercial and industrial leaders, as well as researchers, about the business value of research carried out in biology and biomedicine. The database gives information on the economic value of agriculture, animal production, biotechnology, crop production, diet and nutrition, food technology, forestry, genetic engineering, industrial microbiology, veterinary science, and pharmaceuticals.

B.R.I.N.T. (www.brint.com)

Business Research in Information and Technology (B.R.I.N.T.) has links to many other web sites that may be of use or interest to people in the information and technology fields. B.R.I.N.T. itself has a search engine and a "knowledge map" to facilitate searching. In addition to accepting press releases, B.R.I.N.T. also accepts web documents.

Business & Company ProFile (Foster Grove, CA: Information Access)

A CD-ROM source from Information Access, this product combines the data from the Business Index and Company ProFile CD-ROMs. Also, data are taken from the on-line Company Intelligence and PR Newswire databases.

The compilation of these databases then provides indexing and abstracts of business, management, and trade periodicals in one searchable format. Directory information and full-text newswire releases also are available. National newspapers on the database include The New York Times, The Wall Street Journal, The Asian Wall Street Journal, and Financial Times of Canada. In addition to these publications, articles relating to business from other periodicals are indexed. Several thousand periodicals fall into this category. More than 100,000 private and public companies are covered; however, emphasis is on private companies.

The database can be used for business and market research and to investigate employment opportunities. It is possible to track current industry trends and new or established companies. The database can be searched in seven ways: by subject, industry, company, geographical location, personal name, product, or SIC code. Company directory listings include company address, description, SIC codes, founding date, and number of employees. PR Newswire supplies company press releases. These entries give article title and date along with the full-text of the article. Citations for articles pertaining to current events in the business world provide article and journal titles, authors, dates, and page numbers. Industry reports include information on earnings, distribution, mergers and acquisitions, advertising, commercial policies, and customer relations. Company rankings are available.

Coverage for the database is the current year plus the previous 3 years for periodicals. The most current 12 months are available for the newspapers and 6 months for Asian Wall Street Journal, Financial Times of Canada, and PR Newswire. This CD-ROM is for use on the InfoTrac system (PC terminal, CD module, and printer), but subscriptions are available without it.

Business Data Galore (Omaha, NE: American Business Information) [DIALOG]

Business Data Galore (on CD-ROM and DIALOG) contains business directory information, and is composed of databases from American Business Information (ABI)–American Business Directory and American Business 20 Plus Companies with at least 20 employees. The information is collected from sources such as yellow pages of telephone directories, white business pages, US. Department of Labor and Postal Services material, company annual reports, and telephone researches.

Business Dateline (Ann Arbor, MI: UMI)

UMI is a commercial information publisher featuring a variety of formats including microform, article reprints, on-line, CD-ROM, and magnetic tape.

Access is provided on these various media to UMI's collections of periodicals, newspapers, dissertations, out-of-print books, and scholarly collections. These information delivery systems are marked under the brand name ProQuest in of the following categories: ProQuest Abstract-and-Index Databases, ProQuest Full-Text Databases, ProQuest Full-Image Databases. These databases offer subject coverage for topics such as business, science, technology, arts and culture, politics, commentary, news, current events, education, social sciences, consumer affairs, and health.

Business Dateline is one of the ProQuest Full-Text Databases that offer business news. Compiled from more than 450 city, local, state, and regional business-focused news wire services, this database offers local and regional business coverage. Each record includes a bibliographic citation, indexing, and geographic information as well as searchable full-text, ASCII format articles. The user can search by subject, title, keyword, or author. An on-line thesaurus and multiple indexes provide user access to all subject terms. Features of the search engine include capability to use Boolean logic, proximity operators, truncation, field limiting, and reuse of searches. Users can choose individual records for printing and downloading.

This database is available as an annual subscription that includes current disks and monthly updates to search and retrieval software. Any combination of ProQuest databases can be utilized in either stand-alone or network systems running MS-DOS 3.3 or higher. Users are provided with documentation and toll-free technical support.

BUSINESS (Heidelberg, Germany: BUSINESS Datenbanken GmbH)

BUSINESS is an on-line database founded in 1983 and lists promotional materials sent in from subscribers. BUSINESS accepts promotional advertisements, company profiles, and product lists. It also accepts advertisements for goods or services wanted, as well as inquiries about licensing and representations, joint ventures, mergers, and acquisitions.

BUSINESS is available to businesses, promotion agencies, financial institutions, publishers, chambers of commerce and industry, trade associations, and consultants.

BUSINESS currently has over 30,000 records. It is available in over 70 countries and is continually updated. It can be searched by products, sectors, institutions, countries, and types of business contacts. It is available for on-line searching 24 hours a day, or searches can be ordered, including ongoing searches. It is available through four search services; DATA-STAR Radio Schwiez AG, Fachinformationszentrun Technik e.V., GENIOS-Wirtschaftsdatenbanken, Btx Südwest Datenbank GmbH (German Videotext).

Business Index (Forest City, CA: Information Access)

A CD-ROM product, this source provides indexing to business information from newspapers and journals. Sources include almost 1000 business, management, and trade journals. Indexing also covers Barron's, The Wall Street Journal, and The New York Times' Business and Financial Section. In addition to business materials, a large number of business-related journals are indexed. More than 3000 general, legal, and computer periodicals are cited. Business Index is also part of the Business and Company ProFile CD-ROM and General BusinessFile CD-ROM.

Current information can be found on a variety of business concerns. Topics include new products and technologies, consumer surveys, management theories, industry trends, taxation, mergers, and banking and investments. Citations provide article and publication titles, authors, issue dates of the periodicals, and page numbers. Abstracts are provided for articles from selected management and computer periodicals. Also, a number of articles are available in full-text on Information Access Company's Business Collection (microfilm), which records approximately 400 periodicals. A notation is made in the bibliographic citations of those articles that are available in full-text.

Annual subscriptions provide software, 12 monthly updates, the InfoTrac handbook, and the InfoTrac system (PC terminal, CD module, and printer), including maintenance and service. Customer support is also available via a toll-free telephone number. Subscriptions are available without the InfoTrac system.

Business Information Alert (www.alertpub.com/hpbia.html)

This newsletter provides up-to-date information for business researchers. It contains in-depth articles on new and emerging research techniques, new product reviews, industry updates, and reports from on-line databases and CD-ROMs.

Business Information Network

This organization creates pages for governmental agencies, companies, and other organizations for the World Wide Web.

Business Software Database (Berkeley, CA: Information Sources)

This on-line directory provides descriptive listings for software products for micro-, mini-, and mainframe computers. It covers software for businesses and professionals, technical and system software, and various other products. There are two types of entries: directory and review records.

The directory record contains descriptive information about individual software packages and vendors. It includes information supplied by the software producer as well as company names, addresses, telephone numbers, and contact people. It also includes system requirements, documentation, and user support supplied. The review record presents analytical, evaluative, and comparative discussions of the software drawn from selected articles in trade and consumer publications. It includes abstracts that reflect the author's comments about the software.

Businesswire (San Francisco, CA: Businesswire)

Businesswire is an international wire service, available 24 hours a day, 365 days a year. This service electronically delivers press releases to local, regional, state, national, and international media. Countries covered are the United States and Canada, and media throughout Latin America, Europe, Asia, and Australia. Businesswire allows clients to customize their own media circuit, including what kind of information will be sent and to whom. It offers specialized wire services by subject, geographic outreach, or type of media serviced, including specific investment, corporate, sports, entertainment, automotive, global, radio, and television wires. The service also offers photo, fax, direct mail, and television graphics services.

In addition, the service sends current information from various industries to clients periodically. It also has a research service with newswires, more than 500 databases, and thousands of publications covering information on companies, people, products, and trends. Services include sending clients' profiles to hundreds of dailies, opportunities to attend a number of seminars in the area of communication professionalism, newsletters, and job placement assistance.

CD/Private+ (Cambridge, MA: Lotus Development)

This CD-ROM source provides data on the activities of more than 110,000 private and 10,000 public parent companies, subsidiaries, and divisions. This information includes the company's annual revenues, number of employees, chief executive officers, description of its business, its primary SIC code, import/export activities, and subsidiaries. The user can also search for these summaries by industry, revenue range, or geography. The disks are updated quarterly.

CD/Private + has three levels of menus. The main menu presents the categories of information. The user can select from Company, Portfolio, Industry, Line of Business, SIC Code, Screen all Companies, Screen Public Companies, and Quit. The next menu provides subject choices and the third menu provides types of information such as reports, profiles, and summaries.

The left side of the screen lists the various options under the menu name and the right side lists an explanation of the kinds of information the user can retrieve with each option. CD/Private + , in addition to menus, has a function key interface.

A useful feature of this CD-ROM product is the reporting feature. The user is able to produce a variety of reports. The search choice determines the content and format of the report. After selecting the report option, the user selects the companies he wants included in the report. Reports available include company summaries, company profiles, comparative financials, companies ranked by total sales, and mailing addresses.

CD-ROM Directory (Brussels; Paris: BUREAU van DIJK)

More than 60 CD-ROM databases made available by the management firm BUREAU van DIJK are profiled in this source. The databases fall into four categories: financial, marketing, statistical, and reference. The financial databases cover the accounts of more than 600,000 Western European companies and over 7000 banks, both U.S. and Western European. The marketing databases offer marketing data for more than 2,000,0000 Western European companies. The statistical databases cover topics such as European Economic Community trade, the European agricultural community and international trade. The reference databases include a French language reference text, a chess encyclopedia, and French legal and regulatory information.

CEO Express (www.ceoexpress.com)

CEO Express provides a directory of business-related web sites. It was developed by the AlphaSight Online Strategists Consulting firm targeting executives who have little time to search and organize the frequently used on-line resources. The links are useful for quick reference for business decisions and business trips. They range from major newspapers and corporation search to airline schedules. It also gives users a variety of "break time links," including Amazon Books, Car Talks, GolfWeb, Send Flowers, and Sierra Club.

Census (Washington, DC: Government Printing Office, U.S. Bureau of the Census)

The 1990 Census and the 1987 Economics Census are available on CD-ROM. The data are, in part, in a common format for statistical data for micro-computers (dBase III) and do not require a specific software package. Population, trade, housing, and agricultural information are available. Subjects including sex, race, age, education, disability, and income are represented.

Metropolitan areas, urbanized areas, and ZIP codes are examples of geographic divisions in the Census. Maps can be made to represent divisions and census data by using a software package called TIGER/Line ™. The data are on-line, as well as in print, on computer tape, and on microfiche. The on-line data are provided through DIALOG and CompuServe. Daily updates of certain types of economic information, such as manufacturer's shipments and inventories, are available through the CENDATA file on DIALOG.

Center for Research in Securities Prices (Chicago, IL: Center for Research in Securities Prices)

Information from NASDAQ (1972–present) and from NYSE (1925–present) are part of this database, which is stored on magnetic tape. Daily information from the ASE and NYSE (1962–present) and bonds (1925–present) is also available. During the summer, the system is updated for the previous year. The tapes cover 12,000 publicly held companies and major stock market indices and include stock prices and returns, shares outstanding, dividends, and other distributions. Previous names of companies are identified and information is also given on government bonds.

Chicago Board of Trade (www.cbot.com)

This site provides a variety of business-related information including current economic trends, price indices, market commentaries, bond markets, and the U.S. Treasury. The MJK link provides daily closing prices from commodity exchanges worldwide. There are also a number of news and commentary links including: @griculture on-line, Global Finance, and the Futures Industry Institute (education and information for the futures and options professional). The Financial Place provides news and updates relating to global capital markets, as well as numerous investment-related links (providing information on many forms of long-term and short-term securities.

CIA World Fact Book (www.odci.gov/cia/publications/nsolo/wfb-all.htm)

This is an on-line version of the CIA World Fact Book, which also contains links to downloadable versions. The World Fact Book is published annually by the Central Intelligence Agency for the use of U.S. Government officials. The information contained in the World Fact Book is compiled from various U.S. government sources such as the Bureau of the Census, Department of State, and the U.S. Coast Guard. The printed version is published in August, with the on-line version preceding it in March.

Both versions organize information alphabetically by country and by topic headings within country. Two hundred and sixty-six entries cover countries, oceans, and entities such as the Gaza Strip. The topic headings are map and flag—graphics and description; geography—typical atlas information with the addition of maritime claims, international disputes, environmental issues; people—general population data including ethnic divisions, religions, languages; government—organization, holidays, political parties, other political or pressure groups, international organization participation, U.S. diplomatic relations; economy—labor, budget, industries, imports, exports, illegal drugs, debt, currency; transportation—rail, road, water, air; communication—telephone, radio, television, and defense—branches, manpower, expenditures.

Additional information can be found in the eight appendices: Abbreviations, The United Nations System, International Organizations and Groups, Selected International Environmental Agreements, Weights and Measures, Cross-Reference List of Country Data Codes, Cross-Reference List of Hydrographic Codes, and Cross-Reference List of Geographic Items.

The on-line version further allows geographic division of the world into sections or can limit the information retrieved based on topic headings. Navigation can be by country or by section with returns to the Table of Contents by region or for all countries available after each section. Keyword searching is not an option. The table of contents indicates the size of each country's entry in kilobytes. All graphics are available in several formats, with maps also available in an Adobe Acrobat format.

Corporate and Industry Research Reports on Disc
(New Providence, NJ: Bowker Business Research)

Corporate and Industry Research Reports (CIRR) on Disc is a CD-ROM index with brief abstracts to research reports by brokerage houses and investment firms on thousands of companies and hundreds of industries. It also includes presentations on companies and industries done before the New York Society of Security Analysts. Topics covered are businesses, industries, economics, finance and stock market trends, product development, acquisitions, potential takeovers, market shares, and growth strategies. Information contained is from 1979. Access points include company name, product, industry, and topic. The database is available on-line through various vendors such as BRS Information Technologies and is part of PTS PROMPT. The CIRR Index is the corresponding print format and is issued quarterly.

CitiBase (New York, NY: Citicorp Database Services)

Citibase contains daily, weekly, monthly, quarterly, and annual macroeconomic time series for more than 100 federal government and private sources.

Data coverage includes such topics as business formation, construction, manufacturing and trade prices, industrial production, population, productivity, labor statistics, national income, projections, business conditions, and energy. Information covered is from 1947 to date for most data. The database is available on-line, with daily updates and on magnetic tape or diskette with monthly, quarterly, or annual updates.

Clarinet (www.clari.net/index.html)

This site has been coined as "your on-line clipping service," which is exactly what it is. Featuring complete access to all business information, this site includes business news, updates on technology as it relates to business, an e-news stock report, and other information to include links to job opportunities. This site is hosted by Clarinet Communications Corporation. This site is updated daily, constantly throughout the day, and is very clear and concise.

Commerce Business Daily (Chicago: Commerce Business Daily, U.S. Department of Commerce) [DIALOG]

Commerce Business Daily is a source of on-line information on procurement. The topics covered by the database include (1) U.S. Government procurement services; (2) U.S. Government procurements—supplies, equipment, and materials; (3) contract awards—services; (4) contract awards—supplies, equipment, and material; (5) foreign government standards; (6) business news; (7) special notices; (8) surplus property sales; (9) research and development resources sought or numbered notices.

CompareNet (www.compare.net)

This free web site provides consumers with information about models available for products. Categories of these products include electronics, automobiles, home appliances, home office, services, software, and peripherals, as well as products used predominantly in the summer such as personal watercraft and air conditioners. Within each category, the consumer may choose a product, indicate a price range, and choose the features to be included. After completing a list of preferred features, the web page then provides a list of models that meet the criteria. The results can be included in a comparison chart or compiled in a "wish list" and sent to the user by e-mail.

Compact D/Sec (Compact Disclosure USA) (Bethesda, MD: Disclosure)

Compact D/Sec is a CD-ROM source containing business, financial, and stock ownership information extracted from annual reports and SEC documents. It includes financial and management information on over 12,000 publicly held U.S. companies and stock ownership information on more than 5500 publicly held companies. Each disk includes the last 5 years of annual data and the last 3 years of quarterly data, as well as the most recent textual management statements. The historical disks contain annual data from 1983 and quarterly data from 1985.

The information provided includes name, address, SIC code, legal counsel, auditor, and Forbes and Fortune ranking for each company. Financial data, taken from SEC filings, list eight quarters of quarterly financials, ratios, and price/earnings, 5-year summaries and growth rates for sales, net incomes, and earnings per share, 3 years of annual cash flow data, and the full-text of the footnotes to financial statements. Full-text of the letters of presidents, management discussions, and auditors reports are also available. Finally, lists of subsidiaries, corporate earning estimates from over 120 brokerage firms on more than 4000 companies, abstracts of corporate events, lists of documents filed with the SEC, ownership profiles, and the names, titles, ages, and salaries of top officers are included. The data are taken from 10-Ks, 10-Qs, 20-Fs, 8-Ks, proxy statements, registrations, statements, and annual reports to stockholders.

Company Intelligence (Foster City, CA: Information Access)

Combining company information with news stories, Company Intelligence reports on more than 115,000 private and public companies in the United States. Coverage of companies includes company divisions, subdivisions, affiliates, and joint ventures. Information is updated daily and citations come from approximately 4000 periodicals that are checked for current company news references. New companies are added as they appear in the news and approximately 3500 new companies appear monthly in the database. News stories are taken from newspapers, journals, and newswire services that are indexed by Information Access Company. These include The New York Times, Wall Street Journal, Barron's, and UPI.

Each record provides a maximum of 10 citations; sources and availability of additional citations are also recorded. The date of the latest citation is recorded. Each citation provides article and publication titles, author names, publication dates, page numbers, source files, and the availability of full-text articles on other Information Access databases. Search options include company names, officer names, telephone area codes; stock exchange, SMSA and SIC codes, ticker symbols, revenues, parent company names, and the number of citations.

Company directory information is updated monthly and is confirmed by telephone, questionnaires, annual reports, or 10-K reports for each company. Companies are included regardless of revenue or net worth if they appear in the news. Revenues, actual or estimated, are available for all companies. Each company record provides addresses and telephone numbers, along with a brief description of the businesses, number of employees, names of key personnel, dates of founding, and revenues. Parent company names are recorded when appropriate. Sources of revenue and employee data are given. The revision date of the company data is also reported.

Company ProFile (Foster City, CA: Information Access)

Combining directory information and full-text news articles, this CD-ROM source covers both private and public companies. As with other information Access Company products, this CD-ROM combines existing products, the Company Intelligence and PR Newswire databases. Directory information can be found for more than 100,000 companies, the majority being private businesses.

The CD-ROM provides information on current industry trends, company profiles, new companies, and industry data by city and state. Company directory information comes from Ward's Business Directory. Company information includes brief business descriptions, addresses, contact names, sales volumes, founding dates, number of employees, and special features. The PR Newswire service supplies current news releases. Tables covering industry rankings by volume of sales are also available.

Users can search the database one of six ways: by company, industry, city, state, SIC code, or product. As with other Information Access Company CD-ROMs, Company ProFile is available by annual subscription, which includes 12 monthly updates and the InfoTrac system (PC terminal, CD module, and printer) with software. Maintenance, service, and customer support are also included with a subscription. Subscriptions do not require the use of the InfoTrac system.

CompuServe (Columbus, OH: CompuServe)

CompuServe is an on-line computer communication network. Basic services include information resources such as news, entertainment, financial, communications, shopping, reference/research, and travel. It was designed for a general audience with consumer-oriented, business, and professional needs. Business sources are extensive and include stock quotes, exchange values, and other data. Business-oriented databases are accessible as are databases in other disciplines. Approximately 850 databases are on-line and many are full-text. It is relatively simple to navigate in the CompuServe system, and a 24-hour customer service representative is available to assist subscribers.

A subscription to CompuServe is on a monthly basis and includes bonus software and a trial period. Lifetime membership is available. However, there are fees for optional services such as Forums on topics including investments, genealogy, health, military veterans, and aviation, as well as access to library catalogs and faxing and telex services.

Compustat (Englewood, CA: Standard & Poor's Compustat Services)

Compustat is an on-line database that contains information on over 7000 publicly held companies, 5200 inactive companies, 200 industry composites, and over 3000 research companies. Most of the companies covered are American. It includes balance sheets and income statements, as well as bond ratings. It also provides yearly, high, low and closing stock prices, and the number of employees. The database supplies 15 years of annual data, 5 years of quarterly data, 7 years of business segment information, and 10 years of monthly market data for each company. Information is taken from company annual reports, reports filed with the SEC, government reports, and news services.

Congressional MasterFile

This CD-ROM product provides bibliographic access to a large number of Congressional publications available on microfiche from 1789 to the present. This access is also available in comparable paper indexes. The CD-ROM product is divided into two disks representing a chronological breakdown of the paper indexes: the first disk represents a variety of indexes that collect Congressional publications from 1789 to 1970, e.g., Congressional Information Service United States Serial Set Index and Congressional Information Service United States Congressional Committee Prints Index; and the second disk represents the Congressional Information Service Congressional Index, which indexes Congressional publications from 1970 through the present.

The CD-ROM product provides a user interface that is relatively easy to use. A series of pop-up menus allow the user to negotiate the process of searching and printing search results. The search engine allows both free-text Boolean searching and controlled vocabulary searching, and also allows the user to combine these two search strategies. The user can browse through the controlled vocabulary to select appropriate terms. Once the search results have been identified, the user may scan a title list before accessing the full bibliographic record of any single search result. The user can easily move through the record by searching for a particular word. While not completely intuitive, there is enough information on the interface to allow a novice to search after a short period of familiarization.

The bibliographic information available includes the accession number to the fiche set that accompanies each of these indexes; standard bibliographic information such as title, date, and source; any numbers associated with the publication, such as the Superintendent of Documents number, item number, and Library of Congress card number; and a concise abstract which, for hearings, includes all witnesses and their affiliation. The user may print or download the results of a search in a variety of formats, including the title list, a brief citation, text that the user has marked, the bibliographic information, or the full record.

All these features provide the user the ability to search historically much more quickly than is possible with the paper format. The paper product consists of seven indexes, which are cumulated every 5 years. The user also has the ability to pull up bibliographic information on all documents relating to any public law passed by the Congress, thus creating a legislative history of that law. The producer also makes sure the CD product is kept as up-to-date as the paper product. The CD is updated quarterly with print updates on a monthly basis between CD updates. There is also a toll-free support line.

Consumer Law Page (www.yahoo.com/Government/Law/ Consumer)

The Consumer Law Page can help the user find a lawyer. The site is broken down into three areas that contain information for consumers. The three main areas are Articles, Brochures, and Resources. Consumer-related articles, consumer brochure information, and links to other helpful sites can be found in these categories. One of those sites is the Alexander Law firm, which specializes in consumer damage cases and personal injury. Its purpose is to serve small businesses and consumers.

Consumer's Guide to Electronic Payments (www.paytips.org)

This web site is maintained by the "Mid-American Payment Exchange" (MPX), which is a nonprofit organization providing information on the appropriate utilization of electronic payments. Currently, MPX serves thousands of banks, credit unions, savings and loan associations, as well as individuals. The web site educates financial institutions through the promotion of seminars, conferences, and the introduction of reference books. Besides, consumers can find out news about direct deposit, direct payment, consumer tips, consumer rights, and related links on the web site. Consumer's Guide supports electronic payment systems through public education on the Internet, while MPX's main job is to improve system efficiency, reduce risks, and maximize profits.

Current Contents (Philadelphia: Institute for Scientific Information)

This CD-ROM database provides bibliographic citations and abstracts in seven different disciplines, including life sciences; agriculture, biology, and environmental sciences; physical, chemical, and earth sciences; clinical medicine; engineering, computing and technology; and social and behavioral sciences. A total of over 7700 scholarly journals and 1700 books are represented. The engineering, computing and technology data set alone covers over 1000 journals, including the American Business Law Journal, Business Week, the Harvard Business Review, and the International Journal of Advanced Manufacturing Technology.

The database is updated weekly to reflect new articles and new research in each field, and is available with or without abstracts. Each discipline can be purchased separately or together to customize coverage. The database is searchable in 18 different fields, such as author, title, journal name, keyword, language, and ISSN/ISBN. Contact information is also provided to aid in obtaining reprints of articles. The CD-ROM supports Boolean logic, citation sorting, and both Windows and MS-DOS platforms.

Consumer Information Center (www.pueblo.gsa.gov)

The Consumer Information Center was established to help federal agencies and departments develop, promote, and distribute information of interest to consumers. Their web page includes a copy of the Consumer Information Catalog, which describes documents available to the public from governmental sources. Directions are provided on how to obtain items, which cannot be ordered on-line. Other resources on the site include the full text of documents, the Center's Consumer Resource Handbook, and links to other federal agencies' web pages and materials geared toward consumers. The catalog can be ordered and downloaded on-line. A search engine is also available.

DataWorld Infodisk (Pennsauken, NJ: Faulkner Information Services)

This CD-ROM source contains the full text and images of all four volumes of the DataWorld reference publication. This monthly publication provides more than 1000 product reviews, evaluations, recommendations, and reports on computer products, specifically data processing hardware, software, and data communications products. Subjects covered include hardware, software, systems, peripherals, and communications products for mainframe, mid-range, and micro-based computer environments. The data given includes pricing, product comparison charts, tables, diagrams, and graphic images, as well as news summaries and feature articles on trends in the computer industry from the Faulkner newsletter Perspectives. Coverage includes only current information, and the CD-ROM is updated quarterly with back editions available.

The language used is English, although coverage is international. The CD-ROM system has a simple search interface with broad fields to search free text. It has some preset keywords to narrow down searches. Adjacency terms are not available. Valuable features include a manual and a help key, as well as a troubleshooting file. The format is ISO 9660 with KAware search software by Knowledge Access International. An IBM or any compatible PC with an MS-DOS 3.1 operating system plus 640K of RAM and a minimum of 1 megabyte of hard drive space is necessary. A CD-ROM drive is also needed. Demo copies are available.

D&B-Dun's Electronic Business Directory (Parsippany, NJ: Dun and Bradstreet Information Services) [DIALOG]

Dun and Bradstreet—Dun's electronic business directory has on-line information on U.S. companies, businesses, and professionals. Each listing includes address, telephone number, SIC codes, and descriptions and number of employees. The business categories covered are agriculture, business services, communication, construction, finance, insurance, manufacturing, mining, professional services, real estate, retail, transportation, utilities, and wholesale. The information is compiled through interviews, telemarketing, and direct mail surveys.

D&B-Dun's Business Update (Parsippany, NJ: Dun and Bradstreet Information Services) [DIALOG]

Dun and Bradstreet Business update is a directory of U.S. enterprises that are either new companies, new legal entities, or new to Dun and Bradstreet. These changes are brought about by new ownership, chief executives officers, company name, address, and telephone numbers.

D&B-Million Dollar Directory (Parsippany, NJ: Dun and Bradstreet Information Services) [DIALOG]

Dun and Bradstreet-million dollar directory contains business information on companies with at least $25 million annual sales, 25,000 employees, and $500,000 net worth. Each entry includes company name, address, primary and secondary SIC codes, annual sales, number of employees, and names of executives.

Datapro Product Specifications (Delron, NJ: Datapro Information Services Group) [DIALOG]

Datapro Product Specifications describes products made by computer, communication, and office technology industries. The descriptions include product design, system compatibility, network characteristics, standards adherence, service and support, performance, security features, price, and vendors.

DIALOG Information Retrieval Service (Palo Alto, CA: DIALOG Information Services)

DIALOG is a broadly based reference source and does not specialize in one particular subject area. DIALOG is a commercially available computer database service. The Catalog of Databases lists over 400 different databases that are available. Databases are collections of records maintained by computer mainframes and accessible via phone lines. Some DIALOG files are also available in CD-ROM or print forms. However, on-line versions are more up to date.

DIALOG databases are generally citations and abstracts, although sometimes full-text (a complete record of a journal article) version is available for a higher fee. Rates for the use of DIALOG services vary, depending on the institution subscribing to the service, the databases accessed, and the connect time. Additional fees are assessed for viewing the records retrieved by a search or having these records printed offline and mailed to the searcher.

Searching on these databases is performed by using Boolean operators and a set of standardized commands that are listed in either the DIALOG Blue Sheets or White Sheets. The Blue Sheets are 2- to 4-page descriptions of the available databases, listing their contents and organization. The White Sheets are an expanded version of the Blue Sheets, offering tips on search strategies and giving examples.

The Database Catalog available from DIALOG is an important tool for determining which databases should be used. It is an alphabetical listing of the databases. Dates of coverage, the number of records in the database, the frequency of updates, and the File Numbers (for use in accessing the database for searching) are given. A description of the databases and the name and location of the organization/agency/company providing the database are also included. The Catalog is indexed by data type and subject and has an alphabetical listing of full-text sources.

DIALOG Company Name Finder (Palo Alto, CA: DIALOG Information Services) [DIALOG]

DIALOG company name finder is used for searching company information in the DIALOG databases. The searches are done by using company names that are used as index terms.

DIALOG Ondisc U.S. Business Reporter (Palo Alto, CA: DIALOG Information Services)

DIALOG Ondisc U.S. Business Reporter contains information from business sections of newspapers and company news releases. The topics covered include company executives, marketing, and business conditions.

DIALOG Product Name Finder (Palo Alto, CA: DIALOG Information Services) [DIALOG]

DIALOG Product Name Finder assists in searching product information from other DIALOG databases.

Disclosure Inc. of Bethesda

This service provides documents from the Securities and Exchange Commission on CompuServe and America Online.

Disclosure Laser D/SEC (Bethesda, MD: Disclosure, Inc.)

This CD-ROM database is a collection of important corporate documents filed with the U.S. Securities and Exchange Commission, as well as other government regulatory agencies. Approximately 11,000 corporations are included on this CD-ROM, along with the complete 10-K reports, annual shareholder reports, proxy statements, and 8-K reports filed by each. Information available within these reports include company name, address, phone and fax numbers; fiscal year-end date; stock exchanges on which the company's stock is traded; public disclosures of mergers and acquisitions; notification of pending litigation; financial information, including statements of cash flows, statements of earnings, and outstanding loan amounts; the full-text of the company's annual report to shareholders; power of attorney letters; and lists of the company's subsidiaries and branch offices.

The Laser D/SEC CD-ROM consists of U.S. companies that trade on the major U.S. stock exchanges: the New York Stock Exchange, NASDAQ, Over-the-Counter, and the American Stock Exchange. Listings and filings are continually updated, with daily updates occurring during peak periods and the weeks surrounding a filing deadline. The filings are obtained through the U.S. Securities and Exchange Commission's Electronic Data Gathering, Analysis, and Retrieval (EDGAR) system, the paperless, electronic filing system to which corporations submit their reports and other public documents as required by law.

Disclosure/Worldscope Global

The CD-ROM Disclosure/Worldscope Global is published by Disclosure, Inc. This database has information on many international companies. This

CD-ROM is mainly for people who are researching foreign firms or who are interested in international investing. Disclosure/Worldscope Global gives basic corporate information such as the company's business address and number of employees. The CD-ROM also provides company financial data with income statements and balance sheets. Based on the type of subscription chosen, Disclosure/Worldscope Global is updated monthly, quarterly, or annually.

Dow Jones News/Retrieval (Princeton, NJ: Dow Jones)

Dow Jones News/Retrieval is an on-line source of information and news about the business world. It is a composite of a variety of services and Dow Jones databases for managers, personal investors, and information specialists.

The service consists of current and historical data on publicly held companies and businesses. Current news, facts, and analyses of financial, economic, and political matters are available as well. It has quotes and news services and a variety of full-text newswires on both the domestic and international levels. Data are gathered by Dow Jones and taken from investment reports and Federal reports. Updates on news-oriented services are daily. The full-text of The Wall Street Journal is on-line, as are articles from Barron's, Business Week, Forbes, Fortune, The Los Angeles Times, and The Washington Post.

News/Retrieval provides general services, such as on-line information on travel and electronic mail, and access to general news and reviews. It is a menu-based system and is searchable by personal names, company names, company stock symbols, industry, and government codes and miscellaneous codes.

Dissertation Abstracts International (Ann Arbor: University Microfilms International) [DIALOG, BRS]

This work has abstracts available starting in July 1980. This publication includes Dissertation Abstracts International, Comprehensive Dissertation Index, American Doctoral Dissertations (ADD), and Masters Abstracts.

Dissertation Abstracts/Dissertation Abstracts Online (Ann Arbor, MI: University Microfilms)

Dissertation Abstracts contains references for many doctoral dissertations accepted at accredited American institutions in approximately 3000 subject areas since 1861 and master's theses. It contains some citations for doctoral dissertations from Canada, Great Britain, and Europe since 1988.

Each entry contains all or some of the following information: adviser, author, date degree awarded, degree, International Standard Book Number, language, location of reference copy, publication number, publisher, subject, subject code, school, school code, source, title, availability information, and an abstract. The abstract, when available, is 350 words written by the author and describes the original research project on which the dissertation was based. Abstracts are available from July 1980 to present and bibliographic citations are available from 1861. Masters' theses bibliographic citations are available from 1962 and abstracts are available from 1988 to the present.

Users may search for records by author, title, UMI order number, date, institution, or university, supervisor of the thesis, and by descriptive topic or keyword.

The on-line database is available through DIALOG, BRS Information Technologies, and OCLC EPIC, and is updated monthly with the edition of approximately 3500 records. The database is also in CD-ROM format. Dissertation Abstracts International is the printed source for abstracts of doctoral dissertations, and Masters Abstracts International is the printed source for masters' theses.

Dun's Reference Plus (Murray Hill, NJ: Dun & Bradstreet)

The Dun's Reference Plus is a CD-ROM source containing the name, address, founding date, alternate name, headquarters, parent company, D&B rating, D-U-N-S number, and SIC codes for over 4,000,000 American businesses. The software also makes it possible to dial into the Dun & Bradstreet database to update records. The disk is updated on a bimonthly basis.

Dun's Million Dollar Disc (Parsippany, NJ: Dun & Bradstreet)

The Million Dollar Disc is a CD-ROM source that contains information on U.S. companies worth $500,000 or more. Many types of commercial, manufacturing, and service industries are represented. Records include company names, addresses, top executives, founding dates, amounts of sales, numbers of employees, D-U-N-S numbers, stock exchange, and SIC codes, their accounting and banking firms, and whether they import or export. Biographical information is included for executives. The disk is searchable by company name, by location, amount of sales, number of employees, import/export indicator, and public/private indicator. The disk is updated quarterly.

Dun & Bradstreet (Dun's Business Identification Service)

This service identifies organizations in the United States. Listings include a Data Universal Numbering System (D-U-N-S) number, company name, and company address. The D-U-N-S number is similar in nature to a social security number of companies and is issued by Dun and Bradstreet. The listings are arranged alphabetically by company name on microfiche cards.

E-Trade

This service, available on CompuServe, permits on-line trading with money-management software.

EconData (A Source of Economic Time Series Data from the University of Maryland)

telnet://gopher@info.umd.eduUSA/Maryland/University of Maryland/ Educational Resources/AcademicResources/Academic Resources by Topic/ Economics Resources/EconData

ftp://info.umd.edu/inforM/Educational_Resources/AcademicResourcesByTopic/EconomicsResources/EconData

gopher://info.umd.edu:901/11/inforM/Educational_Resources/ Academic ResourcesByTopic/EconomicsResources/EconData

This database, collected by INFORUM, a project building an interindustry model of the U.S. economy, processes a wide variety of macro data and places it in a common format. Data include the National Income and Product Accounts, balance of payments, flow of funds, monthly employment surveys, CPI, PPI, Business Conditions Indicators, blue pages from the Survey of Current Business, industrial production, the Penn World Tables, and state and local data including employment, earnings, GSP, and state personal income.

The following G data banks are available:

A. USNational:

U.S. national data are placed under four subdirectories—Accounts, Labor, Price, and BusInd.

Files in "Accounts":
NIPAA.ZIP—Annual National Income and Product Accounts
NIPASA.ZIP—Annual NIPA Supplementary Tables
NIPAQ.ZIP—Quarterly National Income and Product Accounts
NIPASQ.ZIP—Quarterly NIPA Supplementary Tables
FDI.ZIP—Foreign Direct Investment in the U.S.
BOP.ZIP—Balance of Payments of the U.S.(follows federal org?)A.
FOFLEV.ZIP—Flow of Fund Accounts
FOFNSA.ZIP—Flow of Fund Accounts
FOFSA.ZIP—Flow of Fund Accounts

Files in "Labor":
  EHENSA.ZIP—Monthly National Employment, Hours, Earnings and Diffusion Indices; Not Seasonally Adjusted
  EHESA.ZIP—Same as above, yet is Seasonally Adjusted

Files in "Price":
  PPI.ZIP—Producer Price Indexes
  PPIR.ZIP—Producer Price Indexes, Revised
  CPIW.ZIP—Consumer Price Indexes, Wage Earners
  CPIU.ZIP—Consumer Price Indexes, Urban Workers
  XMPI.ZIP—Export/Import Price Indexes

Files in "Buslnd":
  BCI.ZIP—Business Conditions Indicators
  SCB.ZIP—Blue Pages of the Survey of Current Business
  IPISA.ZIP—Industrial Production Indexes, Seasonally Adjusted
  IPINSA.ZIP—Industrial Production Indexes, Not Seasonally Adjusted
  KWHSA.ZIP—Kilowatt Hours, Seasonally Adjusted
  KWHNSA.ZIP—Kilowatt Hours, Not Seasonally Adjusted
  MFG.ZIP—Manufacturing retrospective

B. StateLocal:

Employ—State and Area Employment, Hours, Earnings. This directory contains several archives organized by region.
UNLFC.ZIP—Labor force and Unemployment from household surveys.
GSP.ZIP—Gross State Products
SPI.ZIP—State Personal Income

C. International:

PWT.ZIP—Penn World Tables

The data on EconData is provided by INFORUM as a service to the general public. Data are in the form of archived G-banks due to data storage efficiency. Anyone using this database will need decompression software and the public domain version of the G software (PDG). All files have data stamps to show when the information was updated.

EdgarPlus (Bethesda, MD: Disclosure Inc.)

EdgarPlus is the Security Exchange Commission's Electronic Data Gathering, Analysis, and Retrieval system. This version contains the original and additional non-EDGAR filing and other documents. Also, with the new version, the user is able to link to Disclosure's public companies' databases. Unlike the older version, EdgarPlus does not use American Standard Code of Information Interchange text; hence it can be formatted and easily navigated. EdgarPlus is compatible with the SEC's on-line service; the information can be integrated fully into EdgarPlus format. The Access Disclosure database contains filings by the SEC. Some information is obtained directly from the stock exchanges or the companies. The database also reaches overseas to thousands of companies. Access Disclosure also receives information from several other federal offices. EdgarPlus is available on the Internet, CD-ROM, and direct feed.

Edgar ftp town.hall.org (login: Anonymous)

This database contains thousands of 10-K reports for businesses and investors. The site has its own search engine organized according to company name or ticker number. Its listings include those companies with current files at the U.S. Securities and Exchange Commission.

Electronic Data Gathering and Retrieval (Edgar)

Files of the Securities and Exchange Commission may be ordered by electronic mail by sending a message to the Internet Multicasting Service mail@town.hall.org), requesting an index of documents and a list of commands. It can be accessed also by using Mosaic, the World Wide Web, American Online, or CompuServe. The Edgar documents are available through many services, such as Mead Data Central, Disclosure, and Dow Jones.

Entrepreneurs on the Web

Entrepreneurs on the Web is a labyrinth of hypermedia documents on the World Wide Web bursting with information. This wedge of cyberspace, complete with graphics, text, sound, and quick-motion videos, is dedicated to the exchange of business information, goods, and services. The spectrum of clients/users of this document may range from computer-literate children to serious business professionals.

The diverse activities available through Entrepreneurs on the Web include ordering merchandise on-line, placing an advertisement, viewing vacation real estate, and accessing business statistics and graphs. Clients can order flowers, books, and videos; take a virtual tour of Malaysia, Paris, and Montreal; gain quick access to an abundance of reference resources such as Library listings, Index to Multimedia Information Sources, and a Directory of Research at MIT. Not only are resources being continually added, but this document also contains Gopher menus, which serve as jumping off points to documents such as Bureau of the Census, National Archives, National Science Foundation, and Social Security Administration.

To successfully navigate Entrepreneurs on the Web, start at the home page, which offers two major departments: Business Information Resources and Goods and Services. Business Information Resources divide into areas such as The Internet Business Center, Brookfield Economics Institute Newsletter, Free Listings in a National Directory of Consultants and Consulting Firm, Free Listings in a National Directory of Telecommunications and Related Services, Laws Concerning Unsolicited Faxing. The Internet Business Center has interesting subdivisions such as Valuable Stats, Travel Sites, LISTSERVEs, Internet Marketing Archives, and entertainment establishments such as MPEG Movie Archive featuring 200 Kb to 2 Mb stop–motion video clips.

The second of the major departments, Goods and Services, contains The Computer Tailor, Dellen Leasing, The Reference Press, and the Branch Mall. Would you like to "Stop Smoking in 5-Days?" Visit the services section in the Branch Mall. Vacuum cleaners, T-shirts, and fabulous flags are also on the list of merchandise available at the mall.

Entrepreneurs on the Web is most easily accessed by using Mosaic software on a Macintosh computer. Simply open the Universal Resource Locator (URL) under Mosaic's "Find" menu, then type in sashimi.wwa.com/ ~notime/eotw/EOTW.html.

ESPN Sportszone (ESPN.Sportzone.com)

ESPN Sportszone is a web site comprising of daily sports-related information. Users can traverse the web site for National Basketball Association (NBA), National Hockey League (NHL), National College Athletic Association (NCAA) basketball, National Football League (NFL), professional baseball, golf, soccer, auto racing and tennis scores, highlights, and related stories. Direct links are available to daily columns, features, and sports polls. Further links include ESPN live audio, ESPN studios, Sportszone games and stores, health and fitness, a sports almanac, and a sponsor index. A score tracker is provided for up-to-the-minute sports scores. An index of all the sections and features of the site is provided.

European Union Official Site (europa.eu.int/index-en.htm)

The official web site of the European Union provides update news about the official press releases and information on upcoming events. Links to different institutions and other bodies of the Union are listed. Information on the Union's economic, social, security, and foreign policies are provided.

EXEGY

Covering most countries of the world, EXEGY offers current information on numerous subject areas such as politics, sports, business, laws, and cultures. This CD-ROM database provides information in various formats: statistical figures, atlases, photographs, and texts. Whether the user is searching for information on popular sports players in Asia or on the latest documents (e.g., major speeches, treaties, legislation) released by European political parties, EXEGY enables the user to retrieve not only the information he/she needs but also related information to maximize the search effectiveness. EXEGY is updated bimonthly.

FBR Asian Company Profiles (Taipei, Taiwan: FBR Data Base Inc.) [DIALOG]

FBR Asian Company Profiles is source of information on companies that have English names and are involved in manufacturing, international trade, exporting, importing, investment, and support international business. Details about each company include address, chief executive officer, number of employees, product, subsidiaries, financial information, market, and factory facilities. Information about the companies is collected through credit investigations and surveys.

F&S Index Plus Text/International and United States (Cleveland, OH: Predicasts)

This CD-ROM source is the equivalent to F&S PROMPT on-line and F&S Indexes PROMPT in print. It covers worldwide business activities from over 1000 trade, business, and government publications. The database gives references on topics from many areas of the manufacturing and service industries but focuses on companies, products, markets, and applied technology. Most references include either an abstract or article excerpt averaging 350–450 words. In the case of shorter articles, the full-text is often included. Market trends and forecasts, economic climates, mergers, government regulations, emerging technologies, and consumer attitudes are some of the subjects covered. Information contained is from 1990 to the present, with updates added monthly.

The product comes with two disks. One covers the United States and the other covers international businesses. Boolean searching is available as is searching by industry, product, and geographic area.

Federal Express (www.fedex.com)

Federal Express hosts its own well-organized web site. A complete list of services includes services-on line, free software, info central, what's new, and help/search. An added feature includes a homepage for each of the areas in which FedEx provides services, including Canada, Asia, Europe, Africa, Middle East/India, and Latin America. This site also offers an Express Menu for tracking orders, delivery options, and shipping information. This entire homepage is indexed under the help/search option.

Federal Grants and Funding Locator (Mount Vernon, VA: Staff Directories)

This CD-ROM source is used for locating Federal grant money, indexing 1300 grant programs. The searchable fields are Program name, Federal agency, Grant requirements, Dollar amounts, Deadlines, Funding guidelines, and Past funding data. This is a good database for any entity seeking funding and evaluating the potential of a grant program.

The CD-ROM is updated twice a year and it is available with network options.

Federation for Enterprise Knowledge Development (www.fend.es)

The Federation for Enterprise Knowledge Development web site offers information and services designed for efficient knowledge management within an organization. FEND is a federation of companies and universities working in collaboration to research, test, and develop enterprise knowledge and innovation. FEND provides independent diagnoses of organizations and integrates companies in a network of knowledge organizations. The site allows users to join the mailing list, receive the newsletter, and access a number of useful web sites; it also provides information and an application for joining.

Fedworld (www.fedworld.gov)

Fedworld is a web site for users of a wide array of governmental information. It holds a keyword search engine, which is helpful in locating rather specific items within its large database. One can also traverse a variety of links to many beneficial pages including the Internal Revenue Service, the National Performance Review, the United States Business Advisor, and the United States Treasury. Furthermore, it contains the "Davis–Bacon Act" database, which maintains more than 2000 records, each with wage information for numerous careers. The "Davis–Bacon Act" database, however, requires a small fee for usage. Another useful link is the "World News Connection," providing current news from a variety of global sources.

FEDNet—Home Page of the Foundation for Enterprise Development (www.fed.org/fed)

The Foundation for Enterprise Development (F.E.D.) is a nonprofit organization that focuses on providing information and assistance to companies interested in equity-based compensation and methods of involving employees in improving business operations.

The F.E.D. has created a home page describing their activities and disseminates information. FEDNet has three main sections. The first section, The Foundation for Enterprise Development, includes information about the foundation, its publications, and its members. Full text of Foundation newsletters, which cover topics such as recent legislation, trends, and tips from other entrepreneurs, is available from August/September 1993 to the present. The full text of 1992 and 1993 conference proceedings is also available.

Other information available includes a listing of the officers and staff of the F.E.D., the annual report, a calendar of events, and a list of corporations and individuals making financial contributions to the organization.

The second main section of FEDNet is called The Entrepreneur's Network and has sections on frequently asked questions, the most recent newsletter of the foundation, and the "question of the week" (a question posted to the readers to elicit reader responses and ideas). A calendar of events is available both as a complete listing of events and as a geographic listing by regions of the country. A "Discussion Forum" is available for readers to share ideas on management and organization issues. The "What's New" section has articles about employee compensation and the historical files for the section.

The third main section of the home page is called The Business Resource Library and includes information on new developments in employee ownership and equity compensation, methods of equity compensation, employee motivation and empowerment, international employee ownership, case studies of successful companies, government policy and legislation, and employee ownership research. From the Business Resource Library, it is also possible to access the "What's New," "Discussion Forums," and "Business Updates" sections of the Entrepreneur's Network section.

FEDNet is searchable from a number of screens. It is designed to search for the occurrence of a word in any title, and will retrieve a list of documents meeting the entered search string. An index is also available. It is arranged by broad categories that appear within the home page, such as "What's New," "Business Updates," and "Newsletters," with the individual articles listed beneath the section heading. The index is most useful for browsing to see what types of information are available in this database. FEDNet also provides a form for giving feedback, and has compiled a useful list, with hypertext links, of related resources available on the World Wide Web.

Fedmarket Database (Mount Vernon, VA: Staff Directories)

This source is available for information technology businesses wanting to expand their market share and receive increased funding for their information technology from the federal government. This source lists government decision-makers who purchase technological products and services. Compiled from sources such as the Federal and Congressional Staff directories, this database leads the user to government individuals anxious to receive information on technological commodities and services needed by governmental agencies. Prices for this database are quoted individually.

Findout's Consumer & Legal Affairs Library (www.yahoo.com/Government/Law/Consumer)

The Legal & Consumer Affairs site provides information about your rights as a consumer and potential client. The site possesses a library containing articles, books, periodicals, software, pamphlets, and on-line resources for you to read. This web page's objective is to increase consumers' awareness of their rights.

First Search (Dublin, OH: OCLC Online Computer Library Center)

First Search is an on-line union catalog provided by OCLC. This bibliographic database offers access to an assortment of database systems. Approximately 30 databases are available, that ranging from general library catalogs to humanities, social science, science, and engineering indexes. Legal, business, and medical indexes are also included.

The catalog can be accessed by either an OCLC workstation or a personal computer. It can be linked to an existing computer system by dial access, Internet, or an OCLC-designated line. It provides on-line help for inexperienced users and a printed guide for more in-depth instruction.

FINWeb—A Financial/Economics World Wide Web Server

Finweb has been created and is managed by Professor James R. Garvin of the University of Texas. It contains 4 pages of links to other web sites, 91 in all. These include working papers, databases, other financial/economic web servers, miscellaneous related links and a list of web tools, guides, and services.

The majority of the links are connections to a variety of financial services. There are one or two sentence definition(s) for most links.

Finweb offers the opportunity to browse through a diverse group of sources on the subject and to keep abreast of WWW projects in the field. Its primary use is likely to be for the curious and those who already know the potential resources well.

Franchise Network (www.frannet.com)

This web site provides help in buying and selling a franchise. It has data on the history of franchising, as well as why and how to select one. Franchise Network has developed two self tests for determining whether users are suited for ownership and what type they should purchase. An alphabetical listing of franchises with their telephone numbers is included. Franchise Network has a home page for many companies, explaining the nature of the businesses, their history, investment information, financing, and qualification requirements. Interested parties can receive brochures and videos about the franchise by electronically submitting the form at the bottom of each home page.

Global Business Network (www.gbn.org)

Global Business Network (GBN) is a web site of a consulting firm, the Global Business Network, for users interested in planning corporate management strategies. The Network was created to offer members consulting, scenario developments for business strategies, and learning opportunities on current issues which influence business management. It provides users a network of companies and individuals from science, the arts, business, and academia. The members are linked electronically and share ideas through on-line conferences. This web site gives users summaries of the company's services: consulting, scenario reports, news, a book club, and bibliographies by their staff.

Global Contact (www.globalcontact.com)

Global Contact offers help to companies in locating products and services worldwide. They give access to the latest news and information regarding to the world of International Trade and Transportation. In the section on International Trade News and Information, information sources in the United States and abroad are made available. One can find news and information that affects business. In another part of the page, one can find out more about the U.S. labeling law, which is worth reading for any manufacturer providing products sold in this country or overseas. There is also a database to locate companies that specialize in products of the user's interest. Direct links to products and services are accessible.

GLOnet (www.glonet.com)

The global business network is a full-service corporate Internet provider. They serve many of today's leading corporation and educational institutions. The page offers business solutions using the Web, mainly advertising their own services as to how they can help in analyzing one's business and advise how the Internet will add to business growth. There is also a directory of corporations and links to web sites in the areas of business and government. One can print news articles from such papers as Wall Street Journal, USA Today, and New York Times. Also accessible is on-line news at Newslink and broadcast stations such as CNN, NPR, and ABC.

Gopher.Medsearch.Com

The Medsearch.com on-line database is a commercial site that is organized using gopher software. It is accessible by using TurboGopher or any World Wide Web browser. The Medsearch.com gopher address provides a link to information pertaining to the Msen gopher. The Msen World Headquarters are in Ann Arbor, MI. The Msen gopher directory provides access to news service, Internet reviews, business page listings, a marketplace, a directory of professionals, ftp sites for software, Ann Arbor/Detroit weather, Ann Arbor Civic Information, and the Online Career Center for the Internet community.

The Internet Business Page directory (IBP) provides the Internet user community instant access to basic information about businesses around the world including street address, email address, sales phone number, and fax number. In order to be listed in this directory, the business has to complete a registration form. An index is provided that lists the businesses registered with Msen, Inc.

The Msen MarketPlace is a directory of a variety of approximately 20 vendor gophers, ranging from an Internet catalog of gourmet food to a discussion group of Twin Cities Area Libraries and Information Centers. Most of these vendors have gophers that are under construction. A few of the gophers that actually provide some kind of information include:

- the Detroit Free Press—provides a listing for departmental phone numbers and e-mail addresses, phone numbers for press reporters and editors, explains how to obtain back copies and articles, provides weather information for the Detroit area and Michigan, and also gives a listing of library catalogs in Michigan, and more.
- MedSearch America—provides employment advertising and communications networking designed specifically for the healthcare industry. Job announcements are résumés are posted here. Job announcements are searchable by keyword. Articles on the healthcare

industry as well as the healthcare industry outlook are also provided in this gopher.

• Online Career Center—the Online Career Center is basically a not-for-profit organization that develops, manages, and distributes electronic employment advertising and communication systems for human resource management. The job postings listed here are predominantly for computer programmers and analysts and are searchable by geographic location, and keyword.

Medsearch.com is not a very reliable database because the connection does not always work. In addition, many of the resources are still under construction and completion dates are not provided.

This Internet file can be reached by more than one method. It can be reached through Mosaic by opening the URL: gopher://gopher.uoregon.edu/77/Reference/.index/zipcode. It can also be reached through gopherspace by following this procedure:

um-ulibrary
   Other Gophers and Veronica
     United States
       Oregon
         University of Oregon < menu >
           Index: Titles in this Gopher Server < index >
Search under the term [zip codes]
Use the first title in the list, U.S. Postal Zip Codes

This is a searchable file. There are several ways to search on this. Search on a city name alone and all cities with that word (or words) in them will appear, along with their corresponding zip codes and states. This can be limited by searching on a city name followed by a two-letter state abbreviation. This will produce a list like above, only it will contain all the cities within the given state and the city that was searched will be on top. A search can be carried out by state names as well. By doing a search like this, a list is produced containing all the cities within the state, in alphabetical order, with their corresponding zip codes. A search can also carried out by using the zip code. Corresponding city name(s) and the state appear.

This file can be used in several ways. If the city and state are known, the zip code is easily retrieved. If the city and zip code are known, the correct state is given. And, lastly, if only the city or state is known, large lists come up for the patron to scan. A list of cities with the search word(s) is brought up so that variations can be viewed. A list of cities within a state can help by allowing the patron to browse and hopefully find the one desired.

H.E.A.R.T. Career Connections Online Interactive Employment Network

H.E.A.R.T. is a free on-line database that is a fully menu-driven, graphical system that allows clients to search for jobs in various disciplines. Potential clients may access the service by registering and then creating his/her employment profile. The database can generate résumés for the client based on information that is given in the profile—or the client may opt to upload an ASCII text version of a résumé into the system for storage and continuous use.

By using H.E.A.R.T., clients may connect with potential employers on-line, view career opportunities, write electronic cover letters, and respond to job recruiters. The system also allows employers to conduct on-line interviews with applicants. The employers are responsible for updating positions that appear in the database, which are removed when positions are filled. Some job listings appear outdated but may still be active. Clients must forward all information and résumés to employers of their choice because all résumés and profile data are kept confidential.

Clients may access job listings through three relational files: the company file, which displays the potential employers and contact persons; the discipline file, which lists the positions and job descriptions; or the geography file, which lists employment by city and state. Other features of the system include the public bulletin board, which allows participating clients to communicate with each other, and clients can use the electronic mail to post comments, questions, or suggestions.

H.E.A.R.T. information and text may be downloaded to a disk, a printer, or other transfer protocols. H.E.A.R.T. may be accessed via telnet (telnet career.com) or by using an IP address (telnet 157.151.160.1). The H.E.A.R.T homepage may be reached on the World Wide Web (URL: www.career.com:8500) via Mosaic. Because job postings are geared toward experienced clients, H.E.A.R.T. maintains a separate database for new college graduates.

Harvard Business School Publishing Gopher

This gopher provides a catalog of material available through the Harvard Business School (HBS) Publishing program. Included are Harvard Business School titles, reprints from the Harvard Business Review, and other materials from Harvard Business School such as case studies, background notes, videos, teaching notes, and software. Search capabilities are possible through entries in the Harvard Business School case studies and press catalogs and the

Harvard Business Review. Each search will provide title, author, and publication information, as well as abstracts for each citation. Also included are price lists and listings of international distributors of HBS publications. An order blank can be produced from the screen for ordering materials and toll-free telephone numbers are also available.

Home Office Internet Resources (www.hoaa.com/links.htm)

The Home Office Internet Resources Web page assembles a list of what they believe are the worthiest combination of World Wide Web links available for home office professionals. They also renew their list frequently.

Hoover's Business Resources

This service provided by America Online provides facts and statistics for industries, as well as rankings and profiles for companies.

Hoover's Online (www.hoovers.com)

This site provides information on over 10,000 publicly traded companies. Many links are available including company information, corporate web sites (with over 4000 available listings), company profiles, and current information on companies about to go public. Other valuable tools include: Hoover's Business Tools (a list of business-related books and periodicals for sale), Cyberstocks (a site dedicated to current stock prices), Earnings Central (providing the latest quarterly earnings, and a portfolio in which to monitor ones personal stock activity.

Hoppenstedt Directory of German Companies (Damstadt, Germany: Hoppenstedt Wirtschaftsdatenbank) [DIALOG]

The directory provides information on German companies whose sales are worth at least 2 million Deutsche marks or have at least 20 employees. Information about each company includes address, line of business, number of employees, sales, capital stock, branches and subsidiaries, executives and directors. The records are written in German and English.

HRIM MALL (www.hrimmall.com)

HRIM MALL provides the service of consolidating Human Resource Information Management and Technology. This one-step service offers analytical information from companies around the world that offer Human Resource Management Information. The Marketplace link offers two links that specialize in the products and the latter in the product reviews. Another link is that of the Products and Services Guide. This link offers shopping information on HRIM topics. Other links are the Search The HRIM MALL and HR Sites, which offer information on other groups that also provide human resource information. Direct links are available to all HRIM MALL services.

ICC British Company Annual Reports (London: ICC Information Group) [DIALOG]

ICC British Company Annual Reports are a source of full-text annual reports as well as accounts of UK quoted companies. Each record provides the following information, company name and address, company organization, board of directors, bankers and auditors, profit and loss accounts, balance sheets, operating results, future plans, product data, and research and development.

IHS International Standards and Specifications (Englewood, CO: Information Handling Services) [DIALOG]

IHS International Standards and Specifications provide information about industry, engineering, government, and commercial standards and specifications.

IEEE/IEE Publication Ondisc (Ann Arbor, MI: University Microfilms)

Providing data on electronics and computing, this CD-ROM product covers the publications of the Institution of Electrical and Electronic Engineers (IEEE) and the Institution of Electrical Engineers (IEE). It covers approximately 80 journals, 500 standards, and 350 conference proceedings. Twenty-five disks are added to the collection every year, with approximately 15,000 page images added each month.

The database provides indexing and abstracting and full-text articles. Users can find information on such subjects as telecommunications, image processing, software engineering, and electronic devices. All materials from publications are scanned, so text, formulas, charts, diagrams, photos, and illustrations are available. The index can be searched and the abstract viewed before retrieving and printing the article. Publications can also be retrieved by searching the Periodical Directory and entering the title, issue, and page number.

IEEE/IEE Publications Ondisc is part of University Microfilms' Pro-Quest image database system. Subscriptions include the CD-ROM and updates, software, documentation, equipment, and workstation.

Information Professional's Career Page
(www.brint.com/jobs.htm)

Information Professional's Career Page is a web site profiling key issues relevant to the Information Systems Professional's career. The site offers a word search to navigate the contents of the site. Users may access the on-line library of books and articles covering many aspects of jobs and business. Extensive information is available on employment, interviewing skills, professional development, and executive information. Links are provided to other career employment site on the Web.

International Federation of Building and Wood Workers
(www.ifbww.org)

The site for the International Federation of Building and Wood Workers (IFBWW) is directed to members of its organization. Included on the page is news from the IFBWW 20th World Congress, press releases, links to related sites, and "Events of the Year." The home page contains some information about trade union rights and the development of labor unions, but is primarily focused on issues affecting IFBWW only.

Internet Publicity Resources
(www.olympus.net/okeefe/Pubnet)

The Internet Publicity Resources allows people to view information from Steve O'Keefe's book, Publicity on the Internet. Articles found on this site by Steve O'Keefe, are about Online Marketing and covers items such as: Book Publicity in the Internet, E-Mail Basics, Internet Demographics, The Art of Free Sample, Getting Ready for chat, and Online Publicity for Authors. Links are resources (or sites) that contain further beneficial information for various categories. Self-Promotion Resources and SuperSite Finder Resources are just examples of the many links available.

InfoTrac SearchBank

InfoTrac SearchBank offers unique features that are designed to assist the user in many ways. InfoTrac SearchBank can be accessed through various platforms including Z39.50, and unlike other commercial on-line services, it offers Web access as well. Easy accessibility is further enhanced by easy user interface, and InfoTrac SearchBank claims that user training is unnecessary.

InfoTrac SearchBank is also rich in terms of its coverage of databases. The databases available via InfoTrac SearchBank include: General Business File, Health Reference Center, Expanded Academic Index, PsychINFO, and Current Contents. Documents can be retrieved in either ASCII text or image articles. InfoTrac SearchBank also offers document delivery service.

Institute of Business and Economic Reports (IBER) (uclink.berkeley.edu:160511)

This gopher site contains a brochure (with general information on IBER) publications (a series of working papers related to finance, economics, and real estate), a bulletin (containing the most recent newsletters and information relating to IBER), economic history (announcements and lists of papers from recent group conferences), tax policy/public finance (announcements from the Robert D. Burch Center for Tax Policy and Public Finance at UC Berkeley, and current news and tools for economists). The site can be searched using keyword or subject.

Internet Business Center (Pittsburgh, PA: The Internet Group)

The Internet Business Center (IBC) on-line database was created by The Internet Group (TIG), Mike Walsh of Internet Info, and Jayne Levin of The Internet Letter. TIG helps companies optimize their use of the Internet through a range of Internet services. IBC is a World Wide Web source for information about conducting business on the Internet. This source offers businesses a variety of information on such areas as Breaking News, Internet statistics, Internet Business Sites and Services, and Commercial Internet domain growth statistics.

Marketing on the Internet gives businesses valuable information on using the Internet to market their products, services, and corporate needs.

IBC also includes publications from corporations and associations that may be of interest to its users. For example, the August 1, 1994 issue of The Internet Letter was included in IBC. Its focus was on the NSF transition.

IBC lists the statistics of the commercial Internet domain growth. IBC gives the domain names and company owners of some of the more notable registrants. Companies listed include Kraft General Foods, Microsoft, Inc., and Master Card International.

IBC also provides users with a survey to fill out regarding use of the Internet and IBC. An e-mail address is also included for IBC users who wish to communicate their comments and questions.

IBC can be found at: tig.com/IBC/ on World Wide Web.

Info-South: Latin American Information System (Coral Gables, FL: University of Miami)

Info-South is an on-line database of current information on economic trends, political events, and social change in Latin America. Citations are drawn from more than 1500 journals, news magazines, newspapers, and newsletters published in Latin America, Europe, the United States, and elsewhere. Sixty-four publications come from Latin America, and represent 22 countries. The database is supported by an archive of all materials cited in the database. Coverage of journal articles began in January 1988; newspaper and news magazine coverage began July 1988. Topics covered include the following: agriculture, banking, commerce, crime, demography, development, drug trafficking, economics, environment and ecology, education, politics and elections, government and finance, foreign investments and trade, health, human rights, intelligence activities and defense, international relations, marketing, privatization, refugees, science and technology, sociology, terrorism, and transnational corporations. Full-text copies of all the documents in the database are available for document delivery by mail or fax.

Info-South contains abstracts with full bibliographic elements, including English language titles for non-English articles, descriptors, identifiers, and abstracts. Abstracts range from 50 to 100 words each. The database is updated weekly with a lag of 5 to 6 weeks between publication of an article and its inclusion in the database. Subscriptions include an on-line thesaurus, documentation, customer service lines, and a year's subscription to Info-South Abstracts, a printed serial index based on the database and issued quarterly. Training is available in Miami and onsite.

Infomat International Business (Cleveland, OH: Predicasts)

This on-line database covers worldwide business events and conditions, with a focus on Europe. It provides English language abstracts of business news articles from over 600 international business newspapers and other press sources. Subjects covered include market information, technology, industry trends, legislative activities relating to business and the economic environment. Sources originate in over 20 countries, including Germany, France, Canada, Australia, and Japan. Approximately one-third of the sources is published in the United Kingdom.

The majority of database users are in major industries such as communications, electronics, food and beverages, plastics, and financial services. The selection of abstracts is based on the information needs of these companies. Coverage dates from April 1984. Updates are done weekly and add about 200,000 abstracts a year.

ISBM Business Marketing Web Consortium (www.smeal.psu.edu/isbm)

The Institute for the Study of Business Markets (ISBM) is an industry-supported center in the Smeal College of Business Administration of Penn State University, founded in 1983. A coalition of academic and corporate members, the Institute draws support from corporations such as Amoco Chemical Co., AT&T, Eastman Kodak, and IBM.

The Business Marketing Web Consortium was developed to explore the use of the World Wide Web as a tool and to provide a community of practice for marketing strategists. The web site provides information about ISBM seminars, publications, and research projects. It includes a profile of ISBM, a directory, a calendar of scheduled seminars and conferences, membership information, a newsletter, priorities in research and funding opportunities for graduate students. Abstracts of the Institute's publications are available on-line, and full-text copies may be ordered. Links provide access to marketing resources, associations, events, list-serves, on-line publications, and the home-pages of members.

Kiplinger Online (www.kiplinger.com)

This site provides business forecasts and personal financial advice. News of the day displays selected consumer, business, and financial news. Other sites include business forecasts (predictions of future economic trends and business cycles), personal finance (professional on-line financial advice), top funds (a list of the top performing mutual funds), retirement advice, as well as a list of other business-related web sites.

KR Information OnDisc

KR Information OnDisc is the new name for DIALOG OnDisc. The product is for people who need to find certain business-related information.

Specific databases, such as Corporate America or Directory of U.S. Importers and Exporters, can be selected and searched. KR Information OnDisc's built-in search mechanism allows information to be located through a host of options, such as author, key word, or subject heading.

LegalEagle (www.yahoo.com/Government/Law/Consumer)

LegalEagle has been practicing law for 25 years, and this web site is asking for a description of legal problems. This site provides LegalEagles professional qualifications and will be helpful in finding a lawyer.

Links to Business Journals from "A Business Researcher's Interests" (www.brint.com/journals.htm)

A list of links to major business academic journals and publications is provided in alphabetical order. This site is maintained by Yogesh Malhotra.

Lotus One Source (Cambridge, MA: Lotus)

Lotus One Source is a collection of CD-ROMs that cover business-oriented topics and provide financial analyses. It is a source for information on trends, acquisitions, mergers, investments, and other critical business decisions. The Lotus Corporation has gathered information from companies that track the market. With a subscription, Lotus provides the CD-ROMs and a CD-ROM reader. The subscriber must have a personal computer.

Lotus One Source has four major categories of disks: CD/Investment, CD/Corporate, CD/Banking, CD/Insurance. Within each CD category, there are more specific subdivisions relating to the business topic addressed. For instance, on CD/Investment, there are four databases pertaining to investment. It includes information on U.S. Equities, International Equities, the Russell Profile, and Fixed Income. The other three types of disks are arranged in a similar manner with specific subdivisions. Lotus Corporation allows the subscriber to select the disks he or she wants, making the set customizable to the user's needs.

MapQuest (www.mapquest.com)

MapQuest is an on-line mapping service offered by GeoSystems Global Corporation through their division, MapQuest Publishing Group. MapQuest offers three primary mapping services: TripQuest, Interactive Atlas, and Personalized Maps.

TripQuest provides a form to enter origin and destination information from which it provides door-to-door directions instantly for routes. The directions are broken down into street-by-street items giving the distance for each item in tenths of a mile. At the bottom of the list of directions it provides total distance and estimated driving time by minutes. On the same page, results include a map sidelined with two other maps of the origin and destination of trips.

The Interactive Atlas Service provides a graphical map of a location entered. The map is interactive because it can be customized according to zoom level and places of interest, including points for shopping, banking, recreation, lodging, health care, dining, education, transportation, and personal addresses. A customized map can then be printed. Personalized Maps offers a MapQuest membership, which is free and allows the saving of maps on their server and placing icons on maps to indicate the kinds of points of interests listed above.

Materials Business File (London: Materials Information) [DIALOG]

Materials business file provides information on technical and commercial value of iron, steel, nonferrous metals, and engineered products. The information is obtained from magazines, trade publications, newspapers, and conference proceedings.

Marquis Who's Who on CD-ROM

Marquis Who's Who on CD-ROM allows instant access to 18 Who's Who titles including Finance and Industry, Science and Engineering, and Emerging Leaders in America. Searches may be made using 30 criteria. Placement in Who's Who relies not only on notoriety or social status, but also by contributions to society through achievement.

This CD-ROM includes not only the most recent editions of the Marquis Who's Who series, but biographies printed since 1985, including almost 750,000 figures of national and international importance. Information in the biographies includes birth, education, career achievements, address, and other facts of importance.

Marquis Who's Who (New Providence, NJ: Marquis, a Reed Reference Publishing Company) [DIALOG]

The database is a source of biographies of business, entertainment, and technology professionals. Each entry provides details about career history, education, creative works, publications, family background, current address, political activities and affiliation, religion, and outstanding achievements.

MarketPlace Business, MarketPlace Information

This CD-ROM is designed for prospecting and analyzing markets and is intended for marketing and sales professionals. The database contains information from Dun & Bradstreet Information Services on over 7,000,000 businesses in the United States and includes names, telephone numbers, addresses, contacts and titles, and summary market statistics. The database is searchable by type of business (SIC Code), geographic area, annual sales, number of employees, year founded, and type of ownership. To assist in locating customers, information can be used for generating prospect lists, targeting niche markets according to SIC Codes, and tabulating list counts. The resource can be used for test marketing purposes by generating small random samples from larger lists, developing new lists according to test results, and creating new target markets with different criteria. Information can be exported to other software packages and the database is available for IBM or Macintosh systems. Updates are made quarterly.

MEDLINE (PubMed) (www.nlm.nih.gov)

In June 1997, the National Library of Medicine began offering MEDLINE free on the World Wide Web. MEDLINE is a gigantic database of references to articles published in the field of medicine and related fields. Users with a variety of skills can search the database successfully because it offers a variety of search interfaces, which range from allowing simple keyword entry to complex Boolean searches. Another useful feature of the interface is that it offers a link to related articles for each citation that the user finds. MEDLINE contains many topics that are important to businesses and industry. Industries that may find MEDLINE useful are agricultural, pharmaceutical and medical equipment industries. The database includes articles on changing trends, product comparisons, new products, and procedure comparisons for these industries; it also contains other entries that are pertinent to more companies. The database, for example, contains many entries on health insurance and health care. MEDLINE also covers topics such as workplace safety and work-related injuries. Articles on these issues can help companies to make better decisions about work conditions for their employees. The database offers citations to articles about the environment and pollution as well as the effects of environmental legislation on industries. The Medical Subject Heading (MeSII) hierarchy, the controlled vocabulary thesaurus for MEDLINE, contains the major category "Technology, Industry, Agriculture," which further breaks down into a variety of industries. Access to MEDLINE would be beneficial for many businesses and industries.

Mercury Center (www.mercurycenter.com)

Mercury Center is the official web site of the San Jose Mercury News. The site is divided into sections that include news, business and stocks, technology, sports, opinion, living and comics, and weather. A classifieds and services section is also provided. Direct links are available to breaking news information, daily highlights, employment information, and the Yellow Pages. Further links include a site index, search engine, feedback, and customer service.

Microcomputer Index (Santa Clara, CA: Microcomputer Information Services)

The Microcomputer Index is a CD-ROM source that is issued quarterly and contains more than 10,000 abstracts of publications on personal computer software, periodicals, corporate events, corporate information, and databases. Information on thousands of companies is provided.

There are seven categories of abstracts in the Microcomputer Index. The categories are book reviews, buyer guides, news, consumer product announcements, a listing of programs, and hardware and software. Each category is listed in alphabetical order by primary subject. The program includes indexes by author, name of the company, name of the product, and hardware and software compatibility. The hardware and software compatibility index informs the user what products are compatible with each other and what "add-on" equipment and software is compatible with a particular system.

Military Contracts/Procurement Locator (Mount Vernon, VA: Staff Directories)

This CD-ROM provides detailed information on military contracts, contractors, and subcontracting opportunities with the military. This source searches contracts by product sold, company name, contracting agency, weapons system, SIC code, product service code, and Congressional district. There are five databases in this product. The first, Military Contracts Locator, lists every Department of Defense contract awarded in the last 12 months. The second, Military Dictionary of Terms/Acronyms, contains over 80,000 dictionary entries of military jargon. The third, Small Business and Subcontracting Locator, contains data about opportunities for subcontracting at military installations. The fourth, SIC Code Database, locates the correct SIC code for searching any subject. The fifth, Contractors Currently Barred from Department of Defense Contracts, lists contractors who are currently barred from receiving contracts and lists the reason, terms, and length of disbarment. The CD-ROM is updated quarterly and is available for network contracts. This information would be helpful to businesses seeking opportunities to contract with the Department of Defense.

Military Personnel/Base Locator (Mount Vernon, VA: Staff Directories)

This CD-ROM contains three databases. The first, Military Personnel Locator, lists over 128,000 military and civilian personnel. The list includes biographies of the top U.S. military leaders. The second, Military Base Locator, gives information on over 1000 military bases from around the world. Information includes, but is not limited to, base function, base closure data, history, names, and community information. The third database, Military Dictionary of Terms/Acronyms, contains over 80,000 entries of military jargon. The CD-ROM is updated three times a year and is available with a network contract.

MLM Software and Resources (mlmstartup.com/index.vs)

Multi Level Marketing (MLM) Home Page offers opportunities to download Shareware Internet and MLM software, read articles that are aimed toward start-up MLM companies and their distributors, and access information about Wildlife Corporate MLM Software for Network Marketing Companies.

Money Hunter (www.moneyhunter.com)

This site provides weekly business information to the user. This site is updated weekly, with the most current business news. In the middle of the home page there is a big cigar that leads to other links. This site provides business information for the small business owner and has different business strategies laid out for the user. This site also has business surveys. Mentors are offered to the users of the site. Several back issues of business magazines are also available to the user. Money Hunter also provides a segment called the pick of the week, where they pick the best business summary that they receive and publicize it. Apparel is also sold through this site.

Moody's Company Data (New York, NY: Moody's)

This CD-ROM source contains information on more than 10,000 public companies. The history, business, product line, recent developments, and finances of a company can be accessed. Reports can be printed by the company or the information can be accessed by topic. Reports can also be customized to provide a specialized report for the user. The system has menu-driven software, and searches can be conducted with Boolean logic by words or phrases and ranked or sorted by selected variables. The searching capabilities allow the user to track financial performances and to analyze competition. An annual subscription to this CD-ROM includes monthly updates, a tool-free support hotline, CD-ROM reader, and a time tracker for billing purposes.

Moody's Corporate News—U.S. (New York: Moody's Investment Services) [DIALOG]

Moody's Corporate News—U.S. provides business and financial data for U.S. public organizations, industrial enterprises, banks, savings and loan institutions, insurance companies, real estate companies, investment trusts, and public utilities and transport companies. The information is gathered from news releases, reports, and journals.

Moody's International Plus/Moody's Corporate News International, Moody's Investors; Dun and Bradstreet [DIALOG]

Moody's International Manuals (on DIALOG and CD-ROM) contain data on over 5000 non-U.S.-based companies. The information includes history of each company, business section, financial statement, and detailed bond description.

Moody's International Plus (New York, NY: Moody's Investors Service)

This CD-ROM contains descriptions of over 5000 non-U.S.-based companies operating in 100 countries. It provides current and historical financial data from 1989 to the present. It also includes Moody's international news reports that cover recent business and financial developments. For each company, information includes a detailed company history as well as in-depth coverage of the company's financial statements and long-term debt and capitol stocks.

National Automated Accounting Research System (Dayton, OH: Mead Data Central)

The National Automated Accounting Research System (NAARS), an on-line source, contains full-text articles covering accounting literature, corporate annual reports and financial data. Over 4000 publicly held company annual reports, including footnotes, are covered. The literature file is composed of all current and superseded authoritative and semiauthoritative promulgations of the AICPA, FASB, GASB, and the SEC. The most recent reports are about a year old, with the accounting database literature file encompassing more recent information. The database coverage ranges from 1972 to the present. Access points include company names, words of phrases, and financial statement items. The database is available through Mead Data Central and Nexis.

National Bureau of Economic Research (www.nber.org)

The National Bureau of Economic Research (NBER) is a private, nonprofit, nonpartisan research organization dedicated to promoting understanding of how the economy works. In keeping with its mission, the organization maintains a free, public-access, English-language web site for the dissemination of its economic information.

Among the resources available at the NBER site are searchable databases of NBER Working Papers, NBER books, and the organization's membership. Search is by keyword, with the ability to narrow results by month, year, and number of matches. Search results may be displayed by relevance or by reverse chronology.

In addition to the searchable databases, the NBER site contains economic data of interest to economic professionals, broken down into four categories: macro, industry, individual, and other data. Files are accessed by selecting highlighted links.

Descriptive links are also available on the NBER web site. One can access informational pages regarding the history/mission of the bureau, major programs and projects, funding, publications, and staff.

National Institute of Standards and Technology (telnet://gopher.nist.gov)

This Gopher site, maintained by the U.S. Department of Commerce, describes the National Institute of Standards and Technology's (NIST) goals, operations, and services. Before users are permitted to view the gopher menus, they must first read the first item, the server access restriction document. This site furnishes information about NIST's special programs, for example, Advanced Technology, Campus Information, and Laboratory programs, as well as information about awards, budgets, and consultation services that NIST provides. This site also provides funding information for small and midsize businesses regarding innovative research grants.

The site is kept up-to-date and provides access to current NIST newsletters and press releases. A menu item search engine to facilitate finding relative information is also provided. Users can search the full text of NIST documents by keyword. The information is directed at NIST's employees and member organizations as well as toward users knowledgeable or interested in standards and measures and how they relate to different fields. This site is useful for businesses in fields that use government standards, for example, those involved in manufacturing, utilities, or technology.

Nikkei Economic Electronic Databank System (Nihon Keizai Shimbun)

The Nikkei Economic Electronic Databank System (NEEDS) is an information service available on-line and on magnetic tape. It provides business- and economic-related data and includes numerical and bibliographic information databases. The numerical database contains financial, industrial, international, and national data. The bibliographic database offers information from Nikkei publications. The information can be used for corporate analysis, forecasting, portfolio selection, and investment analysis and is updated continuously. Types of databases focusing on Japan include corporate information (e.g., Nikkei Who's Who), financial statements, macroeconomics (e.g., Consumer Statistical Data), monetary data, energy, marketing, news, and data on stocks, bonds, and commodities. Non-Japanese focused information can be obtained from Lexis/Nexis, Asian Corporate Profile, REUTER TEXTLINE, and EXTEL Extat.

NewsNet

NewsNet is a company that provides current on-line news. It receives and transmits information from hundreds of sources including United Press International (UPI), Associated Press (AP), Xhinghua News Services, trade news lines, major newspapers, congressional transcripts, and corporate annual reports in their entirety. NewsNet provides access to both national and international newswire services. A full listing of the news sources available is provided with the subscription to be kept by the subscriber, and is updated quarterly in a newsletter announcing new services.

NewsNet provides two main types of services. The first is on-line searches directed by the user. The user directs the search by subject, topic, personal name, corporate name, or date range, The services can be searched for only the prior year in information and can be by month, week, or specific day.

The second type of search is a service provided by NewsNet (at extra cost). It allows a user to establish a folder into which NewsNet will automatically dump all items on a user-chosen subject. In this way, the user can access NewsNet and not waste time in a search. All current hits pertinent to the user's prescribed topic are immediately available. NewsNet displays the titles of each article (or a one-line topic description), the number of words and lines, of each article, and a symbol denoting which publication originated the article. At the user's discretion, these articles may be downloaded directly into MicroSoft Word or other word processing software to be perused at the user's leisure (and lower cost).

NewsNet is a subscriber-based service ideal for Communications and Marketing fields as it is constantly updated. A newsletter is sent out quarterly announcing newly acquired newswires. NewsNet is accessible by using ProComm Plus or Telnet.

Newspaper and Periodical Abstracts (Louisville, KY: University Microfilms/Data Courier)

Combined here as one on-line source, Newspaper Abstracts and Periodical Abstracts are available separately on CD-ROM and through magnetic tape leasing. The database provides business, general reference, and academic information from 25 newspapers and 950 journals. Bibliographic citations, indexing, and abstracts are recorded for national and regional newspapers, academic journals, popular magazines, and business publications. More than 1,500,000 records are on the database. Newspaper coverage began in 1989 and coverage of periodicals began in 1986.

Subjects covered are political parties and systems, science, current events and trends, editorial cartoons and commentaries, academic research and opinions, and reviews of products, films, books, and concerts. Periodicals include Foreign Policy, Forbes, Nation, and Business Week. Newspapers include The Wall Street Journal, The New York Times, the Chicago Tribune, and the Boston Globe. Citations include article and periodical titles, authors, company names, controlled vocabulary subject terms, article lengths, and 25-word abstracts. The newspaper citations describe the type of article. All fields can be searched. Although only abstracts are available on-line or on CD-ROM, it is possible to order full-text articles from University Microfilms' Article Clearinghouse for most of the articles cited in Newspaper and Periodical Abstracts as well as articles from more than 12,000 other periodicals.

On-line searching is available only on DIALOG. Part of UMI's ProQuest system, CD-ROM subscriptions for Newspaper Abstracts and Periodical Abstracts include the initial disc, monthly updates, software, and documentation. A thesaurus can be obtained for the controlled vocabulary and publication lists to aid searching. In addition to the electronic versions, several printed indexes are available for individual newspapers.

Newswire ASAP (Foster Grove, CA: Information Access)

Newswire ASAP is an on-line database that provides indexing and full-text articles from newswire services in the United States and around the world. Services in the United States include Comtex, Federal News Service, and Market Consensus Surveys. Foreign newswire services originate from the Russia, Japan, China, Germany, and Spain. Other international news services are OPEC News Agency, UPI, PR Newswire, Newsbytes News Service, and Reuters Financial Report. New records are added daily to the database. Generally, news is available on the database in less than 36 hours. Many of the newswire services include analyses in addition to news and business coverage.

Beginning dates of coverage depend on the newswire service. PR Newswire, which provides news releases from companies, government agencies and trade unions, dates to 1985. Reuters Financial Report and Kyodo News Service coverage began in 1987. Reuters reports on international business, political, and financial news, and analyst reports are included. Coverage of Reuters, however, ended in 1990. Kyodo News Service covers Japanese companies, products, trends, and government activities, as well as business news for Asia. Beginning in 1989, Newsbytes News Service covers the international computer industry.

Coverage of other news services began in 1991. The OPEC News Agency covers news and information dealing exclusively with OPEC member countries. TASS, covers internal news of Russia as well as Eastern Europe. Specialized coverage of Latin America is provided from Agencia EFE, the Spanish international news service. The German agency, Deutsche Press-Agentur, also supplies international coverage of economic, political, and general news. The exclusively American services, Comtex and Market Consensus Surveys, cover corporate news such as trading activity, earnings, and mergers and acquisitions and provide analyses and summaries of the U.S. economy and financial markets. The third American newswire, the Federal News Service, covers federal policy statements, Congressional hearings, and White House transmissions.

The database can provide information on new companies and products, stocks and commodities, political and economic news, events, as well as mergers, and acquisition activities. Because the database is composed of news sources from around the world, press coverage in the United States can be compared with overseas coverage. Searches can be conducted in a variety of ways. Index groupings include authors, article titles, journal titles, publication dates, SIC codes, line counts and updates. Entries then provide this information plus subject and industry information and abstracts. Full-text articles are also accessible.

Newswire ASAP is available from DIALOG.

Nexis, Mead Data Central

The Nexis library is an on-line database that contains the full-text of business, financial, news, and general-interest publications as well as wire services. It also contains the full-text of scripts from radio and television news broadcasts.

The database is updated on a continuous basis. The earliest material dates to the mid-1970s. There is not a standard length of time from publication date to inclusion on Nexis, although the range is 1 week to 2 months depending on the publication and the speed of delivery.

It is possible to search all files at once, either for current material published in 1989 or after, for pre-1989 material, or for all material. Specific sets of files or libraries are also searchable. The material can be displayed in four formats: citation only, segments, citation plus enough text to include material containing the search, and full-text. The last two include the name of the publication, length in words, headline, byline and body, and a piece of or the entire text.

North American Industry Classification System (www.census.gov/pub/epcd/www/naics.html)

Common industry definitions for Canada, Mexico, and the United States can be found in this web site for the North American Industry Classification System (NAICS). It is jointly developed by U.S. Economic Classification Policy Committee, Statistics Canada, and Mexico's Instituto Nacional de Estadistics, Geografia e Informatica. Many documents listed on the site are saved in Portable Document Format (PDF).

Office of the Comptroller of the Currency (www.occ.treas.gov)

The Office of the Comptroller of the Currency (OCC), an independent bureau of the Treasury Department, is the oldest federal financial regulatory body and oversees the nation's federally chartered banks. Providing information about the workings of the agency and the history of banking, OCC's web page includes information for individuals heavily involved with national banks and novices interested in a cursory overview of the subject. With few pictures and graphics, the site provides a straightforward table of contents with numerous links to additional information. The resources cover everything from the history of the OCC, its regulatory duties, legal interpretations, and publications, to consumer information. Special emphasis is made on OCC's duties under the Community Reinvestment Act. Finally, the page includes a subject index and is keyword searchable.

Online Computer Library Center (www.oclc.org)

Online Computer Library Center is an organization providing information on computer systems for libraries requiring international, electronic databases. This information is available in English, Spanish, and Chinese. The OCLC divisions include Asia Pacific, Europe, Forest Press, Latin America and the Caribean, Pacific, Information Dimensions, Inc., and Preservation Resources.

On-Line Job Services (rescomp.stanford.edu/jobs.html)

On-Line Job Services is a server that provides access to a number of Internet-accessible job-listing databases. The server includes job listings available through World Wide Web, Gopher, Telnet, Dial-Up, UseNet Newsgroups, or Other Meta-Lists. Within each of these categories, a number of different job databases are listed and briefly described. Some are related to specific fields, such as the American Astronomical Society Job Register and NCSA Job Announcements. Others, such as The Job Board and The Monster Board, list employment opportunities across a broad range of disciplines.

The individual databases are set up differently. For example, the American Astronomical Society Job Register automatically lists all jobs when it is opened, whereas The Monster Board allows the user to narrow a job search based on selected industries, disciplines, geographical areas, or job titles. The Philanthropy Journal organizes job listings by date posted. The Online Career Center and The Chronicle of Higher Education offer more detailed indexes, and Career Mosaic provides a searchable index.

In addition to job listings, many of the databases offer full-text articles from related publications. Some, such as The Chronicle of Higher Education, also provide additional material of interest in the field, ranging from facts and figures to book reviews to organizational information.

The job listings portions of these databases provide full job descriptions, including required qualifications, salary information, and application procedure. Several databases also allow users to post their résumés on the service to be viewed by potential employers, although some of these require membership before full privileges are available.

The job listings provided by the databases offered through On-Line Job Services are updated regularly, in many cases weekly. Several of the databases list jobs by date, allowing the user to read only the most recent notices.

OPENAIR-MARKET NET (www.openair.org)

OPENAIR-MARKET NET: The World Wide Guide to Farmers' Markets, Street Markets, Flea Markets, and Street Vendors is a site maintained by educators for the promotion of open-air markets. This web site was created and is maintained by two professors from Roosevelt University and the University of Arizona. The intended audience of this web site includes shoppers, vendors, farmers, and scholars. One page on this web site defines the open-air market and explains the value of open-air markets to both vendors and consumers. This web site offers a searchable list of links to over 100 open-air markets from around the world that are on the World Wide Web. The list is arranged by the location of the market. In addition, the site highlights an open-air market each month, and posts comments from users about their favorite open-air markets. OPENAIR-MARKET NET posts alerts about markets or vendors that are in danger of being closed. Other features include a searchable list of marketplace images and Openair Cyber-Journal, the site's compilation of reports, guides, essays, articles, reports, book excerpts, and poems about open-air markets.

Oppnet.com (www.oppnet.com)

Oppnet.com is produced by the Opportunity Network based in Massachusetts. The objective of the site is to provide resources for the independent businessperson. Included are data on opportunities for business, services, alliances, networking, positions, and education. Within each category is a listing of titles, descriptions, and contacts. It is possible to find information on businesses that are for sale or that are looking for employees or partners, companies that offer financial or technological support, and educational experiences for entrepreneurs. Oppnet.com charges a fee for submissions.

Packaging Science and Technology Abstracts (Frankfurt: International Food Information Service) [DIALOG]

Packaging Science and Technology Abstracts offers data about packaging science, materials, equipment, packs, transport, storage, and testing. The information is obtained from many sources, which include books, journals, standards, patents, and conference proceedings.

The Paladin Group (www.silcom.com/~paladin)

The Paladin Group is a web site containing information regarding the services that The Paladin Group provides, such as social services, criminal and justice system, and drug abuse. Users interested in establishing a program involving great collaboration and making project proposals can browse through the given links in the web page. In addition to that, users can browse through the FAQs and can contact the E-mail address given in the web site.

PAPERCHEM (Atlanta, GA: The Institute of Paper Science and Technology) [DIALOG]

PAPERCHEM is a source of patent and periodical data about pulp and paper technology, chemistry of cellulose, hemicellulose, carbohydrates, lignin, and extractives, engineering and process control, equipment, packaging, and graphic arts. The database is the on-line version of the print Bulletin of the Institute of Paper Science and Technology.

PC-SIG Library (Parsippany, NJ: Bureau of Electronic Publishing)

This CD-ROM contains shareware computer programs including word processing programs, databases, games, spreadsheets, telecommunications programs, educational programs, desktop publishing packages, and utilities. Specialized programs, such as one that creates survey questionnaires, are also included.

The software the disc uses is a hypertext program. The user may browse through the program lists arranged by subject or through a "favorites" program listing. When the user selects a program, an abstract describing the program is accessed, complete with downloading options and official registration fee information. For those programs in the "favorites" listing, it is possible to run the individual programs directly from the CD before deciding to download it.

Netherlands, Norway, Portugal, Spain, Sweden, Switzerland, Turkey, and the United Kingdom. Three loose-leaf binders are updated quarterly.

Taxation and Investment in Central and East European Countries covers companies and individuals in the following countries: Bulgaria, Croatia, the Czech Republic, Poland, Romania, Russia, the Slovak Republic, Albania, Belorussia, Estonia, Hungary, Kazakhstan, Latvia, and Ukraine. Two loose-leaf binders are updated three times a year.

The Taxation of Individuals in Europe details the taxation of the individual in Austria, Belgium, Denmark, Finland, France, Germany, Greece, Ireland, Italy, Luxembourg, the Netherlands, Norway, Portugal, Spain, Sweden, Switzerland, Turkey, and the United Kingdom. Two loose-leaf binders are updated annually.

Supplementary Service to European Taxation contains most treaties on the avoidance of double taxation in European and non-European countries. Summaries on taxation in individual countries in Europe are given. Fourteen binders with a bibliography are updated monthly.

Taxes and Investment in Asia and the Pacific is a guide to international and local taxation and investment in Afghanistan, American Samoa, Australia, Bangladesh, Bhutan, Brunei, People's Republic of China, Cook Islands, Fiji, Guam, Hong Kong, India, Indonesia, Japan, Kiribati, Korea (rep.), Macao, Malaysia, Maldives, Myanmar, Nauru, Nepal, New Caledonia, New Zealand, Pakistan, Papua New Guinea, Philippines, Singapore, Solomon Islands, Sri Lanka, Tahiti, Taiwan, Thailand, Tonga, Trust Territory of the Pacific Islands, Tuvalu, Vanuatu, and Western Samoa. It includes a bibliography and takes up 10 binders that are updated monthly.

Taxes and Investment in the Middle East covers taxation and investment of companies and individuals in Bahrain, Egypt, Iran, Iraq, Jordan, Kuwait, Lebanon, Oman, Qatar, Saudi Arabia, Syria, the United Arab Emirates, and Yemen. It is contained in two binders that are updated quarterly.

Taxation and Investment in Canada is a comprehensive guide for professionals. Taxation of companies and individuals is covered. Governmental laws and systems are outlined. It is written by Blair P. Dwyer, a Canadian. One complete binder is updated semiannually.

PR Newswire (www.prnewswire.com)

The PR Newswire offers full coverage of the general media, industry publications, financial community, and entertainment. The Today's News enables the user to search for keywords or any company and provides the latest news about the company. The Company News offers the revenue and incomes and quarterly dividends for the past year of a given company. Other fields that are available are car connection, health/biotech, technology, financial, energy, automotive, entertainment, investment profiles, and government.

Predicasts Terminal System, Marketing and Advertising Reference Service (PTS MARS) (Cleveland, OH: Predicast)

This source is intended for use by professionals in the advertising and marketing business. It is a national database containing over 700,000 records and is updated weekly. It covers all aspects of advertising and marketing and is used for in-depth research. The coverage is of a wide range of consumer goods and services, market share and size, evaluation of new product launches, and the strategies of competitors. Predicasts gathers information from six types of sources: major national newspaper articles and sections on advertising and marketing, business journals, professional trade periodicals, consumer-oriented trade publications, market research studies, and newsletters.

Examples of subject types covers are advertising media, theory and research, agencies and campaigns. A basic subject index is provided as well as additional indexes. The database contents can be searched by text word, subject words, and phrases. The database is available through DIALOG.

President@whitehouse.gov

President@whitehouse.gov is the public E-mail address of the President of the United States. Because of the volume of messages sent to the White House it is not possible for the President to review each one. E-mail sent to this address is read by White House staff, who communicate a representative sample to the President. An automated response beginning "Dear Friend" is returned to the E-mail address from which the message to the President was sent. The automatic response is the only message sent from whitehouse.gov, and no other message purporting to be from whitehouse.gov is authentic.

The automatic response also lists the postal mail address for the White House, the uniform resource locator (URL) of the White House World Wide Web home page, an address from which White House documents can be retrieved by E-mail, and an E-mail address that automatically sends back a White House public access E-mail frequently asked questions (FAQ) document. The FAQ document explains how to retrieve the State of the Union Address and a list of accomplishments. Directions are also given for access to non-White House sources of governmental information by E-mail, World Wide Web, Gopher, and file transfer protocol (FTP). These sources include the Senate, House of Representatives, Library of Congress, and many other federal agencies.

ProPhone—National Edition (ProCD, Inc.)

This CD-ROM source is made up of three discs: business, Western residential and Eastern residential. The business disc is comprised of the names, addresses, and telephone numbers of nearly all businesses in the United States and includes over 8 million numbers. It can be searched by name, heading, or SIC code. The Western and Eastern residential discs list most American home phone numbers and can be searched by name, address, city, state, and zip code. It includes over 60 million home phone numbers. The software that comes with the CD-ROM allows the user to dial a highlighted entry. Together, the three discs represent published directory listings in the United States.

System requirements are an IBM-compatible machine with 512K and MS-DOS 3/1/+. The CD-ROM is updated annually.

ProQuest Direct

ProQuest Direct is an on-line product from UMI that is intended for people who need access to current business information. A large variety of publications containing industry and company related material is accessible via a modem. Once a search is completed, relevant articles are available in different formats such as abstracts and full-text documents with illustrations. Facsimile machine and regular U.S. mail are included in the list of article delivery methods used by ProQuest Direct.

PsycINFO (Arlington, VA: American Psychological Association)

This information source is available on-line as PsycINFO, on CD-ROM as PsycLIT, and in print as Psychological Abstracts. It provides material on psychology and related subjects. The database covers over 1300 psychology and psychology-related journals, dissertations, book chapters, books, and technical reports in English and other languages. Coverage begins in 1967 and the source is updated monthly. Aspects of applied psychology that are business related include management, organizational behavior and change, human resources, employee issues, training, marketing, and advertising. Reports on leadership style, education, attitudes of consumers, work environment, and productivity can be found under these topics. Some business journals included in the database are Group and Organizational Studies, Journal of Advertising, Journal of Organizational Behavior Management, Personnel Administrator, and Training and Development.

Formats available include abstracts, citations, indexing terms, and full-text articles. Abstracts are not available for dissertations. Citations are all in English and include article title, author name, source title, language, and document type. Abstracts are followed by major and minor subject descriptors and a general classification code. The database can be searched four ways. A controlled vocabulary can be used to search subject descriptors. Free text searching is available as is subject code and author searching.

PsycINFO is available on-line through DIALOG, BRS Information Technologies, DIMDI, Data-Star, and the Human Resource Information Network (HRIN). Necessary equipment is a PC terminal, a modem, and communications software. Searching help is available for users through a manual and a toll-free line. A quarterly user newsletter and a thesaurus of search terms are also available.

PTS Annual Reports Abstracts (Foster City, CA: Information Access Company) [DIALOG]

PTS Annual Reports Abstracts is a source of information on company annual reports. The database contains details about statistics, performance, developments, acquisitions, changes in company structure, product line profits, and parent company records.

PTS New Product Announcements/Plus (Foster City: Information Access Company) [DIALOG]

PTS New Product Announcements Plus is a source of full-text press releases for new products and services. Furthermore, the database provides characteristics for new products. These are technical specifications, availability, uses, licensing agreements, distribution channels, and prices. Other type of information available includes new facilities, mergers and acquisitions, contracts, litigation, and business events.

PTS PROMT (Foster City, CA: Information Access Company) [DIALOG]

Predicasts Overview of Markets and Technologies (PTS PROMT) database is a source of information on companies, products, markets, and applied technologies. The information is gathered from a variety of sources that include journals, newspapers, business newsletters, reports, and statements.

International PSI (www.world-psi.org)

Presented in English, French, Spanish, German, or Swedish, Public Services International's (PSI) home page is minuscule, with the focus being on PSI news and PSI history.

Prime Marketing Publications (www.pmp.co.uk)

Prime Marketing Publications is an on-line magazine covering many aspects of sales, marketing, and management systems. The site has four sections: Conspectus, News, Internet Services, and General. The Conspectus section contains articles designed for decision makers and consultants who are interested in current developments in information technology. The News section provides articles published from "Management Consultant News." Users are provided with Internet services such as web authoring, security, access management, and consultancy. The site provides information covering training courses, glossaries, research, and other areas of interest.

Résumé Net (www.resumenet.com)

Résumé Net is dedicated exclusively to assisting individuals publish their résumés on the World Wide Web. This Internet Source's staff is comprised of skilled résumé counselors and web page design specialists.

SIRS (www.sirs.com)

SIRS is a set of databases that covers social, scientific, historic, economic, political, and global topics. The entries come from 1200 domestic and international newspapers, magazines, journals, and publications of the government and give the complete text and bibliographical information; some articles have graphics, maps, and charts. The systems are available in CD-ROM, on magnetic tape, and by way of the Mandarin Library Automation System. The on-line versions are connected also to Newsline, which gives concise descriptions of major news events since January 1995 and a link to related articles, and the Directory of Publications, which gives background information about the sources used and other resources.

SIRS Researcher is a database for general information. Searches are done by topic, keyword, title, author, and Library of Congress subject heading.

SIRS Government contains selected full-text articles and several almanac features such as U.S. Supreme Court Decisions of recent and monumental cases, a directory of the U.S. Supreme Court Justices, Historic Documents, data on members of the Senate and the House of Representatives, and a directory of 400 Federal Agencies and departments.

Other systems provided are SIRS Renaissance for information in the Arts and Humanities, SIRS Discover for elementary and middle students, and the Book Brain/Book Wiz format.

Standard Industrial Classification Search (www.osha.gov/oshstats/sicser.html)

This web site is a searching engine for the Standard Industrial Classification manual (SIC). A specified four-digit SIC can be used to get more descriptive information. The site is sponsored by the U.S. Department of Labor Occupational Safety and Health Administration.

Switchboard Internet Directory (www.switchboard.com)

Switchboard allows Internet users to find friends, family, and colleagues as well as businesses. Switchboard provides residential and business listings in the United States. Corporate web sites, special-interest groups, and associations are also included. In a matter of seconds, anyone with a Web browser can look up the names, phone numbers, and street addresses of friends, colleagues, and businesses. Switchboard information is publicly available.

Business listings are similar to the yellow pages of a telephone directory. Users can search by company name or category (e.g., automotive, brake services, and churches). If you search by category, the city and state information is required. The business listing includes the company name, phone number, and fax number. Once you locate the business, there is a link to MapQuest (http://www.mapquest.com), which provides a city and street map of the location. MapQuest can calculate the driving distance and provide driving directions.

Residential listings are similar to the white pages of a telephone directory. Searching for someone requires only a last name. The residential listing includes the address and phone number. Individuals can personalize their own listing by adding an E-mail address, information about their personal interests, and association memberships. If the person has an E-mail address, you can send them a message directly from your Web browser. Users can link to OutPost Network (http://www.outpostnetwork.com) for sending greeting cards, postcards, or letters. OutPost Network is an Internet Post Office, and for a small fee you can send someone a greeting card or letter. Other features of Switchboard include a résumé builder, job searching, and job posting.

Exposition of High Technology (techexpo.com)

This web site is an "Exposition of High Technology Companies and Products on the World Wide Web." It is geared to show off sites on high-tech engineering and the medical/life sciences.

The American Business Disc

The American Business Disc is a CD-ROM from American Business Information that runs on IBM-PC compatible computers. The product is intended for people who need data on companies and organizations that operate in the United States.

The 10 million businesses on the CD-ROM are accessed through a variety of search options. Choices include searches by geographical area and by Standard Industrial Classification (SIC) code. Each company profile provides data such as company address, estimated sales volume, and stock exchange information. The files can be downloaded and printed. In addition, The American Business Disc is updated two times each year.

The Financial Post (www.canoe.ca/pp)

The Financial Post is a business newspaper that presents daily happenings in the Financial Market. One can view currency rates of all the countries in the world from the Money Rates, the Market Watch that shows how the market is doing, and Daily Mutual Funds. Direct links to Canoe Money and FP Services are available. Users can search for companies of their interest through BRE-X Archive Search and Bizlink. In addition, this site presents the Financial Post Top 50 Companies.

The Free On-Line Dictionary of Computing (wombat.doc.ic.ac.uk)

This resource is a dictionary of terms related to computing. The Free On-Line Dictionary of Computing (FOLDOC) includes acronyms and jargon, as well as terms from operating systems, conventions, standards, and electronics. Entries are cross-referenced to each other and to related resources on the Internet.

The dictionary has an introduction describing what it is and what it contains and a list of contents, which are linked to more specific information. The dictionary is searchable from a number of locations, including the introductory page, the contents page, and from within entries. Users can search by terms, subjects, subject headings, subject headings grouped by first letter, other characters, or subject areas.

Each entry gives pronunciation, definitions with links to other terms, the date the entry was established, and links to the previous term and the next term in alphabetical order.

The Freep (www.freep.com)

The Freep is the official web site of the Detroit Free Press. Users can traverse the web site for daily news, sports, and business information. Direct links are available to top stories, personals, help wanted, classifieds, news library, comics, forums, services, and home delivery. Further links include auto, browsing, voices, photos, and real estate. A search engine is provided for further information.

The Haystack Group, Inc. (www.haystack-group.com)

The Haystack Group, Inc., is a Retained Executive Search advisory that provides Executive Search and Search Research to firms employed in industries of the following areas: Biotechnology, Healthcare Information Technology, Medical Devices, and Pharmaceuticals. Inside these industries, their skill and experience lies in the areas of Clinical, Scientific and Regulatory Affairs, Competitive Intelligence and Market Research, Sales, Marketing and Product Management, and Research Development. The Haystack Group, Inc., allows people to send their résumés and any request for information directly to them for more detail about their firm.

The Institute of Management and Administration (www.ioma.com)

The Institute of Management and Administration web page provides information on news and issues affecting the business world. Under the "Business Directory" the site provides links to over 600 useful outside pages, such as the Investor's Business Daily and the CNN Financial Network, which are organized into 16 major categories. This site also provides access to several discussion groups covering major issues in business such as the Report on Salary Survey's Compensation Bulletin Board and the Legal Bulletin Board. It also includes a list of over 30 newsletters published by the Institute in various subjects, such as Insurance and Risk, Public Accounting, and Corporate Financial Management. While the site provides access to the texts of the recent top articles for each newsletter, there is a free subscription to receive the complete newsletter. In addition, the site allows users to browse the IOMA archives with a keyword search engine.

The Journal of Commerce (New York: The Journal of Commerce) [DIALOG]

The Journal of Commerce is an on-line database that contains full-text articles of business newspapers. The topics covered are transportation, banking, finance, foreign trade, insurance, communication, plus commodities. The database is available in selected cities.

The Tenagra Corporation (www.tenagra.com/net-acceptable.html)

The site informs Internet users of how to correctly market their products or services on the World Wide Web. Net.acceptable also discusses the consequences of inaccurate use of the Internet—which is not net.acceptable.

Tiger Mapping Service (tiger.census.gov)

Topographically Integrated Geographic Encoding and Referencing (Tiger) is the name of the system and digital database developed at the U.S. Census Bureau. The Tiger Mapping Service (TMS) allows the user to generate street-level and regional maps anywhere in the United States. The maps have Geographic Information Systems capabilities such as point display and statistical choropleth mapping. The version currently available is TMS Version 2.5, but they also offer use of Version 1.3.1 for browsers not supporting the table functionality of Version 2.5.

The user completes a brief search form on-line indicating, locations with the name of a city, town, or zip code area. A map is then generated providing a zoom function. Map Census statistics and the option to enter precise latitude and longitude coordinates are provided. Users can also avail themselves of a layering function that provides information regarding Congressional districts, Native American Reservations, zip code points, water bodies, parks, shorelines, Census tracts, and highway labels. The mapping service does not offer any commercial locations. Once generated, the user can print out the map or incorporate it into other existing documents. Besides the map, search results generate a list of geographic entities that match the name given with precise coordinates, corresponding zip codes, and information for Census tables.

Transport Web (www.transportweb.com)

Transport Web is a web site that helps the user identify information and services available to the Transport World. The site is categorized into four main sections: Databases that include Software Guide, Magazines/Periodicals, General Publications, and Official Bodies; Resources that include

Transport Links and NewsGroup; Diary that includes Conference Guide, Exhibition Guide, and Training Courses; finally, the General that includes Enquiries, Customer Services, and Internet Services. When a user enters the Databases, one will find various categories where users have to type in Category, Country, Product, and Keyword to find software products, and Publisher and Publication to find magazines and periodicals. The Diary section provides users Conference, Exhibition, and Training Courses date, location, and E-mail address so they can get more information if desired. The General section offers information on how to use this site more effectively, and an E-mail address is also offered for comments and help if needed. Finally, the Resources offers Links in Transport World and Newsgroup.

United States Postal Service Consumer Information (www.usps.gov/consumer)

On the United States Postal Service Consumer Information home page, users can find information on the postal service. The consumer information section includes frequently asked questions (FAQs), mailing tips, postal publications, and tips on how to protect oneself from mail fraud and scams. Users can also search for zip codes and post office locations. The stamp center has a link to Stampsonline, which provides an index of issued stamps, recent releases, and stamp news. The passport section, furnished by the State Department, contains general information about citizenship, passport applications, and agency locations. The link to MoversNet offers consumers tips on packing, moving, and changing their addresses.

United Parcel Service (www.ups.com)

This site, hosted by the United Parcel Service of America, Inc., offers on-line information to businesses for package tracking; drop-off locator; quickcost calculator, and request pickup. As an added feature the site offers web sites for international business needs to include Canada, Asia/India, Europe, Latin America/Caribbean, Middle East, and Africa. Also included in the web site is a what's new section, services, software/utilities, news, and an index. The index allows the user to search the site for everything contained in the entire home page.

University of California Berkeley Libraries (www.lib.berkeley.edu)

This is the web site of a major research library system and, as such, provides access both to its book catalogs and to newly developed digital materials. The home page is designed to accommodate both the first time and experienced users. A table of contents includes Help/Search, CyberSemester, Your Comments, About the Libraries, Collections and Resources, Library Catalogs, Map of the Libraries, UC Berkeley, and Digital Library SunSITE. The experienced user has the option to use keyword queries for direct access to digital materials.

Each table of contents item is specific to the on-line world. CyberSemester is a list of technology activities and courses on campus. Collections and Resources lists Internet sources for reference use. Library Catalogs accesses not only Berkeley's library catalogs, but also other research catalogs in the United States and the world. The Digital SunSITE links to Berkeley's and other digital library developments and include image collections and software tools.

At the bottom of each page are graphical buttons to facilitate return to the home page or entry to the library catalog. Links are designed as part of the line of text, so that as one reads an item of interest, one can click to it directly.

Uncover (www.carl.org/uncover)

Uncover is an on-line periodical article delivery service and a current awareness service. The large database contains nearly 17,000 English-language periodicals. The service is updated rapidly, at the same time periodicals are delivered to local libraries and newsstands. The Uncover Reveal Alert service delivers tables of contents from the latest periodical issues directly to a selected E-mail box. Searching the database is free; however, users must pay for each article ordered.

Ulrich's PLUS

Ulrich's PLUS lists many periodicals and annuals. Citations include publisher, circulation, subscription prices, and advertising prices. In addition to periodicals, Ulrich's PLUS includes data about newspapers. Details are included on numerous publishers.

It is possible to search 24 criteria. It is also possible to copy records from this quarterly updated publication to any system that reads American Standard Code for Information Interchange (ASCII) text format.

USA DATA (www.usadata.com)

USA Data company is made of a team of professionals who specialize in database design, technology, and information research. Their greatest ability is to supply companies with reliable market and consumer behavior specific data in the United States. To provide the most comprehensive information solutions, they work closely with the nation's leading data and information companies.

WhoWhere? (www.whowhere.com)

This web page provides a quick way to look up E-mail addresses, residential, and governmental phone numbers and addresses, as well as company web pages. The site includes numerous search engines; users supply the name, location, or category of the person or organization in which they are interested and the search engine produces matches. In addition, WhoWhere provides business yellow pages, which include maps and directions to the locations of the companies. Other items of interest to businesses include Securities and Exchange Commission filings (through Electronic Data Gathering Analysis and Retrieval or EDGAR filings); "Business News," with short articles and stock quotes; as well as toll-free numbers. Finally, the page provides links to free web E-mail and assistance in creating an individual home page.

World Trade Organization (www.wto.org)

This web page deals with the functions of the WTO. These functions include administering trade agreements, trade negotiations, handling trade disputes, monitoring trade policies, and offering technical assistance for developing countries. WTO is run by member governments. The WTO has an impact on the lives of various people in the nation. Many trade topics are available for exploration.

Yahoo! Finance (quote.yahoo.com)

This site includes a stock chat, portfolios currency exchange rates, The Motley Fool, upgrades and downgrades, and Security Exchange Commission (SEC) filings. Featured also are economic and earnings calendars as well as stock surprises and links to articles on market news, updated hourly by Reuters Wire Service. Current stock market rates are posted at the top of the page as well as a search tool that allows users to obtain quotes, profiles, and growth forecasts for companies, stocks, and mutual funds.

Yakscorner (www.yakscorner.com)

Yakscorner is the official web site of Yak's Corner Magazine, a newsmagazine for children. Users can traverse the web site for child-related news and information. Direct links are available to kid news, animals, activities, top stories, fun and games, art, and Yak on the road. An E-mail address is provided for further information.

ZDNet (www.zdnet.com)

The world's leading publisher of computer magazines and newspapers offers a web site complete with features from all their publications. The web site, although full of graphics, allows the user to check out the following: today's news; Software Library; products; on the net; home computing; Macintosh; and the Community Center. The Community Center is an on-line chat room/ discussion group. This site is updated daily and is hosted by Ziff-Davis Publishing Company.

INSURANCE

Best's Insurance Reports on CD-ROM (Oldwick, NJ: A. M. Best)

Since 1899, the A. M. Best Company has been compiling and publishing information on various aspects of insurance company operations, including the Best's Ratings. With its involvement in the insurance industry, the company's understanding of the information they sell is the backbone of its product line. Best databases are available in a variety of formats including printed references, on-line service, mainframe tapes, and personal computer diskettes. The CD-ROM format is now available for most of Best's databases, including Profile, Underwriting Analysis with Ratios, and Experience by State, by Line. Many of these CD-ROM databases are also available in 1- or 5-year application versions.

Best's Insurance Reports on CD-ROM is available in either Property/ Casualty or Life/Health editions. Virtually the entire contents of the printed volumes are presented with full text and search capabilities. The product is made up of three separate databases. The Preface database contains information such as an explanation of Best's Ratings. The Best's Insurance Reports database provides data, financial analyses, and commentary on thousands of insurers. Information provided in this database includes company names and addresses, assets, liabilities/surplus/and other funds, summaries of operations, investment data, company histories, names of company officers and directors, premiums and losses, operating comments, Best's ratings, Best's financial performance indexes, and comparative financial and operating exhibits. Finally, the Retired Companies database is a directory of mergers, voluntary liquidations and retirements, and other company changes during the most recent 5-year period.

E-Benefits (www.e-benefits.com)

E-Benefits (EB) provides insurance and human source solutions. EB assists with software for payroll processing, record keeping, and retirement administration. The Virtual HR software assists in the administration of employee information. On the other hand, the Quote Wizard enables companies to select and manage employee benefit packages. Direct links are available to EB's various services.

Insurance Periodicals Index (Chatsworth, CA: NILS Publishing Company) [DIALOG]

Insurance Periodicals Index provides indexes and abstracts for journals on the insurance industry. Some of the topics covered by the database are accounting, advertising, insurance, bank bonds, financial services, pensions, stocks taxation, property insurance, mergers and acquisitions, and investments.

Insurance and Workers' Compensation Research, on Westlaw (St. Paul, MN: West Publishing)

The database vendor WESTLAW provides access to five databases that cover the subject areas of insurance and workers' compensation. The databases may be accessed through a user interface that utilizes the same searching commands and screens for each database.

The databases allow users to access information about laws and regulations, claims and court rulings, updates on recent developments in the insurance industry, corporate and government profiles, interpretations of insurance policies, technical advice, and locating expert witnesses.

The databases are as follows:

National Insurance Law Service (NILS)—This database consists of seven files covering insurance company publications, circulars, and bulletins; state regulations; attorney general opinions; insurance statutes; and a list of subject headings for the INSURLAW file.

Case Law and Administrative Decisions—Seven files make up this database and they cover court decisions, insurance cases from specific states, and individual and multistate workers' compensation cases and administrative decisions.

Specialized Databases—This database contains seven files that include biographical data on medical malpractice and personal injury; scientific and technical experts; specialized literature about life, property, and liability insurance; abstracts and citations to industry journals; and recent legal developments within the insurance industry.

Texts and Periodicals—Eight files contribute to this database's coverage of journals, periodicals, indexes, handbooks, texts, treatises, and law reviews.

Gateway Databases—This database contains two files. One is the full text of 70 newspapers plus several magazines and journals, and the other has information on both existing and proposed state and federal regulations.

INTERNATIONAL FINANCE

International Business Form (www.ibf.com)

The International Business Form provides business information about international marketplace opportunities. The web site has a section about business opportunities and business meetings (which includes trade shows and other events). The links section of the web site includes an international business directory which is classified by the type of business, for easy use. An interesting feature of the International Business Form is their education section, which includes information about masters' programs in business and other business courses. Finally, this Internet web site includes a business resources page and a search directory to quickly find information.

INTERNATIONAL TRADE

Foreign Trade Division, U.S. Census Bureau (www.census.gov/ftp/pub/foreign-trade/www)

This web site on official U.S. international trade statistics is under the Office of the Associate Director for Economic Programs at the U.S. Bureau of the Census. It includes, among other things, a profile of American exporting companies from 1992, historical trade data, and trade balances with U.S. international trading partners. There is an official international trade bookmarks page with web site links to over 25 major trade web pages, including the United Nations trade-related organizations web page. Another popular feature is the Schedule B Codes which can be obtained from this web site. In addition, on the Foreign Trade Division web site, information can be obtained about a specific product or a specific country.

IMEX Exchange, Inc. (www.imex.com)

The IMEX Exchange that promotes international trade on the Internet helps international-focused companies, organizations, and countries develop and implement their Internet strategies through web page design, marketing, networking, and education. What's New section keeps you posted of new offerings and information on the IMEX Exchange and the Internet. Links for Cyber Trader Column that contains the hyperlinks referred to the biweekly column CyberTrader with additional resources can be found in the Journal of Commerce Cyber Trader Links. Global Trade Shows allows users to locate trade shows by any combination of industry, city, month, and name. It provides an executive summary including event descriptions, histories, exhibitor information, attendee information, press releases, conference information, and much more to help comparing the alternative. Also available is the IMEX's Trade Lead Board that is made to post and locate up-to-date trade offers from around the world in only a few seconds. The IMEX Search Engine allows visitors to post their own Trade Lead offer immediately. Submit URL section gives users the opportunity to receive a free listing of IMEX Exchange Inc. and to be updated on what is happening in international business.

Import/Export Directory, Serra International Inc. (www.serraintl.com)

This web page is made for international trade and transportation professionals in mind. The user can link to a site and see the 10 best air cargo sites. One can explore markets, find buyers and sellers, obtain transportation costs, review regulations of the government, and arrange for the import or export of goods. This page also gives sites that offer free searching of import and export trade leads. A chat room and bulletin board are options on this site. In the import/export directory, an extensive list of links on international trade and the transportation industry are available.

International Trade Administration (www.ita.doc.gov)

This resource is a collection of the International Trade Administration's web sites organized by the U.S. Department of Commerce. Users are informed of basic facts about the ITA, the latest additions to ITA sites, and its press releases and other media information. Links are categorized by region and country of market, industry or service cluster such as technology and aerospace, tourism, environment technology, finance, and consumer goods. Highlighted connections include the Office of Trade and Economic Analysis, which entails worldwide publications about trade statistics, exports, and foreign markets; a section on cross-cutting export programs, like Free Trade Area of Americas, Big Emerging Markets on the Internet, and the Advocacy Program to win major projects abroad; and the Trade Information Center for a guide to the 19 federal agencies which help develop export strategies. There is also an Export Assistance Center which helps businesses as they emerge into the global market that is broken into categories based on the users' needs including to locate market research and to learn about promoting products and services abroad and how to pinpoint export prospects. In addition, information on law enforcement of fair trade, exchange rates, foreign-trade zones, and policy bulletins is provided.

J + W Commdisc International (Birkenweg, Germany: Telex-Verlag Jaeger + Waldmann GmbH)

J + W Commdisc International is an international communications database on CD-ROM. It is a reference directory of businesses and products and is updated twice a year. The database is cross-referenced by name, country, product, and service. Each full entry consists of complete address, phone, telex and fax number, trade code, and is in English, French, German, and Spanish. Coverage is international in scope, and there are distributors and associates located in Europe, North America, South America, the Middle East, and the Pacific Rim. The database uses International Retrieval Software that conforms to most computer languages and special transcription characters developed for end users and professional searchers, including ASCII downloading to disk or printout. A demo disk is included in both 5.25 and 3.5 formats.

National Newspaper Index (Foster Grove, CA: Information Access)

National Newspaper Index is a CD-ROM source available for use on the InfoTrac system. Indexing is done for five national newspapers: The New York Times, The Wall Street Journal, Christian Science Monitor, The Los Angeles Times, and The Washington Post. The Los Angeles Times home edition and The Wall Street Journal eastern and western edition are indexed. The other three newspapers national or final editions are indexed. Indexing is cumulative and is updated each month. The coverage includes world affairs, politics, business news, and scientific news. All news reports, articles, editorials, columns, letters to the editor, obituaries, reviews, product evaluations, biographical pieces, cartoons and illustrations, poetry, and recipes are indexed.

Since this database is comprised of these five newspapers, searches result in citations from all of them. Citations indicate the length of the articles in column inches. A subscription covers the CD-ROM, the InfoTrac system, software, monthly updates, handbook, and maintenance and service. Software can be customized and software upgrades are provided at no cost to subscribers. Subscriptions are available without the InfoTrac system. Coverage is of the current and previous 3 years. Backfiles are provided upon request. Customer support for both the database and the system is available through a toll-free line from Information Access. In addition, a thesaurus of search terms and headings is available to aid searching. A microfilm version is available and an on-line version is accessible through BRS Information Technologies and DIALOG.

Saludos Web (www.saludos.com)

Saludos Web was created to provide a starting point for Hispanic people who are seeking jobs. It is supported by Saludos Hispanos, a journal for careers for Hispanic people. This Internet web site includes a listing from various not-for-profit organizations, universities, and companies. It has a section for posting résumés for recruiters to view. Saludos Web also includes numerous articles from the Saludos Hispanos magazine, national job listings, and a Hispanic resource center.

Sirat Development (www.sirat.com)

This business deals with international trade and export management. The user can browse and search through any trade leads that they have. One can also post any trade offers or requests. A translation service (English, German, and Turkish) is available. Sirat Development specializes in business, scientific, legal, and personal documents.

TradePort (www.tradeport.org)

This international trade web site gives the user the basics of exporting, where one can learn the terminology and read a business guide to exporting. An area of market research can be found. One can develop an export plan, identify markets, find out about the trade outlook, and evaluate the target market. A list of laws, regulations, and standards is available. In another area, the user can find out more about shipping and transportation, schedules of shipping companies, search for companies that specialize in certain area of shipping (i.e., air, ocean, storage packaging), and look at a list of shipping companies. A trade events calendar, special events, job opportunities, and newsgroups and mailing lists can also be found at this site. One can link to radio stations and newspapers across the country to find out about world news. In the Trade Expert section, TradePort gives advice in order to help companies get started in the field. Links to international trade sites are accessible.

United States International Trade Commission (www.usitc.gov)

This page first includes an explanation of what the United States International Trade Commission (USITC) does. At this site, one can find out the latest news and read about recent petitions and complaints filed with the commission. Also included are a calendar of deadline dates, hearings, and the status of the investigation. The user can download files on tariff affairs. One can also find out more about the trade commissioners, by reading a brief biography about them, and other statute information. Links to trade-related sites are available.

World Trade Plan (www.tradezone.com/wtp.html)

World Trade Plan is a site designed for users interested in international trade. It provides indexed resources on banks, government, exports, global travel, law, statistics, and other topics from countries offering business opportunities. After an initial bulleted list, there follows five large sections of information on Trade Zones, International Traders, International Business Opportunities, What's New, and Company Profiles.

"Trade Zones" provides an index to clustered hot links including, but not limited to, banks, embassies, clickable maps, trade references, statistics, law, and world weather. The link to clickable maps offers the user links to other web sites indexed by country. The first page on Antarctica is an image map offering the user a choice of information on its environment, education, images, science, news, treaty, history, tourism, and logistics. Within the environment section, the user has a choice of sources of Web information on subjects ranging from ozone depletion to protected areas.

"International Traders" presents a list of the web sites of International Traders indexed alphabetically by product names from agriculture to textiles. Traders may also discuss their mutual concerns at the Live Conference Room and pin their advertisements on the Web Board.

"International Business Opportunities" provides leads to established wholesalers who wish to establish long-term opportunities to traders. The companies are indexed by the type of products, and each one makes a general statement about its business and its products. Some of the information is more detailed here than in the traders index mentioned above.

"What's New" informs users of the new features and sources recently added to the web site.

"The Company Profiles" tells the story of four generations of Mellinger men who founded the international mail order trade business 90 years ago and, more recently, the club which provides trade agreements, product sources, the bimonthly Trade Opportunities Magazine, and sample imports.

The primary audience for the site is individuals who wish to become world traders. It offers a wide variety of information that would be of interest to all of those who wish to know about other countries.

INVESTMENTS

Alpine Technology Ventures (www.alpineventures.com)

Alpine Technology Ventures is an investor group that is based in California. ATV investors' group focuses on investment ventures throughout California's Silicon Valley area. Alpine Technology Ventures group seeks for ventures in emerging information technology. Technology market items include hardware, software, semiconductors, or communication tools. Direct links are available to Alpine's various services.

InvestinginBonds.com (www.investinginbonds.com)

This site offers consultation and planning services in securities, the markets as well as finance and politics. This site also offers information on bond-related topics and how to read the bond guide in the newspaper.

Investment, Information Access Company

Investment is one of the larger databases covering companies and industries analyses reports. The information provided includes full texts of investment reports, indexes, and abstracts.

Investor's Galleria (centrex.com)

This site contains information resources for a wide range of investors. A link to Barron's Online provides current market information and news. Free stock quotes are available via a ticker symbol search engine. Company news and profiles can also be accessed. Programming services and Internet services (consulting, training, and seminars) are also available. Links to top-selling financial software are available for downloading, and investing books and CD-ROMs can be ordered electronically. The Infoseek link provides news headlines, technology reports, stock information, and political news. The Infocenter contains a number of links including stock symbols (ticker symbols for the top 400 U.S. corporations), Technical Analysis Terms (a glossary of terms used with the analysis of stocks), and links to other financial servers.

Investment Resources (infomanage.com/investment)

This site contains a wealth of investment resources including information on bonds and debt securities (a variety of links and resources are available), brokerages (a comprehensive list of brokerage firms), computers and technology (Internet-related stocks, computer company links, Silicon Valley stocks, database-related companies, and computer technology stock prices), financial news (Investor's Business Daily, Wall Street Journal, Money Magazine, and Money$earch), investment banks (a list of prominent investment banks and links to home pages), stock quote, and a list of other related web sites. Other resources include CNN Business News, NASDAQ, and various stock exchanges on the World Wide Web.

Microsoft Investor (www.investor.msn.com/home.asp)

Microsoft Investor was designed to help investors improve their respective portfolios. To accomplish this, this Internet web site has a portfolio manager, market update section, and an investment finder. Microsoft Investor also contains numerous news articles about investing and business-related events. In addition, this Internet web site contains a tips and tricks section. Finally, Microsoft Investor has a research central section that allows the viewer to view a summary and some economic facts about numerous firms on the stock market.

The Street (www.thestreet.com)

The Street is a financial information Internet web site offered by James Cramer and other Wall Street businesspeople. In addition to their informative newsletter, this web site offers trading advice and stock market opinions about specific stocks. This Internet web site also contains news articles concerning different investment opportunities and possible investment ideas. Finally, The Street contains a resource page with a portfolio tracker to inform viewers on how their particular stocks faired in the market.

LABOR

American Federation of Labor-Congress of Industrial Organizations (AFL-CIO) (www.aflcio.org/home.htm)

Their goals are to improve the lives of working families and to bring economic justice to the workplace and social justice to the nation. In the What's New section, one can find out what is going on with unions this week, look at the shareholder alert, and get more information on upcoming conventions. The user can also access information on how to form a union at the workplace or how to become a trained union organizer. The latest boycott label, label letter, and a place as to how to locate union-made products are available. One can search the AFL-CIO archives and also find out about summer activities. Links to unions and other organizations can be found.

American Federation of Labor (www.aflcio.org)

The American Federation of Labor home page is larger than most other labor union pages. The contents of the page include links to other labor unions, public documents (press releases, speeches, and archives) concerning labor unions, and information about how to contact the AFL-CIO and your state representative. A feature of this page is the AFL tribute to the working woman. This page is resourceful and more educational than the typical labor union site.

The Bureau of Labor Statistics' LABSTAT Data Server (stats.bls.gov/pub)

The Bureau of Labor Statistics' (BLS) Public Directory contains the plain text file of "Economy at a Glance," a current register of BLS news releases, miscellaneous BLS documents, and a "Special Requests" directory. The "Economy at a Glance" has tables about the U.S. Labor Market. The most current BLS news items are stored in the directory.

The "Documents" folder contains miscellaneous reports from the Bureau of Labor Statistics; some examples are the consumer price index, the international price index, and the employment cost index. The "Special Requests" repository consists of BLS Regional office subdirectories and survey-specific subdirectories. The "Time Series" folder contains files of current statistical data.

Institute for Global Communications (www.igc.org)

This Progressive Directory site, known as the Institute for Global Communications (IGC), is visually stimulating and easy to browse. The page contains links to its five sister sites: PeaceNet, EcoNet, ConflictNet, LaborNet, and WomensNet. These sites are the IGC's on-line communities of activists and organizations. The IGC newsletter and members directory can be found on the home page, along with information about jobs at IGC. This site, as a whole, does not focus mainly on labor unions, although LaborNet provides useful information about the working world.

International Transport Workers' Federation (www.itf.org.uk)

The International Transport Workers' Federation (ITF) home page is unlike most other labor union sites. It is available in French, Spanish, German, Japanese, Swedish, and English and contains various pictures and unique thumbnails. The site revolves around inland, maritime, and aviation transportation. Included on the page is information about ITF history, ITF publications, and a feature on women transport workers. There are also links to tourism services affiliated with ITF.

Labor Law I (Washington D.C.: Bureau of National Affairs) [DIALOG]

Labor Law I contains concise information on decisions and references contained in publications about labor relations, fair employment, wages, as well as hours, occupational health, and safety. The database is composed of seven subfiles that are on-line versions of U.K. Kompass register, Kelly's directories, Dial industry, British exports, U.K. trade names, and Directory of Directors.

National Hispanic Employee Association (www.yahoo.com/ Business_and_Economy/Organizations)

National Hispanic Employee Association (NHEA) is a web site comprised of Hispanic employee association professionals from Fortune 500 corporations and government agencies dedicated to the development, advancement, and upward mobility of its members. Direct links are available to information about NHEA, members, breaking barriers awards, news, and conferences.

Saludos Web: Careers, Employment, and Culture (www.saludos.com)

Saludos Web: Careers, Employment, and Culture is a World Wide Web site that provides career and education opportunities for Hispanics. Users can choose links to further explore what the web site has to offer. These links include Articles, Careers, Education, FAQ, Hispanic Resources, Internet Resources, Job Listings, and Résumé Pool. Under Articles, this web site has up-to-date stories on certain careers in different fields; the articles change periodically. The Careers link provides job listings for users, while the Education link provides internships and scholarship listings as well as education centers throughout the country for Hispanics.

U.S. Department of Labor (www.dol.gov)

The U.S. Department of Labor home page is loaded with facts and figures about labor in America. The page includes news and past articles about minimum wage, divorce and pensions, welfare, America's job bank, a pension search, and "small business retirement solutions." Also, there is a "What's New" section and an archive of media releases. Information about job openings at the Department of Labor is also provided.

LIBRARIES

Academic Business Libraries' Web Sites (weber.u.washington.edu/~balib/abl.html)

This site, maintained by the Business Administration Library of the University of Washington, provides links to the business libraries of academic institutions in the United States.

MANAGEMENT

ASCOT (Australian Securities Commission's National Corporate Database), INFO-ONE International

This electronic database provides current and historical information on Australian companies and their organizational relationships. Company information includes names, addresses, details of key positions, share structures, names of shareholders, charges against the organizations, and lists of documents and annual returns as filed by the organizations. Other types of searches, like by registered auditors, official liquidators, securities dealers, and banned futures authorities, are also available. ASCOT is maintained by the Australian Securities Commission.

Compact D/SEC

This CD-ROM database contains financial and management information spanning over 10,000 publicly traded companies. The data contained within the database are derived from annual reports filed with the U.S. Securities and Exchange Commission. The database can be searched using a variety of methods including company name, type of business, geographic location, financial information, number of outstanding shares, number of employees, or Fortune number. Once a company is located, information is available about the company's past performance, earnings, stock issuance, financial reports, ownership and subsidiaries, company profiles, and mailing address.

The Institute of Management and Administration (www.ioma.com)

The Institute of Management and Administration web page provides information on news and issues affecting the business world. Under the "Business Directory," the site provides links to over 600 useful outside pages, such as the Investor's Business Daily and the CNN Financial Network, which are organized into 16 major categories. This site also provides access to several discussion groups covering major issues in business such as the Report on Salary Survey's Compensation Bulletin Board and the Legal Bulletin Board. It also includes a list of over 30 newsletter published by the institute in various subjects, such as Insurance and Risk, Public Accounting, and Corporate Financial Management. While the site provides access to the texts of the recent top articles for each newsletter, there is a subscription fee to receive the complete newsletter. In addition, the site allows users to browse the IOMA archives with a keyword search engine.

Management Contents (Foster City, CA: Information Access Company) [DIALOG]

The Management Contents is a source of information about business and management. The subjects covered by the database include accounting, decision sciences, finance, industrial relations, managerial economics, marketing, operations research, and organizational behavior.

Off the Record (www.yahoo.com/Business_and_Economy)

This site deals with the web-based radio show. The show is directed towards business and technology professionals. The show has news and interviews with people involved in information-technology management. The site also has transcripts for those viewers who do not have audio. Once the viewer has seen what they wanted, it is possible for him/her to react to what was viewed.

MANUFACTURERS

Industrial Technical Institute (www.yahoo.com/Business_and_Economy/Organizations)

Industrial Technical Institute is a web site dedicated to assist manufacturers in increasing productivity, quality, and consumer satisfaction. Direct links are available to performance benchmarking service, center for electronic commerce, energy and environment center, Michigan manufacturing technology center, electro-optics engineering, and financial solutions. Further links are available to services, frequently asked questions, news, maps, and related web sites. An E-mail address is provided for further information.

MAPS

Mapblast (www.mapblast.com)

This site is maintained by Vicinity Corporation. Detailed maps, even street maps, from anywhere in the United States can be provided. Maps can also be e-mailed to anybody or added into any home page from this site.

MARKETS

Dun's Market Identifiers (Murray Hill, NJ: Dun & Bradstreet)

Dun's Market Identifiers, otherwise known as DMI, is a directory file produced by Dun & Bradstreet Information Services. It is available from DIALOG as file number 516. The files consist of executive names and titles, corporate linkages, D–U–N–S numbers, basic company data, and organization status. They also contain more marketing information on over 7.6 million U.S. business establishments, including private, public, and government organizations.

The subject coverage of this source consists of U.S. businesses. The commercial, industrial, and service industries are indexed with over 15,000 of the unique D & B SIC codes. The information comes from more than 9 million U.S. businesses.

Search options are varied when searching through DIALOG. Some of the search options include company name, executive name, SIC code, street address, and net worth. There are also options available to limit searches, sort output, map output, and reports listed by city, total employees, telephone numbers, etc.

Foreign Marketing (www.lib.lsu.edu/bus/marketin.html)

This web site provides and organizes annotated links to other web sites composed primarily of primary and secondary materials. The annotations sometimes indicate the source of the materials as well as if the link is to information or to a collection of links. It is intended to serve as a reference and research tool for an academic audience and is authored and maintained by Tom Diamond who is a Business Librarian at Louisiana State University-Baton Rouge.

A table of contents is the primary navigation tool and also provides the organizational structure. No keyword searching is available beyond the native browser level. The headings in the table of contents are Advertising, Country Reports (A–H), Country Reports (I–P), Country Reports (Q–Z), Country Reports (U.S./Global), Foreign Policies, Internet, Journals and Scholarly Publications, News, Organizations, Statistics, and Trade Agreements and Impact. The entries under the Country Reports headings are organized by country or region. Some locations provide only specific marketing and business information, while others also include geography, history, maps, art, or culture as well. The U.S./Global section is more tightly targeted to foreign marketing, with the majority of the entries tied to information collected by the U.S. government. The Internet heading covers issues related to the use of the Internet and marketing issues that are unique to this medium. The majority of the journals mentioned provide tables of contents with some including abstracts or indexes. The news listings are heavily weighted toward Eastern Europe. The organizations include the American Marketing Association, the World Trade Organization, and others targeting the Pacific Rim. Statistical data are found for many countries via governmental or major international bank links. Trade agreements include references to international trade but are primarily targeted to North America.

The author adds updates and deletes links on a regular basis. Link selection is based primarily upon utility to the intended audience. New Internet sources are located using services such as MidNet, Newsbytes Pacifica, and Scout Report as well as user suggestions. Sites that are collections of links with no informational content of their own are typically not included unless they complement the sources included here. Typically included sites contain public information, with a minimum of fee-based sites. The majority of the references are in English but may contain pointers to foreign language sites. Details of the selection criteria can be found athttp://indigo.lib.lsu.edu/bU.S./criteria.html.

/MouseTracks/(nsns.com/MouseTracks)

/MouseTracks/ is a web site produced by New South Network Services. /MouseTracks/ lists several marketing and entrepreneurial resources that can be found on the Web. "The List of Marketing Lists" is a collection of web sites and E-mail discussion lists maintained by marketing organizations and companies. "MetaMarket" provides links to advertising, research, and design companies, as well as to further commercial resources. Upcoming meetings and conferences of interest to businesspeople can be found in "Conference Calls." Course listings and syllabi from business-related classes are listed in "Syllabits." The budding entrepreneur can find links to basic information about conducting business on the Internet in "Nuts and Bolts." "The New Medium" provides links to on-line business and marketing publications. Business instructors and other interested parties can find summaries and links to academic resources and theoretical information in "Of Academic Interest."

Point of Purchase (www.popmag.com)

Point of Purchase is an on-line magazine offering information for retailers and brand marketers covering the aspects of the point of purchase industry. The site offers information covering recent news events, along with reviews of new products every month. Links are provided to sites of sponsors and suppliers. Users also have access to information about available employment positions in the point of purchase industry.

Standard and Poor's Current Market Perspectives (www.standardandpoors.com)

Current Market Perspectives is published monthly and provides facts and action on hundreds of stocks.

MERGERS

M&A Filings (Washington, D.C.: Prentice-Hall Legal and Financial Securities and Exchange Division) [DIALOG]

M&A Filings provides abstracts of merger and acquisition documents made available by the U.S. Securities and Exchange Commission (SEC). The documents covered are 13a (15% purchase), 14a-1 (tender offer), 14a-9 (management response to a tender offer), 13e-3 (leverage buyout), and 13e-4 (issuer tender offer).

World M&A Network (www.worldm-anetwork.com/index.htm)

This site offers hundreds of listings for merger and acquisition opportunities which are updated on a daily basis. It offers an opportunity to identify corporate acquisitions and buyers. Its main focus is the U.S. market with companies for purchase $5–100 million. Once you obtain a subscription (a few hundred dollars per year), you not only get thousands of listings, but also the opportunity to place listings. M&A Network provides numerous sources of information, although transactions are not part of their practice. The link Done Deal Info, a subgroup of M&A, provides many details on transactions for private and closely held public companies for a subscription fee.

World M&A Network (www.worldm-anetwork.com/index.htm)

World M&A Network is published monthly and updated weekly on the Internet. It is also published in print and has hundreds of listings for companies for sale, merger candidates, corporate and strategic buyers, and sources of financing in the United States and worldwide. Each of the leads that they publish is created by a M&A professional.

METALWORK

ADCO (www.adcodiecast.com)

This site stands for "Aluminum Die Castings." This is a very general web site. The site mainly explains what ADCO works on. They are a company that is concentrated on making die castings. They explain that they rely on tooling, casting, machining, and painting in order to get the goal of making die castings accomplished.

MONEY MARKETS

Smart Money (www.dowjones.com/smart)

Smart Money is an on-line magazine offering users insight on many aspects of investing, saving, and spending. The site serves as a tool to allow users to browse the current issue and subscribe to get others. The site contains summaries of the current month's cover stories and highlights important current issues. The "Media Kit" section features editorials, circulations, research, and advertising information.

MUTUAL FUNDS

FRONTLINE: Betting on the Market (www2.pbs.org/wgbh/ pages/frontline/shows/betting)

FRONTLINE is an award-winning series, which has produced documentaries on public television (PBS) for more than 15 years. On-line presentations of some programs are available on FRONTLINE's web site.

Betting on the Market aired on January 14, 1997. This on-line version provides an analysis of American investment in the stock market, either directly or through mutual funds. The program looks at the risks involved for the individual and the implications for the nation. This site presents full-text interviews with experts, descriptions and analyses of famous bear markets, musings by professional money managers on the possibility of a downturn, and a series of special reports which provide additional commentary. In the discussion section, money managers answer questions and visitors to the site may record comments.

Morningstar

This service on America Online provides rankings for mutual funds.

NetEc (netec.wustl.edu/NetEc.html)

This site is a collection of resources available for electronic research on Economics which is mirrored in Japan, Finland, and the United Kingdom. It includes connections and information on BibEc, for printed working papers, and WoPEc, for electronic working papers, which allows the user to search by title, author, or subject. Additionally, there are CodEc, on codes for economics and econometrics, WebEc, for economic resources on the World Wide Web, HoPEc, on home page papers in economics, and BizEc, for selected resources in business administration including subdirectories for each subject on daily, weekly, and monthly or long-term publications.

NEWSPAPERS

American Banker–Bond Buyer (New York, NY: American Banker–Bond Buyer)

This source provides current financial information in two daily newspapers, the American Banker and The Bond Buyer, and in over 20 weekly newsletters. The newspaper and most of the newsletter are available on-line through numerous services, including NewsNet, DataTimes, Nexis-Lexis, and DIALOG. Newsletters include Asset Sales Report, High Yield Report, Mortgage Marketplace, The Bond Buyer's Public Finance Watch, Regulatory Compliance Watch, and The Thrift Regulator.

General News and Newspapers

Asiaweek (www.asiaweek.com)

This site, produced weekly by Asiaweek magazine, provides the articles included in the current issue, a newsmap which searches for the articles about the place chosen, information for putting advertisements on subscribing Asiaweek, and the profiles of 20 great Asians.

Boston Globe (www.boston.com)

This site provides information on Boston in terms of news/media, arts/diversions, sports/outdoors, business, weather/traffic, autos, homes, and jobs.

After choosing one of the fields, a keyword can be entered, then the relevant information will be provided.

Business Dateline (Ann Arbor: University Microfilms International) [DIALOG]

This CD-ROM contains records from U.S. and Canadian regional business publications that include newspapers and wiretap services. Some of the specific sources are Crains Chicago Business, San Francisco Business Times, and Washington Post.

Business Post (www.scmp.com/news/business/topbiz.idc)

This daily on-line newspaper is a supplement to the South China Morning Post, a leading English newspaper in Hong Kong. The post covers daily Asian and international business news. Market information and data are updated throughout the day. Free registration is needed for access.

Chicago Tribune (www.chicago.tribune.com)

This is an on-line newspaper. It provides news in Chicago and also national and international news. News on sports, stock exchange, technology, tempo, travel, jobs, homes, autos, weather, and TV listings are also included.

Christian Science Monitor (www.csmonitor.com)

This site, maintained by The Christian Science Publishing Society, provides daily news, access to Monitor Radio including hourly news, topic search, links to different sites, a forum, headlines of associated press, E-mails from people of different places of the world, and information on different areas such as food, books, and film.

CNN (www.cnn.com)

This site, maintained by Cable News Network, Inc., provides daily news, information on science and technology, travel, health, earth, entertainment, finance, employment opportunities, and many different topics. There is also a link to Allpolitics, and to Pointcast, where an Internet news network program can be downloaded for free.

Crain's Detroit Business (www.crainsdetroit.com)

This web site contains daily news stories as they pertain to the business world as well as a variety of other business-related tools. The editorial section provides an outlet for user voices. Executive Recruiters is a link containing advertisements from employers looking for experienced employees. BizServe, an on-line business guide for the state of Michigan, is also accessible from this site.

Detroit News (www.detnews.com)

The Detroit News Home Page provides daily news, editorials, horoscope, lottery, weather, death notices, and up-to-date information on areas such as sports, business, lifestyles, college, and media. Contacts to staff and departments and for home delivery and advertisement postings are listed.

Electronic Mail & Guardian (www.mg.co.za)

This site deals with one of the on-line newspapers in Johannesburg. Included are political news, sports news, and business-related news. Also listed on the page is information about entertainment, travel, and job openings. This is one of the many ways the web provides services about one place to many places all over the world.

Los Angeles Times (www.latimes.com)

The Los Angeles Times Home Page provides daily news, up-to-date information on areas such as sports, business, homes, jobs, and automobile. PointCast and Netscape can be downloaded here.

National Business Employment Weekly (NBEW) (www.nbew.com)

A table of contents of the current issue of NBEW at newspaper stands is available at this web page. Also at this site are feature articles and selections from previous issues, which range in subject from salary, interviews, and jobs. The Best-of section has articles on cyberstrategies, search tactics, résumés, networking, and interviewing. A link to find jobs outside of the United States is accessible. Reader services and subscriptions and a link to find out more about National Business Employment Weekly are included at this page. Advertising opportunities are offered to the user.

Financial Times Fulltext (London: Financial Times Business Information) [DIALOG]

Financial Times Fulltext provides entire articles published in Financial Times newspaper and its editions. The subjects covered by the articles include company information, government regulations, labor, industry information and developments, management, markets, technology, and international trade.

National Public Radio (www.npr.org)

National Public Radio Online, sponsored by Federal Express, provides hourly news which require Real Audio to listen to. It also has a listing of programs, as well as commentaries and contact E-mail address. Transcripts and tapes of the programs of the National Public Radio can be ordered and sponsors can be met on-line.

The Wall Street Journal Interactive Edition (www.wsj.com)

The WSJ Interactive Edition is a currently updated newspaper that also provides links and access to a multitude of information and opinions. The special feature of The Interactive Edition is that most of the companies mentioned will be linked to its Briefing Book, or financial summary, and other relevant articles which may appear in the printed edition of The Wall Street Journal. The user can also utilize the "Search Page" to be connected with information on a specific company. Certain information may also be available in audio reports that come from the Dow Jones Investor Network or special reports that include actual data along with news coverage. Another component of The Interactive Edition is the "Personal Journal," which allows the user to create an index of personal words, phrases, or companies which will automatically be searched for and compiled from each edition. The "Personal Journal Portfolio" can also be used to track the status of selected stocks and mutual funds.

Time (www.time.com)

This site of the magazine Time provides daily news, the U.S. edition and the international edition of the magazine, chat and forum section, politics, international and national news, science and technology, and sport and entertainment columns, and subscription information and services are provided on-line.

US News and World Report (www.usnews.com)

The US News and World Report Home Page provides news, mainly U.S. news, and up-to-date information in areas such as business and technology, culture, and ideas. There are also editorial and forum sections.

USA Today (www.usatoday.com)

The USA Today Home Page provides daily news and up-to-date financial and political information. There are also information in travel, shopping, lotteries, jobs, and many other areas.

Washington Post (www.washingtonpost.com)

The Washington Post Home Page provides daily news and up-to date business and sports information. There is also information on travel, shopping, lotteries, jobs, and many other areas.

Wall Street Journal Shopping (shop.wsj.com/catalog)

This page is an on-line catalog of Wall Street Journal gifts and accessories. The items that can be ordered include a baseball cap, travel bag, sweatshirt, T-shirt, baby bib, golf shirt, and golf balls. Orders are only accepted by fax.

OCCUPATIONS

America's Job Bank (www.ajb.dni.us)

America's Career InfoNet is a prototype system. This site has occupational information that helps employment search and develop one's understanding of the job market. There are options available that provide information concerning employment, careers, and more.

Career Management International (www.cmi-lmi.com)

Career Management International web site is an on-line resource for information covering outplacement, relocation counseling, employee assistance programs, and management interventions. The main focus of the site deals with career transitions and common business problems. Programs are described for both firms and employees to help make job searching more successful. Individual programs cover such topics as resource recovery, stress management, and retirement preparations. Group programs include conflict resolution, team building, and succession planning. Links are provided to job posting sites, résumé planning resources, and relocation assistance resource on the web.

CareerNet (www.careers.org)

Career Resource Center is an index of career-related web sites on the Internet. At this site, a huge number of links to jobs with major employers, Internet newsgroups, and newspapers can be viewed. They also provide links that concern career advice, colleges and libraries, employment agencies, outplacement firms, state employment offices, and more information about jobs and employment.

CareerSite (careersite.com)

CareerSite allows users to search for available jobs in their field of interest and view company profiles. Users may develop a personal profile, providing employers with information, qualifications, interests, and expectations. Users may then use this profile to search the job database for available positions and receive messages when any job positions match their profile. Users may submit their profiles and résumés to any of the available employers. Extensive information is available on all the participating companies.

CareerWEB (careerweb.com)

CareerWEB is an extensive web site composed of resources and information for employees to find jobs, and employers to hire applicants. The site offers a keyword search to help locate several jobs in many fields of interest, such as accounting, education, engineering, law, and retail. Users may search for jobs by state or even by city. Users may research all the employers on the site from the "Employer's Page" section. Employers may search all the posted résumés and advertise their companies on the site. Employees may file their résumés on the site for employers to search, or be notified of opportunities that match their résumés in the "Job Match" section. The site offers information on career employment, and helpful articles are available in the "Career Doctor" section. Links to other career resources are offered such as books, videos, and software. The "Career Inventory" section allows users to fill out a survey, have it evaluated, and receive feedback and suggestions on the job search process.

Chancellor & Chancellor (www.chancellor.com)

Chancellor & Chancellor is a placement service for companies and individuals in the computer technology industry. With its "Passthru Services," companies are assured compliance with Internal Revenue Service regulations when hiring and paying consultants such as classifying them as 1099 Independent Contractors or W2 Temporary employees. Job openings are listed for contractors and full-time employment with connection to other resources for contractors. Chancellor & Chancellor also provides a service that will send job hunters specified job openings over electronic mail.

Corporate Jobs Outlook! (Boerne, TX: Corporate Jobs Outlook!)

Corporate Jobs Outlook is a bimonthly newsletter available in hard copy and on-line with Newsnet on the Human Resources Information Network (HRIN). The newsletter is written for job seekers and reports on large companies, usually with at least 5000 employees and nationwide operations. Each issue profiles 16 to 20 employers. For each corporation, the following information is provided: name, addresses, phone numbers, contacts, sales and earnings (in dollars and percent change), salaries/benefits (on a five-point scale), financial stability (on a five-point scale), industry and company out-look (on a five-point scale), locations, and business. Also given are multi-paragraph narrative descriptions of the company outlook and opportunities. Suggested readings for each company are often included. Each issue has a cumulative index that lists reports according to industry.

Equal Opportunity Publication (www.eop.com)

Equal Opportunity Publication web site is a career center for workforce diversity for minorities, women, and people with disabilities. The "Career Center Opportunities" section provides career opportunities offered by companies, government agencies, schools, and hospitals. The site contains an on-line library of diversity career magazines dedicated to helping career searches. The site offers tips and trends in diversity career searching. Users may post their résumés on-line and have them sent to all the companies advertising on the site who are seeking to recruit.

Office of the Comptroller of the Currency (www.occ.treas.gov)

The Office of the Comptroller of the Currency (OCC), an independent bureau of the Treasury Department, is the oldest federal financial regulatory body and oversees the nation's federally chartered banks. Providing information about the workings of the agency and the history of banking, OCC's web page includes information for individuals heavily involved with national banks and novices interested in a cursory overview of the subject. With few pictures and graphics, the site provides a straightforward table of contents with numerous links to additional information. The resources cover everything from the history of the OCC, its regulatory duties, legal interpretations, and publica-tions, to consumer information. Special emphasis is made on OCC's duties under the Community Reinvestment Act. Finally, the page includes a subject index and is keyword searchable.

RadioSuisse Services, RadioSuisse AG

This on-line information service provides access to Data-Star, TRADSTAT, Data-Mail, bulletin boards, and gateways. Data-Star contains more than 250 databases, providing global coverage with an emphasis on Europe. Types of business databases include banking such as Investext Broker Research; business opportunities such as Advertise; EC companies such as French Importers and Exporters; industry analyses such as INFOMAT International Business; management such as Harvard Business Review Online; markets and technology such as Predicasts PROMPT; market research such as Euromonitor Market Direction; materials such as Materials Business Information; and trade journals such as Company Intelligence. TRADSTAT provides world trade statistics. Data-Mail is an electronic mail service, and gateways allow access to other RadioSuisse associated services. The bulletin boards are a forum for group communication and discussion.

ORGANIZATION

Outside Insights (www.outside-insights.com/index.html)

This site provides information about Outside Insights that customizes retreats and workshops to increase personal, team, and organizational effectiveness in the business world. It relies on the expertise of a team of highly qualified professionals to custom-design and implement leadership programs for business and organizations worldwide. The site includes a half-day team-building program, maximize, which is a three-hour learning activity of 20 to 100 people competing and collaborating through the program. The cofounders Kelly Andrews and Greg Ranstrom and the facilitators are introduced in this site. Also provided is the list of favorite facilities chosen by the organization.

PARTNERSHIPS

Venture Web (www.venture-web.or.jp)

Venture Web is a web page consisting of information regarding prospective business partnership. This web site is dedicated for users that are interested in searching for business partners in an electronic business forum. Users can discuss the development of their business in the chat rooms available in this web page. Users can also browse through the given links in the web site. For further information, they can contact Venture Web by the address and e-mail address provided in the web site.

PERIODICALS

Business Insurance (www.businessinsurance.com/default.html)

This weekly newsmagazine covers information on corporate risk, employees benefits, and managed care news. It includes analyses of industry issues and state, national, and international news. It also provides links to other related resources and dated Internet articles.

Business Periodicals Index, H. W. Wilson

The database (online and on CD-ROM) indexes leading business magazines that deal on accounting, acquisitions and mergers, advertising, banking, building and construction, communications, computers, economics, electronics, engineering, finance, investments, and government regulations. Some of the countries covered by the database are the United States and most of the European countries.

Business Periodicals Online

This database provides abstracts and keyword searching for over 800 professional periodicals relating to the business and management industry. Once a keyword is entered into the search engine, a list of related articles are derived. A detailed summary of the article including date, publisher, and bibliographic information is then available. The two compact disc set is updated monthly, providing relevant current information. The content and search methods are similar to ABI/Inform Global.

Business Periodicals Select, Research, Global

Business Periodicals encompasses three ProQuest full-image databases:

1. Business Periodicals Select
2. Business Periodicals Research
3. Business Periodicals Global

All three databases offer full images of articles to citations from ABI/INFORM® Select, Research, Global, therefore, allowing the user to locate and review relevant citations and abstracts and then retrieve, view, and print full images. Records include abstracts, indexing, and bibliographic citations. Each database also allows the user to search by subject, title, keywords, author, and publication. An on-line thesaurus and multiple indexes provide user access to all subject terms. Features of the search engine include capability to use Boolean logic, proximity operators, truncation, field limiting, and reuse of searches. Users can choose individual records for printing and downloading.

Select features articles that are more of a general business topic. Abstracts and article indexing is provided. More than one-third of the indexed titles are imaged cover to cover. Research is a database geared toward corporate and academic researchers, managers, librarians, executives, students, and government officials. In contrast to Select, this database offers cover-to-cover images from more than one-half the indexed titles. Global contains abstracts and indexing to articles from outside the United States.

Each database is available as an annual subscription that includes index and full-image databases, monthly updates, and search and retrieval software. These databases can be utilized on a stand-alone system running MS-DOS 5.x or higher (6.22 recommended). Users are provided with documentation and toll-free technical support.

Card Technology Magazine (cardtech.faulknergray.com/ index.htm)

The Card Technology Magazine web site is a companion to a print magazine by the same name that is published by Faulkner & Gray, Inc. This site is devoted to news and issues of the card payment systems industries and card applications. The main page offers news bulletins that are updated weekly. The Card Technology Buyer's Guide offers alphabetical lists of resources by category for a variety of services and products that users of advanced card technologies may need, including software and hardware companies as well as advertising companies. Businesses just beginning to become involved with card payment systems would benefit from the list of associations and industry contacts. Tables of industry rankings are organized by company, technology, and region and include market share statistics as well as projections for the future. A list of Internet resources features links to card-technology-related information. The conference calendar is an extensive list of future conferences in cities around the world. Several on-line forums allow users to discuss hot topics. Faulkner & Gray, Inc. lists links to related web sites that it has created and offers descriptions and ordering information for the print magazines and directories that the company publishes.

Computer Database (Foster City, CA: Information Access)

Computer Database is a bibliographic database containing citations and abstracts of journal articles, published proceedings, and research reports from more than 360 journals, newsletters, and newspapers covering computers, the computer industry, telecommunications, and electronics. Topics covered include businesses, home and industry applications, software and hardware reviews, product evaluations, technical reports, and consumer information. Coverage starts in 1983, with full-text access for 70% of the articles beginning in 1987. Updating occurs daily with some 6000 records added to the database each month.

The database is available on-line through DIALOG, BRS Information Technologies, Data-Star, Nexis, and Compuserve. A CD-ROM version is also available, covering the last 3 years only. Subject headings for searching are supplied in Access to Access: An Online User's Guide to IAC Databases, a thesaurus available from Information Access Co.

Computer News Fulltext (Boston: I D G Communications) [DIALOG]

Computer News Fulltext provides articles about computer-related technologies and companies, products, marketplace, developments, systems and software, networking, data communications, management, and telecommunications.

Consumer Reports (Mount Vernon, NY: Consumers Union) [DIALOG]

Consumer Reports are available in three editions, Consumers Reports, Consumer Reports Travel Letter and Consumer Reports Health Letter. The purpose of the reports is to provide consumers with results of tests and ratings of goods and services such as automobiles, appliances, financial services, money management enterprises, health, nutrition, laws that affect consumers, as well as product recalls.

Fast Company (www.fastcompany.com)

This web site is a magazine on-line. The magazine provides many options and tools that are available to the user through this site. The user can access back issues of the magazine of Fast Company. Customers are able to access services that are available through the company on this site. This site gives current and background information on this company. Through this site, the user can research who is associated with this company. There is also late-breaking business news that is available to the user.

Harvard Business Review (New York: John Wiley and Sons) [DIALOG]

Harvard Business Review is an on-line database that provides full-text articles of the print edition as well as abstracts and citations. It covers the following subjects: accounting, automation, business ethics, industry analysis, strategic planning, and trade.

Independent (London) (London. Newspaper Publishing) [DIALOG]

Independent (London) is an on-line full-text edition of the Independent newspaper. Subjects covered by the database include business, finance, government, legislation, technology, trade, and industry.

InfoTrac (Foster City, CA: Information Access)

InfoTrac is a CD-ROM source that provides bibliographic citations, abstracts and some full-text articles from periodicals, newspapers, and other sources. It is designed to meet the research needs of readers in academic and public libraries. It is a menu-driven system that searches by keyword or subject with Help functions in all screens. Subject headings are taken from the Library of Congress Subject Headings and are arranged alphabetically. Information may be printed or copied to a disk. Software is also available that would indicate on each entry whether or not that reference is available in a specific library. The CD-ROMs are updated and cumulated monthly. The data covered is for 3 years plus the current year unless otherwise noted. Backfile databases are also available.

Information Access Co. maintains customer service lines, a newsletter, and continual upgrades to meet customer needs. The system is capable of downloading usage data that includes time of day, day of week, usage histograms, and the number of times information from a specific journal was printed or downloaded.

Over 15 different customized databases are now available for use with InfoTrac:

General Periodical Index—Public Library Version—an index to 1100 popular magazines and journals plus The New York Times, The Wall Street Journal, and The Christian Science Monitor. All titles from Magazine Index Plus and Business Index are included.

Magazine ASAP Select—an index for smaller libraries. It provides full-text of 50 of the most requested titles indexed in Magazine Index Select over a 2-year period.

Business Index—contains over 700 business, management, and trade journals with references to over 3000 other sources.

Business ASAP—contains full text of 350 popular business titles.

Company ProFile—combines directory information and text of newswire releases for over 140,000 private and public companies. It includes newswire releases for the most current 6 months.

Investext—provides indexing and full text of company and industry research reports prepared by over 60 leading Wall Street firms. Reports cover 8,000 U.S. companies and 2000 publicly held foreign companies. It includes the most current 12 months plus the previous year.

InfoTrac EF/General BusinessFile

This CD-ROM database contains abstracts for nearly 900 business, industry, economic, and management periodicals. Furthermore, it provides indexing to the Wall Street Journal and selected sections of the New York Times. Company, products, industry, and economic information is also provided, using either a keyword or subject heading search. The subject guide search permits browsing of company listings, industries, topics, geographical locations, and people.

Magazine Index Select (Foster City, CA: Information Access)

Updated monthly, this CD-ROM source provides 3 years plus the current year of indexing and abstracting to more than 200 of the periodicals most requested in small public and academic libraries. It provides assistance in research on current issues, business, health and fitness, travel and leisure, arts and entertainment, people, products, world affairs, and personal finance. The Expanded Search mode available allows for combining multiple search terms and concepts, keyword searching, and the display of subject terms in each citation. As an option, the citations can be linked to a holdings catalog, allowing the searcher to display journal holdings information. Included with the indexing of periodicals is coverage of The New York Times.

Magazine Index/Plus (Foster City, CA: Information Access)

Indexing more than 430 periodicals, Magazine Index/Plus is a CD-ROM source. In addition to journals, indexing of The New York Times and The Wall Street Journal is done. Coverage encompasses data from the current year, a cumulation of the previous 3 years and the past 60 days of The New York Times and The Wall Street Journal. The monthly updates are cumulated. The Magazine Index/Plus backfile covers the periodicals and newspapers back to 1984. Approximately 300 of the periodicals date back to 1980.

Subject areas include current national and international events, business, computers, and consumer information. Among the business-related journals are The Economist, Barron's, Journal of Small Business Management, and Financial World. Each citation provides article and journal/newspaper title, author, volume number, date, and page numbers. Many of these periodicals are available in full text on Magazine Collection, a microfilm product from Information Access. Coverage on Magazine Collection begins with 1980. Searches on Magazine Index/Plus can be done using controlled keywords or subjects. The search results report the number of citations before listing them out.

The CD-ROM was intended for use on the InfoTrac system. A subscription covers hardware, software, monthly updates, a handbook, and maintenance and service. Software can be customized and software upgrades are provided at no cost to subscribers. Subscriptions are available without the InfoTrac system. Subscriptions normally begin with coverage of the current and previous 3 years. Backfiles are available on request. Customer support services are available through a toll-free line.

McCarthy on CD-ROM

This is a compilation of company, industry, and market information and news from over 50 international newspapers and business magazines. Some of these include The Financial Times, The Economist, Middle East Economic Digest, Business and Finance, Euromoney, and Lloyd List. The database includes the full text of more than 600 articles per day chosen for their authoritative worldwide coverage of company and industry information. The articles and headlines are indexed to enable precise searching on company names, industries, and countries, in addition to free text searching.

McGraw-Hill, Inc. (New York: McGraw-Hill, Inc.)

McGraw-Hill publishes over 40 business-related magazines and newsletters that are available on-line in full text. Examples of publications include Business Week, Byte, Platt's Oilgram News, Securities Week, Tech Transfer Report, Inside N. R. C., and Data Communications. Information retrieval services that can access the sources include DIALOG, Dow Jones News/ Retrieval, FT Profile, and NewsNet. McGraw-Hill also offers business CD-ROMs such as PC Plus GLOBAL Vantage, PC Plus Corporate Text, and Standard & Poor's Corporations.

Predicasts Overview of Markets and Technology (Cleveland, OH: Predicasts)

The Predicasts Overview of Markets and Technology (PROMPT) is a source available in various formats. It includes information on such topics as market trends, new products, sales and consumption, financial reports, market plans and strategies, international product research and development, and industry and business issues. The database covers more than 60 manufacturing and services industries, including agriculture, apparel, computers, transportation, and wholesale and retail trade. PROMPT contains abstracts or the full text of journals, newspapers, newsletters, investment analysts' reports, annual reports, research studies and SEC registration statements. The information is from 1972 to present with updates added daily.

The database is available on-line through BRS Information Technologies, Data Star and DIALOG (file #16) and is updated daily. It is also available on magnetic tape and through batch access (1978 to date) and on CD-ROM. Finally, various print publications correspond to the database, including one called PROMPT.

PTS Newsletter Database (Foster City, CA: Information Access Company) [DIALOG]

PTS Newsletter Database provides full-text newspaper articles on business enterprises such as broadcasting and publishing, computers and electronics, in Europe, Japan, Latin America, and Pacific Rim. The articles provide data about company activities, new products, technologies, market conditions, government policies, and market and business developments.

PHARMACEUTICAL COMPANIES

IMS World Patent International (London: IMS World Publications) [DIALOG]

IMS World Patent International is a source of information on pharmaceutical compound patents. The details provided are patent entry, approximate expiration, CAS registry numbers, original patentee, patent family, therapeutic class, patent code and marketing.

POPULATION

Big Book (www.bigbook.com)

Big Book is an on-line yellow pages for the United States and works with even small towns. It has an intuitive search engine, which enables one to search for a kind of business in a particular city and state. One simply fills in the three boxes (type of business, city, state). One can also limit one's search to a zip code, and area code, or a street name.

PORTFOLIO MANAGEMENT

Quicken.com (www.quicken.com)

This site is a portfolio tracker that informs of stocks that made news on a particular day, was upgraded by a Wall Street pro, or achieved an annual high or low.

PRIVATE COMPANIES

CD/Corporate: U.S. Private +

This CD-ROM database provides information on over 100,000 private companies, subsidiaries, and other related firms. It can be searched via company name, industry, SIC code, or by simply browsing the database glossary. A variety of reports are available for each company including a company summary (a brief description of the entity including sales data, number of employees, history, ownership, stockholders' interest, etc.), a corporate family report (discloses information relating to subsidiary firms as well as parent companies), abstracts of current articles relating to the firm or industry, and a mailing list.

Small Business Information (www.sec.gov/smbus1.htm)

This web site, operated by the United States Securities and Exchange Commission, is designed to help small businesses in raising capital, while at the same time complying with federal securities laws. It gives a general overview of the Federal Securities Laws and some advice about registering with the commission. It includes a compelled initiatives page for small business and a pending initiatives page that include recent revisions to various laws. There is also a page that has links to other business sites, both governmental and nongovernmental. Finally, this web site contains various links to other divisions of the Securities and Exchange Commission.

PRODUCTION CONTROL

Derwent World Patents Index (London: Derwent Publications) [DIALOG]

Derwent World Patents Index has information on pharmaceutical, agricultural, chemical, polymer, and plastics patents. Each patent entry provides an abstract, International Patent classification codes, and Derwent subject codes.

PRODUCTION MANAGEMENT

Industrial Technical Institute (www.yahoo.com/ Business_and_Economy/Organizations)

Industrial Technical Institute (ITI) is a web site dedicated to assist manufacturers in increasing productivity, quality, and consumer satisfaction. Direct links are available to performance benchmarking service, center for electronic commerce, energy and environment center, Michigan manufacturing technology center, electro-optics engineering, and financial solutions. Further links are available to services, frequently asked questions, news, maps, and related web sites. An e-mail address is provided for further information.

PUBLIC RELATIONS

AP News (New York: Associated Press) [DIALOG]

Associated Press News has full-text information on national, international, commercial, and business issues. Information from the database is obtainable 24 hours after it has been brought into the DataStream Service. It is also a source of general interest news from international media.

REAL ESTATE

Homebuyers' Fair (www.homefair.com/home)

This web site is maintained by The Homebuyer's Fair, LLC. It provides information needed for buying a home. It has information on mortgage finance resources, relocation, apartments; and also some useful tools such as The Moving Calculator, The Salary Calculator, The Insurance Calculator, and Mortgage Qualification Calculator.

International Real Estate Directory (www.ired.com)

This web site provides information for apartment buyers. It provides relevant links, information on mortgage, agency law, funding, and information for first-time homebuyers.

It also has a region list of different places in the world, and it provides information on real estate companies of that place.

MetroScan, Transamerica Information Management Services

This CD-ROM source contains real estate information obtained from public records, such as county assessors. Area information includes street address, subdivision name, map grid coordinates, census tract, and tax rate area. Among the property characteristics provided are land use code, property assessment, year built, lot size, square footage, style, heat type, number of units, and taxes. Owner name and transfer information (e.g., sale price, deed type) are also available and can be used when searching. Data can be exported in various formats or used to create mailing labels, property profiles, parcel maps, and custom reports.

Realtor.com (www.realtor.com)

This site offers an index of homes available nationwide. It also gives the user information on buying a home and the selection of realtors.

REGULATION

The European Commission Host Organization
(www.echo.lu)

The European Commission Host Organization (ECHO), a non commercial host organization, draws together databases in English, French, German, Italian, Spanish, Dutch, Danish, and Portuguese. Not all sources are available in all eight languages; some are limited to English. This multilingual database offers sources in bibliographic, full-text, and numerical databases. Databases range in size from 250 to 400,000 records. They include an international database in the social sciences (DARE), a catalogue of periodicals (EUROLIB-PER), an on-line directory of more than 15,000 theses and studies (EURISTOTE), a number of research and development programs, thesauri for about 600 European subject thesauri, the Index Translationum (XTRA), a bibliographic database of translated material, an on-line version of European Employment and Industrial Relations Glossaries (EMIRE), and the Directory of European Institutions (IDEA).

Through ECHO, public access is provided to resources usually limited to corporations conducting business in Europe. Passwords or fees are charged for some files; however, most are accessible to the public at no charge.

Numerous forms of assistance are available for using ECHO, including printed sources, videos and on-line help. On-line help and tutorials are available through telnet. Further assistance is available via mail. Common Command Language (CCL) will be helpful to frequent users as it expedites the retrieval of information. Among the search features that CCL employs are Boolean operators, proximity and adjacency operators and truncation. CCL-Train exercises are available on line.

ECHO is available 24 hours a day through telnet or the World Wide Web. Users can login through telnet, European Videotex, direct dial-up, or packet-switched data network. When maintenance is needed, it occurs on Fridays, 6 to 9 AM, Central European Time.

Subjects covered by the databases include social sciences, high technology, energy, transportation, biotechnology, and industry. Periodical databases are included as well as databases covering theses and other university research. Currency exchange rates are offered through the European Union. The databases have their own menus. Searching capabilities and the frequency of updates vary between databases.

The address for ECHO is ECHO, European Commission Host Organisation, B.P. 2373, L-1023 Luxembourg. ECHO can be reached on e-mail at echo@echo.lu or echo.mail@eurokomie. On the World Wide Web, send inquiries to webmaster@echo.lu.

RESEARCH

A Business Researcher's Interests
(www.brint.com/interest.html)

This web page is a compilation of references to and the texts of periodicals, conference papers, and case studies for researchers. The choices are classified into four disciplines: research, management, Internet, and management information systems. Each of these categories is divided into smaller units. Within these subdivisions, links are provided for governmental organizations, current and back issues of magazines and journals, and business school reviews. Users can search this site by keywords or categories.

Institute for the Study of Business Markets Business
Marketing Web Consortium (www.smeal.psu.edu/isbm)

The Institute for the Study of Business Markets (ISBM) is an industry-supported center in the Smeal College of Business Administration of Penn State University, founded in 1983. A coalition of academic and corporate members, the Institute draws support from corporations such as Amoco Chemical Co., AT&T, Eastman Kodak, and IBM.

The Business Marketing Web Consortium was developed to explore the use of the World Wide Web as a tool and to provide a community of practice for marketing strategists. The web site provides information about ISBM seminars, publications, and research projects. It includes a profile of ISBM, a directory, a calendar of scheduled seminars and conferences, membership information, a newsletter, priorities in research, and funding opportunities for graduate students. Abstracts of the Institute's publications are available on-line and full-text copies may be ordered. Links provide access to marketing resources, associations, events, list-serves, on-line publications, and the home pages of members.

Investext (Foster Grove, CA: Information Access)

Investext is a CD-ROM source providing company and industry analyst reports. More than 200,000 reports are available from approximately 100 investment banks and brokerage firms. Information is provided on companies in the United States, the United Kingdom, Europe, Asia, and Australia. Approximately 8000 U.S. companies and 2000 foreign companies are covered. The information is divided into 53 industry groups. Industry groups cover high technology, chemical, medical, consumer goods, and trade industries.

The database can be used to research industry trends, locate present and past financial information, and produce analyses on products or companies.

Marketing data reports supply company and industry information on research and investment possibilities. Within corporate profiles can be found corporate descriptions, properties and equipment, and corporate strategies. The analyst also reports present opinions on corporate management and examinations of employee/labor relations and forecasts of future success. The financial data and forecasts include balance sheets, income statements, sales analyses, and earnings forecasting. In addition, debt and equity information is reported along with P/E ratios and mergers and acquisitions assessments.

The database can be searched by company names, industries, product names, investment bank names, and SIC codes. Both abstracts and full-text reports and forecasts are available. A subscription comes with the InfoTrac system, but it is available without it. In addition, a subscription includes a user manual, software, maintenance and service, and customer support. The database is updated monthly.

Knight-Ridder's Dialog [DIALOG]

This a source of commercial information that is valuable to corporate intelligence. The database collects information such as business articles, corporate news releases, financial reports, criminal records, and factory specifications. These data are used by companies to find out what their competitors are doing, or their future development plans.

Knight-Rider/Tribune Business News (Washington, D.C.: Knight-Rider/Tribune; New York: Knight-Rider Financial Information) [DIALOG]

The database contains full-text articles on business and finance from major U.S newspapers. The subtopics covered are credit markets, foreign exchange, mortgage-backed securities, banking, market analysis, and corporate earnings.

Legal Resource Index/LegalTrac (Foster Grove, CA: Information Access)

Available in two formats, this source offers indexing of legal periodicals. The Legal Resource Index is an on-line database and LegalTrac is the CD-ROM version. More than 900 publications are indexed. The publications covered are major law reviews, bar association journals, legal newspapers, and specialty publications. In addition, related articles from more than 1000 business and general-interest periodicals are indexed, as are major legal publications from other English-speaking countries. Approximately 3500 new entries are recorded each month. Publications both on-line and on the

CD-ROM include the Harvard Law Review, British Journal of Criminology, Legal Times, and Human Rights Quarterly. In either format, the database can be searched by subject, case, or statute. Headings are cross-referenced and easily accessed.

Legal Resource Index is available on-line from four vendors and the equipment necessary is a personal computer, a modem, and communications software. LegalTrac is a CD-ROM intended for use on the InfoTrac system. Subscriptions cover the monthly updates, the workstation, software, and maintenance and service. It is available without the system. Software upgrades are free and Information Access provides a toll-free customer service line. A thesaurus is available to aid users in searching by providing precise search terms. The index is also obtainable in print form although not all the legal newspapers on the database are in print format.

MARKETFULL (Norwalk, CT: BCC; London: Datamonitor) [DIALOG]

MARKETFULL is composed of research files found on DIALOG. It can also be used as file BEGIN MARKETFULL. The subjects covered by the database include products, industries, markets, market share, pricing, consumer attitudes, consumption, and sources of supply.

The following files make up MARKETFULL:

BCC Market Research
Datamonitor Market Research
Euromonitor
Freedom Market Research
Frost and Sullivan Market Research

MS World R&D Focus (London: IMS World Publications) [DIALOG]

IMS World Research and Development Focus contains information on pharmaceutical developments. Data available for each product are generic name, laboratory code, CAS registry number, chemical name, synonyms, therapeutic indications, patents issued, latest development, and marketing potential.

National Bureau of Economic Research, Inc. (www.NBER.org)

The National Bureau of Economic Research, Inc. (NBER) is a private, nonprofit research association whose 450+ researchers (economics and business professors, primarily) produce books and "working papers," publish two journals, and organize conferences in the areas of "statistical measurement, quantitative modeling, and the economic effects of public policy."

The NBER web site reflects the specialized interests of NBER and its main audience: economists in business, government, and academia. Short descriptions of 12 major programs and projects, such as "The Corporate Finance Program" and "The Economic Fluctuations and Growth Program," are followed by a list of participating researchers (each linked to postal and e-mail address, phone and fax numbers). NBER books, papers, and journals are briefly described, with ordering information. General information about the organization is given, and searching can be done for books, working papers, or researchers.

On-line data available may be Gopher files, large data files for downloading, or brief survey or analytical reports; in most cases, there is an introductory explanation. Business cycle measurements, gross domestic product statistics, manufacturing industry productivity, and consumer expenditures are some of the types of information available.

Much of the data was compiled by NBER, but some, like the Economic Report of the President and the Consumer Expenditure Survey Extracts, are from government agencies. Both current and historical data are represented in the selections available. More general information is available through links to business and economic news via CNN, The New York Times, The Economist, Forbes, and other business periodicals; to U. S. government bureaus and agencies, including the Federal Reserve Banks and the Superintendent of Documents; and to college and university economics departments worldwide, financial markets, and resources for economists.

Predicasts (Cleveland, OH: Predicasts)

Predicasts is an on-line indexing and abstracting service that provides access to international business, trade, defense, and government information. It is a source of information about companies and industries, new products and technologies, competitor activities, market trends and forecasts, government policies and regulations, and economic environments. It offers 10 on-line databases including Predicasts Overview of Markets and Technology (PROMPT), Newsletter Database, Marketing and Advertising Reference Service, New Products Announcements/Plus, Infomat International Business, Aerospace/Defense Markets & Technology, Annual Reports Abstracts (ARA), F & S Index and Predicasts Forecasts, U.S. Time Series. These databases cover more than 10,000,000 records from approximately 2000 publications including trade journals, international business newspapers, journals, local newspapers, regional business publications, industry newsletters, news releases, company annual reports, investment reports, research studies, and government publications. The records include full-text articles, abstracts, indexes, and statistical reports. The Predicasts Source Directory Catalog, published annually, provides information about the scope, coverage, and the cost of each database. The annual Predicasts Company Thesaurus lists over 210,000 company names that appear in the on-line databases.

PTS U.S. Forecasts (Foster City, CA: Information Access Company) [DIALOG]

PTS U.S Forecasts provide forecast data about the economy, industries, products, and end use data. The information is gathered from trade journals, newspapers, reports, and studies.

SRI International (www.sri.com)

SRI International was founded as the Stanford Research Institute in 1946. The goal of SRI is to promote and foster the application of science in the development of commerce, trade, and industry. SRI's business units are Engineering Science & Systems Development, Advanced Technologies, Pharmaceutical Discovery, Policy, Information Science & Technology Chemicals, Energy & Materials, Biopharmaceutical Development, and International Programs. With the broad base of expertise in science, engineering, business strategy, and policy areas, SRI provides clients with solutions for competing in today's global markets. Employment opportunities are available in many parts of the SRI organization to qualifying applicants.

US–Japan Technology Management Center (fuji.stanford.edu)

A search option is available to the user to facilitate the user's research process. One can read about current and complete projects by the center. A link to center-sponsored courses and public events can also be found. Also included at this site is a guide to Japan Info Resources where one can find out about the latest news and other various topics including law and regulation, arts and entertainment, science and business. A link to a virtual library is also available.

SECURITIES

Compact D/SEC

Compact D/SEC is published by Disclosure, Inc. Certain portions of publicly traded companies' Securities and Exchange Commission (SEC) filings are found in this CD-ROM database. Compact D/SEC is for people who want basic information about a firm. Included in Compact D/SEC is company information such as the income statement, balance sheet, and financial statement footnotes. Based on the type of subscription selected, the CD-ROM can be updated monthly, quarterly, or annually.

Laser D/SEC

Laser D/SEC is a CD-ROM from Disclosure, Inc. This database has Securities and Exchange Commission (SEC) filings for over 12,000 publicly traded companies. Laser D/SEC is geared toward people interested in knowing detailed information about a company. Reports found on Laser D/SEC include a company's annual report, 10-K, and prospectuses. The CD-ROM is updated throughout the year.

Securities and Exchange Commission EDGAR Database (www.sec.gov/edgarhp.htm)

This site is now hosted by the Securities and Exchange Commission (SEC). The Electronic Data Gathering, Analysis, and Retrieval (EDGAR) system, performs automated collection, validation, indexing, acceptance, and for-warding of submissions by companies and others who are required by law to file forms with the SEC. Its primary purpose is to increase the efficiency and fairness of the securities market for the benefit of investors, corporations, and the economy by accelerating the receipt, acceptance, dissemination, and anal-ysis of time-sensitive corporate information filed with the agency. Special features include general information on retrieving data, the tools and utilities in EDGAR, and news about EDGAR.

Securities Class Action Clearinghouse (securities.stanford.edu)

The first thing on the page is a "Federal Litigation Box Score" where one can see the statistics on the number of companies sued in federal court, federal complaints on line, the most frequently sued industry, most active district court, and the percentages on alleging accounting fraud and insider sales during class period. Information about the Securities Class Action Clearing-house can be found and also significant cautioning language and plans for advancements in the future. One can access class action securities fraud complaints and get links to stock quotes and charts. Summaries of federal complaints can be found by knowing the name of the company sued or the date of filing. Opinions and orders from the Courts of Appeals and the U.S. District Courts are available. Docket sheets can be retrieved for all cases from the Northern District of California. Related documents on settlements, state court cases, securities-related reports, articles, and written testimony are also available categories.

Securities and Exchange Commission Corporate Filings

This work has data on public companies whose stock is traded on the NASDAQ, American Stock Exchange, the New York Stock Exchange, or over-the-counter file reports with the Securities and Exchange Commission. The reports contain a large amount of information, including a description of the business, financial statements, directors and officers, number of employees, and number of shareholders. This information is made available on microfilm. The reports filed include, but are not limited to, the 10-K, the 20-F, the 10-Q, a proxy statement, and a prospectus. Reported contents also include, but are not limited to, portfolio operations, subsidiaries, foreign operations, and underwriting. This source of data contains virtually every substantive fact concerning companies who list with the above public exchanges.

Securities Law (www.seclaw.com)

This home page includes a list of 10 major law firm sites and a link to see the current news headlines that affect the securities laws and those in the market. Also accessible is a security law news update. An option on the page includes a search for all articles in the information centers at the Securities Law Homepage. There is a link to Money Magazine and a financial event calendar. One can also find articles related to topics of arbitration, corporate finance, brokers, investors, law, and compliance.

Small Business Information (www.sec.gov/smbus1.htm)

SEC is an agency that is independent and nonpartisan regulatory. It is responsible for overseeing the federal securities laws. To protect investors in securities markets, which operate evenly, and to confirm that inventors have entrance to uncovering material information regarding publicly traded securities is the purpose of the laws. In addition, the Commission works with firms involved in the purchase or sale of securities, investment companies, and people who offer investment guidance.

SMALL BUSINESSES

American Express Small Business Exchange (www.americanexpress.com/smallbusiness)

American Express Small Business Exchange web site provides users with information covering many aspects of smaller businesses. There is a "Business

Planning" section where users can access a library of information covering aspects such as starting, managing, and expanding a business. Small businesses can promote their services with the business to business directory or the on-line classifieds. Users have access to updated news and information for small businesses. Users can receive expert advice by emailing questions to an on-line advisor, or they may go to the advisor. The site offers a range of products and services to meet the needs of a small business.

Biz Op. the Home Business Opportunity Center (www.bizopp.com)

The Home Business Opportunity Center gives brief explanations of home businesses that can be chosen for a more detailed description. The page is constantly changing to provide a variety of home business information. This site examines every home business opportunity listed.

Computer Edge Business Support Organization (www.yahoo.com/Business_and_Economy/Organizations)

Computer Edge Business Support Organization is a support/service web site for home and small businesses. Direct links are available to feature articles; columns; departments, which include career opportunities, classifieds, worldwide news and product reviews, and users groups; question and answer forums; advertising; and creative corner. A search engine of the web site is also provided for further information.

Entrepreneur Magazine's Small Business Square (www.entrepreneurmag.com)

This web site is geared toward small businesses. It contains several applications that can enhance the performance of small businesses. It has a chat room, where the user can go in and talk to other people running small businesses. A link shows how to create a web page. This site also contains various tips on staying competitive and improving production. There is a link called Daily Features that show tips, weekly features, business news, and current trends. The user is able to download new business software.

Home Business Institute (www.hbiweb.com)

The Home Business Institute (HBI) is devoted to supporting small business entrepreneurs by providing crucial information and services for assistance. HBI also regulated vital research about small and home businesses and their owners. A considerable amount of focus groups, interviews, and seminars are conducted as part of the research. HBI contributes over 25 benefits and services.

Idea Cafe: The Small Business Channel (www.ideacafe.com)

Idea Cafe consists of experienced entrepreneurs. Their main interests are to inform other small business owners of vital information they need to be aware of for maintaining or running a business. Idea Cafe can solve problems and give entrepreneurs the opportunity to network with others who share the same experiences.

Indus Entrepreneurs—TiE (www.yahoo.com/ Business_and_Economy/Organizations)

Indus Entrepreneurs—TiE is a web site established by entrepreneurs with interest in the Indus region, devoted to benefiting all entrepreneurs. The three explicitly established objectives of Tie include the following: to foster entrepreneurship and to nurture entrepreneurs, to network and to facilitate networking among members, and to help membership integrate with the mainstream community. Direct links are available to information postings, TiEcon sponsors, calendar of events, membership, and further information about TiE, which includes objectives and values, programs and activities, membership and benefits, TiE history, and Indus immigrants in America.

Oppnet.com (www.oppnet.com)

Oppnet.com is produced by the Opportunity Network based in Massachu-setts. The objective of the site is to provide resources for the independent businessperson. Included are data on opportunities for business, services, alliances, networking, positions, and education. Within each category is a listing of titles, descriptions, and contacts. It is possible to find information on businesses that are for sale or that are looking for employees or partners, companies that offer financial or technological support and educational expe-riences for entrepreneurs. Oppnet.com charges a fee for submissions.

Siegel Business Services Inc. (www. onix.com/sbs/index.htm)

The Siegel Business Services Inc. web site is designed to provide small and midsize business owners and buyers with brokerage and other related services. This company, which has been around since 1983, helps to move along the process of selling a business by matching owners of businesses with prospec-tive qualified buyers. They also are involved in finding equity investors, franchising opportunities, business appraisals, and other general consulting services. In addition, this web site contains finance links (to stocks and mutual funds) and government and business-related links.

Small Business Administration (www.sbaonline.Sba.gov)

To help America's entrepreneurs form successful small enterprises, the Congress (of the government) created the U.S. Small Business Administration (SBA). SBA offers advocacy, financing, and training for small forms on every state. Their offices also deliver programs to the District of Columbia, Puerto Rico, and the Virgin Islands. SBA also works nationwide with educational and training organizations.

Small Business Advisor (www.isquare.com)

Information International staff have experience in technical management and high-technology product development and over 40 years of blended Federal Government Service. They are dedicated to aiding and guiding individuals who have begun a business already or are considering the idea of starting a business. Their assistance helps others in the form of books, consulting, seminars, and special reports. Information International also supports companies in doing business with U.S. Government agencies.

Small Business: Organization and Operations (www.nolo.com/ChunkSB.index.html)

This site gives all the vital information that informs one of the tasks that should be completed and considered before starting a business. From the Nolo Press Legal Encyclopedia, Small Business: Organization and Operations keeps ones' business on track by including data on corporations, limited liability companies, partnerships, nonprofits, start-up, taxes, and more.

Small & Home-Based Business Links (www.ro.com/small_business/homebased.html)

Small & Home-Based Business Links provides access to web pages containing resources of interest to small and home-based businesses. The links include sites describing services and resources available for individuals with small or home-based businesses, franchise and other business opportunities, and marketing information. In addition, the page provides connections to small and home-based business newsgroups and a bulletin board on which individuals may post announcements, items for sale, and new product releases.

Small Business Innovative Research (www.sbir.dsu.edu)

This web page, supported by the U.S. West Business Project, is a nonprofit organization designed to foster small, technology-based businesses. It operates throughout a 14-state U.S. West service area. Their goal is to encourage the preparation of more Small Business Innovation Research (SBIR) proposals by businesses based in those 14 states for their submission to the two participating federal agencies that reward such businesses. It includes local and state information of the member states, examples of successful (SBIR) proposals, and a news page. Finally, the Small Business Innovative Research page includes a search engine of various federal grants and awards awarded by specific agencies and in specific states.

Small Business Information (www.sec.gov/smbus1.htm)

This web site, operated by the U.S. Securities and Exchange Commission, is designed to help small businesses in raising capital, while at the same time complying with federal securities laws. It gives a general overview of the Federal Securities Laws, and some advice about registering with the commission. It includes a compelled initiatives page for small businesses and a pending initiatives page that includes recent revisions to various laws. There is also a page that has links to other business sites, both governmental and nongovernmental. Finally, this web site contains various links to other divisions of the Securities and Exchange Commission.

SmallbizNet: the Edward Lowe Small Business Network (www.microsoft.com/smallbiz)

SmallbizNet is a web site composed of links to Microsoft software products and on-line tips to improve business management and productivity. This web site is intended to help users expand their business through the World Wide Web and other technological means. Interested users can browse through the given links to search for topics they are looking for. For further information, users can contact SmallbizNet through the given E-mail address.

TimeVista Boardroom (pathfinder.com)

TimeVista Boardroom is brought to viewers by the Marketing Department of TIME Magazine. It contains information and expert advice for small businesses. Articles can be read, and software and network can be downloaded.

STATISTICS

Census International Database
(www.census.gov/ftp/pub/ipc/www/idbnew.html)

The International Data Base (IDB) is a data bank containing statistical tables, demographic and socioeconomic data for all countries in the world from 1950 to the present, and projected data to 2050. The main types of data available in the IDB are population, vital rates, fertility, migration, marital status, family planning, ethnicity, literacy, labor force, and households. The IDB is created by the Census Bureau's International Programs Center.

Charles Schwab Online (www.schwab.com)

Trading on the World Wide Web has been made easy by Charles Schwab. This site allows a person to handle its trading needs wherever there is Web access 24 hours a day. The site offers a full range of Schwab services to include the following: access real-time quotes; get unlimited delayed stock and option quotes plus mutual fund quotes (free); view (free) intraday, daily, and weekly price charts; trade equities and most mutual funds on-line; view order status and change or cancel orders; check account positions; and send E-mail to Schwab customer service.

    The site is hosted by the company and includes pages for stock quoted on-line by entering the ticker symbol. The log on is prompted simply by entering the account number and password, then submitting it. There are also 1-800 customer service numbers. Lastly, if one does not have an account one can fill out an on-line account application for the convenience and control of trading on-line.

Journal of Statistical Education Information Service
(Carnegie Mellon University, A Service of the International
Association of Statistics Educators)

The Journal of Statistical Education Information Service (JSEIS) is provided through the International Association of Statistics Educators (IASE) and is available on the Carnegie Mellon University StatLib Server. It is one of the economics databases that may be accessed through the Ulibrary Gopher. The Journal of Statistical Education is a scholarly electronic journal on post-secondary statistics education, and the JSEIS provides access information for the journal as well as other services relating to the field of statistics and the IASE.

    The primary function of JSEIS is to provide access to the Journal of Statistical Education. The contents of each published issue are available for browsing, and access functions allow users to search specific authors, titles, or keywords in the journal index. Abstracts are provided for each article, as well as a list of keywords for additional cross-reference. Because this is a relatively new scholarly journal, author and data set contributor guidelines as well as submission information are included. The index for the journal is updated with each quarterly issue.

The JSE is not available in hard or paper copy, only in electronic format. The full-text articles are not on-line for browsing, but may be obtained through E-mail. The contents and indexes are available to any person with Internet access using an Ethernet terminal. BITNET users must use electronic mail to gain access to these files. To obtain an electronic copy of any article or one of the other files on the JSEIS, send the name of the file requested to: jse.stat.ncsu.edu.

Other information and services provided by the Journal of Statistical Education Information Service include:

> Software Tools and Information. This menu allows users to browse and download a variety of econometric and statistical software. Included is network navigation software, graphics and general statistics software, as well as an SAS software archive. A frequently asked questions file is provided to help users obtain software through electronic mail, which may be challenging for first-time users.
> Discussion Groups. Users may log onto electronic discussion groups dealing with statistical issues and statistics education. First-time browsers of the service may sign on as guests or monitor the discussions without participating.
> IASE. The related international organization provides to users reports, publication statistics, and meeting information. Reports and files may be obtained through request at the E-mail address stated above.

Key British Enterprises, Dun and Bradstreet International

It contains more than 50,000 company records covering various types of data. The database utilizes the Immediate PC based Access and Count Technology (IMPACT) software, which allows speedy and sophisticated searches.

PAIS International (New York, NY: PAIS International)

Public Affairs Information Service (PAIS) has been an established provider of indexes since 1914. It indexes information from newspaper and journal articles, federal documents, circulatory bulletins, monographs, periodicals, microfiche, and various public and private agencies. The database contains hundreds of thousands of entries and thousands more are added each year. Information provided comes from the international, national, state, and local levels. Foreign-language abstracts are translated to assist users. PAIS provides indexes commonly used by public and social legislators, officials in government, and businesses dealing with financial affairs. It covers a variety of subjects, from business to health.

PAIS indexes are available in English, in foreign languages, and in machine-readable formats. PAIS is available on CD-ROM and can be specialized to fit the needs of the user. Both beginner and experienced user search modes are available. There are several formats for viewing and copying data. It is also available on-line from a number of access providers.

PIERS Exports (U.S. Ports) (New York: The Journal of Commerce) [DIALOG]

Port Export Reporting Service (PIERS) Exports (U.S. Ports) is a directory of shipping activities at U.S. and Puerto Rico seaports.

PTS F & S Index (Foster City, CA: Information Access Company) [DIALOG]

The database is a source of index information on commerce and economics for companies. The data provided include company, product, industry, business and finance, demographics, government regulations, and economics.

Statistical MasterFile

This CD ROM product provides bibliographic access to the following statistical indexes: American Statistics Index (ASI), which indexes the statistical publications of federal agencies since the mid-1960s; Statistical Reference Index (SRI), which indexes the statistical publications of nonfederal entities since 1981; and Index to International Statistics (IIS), which indexes the statistical publications of intergovernmental organizations since 1983. All three of these indexes are, and have been, available in paper. The paper index is associated with a microfiche collection of all the indexed publications.

The CD-ROM provides a user interface that is relatively easy to use. A series of pop-up menus allows the user to negotiate the process of searching and printing search results. The search engine allows both free-text Boolean searching and controlled vocabulary searching and allows the user to combine these two search strategies. The user can browse through the controlled vocabulary to select appropriate terms. Once the search results have been identified, the user may scan a title list before accessing the full bibliographic record. The user can search for a word in a full record to move through the record more efficiently. Although not completely intuitive, there is enough information on the interface to allow a novice to search after a short period of familiarization.

The bibliographic information available includes the accession number to the fiche set; standard bibliographic information such as title, date, and author; any other numbers, such as Superintendent of Documents number and item numbers where appropriate; a list of tables; the associated subject headings; and a concise abstract. The user may print or download the results of a search in any of several formats including the title list, a brief citation, text the user has marked, the bibliographic information, or the full record.

These features provide the user with the ability to search for an index entry much more quickly than would be possible in the paper format. The paper product does not provide the ability to cumulate that is available through the CD-ROM product. The CDs are updated quarterly with print updates on a monthly basis between CD updates.

STOCKS

BigCharts.com (www.bigcharts.com)

This site charts the daily flow of the markets and offers news updates based on the daily transpirings of the markets. This site also offers stock histories and an in-depth tracker entitled BigReports, which offers very specific information on the NYSE, NASDAQ, and AMEX.

ClearStation (www.clearstation.com)

This site offers a multitude of stock charts and offers the visitor the ability to be taught how to read the charts to learn the history of a particular stock.

Daily Stock Market Data (www.stockmaster.com)

This site, formally hosted by The Massachusetts Institute of Technology's Artificial Intelligence Laboratory, is now hosted and maintained by the Marketplace.net Inc. This site has been on-line since August 1993 and serves individual investors. The site offers comprehensive quotes and charts on U.S. stocks and mutual funds. The site boasts that it is all free to end users. Stocks and mutual funds are accessed by entering symbol or part of a company or fund name to view its quote and chart. As a special added bonus, the site offers a list of top stocks and mutual funds most frequently graphed by stock-master.com for the previous day of trading.

Earnings Whispers.com (www.earningswhispers.com)

This site estimates the levels of earnings based on polls issued by the staff of editors to industry experts and analysts to compare their numbers to those estimates published by stock analysts. These estimates often illustrate differences in estimates from published expectations.

Holt Report (wuecon.wustl.edu/holt/011596.html)

The Holt Stock Report web site contains relevant market closing results. There are many links including indices, foreign market information, current lows and highs, up-to-date currency values, gold values and interest rates, and the most active stock exchanges (NYSE, NASDAQ, and AMEX). The site also reports the present day's DOW closings.

Interactive Nest Egg (www.yahoo.com/ Business_and_Economy/Finance_and_Investment or nestegg.iddis.com)

Interactive Nest Egg originated in 1994 as an on-line magazine for the personal investor. Over the last two years it has grown to become a premiere source for up-to-date information on current stock and mutual fund market conditions, initial public stock offerings, and a one-stop source of answers to personal finance questions. The content also includes a section on planning your future, and a Reference Center containing articles and facts in 10 different subject areas ranging from college financing to estate planning. In addition, Interactive Nest Egg contains links to such established financial sources as Baron's On-Line, Smith Barney, and the Wall Street Journal Interactive Edition.

Interquote (www.interquote.com)

Interquote is a site advertising an on-line, real-time quote service that is continuously updated. Users can download the software from the site, but the access is fee-based. Clients register for one of five membership packages offering different levels of service. Links to other financial sites are available, including Financial Chat, Investment Analysis & News, Magazines, and Internet Provider Service Links.

Media General Plus (Richmond, VA: Media General Financial Services) [DIALOG]

Media General plus is a source of financial and stock price data about public enterprises. Some of these are New Stock Exchange, American Stock Exchange, NASDAQ National Market System, and Over-the-Counter companies.

MSN MoneyCentral (www.moneycentral.com)

This site tracks stock portfolios and updates stock prices every five minutes and can point out holes in a personal stock portfolio.

MSN MoneyCentral's Stock Finder (www.moneycentral.com/investor)

A part of MSN MoneyCentral, this portion of MoneyCentral is dedicated to stock screening, which lists stocks according to 100 criteria and is grouped for easy access.

Motley Fool (www.fool.com)

The Motley Fool is an on-line magazine written by a group of people ranging from writers with no experience in investing to business consultants and certified public accountants. This newsletter is intended to help individuals invest in stocks. Beginners can start with the section titled "Fool's School." This part includes articles designed to help a person prepare his finances for investing and to understand how the stock market works. The titles include "The Thirteen Steps to Investing Foolishly" and "How to Value Stocks." Different methods for valuing and choosing stocks are described in "The Dow Dividend Approach" and "Valuing Stocks." Once they have begun, investors can monitor the market with the "Lunchtime News" and "Evening News." These areas give the daily performance of the stock market and news articles covering noteworthy events. The stocks of the major companies are covered in "The Daily Dow," and weekly updates for the various industries are provided by "Industry Updates." "Daily Double" and "Daily Trouble" spotlight companies that are doing exceptionally well or poorly. The writers describe the performance of their own selections in "Fool Portfolio," while less risky choices are covered by the "Boring Portfolio." One of the more unusual features of this site is the "Conference Calls" section. This division provides synopses of the conference calls many companies use to inform analysts and investors of the company's financial status. This page also includes several message boards to allow investors to post comments or advice to the editors and each other. The entire magazine is written with a surprising amount of humor. The Motley Fool even includes a section titled "The Fribble," which contains amusing stories and anecdotes contributed by both writers and readers.

Laser D/SEC

This Windows version CD-ROM database contains SEC filings from publicly traded companies. Filings include those from NASDAQ, the American Stock

Exchange, the New York Stock Exchange, and Over-The-Counter. Searches can be performed using keywords, company title, and/or U.S. ticker number. The continually updated database allows one to view actual annual reports and 10 K's. It also provides company information including the entity's U.S. ticker number and SIC codes.

News Alert (www.newsalert.com)

The News Alert is a web site that offers latest stock markets and corporate earning announcements. The user can obtain comprehensive national, international, financial, and business news. The News/Quotes presents information on Mutual Funds, Merger/Acquisition, Global Stocks, and more. Through the Research, the user can obtain Company's Digest and Earnings Surprises. However, to get these services, one needs to subscribe and become a member. Free 30-day trial periods are offered.

Nikkei Telecom II, Japan Financial News & Data (Nihon Kiezai Shimbun America)

Nikkei Telecom II is an English-language database that provides information on Japanese business and financial markets. There are a variety of news files that offer economic, financial, and industrial news from Japan. These files contain articles from many of the leading Japanese newspapers, including The Japan Times, The Japan Economic Journal, and Nikkei Financial Daily.

The Tokyo stock market is another area covered by the database. Current information is available on stocks, bonds, money markets, forex, and commodities. In addition, historical data is available for researchers interested in business or corporate information about Japan. The source allows the user to create charts and graphs using stock information. International electronic mail capabilities are also available.

Oz on Disc

Oz on Disc is a CD-ROM source that provides the user with access to business and residential directories of Australia. The two sets of discs that come with the product are the Business Discs and the Residential Discs and they can be searched individually or together. Information provided for each entry includes location, state, company name or individual's surname, street address, suburb name, post code, STD code, telephone number, advertising code, and business classification.

The source can be used to locate directory information or to create mailing lists. The database has various search capabilities that can be used on both directories. The search can be general or it can be limited by searching one or more of the fields. These fields include company name, surname, post code, and advertising code. The database is compatible with IBMs and Macintoshes.

Public Affairs Information Service International [DIALOG]

Public Affairs Information Service (PAIS) International provides bibliographic indexes with English abstracts and index headings to public policy literature of business, economics, and government. It covers all material in English, French, German, Italian, Portuguese, and Spanish.

Quicken.com's Stock Screener (www.quicken.com/investments)

This site is a part of Quicken.com; its focus is stock screening. This site offers only 33 screening criteria that allow for simple and quick searches. This site also offers investing tools to aid the investment newcomer and aids in planning for retirement.

QuoteCom Business Wire (www.quote.com)

QuoteCom is a customized service to track real-time news, stock quotes, and financial information for Internet users. The financial news includes stock options, commodity futures, mutual funds, and indices for U.S. and Canadian markets, earnings forecasts and reports, market analysis and commentary, balance sheet data, annual reports, intraday and historical charts, weather information, and company profiles. QuoteCom also provides direct E-mail of news stories. The search engine requires the stock market ticker abbreviation. Translation of a company name to ticker abbreviation is available. Charts and graphs can be customized to a variety of time periods, as small as 15-minute intervals.

QuoteCom offers a number of free services, such as access to unlimited delayed-security quotes, retrieval of limited balance sheet data, information on earnings, P/E ratio, yield, and 52-week price ranges, ticker symbol and company name searches, customizations of and unlimited updates for 1 Portfolio of up to 1, securities, real-time and historical news headlines, noncustomizable charts, real-time Market Index charts, Market Movers, major Industry Groups, and Foreign Exchange Rates. Subscriptions are available that in addition to the free services add more portfolios, E-mail of relevant news stories, and the ability to access stock market news providers. There is a demo company, which can be used to create the available reports to determine whether a subscription is desirable.

QuoteCom uses many different sources for the information provided. One of the sources is Business Wire. The URL was formally http://www.quote.com/bwire.html. BusinessWire is one of the nation's wire services, used by more than 12,000 organizations to disseminate information to the news media and investment community worldwide.

Philadelphia Stock Exchange (www.phlx.com)

This site is maintained by the Philadelphia Stock Exchange and includes information on publications, products, and events of the exchange. It also includes information about the national market, and it is updated daily. The link called "Marketplace" is an index of kinds of data about the stock exchange and other markets with figures provided by Quote.com. Here one can find daily quotes on various markets and specific stocks, the daily market bias with speculations for the following day, rankings of mutual funds, the biggest gainers and losers of the day, currency figures, news headlines, and charts on market activity. In "Portfolio" one can create a portfolio via a form in which the volumes and prices of up to 20 securities can be entered, and the value will be computed at the site.

Standard & Poor's Corporations

This CD-ROM source is a compilation of three databases: Public Companies, Private Companies, and Executives. It provides corporate information such as financial and marketing data for more than 50,000 public and private companies. Additionally, it presents profiles of business executives in public and private corporations and recent corporate news. There are several search modes that allow searching by fields, sorting data by variables, customizing outputs, and creating comparative tabular reports. System requirements include an IBM-compatible computer or a Macintosh with 640K of RAM and 5MB of free space on the hard drive. This product is updated six times a year.

The CD-ROMs come in three parts. The first is Corporate Text that provides the Annual Reports, 10-Ks, 10-Qs, 20-Fs, and Proxy Statements for New York Stock Exchange companies. It also provides full-text documents filed with the SEC since July 1987. Software features allow searching with Boolean logic and specific criteria such as state or SIC code.

Global Vantage is the second disc. It is an international database containing information on over 7220 companies from 30 countries. Data are from 1982 to the present. There are four files in this database. They are Annual Data, Financial Services, Currency, and Issue. Data included are general company data, income statements, balance sheets, flow of funds statements, insurance business line data, and Japanese Trust Bank supplemental data.

Finally, there is Stock Reports on CD-ROM. This file is composed of companies from the NYSE, ASE, and selected OTC companies. It provides an overview of companies including in-depth financial information like the financial strength of a company and a text analysis. Some of the features include searching by keyword or item, printing and downloading for selected text, and automatic filing of documents.

Standard and Poor's Daily Action Stock Charts (www.standardandpoors.com)

Daily Action Stock Charts provides data on the prices and volumes of popular stocks on the American and the New York Stock Exchange on a weekly basis.

Standard and Poor's Outlook (www.standardandpoors.com)

Articles of interest to investors and information on stock markets are provided weekly on this home page. Analyst reports and recommendations for particular stocks are also available.

Standard and Poor's Stock Guide (www.standardandpoors.com)

Stock Guide provides statistics on thousands of stocks. The data include price ranges, volumes, earnings, and dividends. Another element of this work is its rankings and ratings.

Stock Market Timing (www.firstcap.com)

Stock Market Timing, a weekly stock commentary, is made available by FirstCapital Corporation each Saturday at 5 o'clock PM Mountain Standard Time (MST). The site does not contain listings of individual stocks but rather is broken down and tracked by 78 segments charting the trends the stocks have been taking, a 1 being the strongest and 5 being the weakest. The theory behind it is to accurately measure the pulse of the market and make money from it, not in massive payoffs, but in consistent gains, therefore, attracting experienced investors who are not interested in holding onto their stocks and bonds for the long term but who are willing to follow the underlying market trends and trade frequently.

The site is straightforward. The only options on the home page are for stock and bond commentary, the market segments breakdown, interesting stocks, and the Weintraub Breadth Oscillator, in which the author comments on the weekly happenings of the stock market. One additional bonus is the large graphs on each of the pages detailing the markets as a whole, including the stock and bond markets.

Stock Smart (www.stocksmart.com)

Stock Smart is a free service to people who want to follow the markets, watch patterns and trends, as well as create their own portfolio. "Industry Watch" depicts the largest industry changes by percentage, the winners and losers by dollar values and change, along with a graph illustrating the past 90-day activity. From the home page, there are links to company information such as address, phone number, executive officers, EDGAR filings, stock options, and technical analyzes. Company spreadsheets show the ticker symbol, the last price, net +/−, opening price, the high, low, and volume sold. Quotes are generated by the ticker symbol or by company name. StockSmart reports upcoming stock splits, distributions, and dividends. One can find spreadsheet comparisons and graphical representations of the year-to-date performance by mutual fund. "Fund Wizard" contains questions about what people are looking for in a mutual fund and uses their preferences to find funds that best match their specific needs. The global currency exchange rates table displays the exchange rates from more than 70 countries and converts monetary units. Worldwide market information is provided for 40 countries, plus indexes and quotes. A link to Businesswire.com offers news articles about companies and the market.

STREETnet Online Investors Guide (www.streetnet.com)

STREETnet provides resources for individuals wanting to learn more about the stock market. Stock quotes can be found for companies as well as a listing of "hot stocks" and stocks categorized as "losers." In addition, the site includes articles on industries, recommended stocks within sectors of commerce, and data on public companies; however, to receive more than rudimentary information on companies a fee is assessed. The web page includes additional articles, such as profiles of money managers and information on global investing, and links to commercial sites that provide research on companies. An index of articles also is available.

Wall Street City's ProSearch (www.wallstreetcity.com)

This site offers features on international markets as well as Wall Street. This site also offers advice as to stock growth that may be undervalued.

STORAGE OF INFORMATION

EMC^2 (www.emc.com)

EMC^2 offers information storage services, both on hardware and software, their claim being that greater efficiency and success will be achieved with better information storage. Their services include:

- EMC Storage systems: These are hardware systems that they offer for the purpose of storing information, for example, the EMC Data Manager (EDM).
- Storage Networking: These hardware systems allow businesses to create a network in which their information can be accessed internally.
- Storage Software: A broad range of software for operations like information backup, data protection, data management and recovery.
- Storage Management: Provides solutions to management of data, and improving what they call "e-infostructure."
- Infrastructure Services: These include professional services and Internet solutions for better management of data.

The company's annual report is on the web site, as well as news on the company and the some of the projects that they have been contracted to do. On its Investors Relations page, it allows investors to receive proxy information electronically, as well has holds information on annual stockholders' meetings and investor earnings. It quotes its own real-time stock value and gives potential investors its financial background.

TAXATION

Daily Tax Report covers developments in areas effecting accounting, taxation, policies on budgeting, and policies on pensions. It provides in-depth coverage of legislation on taxes, rulings of the courts, summaries of the courts, decisions on both the federal and state levels, IRS summaries and rulings, the latest additions to items like the IRS manual, and developments of reports on state and federal budgets.

Securities Regulation and Law Report provides weekly coverage of legal, regulatory, and legislative developments. It reports on the activities of Congress, the SEC, the administration, the CFTC, the FASB, and various regulatory accounting agencies.

Taxsources is an on-line tax package provided by a mixture of companies. It provides a combination of tax-related news reports and coinciding court cases, rulings, and regulations. It provides full-text portfolios of many of the aforementioned databases and information on statutes, state case laws, and IRS documents.

Tax Management Portfolios are a series of handbooks provided by reputable tax attorneys and accountants. The reports cover topics ranging from tax-related problems to foreign income. Each report contains discussion of a selected tax problem, forms, worksheets, checklists, and a bibliography of official and unofficial sources.

Tax Management Journals is a series of databases that provide coverage of issues ranging from real estate to compensation and planning. These journals are updated both weekly and monthly.

Idea Cafe's Blue Plate Specials (www.IdeaCafe.com/html/BP.html)

Idea Cafe's Blue Plate Specials is a web site that provides browsers with helpful tax tips and techniques. Users can find information on reducing their taxes, depreciating property, and prevention on becoming audited. Questions on deductibility of items are also answered.

National Association of Computerized Tax Processors (www.nactp.org)

National Association of Computerized Tax Processors is a web site that provides a number of services to taxpayers. Users have access to a variety of links to the Federation of Tax Administrators, the American Institute of Certified Public Accountants, the TaxChannel Web, and the IRS and state sites, which have tax forms available for download.

Navatar Canada Inc. (www.navatar.ca)

This site provides information and resources available from Navatar Canada Inc. (NCI), a Canadian organization responsible for providing consulting support to improve organizational effectiveness in public and private businesses, organizations, and agencies. Consulting services include performance enhancement, process innovation, organizational recovery, and project management. An information page is available along with an E-mail address for client and prospective client information and questions.

Nolo's Legal Encyclopedia: Tax Problems (www.nolo.com/chunkTAX/TAX.indes.html)

Nolo's Legal Encyclopedia: Tax Problems is a web site comprised of links providing suggestions and strategies for dealing with the IRS: audits, tax bills, and tax returns. Users can find helpful tips on tax deductions, buying a small business, and owning shares of stock.

Latin America Taxation (Amsterdam, The Netherlands: IFBD Publications)

A joint project of IBFD and the Inter-Centre of Tax Administration, this CD-ROM source provides surveys of the tax systems for Latin American countries. Business-related information includes descriptions of the economic and political systems, business organizations, and regional agreements. Corporate and individual tax systems are profiled and topical information (e.g., capital transfers, tax incentives) is provided. The surveys are offered in English and Spanish. The software features a full index, subject outlines, and a split screen option for viewing two documents at once. In addition, a standardized format facilitates comparisons between countries. The database is updated twice a year through replacement discs.

OneDisc

OneDisc is published by Tax Analysts. The full-text databases on this CD-ROM provide information about the U.S. tax system. It is primarily intended for tax professionals. Included on OneDisc is the Internal Revenue Code with amendments, Internal Revenue Service (IRS) Publications, IRS Revenue Procedures, and U.S. Court Decisions on tax matters from 1990 to the present. Names, addresses, and phone numbers of tax officials are also given. The information in OneDisc can be accessed by keyword searches and can then be printed or saved to another file.

Online Career Center (www.occ.com)

To develop the most economical effective network possible for employment advertising, outplacement services and communications is the Online Career Center's (OCC's) purpose. This must be done by working with America Online, ComuServe, GEnie, Internet, Prodigy, and other national on-line networks. To effectively assist employers and applicants, OCC provides on-line search software and job and résumé files. Online Career Center is available in the United States and in other countries through the Internet.

Tax Analysts (www.tax.org/default.htm)

Tax Analysts is a web site comprised of information for tax professionals. The links of this web site provide federal, state, and international tax laws and policies to individuals. Users have access to Taxnews, which provides information on IRS restrictions and reform policies. Tax clinics, where forums for discussion groups with topics on accounting exempt organizations and tax practice and procedures, are also available.

Tax Planet.com (www.taxplanet.com)

This web page based on taxation policy provides information on changes for the upcoming tax-reporting period. This site also includes various tax forms and tips on preparing forms.

TaxWeb (www.taxweb.com)

TaxWeb is a consumer-oriented source for federal, state, and local tax-related developments. Users have access to a variety of links that will answer general tax questions on refunds, filing extensions, and federal and state legislation. This web site also provides current federal and state-sponsored tax sites to allow more comprehensive tax research by individuals.

TECHNICAL ASSISTANCE

Data Interchange Standards Association (www.disa.org)

This web site, sponsored by Data Interchange Standards Association (DISA), is a nonprofit organization that supports the development and use of electronic data interchange (EDI) standards in electronic commerce. From the home page, one can access meeting dates, meeting minutes, and membership information pertaining to national and international standards development activities. "News @ DISA" provides news about educational seminars, conferences, press releases, as well as related informational services. "EDI Reference Desk" contains a glossary of terms and acronyms related to the industry. One can search for a specific acronym, browse the full glossary, or select additional glossaries such as BABEL. The latter can be used over the Internet or downloaded as a stand-alone database to search for computer-oriented abbreviations and acronyms.

Global Land Information System

The Global Information System (GLIS), located in Sioux Falls, South Dakota, is an interactive computer system developed by the U.S. Geological

Survey for scientists seeking sources of information about the Earth's land surfaces. GLIS contains metadata, that is, descriptive information about data sets. Through GLIS scientists can evaluate data sets, determine their availability, and place on-line requests for products. Available on-line are samples of earth science data to assist scientists in choosing the appropriate data sets for their needs.

Scientists can use GLIS to bring up outlines of the geographic areas covered by the data sets. Using digital browse functions to manipulate the data, they can determine information such as the amount of cloud coverage or the quality of images in which they may be interested.

On-line requests can be placed via GLIS for earth science data. The producing organizations will receive the request and provide the user with the price and ordering information.

GLIS contains references to regional, continental, and global land information including land use, land cover and soils data; cultural and topographic data; and remotely sensed satellite and aircraft data. GLIS is routinely updated with new data set descriptions as they are contributed by the global change scientific community. GLIS inventories are reviewed daily to assure access to the most current information. The system operates 24 hours a day, 7 days a week for worldwide connectivity and availability.

Users wishing to perform graphic-based query functions can use an X terminal or X terminal emulator package on a PC and access via the GCRIO Gopher. Users wishing to perform text-based query functions can use an alphanumeric terminal or a terminal emulator package on a PC and access via the X-GLIS interface.

Access via the Internet:

Telnet-URL: telnet://glis.cr.usgs.gov
Anonymous FTP: ftp://edcftp.cr.usgs.gov
WWW-URL: http://sunl.cr.usgs.gov.glis/glis.html
Dial-up Access: (605) 594-6888 (set modem to * bits, no parity, 1 stop bit)

The Task Analysis, Synthesis and Execution Group (www.tase.com)

The Task Analysis, Synthesis and Execution (TASE) Group was founded by technology professionals for technical professionals. The TASE Group is a contact service firm corresponding to client needs with skilled technical professionals. Their method is thoroughly understanding the needs of their clients.

TELECOMMUNICATIONS

AT&T (www.att.com)

This web site hosted by the American Telephone and Telegraph Company (AT&T) is an enormous site with main features, secondary features, products and services, tops and navigation links to include a search engine. The directory, which is found under topics, adds a bonus to this site and includes an area code finder and a white pages directory for worldwide E-mail addresses. There is, for computers with nonbrowsing capabilities, a text-only version.

AT&T 800 Directory (att.net/dir800)

AT&T Directory is a composite of companies with Nation 800 or 888 services. Users can browse the toll-free numbers by categories or perform quick searches that create lists based on company names, cities, and states. The two main categories of travel and gifts are broken down more extensively and connected to related information such as weather and road maps on a state-by-state basis or anniversary gifts and birth stones correspondingly. In addition, the search can be done with Personal Library Software (PLS) which the site will teach the user how to use or an Easy Search if the toll-free number is known. Information for potential buyers of AT&T 800 services is provided under the Advertiser's Index.

Builder.Com (www.builder.com)

This web page deals with web-site construction. Information about authoring, programming, graphics, and servers is located on this page. Links are available for ideas about shortcuts and other topics for a web site. This is another reference for people to look at when trying to create web.

MCI (www.mci.com)

This comprehensive site hosted by the MCI Telecommunications Corporation allows businesses to tap into the latest information in communications. This site, although full of graphics offers information on network MCI, MCI one, Friends & Family, MCI World, Product Overview, On-Line Tools & Customer Service, Global Communications, About MCI, and Find It. Because this site is large, the "Find It" section is an index that allows the user to search for information contained in the site.

Small Business Knowledge Center (www.bell-atl.com/sbs)

Bell Atlantic is a company that is a market leader in the wireless services, and a principle provider of leading wireline and data services. Formed through the wield of Bell Atlantic and NYNEX, Bell Atlantic is also one of the world's investors in communications markets with investments and operations in other countries.

TELEPHONES

MetroSearch Library (1-800-234-1489)

MetroSearch Library is a telephone book on CD-ROM that includes 80,000,000 residential and business white pages. It comes on four network accessible discs that are updated every three months. The listings can be found by using a last name or a company name.

TRAVEL

MapQuest (www.mapquest.com)

This site is maintained by GeoSystems Global Corporation. Detailed maps of places anywhere in the world and driving directions in the United States can be provided. Maps can also be personalized for registered members.

TREASURY BILLS

The Public Debt (www.publicdebt.treas.gov/opd/opd.htm)

The web site is provided by the Department of Treasury, Bureau of the Public Debt. For each calendar day, this on-line resource reports the debt of the United States. Because of frequent updates, users can observe the dynamics of the growing liability. In addition to daily reports, the site offers monthly and yearly accounts of the subject. Pages of summaries are available for downloading the data in several formats. The site also presents historical information concerning the public debt and a list of Frequently Asked Questions. A link to The Monthly Treasury Statement of Receipts and Outlays of the U.S. Government (MTS) provides information about the government's budget and financial operations.

ZIP CODES

CEDAR National Address Server (www.cedar.buffalo.edu/adserv.html)

When entering a valid U.S. postal address, this server will attempt to rewrite the address in proper format along with ZIP + 4. This site claims to possibly be able to retrieve a Postscript or a GIF file of the address for printing, with a bar-code. Another added bonus is the possibility of viewing a street map from two different sites (Yahoo and MapQuest). This site is hosted by CEDAR-Center of Excellence for Document Analysis and Recognition through State University of New York at Buffalo.

Section II

Printed Sources

AI—INDEXES

AI 15 .L65 (Russian Newspapers—Indexes—Periodicals)

Letopis Gazetnykh Statei (Moskva: Vsesoiuzhnaia Palata)

This source is the most comprehensive general index to Russian central and republic-level newspapers. About 40,000 bibliographic entries are added annually on documentary materials, articles, and works of fiction from nearly 40 newspapers. The title is translated as the *Chronicle of Newspaper Articles*.

AI 15 .L66 (Russian Periodicals—Indexes)

Letopis Zhurnalnykh Statei

This source is a weekly listing of publications of universities, research institutes, and academies of the sciences, social sciences, and humanities. The contents are arranged by a classification in 31 sections and are indexed in a bimonthly issue. It is cumulated annually by *Spisok Zhurnalov*. The title translates as the *Chronicle of Magazine Articles*.

AI 21 .N44 (New York Times—Indexes)

New York Times Index (New York, NY: New York Times)

This source indexes the contents of the Late City edition of the *New York Times*, a daily news publication. Its purpose is to serve as an index to the *New York Times*'s contents, but it can also serve as a basic chronological overview of the news or as a guide to articles in other daily news publications. The entries include brief synopses of each significant news article, editorial matter, and special features, as well as the date, section, page, and column of the paper in which the article appears. The length of the articles and types of accompanying illustrations are also indicated.

This is a bimonthly publication, with quarterly cumulations published for the first three quarters and an annual cumulation published in the fourth quarter. The index includes subject, geographic area, organization name, and personal name headings arranged alphabetically, word by word. The entries beneath these headings are arranged chronologically, with the exception of subjects that are easier to use in an alphabetical arrangement, such as "Deaths," "Book Reviews," and "Motion Pictures." The use of cross-references (See also and Use) refer the user to other relevant or preferred headings. Special features of the index include the use of bold-face type to indicate entries of unusual interest and "How to Use" instructions in the bimonthly and annual editions.

AN—NEWSPAPERS

AN 107 .M9 M88

Moscow News

The *Moscow News*, known as the "People's Newspaper," has been published since 1930 and became an independent weekly in 1990. It is international in scope, covering local and world news. Interviews and political speeches are included, as well as sections on the economy, politics, and literature and the arts. A highlights sections features detailed coverage of a current topic, while a "Way We Live" section examines current trends in society. "Three Voices," a regular feature column, contains world, national, and personal views of scholars, journalists, and authors. *Moscow News* is published in English, French, German, Greek, Hungarian, Italian, Russian, and Spanish.

AP—PERIODICALS

AP 2 .C9752 (World Politics—1945—Periodicals)

Current Digest (Columbus, OH: Ohio State University)

Founded in 1949 be the American Council of Learned Societies and the Social Science Research Council, this publication is published by non-profit corporation affiliated with these organizations and the Ohio State University.

At the beginning of each article, it is stated whether the article is printed in its entirety or if it has been condensed. Each article begins with a citation providing the name of the author, title of the original newspaper or magazine, date, and page numbers, if condensed. The article citation also includes the number of works in the original article.

Articles are selected from approximately 120 publications and cover a variety of subjects, including news, politics, economics, environment, and industry. Selections from *Pravda* and *Izvestia* are printed each week, while other newspaper and magazine selections vary. A number of government publications are also covered.

Indexing of articles is done on a quarterly basis and a cumulation is done annually. The index is in two sections. The first is arranged by subject and the second is arranged by personal names. Both sections are alphabetically arranged with articles listed in chronological order following the main index heading. A list of publications from which the articles have been selected is provided at the beginning of the index.

AP 4 .N57 (World Politics—Periodicals)

New Times (Moscow: Moskovskaya Pravda Press)

This weekly newspaper is published in Russian, English, German, and Italian, with emphasis on politics and economics. Most of the articles are by Russians, but a few are written by foreigners. Writers include professors and experts in the field in addition to the staff writers and correspondents.

Topics include the economic burden of uprisings and human rights. News articles are accompanied by political analyses and commentary. Interviews appear as well as profiles of politicians, business people, educators, and filmmakers.

AS—ACADEMIES AND LEARNED SOCIETIES

AS 22 .E56 (Associations, Institutions, etc.—Directories)

Encyclopedia of Associations (Detroit, MI: Gale Research)

This comprehensive reference book provides information on a wide variety of nonprofit American membership organizations. The organizations outlined are categorized in eight groupings: national nonprofit membership associations; international associations that are generally North American in membership and activity; local and regional groups whose goals are of national interest; nonmember organizations that provide information to the public; and for-profit associations whose names suggest nonprofit status. Informal organizations (no national headquarters), inactive and defunct organizations, and untraceable organizations appear only in the index with the appropriate annotations. The listed information in this directory comes primarily from the associations themselves.

Entries are divided into subject sections with organizations arranged alphabetically within each section. Entries provide addresses, chief officials' names, and membership, budget, and staff information. In a brief description, the purpose, activities, and types of memberships of each association are outlined. In addition, computerized and telecommunications services are reported. These include on-line and database services, bibliographic services, electronic publishing capabilities, electronic mail, and toll-free hotlines. Each organization's publications are listed with details on prices and circulation. The internal committees, divisions, and affiliations as well as regional, state, and local groups are also noted.

This directory of associations has three volumes. The first volume covers national organizations in the United States with a name and keyword index. The index serves as a quick reference guide, providing addresses and phone numbers after organizations' primary references. The second volume is the Geographic and Executive indexes, and the third is a supplement of newly formed and founded associations not listed in the main volume. Major changes that occur between editions such as mergers, address changes, and turnover in executive staff can also be found here. Other parts of the series are a volume on international organizations and five volumes on regional, state, and local organizations. These five volumes have little overlap with the volume of national associations.

AS 29.5 .R43 (Research—United States—Directories)

Cichonski, Thomas J. Research Centers Directory
(Detroit, MI: Gale Research Inc.)

Research Centers Directory chronicles the efforts of North America's premier nonprofit research organizations. The *Directory* lists and describes nonprofit laboratories, operating foundations, and centers.

The *Directory* is published in two volumes. There are 17 sections arranged by subject; these sections are further grouped into five broad categories. Volume one contains seven sections in the areas of physical sciences and life sciences and engineering, plus the "Business and Economics" section. Volume 2 includes nine sections in the areas of public and private affairs and policy, cultural and social studies, and research and multidisciplinary coordinating centers. Within each section, entries are arranged in alphabetical order by the sponsoring university name (if applicable) and then by center name.

Volume 2 also contains three other indexes that help locate listings. The Master Index combines all research centers, programs, and parent institutions alphabetically. This index also contains the names of defunct and inactive centers. The Geographic Index lists in alphabetical order centers by the city and state in which they are based. This index also includes complete contact information. The Subject Index includes over 5000 cross-references and terms that classify the research centers by the main field of study.

AS30 .M63 (Dissertations, Academic—Abstracts)

Dissertation Abstracts International

Dissertation Abstracts International is a publication that includes concise, author-written abstracts of dissertations accepted for doctoral and post-doctoral degrees at institutions worldwide. *Dissertation Abstracts International* is published in three sections. Section A is *The Humanities and Social Sciences*, Section B is *The Sciences and Engineering*, and Section C is *Worldwide*. Sections A and B are published monthly and include dissertations accepted at institutions throughout North America and the world. Section C is published quarterly.

Entries are arranged by subject. Within each subject, the works are in alphabetical order by author. At the head of the entry is the bibliographic data relating to the dissertation. The bibliographic information contains at least the title in the original language, the author's name, the year of award, and the institution granting the degree. There are instances when other information is provided.

The abstracts come from a variety of sources. Usually, they are printed the way they are received.

Each issue has two main indexes. They are the Keyword Index and the Author Index. The Keyword Index is a list of all of the abstracts by an important word in the dissertation title. The Author Index is used by finding the author's name in the end of the year Cumulative Author Index and cross-referencing the number that goes with the abstract.

A relatively new feature of *Dissertation Abstracts International* is the ability to search the dissertation database using *Dissertation Abstracts Ondisc*. Using CD-ROM technology, researchers can find the bibliographic citations and abstracts from 1980 and on.

AY—YEARBOOKS, ALMANACS, AND DIRECTORIES

AY 754 .W6

Whitaker's Almanac

It provides current statistical data on subjects like economy, trade, investment laws, population, judicial system, currency and exchange rate, finance, and development for each country. This information is useful to business professionals, investors, and international organizations such as International Monetary Fund and United Nations.

AY 2001 .D542
(Directories—Directories; United States—Directories)

Directories in Print (Detroit MI: Gale Research)

Information on directories covering many subject areas is provided in these directories. Subject areas include, but are not limited to, computers and telecommunications, health and medicine, arts and entertainment, and law. The tens of thousands of directories listed include directory databases, guides, rosters, and other lists. A possible 26 points of description are provided for each directory arranged by 26 additional subject categories. Listings are arranged alphabetically within the categories. Subject, title, and keyword indexes locate directories by their areas of primary interest and alphabetically list all directories in the current edition, including inversions of keywords in the directory titles.

BJ—ETHICS

BJ 1725 .C67 1994 (Professional Ethics—United States)

Gorlin, Rena A., Editor. Codes of Professional Responsibility,
3rd Edition (Washington, DC: Bureau of National Affairs) 1999.

This book contains the official codes of ethics of numerous professional organizations in the fields of business, health, and law. Although most are complete, some are excerpted. Basic information about each organization and the implementation and enforcement of the codes precedes every text section. Also found here are institutional, periodical, and bibliographic (including nonprint) resources. There are three indexes: issues, professions, and organizations.

D—HISTORY (GENERAL) AND HISTORY OF EUROPE

D 2 .E92 (World Politics—1945—Periodicals; International Organizations—Periodicals)

Europa World Yearbook (London, UK: Europa Publications)

This source gives detailed information on the political, economic, and commercial institutions of the world. The first volume begins with information on the United Nations, its agencies, and other international organizations. The rest of the volume and volume two contain detailed information about each country in alphabetical order. Information given is an introductory survey, a statistical survey, and a directory that contains information on the government, political parties, the constitution, religion, press, publishers, radio and television, finance, trade and industry, transportation and tourism, and atomic energy.

D 847 .A13 (Soviet Union—Abstracts—Periodicals; Europe, Eastern—Abstracts—Periodicals; Communist Countries—Abstracts)

ABSEES: Soviet and East European Abstracts Series
(Oxford, UK: Pergamon Press)

ABSEES is a mixed media journal published three times a year. The print journal contains summaries of articles and reports from newspapers and periodicals and refers the user to the complete abstract on microfiche that is contained in an inner pocket of the journal. Contents are classified by country of origin and are indexed by subject. Each entry contains the topic of the material, a complete bibliographic citation, a brief summary, and a cross-reference to the full abstract on microfiche. Subjects of the journal include economic planning and theory, trade and services, management, science and technology, foreign trade, labor and wages, and social issues. *ABSEES* is indexed in *Current Contents.*

DJK—EASTERN EUROPE (GENERAL)

DJK 1 .I62
(Europe, Eastern—Study and Teaching—Periodicals)

International Newsletter (Glasgow, UK: International Information Centre)

A Library News section provides information on new acquisitions and special collections; a Publications section announces upcoming books and periodicals; and a Conference News section gives names and dates of upcoming events. The newsletter is printed in English, French, and German. *International Newsletter* is published three times a year.

DK—RUSSIA, SOVIET UNION, FORMER SOVIET REPUBLICS, AND POLAND

DK 1 .I43 (Soviet Union—Periodicals; Soviet Union—Politics and Government—Periodicals)

Glastnost News and Review (New York, NY: The Center for Democracy)

This source, formerly *Glastnost*, is a bimonthly newsmagazine that provides a selection of articles from emerging independent presses. The Center for Democracy collects and translates selected articles from independent journals. There are feature articles that range in length from a few paragraphs to several pages and regular departments such as "GNR Rightswatch," "Observations," "The Press," "Chronicle," and "Letters and Documents." Each article contains an editor's note detailing when and where the article was first published. The sources of the articles are listed on the last page with a brief description of each, including when it was founded, circulation statistics, and political ideology.

DK 1. R241

Radio Free Europe/Radio Liberty (New York. NY: Radio Free Europe/Radio Liberty Research Institute)

This weekly publication provides the results of research conducted on developments in Russia. Contributors are usually staff members of the Institute, but articles from others are encouraged.

The publication has three main sections. The first section, "All-Union Topics," deals with developments affecting Russia. The second section, "In the Republics," reports on issues of importance in a republic. The third section, "In the Baltic States," provides information on subjects relating to this area. In addition, articles on economics, trade unions, trade, agriculture, politics, religion, history, and foreign relations are provided. Each issue also provides a day-by-day account of the week's events.

An annual index is available. Each article is given a chronological identification number that is used in the index. This index consists of two parts. The first part is an alphanumeric list of entries by subject, and the second part is an alphanumeric list of entries by author.

DK 1 .R9855 (Russia—Periodicals)

The Russian Review: An American Quarterly Devoted to Russia
Past Present (Columbus, OH: Ohio State University Press)

This quarterly publication includes feature articles on art, education, politics, religion, law, and economics. A large book review section examines recent publications, and a bibliography is included at the end of each issue. The *Russian Review* is indexed by *Current Contents* and the *Humanities Index*. Each April issue has a bibliography of major new reference works on Russia published in all Western languages and in Russian.

DK 1 .U53 (Russia—Periodicals—Index)

Daily Report: Soviet Union (United States: Foreign Broadcast Information Service)

Daily Report is a publication of the U.S. government containing translations of foreign radio and television broadcasts, periodicals, newspapers, and governmental decrees. The report is divided into categories of national and international affairs and features political, social, economic, and technological news. Monthly indexes arrange contents alphabetically by country, organize information by subject and personal names, and refer the user to the date and page of the information in the report. Each entry in the report provides the original source, date, and author of the broadcast or document and contains the full translated text. *Daily Report* is published in print and microfiche formats.

DK 65 .U14
(Developing Countries—Foreign Relations—Periodicals)

This bimonthly publication charts current developments in foreign and domestic policies. It is arranged geographically with a name index.

DK 266 .A2 R37 (Russia—Periodicals)

Reprints from the Russian Press (New York, NY: Compass
Point Publications)

This biweekly publication contains current, unabridged translations of
speeches, interviews, reports, documents, and articles. Topics covered include
economics, foreign trade, politics, technology, law, and agriculture. It is
indexed in *International Political Science Abstracts* and *Middle East Abstracts
and Indexes.*

DU—OCEANIA (SOUTH SEAS)

DU 10 .P77 1989
(Pacific Area—Dictionaries and Encyclopedias)

Segal, Gerald, Ed. Political and Economic Encyclopedia
of the Pacific (Chicago, IL: St. James Press) 1989.

This encyclopedia provides information on the politics, economics, security,
trade, ideologies, cultures, and resources of the nations in the Pacific. In
addition, it tries to organize the information in such a way as to understand
the subregional and global connections that exist within the Pacific region.
Emphasis has been on the post-1945 Pacific.

The articles range in length from short paragraphs to several pages. The
encyclopedia arranges the material by having separate headings for smaller
topics instead of grouping them under general headings.

E–F—HISTORY: AMERICA

E 154.5 .N28
(Business—United States—Directories—Telephone)

The National Directory of Addresses and Telephone Numbers
(Detroit, MI: Omnigraphics)

The National Directory of Addresses and Telephone Numbers contains
listings of corporations, government offices and institutions, and organizations in the United States. Listed in alphabetical order, there are two parts:
the Alphabetical Section and the Classified Section.

The Classified Section contains listings arranged according to the type
of business. Similar to ordinary yellow pages, it is based on major business
categories ranging from Agriculture, Forestry, and Fishing to Wholesale

Trade. Each section is further divided into subsections based on even more specific descriptions of the business. Again, these are arranged alphabetically.

The Alphabetical Section is much like the white pages of any local phone book. There are several other additional features such as fax and toll-free number and the complete official name and address.

In addition to the Classified and Alphabetical Sections, there are other useful features. Some include Charts and Maps (that include an area code and time zone map) and Profiles of some Top U.S. cities.

G—GEOGRAPHY

G 59 .U58 (Geography—Collections)

United States, Department of State, Background Notes
(Washington, DC: Bureau of Public Affairs,
Department of State)

This government publications provide background information on many nations. A general profile outlines the geography, the people, the government, the economy, and membership in international organizations. Following this is a narrative description of the geography; culture; history; government and political conditions with a list of principle government officials; the economy in terms of gross domestic product, agriculture, natural resources, transportation, and communication; defense; foreign relations; relations with the United States; and a list of key U.S. officials with embassy and consular information. A bibliography of further reading is included.

G 1201 .E1 G45 (Sex Distribution (Demography)—United States—Maps; Women—United States—Statistics)

Fast, Timothy H., and Cathy Carroll. The Women's Atlas
of the United States (New York: Facts on File) 1995.

The *Women's Atlas of the United States* is a pictorial and graphical atlas on women in the United States. The *Atlas* shows that there are differences between men and women, as well as regional differences between the women of the North and South, and the East and West with regards to everything from health to politics. The further reading suggestions are to help explain questions the user may have while exploring the *Atlas*, mainly, why are there differences? Issues profiled are demographics, education, employment, family, health, crime, and politics. Included at the end are an appendix, notes, a bibliography, further reading suggestions, and an index.

G 1797.2 .E21 1992

The Economist Atlas, The Economist Books Ltd
(New York: Henry Holt) 1992.

The atlas is composed of maps, charts, graphs, and profiles that show
political, economic, and geographical data of many countries and cities of
the world. Section one of the atlas shows political as well as physical maps;
Section two deals about "World Comparisons" on topics such as foreign
debt, energy, education, the environment, industrial production, and mineral
wealth; and the final section is about country profiles with emphasis on capital
city, population, religions, language, educational requirements, currency,
public holidays, and geographical features.

H—SOCIAL SCIENCES

**H 72.5 .U5 G94 1989 (Economics—Study and Teaching
(Graduate)—United States—Directories; Economics—
Study and Teaching (Graduate)—Canada—Directories;
Agriculture—Economic Aspects—Study and Teaching
(Graduate)—United States—Directories; Agriculture—
Economic Aspects—Study and Teaching (Graduate)—
Canada—Directories)**

Owen, Wyn F. and Douglas A. Ruby, Editors. Guide to
Graduate Study in Economics, Agricultural Economics,
Public Administration, and Doctoral Programs in Business
Administration in the United States and Canada, 8th Edition.
(Boulder, CO: The Economics Institute) 1995.

Using data provided by the respective departments, this guide describes 136
out of 220 economics programs in the United States and Canada, 44 of 65
agricultural programs, as well as 29 Ph.D. programs and 14 in public
administration. The descriptions include contact information, chairperson,
brief descriptions of schools, programs offered, number of degrees granted
over a 5-year period, admission policies and procedures, student enrollment
profile, and a list of faculty with information about them. Preceding the
descriptions of individual programs is a useful chapter containing general
information for prospective students. There is a helpful chapter of additional
information specifically for foreign students. A final chapter describes the
Economics Institute. The index consists of an alphabetical list by state or
country covering all departments.

HA—STATISTICS

HA 40 .I6 O68 (Industrial Statistics—Periodicals)

Organization for Economic Cooperation and Development,
Indicators of Industrial Activity (Paris, France: Organization for
Economic Cooperation and Development, Publications Service)

This periodical provides an overview of short-term developments in diverse industries in the 25 member nations of the Organization for Economic Cooperation and Development (OECD). There are two main sections. The first section contains graphs and tables as quantitative indicators. The tables present data on total industry, mining and quarrying, and manufacturing. The manufacturing section is subdivided into food, beverages, and tobacco, textiles, wearing apparel, and leather, wood and wood products, paper and paper products, printing and publishing, chemicals, nonmetallic mineral products, basic metals, fabricated metal products, machinery and equipment, and electricity, gas, and water. Detailed notes on the production indexes complete section one.

Section two provides qualitative indicators for manufacturing activities such as food, beverages, and tobacco and electricity, gas, and water. Rounding out the publication are International Standard Industrial Classification (ISIC) definitions and country/industry weighting tables. All tables in the main sections deal with output, deliveries, new orders, unfulfilled orders, prices, and employment. Data are presented in monthly, quarterly, and yearly increments and follows the ISIC format. The text is in both English and French.

HA 40 .I6 U58 1987 (United States—Industries—Classification—Handbooks, Manuals, etc.)

U.S. Office of Management and Budget, Standard Industrial
Classification Manual (Washington, DC: Government
Printing Office)

The Office of Management and Budget's Standard Industrial Classification (SIC) provides the classification standard for all federal economic statistics that are establishment-based. Organized by industry, the manual's structure facilitates the comparability of federal statistical data. Covering all economic activities, the manual defines industries via the economy's composition. There are 11 sections: agriculture, forestry and fishing; construction; finance, insurance, and real estate; manufacturing; mining; public administration; retail trade; transportation; wholesale trade; and nonclassifiable establishments.

Periodic revisions will reflect institutional and technological changes as well as growth and decline in any facet of the economy. The manual uses a numeric classification system accessed with an alphabetic index.

HA 40 .I6 U463

United Nations Industrial Statistics

This two-volume book is a source of statistical information on industries of various countries. The first volume deals with statistics of countries, the source of information, and a bibliography of each country covered. Some of the topics where statistics are given are number of employees, wages, gross output, and value of stocks. Whereas the first volume covers the first 5 years, volume two has statistics for the past 10 years.

HA 42 .I62 (Statistics—Periodicals; Economic History—1945—Periodicals; Commerce—Periodicals)

Euromonitor, International Marketing Data and Statistics
(London, UK: Euromonitor Publications Limited)

This publication provides statistical data pertaining to international market planning. Major and minor markets in Africa, North and South America, Asia, and Oceania are covered. Information is provided on socioeconomic trends, consumer marketing parameters, consumer spending, retailing, consumer market size, agro-industrial trends, advertising, and housing composition. Specific topics are covered in 25 sections, such as defense, finance and banking, literacy and education, automotives, and transport infrastructure. Individual sections are further subdivided into specific tables such as defense equipment. Tables, or databases, are organized by world area with country subdivisions and have 10- to 11-year coverage as well as notes. A user's guide, information source section, marketing geography section, and alphabetic subject index are also provided.

HA 155. H24 (Economic History—1971—Statistics)

Central Intelligence Agency, U.S.A. Handbook of International Economic Statistics (Springfield, VA: National Technical Information Service)

The primary categories for the majority of the tables in this book, with the exclusion of aid, are "OECD" (Organization for Economic Cooperation and Development), "Eurasia," and "Other." The "Eurasian" category contains entries for the 15 new republics of the former Soviet Union and the East European countries including the newly independent countries of the former Yugoslavia. The "Other" category includes, when suitable, Organization of Petroleum Exporting Countries (OPEC), newly industrialized economies, and additional countries not in the first two categories.

HA 202 (United States—Bureau of the Census;
United States—Economic Conditions;
United States—Social Conditions)

Statistical Abstract of the United States (Washington, DC: U.S. Department of Commerce, Bureau of the Census)

This publication was designed to serve as a general statistical reference guide as well as serving as a guide to other statistical sources and publications. Most of the data come from government agencies, although some are provided by private sources. Primarily, national data are given, but some tables cover regions and individual states. A few provide statistics on metropolitan cities and areas. The data generally are gathered from the most recent year or from the period available by the date of publication.

Statistics are arranged by subject and cover a wide range of topics of social, political, and economic importance. Commerce-related facts are found in chapters covering banking and finance, the labor force, income and expenditures, and other business enterprises. Data on specific industries such as manufactures are also available. Domestic trade and services and foreign trade are also recorded. Tables include such information as prices, profits, income tax returns, shipments, production, and employment.

The first appendix is a source of other statistical publications, providing listings of guides to state statistical abstracts and foreign statistical abstracts. Other appendices give some additional information relating to metropolitan areas and explain the methods of obtaining the statistics reported and their reliability. An index to tables with historical statistics is also included.

HA 203. A2235
(United States—Statistics; Time-Series Analysis)

United States Bureau of the Census, Long Term Economic Growth (Washington: United States Bureau of the Census)

This report is a revised and updated edition of "Long Term Economic Growth, 1860–1965" which was published in 1966. It displays conveniently the principal economic time series for the study of economic growth. It includes a wide base of information including a new economic time series on fixed business capital. This report also supplements "Business Conditions Digest" which analyzes short-term business conditions and prospects.

HA203 .S722 1991
(United States—Population—Statistics—Periodicals;
Income—United States—Statistics—Periodicals;
Purchasing Power—United States—Statistics—Periodicals;
United States—Commerce—Statistics—Periodicals;
Zip Code—United States—Periodicals)

The Sourcebook of Zip Code Demographics, Census Edition
(Fairfax, VA: CACI) 1990.

This special 1990 Census edition of the sourcebook covers the latest demographic information from the census. Volume one contains data from the 1990 Census Summary Tape File No One. It includes housing, household, and population data. The book is organized into two main sections where demographics on residential and nonresidential zip codes are listed.

HA 1107 .E87 (Europe—Statistics—Periodicals)

Euromonitor, European Marketing Data and Statistics
(London, UK: Euromonitor Publications Limited)

This publication is essentially a yearbook of statistical information on business and marketing in European countries, including those in the east for the 1990 edition. The book begins with a user guide, an overview of the European market, and an extensive bibliography of data sources. The data sections contain 24 databases providing graphs, tables, or narrative on a wide variety of topics covering market parameters, background information, and socio-economic trends and forecasts. Examples of specific topics are demographic trends and forecasts, defense expenditures, advertising patterns and media access, literacy and education, and tourism and travel. Data coverage is either for the latest year available, 10, or 11-year periods. Thirty-three countries or principalities are covered in the 1990 edition, organized under European Economic Community (ECC), European Free Trade Association (EFTA), Community of Mutual Economic Assistance (CMEA), and "other" groupings. An alphabetic subject index is included.

HA 1432 .N23 (Soviet Union—Statistics)

Narodnoe Khoziaistvo: Statisticheskii Ezhegodnik
(Moskva: Gos. Statisticheskoe lsd-vo)

This annual publication contains information on social and economic development during the year covered. It provides statistics on economics, population, industry, education, and agriculture. It also contains data of the most recent census. Most of the data are presented in comparison with the one for the two previous years and with the data collected for the preceding 5-year periods. Some data are provided with international comparisons. The title of the publication translates as *Peoples Economics: Statistical Yearbook*.

HA 1449 .M8 A54 (Moscow (R.S.F.S.R.)—Statistics)

Moskva v Tsifrakh (Moskva: Finansy i Statistika)

This annual publication contains statistical information on social and economic development of the city of Moscow during the year covered. The publication presents data characterizing the development of economics of the different districts of the city and the suburbs. The title of the publication translates as *Moscow in Numbers*.

HB—ECONOMIC THEORY

HB 34 .D55 1984 (Economics—Quotations, Maxims, etc.)

A Dictionary of Economics Quotations (Totowa, NJ:
Barnes and Noble)

This source is a progressive assortment of quotations in the areas of history of the economy, legal matters, mathematics, political science, and statistics. The arrangement of the contents is by topic. An index of key terms is included as a means of simplifying the process of finding a quote. The key term index is devised of a system that gives each quotation a two-figure reference; the first figure is the topic indicator and the second is the verse itself. Portions of the verse are also given as indicators of context. In addition to the initial arrangement by the topic, the entries are also arranged by authors or sources.

The text contains an index by author to help look for quotations. All works used in the text are cited. Quotations that are used heavily have been expanded upon. Where available, information pertaining to the births and deaths of deceased authors has been provided. No dates are given for living authors.

HB 61 .A52 1984
(Economics—Dictionaries; Business—Dictionaries)

Dictionary of Business and Economics (New York, NY:
Free Press) 1984.

This source covers a large amount of material under many topics. The topics range from past and present applications of economic theory to bibliographies emphasizing the works of important economists. Charts are used to cover pertinent legislation. Graphs and tables are used as illustrations of both academic and modern business management concepts. The major sources of the economic and financial data in the book are found in the appendix. A selected bibliography of economic and business works is included. Difficult concepts are covered more fully than simpler concepts.

All terms in the dictionary are alphabetized letter by letter regardless of length or spelling. Words containing cardinal numbers are alphabetized by the spelling, and phrases are alphabetized up to the comma in cases of inversion.

HB61 .E56 (Economics—Encyclopedias)

Greenwald, Douglas. The McGraw-Hill Encyclopedia of Economics. 2d Ed. (New York, New York: McGraw-Hill) 1993.

The *McGraw-Hill Encyclopedia* combines the knowledge of experts from academic, business, and government sectors. It provides meaningful and useful articles on several important sectors, such as economics and finance.

The new edition of the *Encyclopedia* has undergone some changes since the first edition was published. Since that time, there have been major changes in the economies of many nations. The new encyclopedia has evolved and adapted to the changes that these incidents have caused in several ways. The primary way is seen in the vocabulary that it uses. It has also changed to include articles that current political campaigns have dealt with; some of these topics include economic growth, federal debts and deficits, the outcome and effectiveness of fiscal and monetary policy, and the difficulties the banking industries have had. All of these issues are discussed in depth in the new edition of the *Encyclopedia*.

The level of complexity of each of the articles varies widely. They all vary in the amount and complexity of mathematics and graphs that are used. The majority of the articles were intended for the graduate level or higher.

The articles are arranged in order alphabetically. The *Encyclopedia* is extensively cross-referenced and indexed. For example, if someone were to look up "growth rate," it would say "see rate of growth."

The *McGraw Hill Encyclopedia* is an excellent reference for anyone from the practitioner to the undergraduate student.

HB 61 .F671 1993 (Economics—Encyclopedias)

Henderson, David R., Editor. The Fortune Encyclopedia of Economics (New York: Warner Books) 1993.

This attractive book contains numerous signed articles by leading economists and economic journalists. The editor reflects areas of disagreement among economists (particularly in the area of macroeconomics) by including articles that clearly set forth their thinking. We also find the shades of thinking that exist in the area of microeconomics (where there is more general agreement among economists). Both positive and normative positions are clearly identified and differentiated, revealing the role economic analysis can play in making sense of issues faced by everyone in daily life. Entries are brief and to the points, followed by a capsule biographies of the author and short bibliographies. Following the 14 chapters of encyclopedia, entries are lists of Nobel prizewinners in economic science, chairmen of the Council of Economic Advisors, and a section devoted to biographies.

HB 61 .K571 (Economics—Encyclopedias)

Knopf, Kenyon A. A Lexicon of Economics (San Diego, CA: Academic Press) 1991.

This 314-page book contains more than 800 terms and provides an up-to-date and clear explanation of the language used in economics. Both everyday terms and definitions of terms specific to the topic are included. Knopf, an emeritus professor of Economics at Whitman College in Washington, has written for the layperson. The work is readable and does not assume any prior knowledge of the subject. The definitions include very basic economic terms with some graphs and formulas as illustrations. Entries vary in length from a few lines to several pages.

A list of abbreviations, acronyms, and foreign phrases that are common to economics is located in the front of the book. The terms included here are also defined in the main body of the text. References to alternate or related terms are used. No bibliography is provided.

HB 61 .P36 1992 (Economics—Dictionaries)

Pearce, David W., Ed. The MIT Dictionary of Modern Economics. 4th Ed. (Cambridge, Mass.: MIT press) 1992.

This dictionary is aimed primarily at the "average" undergraduate. Although primarily concerned with explaining and defining terms and concepts, there are entries dealing with economists past and present and economics institutions. Many of its 2800 entries are cross-referenced to assist the reader in obtaining a picture of a particular branch of economics. Mathematical symbolism appears in some entries, but is not extremely complicated and is explained when it does appear. A goodly number of Scottish economists are among the contributing authors, insuring the U.K. viewpoint gets a hearing. This edition also gives representation to East European Economic thinking. Other features include a list of acronyms, economic performance data for major countries, and bibliographic references with some entries.

HB 61 .S46 1991
(Economics—Dictionaries; Statistics—Dictionaries)

Seplaki, Les. Attorney's Dictionary and Handbook of Economics
and Statistics (New York, NY: Professional Horizons Press) 1991.

This lexicon is designed to be a time saver for the user by being deliberately concise and to the point as much as possible and still be comprehensible. The principal subject areas covered include economics, finance, and statistics; contained also are a considerable number of accounting, management, and healthcare terms. An appendix contains a wide array of financial and statistical tables, formulas, and historical, as well as current statistical data. A specific purpose of the volume is to render to professionals, in a readily accessible format, those concepts, data, and materials which they do not routinely encounter within their own professional literature. Following some definitions, there are designations for reference, related, or alternative terms. Annual Statistical Update and Supplement volumes are available upon request from the publisher.

HB 72 .A78 (Economics—Moral and Ethical Aspects;
Capitalism—United States; Capitalism—Moral
and Ethical Aspects; Externalities (Economics);
Environmental Economics)

Goodwin, Neva R. Ed. As if the Future Mattered; Translating
Social and Economic Theory into Human Behavior (Ann
Arbor: The University of Michigan Press) 1996.

This book contains essays which are divided into two parts. The first part deals with the issue of investment in the future and also the question of how much will one invest in his or her future and what circumstances will he or she invest and which encourages long-range or socially beneficial investments. Part two deals with how political and activist people approach economic investment and deals with relatively theoretical papers from part one.

HB 72 .P88 (Economics—Moral and Ethical Aspects;
Social Problems; Social Politics)

Powelson, John P. The Moral Economy (Ann Arbor:
University of Michigan Press) 1998.

The idea of this book is to show how economic prosperity is mutually reinforcing with a moral economy. The work proposes solutions to how a greater balance of power among social groupings and their social problems are sought in them. It talks about how a desirable world can be possible if certain trends of the past millenium are continued and also if worked power becomes more diffuse. It also explains how conflicts will be resolved fairly and peacefully through designs of institutional structures.

HB 72 .V64 (Economics—Moral and Ethical Aspects)

Vickers, Douglas. Economics and Ethics: An Introduction to Theory, Institutions, and Policy (Westport, CT: Praeger) 1997.

This work tries to bring forward a greater conversation between moral philosophers and economists. Three main issues are addressed in the book with the first being historical aspects of how most economists gave up their association with ethical categories and criteria. The second part deals with how the vocabulary of ethical theory and its thought forms needs to articulate in a nonethical manner. The third part deals with how ethical awareness should be allowed to show influence in areas of economics when desirable. The book is divided into two parts with the first discussing economic and ethical theories' present status. The second part deals with three main issues, the first being ethical criteria of relevance on the supply and demand side of economics. The second deals with the distribution of income and wealth, and the third deals with issues involving macroeconomic policy and performance and how they are related.

HB 74 .G95 1989 (Economics—Study and Teaching (Graduate)—United States—Directories; Economics—Study and Teaching—Canada—Directories; Agriculture—Economic Aspects—Study and Teaching (Graduate)—United States—Directories)

Guide to Graduate Study (Boulder, CO: Economics Institute)

The series is designed to help prospective graduate students find information about various masters and doctoral study programs in both the United States and Canada.

Within the guide, there are numerous descriptions of hundreds of economic studies programs in the United States and Canada. The book also lists programs in the area of agricultural economics and doctoral programs in business and public administration. The guide is aimed at the needs of a multinational group of students and stresses the need to have earned economic degrees in the United States. A special information section for foreign students is included.

HB 95 .K37 (Free Enterprise; Competition; Economic Policy; Comparative Economics)

Kenworthy, Lane. In Search of National Economic Success: Balancing Competition and Cooperation (Thousand Oaks: SAGE Publications) 1995.

This work attempts to portray a convincing theory of comparative economic success. It also examines market liberalism and the thoughts behind it. This book tries to form a comparative prospective of how the performance of an economy is impaired by income equality, government intervention, labor organizations, and nonmarket constraints on freedom of choice. Finally, the author offers his own explanation for why some national economies do better than others.

HB 119 .A2 N28 (National Association of Business Economists (U. S.)—Directories; Economists—United States—Directories; Business—Directories)

National Association of Business Economists (U.S.). Business Economics: Membership Directory (Cleveland, Ohio: The National Association of Business Economists)

This professional journal features information helpful to the business economist. Each issue includes a brief history of the National Association of Business Economists (NABE), an up-to-date membership list, a list of chapter affiliates with their addresses, book reviews, a list of membership criteria for the NABE, and several articles dealing with the business economy. This publication is released four times per year to benefit the economists working in business, government, and universities, as well as students in economics.

HB 126 .J2 E19 (Economics—Japan—History; Japan—Economic Policy)

Sugihara, Shiro, Tanaka, Toshihiro, Ed. Economic Thought and Modernization in Japan (Cheltenham, UK; Northampton, MA: Edward Elgar) 1998.

This work is a collection of essays translated from Japanese to English about economic thought and modernization in Japan. The goal of the work is to provide a better understanding of the history of economic thought in Japan. The book keys in on the Meiji Restoration of 1867 and the Japanese surrender of World War II in 1945 as two major changes that impacted the modernization of Japan. All topics are concerned with how economic and social issues are perceived in their time. Some are in relation to policy and history and others theoretically. Chapter one deals with economic thought during the Tokugawa period. Chapters two and three deal with economic thought in the Meiji period. Chapters four and five deal with interwar period and Chapters seven through nine deal with the period during and after World War II.

HB135 .A34 (Economics, Mathematical; Statistics and Dynamics (Social Sciences); Computational Complexity)

Albin, Peter S. Barriers and Bounds to Rationality: Essays on Economic Complexity and Dynamics in Interactive Systems (Princeton, NJ: Princeton University Press) 1998.

This book deals with economic complexity and dynamics in interactive systems. It focuses on the rigorous analysis of an advanced economy's supportive and connective structures and the evolutionary, informational, and adaptive processes that occur within. The author plays several roles beyond that of a researcher for setting out an automata-theoretic design for the study of complex economic structures. "Structure" and "Complexity" are presumed to be well understood by the reader of this book. Discussed within are microeconomic foundations of cyclical irregularities, qualitative effects of monetary policy, prisoner's dilemma, and the complexity of social groups and social systems.

HB 135 .C74 (Economics, Mathematical—Study and Teaching; Econometrics—Study and Teaching; Computational Learning Theory)

Brenner, Thomas, Ed. Computational Techniques for Modeling Learning in Economics (Boston: Kluwer Academic Publishers) 1999.

This work gives an overview of recent developments in the research of the learning processes and experimental study of it, learning models and the analysis of its characteristics, and application to an economic context of the learning process. The work discusses three main techniques: evolutionary algorithms, neural nets, and cellular automata. The main focus of the work is to give examples, to discuss advantages and disadvantages, and to describe the computational techniques used in modeling learning economics. The work is broken up into five sections with the first looking closely at the use of simulations in economics. The second section deals with biological evolution and approaches inspired by it. The third deals with local interaction models in economics and neural nets and the uses behind them. The fourth deals with examples of rational learning models and boundedly rational which are used in economics. The fifth section deals with the subject of cognitive learning and contains three papers about it.

HB135 .F35 (Economics—Mathematical Methods; Econometric Models; Economics—Methodology; Statics and Dynamics (Social Sciences)—Mathematical Models)

Ferguson, Brian S. Introduction to Dynamic Economic Models. (Manchester, UK; New York: Manchester University Press; Distributed in the U.S.A. by the St. Martin's Press) 1998.

This work deals with dynamic models which incorporate equilibrium, specifically where equilibrium is defined as zero disequilibrium. Examples are taken from a broad area including resource economics, open-economy macromodels, and industrial organization. The main focus is on the economics. Examples are taken from the literature which makes it easier for readers to move into reading professional journals of interest.

HB 137 .J92 (Economics—Statistical Methods)

Judd, Kenneth L. Numerical Methods in Economics (Cambridge, Mass: MIT Press) 1998.

This work presents techniques from the numerical mathematics literature and also shows the usefulness of these techniques when using economic analysis. It was written in order to teach economist the power of computers and technology. The book, intended for second-year doctorate students, draws on the subjects of the basics of linear algebra, multivariate calculus, probability econometrics, optimization competitive general equilibrium theory, Nash equilibrium, optimal control, and dynamic programming as examples. The book is divided into five parts with Part I being the introduction. Part II reports on basics from numerical analysis. Part III reports the methods for dynamic programming. Part IV reports asymptotic solution and perturbation methods, and Part V deals with applications to dynamic equilibrium analysis.

HB 139 .D68 (Econometrics; Bayesian Statistical Decision Theory)

Dorfman, Jeffrey H. Bayesian Economics Through Numerical Methods: A Guide to Econometrics and Decision Making with Prior Information (New York: Springer) 1997.

This book talks about the subject of Bayesian economics. The two goals of this book are to convince the reader of inherent advantages and usefulness of Bayesian statistics compared to the sampling theory or classical approach and, second, to provide economic questions that can be answered empirically using Bayesian methods. The work demonstrates many economic topics which can be investigated using the Bayesian approach. Also, a wide variety of empirical applications are presented. Included is a list of references of treatments of theatrical issues involved, and empirical studies proving Bayesian methodology are successful in solving problems in economics in the real world.

HB 141 .C73 (Econometric Models—Congress; Econometrics—Congresses)

Gilli, Manfred Ed. Computational Economic Systems: Models, Methods Econometrics (Dordrecht; Boston, MA: Kluwer Academic Publishers) 1996.

This work presents a collection of papers from the IFAC-Meeting on "Computational Methods in Economics and Finance." They were organized by Hans Amman and Berc Rustem in Amsterdam in June 1994. It discusses the use of computing techniques and new computational methods. The work is broken up into two parts with part I dealing with modeling computational economic systems. Part II deals with new computational approaches to econometric problems.

HB 141 .T37 (Econometrics Models; Purchasing Power Parity—Econometrics Models; Gross Domestic Product—Econometrics Models; Consumption (Econometrics)—Econometric Models; Demand Functions (Economic Theory))

Theil, Henri. Studies in Global Econometrics (Dordrecht, The Netherlands; Boston, Mass: Kluwer Academic Publishers) 1996.

This work discusses the use of cross-country data which relies on purchasing power parties which are all comprised of a collection of essays. Two major points are discussed throughout with the first concerning per capita gross domestic products and the development over time. The second idea is broad groups of consumer goods and the fitting of cross-country demand equations for them. A list of figures and tables are shown throughout the book in order to help understand the ideas.

HB 171 .H46
(Economics; United States—Economic Conditions—1945–)

Heilbroner, Robert L. Economics Explained: Everything You Need
to Know About How the Economy Works (New York, NY:
Simon & Shuster) 1998.

This work tries to explain the economic trends happening due to newer and
better technology. It tries to simplify and clarify the concepts and vocabula-
ries of economics and also to help understand the economic world and
whether it is working or not working smoothly. The book is broken up into
four parts with Part I describing economic background. Part II describes
macroeconomics and the analysis of prosperity and recession. Part III
describes microeconomics and the market system and Part IV discusses
problems dealing with economics.

HB 171 .V82 (Economics Abstraction; Structural
Adjustments (Economic Policy); Economic Policy;
Economic Development; Capitalism; Economic Man)

Carrier, James G. Ed., Miller, Daniel Ed. Virtualism: A New
Political Economy (Oxford, OX, UK; New York: Berg) 1998.

The main focus of this book deals with Western Capitalist economic thought
and practice and the continuing evolution of it. Two notions are used to
describe this, which are abstraction and virtualism. Both of these operate at
conceptual and practical levels. The book begins by sketching the lineage of
abstraction and virtualism. Then it gives support of different arguments of
what they are about.

HB 172.5 .K36 (Macroeconomics; Economic Policy)

Kennedy, Peter. Macroeconomic Essentials for Media
Interpretation (Cambridge, Mass.: MIT Press) 1997.

This book discusses three kinds of economics: curve shifting, pop art, and
media. The work describes each of these through the microeconomic view and
the macroeconomic view. The first part looks at the behavior of individual
firms and consumers. It focuses on such issues as how firms determine prices,
how consumers make choices, and sales tax and quotas. The second part deals
with inflation, unemployment rate, interest rate, exchange rate, and business
cycles.

HB 172.5.M28 (Macroeconomics)

Mankiw, N. Gregory. Macroeconomics (New York: Worth
Publishers) 1997.

This book deals with the subject of macroeconomies. Four main points are
given with the first being short-run and long-run issues in macroeconomics.
The second deals with Keynesian and classical economics and integrates the
insights of both. The third issue uses a variety of simple models to discuss
macroeconomics. The fourth issue emphasizes how macroeconomics is an
empirical discipline that is brought forth through a wide array of experiences.
The book is broken up into four parts. Part one is the introduction. Part two is
the economy in the long run. Part three is the economy in the short run and
part four deals with issues on the microeconomics behind macroeconomics.

HB172.5 M54 (Macroeconomics; Control Theory)

Herbert, Ric D. Observers and Macroeconomic Systems:
Computations of Policy Trajectories with Separate Model
Based Control (Boston, MA: Kluwer Academics) 1998.

This work focuses on the computational aspects of using a control theoretic
approach. The author uses separate models for the development of the
control policies. Also included are visual simulations software tools which
may be used for policy analysis with dynamic macroeconomic systems. The
observer-based approach can be used to learn the forward-looking behavior
of economic actors and also shows how it can be used with low-order models.

HB 221 .A83 (Prices—Mathematical Models;
Business Cycles—Mathematical Models)

Blinder, Alan S. Asking About Prices: A New Approach
to Understanding Price Stickiness (New York, NY: Russell
Sage Foundation) 1998.

This work is divided into four parts. Part I is concerned with the methodology
of study and the motivation for it. Part II summarizes the facts of price
stickiness and main findings form respondent evaluations. It also deals with
various theories from those respondents. Part III discusses in great detail the
findings on a particular theory. Part IV draws some final conclusion and
wraps up the book. Included at the end of each chapter is a brief summary of
that chapter.

HB 235 .U6 V22 1999 (Finance)

The Value of a Dollar (Lakeville: Grey House Publishing) 1999.

Compiling information from over 500 sources, including newspapers, magazines, and catalogues, this book contains prices of products from the Civil War until 1999. The five chapters contain information on 20-year periods and also discuss economic and social forces of the time.

HB 236 .A3 C84 (Prices—Government Policy—Congresses; Price Regulation—Congresses; Monetary Policy—Congresses; Inflation (Finance)—Congresses)

Fledstein, Martin Ed. The Cost and Benefits of Price Stability (Chicago: University of Chicago Press) 1999.

This book is a collection of papers focusing on the appropriate monetary policy in a low-inflation environment. The major focus is on price stability and the gains that would result from them because of interaction between the tax system and inflation. Price stability has not yet been experienced in the United States and cannot be tested directly but rather ideas are discussed through low inflation. Three questions are addressed in this work: "How should the Federal Reserve respond if some nonmonetary force causes a rise in inflation?" "How should it respond if economic activity slows. . .?" Finally, "What risk of excess tightening and resulting economic decline should the Federal Reserve be willing to take as it contemplates the probability that the current low rate of unemployment is below the level that is consistent with stable inflation?"

HB 238 .I37 (Competition, Imperfect; Economies of Scale; Classical School of Economies)

Arrow, Kenneth J., Ng, Yew-Kwang, Yang Xiaokai, Ed. Increasing Returns and Economic Analysis (New York, NY: St. Martin's Press) 1998.

This work is a collection of essays from The International Conference on "Increasing Returns and Economic Analysis" which was held in September 1995. The essay deals with increasing returns and economies of specialization and the associated nonperfect competition. The work is broken up into three sections. Part I contains essays dealing with the new classical framework. Part

II deals with the associated deviations from perfect competition and various implications of increasing returns. Part III deals with the implication of information on increasing returns and increasing returns on issues of international trade.

HB 241 .M29 (Production Functions (Economic Theory)—Econometric Models; Industrial Productivity)

Harrigan, James. Estimation of Cross-Country Differences in Industry Production Functions (New York, NY: Federal Reserve Bank of New York) 1998.

This work gives differences of total factor productivity in groups of industrialized countries in the 1980s. The work examines two hypotheses to account for total factor productivity differences. The first examines constant returns to scale production dealing with specific technological differences. The second deals with industry-level scale economies dealing with identical technology. Total factor production indexes are calculated and total factor production differences across countries are statistically examined.

HB 241 .W24 (Industrial Productivity—Mathematical Models; Industrial Productivity—United States—Case Studies; United States—Manufacturers—Capital Productivity—Case Studies; Research, Industrial—Economic Aspects—United States—Case Studies)

Wang, Doris Yi-Hsin. Productivity Analysis: An Empirical Investigation (New York: Garland Pub.) 1996.

This work deals with the concept of productivity. It is about a study of productivity analysis focusing on reasons for improvements in U.S. manufacturing industries. The study examines empirically relationships between productivity/profitability changes and changes in catalyst financial commitments and also examines the relationship between profitability changes and productivity changes in selected companies and manufacturing industries. The study attempts to answer the questions of what are the impacts of changes in catalyst financial commitments on productivity changes, if there are any relationships between productivity changes and profitability changes, what are the impacts of changes in catalyst financial commitments on profitability changes, and if time lags exist between these changes for the first and second year after the year of investment.

HB 501 .C92
(Capitalism; Industrial Revolution; Economic History)

McCraw, Thomas K. Ed. Creating Modern Capitalism: How
Entrepreneurs, Companies, and Countries Triumphed in
Three Industrial Revolutions (Cambridge, MA: Harvard
University Press) 1997.

This work gives a perspective on the idea of capitalism, how it evolved over
time, and why entrepreneurs, companies, and countries make it work while
others fail. The work covers the history of capitalism and also examines the
economic development of Britain, Germany, Japan, and the United States. It
talks about the leading people of capitalism and also talks about some notable
companies. The work contains the systems that worked and the ideas involved
in the creation of modern capitalism.

HB501 .H24
(Capitalism—Moral and Ethical Aspects; Values)

Handy, Charles B. The Hungry Spirit: Beyond Capitalism: A Quest
for Purpose in the Modern World (New York: Broadway Books)
1998.

The main focus of this book deals with capitalism. The work is broken into
three parts. Part one deals with capitalist societies and the puzzles and
worries of them. The market, competition, and efficiency are all discussed.
Part two examines the quest for a purpose in our own lives from a philo-
sophical point of view. The third part deals with how capitalism needs to be
reinterpreted to make it decent and so values would dictate the way things
worked.

HB 523 .J82 .v1 (Income Distribution; Consumer Behavior;
Economic Policy; Public Welfare)

Jorgenson, Dale Weldeau. Welfare (Cambridge, Mass.: MIT
Press) 1997.

This work deals with consumer behavior and the empirical studies behind
them. It contains econometric models of demand, which were obtained from a
population of consumers with heterogeneous preferences. These are unified
through cross-section data for households and pooling of aggregate time
series data. Included in this work is a collection of essays already printed
describing consumer behavior throughout various chapters.

HB 615 .E632 (Entrepreneurship—Congresses; New Business Entrepreneurship—Management—Congresses)

Sexton, Donald L. Ed., Smilor, Raymond W. Ed., Entrepreneurship 2000 (Chicago: Upstart Publishing Co.) 1997.

The goal of this book is to address issues to help understand what contributes to business growth and success through cause and effect relationships. It also explores entrepreneurial issues directly involved in the current economic revolution. Five areas of Entrepreneurship are discussed being Financial growth, Growth Strategies, Entrepreneurship education, Dimensions of Entrepreneurship, and research applications and issues.

HB 615 .E6445 (Entrepreneurship—Congresses; Small Business—Congresses; Competition—Congresses; Macroeconomics—Congresses; Comparative Economics—Congresses)

Acs, Zolton J., Carlsson, Bo, Karlsson, Charlie, Ed. Entrepreneurship, Small and Medium Sized Enterprises and the Macroeconomy (Cambridge, UK; New York: Cambridge University Press) 1999.

This work contains papers which were presented at the international conference, Entrepreneurship, Small and Medium Sized Enterprises and the Macroeconomy at Jonkoping International Business School, Jonkoping University, Jonkoping Sweden on June 13–15, 1996. Some topics discussed include productivity and economic growth, innovation, technological change, employment, income distribution, and finance. Large and small advanced economies are discussed through theoretical and empirical research.

HB 701 .G26 (Property; Capitalism; Property—United States; Capitalism—United States; Comparative Economics)

Gates, Jeffrey R. The Ownership Solution: Toward a Shared Capitalism for the Twenty-First Century (Reading, MA: Addison-Wesley) 1998.

The main goal of the work is to make visible the world of finance and its operations-capital ownership and to give a new way for people to think. The work describes how the rich-get-richer legacy of primitive capitalism happened, identifies the policymakers who put it into action, and also shows why it is unsustainable. The work also explains how modern-day capitalism can be changed to give real security, abundant leisure, and broad-based prosperity.

The work is more of an overview rather than a detailed study of capital ownership. Endnotes are provided in this work for those who wish to perceive a more in-depth analysis.

HB 849.41 .P765 (Demography; Marketing Research; United States—Population; Decision Making)

Pol, Louis G. Demography for Business Decision Making
(Westport, Conn.: Querum) 1997.

The main topic this book discusses is demography and decision making in business. The work describes the role of demography in business decision making and also describes how employment of demographers as consultants in business organizations is increasing. The ways which demographic input contribute to the decision-making process are emphasized. The work finally discusses how demography and business will evolve even further in the future.

HB 864.8 .U18
(Social Choice; Economics—Sociological Aspects)

Udehn, Lars. The Limits of Public Choice; A Sociological Critique
of the Economic Theory of Politics (London; New York:
Routledge) 1996.

The main goal of this book was to critique the economic approach to politics. The foundation of the economic theory of politics is the main critique by way of limits to analyses. The focus of the book deals with the economic approach and what is lost from making assumptions. The most basic assumptions of economic approach are explored.

HB 881 .A2 V5 (Population—Statistics—Periodicals)

United Nations Statistical Office, Demographic Yearbook
(New York, NY: Department of International Economic and
Social Affairs, Statistical Office, United Nations)

Written in both English and French, this United Nations publication provides a comprehensive data source for demographic statistics covering over 200 nations. Each issue has two sections. The first section consists of 25 basic tables. The first four of these are a world overview of population statistics, such as rate of increase for selected years, percentage of distribution for a given year, population by sex, and natural increase rates based on the latest census and selected mid-year figures and expectations of life at birth for the latest available year. The remaining basic tables provide statistics on birth, divorce, fetal mortality, general mortality, infant and maternal mortality, legally induced abortion, and population. Coverage spans 4 to 9 years. The second part is always a special topic covered in depth, such as 1988's 28 tables of census results covering demographic, economic, social, geographic, and education characteristics.

Demographic Yearbook also contains a list of special topics dating back to 1948, tables on census dates by world region and country, technical notes on the statistical tables, descriptions of the tables, and copious general notes and footnotes for the tables. A subject index accesses the statistics by subject matter, year of issue, and time coverage.

HB 2711 .R37 (Business Cycles)

Reiter, Michael. The Dynamics of Business Cycles: Stylized Facts, Economic Theory, Econometric Methodology and Applications (Physica-Verlag) 1995.

The work identifies the principal parts of business cycles without going into details. The stylized facts of economic theory are explained using the simplest equation dealing with it. Business cycle analyses are addressed through methodological questions and models. The work contributes answers to a number of questions concerning economic fluctuations and the business cycle.

HB 3608 .M8 V98 (Moscow (R.S.F.S.R.)—Population)

Moiseenko, V. Naselenie (Moskvy: Proshloe, Nastoiashchee, Budushchee. S. 1. Isd-vo Mosk. un-ta) 1992.

This publication deals with past, present, and future issues of the population of Moscow. The source covers topics such as the history of Moscow's population, population growth, mortality, and migrations. The studied tendencies of the dynamics of population growth in Moscow and the Moscow region are included. The title of this publication translates as *Population of Moscow: Past, Present, Future.*

HB 3608 .U5 D38 (Demography—Ukraine—Periodicals; Ukraine—Statistics, Vital—Periodicals; Ukraine—Population—Periodicals)

Demograficheksie Issledovaniia (Kiev: Naukova Dumka)

This serial covers the problems of contemporary theory and practice in demography. It deals with the demographic issues of Ukraine. Subjects such as population growth, birth, mortality, and migration are included. The title of this publication translates as *Research in Demography*.

HB 3711 .D56 (Business Cycles—Statistical Methods; Business Forecasting—Statistical Methods)

Diebold, Francis X. Business Cycles: Durations, Dynamics, and Forecasting (Princeton, NJ: Princeton University) 1999.

The main idea of this book deals with business cycles and putting recent empirical business cycle research in perspective. It includes much research dealing with applications of modern econometric techniques from problems of business cycle analysis. Many topics are covered including business cycle measurement, modeling, fractional integration, regimeswitching models, and nonparametric analysis. The work is divided into three broad categories. The first deals with business cycle duration or length of contractions and expansions. The second looks at business cycle dynamics, and the third section deals with forecasting business cycles and many issues relating to them.

HB 3711 .M67
(Seasonal Variations (Economics); Business Cycles)

Miron, Jeffrey A. The Economics of Seasonal Cycles (Cambridge, MA: MIT) 1996.

Two main goals are discussed in this book. The first tries to prove to the macroeconomists how seasonal fluctuations is an interesting area to study. The work reveals how they are compared to the nature of business cycles. The second goal of the work is to prove how they can be used to learn about aggregate fluctuations through summarized evidence. The work reviews research of them, which provide information about seasonal and nonseasonal economic phenomena.

HB 3730 .K57 (Economic Forecasting; Business Forecasting; Twenty-First Century—Forecasts)

Kiplinger, Knight A. World Boom Ahead: Why Business and Consumers Will Prosper (Washington DC: Kiplinger) 1998.

This book attempts to answer the question of whether the positive trends of accelerating economic openness and openness and integration, which leads to higher growth in the future, will continue. The book is intended to help people in management and give them a view of the future of business, demographics, U.S. government, world markets, technology, and key industries. The basis of the book comes from a combination of historical analysis and current readings.

HB3730 .W93 1995 (Economic Forecasting—Directories)

World Index of Economic Forecasts: Including Industrial Tendency Surveys, Edited by Robert Fildes (Aldershot, Hampshire, England; Brookfield, Vt.: Gower) 1995.

World Index of Economic Forecasts includes information about 217 organizations that provide forecasts, plans, and surveys for over 100 countries. Each organization profile contains an address, contact data, a checklist of the coverage of the forecasts and surveys, technical notes, methodological commentary, and the forms in which the forecasts are made available. Separate sections discuss macroeconomics forecasts and CIRET surveys, specialist forecasters (i.e., experts in commodities, labor and population, energy, political risk, and shipping industry, trade cycle), and tendency analyses. The work is indexed by organization, country, exchange rate, interest rate, and subject.

HB 3743 .L52 (Business Cycles—United States; Economic Indicators—United States)

Lehmann, Michael. Using the Wall Street Journal (Chicago: Irwin) 1996.

This guidebook was published to help the reader make better financial decisions using the business section of the *Wall Street Journal*. The text provides background information on the United States economic climate, world markets, and different types of investments including, stocks, commodities, money markets, and long-term interest rates. The book is written in a nontechnical manner and sample *Wall Street Journal* entries are examined to facilitate a better understanding of statistical reports and the business economy. Investor's tips, charts, and economic formulae are included as well. Being able to effectively use the *Wall Street Journal* gives the reader an up-to-date look into the business world and helps the reader manage his or her own economic affairs.

HB 5607 .P74 (Soviet Union—Population)

Naselenie SSSR. Istoriia, Sovremennost, Prognoz. S. 1.
(Moskva: Nauka) 1992.

This publication presents a comprehensive, detailed analysis of demography and population dynamics in the Soviet Union. It contains reconstructed demographic data of the Soviet Union prior to the Second World War, data on human loses inflicted by the War (1941–1945), and analyses of the dynamics of population growth in the postwar period. It also includes comparative analysis of the 1989 census data and analysis of the national demographic situation and its changes within the decade. The source details the result of the multivariant demographic prognosis of the Soviet population and covers the aspects of population growth and mortality. The title of this publication translates as *Population of the USSR: History, Modern Day Situation, Future.*

HC—ECONOMIC HISTORY AND CONDITIONS

HC 10 .B98 (Finance—Statistics—Periodicals; Investments, Foreign—Statistics—Periodicals)

The Business One Irwin International Almanac (Homewood, IL:
Business One Irwin) 1993.

This reference book is a guide to businesses and investments abroad. Background information is provided for major developed countries and for developing countries in Asia and Latin America. The text also includes information on such topics as foreign securities, international economic trends, foreign real estate, international companies and markets, and foreign trade fairs. A list of chief international business contacts with their addresses and phone numbers is provided. Charts, maps, and diagrams are used, along with the text, to represent the data clearly.

HC 10 .E348 (Economic History—1945; Economic Indicators; United States—Foreign Economic Relations)

United States. Department of Commerce. International Trade Administration. Foreign Economic Trends and Their Implications for the United States (Washington, DC: Government Printing Office)

A series of over 100 pamphlets, each pertaining to a nation, this government publication covers foreign markets utilizing U.S. goods either presently or potentially. Each issue has a table of key economic indicators, differing for each nation, covering the percent of change over a number of years. A summary of recent economic and business developments and trends is provided as well as more specific analysis. Also included is a section on the implications of these developments in the United States.

HC 10 .I38 1998 (Industry)

Industrial Structure Statistics, Organization for Economic Cooperation and Development

Annual statistics, for manufacturing and nonmanufacturing sectors, on production and exports/imports are provided in Volume 1. The second volume contains data on energy consumption in manufacturing sectors. The data are prepared by the International Energy Agency for the assessment of the OECD member countries.

HC 10 .U83 (Economic Forecasting; Economic Indicators; Social Indicators; Social Predicting; Environmental Indicators)

Brown, Lester A., Renner, Michael, Flavin, Christopher. Vital Signs (New York: W.W. Norton and Co.) 1998.

This work shows both key indicators and special features of today's environment and its effect on the economy. Part one gives information on atmospheric, food, agricultural, energy, transportational, social, and military trends. Part two goes into more depth on some of the aforementioned areas, with special focus being given to the environment, the economy, the social, and the military features. Also included is a special section discussing new areas which must be considered when dealing with today's world.

HC 10 .V83 1998 (Economic Forecasting; Social Prediction; Environmental Indicators; Social Indicators; Economic Indicators)

Brown, Lester R., Michael Renner, and Christopher Flavin. Vital Sign: The Environmental Trends that Are Shaping Our Future (New York: W.W. Norton) 1998.

This book is volume seven of a series that illustrates trends that could possibly predict the future. The text presents relevant information for broad insights for the world. Trends considered insignificant in some sources are thoroughly explained. The book has been published in 21 languages.

HC 10 .W92 (Commercial Products—Periodicals)

Predicasts, World Region Casts (Cleveland, OH: Predicasts)

A companion to *World Product Casts*, this source presents abstracted figures from a variety of sources, mostly journals, and covers commercial activity in seven world regions. The Standard Industrial Classification (SIC) is again used to provide product breakdowns. Data are presented for consumption, production, and sales. In addition, related data are included for such topics as population characteristics, labor force composition, national government administration, and finance. Information for each product is given in terms of what happens to it, e.g., consumption; what other products it effects, when appropriate; base period data for year and quantities with long-range forecasts; unit of measure; journal source; and annual growth. Each volume provides data for a region of the world and each major nation within it. Following the statistics is an alphabetic guide to SIC and a guide to source abbreviations. There are four volumes with one published per quarter. Volume R-1 covers Western Europe; R-2 covers Eastern Europe, Africa, and the Middle East; R-3 covers the Americas, excluding the United States; and R-4 covers Asia and Oceania. A volume designated RC covers world regional forecasts for all regions and issues and is published quarterly.

HC 10 .W93 1998/1999 (World Resources—Periodicals; Economic History 1971–1990—Periodicals)

The World Resources Institute, et al. World Resources
(New York: Oxford University Press)

The series was formed by a joint effort of international organizations. The volume is different from the previous volumes because it gives a new layout allowing the data to be read easier. The book presents accurate data for prediction of trends. The book is currently in over eight languages.

HC 14 .C6 (Commercial Statistics; United States—Economic Conditions; United States—Commerce)

Commodity Yearbook (New York NY: Commodity Research Bureau)

Published since 1939, this comprehensive statistical yearbook annually appears. The sources for the yearbook are primarily government agencies and major trade organizations. It begins with a brief general overview of the past year's events such as commodity price increases or decreases, the state of the U.S. economy and futures market trading volume. Also included before the main listings is a short synopsis of commodity price trends. This section is separated into industrials, precious metals, livestock, grains and oilseed, and imported commodities. Charts of price indexes follow and offer comparisons for the past 6 years.

Divided by industry, the commodity listings are alphabetical and present synopses of each commodity's production, stock trades, consumption, and retail prices for the year as well as the exchange where it is traded. Comparative statistical tables comprise the central part of the yearbook. These tables provide more detailed information on production, prices, exports and imports, consumption, and the volume of trading. Inventory, distribution, and shipping data are also reported. Data are primarily for the U.S. industry market, but world statistics are given for such areas as production, stocks, and consumption.

Supplements are published three times during the year. Each is arranged in three sections: monthly tables, annual tables, and cash price charts for selected commodities. The charts cover 10 years of price activity.

HC 14 .C73
(Commercial Products—Statistics—Periodicals; Commercial Prices—Statistics—Periodicals; Commercial Statistics— Periodicals; Commodity Exchange—Statistics—Periodicals)

Bridge Information Systems, The CRB Commodity Yearbook (New York: John Wiley and Sons, Co.) 2000.

This appendix of statistics contains information on more than 100 commodities with figures dating back as far as 1988. Also included are futures volume highlights, interest rates, and stock index futures for both the United States and the rest of the world.

HC 57 .A1 M79 (Economic History—1945; Social History—20th Century; Statistics—Periodicals)

United Nations, Statistical Office, Monthly Bulletin of Statistics (New York, NY: Department of International Economic and Social Affairs, Statistical Office, United Nations)

This United Nations periodical, written in both English and French, updates the annual *Statistical Yearbook* that provides data on international socioeconomic issues. Each issue provides statistical tables on population, man-power, forestry, industrial production, mining, manufacturing, electricity and gas, external trade, transport, wages, and prices and finance. Coverage is by nation with time series varying and some monthly data. Each issue also contains special topics, outlined in the table of contents, in a special topics section and interspersed in the following tables: industrial production, construction, internal trade, external trade, transport, wages and prices, national accounts, and miscellaneous. Data coverage ranges from individual countries to collective economic communities to status of economic development, with rage of years varying from 2 to 15 years and some monthly and quarterly statistics. Annexes on conversion coefficients and factors, a cumulative list of additions and changes in the bulletin, and new and revised series complete each issue.

HC 58 .U38 1997 (Statistics—Periodicals)

Department of Economic and Social Affairs Statistical Division, Statistical Yearbook (New York: United Nations)

The volumes contain information from national and international sources. The references that provided the information are listed in the back of the text. The publisher distributes a bulletin of statistics monthly. The information is listed on-line and on CD-ROM.

HC 58 .U58 (Statistics—Yearbooks)

United Nations, Statistical Office, Statistical Yearbook (New York, NY: Department of International and Social Affairs, Statistical Office, United Nations)

Written in both English and French, this United Nations publication provides a statistical abstract uniting data from a variety of U.N. sources. The book attempts to provide information on a wide range of international socioeconomic issues such as assistance to developing nations and the alleviation of hunger via the expansion of world trade. There are three broad kinds of tables: world summary, general socioeconomic statistics, and basic economic activities statistics. The world summary tables provide information highlighting major world economic trends and developments. Such topics as population, world railway traffic, world production of primary commodities and manufactured goods, and index numbers of industrial production are covered. Data are generally organized by world area and/or status of economic development, with time period covered varying from table to table. The general socioeconomic tables narrow the scope of coverage to the national level. These tables deal with the broad areas of national accounts; population and manpower; wages, prices and consumption; government sector statistics; balance of payments; finance; education; culture; science and technology; development assistance; and industrial policy. The range of years covered is between 10 and 13 when provided. The basic economic activity tables cover major facets of the world economy. Included are statistics on agriculture, manufacturing, energy, wholesale and retail trade, external trade, transport, communications, and international tourism. Data is provided by world area with national subdivisions and time series, again, varying from table to table. Generally, the time series is 10 years when provided. Rounding out the book are notes on statistics, an appendix on country nomenclature, and an appendix on conversion coefficients and factors.

HC 59 .E165 2000 (Economic History—Periodicals)

Department of Economic and Social Affairs, World Economic and Social Survey: Trends and Policies in the World Economy (New York: United Nations) 2000.

This document is written to help decrease deficiency in poor countries. The purpose of this record is to bring attention to this poverty so that nations are able to reduce deficiency. This book shows nations how to use their resources to accomplish this goal. The survey is divided into two parts.

HC 59 .G88
(Industry—Periodicals; Commercial Products—Periodicals)

United Nations, Statistical Office, Industrial Statistics Yearbook (New York, NY: Department of Economic and Social Affairs, Statistical Office, United Nations)

Previously entitled the *Growth of World Industry* (1963–1973) and the *Yearbook of Industrial Statistics* (1973–1982), this United Nations publication presents data on industrial activity for the majority of the world's nations. Volume one contains general industrial statistics with each country receiving individual tables. Users are provided with country notes giving information on how the data was procured and is presented. A bibliography of related national publications is also provided. Products are arranged under the International Standard Industrial Classification (ISIC). Twenty indicators are available, but not all are used by each nation. In general, the indicators pertain to the number of establishments; employment; wages and salaries; hours of the day worked; quantity of electricity consumed; gross output in producer's prices; value added; gross capital formation; cost of services, supplies, and electricity; and the value of stocks. Figures generally cover 5-year periods. Index numbers of industrial production covering 9-year periods are included in all national tables. Volume one concludes with special indexes on numbers of industrial production and employment for the world, world regions, and type of economic system utilized encompassing the 10-year period up to the present. Volume two presents industrial activity over 10-year periods for mining and quarrying, manufacturing, and electricity and gas. Breakdown is by world area, with individual nations represented, and the ISIC. A section on conversion coefficients and factors and an index of commodities are also provided. Beginning in 1982, volume two is written in both English and French.

HC 59 .H24

World Tables (Baltimore Published for the World Bank
by the Johns Hopkins University Press)

This annual report provides economic and social statistics for 160 countries. All of the data are presented in a table format and are separated into two sections. Section I furnishes data on gross national products, gross domestic products, agriculture, industries, the service sector, imports and exports, and poverty-related social indicators. Section II deals with conversion factors and economic classifications, which are determined according to geographic region and level of gross national product per capita. The text is supplemented by an explanation of methods and sources and a glossary of terms. This publication also is available on diskette and magnetic tape.

HC 59 .H67 (Economic History—Statistics)

Organization for Economic Cooperation and Development,
OECD Historical Statistics (France: OECD) 1999.

This work, divided into three parts, provides historical statistics on the 29 member nations of the OECD. Part one includes benchmark data from 1997 with other national figures and exchange rates. Part two provides analytical tables showing the growth structure and profit of international trade. Part three has a broader focus, showing the progress and cyclical behavior of OECD economies.

HC 59 .S82 (Economic Policy—Periodicals; Economic History—Periodicals; Population Policy—Periodicals; Environmental Policy—Periodicals)

Brown, Lestor, Flavin, Christopher, et al. State of the World 2000. (New York: W.W. Norton and Co.) 2000.

While looking at economic conditions across the world, the authors tried to find alternative economic systems that could sustain our way of life without throwing earth's ecology into ruin. Various charts and tables are included throughout the text with a section of authors' notes at the conclusion.

HC 59 .U57 E38 (Economic History—1945)

United Nations, World Economic Survey: Current Trends and Policies in the World Economy (New York, NY: Department of International Economic and Social Affairs, United Nations) 1990.

This source is an annual publication of the United Nations that analyzes current economic issues within the international community. It is divided into chapters that are each devoted to a different aspect of world economy. Chapter I reviews world economic conditions of the previous year, identifies topics of current interest, and proposes an international economic agenda for the upcoming year. Subsequent chapters address international trade and economic policies, oil consumption, inflation, developing market economies, and special conditions effecting international economic activities. Tables and figures are extensive throughout the survey and are indexed at the front of the book. Articles are lengthy and conclusive, providing relevant statistics and footnoting further sources of information. The 1990 edition places special emphasis on the evolving economies of Eastern Europe.

HC 59 .W897 (Economic History—1945—Statistics— Periodicals; Economic Indicators—Periodicals; Social Indicators—Periodicals)

International Bank for Reconstructions and Development, World Tables, from the Files of the World Bank (Baltimore, MD: John Hopkins University Press)

This publication provides data on economic and social developments in developing and industrialized nations that are members of the World Bank. Economic data for some nonmember nations is also included to provide comparable statistics. The work is divided into a topical-pages section and a country-pages section. The topical-pages section is 20 tables covering such topics as gross national product per capita, gross national income, services, contribution to gross domestic product, private consumption, and growth of merchandise exports. Each table covers developing countries over a 10-year period and is organized by world area and subdivided by country. The country pages are the bulk of the book. Indicators presented for each nation are current GNP per capita in U.S. dollars, population, origin and use of resources, domestic prices (deflators), manufacturing activity, monetary holdings, government deficit or surplus, foreign trade (custom basis), balance of payments, external debt, and social indicators such as total fertility rate. Included are codes for general and country lists and base years for national accounts. A glossary of terms is provided as well.

HC 59 .W915 (Economic History—Periodicals; Economic Policy—Periodicals; Economic Projection—Periodicals)

International Monetary Fund, World Economic Outlook; Asset Prices and the Business Cycle (Washington DC: The Fund) 2000.

This survey chronicles the economic advancement of the world's 50 largest economies that represent over 90% of the world's gross output. Biannually updated, this work discusses North America's continued expansion, the reemergence of Asian economies, and the prospect of recovery in failing economies. Graphs and tables are provided. The latest discoveries in 20th-century economies of the world and the ongoing recovery in emerging market economies are discussed. Also included is an 89-page statistical appendix.

HC 59.15 .W89 (Economic Development—Statistics— Periodicals; Economic Indicators—Periodicals; Social Indicators—Periodicals; Economic History— 1971–1990—Statistics—Periodicals; Economic History—1990—Statistics—Periodicals)

The World Bank, World Development Indicators 2000 (Washington: The World Bank) 2000.

This book was published to vividly, quantitatively, and accurately illustrate its subject. Colored charts are given that easily show data for comparisons to be made. The book was developed by a collaboration of over 90 countries with a goal of increasing the statistical accuracy of reported data. The span of the book includes data beginning in 1980.

HC 59.69 .S67
(Economic Indicators—Developing Countries—Periodicals; Social Indicators—Developing Countries—Periodicals)

Social Indicators of Development (Baltimore: World Bank)

This work attempts to address the most urgent problem currently confronting the World Bank and its member countries: how to alleviate poverty. Priority Poverty Indicators (PPIs), presented in the Bank's Poverty Reduction Handbook, are shown on the first page of every country's table. Priority Poverty Indicators are employed for checking extents and trends in poverty and, together with associated social factors, give a framework for estimating human welfare in low- and middle-income countries. "Supplementary poverty indicators" has access to, expenditure on, and coverage of social security for basic public goods such as health care and clean drinking water.

The economies shown in the country pages consist of both bank members and nonmembers, highlighting a broad range of political, social, economic, and cultural conditions. New modifications in national boundaries influence the presentation of data in some ways. The technical notes and demographic parameters are an essential section of this report. Readers are encouraged to read them before attempting to derive conclusions from the data.

HC 59.69 .W93 (Developing Countries—Economic Conditions; Developmental Economies; Developing Countries—Economic Policy)

Pleskovic, Boris and Stiglitz, Joseph. Annual World Book Conference on Developing Economies (Washington DC: World Bank)

This four-part work examines developmental policy and the global economy. Part one examines the role of geography in development. Parts two and three provide info on developing countries dealing with competition, regulatory policy, and financial market liberalization. Part four details ethnic conflicts and what steps can be taken to avoid them for the good of the economy of the world.

HC 59.7 .A1W93 (Economic Development—Periodicals; Developing Countries—Economic Conditions—Periodicals)

World Development Report (New York: Oxford
University Press)

This report sets out to explain how there can be unusual differences in labor outcomes in different parts of the world and how sound policy choices can result in changing the lives of workers for the better.

Part 1 examines the long-run development experiences of various countries from the view of what impact they have on workers. This is achieved through analysis of the relationship between the determinants of growth and policies affecting demand for labor and human resource development as well as the relationship between inequality and the path of development.

Part 2 evaluates the effects of ongoing international developments for workers while emphasizing their probable future course. Part 3 looks at the role of government policy in labor markets and assesses what kinds of policies are applicable in an increasingly open and democratic world. Part 4 investigates the consequences for workers in countries that are experiencing economic reform as they move away from central planning to market systems, and from protectionism to openness.

HC 59.7 .I43 (Economic Development—Periodicals; Industrialization—Periodicals; Developing Countries— Industries—Periodicals)

Industry and Development: Global Report
(New York: United Nations)

This annual report focuses on the dynamics of our global industrial economy. The major areas of investigation include economic growth as it relates to human well-being, the extent of industrialization, analysis of 13 manufacturing industries, technological and environmental impacts, and the emergence of large trading blocks. Short-term economic forecasts are provided for the entire global economy, as well as for 10 specified geographic regions. Charts, maps, and graphs are used for a clear presentation of the statistical data. This information is especially helpful for industrial and governmental decision-makers.

HC 60 .1625 (Economic Assistance—Abstracts; Technical Assistance—Abstracts)

World Bank Research Program: Abstracts of Current Studies (Washington: World Bank) 1992.

This book deals with World Bank research programs aimed at generating results that are pertinent across countries and regions. The main objectives of the research are to assess the progress of member countries, clarify the development process, measure the effectiveness of the bank's ability to give advice, and nurture research ability within member countries. The information is presented in abstract form and grouped by research objective headings. The programs cover topics from poverty and the environment to trade, economic management, and urban development. Each abstract includes the project's objectives, techniques, and discoveries. A list of other helpful publications, the project's date, and the researchers' names are supplied as well. The work is supplemented by an appendix, which lists other publications produced as a result of this research.

HC79 .I5 N27 1988/89 (Statistik Pendapatan Nasional—Periodicals)

National Accounts Statistics, Analysis of Main Aggregates (New York: United Nations)

This source shows detailed national accounts estimates for 184 countries and areas. Information prepared by the Statistical Division of the Department for Economic and Social Information and Policy Analysis of the United Nations Secretariat with data supplied by national statistical services. National account estimate data are presented in table format under four main headings: summary information; final expenditures on gross domestic product: detailed breakdowns and supporting tables; institutional sector accounts: detailed flow accounts; and production by kind of activity: detailed breakdown and supporting tables. Each heading is divided into smaller headings and those into more detailed ones. The reference source is issued in accordance with the directive by the Statistical Commission that only recent available information on national accounts be regularly published for all countries and areas. Updated by the United Nations Monthly Bulletin of Statistics.

HC 79 .T4 H63
(High Technology Industries—United States—Directories;
High Technology Industries—United States—Statistics)

Jacob, Susan. High Technology Corporate Affiliations Market
Place Guide (Middlebush: Princeton Hightech Group)

This work, divided into five parts, provides information on high-technology
industries. Part one gives a ranking of companies based on their sales and
market position. Part two has product shipment information. Part three
showing import and export statistics. Part four shows a list of the leading
companies in terms of their exports. Part five is a list of data of the leading
producers in 10 major sections of high-technology industries. Also included
are eight sections of information on some of these companies and their place
within the international business hierarchy.

HC 79 .T4 H64 (High Technology Industries—Directories;
High Technology—Marketing—Directories; Biotechnology—
Marketing—Directories; Robotics—Marketing—Directories)

Jacob, Susan. High Technology Marketplace Directory
(Middlebush: Princeton Hightech Group)

This work, divided into three parts, has information on the emerging technology sector of companies in both the United States and the rest of the world.
Part one provides information ranked by sales or market position of companies in 19 different types of technology. Part two gives profiles on businesses
both public and private with their websites, financial data, and industry type
along with many other pieces of information about their company. Part three
provides indexes of high-technology companies ranked by five different
indicators including net sales, SIC code, and geography. Also included is an
index of SIC codes and their meanings.

HC 101 .A13 (Commerce Statistics—Periodicals; United
States—Economic Conditions—Periodicals)

Business Statistics (Washington, DC: US Government
Printing Office)

This guide, written by the U.S. Department of Commerce, provides statistical
data of approximately 2100 series for the years 1963–1991. Information is
drawn from public and private sources. An appendix describing historical

data for selected series and an index describing quarterly statistics for selected series are also included.

HC 101 .A14 (Industries—United States)

United States Department of Commerce, County Business Patterns (Washington DC: United States Printing Office)

This 53-volume work chronicles county business patterns for every county in the United States and its territories. For each state, there are 10 sections covering sources of data, geographic classifications, abbreviations, symbols, and maps. There is also a section of data tables for the state as a whole and then the breakdown of statistics on a county-by-county basis.

HC 101 .A45
(Economic Indicators—United States—Periodicals;
Social Indicators—United States—Periodicals; Metropolitan
Indicators—United States—Statistics—Periodicals)

ACCRA Community Profiles (Charlotte: ACCRA)

This work, divided into six sections, provides economic information on counties across the United States. Section one provides the reader with an introduction and background to the purpose this work tries to accomplish. Section two gives background information on the members of ACCRA. Section three shows rankings for selected counties included in this periodical. Sections four, five, and six provide summary reports for counties, metropolitan areas, and states. Also included are six sections of appendices with information on community profiles and FIPS code lists.

HC 101 .C75 (Consumption (Economics)—United States—
Periodicals; United States—Manufactures—Periodicals;
Market Surveys—United States—Periodicals)

Euromonitor, Consumer U.S.A. (London: Euromonitor)

This work, divided into three sections, provides data on the consumption habits of the consumers of the United States. Section one provides the reader with an overview of the market and economy of the United States. Section two shows parameters and indicators of marketing. Section three summarizes the 15 largest markets for consumer goods. Included are over 1100 tables showing figures on consumption of major products.

HC 101 .C85 2000
(Cities and Towns—United States; Statistics—Periodicals; United States—Economic Conditions)

Gaquin, Deidre A., and Katherine A. DeBrandt, Eds. 2000 County
and City Extra: Metro, City and County. Ninth edition
(White Plains, New York: Bernan Press)

Statistical data are segmented into counties, states, and congressional districts. The text includes information from cities and towns with a population
of over 25,000 residents in 1990. A separate volume contains cities and towns
with a population of under 25,000 residents in 1990. The 1997 Economic
Census is presented for the first time with this volume. This source can be
considered authoritative because of its constant updating for statistical
accuracy.

HC 101 .C85 (Cities and Towns—United States—Statistics—
Periodicals; United States—Economic Conditions—
Statistics—Periodicals)

Gaquin, Deirdre and DeBrandt, Katherine. 2000 County and City
Extra (Lanham: Bernan Press)

This work, divided into five tables and six appendices, provides information
on many statistics of the United States. The five tables, separating data by
states, counties, metropolitan areas, cities, and congressional districts, provide data on trade, income, population, health care, crime, employment, and
many others. The six appendices give maps and graphs showing the separation of counties, districts, and their regions.

HC 101 .S77
(Securities—Prices—United States—Statistics—Periodicals; Stocks—Prices—United States—Statistics—Periodicals)

Statistical Service (New York, NY: Standard & Poor's)

The first section of this statistical reference is composed of current and basic
statistics. The current statistics record daily high, low, and close of the
Standard & Poor's stock price index for a full 12-month period. Also included
are indexes by industrial groups for the same 12-month period. Following are
the basic statistics that provide data on banking and finance, productions and
price indexes, labor statistics, income, and trade. Basic statistics depend on
the industry, but generally include prices, production, exports and imports,
and costs. Banking and financial basic statistics cover interest rates, exchange
rates, and government securities. Industrial groupings follow the basic

statistics. These record industry activity such as production, earnings, and trade as well as employment statistics such as number of employees, hours worked, and payroll. Cost of living indexes are also recorded. Finally, stock price indexes aim to record the pattern of the common stock price movement. This collection of data is divided into industry group indexes that can be used to compare individual stocks within each group. Data for the whole economy (all industries together) completes the first section.

Indexes are broken down into weekly, monthly, and yearly tables. Additional statistics are given on quarterly earnings, dividends, and price-earning ratios. In the latter half of the price index supplement are daily stock price indexes, Dow Jones stock price averages, New York Stock Exchange daily stock sales (1922–present), as well as New York Stock Exchange monthly stock transactions (1885–present). Information on bonds is also provided. This includes monthly transactions, weekly indexes, U.S. government bond yields, and municipal bond yield indexes.

HC 102 .E56 (Industries—United States—Encyclopedias)

Kevin Hillstrom, Ed. Encyclopedia of American Industries
(Detroit, MI: Gale Research) 1994.

The *Encyclopedia of American Industries* is comprised of two volumes. Volume one contains in-depth essays of 460 manufacturing industries. Volume two contains individual essays on 544 service and nonmanufacturing industries. Every industry, with a U.S. Governmental Standard Industrial Classification (SIC) code is represented. The essays may contain historical information, organization, industry leaders, and a bibliography for further reading. The Encyclopedia contains two indexes. The General Index is an index to all key associations, companies, government agencies, and specific legislation mentioned. For example, the passage of the Food, Drug, and Cosmetic Act of 1938 is indexed. The Industry Index is an index to business services and products offered in the United States. SIC codes are included.

HC 102.2 .I43 1998 (Information Industry Association— Directories; Information Services—Directories)

Lewon, Paul, Ed. Information Sources (Washington: Information Industry Association)

This book lists companies with membership in the Information Industry Association. The groups included have over 550 members that actively participate in logistics of information. The members listed range from entrepreneurial companies to Fortune 500 corporations. The members included are in areas such as publishing, telecommunications, finance, and the Internet.

Special groups and committees are established focusing on specific areas such as public policy, marketing, and global strategies.

HC 102.2 .M65 2000
(Industries—United States—Directories; Corporations—United States—Directories; Industrialists—Directories)

Dun and Bradstreet Million Dollar Directory: America's Leading Public & Private Companies (Bethlehem, Pennsylvania: Dun and Bradstreet)

This book is a directory of companies that meet the criteria to be included. The first criterion regards the number of employees. The second criterion concerns sales volume. The sales volume of the company must be at least $9,000,000. Listed in the book are over 160,000 companies in the United States from a broad range of industries. The book is published in five volumes: three volumes called Series A–Z, a series cross-reference by geography, and series cross-reference by industry.

HC 102.5 .A2 I521 1994
(Afro-Americans in Business—Biography—Dictionaries)

Ingham, John N. African-American Business Leaders: A Biographical Dictionary (Westport, Conn.: Greenwood) 1994.

This work gives rich biographical information for 123 individuals in America from early days to the present with particular emphasis on the period 1880–World War II. The author has also noted the availability of archival material to facilitate in-depth study. A bibliographic essay at the end of the volume aids the reader in contextualizing the biographies in terms of history, writings on Blacks in the main cities covered, and within relevant industries. Some very important areas are given rather light coverage: New England, Cleveland, Detroit, and Buffalo. It should be noted that although 123 individuals are covered, there are only 77 entries. This is because individuals are sometimes grouped together on the basis of family or business association.

HC 102.5 .A2 H22 1999
(Businesspeople—United States—Biography—Dictionaries)

Hamilton, Neil. American Business Leaders: From Colonial Times to the Present (Santa Barbara, California: ABC-CLIO, Inc.) 1999.

This book covers over 400 men and women that helped to create the national economy. Biographical information and his or her contributions to economic development are both included. The choice of whom to involve included prominent and influential leaders. The individuals are taken from various careers such as finance, banking, entertainment, communications, and technology.

HC 102.5 .A2 L371 1985
(Women Executives—United States—Biography)

Leavitt, Judith A. American Women Managers and Administrators: A Selective Biographical Dictionary of Twentieth-Century Leaders in Business, Education, and Government (Westport, Conn.: Greenwood Press) 1985.

This exemplary work identifies and profiles 226 women who have achieved prominence as managers, administrators, and leaders. Although a number of the women profiled were born in the early to mid-19th century, the emphasis is on 20th-century figures. About half of the entries represent women who were "firsts." The author expresses the aim of holding up these women as role models for girls and young women beginning careers, and offers it as a reference tool for public libraries and school libraries at every level. The alphabetically arranged biographies average about a page in length and most them are followed by bibliographies of writings about and by the subjects. An appendix classifies the biographies as follows: firsts, founders, presidents, vice-presidents of major corporations, positions of national prominence. The general bibliography is divided into the areas of business, education, and government. The Index primarily consists of name, but also includes organizations.

HC 103 .E12 1996 (Economic Indicators—United States; United States—Economic Conditions)

Darnay, Arsen, Compiler and Editor. Economic Indicators Handbook: Times Series, Conversions, Documentation, 3rd Edition (Detroit: Gale)

This is a major compact resource for 254 statistical series useful for economic measurement in the United States grouped as follows: GNP 1869–1995 and GDP 1959–1995, business cycle indicators, cyclic indicators (leading, coincident, and lagging), economic series, prices (consumer and producer—in great detail), selected stock market indexes. Numerous subdivisions result in a collection of 792 tables. Clear and succinct explanations precede and accompany illustrative material. Text and tables are both thoroughly covered in the keyword index.

HC 103 .F91 (Economic Indicators—United States; Business Cycles—United States—Statistics; United States—Economic Conditions—Statistics)

Frumkin, Norman. Guide to Economic Indicators
(Armonk, NY: M.E. Sharpe)

This book is designed to help people without specialized training in economics to make sense of the main characteristics of economic indicators they are likely to encounter in reading of magazines and newspapers. Toward that end, it concisely describes more than 60 economic indicators. While it emphasizes those developed by U.S. government agencies, it also includes those coming from private and international organizations. The introduction provides guidance for understanding how these indicators are used as well as their interpretation and evaluation. The text is supplemented by many tables and includes references from primary data sources.

HC 103.R66
(United States—Industries—History; Business Enterprises—United States—History; Businessmen—United States—History; Women in Business—United States—History)

Robinson, Richard. United States Business History, 1602–1988
(New York: Greenwood Press) 1990.

This chronology of business presents a calendar of representative events that took place in the evolution of business in the United States. The historical data are classified into two categories: General events and Business events. General events gives an overall background of business by showing changes in living conditions and lifestyles for possible impacts on the marketplace. Business events are those that depict the rise and fall of enterprises engaged in producing goods and/or providing services.

HC 106 .A1 E18

OECD Economic Surveys

This book attempts to address the economic concerns of the major countries of the world. The book briefly reviews recent supply and demand trends in Part I; the stance of monetary policy is analyzed in Part II. Part III deals with fiscal policy, while part IV discusses the prospects for medium-term adjustment of external imbalances. Part V reviews developments in U.S. industrial and trade competitiveness. Conclusions are presented in Part VI.

HC 106 .J66 (United States—Economic Conditions—Statistics Services—Handbooks, Manuals, etc.)

Johnson, David B. Finding and Using Economic Information (Mountain View, CA: Mayfield Publishing Co.) 1993.

This book is intended to explain how to interpret and explain the plethora of economic data that is produced daily. It is intended for anyone who needs or chooses to interact with economic data, and is arranged and written very simply. The first two chapters contain useful information about data series and how they are constructed as well as other important information about the collection of data. Subsequent chapters are organized by major topics such as national income, money, credit, and interest rates; financial markets and instruments; capital markets: price indices; labor markets; and regional, international, and commercial economic data. At the beginning of each chapter is a "Read Me First" section that provides an overview and possibly some analysis of the data series in that chapter. The major topics and the data series within them are arranged in alphabetical order. If you need to look up a particular term, the Table of Contents or Index will help. There is also a "Quick Look" section that summarizes the data series and explains the terms and numbers used in the series. The "Closer Look" section provides a minicourse on the data series and the subjects that relate to it. There is also information on historic data that is helpful.

HC 106.5 .A3 (United States—Economic Conditions; United States—Economic Policy)

Council of Economic Advisors. The Economic Report of the President (Washington DC: United States Government Printing Office) 2000.

This reference work, divided into two sections, provides information on the state of the economy of the United States from the perspectives of both the president and his council of economic advisors. Included are chapters sustaining the record-breaking economy, economic policy, technology, the global economy, and changes that are occurring. Also included is an appendix of statistical tables relating to income, employment, and production.

HC 106.5 .A22 (United States—Industries)

U.S. Industrial Outlook (Washington, DC: U.S. Department of Commerce, Industry and Trade)

Annually published, this work provides industry review and forecasts. It offers overviews of research and development, public policy, product manufacturing, shipping, and consumption. Tables containing 5 years of data provide additional information on trends and forecasts for each industry group.

Short-term forecasts begin each chapter and are followed by descriptions of the industries discussed in the chapter. Domestic market concerns constitute a major section of each chapter. These concerns include rates of change, trends and developments, product research, and public policy issues and legislation affecting the industry market. In some cases, such as advanced technologies, the dependence on Federal Government funding is also discussed. Finally, international trade or competitiveness is examined. International trade concerns include trade agreements, rates of exchange, joint research, trade barriers, and licensing agreements.

HC 106.6 .A88 (United States—Economic Conditions—Maps; Economic Forecasting—United States—Maps; Population Forecasting—United States—Maps; United States—Population—Maps; United States—Economic Conditions—Statistics; Economic Forecasting—United States—Statistics; Population Forecasting—United States—Statistics; United States—Population—Statistics)

NPA Data Services. An Atlas of U.S. Economy, Technology, and Growth (Washington, DC: NPA Data Services) 1996.

This reference work, divided into five chapters, provides information on the economy and future of the United States. Chapter one provides data on the geographic structure and growth of the economy. Chapter two provides statistics on jobs and earnings. Chapter three gives a composition of population and population change. Chapter four shows the effects of science and technology on regional economies, and chapter five shows housing and government expenditures. Provided in each chapter are maps and data tables pertinent to the information included within. Also included are appendices of states, counties, and relevant important definitions.

HC 106.6 .S74 (United States—Industries)

Standard & Poor's Industry Surveys (New York, NY: Standard & Poor's)

Distributed by the Standard & Poor's Corporation, this two-volume reference guide is divided into basic and current analyses covering major industries. Each industry's basic analysis contains information concerning trends and statistical tables including a comparative company analysis. It also deals with specific details and prospects for each industry. The current analysis supplies the most recent developments along with statistics for each industry and company.

Updated quarterly, the Earnings Supplement provides current revenue and earning lists for companies. Company rankings are also listed. Another supplement concerns trends and projections of the economy as a whole.

HC 106.6 .S77

Standard and Poor's Industry Surveys

Industry Surveys provide data on industries and hundreds of companies. A *Basic Survey* published each year is supplemented by *Current Surveys* published three times a year. In the *Basic Surveys*, the industries are discussed within the context of their future in the economy. In the discussion of the financial condition of the industries and their companies, charts and tables are provided. The Current Surveys describe recent developments and make projections. The latter provides information on sales, profits, dividends, and recommendations on investments for various companies. Another part of the *Industry Surveys* is the *Trends and Projections Bulletin*. Not only are leading economic indicators evaluated, but many projections are included. In charts, trends are presented on bond and treasury note yields, employment, housing, production, and sales.

HC 106.6 .S79 (United States—Industries—Periodicals)

Standard and Poor's Industry Surveys (New York: Standard and Poor's)

This guide, published in two volumes, provides information concerning all major domestic industries. A Basic Analysis and a Current Analysis are given for each industry. An industry's Basic Analysis discusses the prospects, trends, and problems for that industry. Statistical data supports the text. An industry's Current Analysis details the most recent developments in that industry and provides updated statistical figures. S&P analysts discuss the investment prospects for that industry. An Earnings Supplement, listing the latest revenues and earnings of more than 1000 companies, is also included.

HC 106.7 .B965 (Economic Forecasting—United States— Statistics; Economic Forecasting—California—Statistics; United States—Economic Conditions—Statistics; California—Economic Conditions—Statistics)

Leamer, Edward E. The UCLA Anderson Forecast (Los Angeles: University of California) 2000.

This reference work, produced quarterly by the University of California-Los Angeles, provides information on the economic well-being and future of both

California and the United States. Included are charts of recent evidence to support claims made, and forecasts for the future. Also included are charts summarizing the information along with a section of detailed data that was less-thoroughly explored in earlier chapters.

HC 106.8 A53 (Economic Indicators—United States; Economic Forecasting—United States; United States—Economic Conditions)

The Ameritrust / SRI Indicators of Economic Capacity

This publication studies economic conditions of the geographic regions of the United States in regards to human resources and economic output. Regions are assessed in the areas of: (1) Accessible Technology—the number of colleges and universities conducting industrial research; (2) Labor—quality and educational levels of the work force; and (3) Capital Availability—potential capital from financial institutions and state initiatives.

Indicators of each region are graphed and ranked accordingly. Further sections examine regions in detail, outlining strengths and weaknesses. Appendices contain regional comparison tables and state scores.

HC 106.8 .H24
(United States—Economic Conditions—1981—Statistical Services—Handbooks, Manuals, etc.; Economics— Statistical Services—Handbooks, Manuals, etc.; Finance—Statistical Services—Handbooks, Manuals, etc.; United States—Statistical Services—Handbooks, Manuals, etc.)

Fabozzi, Frank and Greenfield, Harry. The Handbook of Economic and Financial Measures (Homewood, IL: Dow Jones-Irwin) 1984.

This handbook originates from the authors' observation that business and financial reporting in the media is becoming more sophisticated resulting in the creation of an information gap. Further clarification in the measures of economic activity of gross national product is needed. The measures of economic activity that are most probably encountered in business reporting are selected. Professionals who are familiar with the material were asked to provide in-depth explanations of the background, construction, and uses of these measures. On the whole, the level of exposition is neither too technical nor too simple.

HC 106.8 .K44
(United States—Economic Conditions—Statistics; Economic Forecasting—United States—Statistics)

NPA Data Services, Key Indicators of County Growth 1970–2025 (Washington DC: NPA Data Services) 1998.

The reference work, divided into two sections, gives key economic data meant to help indicate the amount of growth that counties have experienced and will experience in the future. Part one provides descriptions of the selection of indicators, methods of preparation, and different dimensions of county growth. Part two is comprised mostly of data tables meant to back up the assumptions made in part one. Included are many maps with color overlays to exhibit growth factors, earnings, population, and many other pieces of information. Also included are two appendices with metropolitan statistical areas and state maps to show the individual counties.

HC 106.8 .M34
(United States—Economic Conditions—1981—Statistics; Income—United States—Statistics; Industrial Surveys— United States; Market Surveys—United States)

Conroy, Thomas F. Markets of the United States for Business Planners (Detroit: Omnigraphics) 1996.

This work, divided into 183 sections, based on geographic location profiles the 183 most important markets in the United States on the basis of both production and spending. Within each section is a short, one-page description of the area, with special notice being given to the area's composition, growth, and economic base. Also included are tables and graphs showing the area's economic profile, most dynamic industries, and indices of change.

HC 106.8 .M4311 1991
(United States—Industries—Handbooks, Manuals, etc.)

Mattera, Philip. Inside U.S. Business: A Concise Encyclopedia of Leading Industries (Homewood, IL: Business One Irwin) 1991.

In this one-volume encyclopedia, the author provides basic information on a selection of industries based within the United States. It is intended to provide an orientation to major industries and give guidelines for further research and analysis. He chooses industries important to the American economy that can be discussed in general terms. He pays special attention to the changing nature of industries brought about by new technologies, mergers, and foreign competitions.

Each chapter covers the history of the industry; latest trends in competition, technology, and government regulation; information about leading firms of the industry; and information about the state of labor relations. A source guide to further information lists the industry's leading stock experts, trade associations, and unions, and provides a brief bibliography including directories, on-line databases, trade publications, and books. Also included are charts giving the leading companies of the industry with their yearly revenues and, in some cases, industry-wide revenues or leading brands.

The book is divided into six sections containing chapters for separate industries. Sections and chapters include communications (book publishing, broadcasting, film and video, newspapers and magazines, telecommunications); consumer goods and services (beverages, cigarettes, drugs and health care, retailing, restaurants and hotels, casinos, apparel); electronics (computers, semiconductors); energy (coal, nuclear power, electric utilities, oil, natural gas); finance (banks, stocks, venture capital); and heavy industry and . transportation (airlines, automotive, steel, aerospace, military contracting). A proper-name index listing people and companies mentioned in the text is included.

HC106.8 .O36
(Economic Indicators—United States—Handbooks, Manuals)

O'Hara, Frederick M. Handbook of United States Economic and Financial Indicators (Westport, CT: Greenwood Press)

This work presents information on important economic and financial indicators and functions as a reference tool for researchers, librarians, and economists who need answers concerning indicator types and how to discover their current and historic worth. The 200 economic measures come from 55 sources. Entries are arranged in alphabetical order and each consists of no more than nine elements: indicator name or names; indicator description; indicator derivation or how it is produced; indicator's use; the indicator's publisher or compiler; the source from which the indicator's values appeared; frequency in which the statistics are published; a cumulative historical listing of all national publications that continually publish or project the indicator; and a bibliography consisting of general and technical works that direct users to more information. Three appendixes complement the main entries: Non-quantitative Indicators; Abbreviations List and Guide to Sources; and List of Compilers of Indicators. Indexed.

**HC 106.8 .S79 1995 (Economic Forecasting—United States—
Statistics; Social Prediction—United States—Statistics;
United States—Economic Conditions—Forecasting—
Statistical; United States—Social Conditions—Forecasting—
Statistical Methods; United States—Economic Conditions—
Statistics; United States—Social Conditions—Statistics)**

Pollock Sean R., Editor. Statistical Forecasts of the United States,
2nd Edition (New York: Gale Research) 1995.

Statistics offer a useful source for making sense of the past, the present, and
the future. Using material from governmental, corporate, and private sources,
the book presents such information in more than 800 tables, charts, graphs,
and short narratives. The 14 major topics covered are further subdivided into
subtopics so as to present an extremely broad picture of aspects the future
in the United States. A subject index and index of forecasts by year help the
reader through this vast terrain of information.

**HC 106.82 .U84 (Industries—United States—Statistics—
Periodicals; Industries—United States—Forecasting—
Periodicals; United States—Commerce—Statistics—
Periodicals; United States—Commerce—
Forecasting—Periodicals)**

U.S. Department of Commerce, U.S. Global Trade Outlook
1995–2000 (Washington DC: United States Government
Printing Office) 1995.

This reference work, divided into two main sections, provided information on
the state of the United States export market from 1995 to 2000. The first
section assesses our best markets, and looked to see which of the markets can,
and will be, the most profitable for exporters. Also in this section is a list of
markets that are expected to be emerging over the specified time period. The
second section chronicles expanding opportunities for industries. Included in
this section is a list of expanding industries that include computer equipment,
medical supplies, motor vehicles, automotive parts, and paper products. At
the end of this work are three appendices that provide economic and trade
data by country, and foreign trade highlights.

HC 110 .C3 C83 (Capital Costs—United States—Statistics)

Ibbotson Associates, Cost of Capital (Chicago: Ibbotson
Associates) 2000.

This reference work provides data on the cost of capital to businesses in
different industries. Included is information that helps to perform discounted

cash flow analysis. Financial information included are revenues, profitability, returns, ratios, capital structure, cost of equity, and the average cost of capital. Also included are case studies both real and theoretical. Included are four appendices listing the numerous companies discussed in this edition.

HC 110 .C3 C84 2000
(Capital Costs—United States—Statistics)

Ibbotson Associates, Cost of Capital (Chicago: Ibbotson Associates) 2000.

Standard & Poor's Compustat provides most of the data contained in this text. The book has information on areas in revenues, equity returns, and other industry-related financial sectors. The text is useful in providing discount rates for cash flow and pricing of securities.

HC 110 .C6 M68 (Consumers—United States—Statistics;
United States—Population—Statistics)

Mitchell, Susan. American Generations (Ithaca: New Strategist Publications) 1998.

This work provides data on many of the critical areas of the economy of the 20th century. Divided into 11 sections, this work provides information on generations, attitudes, education, health, household, housing, income, labor force, population, spending, and wealth. Included within each section are highlights of each spectrum of data, and tables showing the pertinence of these data to the economy as a whole. Also included is a glossary of relevant terms, and an index of included information.

HC 110 .C6 M72 (Consumers—United States—Statistics;
Consumption (Economics)—United States—Statistics;
Consumers' Preferences—United States—Statistics; Food
Industry and Trade—United States; Alcoholic Beverage
Industry—United States; Consumer Behavior)

Mogelonsky, Marcia. Who's Buying Food and Drink (Ithaca: New Strategists Publications) 1996.

This work, divided into nine sections, provides data on the spending habits of individuals. Chapter one provides a spending overview. Chapters two to nine provide information on spending based on age, income, household type, region, race, education, and occupation, respectively. Included in each section is an analysis of each group, market shares, and indexes. Also included is an appendix of how each of the groups' spending habits has changed over time.

HC 110 .C6 W45 (Consumers—United States—Statistics; Consumption (Economics)—United States—Statistics; Consumers' Preferences—United States—Statistics; Consumer Behavior)

Wellner, Allsion Stein. Who's Buying for the Home (Ithaca: New Strategist Publications) 1996.

This reference work, divided into 17 sections, looks to chronicle the spending habits of Americans on different types of goods. Chapter one gives a spending overview. Chapters two through seventeen provide data on how much is spent on shelter, utilities, and household operations, with each category cross-referenced by age, income, race, education, and occupation. Also included are two appendices that show how such information was gathered, and descriptions of complex economic principles.

HC 110 .C63 B98 (Consumer Protection—United States— Societies, etc.—Directories; Consumer Education—United States—Societies, etc.—Directories)

Bykerk, Loree. U.S. Consumer Interest Groups (Westport: Greenwood Publishing) 1995.

This reference work chronicles the largest consumer interest groups in the United States. For each interest group discussed, there is a list of the organization and resources, the policy concerns, and the tactics used by each group. Also included is an appendix of these groups and contact information for each of them.

HC 110.D5 E71 (Cities and Towns—United States— Handbook, Manual, etc.; Quality of Life—United States—Handbooks, Manuals, etc.; United States— Industries—Location—Handbooks, Manuals, etc.)

The Ernst & Young Almanac and Guide to U.S. Business Cities: 65 Leading Places to Do Business. Ed. Michael L. Evans and Barry M. Barovick, Ed. (New York: J. Wiley) 1994.

The *Ernst & Young Almanac and Guide to U.S. Business Cities* is a compilation of financial, economical, and social data on metropolitan areas. The purpose of the guide is to evaluate major cities, using socioeconomic, regulatory, and social indicators to help businesses determine good locations for their base operations or branch offices. The book is composed of two major sections and includes an introduction and appendices as well as notes. The introduction describes how the data were compiled and has a detailed bibliography. The appendices and notes provide a breakdown of tax and property issues.

The first major section provides seven regional overviews and city profiles within each. The profiles of the cities contain data on population, labor and employment, education, tax rates and real estate costs, and quality of life indicators. The second section provides detailed methods of analysis for choosing business locations and describes recent trends for specific regions. The analyses describe strategic planning processes, site selection criteria, housing affordability, and trends in U.S. corporate relocation. The guide also includes a subject index and lists state and city names.

HC110. H53 C82

CorpTech Directory of Technology Companies (Wellesley Hills, MA: Corporate Technology Information Services)

The *CorpTech Directory* is an annual compilation of profiles of technological companies and allows its users to search under names of companies, geographical locations, product types manufactured, and names of parent companies outside of the United States. At the bottom of each applicable page is a list of code descriptions. Volume one contains a glossary of abbreviations and acronyms, a technological industry analyses, and indexes. The indexes are categorized as business and products. The former includes a Company Name Finder, a Geographical Index, and a Non-US Parent Company Index. The latter comprises Technology Index, Who Makes What Index, CorpTech Code Index, Company Rankings, and the SIC to CorpTech Code Translation Table. Volumes two, three, and four consist of corporate reports arranged in alphabetical order. The outlines list the companies' names, starting dates, addresses, phone and fax numbers, ownerships, manufactured products, annual sales, numbers of employees, names of executives, and Standard Industrial Classification product descriptions.

HC 110 .I5 A31 (Gross National Product—United States— Statistics; National Income—United States—Statistics)

National Income and Products Accounts of the United States (Washington, DC: U.S. Department of Commerce, Economics, and Statistics Administration)

This reference guide provides statistics relating to the national income of the United States and the gross national product. The text is divided into nine categories of statistical tables. Section one, national product and income, is a summation of all the goods and services provided in the United States. Section two is made up of personal income from wages and investments and outlays statistics. Section three, government receipts and expenditures, is a collection of government transfer payment, net interest paid, dividends received, subsidies, and wage accruals data, and the sum of these receipts. Section four contains statistics on net foreign investment including, exports, factor income, capital grants, and transfer payments. Section five provides data on personal savings, consumption of capital, corporate profits, wage accruals, the overall economic surplus or deficit, capital grants, domestic private investments, and foreign investments. Section six supplies statistics on income, employment, and products by industry. Section seven is a quantity and price index. Section eight is composed of supplementary tables. And section nine provides seasonally unadjusted estimates.

HC 110 .I5 E98 Income Distribution—United States—Statistics; Discretionary Income—United States—Statistics; United States—Economic Conditions—Statistics)

Exter, Thomas G. American Incomes (Ithaca: New Strategist Publications)

This reference work, divided into nine sections, provides information on the income of the American workforce. Chapters one through five give data on the earnings of people in different types of jobs, in different types of households, and ways that income is earned through means other than ordinary jobs. Chapter six gives the highlights of consumer spending, chronicling the spending habits of different types of consumers. Chapter seven shows information on the different amounts of net worth workers accumulate. Chapter eight shows the problems that workers face, and the results that those problems have on their economic stability. Chapter nine provides information on income and poverty based on different geographic regions. Also provided is a glossary of terms pertinent to the understanding of the text.

HC110. I5 R95

Russell, Cheryl L. The Official Guide to American Incomes (Ithaca, NY: New Strategist Publication & Consulting)

This statistical reference work reports on the diversity of American families' incomes and its author has explored the reasons causing these differences, presenting the findings through charts and graphs. The data cover income trends, household incomes, personal incomes, discretionary incomes, household income projections, spending, wealth and poverty trends, as well as geographical trends. Each chapter gives a highlight of the major points of the table in the chapter. A subject index and glossary of terms are also provided. A large percentage of the statistical information has been compiled by the Census Bureau, the Bureau of Labor Statistics, and the Federal Reserve Board.

HC 110 .P63 A88 (Economic Assistance, Domestic—United States—Directories; Economic Assistance, Domestic—United States—States—Directories)

Assistance & Benefits Information Directory (Detroit, MI: Omnigraphics) 1992.

This two-volume reference set acts as a guide to federal and state government programs as well as national organizations that provide aid for individuals. Entries are organized under six major headings, including cultural affairs, education, labor, health services, housing, and the legal system. Volume one provides background information on the programs, including the program's name, the title and address of the organization, a description of the aide, the award amount, eligibility guidelines, application information, and a list of other contacts for the reader's own follow-up inquiry. Volume two focuses on the publications provided by these agencies. The entries include the type of publication and its title, the name and address of the sponsoring agency, a description of the information conveyed, and instructions on how to obtain a copy. Both volumes are supplemented by several exclusive indexes and one all-encompassing index. The goal of these guidebooks is to provide direct accessibility for the consumer. The editors have gathered a collection of the most recent information. However, because of the changing nature of these types of programs, the readers may have to update some of the material on their own.

HC 110 .P63 G72 (Economic Assistance, Domestic—United States—Handbooks, Manuals, etc.; Grants-in-Aid—United States—Handbooks, Manuals, etc.; Administrative Agencies—United States—Handbooks, Manuals, etc.)

Government Assistance Almanac (Washington, DC: Foggy Bottom Publications)

This is a guide on how to obtain financial or nonfinancial assistance from the federal government. There are four parts to the Almanac. Part I makes suggestions on how to use the book and gets the user started on obtaining assistance from the federal government. Part II lists all domestic programs that are available in the most recent years available. Part III shows the amount of funding available for all programs in tables that are unique and only provided in the almanac. It also lists the agencies administering the aid. Part IV gives contact information for field offices. There are more than 3000 of them spread out in 52 different agencies, departments, and bureaus. Then, there are two indexes. A Master Index that includes references, cross-references, and subject headings, and an Agency Index listing all the agencies in alphabetical order. Abbreviations used are defined at the beginning of the book.

HC 110 .P63 G95 (Economic Development—United States— Directories; Economic Development—United States— States—Directories; Industrial Promotion—United States—Directories; Industrial Promotion—United States—States—Directories)

Bartsch, Charles. Financing Manufacturing Efficiency and Growth (Washington, DC: Northeast–Midwest Institute) 1996.

This work, divided into two parts, provides data on the economic development of industries across the United States. Part one gives specific data for the economies of each state, and what type of aid is required to help to spur the growth each economy. Part two supplies data on the state of the federal economy, and shows the economic development programs in place to benefit the country. In each section, there are sections showing the overview of each program, the application of each program, and the effects they have on each geographical area. Included throughout are graphs and tables to give a better understanding of the information shown.

HC111 .A1 M34

Market Research Handbook / Dominion Bureau of Statistics. Merchandising and Services Division = Manuel Statistique Pour Etudes de Marche / Bureau Federal de la Statistique, Divison du Commerce et des Services (Ottawa: Dominion Bureau of Statistics) 1995.

This handbook provides information and references for different levels of Canadian markets: the local, provincial, regional, and national. It is divided into eleven sections. Sections one to six cover data on the national and international markets on manufacturing, labor force, earning and spending, and household facilities. Section seven and eight cover most of the metropolitan markets in Canada. Section nine is devoted to the projection of economic indicators to the year 2016, e.g., price, labor force, investment, unemployment, and population. Explanatory terms and indexes are provided in the last two sections.

HC 241.2 .E97 (European Union—Encyclopedias; European Union—Directories)

The European Union Encyclopedia and Directory
(London: Europa Publications) 1999.

This reference work provides a comprehensive guide to the European Union and the historical information behind its founding. Part one provides pertinent information, giving definitions important to fully understand the European Union. Part two gives essays written about the European Union written by top scholars from across Europe. Part three is a directory of the European Union showing the offices behind the important aspects of its administration. Part four shows a statistical survey of the European Union with information on demographics, industries, and trade.

HC 241.2 .S47 (Associations, Institutions, etc.—European Union Countries—Directories; European Communities—Directories)

Serving the European Union (Luxembourg: Office for the
Official Publications of the European Communities) 1996.

This short reference work gives a full spectrum view of the inner workings of the European Union. Meant to take the reader through every aspect of how the European union works, this work goes into fine detail in areas such as the European Commission, the European Court of Auditors, and the Economic and Social Committee. Within each section is vital information about each office, providing data on each member, and the true function of the office as a whole. Also provided is a color-coded map and a list of useful addresses.

HC 244 .A1 C12 (Council for Mutual Economic Assistance; Communist Countries—Statistics)

Vienna Institute for Comparative Economic Studies,
COMECON Data—1989 (London: MacMillan Academic
and Professional Ltd.) 1990.

This source is a comprehensive handbook of statistical data covering production and distribution, foreign trade, foreign indebtedness, domestic finance, energy, and standards of living in Eastern Europe (including the former Yugoslavia) and the Soviet Union. The information is drawn from original language publications all over Eastern Europe and the USSR and is compiled by many international organizations. The names of the organizations are listed in the "Register of Sources." Many of the tables having to do with foreign trade and debt and import and export matters are provided by Reuters.

Sample tables or graphs are "Net material product in Poland, Romania and MCEA; Average rate of annual growth in %," "Exports and Imports by Region," "Debt," and "Consumption and Retail Trade Turnover." Indexes are included.

HC 244 .A1 C74
(Communist Countries—Economic Conditions—Periodicals)

Center for Research into Communist Economies, Communist Economies and Economic Transformation (Oxfordshire, UK: Carfax Publishing)

This source is a quarterly publication studying the central issues in the changing economies of Eastern Europe. Contributors to the journal include scholars from Europe and the United States. Selections are extensive, research-based studies of such subjects as privatization, taxation, and the capital market. Tables and charts are included and complete bibliographies follow each piece. An annual index is included in the December issue.

HC 244 .A1 E12
(Eastern Europe—Economic Conditions—Periodicals;
Eastern Europe—History—Periodicals; Marketing—
Europe—Periodicals)

Marketing in Europe (London: Economist Intelligence Unit)

This source presents detailed reports on consumer product markets in Belgium, France, Italy, the Netherlands, and Germany. Other markets in Europe are presented occasionally. Each issue begins with background information on the European Community member states, presenting statistics on area and population, gross domestic product, and consumer prices and exchange rates. This is followed by a synopsis of the issue's contents. A trade review is included in each issue and it deals with broad product sections in the five permanent countries covering production, trade, and significant trends and features of the market. Also, usually included are three market surveys that provide an analysis of specific consumer goods for national markets, production, brand shares, consumption, distribution, exports and imports, market policy, profiles of leading producers and brands, trends and prospects, as well as the occasional detailed study on retail distribution and leading retailer profiles. An index of previous market surveys is contained at the end of each issue. There are three different product groups and each one is published four times a year. Group one is food, drink, and tobacco; group two is clothing, furniture, and leisure goods; and group three is chemists' goods, household goods, and domestic appliances. A cumulative index is separately published.

HC 244 .A1 E13
(Europe, Eastern—Economic Conditions—Periodicals)

Eastern European Economics: A Journal of Translations
(New York, NY: M.E. Sharpe)

East European Economics is a quarterly publication containing articles translated from economic journals of Eastern Europe. Selections are unabridged and focus on current developments in the economic theory and practice of Eastern Europe. Articles are lengthy and detailed, with tables, figures, and a reference to the original source of publication. Journal contents are indexed by the Social Sciences Index and PAIS Bulletin and are listed in Current Contents: Behavioral, Social, and Educational Sciences, and Contents of Recent Economic Journals.

HC 331 .A85 (Comparative Economics—Periodicals;
Communist Countries—Economic Conditions—Periodicals)

Comparative Economic Studies (Lake Forest, IL: Association for Comparative Economic Studies)

This journal is published quarterly and focuses on international economic planning and development. Articles are lengthy and scholarly in nature and contain bibliographies. Book reviews are also included. It is indexed in ABI/ Inform, PAIS Bulletin, American Bibliography of Slavic and East European Studies, and the Journal of Economic Literature.

HC 335 .S5881
(Soviet Union—Economic Conditions—Periodicals)

Soviet Economy (Silver Spring, MD: Winston & Son)

This journal is published quarterly in association with The Joint Committee on Soviet Studies of the American Council of Learned Societies. Articles examine Soviet economic trends and issues from an American perspective. Abstracts, charts, and references are included. Soviet Economy is indexed by Applied Social Sciences Index and Abstracts.

HC 331 .T77
(Former Soviet Republics—Economic Conditions; Europe, Eastern—Economic Conditions—1989–; Former Soviet Republics—Economic Conditions—Statistics; Europe, Eastern—Economic Conditions—1989—Statistics)

European Bank for Reconstruction and Development, Transition Report Update (London: ERBD Publications Desk) 2000.

This annual reference work examines the status and growth of the economy of Europe. Divided into two chapters, this periodical provides research on the economies of each country in Europe. Chapter one gives figures from economic reports of all of Europe. Included in chapter one is a section listing the recent developments in Europe's structural reform. Chapter two goes into a bit more depth, listing figures for the major corporations of Europe, and the effects that each has on the economy. Also included to aid the reader are a list of abbreviations, and contact numbers for the European Bank.

HC 340.12 .E53 (Russia (Federation)—Economic Conditions—1991–; Russia (Federation)—Commerce; Investments, Foreign—Russia (Federation))

Kvint, Vladimir L. Emerging Market of Russia (New York: John Wiley and Sons) 1998.

This 10-part reference work provides information on the various systems important to Russia. Parts one through six give an in-depth description of the largest six governmental systems in Russia including the tax system, the legal system, the political structure, and the financial system. Included in each section are articles characterizing each system. Parts seven through ten turn towards the economic infrastructure of Russia showing the profits and losses from international trade, the telecommunications industry, and internal production figures. Also included with this work are a list of helpful resources for doing business in Russia, and a list of notable contributors to the authoring of this work.

HC461 .A1 E18 (Japan—Economic Conditions—1945—Periodicals; Japan—Economic Policy—Periodicals)

OECD Economic Surveys—Japan, Organization for Economic Co-operation and Development

This is annual report on Japan's economy by OECD. It provides analyses and statistics of recent trends and short-term prospects, macroeconomic policies, trade policies, and issues in public finance. The appendix includes a chronology of a economic events and statistics.

HC 461.J365 (Japan—Industries—Directories; Japan—Commerce—Directories)

Japan Company Handbook (Tokyo: Keizai Inc.)

This is a directory of 9997 companies in Japan. It lists addresses, types of business, stock information, financial data, and sales breakdowns.

HC 461 .O68 (Japan—Economic Conditions—1945—Periodicals; Japan—Economic Policy—1945—Periodicals)

Setting up Enterprises in Japan (Tokyo: Compiled by TMI Associates Shimazaki International Law Office Chuo Coopers & Lybrund International Tax Office) 1992.

This is a guidebook on how to set up a business in Japan, with practical information, such as data on incorporating a company, initiating capital transactions, and the taxation system.

HC 462.9.H87 1999 (Japan—Economic Conditions—1945—Dictionaries; Japan—Economic Policy—1945—Dictionaries)

Hsu, Robert C. The MIT Encyclopedia of the Japanese Economy (Cambridge, MA: The MIT Press) 1999.

This one-volume encyclopedia has information on Japan's economy. It also includes definitions of terms commonly used in Japanese business practices. Topical essays using tables of figures discuss important issues and the work including addresses of relevant organizations; with references.

HC 465 .H53 .H63 (High Technology Industries—Japan—Directories)

Mitsubishi Corporation, Japanese Business Glossary (Tokyo: Toyo Keizai Shinposha) 1983.

This provides definitions and usages for words, phrases, and expressions, which are commonly used to describe concepts and behaviors particular to Japanese business practices.

HC461 .I42 (Japan—Economic Conditions—1945—
Periodicals; Japan—Industries—Periodicals)

Japan Economic Almanac (Tokyo. The Nikkey Weekly)

This almanac has a chronology of business events and brief descriptions of other current events. It also contains analyses of the economy, trade issues, finance, defense, overseas investment, taxation, environment issues, and industry sectors. It includes charts and graphs of statistics.

It further has brief descriptions of political parties' members and cabinet members with photographs, and lists addresses of industrial organizations, market share survey by companies, and company directories.

HD—INDUSTRIES, LAND USE, AND LABOR

HD 28 .H85 1990
(Executives—United States—Information Services)

How to Find Information about Executives (Washington, DC:
Washington Researchers Publishing)

How to Find Information about Executives is a guidebook and a sourcebook for those interested in collecting information about a corporate individual. Irregularly published, it provides references on defining the question and strategy to be used when gathering these data as well as a section providing telephone interviewing tips and step-by-step guidelines for performing research on executives, with sample cases as examples. A checklist of sources is included as well. This volume also focuses on published and on-line sources for gathering information about executives, listing major biographical directories, databases, and other publications that include biographical information, divided by geography, industry and profession, and general categories. Another portion of the book provides detailed information about possible sources of executive information, including local community and municipal government sources; state and federal government sources; securities watchers; the U.S. Congress and Capitol Hill; the courts; trade, professional, and special interest associations; labor unions; alumni affiliations; and employers and other pertinent companies. Federal agency and department contacts with addresses and phone numbers are provided, as well as federal and state court information. In addition, both general and industry specific hard copy and online sources for searching business, trade, and professional literature are listed. The Appendix includes a list of publishers, distributors, producers, and vendors cited in the book, as well as a general alphabetical index.

HD 30.15 .F48 (Management—Dictionaries)

Finch, Frank. The Facts on File Encyclopedia of
Management Techniques (New York, NY: Facts
on File Publications) 1985.

This reference book is designed to bring managers together with the technique, or techniques, that are best suited to solving their problem. The
techniques presented in this volume are defined as a framework of formal
or semiformal actions that require expertise in execution and tend to lead
efficiently and consistently to a predetermined objective, or set of objectives.
They are not to be confused with a devise that is defined as a step or a small
number of formal or semiformal steps that lead consistently and repeatedly
to a predetermined objective. Managers use techniques to get from point A
to point B. When approaching a problem, managers generally look at where
the problem first surfaced, or how they would like things to change once the
problem is solved. The first approach leads the manager to approach the
problem from a personal perspective, whereas the second approach will lead
the manager to one or more standard objectives, such as detection of the
problem, specification of the problem, or control of the problem. Management decisions should be oriented toward solving problems through the
careful examination of the problem that includes what resources need to be
applied to solve the problem and what objectives should be set for management after the problem has been solved.

This reference manual has been divided into two main textual section
and five indexes. The manual opens on page one with the entry ABC Analysis
and ends with the entry Zero Defects. This section provides the manager with
an alphabetical list of terms and techniques applicable to their problem
solving method. The second section is "A Note of the General Theory of
Management Techniques." The indexes include an alphabetic listing, techniques classified by function or department, techniques classified by their
objectives, techniques classified by their users, and techniques classified by
resources that they are applied to.

HD 30.15 .J65
(Management—Dictionaries; Business—Dictionaries)

Johannsen, Hano. International Dictionary of Management
(New York: Nichols Publications) 1995.

This dictionary provides definitions for over 6500 general and technical terms
relating to business and management. The text is supplemented by a directory

of business and management organizations, a chart of time zones, and a list of foreign currencies.

HD 30.15.S78 (Management—Dictionaries)

Statt, David A. The Concise Dictionary of Management
(London: Routledge) 1999.

The *Concise Dictionary of Management* is a glossary of terms and a brief biographical dictionary drawn from accounting, advertising, behavioral science, business administration, economics, ergonomics, marketing, psychology, and sociology. Both British and American usages are covered in this dictionary. Terms are arranged in alphabetical order and include a short definition or description with see-also references and illustrations when appropriate. Persons are listed with cursory biographical data, including their contribution to the field of management.

HD 30.27 .N361 (Business Forecasting)

Makridakis, Spyros and Steven C. Wheelwright.
The Handbook of Forecasting (New York, NY:
John Wiley and Sons) 1987.

The authors had three main objectives in putting this source together. The primary objective of this book is to make available to the manager information on what forecasting methodologies are available, how the methodologies available work, and why they do so. The second objective was to provide a reference work that would be tailored to the needs of managers. The third and final objective of the authors was to make available a work that would highlight the importance of the interdependent nature of staff and management in the forecasting process.

This book is divided into four major parts. This first of these is the "Role and Application of Forecasting in Organizations" section. The second section is entitled "Approaches to Forecasting." In this section, various methodologies that are available to managers are listed. Forecasting challenges deal with some of the changes that have already occurred and some that may occur in the business environment for which the manager is forecasting. "Managing the Forecasting Function" section attempts to tie together the preceding sections into a series of methods and concepts for the manager to keep in mind. Primarily designed as a handbook, the authors have presented the materials in an easy to understand and find manner. The source also includes a glossary of terms used in forecasting and an index.

HD 30.28 .H43 (Strategic Planning)

Hayden, Catherine L. The Handbook of Strategic Expertise: Over 450 Key Concepts and Techniques Define, Illustrated and Evaluated for the Strategist (New York, NY: The Free Press) 1986.

The primary objective of this reference work is to provide a source that managers can look to when decisions requiring the use of corporate strategy are to be made. The concepts addressed in this volume are drawn from those developed by individuals in academics, management, and business consultation. In addition, concepts in marketing, finance, operations management, accounting, engineering, and economics are also presented as material relevant to the study of corporate strategy. To help the manager better understand the complicated definitions and examples presented in this volume, the author has attempted to simplify the information while maintaining a comprehensive outlook that the managers will need in learning how to apply the material presented to their needs.

This reference source is divided into four sections: (1) an overview into the history of strategic planning; (2) relevant concepts, examples of application, and techniques for application; (3) a bibliography of relevant materials to be consulted in the need of further information; (4) and the index and cross-reference section that allows the reader to find relevant information throughout the book. To provide the reader with a comprehensive overview on the material available, the author has sought to provide the views of a number of recent practitioners.

HD 30.35 .M391 1983 (Industrial Management—Information Services; Business Information Services; Industrial Management—Bibliography; Business—Bibliography)

Mayros, Van and Michael D. Werner. Business Information: Applications and Sources (Radnor, PA: Chilton Book Company) 1983.

The primary objective of this reference source is to make it easier for managers to acquire needed information. The secondary objective of this source is to present the answers to the various managerial questions along with techniques that can be suitably used as remedies. The sources consulted and listed in this volume have met four criteria. All sources listed must be obtainable in English, be easily accessible through either a library or publisher, be afford-able to the general public, and must be relevant to business. This book is organized according to three major divisions. There is an applications section, a sources section, and an appendix. The applications section consists of 10 chapters dealing with a specific aspect of business. Each chapter has sub-chapters that detail the finer points of the chapter's overall theme. The subchapters list definitions, relevant applications, and a number of source listings. Although a number of relevant remedies are provided, the list is not meant to be exhaustive. It is intended to provide a starting point from which to approach a problem. A list from one to six source title listings will follow the relevant applications. These are arranged in alphabetical order and will appear in the following order: general references, periodicals, databases, information services, U.S. Government agencies and departments, and U.S. Government publication sources. In addition to the six specific source listings, a miscellaneous and a general category are included at the end of each chapter. In these categories, the cross-referenced sources that were either not specific enough to fit into one of the subchapters or that were general enough to fit into more than one of the subchapters are listed.

In the second section, bibliographic and descriptive information is provided on the source listings in the six categories listed in the applications section. The appendix section is concerned with how to locate information through the use of various databases. Three example cases are provided to give the reader a step-by-step guide. In addition to the three sections, a dictionary of database vendors, an index to U.S. government publications, and a subject index are included.

HD 30.4.D62 (Management—Study and Teaching—Catalogs—Periodicals; Business—Study and Teaching—Catalogs—Periodical; Management—Case Studies—Periodicals; Business—Case Studies—Catalogs—Periodicals)

Harvard Business School Catalog of Teaching Materials
(Boston: Harvard Business School Press) 1994.

The *Harvard Business School Catalog of Teaching Materials* is a catalog of teaching materials for business and business-related courses or programs. Its purpose is to provide a detailed listing of materials for business or educational teaching. It provides abstracts for thousands of teaching materials. These summaries include entries for authors, titles, types of material, as well as descriptions of contents and prices. The product listings are organized by 17 headings.

The major sections are suggested course outlines, an annotated listing of course materials, and the indices. It also includes an introduction, a user's guide, a classified list of Harvard Business School courses by discipline, case entry descriptions, definitions of product descriptions, and information on how to order the materials. The indices point to the annotated listings by authors, abstract numbers, software, and subjects. The subject index includes four smaller indices: a list of subjects represented within the catalog, a subject index, a title index, and an index for video products.

HD 30.4 G73 1992/94 (Management—Study and Teaching (Graduate)—United States—Directories; Management—Study and Teaching (Graduate)—Directories)

The Official Guide to MBA Programs, Admissions, & Careers
(Princeton, NJ: Graduate Management Admission Council)
1992.

The heart of this biennial publication is its full-page descriptions presented in alphabetical order of more than 550 schools of management across the United States and throughout the world. These descriptions include information on programs of study, admission, expenses, financial assistance, and contact information. Summary tables by state or country contain additional information. Useful short essays discuss the nature and state of these programs, issues related to choosing a school and gaining admission, finance, issues relative to minority students, and where it all may lead. Many tear-out forms simplify the process of directly getting additional information. Also helpful is the GMAT registration calendar.

HD 30.42 .U5 T77 (Management—Study and Teaching—United States—Directories; Executive—Training of—United Estates—Directories)

Training and Development Organizations Directory
(Detroit, MI: Gale Research Co.) 1998.

This handbook lists 2300 organizations and companies that offers training and development programs in various formats. There are public seminars and workshop for general information and university institute programs for intense management training. Addresses and course descriptions and fees are provided.

HD31 .H235 (Management—Handbooks, Manuals, etc.; Business—Handbooks, Manuals, etc.)

Handbook for Professional Managers (New York: McGraw-Hill) 1985.

This handbook provides detailed explanations of fundamental concepts and practice techniques on professional organization. Advice on how to apply these principles are also given. Areas covered include the primary management functions, major business activities, and environmental resources and constraints. The entries are organized in alphabetical order.

HD 38.25.U6 K44 1991 (Executives—United States— Recruiting—Directories; Executives—Europe—Recruiting— Directories; Business Consultants—Directories)

Key European Executive Search Firms and their U.S. Links (Fitzwilliam, NH: Kennedy Publication) 1991.

Key European Executive Search Firms and their U.S. Links lists many businesses that have representatives in Europe and/or the United States. This source has more than 500 companies stationed in the United States and 24 in Europe, which are classified into three categories: corporations that operate worldwide on their own; networks, which is an independent business in an umbrella organization; and specific affiliations, which operate without any umbrella organization. There are also listings of search companies: European businesses with U.S. links, U.S. organizations with European links, and international corporations with networks and affiliations. There are two indexes: one by organization and one by persons. This book also has a section on how to locate and contact these companies.

HD38.7 .H86

Washington Researchers Publishing, How to Find Financial Information About Companies (Washington, DC: Washington Researchers Publishing) 1990.

This book is designed to give the user a blueprint to compile a set of financial records about a company. The book outlines sources and techniques to compile financial data about a company.

The work is divided into three main parts, "How to use the book," "Strategies to plan investigation," and "How to read financial statements." These three main sections are further divided into areas on sources of information, how to compile a income statement, an expense statement, profit statements, a balance sheet, and liabilities of both domestic and foreign companies. The appendix lists sources of information such as state corporate offices, databases for sale and the vendors that sell them, and a list of regional U.S. commerce offices.

HD 58.7 B78 1990 (Organizational Behavior)

Bowditch, James L. and Anthony Buono. A Primer on
Organizational Behavior, 2nd Ed. (New York: Wiley) 1990.

The excellent organization and clarity of presentation found in this book reflect its origin and development as a classroom tool. It serves to introduce terms and concepts essential for understanding organizational behavior and management; provide the elements of a general survey of the field; and equip readers to read the literature with understanding and evaluate what they read. Topics include the research process in organizational behavior, motivation; perception, attitudes and individual differences; communication; leadership and the manager; macro- and microorganizational behavior; etc. Each chapter includes a summary and notes. An appendix is devoted to statistical analysis and a very useful chapter guides the reader through a reading of an actual research-oriented article. The book is useful not only as a textbook for the classroom, but also for self-study, or as a reference. There is a subject index and an author index.

HD 59.D57 (Public Relations)

Dartnell Public Relations Handbook, 3rd Ed.
(Chicago: Dartnell Corp.) 1987.

This handbook describes how pubic relations have become a marketing tool for many corporations. Much of the information is from people and organizations involved in public relations and looks at the marketplace, internal business, and health care facilities. Another section is an appendix of case studies chosen from the award winners of the Public Relations Society of America and/or from receiving the excellent public relations program award from the International Association of Business Communication. An additional Appendix has reprints of speeches given at the Foundation for Public Relations Research and Education.

HD 59 .N28 1990
(Public Relations—Corporations—Directories; Corporations—United States—Political Activity—Directories; Industry—Social Aspects—United States—Directories)

Close, Arthur C., Gregory L. Bologna, and Curtis W. McCormick. National Directory of Corporate Public Affairs (Washington, DC: Columbia Books) 1990.

Corporate involvement in public affairs is the topic of this directory. This source provides information on the corporate public affairs profession in the United States. Key individuals and principal corporate offices involved are identified. Government and press sources available to the public have been consulted over a 1-year period to provide the information available in this directory. Information is updated annually from the responses of question-naires sent out to the corporations listed.

The directory is divided into two major sections. The first lists compa-nies and the second lists individuals. The first section is a catalog consisting of a listing of 1600 companies of various sizes. Listed in alphabetical order, these companies have been identified as organizations having public affairs pro-grams. Information on the location of corporate headquarters, programs supported by each organization, political involvement, and philanthropic activities is listed. The second section alphabetically lists 12,000 individuals involved in public affairs across the country. Individuals cited are involved in similar activities as the companies listed in the first section.

HD 59 .O27 2001 (Public Relations—United States— Directories; Public Relations—Corporations—Directories)

O'Dwyer, Jack, Editor. O'Dwyer's Directory of Corporate Communications. (New York: J.R. O'Dwyer Company, Inc.) 2001.

Listed in the directory are over 4400 companies in various industries. In six categories, the 50 largest corporations are given in the areas of life insurance, retailing, transportation, commercial banking, and utilities. Most of the businesses included have a formal public relations title; however, the standard has been to use the phrase "corporate communications." The index shows volume of sales, areas of business, and key corporate executives.

HD 62.4 .H24 (International Business Enterprises— Management—Handbooks, Manuals, etc.)

Walter, Ingo, Ed. Handbook of International Business
(New York, NY: John Wiley & Sons) 1988.

This handbook is intended to aid in the interpretation of international developments as they relate to planning effective marketing approaches. An overview of the world business environment provides insight into the driving forces of international trade and competition, policies pertaining to global markets and adjusting economically to international situations. To provide a greater degree of understanding into obscure but important facets of international trade, detailed analyses are provided in the areas of balance of payments, debt, world financial flows, foreign exchange, and international reserves. Each section is written by an individual author and has a bibliography. An alphabetic subject index is included.

HD 62.6 .N825 (Nonprofit Organizations—Management— Handbooks, Manuals, etc.; Nonprofit Organizations— Finance—Handbooks, Manuals, etc.; Total Quality Management—Handbooks, Manuals, etc.)

The Nonprofit Management Handbook: Operating Policies
and Procedures (New York: J. Wiley) 1993.

This reference book acts as a guide to the policies and procedures used by nonprofit organizations. The objective of this book is to organize a list of the most effective guidelines and methods used in dealing with nonprofit organizations and to outline a sturdy foundation for the organization that will ensure quality results. Some of the major headings include leadership roles, quality management, volunteer development, board of directors, employee compensation, fund-raising, marketing, consultants, financial management, and legal issues. The emphasis is placed on the more technical aspects of management and organization. However, some background information is also included. This handbook is aimed at those people involved with the management of nonprofit organizations.

HD 62.6 .O88
(Corporations, Nonprofit—Management—Dictionaries)

Ott, Steven J. and Jay M. Shafritz. The Facts on File Dictionary of Nonprofit Organization Management (New York, NY: Facts on File Publications) 1986.

This dictionary was compiled to meet the needs of those working in and with nonprofit organization. Theory, terms, concepts, laws, codes, practices, and institutions involved in the management of nonprofit organizations are alphabetically listed and defined in this work. It is a comprehensive source of information on all types of nonprofit organizations. Information presented in this source have had to meet two basic criteria. To be included, a term has had to appear in several textbooks, source books, or handbooks dealing with the topic of nonprofit organizations. Terms included in this dictionary have definitions that differ from those found in standard dictionaries due to their association with nonprofit organizations. In addition to these criteria, central to the workings of nonprofit organizations receive more coverage than information that is peripheral to nonprofit operations. Information dealing with terms or concepts in accounting, basic business practices, financial investments, securities, labor relations, or organization theory, personnel management, program evaluation, project or program management, public administration, and public relations may not seem to have relevance to nonprofit organizations, but are included for the frequency that they are encountered when dealing with or in nonprofit organizations.

HD 62.7 .B97 v.1 (Small Business—United States—Planning—Handbooks, Manuals, etc.; Small Business—Canada—Planning—Handbooks, Manuals, etc.; Business Planning—United States—Handbooks, Manuals, etc.; Business Planning—Canada—Handbooks, Manuals, etc.)

Kahrs, Kristin, Ed. Business Plans Handbook (Detroit, MI: Gale Research, Inc.)

The *Business Plans Handbook* (BPH) contains 33 real and successful business plans used by entrepreneurs for the purpose of obtaining a loan. Names, addresses, and products have been changed to protect the contributors' confidentiality. The business plans profiled range from home businesses and restaurants to toy companies and nursing homes. Features in BPH include the following: "Forward: An Introduction to Business Planning" that gives instructional information; 33 real business plans; a directory of all Small Business Development Centers across the country; a glossary; and a bibliography for further reading.

HD 62.7 .B97 v.2 (Small Business—United States—Planning—Handbooks, Manuals, etc.; Small Business—Canada—Planning—Handbooks, Manuals, etc.; Business Planning—United States—Handbooks, Manuals, etc.; Business Planning—Canada—Handbooks, Manuals, etc.)

Kahrs, Kristin, Ed. Business Plans Handbook, Volume II
(Detroit, MI: Gale Research, Inc.)

Business Plans Handbook, Volume II (BPHII) contains an additional 26 business plans, 24 of the original. BPHII shows how to research, compose, and structure a business plan. Businesses represented are a microbrewery, newsletter, and virtual shopping kiosk, among 23 others. Names have been changed to protect the contributors' confidentiality. Features included in Volume II are a template that has all the main elements of a business plan, a directory of all the Small Business Development Centers and 10 Small Business Administration Regional Offices for networking, a glossary, a bibliography, and financial information that was not included in Volume I.

HD 66 .E56 (Work Groups; Organizational Change)

The Encyclopedia of Team-Building Activities (San Diego, CA: University Associates) 1991.

This reference book develops the idea of how to encourage team work among employees. The information is aimed at innovative corporations interested in attaining the benefits of synergy. The introduction outlines the specific differences between a group and a team and is followed by a step-by-step process to make the transformation. Major subject areas include: team effectiveness, values, feedback, role clarification, problem solving, team-member relationships, intergroup activities, and new, temporary, and transition teams.

HD 69 .C6 C76 2000 (Business Consultants—Directories)

Mitchell, Julie A., Editor. Consultants and Consulting Organizations Directory (Farmington Hills, MI: Gale Group) 2000.

Over 24,000 consultant firms are listed in this book in the areas of information technology, electronic commerce, and strategic planning. The text includes companies in the United States as well as Canada grouped into four categories. The indexes are provided, which are geographical, consulting activities, and consulting firms.

HD 69 .C6 D58 (Business Consultants—Directories)

Kennedy, James H. The Directory of Management Consultants (Fitzwilliam, NH: Kennedy Publications)

According to the author, management consulting is by definition an advisory service that an organization contracts to have provided for them by individuals or firms specially trained in the art of identifying, analyzing, and providing recommendations towards the resolution of problems in management.

This directory is meant to serve as a guide to management consultation services. Drawing from a database established in 1970 and from the results of questionnaires completed by firms specializing in management consultation, a list of 1314 firms is provided. Those firms not appearing in this source failed to meet the above definition of what constitutes management consultation, in either their sales practices or in the way they operate their consultation services. Firms are listed alphabetically in the main section of this source. Individual consultants are listed in the Key Principals Index. Four other indexes are included. There is an index for services offered by each firm, an index by industries served, an index by geographic location of the firm, and the Key Principals in management consulting firms index. In deciding which service to use, it is best to first decide whether a generalist or a specialist consultation firm is most suited to the needs of the organization in question.

HD 69 .C6 D93 (Consultants—Directories)

Dun's Consultants Directory (Parsippany, NJ: Dun's Marketing Services)

This directory contains listings for over 30,000 consulting firms. The listings help companies locate a consultant that would be best suited for their needs.

The consultants' profiles are listed alphabetically by the name of the firm, geographically, and by their primary field of consulting activity. The firms range in specialization from marketing and business management to data processing and engineering design. The text is supplemented by a section on how to use the directory, a glossary, a list of abbreviations, and an explanation of the Standard Industrial Classification Codes.

HD 69 .C6 K63 (Consultants—Handbooks, Manuals, etc.)

Klein, Charna and Mardell Moore. Consultants Reference Guide
(New York, NY: The Scarecrow Press) 1989.

This reference book is tailored to fit the needs of those involved in the field of business consultation. The guide is intended for the independent consultant, those consultants in small group practices, consultants employed by large established enterprises, in-house consultants, and those who are training to be consultants. The guide is designed to cut the amount of time needed by consultants to find information necessary to their work. The guide simplifies the consultants' search for information by providing information on where to find a particular reference source, by providing information on what is covered in a particular source, and by providing abstracts on reference works that both rate and evaluate their practical value. The guide also indexes relevant publications. In order to make the amount of information presented easier to handle, information requiring industry-specific expertise has been omitted. The attempt was made instead to provide sources and information that will be valuable to consultants regardless of their field.

The publications listed fall into four main categories. First there are sources pertinent to business management, then sources pertinent to the consulting marketplace, then sources pertinent to the product creation marketplace, and finally, sources that give consultants information on how to consult in specific areas. In total, about 400 sources are abstracted in this work. The sources abstracted can be easily obtained through either a public or college/university library. The sources fall into six categories: information sources, resource guides, directories, key contacts sources, handbooks and guides, and how-to guides or self-help guides. While dictionaries, almanacs, encyclopedias, and magazines have not been abstracted, periodical indexes thought to be relevant have been included. Twenty-five chapters divide this guide into specific subject areas. Works that fall into more than one subject area are listed in the most relevant chapter and are cross-referenced through the general subject index. The abstracts all contain bibliographic information on the source including a rating, a categorization of the publication into textbook, manual, guidebook, etc., a description of the scope, a description of the content, a summary, and an evaluation of the usefulness of the source.

HD 69 .N3 K94 (New Business Enterprises—Indexes; Small Business—Indexes)

Kryszak, Wayne D. The Small Business Index (Metuchen, NJ: Scarecrow Press) 1985.

This index provides a list of publications aimed to help people that are interested in establishing a small business. The major headings include general publications on small business, small business finance, and women in small business. More specific information also is provided on getting started in different states and the role of computers in small business.

HD 69 .P6 B98 (Industrial Management—Environmental Aspects—Information Services; Industrial Management—Environmental Aspects—Case Studies; Environmental Education)

Business and the Environment: A Resource Guide (Washington, DC: Island Press) 1992.

This reference guide provides information on both foreign and domestic environmental management topics. The goal of this publication is to help educators incorporate environmental issues into their courses and to create more research in the area of environmental effects on business. A list of publications focusing on business and the environment, a list of educators that are interested in the relationship between business and the environment, and case studies are provided. The material focuses on the areas of accounting, government, management, marketing, and finance. The text is supplemented by several indexes, a section on how to use the book, and a keyword list.

HD 69 .P6 C81 (Corporations—United States—Environmental Aspects—Directories; Environmental Engineering—United States—Directories; Environmental Protection—United States—Directories; Environmental Indicators—United States—Periodicals)

Corporate Environmental Profiles Directory (Washington, DC: Investor Responsibility Research Center, Environmental Information Service)

This three-volume reference book provides information on the environmental performance of the corporations in the Standard & Poor's 500 index. This information is updated annually and may be useful to investors, analysts, or anyone faced with a financial decision that relates to the environment. Volume I provides background information, statistics, trends, and a description of how to use the book. Volumes II and III contain the environmental profiles for each of the corporations. Each entry includes the full name of the company, the ticker symbol, capital expenditures on environmental matters, legal proceedings concerning the environment, and a list of shareholder resolutions on environmental issues. A table of contents by volume, a table of contents by industry group, and a list of figures and tables are included to make this guide easier to use.

HD 72 .H91 (Economic Development—Periodicals; Quality of Life—Periodicals; Social Indicators—Periodicals)

Human Development Report (New York: Oxford University Press)

This reference book deals with current global problems due to uncontrolled human development and proposes an agenda to change our course for the future. This book focuses on prevention and action at the root of the problems. The major topics include human security, peace and disarmament, foreign aid and cooperation, a framework for global governance, the human development index, and the role of the United Nations in the promotion of sustainable human development. The text is supplemented by boxes of highlighted information, statistical tables, a glossary, a list of country classifications, and relevant essays by Nobel Prize winners. The ideas presented in the book tend to favor people, nature, and jobs.

HD 72 .U58 (Economic Development—Periodicals; Commerce—Periodicals)

Trade and Development Report (New York: United Nations)

This report is issued annually by the United Nations as an overview of the current, major issues affecting the world. The text is divided into three major sections. The first section entitled global trends provides information on the recent performance of the global economy, a short-term economic outlook, developments in international trade, and the current position of international finance markets and external debt of developing countries. The second section, rethinking economic policies, contains information on government interventions in the economy, the effects of global demand on the world's economic performance, and controls on international capital movements. The third section addresses the concerns of developing countries and countries in transition and evaluates the status of global development. Each issue also devotes a section to a specific region in the world that is faced with an interesting problem or has made significant progress over the past few years.

HD 251 .N43
(Real Estate Investment—United States—Directories)

Nelson's Directory of Institutional Real Estate (Port Chester, NY: Nelson Publications)

This directory provides background information and access to real estate firms in the United States. The text is divided into six major areas including real estate investment manager profiles, real estate service firm profiles, pensions and foundations investing in real estate, insurance companies investing in real estate, corporate real estate executives, and real estate investment trusts. Each entry provides the name of the organization, a list of key executives and affiliated organizations, an organizational description, the address and phone number, information on the investment approach, and a list of assets under management. The text is supplemented by a geographical index, an alphabetical index, and an index of services.

HD 253 .N32
(Real Estate Agents—United States—Directories)

National Referral Roster (Cedar Rapids, IA: Stamats Communications)

This directory of residential real estate agencies is aimed to help real estate agents make informed referrals in the United States. Each entry includes the firm name, business address, telephone and facsimile numbers, and a contact name for the firm. The directory is arranged alphabetically by state and the agencies are organized by the major cities in each state. The text is supplemented by a list of the real estate boards and associations in each area.

HD 255 .N421 (Real Estate Business—United States—Statistics—Periodicals; Real Property—Prices—United States—Statistics—Periodicals; Rent—United States—Statistics—Periodicals)

National Real Estate Index (Emeryville, CA: Liquidity Fund)

This reference source is an up-to-date binder of the quarterly reports and special reports published by the National Real Estate Index. Each report contains information on several focus markets throughout the country, a macro market review, a tick report, several brief local market summaries, and a national market overview.

HD 1365 .A75 (Real Estate Business—Dictionaries)

Arnold, Alvin A. The Arnold Encyclopedia of Real Estate
(New York: J. Wiley) 1993.

This encyclopedia features information on the economic, financial, and legal aspects of the real estate industry. The aim of this reference book is to provide explanations of commonly used real estate terms, definitions of legal and banking terms that apply to real estate, and a tool for beginners to become more familiar with the basics of the real estate industry. The text tries to avoid historical references and excessively technical concepts. A list of abbreviations is provided at the back of the book.

HD 1365 .B64 (Real Estate Business—Dictionaries; Real Estate Investment—Dictionaries; Real Property—Dictionaries)

Blankenship, Frank J. The Prentice Hall Real Estate Investor's Encyclopedia (Englewood Cliffs, NJ: Prentice Hall) 1989.

This encyclopedia is aimed at professionals in real estate. Each entry contains a definition of the term followed by advice to the investor and an example. The text includes tips on how to minimize tax liabilities, the procedures for purchasing property, and how to read financial reports to find potential problems.

HD 1365 .F92 2000 (Real Estate Business—Dictionaries; Real Property—Dictionaries)

Friedman, Jack, et al. Dictionary of Real Estate Terms
(New York: Barrons) 2000.

This dictionary is designed to assist in the understanding of real estate terms. Most entries include examples that help to clarify the term. Diagrams, conversions, and abbreviations are shown in the appendix. Mortgage tables are presented illustrating monthly payment calculations based on initial principles.

**HD 1365 .T72 (Real Estate Business—Dictionaries;
Real Property—Dictionaries; Real Estate Business—
Abbreviations; Real Property—Abbreviations;
Real Estate Business—United States—Societies,
etc.—Directories; Real Estate Business—Canada—
Societies, etc.—Directories)**

Tosh, Dennis S. Handbook of Real Estate Terms
(Englewood Cliffs, NJ: Prentice Hall) 1992.

This handbook provides definitions for real estate terms and concepts as well
as buzz words and acronyms frequently used in the real estate industry. The
text is supplemented by a list of abbreviations, a list of real estate organizations and commissions, and sample real estate forms.

**HD1382. 5 .D62
(Real Estate Development—United States—Directories)**

Real Estate Directory of Major Investors, Developers,
and Brokers (Wilmette, IL: Reed Publishing)

The *Real Estate Directory of Major Investors, Developers, and Brokers* is a
guide to major investors, brokers, syndicators, developers, service firms, international real estate, and sources of financial investment. There is a directory
that contains several key headings. These headings are the company index, the
company type index, the geographical index, and the personnel index. There
are complete cross-reference listings whenever appropriate.

**HD1390 .U38
(Real Estate Development—United States—Periodicals)**

ULI Market Profiles (Washington, DC: Urban Land Institute)

The *ULI Market Profiles* uses an outline form to provide a descriptive account
of an area. The information provided includes a map showing development
patterns and is usually divided into six sections. They include the development
climate, the residential market, the retail market, the office market, the
industrial market, and the hotel market. All of these sections are further
broken down to provide additional information. There is a standard form
that is followed for each market profile to allow for comparison between
cities.

**HD1393.5.I43 (Industrial Property—United States—
Statistics—Periodicals; Industrial Buildings—United
States—Statistics—Periodicals; Office Buildings—United
States—Statistics—Periodicals; Real Estate Management—
United States—Statistics—Periodicals)**

Society of Industrial and Office Realtors (SIOR) and Landauer
Associates, Inc. Comparative Statistics of Industrial and Office
Real Estate Markets (Washington, DC: Society of Industrial and
Office Realtors of the National Association of Realtors; New York,
NY: Landauer Real Estate Counselors) 1991.

This market data annual report, compiled by SIOR members, includes a
review and forecast of industrial and office real estate markets. Also included
are both general and detailed analysis of the affect of economic trends on
them.

**HD1394 .I38 (Office Buildings—United States—
Finance—Statistics—Periodicals)**

Income Expense Analysis (Chicago, IL: Institute of Real Estate
Management of the National Association of Realtors)

The purpose of the *Income Expense Analysis* is to act as a database for the
important financial facts of property management. There are four different
versions of income expense analysis. There is a volume on Office Buildings,
one on Conventional Apartments, one on Federally Assisted Apartments,
and one on Condominiums, Cooperatives, and Planned Unit Developments.
    Each entry provides four sections. The "Metropolitan Area Reports"
provide facts on building size, building type, age group, and rental group. The
Regional Reports give more specific information for the Metropolitan Area
Reports. The National Reports compare the information in the Metropolitan
and Regional Reports with National averages. Finally, the Special Reports
provide particular information on energy consumption and leasing fees.

**HD1394.U58
(Real Estate—Management—United States—Directories)**

United States Real Estates Register (Woburn, MA: Barry Inc.)
1993.

The intended goal of the *United States Real Estates Register* is to facilitate the
sharing of information, the marketing of properties, and financial and other

services. There are four sections in the *United States Real Estates Register*. They are the "Managers of Real Estate" section, the "Company Profiles" section, the "Property Digest" section, and the "General Classification Section." The "Managers of Real Estate" section lists the top 1000 largest corporations in America alphabetically. The name, title, address, and telephone and fax numbers are also provided. The "Company Profiles" section alphabetically lists associations, companies, utilities, and government agencies involved in the real estate profession. It is intended for learning more about a company. The "Property Digest" section lists major industrial and commercial properties for sale or lease, arranged by type of property. The "General Classification Section" contains classifications of the various services offered by the industrial and commercial real estate industry.

HD1421 .F64 (Statistics—Periodicals)

FAO Yearbook (Rome: Food and Agriculture Organization of the United States)

The *FAO Yearbook* provides data for the production of foodstuffs. There are countless tables and charts with notes for almost every item. This helps make the *FAO Yearbook* very easy to use. The *FAO Yearbook* is published in English as well as Spanish and French.

HD 2324 .E56 1998 (Industry)

Malonis, Jane A. and Selden, Holly M. Encyclopedia of Emerging Industries (Detroit: Gale)

This book has chapters covering businesses that have been showing growth in recent years, and relatively new industries, namely, telecommunications and artificial intelligence.

HD 2346 .U5 A22 (Minority Business Enterprises—United States—Statistics—Periodicals)

Survey of Minority-Owned Business Enterprises (Washington, DC: U.S. Department of Commerce, Bureau of the Census)

This survey was first done in 1969 and became a regular part of the economic census in 1972. The Census Bureau publishes the survey every 5 years in years ending in 2 or 7. Basic economic data are reported on businesses owned by

African-Americans, Hispanics, Asian Americans, Native Americans, and other minorities. The survey encompasses an entire firm or corporation, not sections of a firm. For the purposes of the survey, a noncorporate form can be categorized as a minority-owned business only if the sole owner or at least half of the partners are of the specified minority. Fifty percent or more of the shares must be owned by persons of the names minority in order for a corporation to be classified as minority owned.

The survey is separated into three parts. The first covers African-American-owned businesses and the second covers Hispanic-owned businesses. Persons of Hispanic descent are asked to identify themselves further as being Cuban, Mexican, Puerto Rican, Latin American, European Spanish, or another group of Hispanic origin and culture. The third part of the survey reports on Asian Americans, Native Americans, and other minorities owning businesses. Again, distinctions are made as to the original ancestral group. Asian ancestral groups are Asian Indian, Chinese, Japanese, Korean, Vietnamese, and others. Pacific Islanders are Filipino, Hawaiian, and others. Native American ancestral groups are Aleut, Eskimo, and American Indian. The statistical tables record these distinctions. The questionnaire used to determine minority ownership appears in the appendices.

The statistical tables are divided into geographic areas, industry, firm size, and the legal compositions of the organizations. Statistics cover the number of firms, sales and receipts, number of employees and annual payrolls. The Hispanic, Asian American, and Native American statistics are broken down into the subdivisions outlined above. For example, the number of Cuban-owned businesses is listed. Statistics for all U.S. firms are reported for comparison. A summary of findings precedes the tables. This discusses industry and geographic characteristics and offers comparisons of minority-owned firms as well as comparisons of minority-owned firms to all U.S. firms.

HD2346 .U5F48 (Small Business—Finance—Periodicals)

Financial Studies of Small Business (Arlington, VA: Financial Real Estate Association) 1993.

The *Financial Studies of Small Business* provides information that allows small firms to be viewed in a more proper perspective by providing guidelines for comparison of financial ratios with firms of similar size. This reference defines a small business as any one making under $1,000,000. Data are selected from a vast array of financial statements, which was processed by Certified Public Accountants.

HD 2346 .U5 N272 (Women-Owned Business Enterprises—United States—Directories)

Frasca, JoAnn, Carollyn M. Barnes and Phyllis M. Devitt, Eds.
National Directory of Women-Owned Business Firms
(Lombard, IL: Business Research Services)

This directory is a source of information for women in the agricultural, industrial and commercial fields. The purpose of the work is to provide an easy reference for women-owned businesses in different fields of interest. It is arranged by the Standard Industrial Classification (SIC) code.

The listings are arranged alphabetically. Included in the entries are the company name, address, telephone number, contact person, fax number, sales volume, references, government contracting experience, number of employees, and business starting date.

HD 2346 .U5 N275 (Minority Owned Business Enterprises—United States—Directories)

National Minorities Business Directories. Try Us: National Minority
Business Directory (Minneapolis, MN: National Minority
Business Campaign)

The guidelines for inclusion in this directory are regional and national sales. The listings are a source of information concerning minority businesses in field relating to commerce, industry, and agriculture. This reference work includes an alphabetical grouping of the companies listed. The index contains headings of the subjects and the names of the companies.

Included in each entry are the name of the company, address, phone number, chief executive officer, the type of customers, and a list of the products.

HD 2346 .U5 N2712 (Minority Business Enterprises—United States—Directories)

Frasca, JoAnn, Carollyn M. Barnes, and Phyllis M. Devitt, Eds.
National Directory of Minority-Owned Business Firms
(Lombard, IL: Business Research Service)

The coverage of this directory includes 35,000 minority-owned business firms in the United States, Puerto Rico, and the District of Columbia, compiled from over 500 separate local, state, and federal directory sources. This source

defines a minority-owned business enterprise (MBE) as a business organization that is beneficially owned and actively controlled by one or more
members of the following groups: a person with permanent residence in the
United States who is African American, Hasidic Jewish, Hispanic American,
American Indian & Native American, and Asian Pacific & Native Hawaiian.
Information for inclusion is based on several criteria including minorities that
own at least 51% of the business, those demonstrating control over the
business, or those who are substantial investors.

In this single-volume directory, the organizations are arranged according to SIC business description in numerical sequence, indicated by the tab
separations and SIC number guides at the top of each page. Each business
listing is first arranged by SIX code and business description, then alphabetically (when applicable) by state, city, and company name. The listing includes
the company name, complete address, telephone and FAX number, LSA
indicator, minority type, business starting date, number of employees, sales
volume, keyword business description and references. Coverage includes
MBE in agriculture, auto repair, business services, construction, health and
legal services, mining, and more. This directory includes abbreviation indexes
for state codes, general and company names, and government abbreviations.
Other indexes include those for SIC numerical codes, alphabetical SIC codes
directory data by SIX code, and alphabetical cross-reference by company
name. This is a companion volume to the *National Directory of Women-
Owned Business Firms*. It is available on magnetic computer tape or diskette
as well.

HD 2346.65 S66 (Small Business—Information Services—United States—Periodicals; Small Business—United States—Bibliography—Periodicals; Small Business—Information Services—United States; Small Business—United States—Bibliography; Small Business—United States—Handbooks, Manuals, etc.)

Dorgan, Charity Anne, Ed. Small Business Sourcebook
(Detroit, MI: Gale Research)

This source is a detailed, annotated guide for the small-business community.
The first volume profiles 163 small businesses and includes detailed source
listings. The companies profiled range from accounting firms to word processing services. Businesses are arranged alphabetically by name. The entries
include address, telephone number, mission statement, association membership, and publications. Comprehensive information is provided for 18 categories on aspects of small business including starting a business, educational

programs, publications, statistical sources, computer resources, associations, and franchises.

The second volume contains general sources for small businesses and sources for further assistance. The nine categories cover federal and state government resources, trade and professional associations, seminars, private venture capital firms, consultants, and available literature. The appendix contains the Standard Industrial Classification (SIC) codes for those small businesses listed. There is an index of information sources listed that is referenced by entry number.

HD 2346 .U5 F48 2000/01 (Finance)

Financial Studies of the Small Business (Winter Haven: Financial Research Associates) 2000.

Financial data on small companies, whose capitalization is less than a million dollars, are studied and compiled in this book. It then provides financial ratios for comparisons between smaller and larger firms, which can be used by analysts for evaluations.

HD2425 .N285 (Trade and Professional Associations—United States—Directories)

National Trade and Professional Associations of the United States (Washington, DC: Columbia Books) 1994.

This directory lists national trade associations, labor unions, professional scientific or technical societies, and other national organizations composed of groups united for a common purpose. The book is composed primarily by an Association Index, arranged alphabetically by organization title. There is also a Subject Index, a Geographic Index, an Acronym Index, a Budget Index, and an Executive Index. Each entry provides the address and phone number of the association, the names of the executive leadership, the number of members, historical data, publications, and meeting dates and times.

HD2709 .B98 (Corporations—United States—Rankings—Periodicals)

Business Rankings Annual (Detroit, MI: Gale Research Inc.)

The *Business Rankings Annual* is a compilation of ranking information collected from over 1500 publications. *Business Rankings Annual* selects the lists that are most in demand by business people, librarians, students, and the public. The reference provides the "top 10" list, along with many other important details.

Business Rankings Annual presents the lists grouped by subject, and subjects are arranged alphabetically. Broad categories are further subdivided. A primary method of subdivision is geographic, although there are other methods. The comprehensive index helps to quickly locate all the rankings in which a given company, person, or product appears. The bibliography provides a complete listing of additional sources on each subject.

HD 2709 .D93 (Corporations—Europe—Directories)

D & B Europa (High Wycombe, UK: D & B Europe)

This reference was originally titled *Dun's Europa* and listed the 35,000 largest companies in the 12 European Community countries, Austria, and Switzerland. User information was provided in six languages and a supplement to the three-volume set indexed the companies by principal U.S. Standard Industrial Classification (SIC) code and by country. The 1993 edition was issued with the present title and different language versions of the User Guide were bound separately. Coverage has been expanded with each edition. The most recent one lists the largest 60,000 companies in all the member states of the European Community and the European Free Trade Association, including Austria, Belgium, Denmark, Finland, France, Germany, Greece, Iceland, Ireland, Israel, Italy, Luxembourg, the Netherlands, Norway, Portugal, Spain, Sweden, Switzerland, Turkey, and the United Kingdom. Distribution of companies between countries is roughly in proportion to their 1991 gross domestic product. Companies are selected from all areas of business. The principal criterion of inclusion for most companies is annual sales. For banks and financial institutions, however, it is total assets and for insurance companies, it is commissions. Data have been obtained from the companies through direct telephone or written inquiry and supplemented by information from company reports and other official sources.

Content arrangement in Volumes 1 through 3 is alphabetically by country according to a two-letter country code. Within each country section, the companies are arranged alphabetically by name in the local language. Entries include DUNS number, unique for each company; address, telephone, telex and fax numbers; lists of principal directors and executives with numeric codes indicating their functions; indication of importer and/or exporter status; details of parent company; nominal capital; number of employees; year started; principal business activity; annual sales and percentage of annual sales going to export; and pretax profit or loss. Net worth figures and company identification number (VAT numbers or equivalents) have been added for the 1994 edition.

Volume 4 contains statistical profiles (sales and SIC codes) by country and for Europe as a whole. Colorful pie charts and graphs provide comparative data such as sales per employee by country and by main business activity. The top 5000 companies are ranked by annual sales, converted to ECUs, and by the number of employees. The top 500 banks are ranked by total assets in millions of ECU. The indexes by principal SIC code and country, published in the supplement to the 1990 edition, are now included in this volume. An alphabetical index by company name has also been added as well as numerical and alphabetical tables of SIC codes. A special feature of each volume is a currency conversion table printed on an attached bookmark. *D & B Europa* is also available from the publisher on tape, diskette, or CD-ROM.

HD 2709.P92 (Corporations—United States—Periodicals; United States—Industries—Periodicals)

Predicasts F. & S. Index of Corporate Change
(Cleveland, OH: Predicasts)

This index is divided into three sections. Section one is used for looking for information by company name. Section two contains consummate information on the company or industry being researched. Section three has information on corporate events, such as bankruptcies, foreign operations, joint ventures, liquidations, name changes, new companies, reorganizations, and subsidiary changes.

HD 2721.I61 (Big Business—History; Business Enterprises—History; Corporations—History)

Derdak, Thomas. International Directory of Company Histories
(Chicago: St. James Press)

This directory provides information on the historical development of over a thousand of the world's largest and most powerful companies. The companies included have met one or both of the following criteria: they have achieved a minimum of $2 billion in annual sales or they are a leading influence in a specific industry or geographical location.

HD2745 .R33 (Directors of Corporations—United States—Periodicals—Executives—United States—Directories)

Reference Book of Corporate Managements (New York, NY: Dun and Bradstreet)

The four volume *Reference Book of Corporate Managements*, is a reference of the officers and directors of the companies in America with the highest revenue. The reference book is divided into several general headings. The companies are first listed alphabetically. This section provides biographical information, company names and addresses, and names of principal officers. They are also classified geographically, by industry classification, and by principal officers.

HD 2746.5 .H22 (Consolidation and Merger of Corporations—Information Services)

Halperin, Michael and Steven J. Bell. Research Guide to Corporate Acquisitions, Mergers, and other Restructuring (New York, NY: Greenwood Press) 1992.

This work provides a basic overview of sources of information and investigative methodologies for the world of corporate acquisitions, mergers, divestitures, bankruptcies, stock filing, and other business changes. Both print and electronic sources of information are described, often with illustrative pages or screens. Some of the topics covered include the monitoring of corporate change, public disclosures of mergers and acquisitions, finding acquisition candidates, identifying corporate parents and their subsidiaries and divisions, international mergers and acquisitions, earnings estimates, joint ventures, and new product announcements.

Special features included are appendices that list on-line databases and vendors described in the text, a glossary of about 50 terms, and a select bibliography of more than 60 items. An alphabetical index is arranged by topic and there is a list of tables and figures.

HD2746.5 .M55 (Consolidation and Merger of Corporations—Periodicals)

Mergerstat Review (Schaumburg, IL: Merrill Lynch Business Advisory Services)

The *Mergerstat Review* is a yearly collection of data on mergers and acquisitions for the year. The reference includes information on deals that are valued over $1,000,000; at least one of the parties is a U.S. entity. The Review is broken down into several categories, such as method of payment, industry highlights, and total dollar value offered. There are also detailed statistics on previous record mergers and acquisitions.

HD2746.5 .M554
(Consolidation and Merger of Corporations—Periodicals)

Merger Yearbook (New York: Securities Data Company)

The *Merger Yearbook* is a comprehensive sourcebook of information about the entire year of U.S. and international mergers and acquisitions. The book lists deals announced during the year in which a majority interest (including tender offers, leveraged buy-outs, and spin-offs) or a remaining interest was involved.

There are four tables of contents and two indexes. They range from the Industry Table of Contents to the Company Index. There are several charts and tables in the "Year in Review Section" that contain valuable composite information. In addition, the "Year in Review Section" provides rankings of targets and acquirers by nation and investment bank rankings.

HD 2746.5 .M57 2000 (Finance)

Mergerstat Review (Los Angeles: Applied Financial Information LP) 2000.

Statistics from publicly announced mergers and acquisitions are collected and published by Mergerstat. Only mergers of over $1,000,000 and involving a party from the United States are listed. This book is useful for investors, teachers, and students at the undergraduate, or higher, level.

HD 2753.A3 C82 (Corporations—Taxation—Collected Works; Corporations, Foreign—Taxation—Collected Works)

Corporate Taxes: A Worldwide Summary (New York, NY: Price Waterhouse)

This directory supplies information about the corporate taxes of numerous countries and territories around the world. The information includes basic explanation and description of the taxes that affect corporations in each country. The directory also contains a sample calculation of taxes to better illustrate the tax configurations.

HD 2755.5 .M44 (International Business Enterprises—Handbooks, Manuals, etc.)

Mattera, Philip. World Class Business: A Guide to the 100 Most Powerful Global Corporations (New York: Henry Holt and Company) 1992.

The major criteria for inclusion in this source are the size of the corporation (as determined by annual revenues and net income) and amount of global activity. All parts of the world are included. Companies that are expected to be "major players" in the future have also been included.

Each profile includes basic information concerning locations of company headquarters, whether or not the company is privately helped, total number of employees, etc. An overview and company history describes how the company developed, its evolution, and future prospects. The operations, top executives, outside directors, and financial data are discussed. The geographic breakdown, labor relations history, and the environmental record are included. Each entry contains a bibliography.

The appendices rank the companies by revenues and by net income. An index lists names of companies, individuals, products, unions and other organizations. Each company profile is written in a general style.

HD 2755.5 .M83371 1987b (International Business Enterprises—Dictionaries)

Hoogvelt, Ankie and Anthony Puxty, Editors, and John M. Stopford, Consulting Editor. Multinational Enterprise: An Encyclopedic Dictionary of Concepts and Terms (London: Macmillan Press) 1987.

This dictionary represents a pioneering response to the special problems of terminology arising in an international business context. The proliferation of voices and languages of analysis can lead to difficulty in understanding it. Terms will be found here that are also treated in dictionaries of conventional related disciplines but are treated differently in this dictionary as befits the emphasis on the international context. Here we have a clear and not overly complicated guide through the multidimensional phenomenon of multinationals. The general readers can use it profitably for information as they read newspapers and magazines. Terminology is mainly confined to the Anglo-Saxon world with very light treatment of the Far East and the developing world. A thoughtful system of cross-referencing permits the reader to derive a reasonably full summary of topics as they cross the boundaries of disciplines. The three appendices cover references, list of bibliographies, and organizations. The somewhat unconventional index contains no page references but organizes entries under topics as an important component of the cross-referencing system.

HD 2755.5 S77
(International Business Enterprises—Directories)

Stopford, John M. Directory of Multinationals (New York, NY: Stockton Press)

This directory provides information about numerous enterprises and corporations. The companies perform a large percentage of their sales outside their base country. The directory describes the economic strategies of each firm and contains financial data, including foreign and domestic sales, that provide a way to compare the performance of each company. It also includes information about many other enterprises that exhibited similar multinational impact, yet provided insufficient data. This directory illustrates the behavior of modern multinational companies and shows their growing importance and power.

HD 2755.5 .W95
(International Business Enterprises—Directories)

Hoopes, Davis S. Worldwide Branch Locations of Multinational Companies (Detroit, MI: Gale Research Inc.) 1994.

Worldwide Branch Locations of Multinational Companies (WBLMC) provides users with directory information on over 25,000 branches, subsidiaries, and offices of 500 influential multinational companies. Users should be able to determine quickly where the company headquarters is located and in which countries it has subsidiaries or branches. For each multinational company entry, the following information is provided when available: name; address; telephone number; fax number; teletype; key officials; relation to parent company; description of business; Standard Industrial Classification (SIC) code(s); the percent owned by the parent company; additional personnel; date of establishment; number of employees; and annual sales. Two hundred of the multinational companies are headquartered in the United States with the additional 300, in no particular order, located mainly in Japan, the United Kingdom, Sweden, Germany, and Canada. The WBLMC contains two sections and four parts or indexes. The first section is an alphabetical list of companies and branches arranged by country. Section two contains an alphabetical list of the company headquarters of the branches listed in section one. The four parts or indexes are a geographical listing of parent company headquarters by country, a numerical list of the SIC codes, a list of branches by SIC code, and an index of parent companies and branches listed alphabetically. A section on how to use the WBLMC and read each entry is also provided.

HD 2756 .C34 1999 (Finance)

Cases in Corporation Acquisitions, Buyouts, Mergers, & Takeovers (San Francisco: Gale Group)

This book contains comprehensive reports on approximately 300 mergers and acquisitions over the past 100 years. These mergers are listed in alphabetic order. The book is useful to business and high school students.

HD 2763 .A2 .M82 (Public Utilities—United States; Corporations—United States; Securities—United States)

Moody's Public Utility Manual (New York, NY: Moody's Investor's Service)

This source is a two-volume reference to over 475 companies providing telephone, electric, gas, and water service to the public. Each entry contains a brief description and history of the corporation, address and telephone number of the main office, and company officials and covers general information relating to company management and production.

The source thoroughly examines the financial activity of the business. The previous years' income figures including assets, liabilities, revenues, and expenditures are reported. Long-term debt statistics and capital stock information are also included.

Companies are categorized into areas of coverage within the manual: Corporate Visibility Plus, Corporate Visibility Ultra, Corporate Visibility Select, and Standard Coverage. Companies subscribing to Corporate Visibility Plus receive the greatest coverage and those choosing Standard Coverage receive the least.

Moody's rates each company from the highest "aaa" to the lowest "c" in regard to stocks and bonds. The rating system is explained in the front of the volume with a key for the user's reference. Companies are arranged alphabetically and indexed at the front of each volume. A definition section, describing terms used in the manual, precedes the index. Public utility maps are scattered throughout the material and are listed alphabetically before the introduction.

An extensive special features section inserted in the center of each volume contains Moody's Public Utility Bond Yield Averages, Moody's Public Utility Preferred Stock Yield Averages, Moody's Natural Gas Common Stock Averages, and various tables regarding stocks and bonds. The manual is updated semiweekly by *Moody's Public Utility News Reports*.

HD 2769.2 .U6 F43 (Federal Aid to Nonprofit Organizations—United States—Periodicals)

Spomer, Cynthia R., Ed. Federal Support for Nonprofits
(Washington, DC: Taft Group)

Federal Support for Nonprofits (FSN) profiles the 750 federal programs of the United States that gives grants and assistance to nonprofit agencies and organizations. FSN explains the types of federal grants available, the federal grant system, and the types of nonprofit recipients. Abbreviations and terms used are explained, as well as the basics to proposing a grant. Over 600 pages are dedicated to profiles of the 750 programs. There are two indexes. The first is a list of Federal Programs by Nonprofit Recipient Type and the second is a Master Index to Federal Programs. An appendix is included that lists, by name, recipients of federal awards.

HD 2771 .D88 (Corporations—United States—Statistics— Periodicals; Ratio Analysis—Periodicals)

Industry Norms and Key Business Ratios (New York, NY:
Dun & Bradstreet)

This annual publication provides information on public and private corporations, partnerships, and proprietorships in the United States. It consists of a series of tables containing statistics for more than 800 types of businesses as defined by Standard Industrial Classification (SIC) codes. Data are collected weekly and maintained daily to keep up to date. The industry norms are calculated using fiscal year (July 1–June 30) figures.

The book is divided into nine sections that cover the main industries of agriculture, forestry and fishing, mining, construction, transportation and public utilities, manufacturing, wholesale trade, retail trade, finance other than banks, and real estate and services. The industry norm table for each industry is headed by the SIC code and short title along with the number of companies in the sample. Each table contains information on accounts receivable, inventory, fixed assets, bank loans, accounts payable, net worth, net sales, gross profits, working capital, and other related data.

The 14 key business ratios cover major areas of performance with indicators of solvency, efficiency, and profitability. The figures are broken down into the median, upper quartile (midpoint of the upper half), and lower quartile (midpoint of the lower half). The key business ratios include fixed assets to net worth, current liabilities to inventory, net sales to inventory, sales to net working capital, return on assets, and collection period.

An appendix provides information on the SIC codes. The print edition supplies general data only, while the expanded sets of industry norms, key business ratios, and other directories for specific industry segments are available in the diskette version.

HD 2771 .H85 (Corporations—Information Services—United States—Directories)

How to Find Information About Companies (Washington, DC: Washington Researchers)

This directory is a guide to ways that a researcher can obtain information about large, small, public, private, foreign, or domestic firms. It is organized into three parts that examine various ways to find data about a company. Part one is organized by type of source and includes over 9000 entries to find information through the government, published material, computers, or human resources. The sources include library services, government agencies, public documents, and company experts. Part two analyzes the specific material that one would need to know about the company and includes questions that a researcher should ask in order to acquire this data. Part three provides the necessary methods to finding information about certain types of companies, such as acquisition candidates, service companies, and subsidiaries.

HD 2771.H86 (Private Companies—Information Services— United States—Periodicals; Corporations—Information Services—United States—Periodicals)

How to Find Information About Private Companies (Washington, DC: Washington Researchers Publishing)

This book provides various ways through which one can acquire information about a specific private company. It gives an efficient and creative format by which data can be obtained by an analyst, researcher, or business executive. The report details how to find information from different resources available in a library, government surveys and data, trade and labor associations, economic analysts, special interests groups, and competitors of the particular private company. It also provides specific data on state offices, vendors, and suppliers where material can be found to research a company.

HD 2771 .H855 (Corporations, Foreign—United States—Information Services—Periodicals)

How to Find Information About Foreign Firms (Washington, DC: Washington Researchers)

This guide provides practical techniques and approaches that can be used to acquire information about business firms around the world. These methods include examining published sources like directories, contacting federal government agencies and international economic organizations, and inquiring at the firm's American connections. It explains also how a researcher must overcome the language and cultural barriers that are present because the firms are foreign.

HD 3611 .I43 (Industry and State—Periodicals)

Industrial Policy in OECD Countries (Paris: Organisation) 1993.

This book reports various industrial information about countries in or involved with the Organisation for Economic Co-Operation and Development (OECD). It describes the industrial policy of each country, including the country's investment promotions, industrial reforms, development policies, environmental regulations, and relations with other OECD and non-OECD countries. Also, it includes a listing of financial figures, comprising the economic trends and changes in wages, investment, productivity, and trade.

HD 3630 .U7 P7611 (Licenser—United States—Directories; Certification—United States—Directories; Government Agencies—United States—Directories; State Government—Directories; Occupations—United States—Legislation)

Bianco, David P. Ed. Professional and Occupational Licensing Directory: A Descriptive Guide to State and Federal Licensing, Registration, and Certification Requirements (Detroit: Gale Research) 1996.

The *Professional And Occupational Licensing Directory* (POLD) gives all the information you need to obtain a license for over 500 occupations and over 1000 different jobs from state and federal boards and agencies. If a license is required for an individual to be able to work at a particular business, or use a professional title, it should be covered in POLD. For each license entry, the following details are listed: the job title; educational or experience requirements; number of licenses that are active; type of exam needed to be taken; authorized activities; reciprocity and exemptions; and required fees. There are five sections: a master list of the professions and occupations requiring licenses; license requirements; an appendix of rarely licensed occupations; an appendix of sources for state licensing information; and a geographical index. Also included is a user guide and sample entry.

HD 4826 .I59 (Labor—Statistics—Periodicals)

Yearbook of Labour Statistics (Geneva: International Labour Office)

This publication is an annual compilation of various statistics related to the labor industry from over 180 countries around the world. The data are divided into different areas of industry, such as community, social and personal services or financing, insurance, real estate, and business services. It includes statistical information about employment, unemployment, wages, hours of work, cost of labor, injuries, consumer prices, and strikes and lockouts. In addition, each edition provides comparative data of the last 10 years for each country.

HD 4839 .R64 (Industrial Relations—Dictionaries)

Roberts, Harold S. Roberts' Dictionary of Industrial Relations (Washington, DC: The Bureau of National Affairs Inc.) 1994.

This book is a listing of numerous terms and expressions that are regularly used in relations between labor and management and communications among industries. The entries include a brief explanation of the term or phrase, a relevant example, and other pertinent information. Each successive volume adds many new entries, and previous definitions are updated and altered to supply the current terminology. The alterations to previous volumes emphasize the trend towards more service-oriented industries and the growing issue of equal employment opportunity. Over 4000 entries are included in the dictionary and source references are provided so that readers can further research a topic. A user's guide informs the reader that the dictionary is alphabetically organized. Labor unions are listed by their formal name and also by their field of industry. A table of the abbreviations and acronyms used in the dictionary follow.

HD 4903.5 .U5 J63 (Discrimination in Employment—United States—Statistics—Periodicals; Minorities—Employment—United States—Statistics—Periodicals; Women—Employment—United States—Statistics—Periodicals)

Job-Patterns for Minorities and Women in Private Industry (Washington, DC: Equal Employment Opportunity Commission)

This directory is a compilation of the employment statistics that the Equal Employment Opportunity Commission requires all companies to file. It serves to provide in-depth and detailed description of the race and gender makeup and distribution of the national employment force. At the national level, the guide organizes the statistics according to the specific industries, for example, department stores, life insurance, and iron and steel foundries. The guide also provides comparative statistics of specific factors of industry, including construction, city services, and manufacturing, at the state and large- and small-city level.

HD 4928.N6 B85 (Employee Fringe Benefits—Dictionaries)

Briggs, Virginia L., Kushner, Michael G., and Schinabeck, Michael J. Employee Benefits Dictionary (Washington, DC: The Bureau of National Affairs, Inc.) 1992.

This dictionary contains a listing of numerous words and expressions that people associated with employee benefits (accountants, lawyers, insurance professionals) often use. These terms have arisen over the years because of increased government legislation in the area of employee benefits. This guide helps a reader to gain knowledge of the terminology in the field. It gives a formal definition of each term or phrase and points out other sources where further information can be found.

HD 5152 .E89 (Business Enterprises—Europe—Directories; Europe—Commerce—Directories)

European Business Services Directory (Detroit: Gale) 1992.

This guide provides contact and descriptive information on over 20,000 European companies that provide essential business services to other companies. The directory is made up of three parts, each of which organizes the listings by a different method. The first section, "Service Listings," arranges companies by primary service provided. The second section, "Geographic Listings," arranges companies by country of operation. The third section, "Company Listings," arranges companies alphabetically by name. Data are collected through questionnaires to companies, chambers of commerce, and trade organizations as well as through related databases and secondary sources. Data include contact information, financial information, services provided, branches, and related company information. The guide also provides an explanation of terms and abbreviations and a listing of SIC codes in several languages.

HD 5415 .B63 1999 (Marketing)

Lewis, Barbara R. and Littler, Dale. Encyclopedic Dictionary of Marketing (Malden, MA: Blackwell Publishers) 1999.

Based on the language used in marketing, this dictionary contains terms in several areas of marketing. Cross-referencing is used because of repetition of common terms.

HD 5715.5 .C2 W7511 (Occupational Training—Canada— Directories; Occupational Training—United States— Directories; Nonprofit Organizations—Canada—Directories; Nonprofit Organizations—United States—Directories)

Wright, Phillip C., Guidry, Josée G., and Blair, Judy. Opportunities for Vocational Study: A Directory of Learning Programs Sponsored by North American Non-Profit Associations (Toronto: Buffalo, NY: University of Toronto Press) 1994.

Opportunities for Vocational Study contains various programs sponsored by the United States and Canadian nonprofit associations for career changers, people who want to upgrade their skills, those who need specialized training, and graduates of high school who do not want to further their education at a college or university. The programs listed give an address and other contact information and the type of training and methods used. The alphabetical list of associations indicates the programs offered, country of origin, and entrance requirements. An index is provided at the end. Health and Medical programs are not listed unless they have a high degree of management opportunities. Most of the associations and programs are business or commerce related.

HD 5723 .O16

Occupational Outlook Handbook (Lanham, MD: Bernan)

This guide provides information on over 300 occupations. Analysts discuss the employment outlooks for each occupation. Contact information for companies within the discussed occupations as well as a list of resources useful in further investigation are also provided.

HD 6983 .A51 (Consumer Price Indexes—United States)

Darnay, Arsen J. and Helen S. Fisher. American Cost of Living Survey (Detroit, MI: Gale Research Inc.) 1994.

American Cost of Living Survey is a collection of reported prices for products and services in 443 cities in the United States. The purpose of *American Cost of Living Survey* is to answer questions on the state of the economy, to allow comparison between cities, and to provide information that is not readily available for smaller communities. *American Cost of Living Survey* is helpful to people considering a move to another part of the United States, to companies trying to determine appropriate levels of compensation for employees, and to parents deciding the costs of education for college-age children.

The *American Cost of Living Survey* covers topics ranging from Alcoholic Beverages and Charity, to Travel and Utilities. *American Cost of Living Survey* is arranged alphabetically by city, and major topics covered are also sorted alphabetically.

HD 7022 .C76 (Consumption (Economics)—Europe— Periodicals; Market Survey—Europe—Periodicals)

Euromonitor, Consumer Europe (London, UK: Euromonitor Publications)

This publication brings together market information on major retail goods purchased in 17 Western European countries from 1982 to 1986. In order to facilitate comparison, the nations are divided into five groups. The major market group consists of the United Kingdom, France, Italy, and Germany; Benelux is Belgium, Luxembourg, and the Netherlands; Iberia consists of

Portugal and Spain; Scandinavia comprises Denmark, Finland, Norway, and Sweden; and the last group consists of Austria, Greece, Ireland, and Switzerland. Data on market share, growth rate, market size, and per capita volume and spending are presented in tables in 16 sections. The sections cover socioeconomic parameters, foods, drinks, tobacco, household cleaning products, over-the-counter health care, disposable paper products, cosmetics and toiletries, housewares, home furnishings, clothing and footwear, domestic electrical appliances, consumer electronics, personal goods, leisure goods, and automotives. Each main section heading is subdivided into specific goods. Also provided in each section are explanatory notes, sources of specific information, and graphs and charts supplementing the tables. In the introduction there is a product classification code and a major information source directory for each nation. An alphabetically arranged index of products is included.

HD 8038 .U5 A48 (Professions—United States—Periodicals)

Dwyer, Edward J. and John W. Wright. The American Almanac of Jobs and Salaries (New York, NY: Avon) 1991.

The *American Almanac of Jobs and Salaries* provides data about the monetary aspects of many areas of occupation, although the largest entries are all aimed at the career minded. It is also useful for the job descriptions, predictions for employment opportunities, and obsolete salary data. The reference also shows information on some emerging trends in jobs and salaries.

The book is broken down into many headings, some as specific as "lawyers," and some as general as "on the public payroll." Under each of these headings, there is a detailed written description about the profession, a table showing the salaries based on position, a table showing starting salaries, a table showing private versus public participation as well as many other statistics.

HD 8051 .A62 (Occupations—Statistics—United States)

United States Department of Labor, Outlook 2000 (Washington, DC: United States Government Printing Office)

The *Outlook 2000* bulletin presents the Bureau of Labor Statistics employment projections for the year 2000. Three alternative growth patterns provide estimates of overall and sector economic growth with consistent industry and occupational employment projections. Part I consists of five articles reprinted from the *Monthly Labor Review*. Part II provides a brief overview of the methodology. Part III represents the assumptions underlying the specific industry and occupational employment estimates. The alphabetical appendix provides more detailed data frequently requested by users.

HD 8064 .S79 1997 (Business)

Statistical Handbook of Working America
(Detroit: Gale Research)

Statistics on employment, salaries and wages, and health and safety are collected from 120 sources. These data are presented on a city, state, and national level. Perspectives on issues that effect the work field also are included.

HD 8064.2 .U58

The Bureau of Labor Statistics Handbook of Methods
(Washington, DC: The Bureau) 1992.

The Bureau of Labor Statistics Handbook of Methods presents detailed explanations of how the Bureau of Labor Statistics obtains and prepares the economic data it publishes. Bureau of Labor Statistics are used for many purposes, and sometimes data well suited for one purpose may have limitations for another. The goal of the *Bureau of Labor Statistics Handbook of Methods* is to allow users the ability to determine the suitability of the statistics for their needs.

Each chapter gives a brief account of the program's origin and development which is then followed by information on concepts and definitions, sources of data and methods of collection, statistical procedures, where the data are published, and their uses and limitations.

HD 8073 .A1 B62
(Labor Movement—United States—Biography)

Fink, Gary M. Biographical Dictionary of American Labor
(Westport, CT: Greenwood Press) 1984.

The *Biographical Dictionary of American Labor* is a compilation of biographies of important and influential men and women in the history of American labor. The introduction provides information on the history of the American labor movement. This is followed by the biographies, which are arranged in alphabetical order. Each biography gives a concise read on the individual, including birth data, childhood, major steps the individual has taken in their career, and finally a listing of either other works they can be found in or have authored.

HD9000.4 .F64 1994 (Produce Trade—Statistics—Periodicals)

FAO Yearbook, Trade = FAO Annuaire, Commerce = FAO Anuario, Comercio (Rome: Food and Agriculture Organization of the United Nations)

FAO Trade Yearbook is an international statistical reference source on agricultural products and related information. The work includes indexes and tables on agricultural trade for each continent, agricultural product trade, trade in the implementation of agricultural production, and agricultural, fishery, and forestry trade values for each country. These data indicate continental and worldwide trends in volume, price, and cost of international trade in food and agricultural commodities. Definitions of the symbols used in the tables and various notes such as classification and definitions and exchange rates as well as remarks concerning various countries, country classifications, lists of countries and continents, standard conversion factors, maritime freight rates for wheat, and exchange rates provide an explanatory framework for the technical data in the main text. FAO collects its statistical facts either through questionnaires supplied by the countries or through their official publications. In the absence of these, data are estimated on whatever is available.

HD 9502 .A1 S82 1986/87 (Energy Industries—Statistics— Periodicals; Energy Consumption—Statistics—Periodicals)

Energy Statistics/Statistique De L'Energie, 1986–1987 (Paris, France: International Energy Agency/Agence Internationale De L'Énergie) 1989.

This source contains comprehensive statistics on energy production, trade, and consumption for the Organization for Economic Co-operations and Development (OCED) member nations. The data pertain to oil, natural gas, solid fuels, manufactured gases, and electricity. The format is both definitional and methodological for the member nations. The source serves as a reference for analytical and policy work related to energy issues. The text is in English and French.

HD 9502 .A2 E534 (Energy Consumption—Economic Aspect; Energy Consumption—Political Aspect; Petroleum Industry and Trade; International Economic Relations; Balance of Payments)

Liscom, William L., Ed. The Energy Decade: 1970–1980, A Statistical and Graphic Chronicle (San Diego, CA: World Energy Information Services) 1982.

This source contains international macroeconomics data on natural gas, hard coal, total domestic primary energy production, consumption, exports, and imports. The statistics material is alphabetically arranged. Graphs are included in the text. The contents of the source include historical data on energy, geographic distribution of resources in a global and regional context, international prices, U.S. domestic politics, international crude oil production, refinery capacities, petroleum products, motor fuel production, and consumption and statistical data on electricity and other energy sources. The data on the United States are arranged by states. A section addresses future energy supplies, economic growth, energy conservation, and dependency of energy and macroeconomics indicators.

HD 9515 .I771 (Steel Industry and Trade—United States— History—20th Century; Iron Industry and Trade—United States—History—20th Century; Steel Industry and Trade—United States—Biography; Iron Industry and Trade—United States—Biography)

Iron and Steel in the Twentieth Century (New York: Facts on File Publications) 1994.

Iron and Steel in the Twentieth Century is part of the *Encyclopedia of American Business History and Biographical* series. It is an encyclopedia of people and companies important to the iron and steel industry. Space reserved for each biography or company increases with their importance to the industry. Historical information on companies are limited to the most important events. In the biographies, individuals' significance to the industry is pointed out as well as their contributions. The entries are listed alphabetically with the company profiles and biographies mixed together.

HD 9560.4 .O65B 1986–1988 (Petroleum Industry and Trade—Europe—Statistics—Periodicals; Petroleum Industry and Trade—North America—Statistics—Periodicals; Gas, Natural—Europe—Statistics—Periodicals)

Oil and Gas Information/Donné es Le Pétrole Et Sur Le Gaz 1988–1989 (Paris, France: International Energy Agency/Agence Internationale De L'Énergie)

This volume contains information on supply, demand, and trade patterns for the Organization for Economic Co-operation and Development (OECD) countries, major market trends for developing nations and centrally planned economies. The information provided also includes statistical data on prices, crude oil reserves, refining capacities, trade, oil production, demand, reserves, and consumption. The same information is given for natural gas.

The book is divided into two sections. Part one is an overview of the world's oil and gas market developments with an emphasis on historical trends. The second part is in tabular form and provides a comprehensive perspective of oil and gas supply and demand for the OECD by region and individual countries. The text is written in both English and French.

HD 9564 .B32 (Petroleum—United States—Reserves; Petroleum Industry and Trade—United States—Statistics; Gas, Natural—United States—Reserves; Petroleum Industry and Trade—United States—Production Standards)

Basic Petroleum Data Book: Petroleum Industry Statistics (Washington, DC: American Petroleum Institute)

This source is updated three times a year. The volumes are independent of one another and contain statistical data compiled from various sources and agencies. The addresses and telephone numbers for the sources are listed under the heading of their relevant sections. The information is divided into 15 sections: (1) energy; (2) crude oil reserves; (3) exploration and drilling; (4) production; (5) financial; (6) prices; (7) demands; (8) refining; (9) imports; (10) exports; (11) offshore; (12) transportation; (13) natural gas; (14) OPEC; and (15) miscellaneous data on the petroleum industry. This includes statistics on service station populations, heat values for different energy products, and information on the number of employees in the industry. Charts and tables are included.

HD 9666.3 P74 (Pharmaceutical Companies—Directories; Pharmaceutical Advertisers—Directories; Pharmaceutical Marketing—Directories)

PMD: Pharmaceutical Marketing Directory (Boca Raton, FL: CPS Communications)

This source is a marketing directory. It is divided into 10 sections with a classified section with eight subsections. It includes a calendar of events for the Pharmaceutical Advertising Council, Inc. (PAC), the Midwest Pharmaceutical Advertising Council (MPAC), and the Medical Marketing Association (MMA). The addresses and telephone numbers for the organizations are listed along with the meeting locations for each event.

The sections are arranged alphabetically. The addresses, telephone number, and fax number are supplied for each listing. The first section contains the names of individuals involved in pharmaceutical advertising, publications, and media. These are cross-referenced to the company section. The other sections are production managers, listed under their company; pharmaceutical companies, including the names and titles of personnel; pharmaceutical companies propriety, a listing of officers and information on markets and sales; advertising agencies with names and phone numbers of officers, account supervisors, account executives, media and creative personnel; medical publications listed alphabetically by title with information on circulation, rates, editorial, administrative, and sales personnel, and publishers' representatives; single-sponsored publications; pharmacy publications; nontraditional media that is a geographical listing of business information specialists in the health care field. The source also contains advertisements.

HD 9676 .R36 S82 (Automobile Industry and Trade—Statistics; Automobile Industry and Trade—United States—Statistics)

Ward's Automotive Yearbook (Detroit, MI: Ward's Reports Inc.)

This annual publication provides a statistical synopsis of events in the global automobile industry over the course of a year. It begins with commentaries on the economic and technological trends of the industry. A listing of each of the types of engines that the numerous automobile companies manufacture follows. Then information about the import, export, automobile registration, sales, production, and various other figures is given for six world markets— Asia, Europe, South America, North America, Mexico, and Canada. A more in-depth analysis and summary of the U.S. domestic auto industry provides data about specific models of automobiles such as cars, trucks, and passenger vans. Retail prices of cars and trucks as well as factory installation rates are also given. Finally, an index contains information about automobile suppliers, advertisers, and products.

HD 9696 .C2 M62 1993 (Computer Industry—Directories; Computer Service Industry—Directories; Microcomputers—Directories)

Microcomputer Market Place (New York: Random House Electronic Publishing)

Microcomputer Market Place is a guidebook for new microcomputer technologies that provides contact information for personal computer (PC) product companies, service providers, sellers and resellers, and other organizations in the field. The primary sections of the book contain telephone numbers and addresses for software and hardware companies, new equipment sources, mail order suppliers, secondary market sources, service providers, information and media resources, microcomputer associations and organizations, educational organizations, computer safety resources, and government agencies. Subsections also contain, where applicable, company product categories, business hours, nonprofit organizations accepting used computer equipment, trade/professional organizations, PC users' groups, schools certified by the Computer Sciences Accreditation Board, listings of products and manufacturers aimed at improving computer safety, and federal agencies that have regulatory jurisdiction over microcomputer products. Subsections contain contact and descriptive information for publishers (electronic and print) and media outlets in the microcomputing field, including publishers of CD-ROMs, computer books, magazines, and newsletters; computer radio and television talk shows; syndicated computer columnists; information brokers; on-line information services; CompuServe computer forums; and electronic bulletin boards. A list of service providers is designed for people who are developing or actively marketing microcomputer products as well as for those who wish to improve staff proficiency and performance with microcomputers, and includes advertising agencies and public relations firms; trade show sponsors; market research firms; market research product and service companies; domestic distributors; international distributors; venture capital firms; computer leasing companies; hardware and software training firms; consulting referral services; and executive recruiters. A comprehensive, alphabetical index is included in the back of the book.

HD 9696 .R36 S82 (Cellular Radio Equipment Industry; Cellular Radio Equipment Industry—United States)

State of the Cellular Industry (Washington, DC: CTIA) 1992.

This guide provides information about the expanding global cellular telephone industry. It is published by the Cellular Telecommunications Industry Association (CTIA), an organization that governs the practices and guidelines of numerous cellular corporations. A brief history and timeline of the cellular industry is followed by a listing of the top 25 carriers in the United States by population. A profile of the owners of each of these companies follows. Then there is a listing of the carriers in each of the over 700 telephone zones in the United States. The cellular systems of Canada, Mexico, and other international countries are briefly reviewed. A roster of the members in CTIA concludes the publication.

HD 9715 .U52 C42 (Construction Industries—United States—Statistics; Building Trades—United States—Statistics)

Census of Construction Industries: Industry Series (Washington, DC: U.S. Department of Commerce, Bureau of the Commerce)

This multivolume guide, published after an economic census every 5 years, provides an in-depth analysis of the American construction industry. The directory is divided into three main categories of the construction industry: (1) building construction by general contractors or by operative builders, (2) heavy construction general contractors, and (3) construction by other special trade contractors. The first section includes contractors who generally build stores, office buildings, or homes. The second section contains industries like the highway and street builders and water and power line companies. The third section is composed of independent construction contractors like plumbers, painters, electricians, and carpenters. Each industry class has its own mini-issue. These volumes contain various statistics that detail the economic activity of each specific industry. It includes data like the values of inventories, assets, expenditures, sales, and employment information. The guide also provides an explanation of terms and listing of SIC codes and geographic divisions.

HD 9718 .E61 (Pollution Control Industry—Directories; Industries—Environmental Aspects—Management)

Meech, Karen Napoleone, Ed. Environmental Industries Marketplace: A Guide to United States Companies Providing Environmental Regulatory Compliance Products and Services (Detroit, MI: Gale Research) 1992.

This work is a guide to companies in the United States that provide products and services enabling industry and business to comply with state and federal environmental regulations. The areas include acid rain, air pollution, asbestos abatement, groundwater pollution, hazardous waste, landfills, noise pollution, recycling, resource recovery, soils, solid waste, spills, wastewater, and water pollution. It is designed for manufacturers, developers, municipal waste control officials, students, and journalists. The source is divided into alphabetical, subject, and geographical listings. The entries include company name, corporate headquarter's address, telephone, fax, toll-free number, brief description of the type of products and services, company products, and company brands.

HD 9720.4 .M31 1998 (Industry)

Manufacturing Worldwide (Detroit: Gale) 1998.

Part I presents manufacturing data from companies worldwide. The information spans more than 400 countries and 37 manufacturing sectors. Part II contains statistics on 141 countries and their leading industries.

HD9723.A84 (Corporations, Foreign—United States—Directories; United States—Manufactures—Directories)

Directory of Foreign Manufacturers in the United States (Atlanta: School of Business Administration, Georgia State University) 1993.

The Directory is a guide to American companies that have more than 10% foreign ownership. The alphabetical listing gives the name, address, phone, type of business, products by Standard Industrial Classification (SIC), parent company, and address of the parent company. This list is indexed by (1) state where the company is located, (2) parent companies, (3) parent companies by country, and (4) products (by SIC) produced.

In addition to this listing, the introduction to the Directory gives a summary of the changing nature of foreign investment in American-based companies and a three-page bibliography. Exhibits are provided on (1) states ranked by the number of foreign-owned American manufacturers, (2) countries of parent companies ranked by number of foreign-owned American manufacturers, and (3) companies by industrial classification.

HD 9724 .A45 1990
(United States—Manufacturers—Statistics)

Census of Manufacturers (Washington, DC: U.S. Bureau of the Census)

This survey is part of the economic censuses done every 5 years. It compiles data on a number of aspects of manufacturing in the United States. Manufacturing, according to the introductory notes, is the "mechanical or chemical transformation of substances into new products." Manufacturing industries covered are those producing for wholesale trade, to order for industrial users and for transfer to other plants of the same company. Service-type activities are included if they are done primarily for trade (such as binding and enameling). Statistics are established through questionnaires, with the list of companies coming from the Internal Revenue Service and the Social Security Administration.

Information is provided on a myriad of manufacturing elements. Included are data on factors of labor: employment, hours worked, payrolls, production, prices, inventories, orders, equipment and machinery investments, and raw material consumption. Price and production indexes are also covered as well as GNP accounts. General statistics, such as hours worked, payroll, material costs, expenditures, and inventories, are gathered for each business enterprise.

Sections of the census are divided into a general summary of the statistics, an industry series, and geographic area series. The general summary contains tables of historical, industry, product class, and geographic area statistics. The industry series further breaks down the statistics. Here, the tables are divided into industry, product, and material. The geographic area series provides information on each state and records summary, industry and employment-size class statistics, as well as historical statistics. The summary statistics are broken down to detail the state and metropolitan areas and counties within that state.

HD9724 .M28 1992 (United States—Manufactures—Statistics—Periodicals; United States—Industries—Statistics—Periodicals)

Manufacturing USA (Detroit: Gale)

Manufacturing USA provides an overview and statistical analysis of manufacturing industries. Tables, graphs, maps, and charts give general statistics, indices of change, ratios, product-share information, and geographic data for each industry profiled. The entries are organized numerically by Standard Industrial Classification (SIC) codes and are indexed by products, companies, occupation, and SIC codes. The information is gathered from federal sources and Ward's Business Directory of Private and Public Companies. A detailed user's guide explains the types of information provided and the organization of the work.

HD 9853 .F16 1994 (Clothing Trade—United States—Directories; Clothing Trade—United States—Statistics; Textile Industry—United States—Directories; Textile Industry—United States—Statistics)

Fairchild's Textile and Apparel Financial Directory
(New York: Fairchild)

This work lists and provides data on textile and apparel companies. It includes outlines of economic and market indicators for the American economy and tables with data on industry shipping information, employment, and foreign trade. It also has lists of statistics for American and Canadian fiber and textile manufacturers. The companies are listed in alphabetical order with information on the addresses, officers, plant locations, directors, business activities, and divisions. For each company data are provided on sales, earnings, assets, liabilities, common stock equity, and revenues. The work also has an index of trademarks, brand names, and company names.

HD 9980.3 D93 (Service Industries—Directories)

Dun's Directory of Service Companies (Bethlehem, PA:
Dun's Marketing Service)

This guide provides a listing of over 50,000 American companies involved in the service sector of the economy. The businesses are grouped into different sections such as auto repair services and garages, motion pictures, health services, social services, and personal services. The directory is divided into three sections that list the enterprises alphabetically, geographically, and by Standard Industrial Classification code. The information contained in each entry includes annual sales and volume, total employment, business address and telephone number, company officers, and bank and accounting relationships.

HD 9981.3 H85 1990 (Service Industries—United States— Information Services—Directories; Corporations—United States—Information Services—Directories; Service Industries—United States—Bibliography—Directories)

How to Find Information about Service Companies, 3rd Ed. (Washington, DC: Washington Researchers Publications) 1990.

How to Find Information about Service Companies explores challenges and opportunities in service company research. The book offers advice in getting the best resources for companies and discusses strategies for producing the best research in service company investigation. It includes address of places to get information. This publication is for people who have experience in service research and for those who have a background in business intelligence.

HD 9981.4 .S44 (Service Industries—United States—Statistics—Periodicals)

Service Industries USA: Industry Analyses, Statistics, and Leading Organizations (Detroit, MI: Gale Research)

This work presents data on the service sector in the United States, including data for over 2000 services grouped into 151 industries. These are primarily in the SIC code 7000s and 8000s. Wholesale and retail trade as well as insurance and financial services are excluded. This source combines statistics from federal sources with facts and figures for leading corporations and representative nonprofit organizations. Six indexes provide access by SIC code, Service, Company, Nonprofit organization, City or Metro Area, and Occupation.

The work is divided into two parts. Part one includes a brief description of each industry followed by national and state level data for 1982–1989, in SIC code number order. Also included are statistics such as number of establishments, percent of U.S. establishments and percent of U.S. employment. Maps show the reader where activity in each service industry is concentrated.

Part two contains data in tables for cities and metropolitan areas in alphabetical order by the name of the city/metro area. The first section of each table contains figures for all services in the city/metro area (e.g., total establishments, employment, payroll, and revenue). Statistics for each industry follow in SIC code number order.

HD 9981.7 .C2 C34 (Service Industries—California— Directories; Industries—California—Directories)

California Services Register (Anaheim, CA: Database Publishing) 1993.

This reference source contains company listings and key executives in business services, communications, entertainment, financial, insurance, health care, real estate, transportation, wholesale, trade, and many other industries.

The book is a good information source for businesses selling products to other service businesses. It includes detailed profiles on 40,000 service companies in northern and southern California. It identifies those businesses that are female- or minority-owned. A complete listing has company name, parent address, telephone, FAX, and WATS numbers, year established, annual revenue, number of employees, plant size, computer system used, primary bank, and legal structure. The listings are printed in both an alphabetic and a geographic section that list SIC code.

HD 9992.U5 S76 (Sporting Goods Industry—United States— Directories; Sporting Goods Industry—Canada—Directories; Athletics—United States—Societies, etc.—Directories; Athletics—Canada—Societies, etc.—Directories)

Sports Market Place (Princeton, NJ: Sportsguide)

This guide contains various information about hundreds of organizations and associations in the sports world. The first section of the book is organized by the type of sport, such as cycling or basketball. Each subdivision includes professional, amateur, and international organizations and media publications for the sport and the manufacturers of related products. The second section has information about multisport associations and periodicals. It is divided into numerous categories including major sports arenas/stadiums, foreign sports media, sports lawyers, and corporate sports sponsors. Each of these sections contains the year the entity was founded, mailing address, and more detailed data about the specific establishment. The third section provides information about hundreds of sports executives and a geographic and alphabetical index of the numerous sports organizations.

HD 9994 .U52 M49 (Medical Instruments and Apparatus Industry—United States—Directories; Medical Care—United States—Directories)

The Medical and Healthcare Marketplace Guide (Miami, FL: International Bio-Medical Information Service)

This annual guide provides a listing of the thousands of companies in the medical and healthcare industry. It is divided into eight sections, the first of which is the Introduction. The second section is an alphabetical index of firms included in the book. Section three, Medical Marketplace, is further divided into three subsections: Pharmaceuticals, Medical Devices, and Medical Services, which present customized reports and overviews about hundreds of categories of companies. The fourth section, Product and Service Classes, lists hundreds of subclasses of companies alphabetically and by market category. Section five supplies a brief profile of each firm. Listed alphabetically by parent company, it provides information like the business address, sales, officers, products and services, and number of employees. The sixth section gives a geographic listing of companies, and the seventh section alphabetically lists the names of the company executives. The last section notes any company name changes that may have occurred since the last edition.

HE—TRANSPORTATION AND COMMUNICATIONS

HE 8.9.N27 (Transportation—United States—Societies, etc.—Directories; Transportation and State—United States—Directories)

National Transportation Organizations: Their Roles in the Policy Development and Implementation Process (Washington, DC: Eno Transportation Foundation, Inc.)

This series of publications aim at the critical decentralized sector of transportation in our economy today. National transportation organizations aid independent agencies within the sector to adjust to changes outside and between each other by playing a significant role in producing information, coordination, and structure needed. This guide provides a ready reference of both private and public organizations, describing the major stakeholder groups and listing about 200 associations which are involved in transportation policy development and implementation. Under the listings are web sites and E-mail addresses of these companies. At the end of the directory are an index of contact names and an appendix of annual meetings and major conferences.

HE 9 .O32 (Hotels, Taverns, etc.—Directories; Tourist Camps, Hostels, etc.—Directories)

Hotel and Motel Red Book (New York, NY: American Hotel and Motel Association Directory Corp.)

This official directory of the American Hotel & Motel Association provides travel and lodging information for hotels, motels, resorts, and condominiums in the United States, Canada, Mexico, the Bahamas, Bermuda, and the Caribbean, as well as limited coverage in Europe, Asia, and the Middle East. The main section details information about accommodations and is arranged alphabetically by state, city, and name of hotel. Information about an individual city is given in preceding each city section, including the county that the city is in, the population, airline service, transportation to and from airports, car rental agencies at the airports, colleges, and points of interest.

Information provided on facility accommodations include the location of the facility (airport, downtown, suburb, etc.), languages spoken, existence of seasonal rates and lodging plans, meetings and convention facilities, as well as the number of rooms, a description, the rates, services available, dining accommodations, and credit cards accepted. The resort and condominiums section and the international section provide similar information. The meeting planning guide gives information detailing meeting facilities. Included is the capacity of the function rooms, exhibit space, audiovisual equipment available, on-site facilities, and rates. A directory of domestic and international airlines, major car rental systems, and domestic and foreign tourism information sources is also included.

HE 9.O33 (Hotels—North America—Directories; Tourism—North America—Directories; North America—Description and Travel—1971—Directories)

Lane, James Max. OAG Business Travel Planner (Oak Brook, IL: OAG Worldwide)

This work is designed for business travelers by providing information on such topics as frequent traveler programs, telephone directories, city guides, and hotel listings in the American Hotel Motel Association. Under each motel and hotel listing, details such as credit card acceptances, the number of rooms, fax machine numbers, and corporate and government rates are provided. This information may also be accessed via the web site http://www. ahma.com.

HE 196.5.M82 (Transportation—United States; Corporations—United States; Securities—United States)

Arnold, Wayne, et. al. Moody's Transportation Manual
(New York: Moody's Investor Service) 2000.

This manual provides detailed statistical data covering the transportation industry in fields such as railroads, airlines, steamship companies, bus and truck lines, oil pipe lines, bridge companies, and automobile and truck leasing and rental companies. Nearly 700 transportation enterprises are represented in this manual. Information from financial statements, such as comparative earnings figures, balance sheets, operating statistics, historical data, management, security descriptions and bond ratings, equipment owned, and routes operated, would be of interest to investors. A listing of board directors, maps, and a glossary can be found at the back of the manual.

HE 196.5.M82 (Transportation—United States—Finance—Periodicals; Railroads—United States—Finance—Periodicals; Securities—United States—Finance—Periodicals)

Moody's Transportation News Reports (New York: Moody's)

This is a publication of statistics from the transportation industry, targeted at investors. The statistical information is categorized into different types of transportation. It contains preferred stock ratings and corporate bond ratings, which would facilitate the reader's understanding of investing in the industry.

HE 2708.I4 1994 (Transportation—Commerce)

Interstate Commerce Commission Annual Report (Washington, DC: Government Printing Office)

The report is a compilation of federal information on railroads, trucking companies, and bus companies during the year ending on September 30. For each of the types of transportation, in-depth coverage is provided on areas such as financial condition, laws that restrict or support the courses of action, as well as federal legislation, consumer protection, and the administration.

HE 5623 A45 T88 1999 (Trucking—United States—Directories; Trucking—Canada—Directories)

National Motor Carrier Directory Organization: TTS—Transport Technical Services (New York: Transportation Technical Services)

Section one has an alphabetically sorted index of trucking company names. Section two sorts the information by the states in which they are located and provides contact information including address, telephone/fax number of each company, as well as what services it offers, the type of trucks owned, as well as when the company was established. Section three sorts the data by zip code and has contact information and references.

HE 6361.N28 (Zip Code—United States—Directories; Postal Service—United States—Directories)

United States Postal Service. National Five-Digit Zip Code and Post Office Directory (Memphis, TN: United States Postal Service)

This directory lists five-digit zip codes and postal offices in the United States and can be found for street names or cities.

HE 7601 .A5 (Telephone—Statistics; Telecommunications—Statistics)

The World's Telephones (Morristown, NJ: ATT International Marketing)

This source is issued annually with varying titles. It contains tables and graphs listing a variety of worldwide telecommunications statistics that may provide necessary information by an analysis of the increasing number of access lines and the ensuing demand for services and products. Some of the tables included are Total PBX and Centrex Access Lines, Total Access Lines by Business and Residence, Local Telephone Traffic, Long Distance Traffic, and Total Exchange Access Lines in the World's Principle Cities and Population. A few of the graphs are Access Lines per 100 Population, Total Households in Descending Order, and Growth of Population and Access

Lines. Some of the tables have 2 years information on facing pages, making a year-to-year comparison easy. There is a two-page section of definitions in the back as well as a section called "Country Notes" that lists by country any omissions or anomalies in the data. The book begins with an explanation of the International Telephone World Numbering Zones and includes a map and a list showing which countries are in what zones. The information in the tables throughout the book is organized according to the nine world zones with the member countries organized alphabetically within each zone grouping.

HE 7601.A62 (Telecommunication—Statistics—Periodicals)

Telecommunication Development Bureau, Yearbook of Statistics: Telecommunication Services (Geneva, Switzerland: International Telecommunication Union)

This yearbook consists of data related to telecommunications for various countries. Comparisons are made across different economies over a span of 10 years. Other information on the countries, such as demographies and economies, is also available.

HE 7621 .I62 (Telecommunication Equipment Industry—Directories; Telecommunication—Directories; Broadcasting—Directories)

Roberts, Steven and Tony Hay, Eds. International Directory of Telecommunications: Market Trends, Companies, Statistics, and Personnel (Essex, UK: Longman Group Limited, Professional and Information Publishing Division) 1986.

This directory attempts to provide access to business information involving the telecommunications industry. Products and suppliers, company statistics, regulatory stance, and market trends are all topics that are included. The book contains a glossary, an index of companies and organizations, an index of product areas, an index of registered trade names, and an index of personal names. Each of the 12 chapters is devoted to one country or geographical area. The areas included are Africa, Asian and Oceania, Australia and New Zealand, Canada, Europe (East), Western Europe (EEC countries), Western Europe (non-EEC countries), Japan, Latin America and the Caribbean, the Middle East, United Kingdom, and the United States. The book covers the United Kingdom more extensively than any of the other areas. Each chapter begins with a description of the telecommunication regulations, the existing networks and services, and the supply industry of the chapter's particular country or area. The chapters covering more than one country contain individual descriptions for several of the countries in that area. The chapter on Africa, for example, begins with a brief description of the telecommunications industry in Algeria, Botswana, Ivory Coast, Malawi, Nigeria, South Africa, and Zimbabwe. Each chapter ends with a directory of company profiles that detail the following information: company name, address, telephone, telex, type of organization, parent, activities, operating sites, operating territories, products, trade names, senior staff, staff at year end, publications, financial year end, and turnover.

HE 7621.T27 (Telecommunication—Directories)

Mueckenheim, Jacqueline K. Telecommunications Directory
(Farmington Hills, MI: Gale)

This work provides information on firms that concentrate in telecommunications and industries that sell equipment, covering a range of areas including cellular communications and access to the Internet. Two indexes are available in this directory: master name and keyword, geography, and personal name.

HE 7771 .F14 (Electronic Mail Systems—Directories; Facsimile Transmission—United States—Directories; Facsimile Transmission—Canada—Directories)

Facsimile Users' Directory: Key Fax Numbers in the U.S. and
Affiliated offices in Canada, Europe and the Far East
(New York, NY: Monitor Publishing Company)

This is a book of fax numbers. It contains an alphabetical index of company names and a chart of time zones and world holidays. A brief explanation of public fax businesses and hotel fax outlets with numbers to call for more information on those services is included. The book is divided into four sections by geographical area: North America, Europe, the Far East, and other regions. Information within each of the four geographical sections is arranged by country. Company names are listed alphabetically within each country segment. Information is not arranged by state or province except in the sections on government, which is further classified by agency. No criteria for the inclusion or exclusion of a company, agency, or organization are given. This directory is weighted towards North America. Its entries are classified by 17 types of businesses: accounting firms; advertising and public relations firms; architectural firms; corporation and subsidiary headquarters; country and municipal governments; embassies, consulates, trade missions, and tourist offices; federal government; financial institutions; foundations; law firms; library facilities; media and publishing firms; museums; real estate firms; state government; trade professional associations; and universities. The sections on Europe and the Far East each have only six subdivisions by business. These are accounting firms, advertising and public relations firms, corporation and subsidiary headquarters, financial institutions, law firms, and media and publishing firms. The section on other regions has only two sections, which are accounting firms and law firms.

HE 8700 .7 .A8 N67 (Television Audiences—United States)

Nielsen Report on Television (Northbrook, IL: Nielsen Media Research)

This report is a compilation of data gathered on television audience behavior. Each section contains one or two brief paragraphs of discussion coupled with an illustrative chart or table. Some of the areas covered include channels receivable per TV household, TV ownership growth, percent of households using television, average hours of household TV usage per day, hours of TV usage per week by household characteristics, audience composition by selected program type, top 20 syndicated programs, top 15 regularly scheduled network programs, and top 20 programs by market.

HE 8700.7 .C6 B87 (Community Antenna Television—United States—Directories—Periodicals; Community Antenna Television—Canada—Directories—Periodicals)

Broadcasting/Cable Yearbook (Washington, DC: Broadcasting Publications)

This yearbook contains nine major sections covering the history and current activity in the broadcasting and cable industry and provides detailed information about individual station and companies. The major sections are the fifth estate, radio, television, cable, satellites, programming, advertising and marketing, technology, and professional services. Each of the major sections begins with an index and a key to the format of its entries. Sections are arranged alphabetically by state, city, and individual radio and television stations where applicable. The editorial and general index provides a guide to the book as well as an index to the short, informative discussions interspersed throughout the book. Sample titles include a short course in cable, anatomy of cable regulation, applying for broadcast stations, and an equipment buyer's guide.

HE 8811 .A88 (Toll-free Telephone Calls—United States— Directories; United States—Directories—Telephone; Telephone—United States—Directories—Yellow Pages; Telephone—United States—Directories)

AT&T Toll-free 800 Directory: Business Edition (Morristown, NJ: AT&T)

This source is a directory of public toll-free telephone numbers. The directory is divided into two main sections; white and yellow. The white section is arranged alphabetically by the name of the business, organization, or government agency. Each entry includes the phone number, the region or states the number can be called from, and a reference to the corresponding product and service heading in the yellow pages under which the listing can be found. The yellow section is arranged alphabetically by product and service headings. Each entry includes the phone number, the region or states from which the number can be called, and where the organization or agency is located. An index lists the various product and service categories found in the yellow section.

HE 8811 .B66 (Toll-free Telephone Numbers—United States—Directories)

Bly, Amy Sprecher and Robert W. Information Hotline U.S.A. (New York, NY: Plume) 1987.

This source is a directory of telephone number for sources of free or inexpensive information from companies, nonprofit organizations, publishers, individuals, and government agencies. Many toll-free numbers are included. Resources for a variety of topics are covered, such as taxes, surgery, child care, small business, insurance, health care, medicine, computers, career planning, and gardening. Resources offered include recorded messages, telephone help lines, on-line information services, free brochures, pamphlets, and newsletters. A cross section of organizations represented includes General Motors, IBM, National Association for the Deaf, Nutrition Action Group, and Smokenders. The book is arranged alphabetically by subject heading. Within this grouping are the name of the organization, the telephone number, and a description of the resource offered. The table of contents is arranged alphabetically by subject heading. The book contains indexes for subject and organizations.

HE 9768 A96 2001 (Aeronautics—United States—Handbooks, Manuals, etc.; Airlines—United States—Handbooks, Manuals, etc.; Aerospace Industries—United States— Handbooks, Manuals, etc.; United States Air Force— Handbooks, Manuals, etc.; United States—Armed Forces—Handbooks, Manuals, etc.; Aeronautics— Handbooks, Manuals, etc.; Aerospace Industries— Handbooks, Manuals, etc.)

The Aviation and Aerospace Almanac (Washington DC: Aviation Week, Group Newsletters, McGraw-Hill)

This is a directory of financial and statistical information gathered from airports, airlines, and other forms of transportation from the aerospace industry. The data are categorized into different sections, for example, airlines, aviation, and military.

HE 9911.A97
(Aeronautics—Yearbooks; Astronautics—Yearbooks)

Aerospace: Facts and Figures (Washington, DC: Aerospace Industries Association of America, Inc.)

This yearbook reports the facts and figures of aerospace activities beginning in 1919. The Aerospace Industries Association of America presented these statistics with a brief overview of the topic followed by a series of tables and occasionally a detailed chart or bar graph. This book covers a variety of issues in the field of aeronautics, such as aircraft production, missile and space programs, air transportation, research and development, foreign trade, employment, and finance. A glossary and an index are included at the back of the yearbook.

HF—COMMERCE

HF 1 .I65 (Executives—Abstracts—Periodicals; Commerce—Abstracts—Periodicals; International Business Enterprises—Abstracts—Periodicals)

The International Executive (New York, NY: American Management Association)

This publication, produced in conjunction with the American Graduate School of International Management (Thunderbird), utilizes a general subject approach to provide information for those engaged in international business. Each issue contains several brief articles on topics of interest to executives and a feature called the reference guide. The guide provides three sections of annotations and bibliographic information for recent books, monographs, and journal articles of substance. The first section features the topics of general management, accounting and taxation, banking, export/import and management, law, and marketing. The international economics and trade sections deal with economic relationships, economic development and aid, monetary affairs, regional economic groups, trade regulations, and world trade. The regional studies section covers the world in general, Africa, East Asia, South Asia, Southeastern Asia, Canada, Eastern Europe and Russia, Oceania, and Western Europe. There is a country and special topic index for the reference guide at the end of every issue. Prior to 1989, this publication provided abstracts of writings rather than original articles.

HF 25 .A52 (Soviet Union—Commerce—Periodicals; Europe, Eastern—Commerce—Periodicals)

Soviet and Eastern European Foreign Trade

This quarterly publication aims to present important Soviet and Eastern European studies articles pertaining to the interests of those concerned with the field. The journal contains translations of articles from scholarly journals and collections of articles pertaining to Eastern European studies.

Each issue is organized on a central term such as the exchange rate policy or aspects of foreign trade and may contain the works of one or more authors. Each article is accompanied by information giving the original language, source, and date of publication. The articles are listed in *Current Contents: Behavioral, Social and Educational Sciences* and is indexed in *PAIS Bulletin*.

HF 53 .W93
(Commerce—Periodicals; Commerce—Directories)

United Nations, Statistical Office, World Trade Annual
(New York, NY: Walker)

The United Nations publishes this five-volume set to provide summarized and detailed trade data for 23 nations. Each volume provides a section of technical notes on such topics as exchange rates. There are three types of tables included in each volume. The first table presents monetary totals on commodities by trading partner with an export and import section. All figures are in U.S. dollars. The other two tables deal with import and export data respectively for specific commodities. These two tables are arranged by product with commodity breakdowns provided by the Standard International Trade Classification (SITC), Revision 2. Monetary figures are again reported in U.S. dollars and quantities are in metric units per each trading partner. Export values are reported as free on board (f.o.b.) and exports as cost, insurance, finance (c.i.f.), except for Canada and Australia, which use f.o.b. for imports.

HF53.W932 1997 v.1–5 (Commerce; Commerce—Directories; Underdeveloped Areas—Commerce—Periodicals; Commercial Statistics—Periodicals)

United Nation Statistical Office, Supplement to the World Trade Annual: Trade of the Industrialized Nations with Eastern Europe and the Developing Nations (New York: Walker)

This guide includes trade statistics for major geographic regions and countries by commodity and trading partner. Within these five volumes, which are differentiated by geographic regions and subregions, each includes total imports, total exports, and re-exports of all commodities reported by the 23 countries.

HF 54.5 .I58 1996 (Business)

The International Directory of Business Information Sources and Services 1996 (London: Europa Publications Limited) 1995.

Every chapter covers one country. Within the chapter, there is information on the Chambers of Commerce, Foreign Trade-Promoting Organizations, Government, Independent and Research Organizations, Sources of Statistical Information, and Business Libraries in the country.

HF 54.52 .U5 .R22 (Business)

Rasie, Lawrence. Directory of Business Information (New York: John Wiley and Sons)

Part I of this book lists sources covering several topics in business. Part II covers topics such as economy, leading companies, and industries. The third part has separate chapters on new and small, international businesses, and topics like antiques. The last section provides information on businesses in different regions and also lists the largest libraries in the countries.

HF 54.56 .D28 (Business)

Deans, Candace and Dakin, Shaun. The Thunderbird Guide to International Business Resources on the World Wide Web (New York: John Wiley and Sons) 1997.

The book is divided into six sections based on geographic regions, and each section contains web sources pertaining to a specific region. Before the section is an introduction describing business practices and cultures of the region.

HF 54.U5 P96 (Commerce—Directories—Periodicals; International Business Enterprises—Directories— Periodicals; Industry—Classification—Periodicals)

Principal International Business: The World Marketing Directory (Parsippany, NJ: Dun and Bradstreet International) 1974.

This book is a listing of thousands of global enterprises. The guide divides these companies into various categories, such as manufacturing wholesale trade, mining, communications, agriculture, and transportation. The directory is divided into three sections that list businesses geographically, by product classification, and alphabetically. Each entry provides data about each. This information includes the name of the parent company, business address, telephone number, number of employees, annual sales, Standard Industrial Classification code, chief executive, and an indicator of whether the company imports and exports. The guide is translated into four languages— English, French, Spanish, and German.

HF54.5.E56 1999 (Business Information Services— Encyclopedias; International Business Enterprises— Encyclopedias; Gale Research Inc.)

Heil, Scott. Encyclopedia of Global Industries (Michigan: Gale) 1999.

This work provides information on worldwide competitors and suppliers, as well as the important trends and enterprises in major industries. It explains the globalization of industry, the direction of future trade, and the integration of the global investment. It gives an overview of relationships among key companies in each industry in addition to an overview of how each industry has overcome the challenges of global integration. It also includes bibliographical references and indexes.

HF54.5.I58 1996 (Business Information Services— Directories; Commerce—Information Services—Directories; Trade Associations—Directories)

The International Directory of Business Information Sources and Services (London, England: Europa Publications Limited) 1996.

This work provides separate chapters with general information on business concerns for each of 23 countries with developed market economies, as well as leading economies of Latin American, Middle East, and Far East, Russian

Federation, Central Europe, and international organizations. It also includes an index of entries.

HF54.5 .P13
(Business Information Services—Handbooks, Manuals, etc.; Business—Bibliography—Handbooks, Manuals, etc.)

Pagell, Ruth A., and Michael Halperin. International Business Information: How to Find It, How to Use It (Phoenix, AZ: Oryx Press) 1998.

International Business Information: How to Find It, How to Use It describes important international business publications and databases and gives the necessary background information for understanding them. The five-part work consists of Introduction, Company Information, Marketing, Industrial and Economic Statistics, and International Transactions, and chapters within each develop a particular theme. The reader can get a quick summary of the material by skimming the chapter's beginning where lists of topics and sources are located. Appendices supplement the main text with specific technical data. Title and subject indexes provide easy access to the work, and lists of tables and exhibits at the front guide the user to exact or truncated facsimiles of printed and electronic business sources.

HF 54.52 .U5 F7411 1991 (Business—Information Services— United States—Directories; Information Storage and Retrieval Systems—Business—Handbooks, Manuals, etc.; Business—Databases—Directories; Reference Books— Business—Bibliography—Handbooks, Manuals, etc.; Government Publications—United States—Handbooks, Manuals, etc.)

Freed, Melvyn N. and Virgil P. Diodato. Business Information Desk Reference: Where to Find Answers to Business Questions (New York, NY: Macmillan) 1991.

The source is a ready-reference handbook and serves as a business information retrieval guide to printed materials (475 entries), on-line databases (138 entries), and selected government agencies and business organizations. This reference tool is designed to be used by people working in the business world, students, researchers, and librarians.

Organized into four parts, parts one and two cover printed business information sources, while parts three and four cover electronic business information sources. It features a question and answer format consisting of

"Where do I find information on. . .?" questions followed by short answers that direct users to the appropriate sources.

The source includes a section on "Guidelines for Finding and Evaluating Business Information" and a section on "Linking the Research Question to the Business Information Source." Also included are three appendixes with publisher information, more on-line databases, and a detailed title/subject index.

HF54.56.L78 (Business/Services—Computer Network Resources—Directories; International Trade—Computer Network Resources—Directories; Economic History—1990—Computer Network Resources—Directories; Business Travel—Computer Network Resources—Directories; Web Sites—Directories)

Liu, Lewis-Guodo. Internet Resources and Services for International Business: A Global Guide (Arizona: Oryx Press) 1998.

This guide covers information from over 25,000 web sites on international business in over 175 countries and regions. The web sites used are all developed, organized, and maintained by businesses, government agencies, or institution of higher learning. The information gathered from these web sites are meant to provide individuals and organizations information on business in over 175 countries. The resources of each country are divided into five categories: General Information, Economy, Business and Trade, Business Travel, and Contact Information. It also includes indexes.

HF 91 .D59 (Commerce—Statistics—Periodicals)

Direction of Trade Statistics (Washington, DC: International Monetary Fund)

This publication presents statistical data on the flow of trade between well over 100 countries. There is no product breakdown. Statistics are aggregate monetary figures for exports and imports. Each issue is organized in two sections of tables. The world area table section provides a breakdown by industrial and developing countries. The industrial nations are listed in alphabetic order; developing nations are subdivided by area and alphabetized. Figures are reported in monthly and quarterly total with recent past years included to facilitate comparison. Import figures are reported in cost, insurance, finance (c.i.f.) values, and exports are reported in free on board (f.o.b.) values. All figures are expressed in U.S. dollars. The second section consists of individual country tables with only major trading partners shown. Values are again c.i.f. for imports and f.o.b. for exports unless otherwise noted. There is no standardization of figure reporting as with the area table. All nations supply monthly totals, but only some provide quarterly or previous year figures. An annual yearbook is published providing 7 years of annual data for over 150 countries.

HF 91 .U48 (Commercial Statistics—Periodicals)

United Nations. Statistical Office, Yearbook of International Trade Statistics (New York, NY: Department of Economic and Social Affairs, Statistical Office, United Nations)

This two-volume United Nations publication gives basic information on the external trade performances of individual countries based on overall trends in present value, volume, and price; trading partner importance; and significance of exported and imported individual commodities. More than 150 nations are covered over 4- to 5-year periods with the most current data available. The first volume deals with each individual country providing country notes and tables. The tables present historical and summary data, trading partners, and flow of trade to and from world areas and countries. Import data are in cost, insurance, finance (c.i.f.) values; export figures are in free on board (f.o.b.) values. The Standard International Trade Classification (SITC) provides the commodity breakdowns. There are also 12 special tables covering such topics as the external trade of nations using a centrally planned economy. All values are in U.S. dollars. Volume two contains two sections. The first one provides tables showing total trade of selected commodities via region and country. The second section provides tables showing a commodity matrix presenting major exporting nations with product volume and value in trade with major importing nations.

HF 105 .A277 (United States—Commerce—Periodicals)

United States, Bureau of the Census, Highlights of U.S. Export and Import Trade (Washington, DC: U.S. Government Printing Office)

Providing a general overview, this government publication, designated FT 990, presents information on U.S. foreign commerce trends. Data are given in seasonally adjusted and unadjusted forms as well as in current and retrospective totals. Section A covers exports. Table 1 deals with Department of

Defense grant-in-aid exports of domestic and foreign merchandise in aggregate form and free alongside ship (f.a.s.) value. The last table provides unit-value indexes with aggregate monthly, quarterly, and yearly figures for selected commodity categories. The remaining tables present selected Schedule E (FT 410, commodity by country) breakdowns for domestic and foreign merchandise via method of transportation; world area of destination; world area and country of destination; and U.S. coastal area, customs district, and method of transportation. All figures are f.a.s. value-based. The section contains data for general imports, imports for consumption, and import charges by month. The final table again provides aggregate unit-value indexes for selected commodities. The tables in between utilize selected Schedule A (FT 135, commodity by country) breakdowns simply for general imports and by method of transportation; world area of origin; world area and country of origin; U.S. coastal area, customs district and method of transportation; and imports for consumption by U.S. coastal area and customs district. Figures are presented in both cost, insurance, finance (c.i.f.) and customs value basis as noted.

HF 105 .A31 (United States—Commerce)

United States, Bureau of the Census, U.S. Exports, Commodity by Country (Washington, DC: U.S. Government Printing Office)

This monthly government publication, referred to as Schedule E, FT 410, provides data reflecting government and nongovernment domestic and foreign merchandise exports. Commodity classification is based on Schedule B and values are given in free alongside ship (f.a.s.) form. There are three tables provided. Table 1 gives the value of commodity groupings for domestic merchandise in current month and cumulative figures. Table 2 presents exported commodities by country of destination for domestic merchandise with net quantity, U.S. dollar values, and current and year-to-date data shown. Table 3 is structured in the same way as Table 2 and covers exported foreign merchandise.

HF 105 .A692 (United States—Commerce)

Guide to Foreign Trade Statistics (Washington, DC: US Dept. of Commerce, Bureau of the Census; For Sale by the Supt. of Docs., US, GPO)

This irregularly published work is a guide to foreign trade statistical sources compiled from the printed and electronic files of the Census Bureau's economic statistics program. It provides background information on the foreign trade statistical agenda and lists the formatted reference materials according to the following categories: merchandise trade (special reports, services, and data products catalog), printed reports, available CD-ROM foreign trade products, magnetic tapes, and microfiche. Also included are conversion tables that translate American weights and measures to the metric equivalents according to the Harmonized Commodity Description and Coding System, information on the countries that are used in compiling export and import statistics along with selected international organizations, and various reference aids such as CENDATA and The Economic Bulletin Board. The last section contains an essay on understanding foreign trade data that is useful for the novice as well as the professional, a chapter that gives various order forms, and an index.

HF 105 .A3443 (Commercial Products—United States— Statistics—Periodicals; United States—Commerce— Periodicals)

United States, Bureau of the Census, U.S. General Imports: Schedule A, Commodity by Country (Washington, DC: U.S. Government Printing Office)

Schedule A, FT 135, presents government data on imports in two tables. Table 1 provides commodity group breakdowns with general imports and imports for consumption data. These statistics are in current month and cumulative form, reported in cost, insurance, finance (c.i.f.) and customs values. Table 2 breaks down commodities by country of origin, presenting information on general imports and imports for consumption. Data cover net quantity with values represented in c.i.f. as well as customs rating, and it is presented in current month and cumulative form.

HF 105 .C2844 (Commerce—Periodicals; United States—Commerce)

United States, Department of Commerce, International Trade Administration, Overseas Business Reports (Washington, DC: U.S. Government Printing Office)

This series of government documents deal with marketing and business transactions with other nations and regions. A wide variety of data are available, but the specific type and nature vary by country. In general, basic and specialized economic data can be found along with foreign trade regulations, market profiles, and trade outlook.

HF 1001 .C75
(Business—Dictionaries; Finance—Dictionaries)

A Concise Dictionary of Business (New York: Oxford University Press) 1990.

This dictionary features definitions of terms used in commerce, taxation, marketing, shipping, insurance, business and personal management, industrial relations, international finance, law, economics, and computing.

HF 1001 .C78 (Business—Dictionaries; Finance—Dictionaries; Banks and Banking—Dictionaries)

Cook, William W. Webster's New World Dictionary of Business Terms (New York, NY: Simon & Schuster) 1985.

This pocket size dictionary contains over 3000 definitions of terms relating to the business side of finance, advertising, banking, accounting, and law.

HF1001.F67 (Business—Dictionaries)

Folsom, Davis. Understanding American Business Jargon: A Directory (Connecticut: Greenwood Press) 1997.

This directory includes terms and expressions used in business, as well as everyday American English phrases often used in the world of business. It also includes bibliographical references.

HF 1001 .F92
(Business—Dictionaries; Finance—Dictionaries)

Friedman, Jack P. Dictionary of Business Terms (New York: Barron's) 1987.

This dictionary contains over 6000 definitions of business terms related to investment, banking, taxes, law, real estate, management, and computers. The text is supplemented by a list of abbreviations and acronyms, compound interest factors, and economic indicators.

HF 1001 .M65 (Commerce—Dictionaries; Foreign Trade Regulation—Dictionaries; Commercial Law—Dictionaries)

Miller, William J. Encyclopedia of International Commerce (Centreville, MD: Cornell Maritime Press) 1985.

This encyclopedia focuses on the terms and concepts of international trade, especially in the areas of marketing, taxation, shipping, law, accounting, and transportation. The text is supplemented by sections on statutes, symbols, directories, textual materials, statistics and financial data, and taxes.

HF 1001 .N72 (Business—Dictionaries)

Nisberg, Jay N. The Random House Handbook of Business Terms (New York: Random House) 1988.

This reference book provides definitions for business terms related to retailing, banking, investing, insurance, economics, manufacturing, marketing, computers, and human resources management.

HF 1001 .R82 1993
(Business—Dictionaries; Management—Dictionaries)

Rosenberg, Jerry Martin. Dictionary of Business and Management (New York, NY: Wiley) 1992.

This source was compiled to present an up-to-date guide of current English word usage in business and management terminology for business specialists, students, and professionals. The scope is an in-depth coverage of how a global perspective has influenced 33 business fields and their practices, to know acceptable meanings, to promote more information sharing, and to aid in stabilizing terminology in international environments. It is meant for practical usage and is not intended to be a scholarly work. In comparison to other business dictionaries, it covers more terms in a wide range of fields with easy-to-understand language and less charts or illustrations to confuse the reader. With more than 7500 entries, a typical entry establishes the most general, widely used meaning and can also develop into a specialized usage information by either a one-sentence definition or an essay explanation to help the expert as well as the novice. Alphabetized word by word, the entry may also clarify related concepts and synonyms, abbreviations, symbols, cross-references, slang terms, and some foreign language terms that are commonly used in English. Syllabication and pronunciation are not provided. The dictionary also contains an appendices section that has a variety of tables and lists.

HF1001.R83
(Retail Trade—Dictionaries; Merchandising—Dictionaries)

Rosenberg, Jerry M. Dictionary of Retailing and Merchandising
(New York: Wiley) 1995.

This dictionary includes terms from marketing, advertising, wholesaling, direct marketing, and buying, as well as other common terms used in retailing and merchandising sector of business.

HF 1001 .R681
(Business—Dictionaries; Management—Dictionaries)

Rosenberg, Jerry M. Dictionary of Business and Management
(New York: John Wiley & Sons, Inc.)

This business dictionary, composed of more than 8000 entries, was designed to provide accurate and present-day definition of commonly used words. It will help people to use words with greater clarity and establish better communications. Broad and core definitions are used in this book to make them apply to diverse areas of specialty. Foreign words, phrases, symbols, abbreviations, and acronyms are included in this book. The dictionary contains terms dealing with accounting, administration, advertising, banking, business, business law, collective bargaining, commodities, computers, distribution, economics, export–import, finance, government, insurance, labor relations, management, manufacturing, marketing, merchandising, operation research, organization, packaging, personnel, production, public administration, public policy, publishing, purchasing, real estate, research methodology, retailing, salesmanship, securities, shipping, statistics, stock market, systems, testing, transportation, and warehousing. Words are organized according to complexity. They are placed in the dictionary by alphabetization, under headings, cross-references, and synonyms. The terms have multiple definitions based on their usage in several fields of study. In order to get the definition that relates to the person's area of specialty, all the terms should be examined.

HF1001 .S33
(Accounting—Dictionaries; Finance—Dictionaries)

Shim, Jae K. Encyclopedic Dictionary of Accounting and Finance
(Englewood Cliffs, NJ: Prentice Hall) 1989.

This source was prepared for business professionals for solving technical problems in accounting, finance, investment, and banking. The dictionary covers 500 topics in financial accounting, financial statement analysis, managerial/cost accounting, auditing, managerial finance, investments, financial planning, financial economics, money, and banking, and 100 more in cognate fields such as computers, quantitative techniques and models, and economics as the subject relates to accounting and finance. Each entry contains precise definitions and step-by-step instructions; checklists; practical applications employing real-life situations; extensive tables and statistical data when needed to elucidate a concept; and appropriate charts, exhibits, and diagrams to clarify an idea. Indexed.

HF1001 .T33
(Business—Dictionaries; Finance—Dictionaries)

Terry, John V. Dictionary for Business Finance (Fayetteville, AR: University of Arkansas Press) 1989.

The *Dictionary for Business Finance* is an encyclopedic reference source for financial professionals, industrial experts, business practitioners, students, and scholars. The work goes beyond the disciplinary boundaries set by specialized business dictionaries and defines terms found in diverse subject areas as investment, insurance, accounting, law, real estate, estate planning, economics, management, communications, social and private employee benefits, banking, and other financial institutions. Definitions vary from brief statements to a paragraph. Extensive appendices supplement the main entries and cover real-estate abbreviations; financial abbreviations; simple analysis of various investment vehicles; national income economic terms and abbreviations; ratios, equations, and formulae used in financial and quasi-financial business institutions; important ratios used to evaluate a business; investment vehicle pyramid; titles and functions of people in various sectors of the business world; sources of financial information (with names and addresses); The 1986 Tax Reform Act; and boundaries of federal reserve districts and their branch territories (map).

HF1002 .O423 (Commerce—Dictionaries; International Economic Relations—Dictionaries; Dictionaries, Polyglot)

Dictionary of International Economics: German, Russian, English, French, Spanish. Edited by Siegfried Kohls, with the Collaboration of Roland Dippmann, Walter Gulich and Jose Valls Ponzoda (Leiden: Sijthoff International) 1976.

This dictionary consists of 6500 alphabetically arranged German entries that define German, Russian, English, French, and Spanish terms dealing with commercial usage, commercial law, customs administration, payment systems, and carrying trade. Excluded are trademarks, geographical names, measuring units, weight units, monetary systems, and industries and trades which the compiler believes should be treated in separate works. The Russian, English, French, and Spanish indexes provide easy access to the desired word which can then be connected to its foreign cognate or similar terms and phrases through a numerical concordance. The indexes also make it possible to prepare translations of particular texts into the four other languages.

HF 1009 .H245 (Trading Companies—Developing Countries—Handbooks, Manuals, etc.; Trading Companies—Developing Countries—Directories)

Handbook of State Trading Organizations of Developing Countries (New York: United Nations) 1983.

This handbook is written in four languages, English, French, Spanish, and Arabic. The text is broken up into two sections. The first section provides an introduction, a list of countries and regional groupings, the exchange rates used to convert currencies into U.S. dollars, a glossary of the listed products, a list of ISO codes, and a list of standard international trade classifications. The second section lists information and statistics on the trading organizations of 70 developing countries.

HF 1009.5 .T92 (Export Marketing—Handbooks, Manuals, etc.; International Trade—Handbooks, Manuals, etc.)

Tuller, Lawrence W. The World Markets Desk Book: A Region-by-Region Survey of Global Trade Opportunities (New York: McGraw-Hill) 1993.

This reference book provides data and analysis on specific markets and trading regions throughout the world. The text includes countries/regions from each of the six continents and evaluates each country/region according to seven criteria including: political stability, economic stability, competition and market size, resource cost and availability, trade barriers to foreign investment, ease of entry into the area, and the location of the country. The text is supplemented by data tables and statistics.

HF1009.6.B28
(Export Marketing—United States—Handbooks, Manuals)

United States Department of Commerce, A Basic Guide to Exporting (New Jersey: Unz) 1998.

This guide includes information on trade, with an emphasis on exports. In an effort to become more accessible to American companies, the Commerce

Department has created this in hopes of assisting the general public with some common questions regarding exporting goods and services. This provides information on how to develop export strategies and marketing plans in addition to export advice. It approaches the subject from a technical aspect of exports as well as general knowledge necessary to conduct business abroad. An export glossary is included.

HF1010 .C95 (Commerce—Handbooks, Manuals, etc.; International Trade—Handbooks, Manuals, etc.)

Croner, Ulrich Horst Edward. Reference Book for World Traders; A Loose-leaf Handbook Covering Information Required for Planning and Executing Exports and Imports to and from All Foreign Countries (Queens Village, NY: Croner Publications)

This work is a guide for international trade and market research people who want to engage in planning and executing importing and exporting programs. Volume 1 covers information sources in the United States, basic rules of U.S. exporting, Domestic International Sales Corporation (DISCS), sources of credit reports in the United States, basic import tariff systems in foreign countries, foreign import and exchange controls, postal information, international telegram and telex rates, decimalization of sterling table, foreign exchange quotations, export credit insurance, insurance of export and import shipments, free zone information, steamship companies and airlines, services of foreign freight forwarders, international trade organizations, agencies providing financing for international trade, and conversion tables. Volume 2 is a directory to categories of information associated with particular countries that would be of interest to the potential businessperson wishing to import and export materials. A sampling of topics for one nation entry includes affiliations, airlines, area, cable rates, capital, climate, currency, electric current, exchange rate, geography, holidays, import and exchange control, language, passport and visas, population, principal hotels, principal exports, principal ports, seasons, shipping lines, time, weights and measures, information sources in the United States, and information sources and services in the foreign country (i.e., banks, collections, credit information, customs brokers and freight forwarders, free trade zone and entrepot, surveyors, chamber of commerce, American consulates, and warehouses.) Export documentation covers bills of lading, certificates of origin, commercial invoices, consular invoices, marking packages, and packing material and shipper's export declarations. A country index is located at the beginning of the volume.

HF1010.W32 (International Relations—Handbooks, Manuals, etc.; Diplomatic and Consular Service—United States—Directories; International Agencies—Directories)

The Washington Almanac of International Trade & Business
(Washington, DC: Almanac Pub. Inc.)

This work provides information on both foreign and domestic contacts that deal with foreign policy and international business. It contains information on international health research efforts, cooperative scientific and engineering research projects, and activities of the Environmental Protection Agency.

HF 1014 .A2 A51
(Balance of Payments—Statistics—Yearbooks)

Balance of Payments Statistics Yearbook/International
Monetary Fund (Washington, DC: The Fund)

This reference guide provides balance of payments data on 140 countries and is divided into two volumes. Volume one presents an aggregated presentation and a detailed presentation of the balance of payments data provided by each country. Volume two supplies data on regional and world totals of the balance of payments. The text is supplemented by a list of abbreviations and definitions and several annexes.

HF 1016 .H24
(Commercial Statistics; Developing Countries—Commerce—Statistics; Economic Indicators—Developing Countries)

Handbook of International Trade and Development Statistics
(New York: United Nations)

This reference guide provides data to help analyze the state of world trade and development. The text is arranged into seven sections including the value, growth, and shares of world trade, the volume, unit value, and terms of trade indexes, the network of world trade, the export and import structures of world trade, the balance of payments, a list of basic development indicators, and a section of special studies.

HF 1040. P92 (United States—Economic Conditions—1971; United States—Manufactures; Business Forecasting; Economic Forecasting—United States)

Predicasts Forecasts (Cleveland, Ohio: Predicasts Inc.)

It provides compilations of forecasts on products, markets, industry, and economic aggregates as reported in the trade and business press.

HF 1041 .C73 1981 (Commercial Products—Classification)

United Nations, Statistical Office, Commodity Indexes for the
Standard International Trade Classification, Revision 2
(New York, NY: Statistical Office of the United Nations)

The Standard International Trade Classification (SITC) was created by the
United Nations to provide statistical classification indexes for merchandise in
international trade, presenting the necessary commodity aggregate data for
analysis and comparison. This edition purposely contains the same headings
and subheadings as the Customs Cooperation Council Nomenclature (BTN),
often used by many countries outside the United States in customs tariff
schedules. Volume one contains an item index for basic SITC headings, a
representative list of articles within said headings and the corresponding
CCCN code numbers. Volume two is an alphabetical index containing
thousands of entries again with related CCCN codes.

HF 1042 .I422 (Commercial Products—United States—Classification—Handbooks, Manuals, etc.; United States—Industries—Classification—Handbooks, Manuals, etc.)

1992 Industry and Product Classification Manual (Washington,
DC: U.S. Department of Commerce, Bureau of the
Census) 1992.

This reference book classifies establishments by their form of industrial activity. The general industry classifications include: agriculture, forestry, fishing, mining, construction, manufacturing, transportation, communication,
electric, gas, sanitary services, wholesale trade, retail trade, finance, insurance,
service, and real estate.

HF1101.I62 v.1–2 (Business Teachers—Directories; Finance Teachers—Directories; Industrial Psychologists—Directories; Economists—Directories; College Teachers—Directories; Business—Research—Directories; Management—Research—Directories)

International Directory of Business and Management Scholars
and Research: 1995–1996 (Mass.: Harvard Business School
Press) 1995.

This directory provides a summary of background, training, career achievements, publications, and current research of 4753 active scholars and author-

ities across disciplines in business and management. The two volumes are separated alphabetically by last names. Where necessary, research titles are listed in both English translation and original language. It also includes bibliographical references and indexes.

HF 1131 .B984 1995 (Business Schools—United States— Evaluation; College Choice—United States—Handbooks, Manuals, etc.; Master of Business Administrations Degree—United States—Handbooks, Manuals, etc.)

Byrne, John A. Business Week Guide to the Best Business Schools (New York: McGraw-Hill)

The use of intensive surveys of students, recent graduates, alumnae, recruiters, and top executives forms the basis of in-depth pictures of strengths and weaknesses of schools and programs, as well as their character and personality. Thus it provides an extremely useful tool for matching up a student's needs with a program that most closely corresponds to them. In addition, there a wealth of practical information on testing, essay writing, interviewing, references, and finances. There is an index of schools by state.

HF1359 .F95 (International Economic Relations— Dictionaries; Economic Development—International Cooperation—Dictionaries; Developing Countries— Foreign Economic Relations—Dictionaries)

Fry, Gerald, and Galen R. Martin. The International Development Dictionary (Santa Barbara, Calif.: ABC-CLIO) 1991.

The International Development Dictionary defines the major concepts of international development and foreign relations employing a interdisciplinary approach that includes a variety of social science and humanistic disciplines. The book's purpose is to provide concise and accurate definitions that are often vague and imprecise because international development discourse often exists in the public domain. The authors believe that the dictionary's users would find the work helpful as a reference source, a study guide, a supplement to a textbook, a review of the subject, and as a general aid in areas of knowledge associated with this particular field.

The dictionary's four sections cover (1) development thinkers who are theorists, leaders, and practitioners; (2) basic concepts of development; (3) analytical concepts; and (4) development movements, projects, and organizations. Each item, except for (3), contains subsections, the most belonging to (2), which comprises the major portion of the book. Entries are alphabetically arranged and numbered in the chapters and each entry consists of two parts. The first is a definition of a the concept or a brief analysis of a particular individual's life and work. The second titled "Significance" places the preceding material within the international development paradigm. The reader can access this classified arrangement in a variety of ways. There are alphabetical list of entries followed by the appropriate numbers and an index that includes references that are defined within the text (indicated by bold entry numbers) and associated ideas (represented by entry numerals in roman type.) Entry texts are cross-referenced. Also included are a glossary of acronyms and a bibliography.

HF 1359 .P93 (International Economic Relations— Encyclopedias; International Finance—Encyclopedias; International Relations—Encyclopedias; Export Marketing—Encyclopedias; International Law— Encyclopedias; Banks and Banking, International—Encyclopedias)

Presner, Lewis A. The International Business Dictionary and Reference (New York: Wiley) 1991.

Though nominally a dictionary, this book approaches the more comprehensive status of an encyclopedia. Reflecting the author's commitment to a cross-disciplinary approach the vocabulary treated comprises business, international marketing, law, economics, banking and finance, and international relations and politics. Vocabulary is divided and arranged topically and geographically in the very useful appendices. A sophisticated system of cross-referencing system and many examples enhance the usefulness of this work. The inclusion of foreign language terms not yet "naturalized" into English usage is a valuable feature. A bibliography at the end consolidates the research sources from which information was gleaned.

HF 1359 .93 (Economics—Research—Directories; Economic Policy—Research—Directories)

Capie, Forrest. Directory of Economic Institutions (New York: Stockton Pr.) 1990.

This directory was compiled on the basis of information provided by 350 economic institutions around the world where research takes place. Its purpose is to help researchers and research institutions to ascertain where particular types of work are being carried out and help individuals in search of funding from institutions. It also serves to alert commercial and government organizations which may wish to commission research. The range of institutions covered goes from university economics departments to large international organizations such as the Organization for Economic Cooperation and Development. Entries include all or part of the following: contact information, parent organization, founding or incorporating date, names of key personnel, nature, objectives, funding, research interests, publications, and other activities.

HF1371.B58 (Marketing; International Trade)

U.S. International Trade Administration, The Big Emerging Markets: . . . Outlook and Sourcebook (Lanham, MD.: Bernan Press and National Technical Information Service)

This guidebook seeks to educate the American businesspeople on the Big Emerging Markets Initiative (BEMs). It also includes a directory of contacts for further information on this initiative.

HF1373 .G52 (International Trade—Dictionaries; International Finance—Dictionaries)

Gipson, Carolyn Renee. The McGraw-Hill Dictionary of International Trade and Finance (New York: McGraw-Hill) 1994.

This dictionary defines concepts and terminology associated with banking, economics, customs, finances, insurance, foreign currencies, shipping, regulations, and legalities. It also elucidates important trade agreements, local trade associations, financial corporations, and stock and commodity exchanges. U.S. federal agencies are included along with related investment programs. The author–compiler, Carolyn Renee Gipson, an international trade attorney, collected her information from banks, embassies, government agencies, and various commodity markets, as well as from published sources.

Main entries are in alphabetical order. When necessary, the author uses subentries to explicate the main concept. Numbered multiple definitions and cross-references including "see also" and "compare" broaden the work's reference base. Definitions consist of explanations and examples and occasionally contain foreign terms, usually in French, German, or Spanish. International corporations and agreements are alphabetized in their native languages.

HF1373 .R82 (International Trade—Dictionaries)

Rosenberg, Jerry Martin. Dictionary of International Trade
(New York: J. Wiley) 1994.

This dictionary on international trade has more than 4000 entries that consist of multiple definitions, current symbols, acronyms, abbreviations, and foreign words and phrases that have become part of English usage. The work brings together terms from the government and private sector and focuses on such regional trading alliances as the European Community, the European Free Trade Association, the North American Free Trade Agreement, and those of Central and South America and the Pacific Rim. Also given special consideration is the nomenclature employed by U.S. governmental agencies and by the General Agreement on Tariffs and Trade. The author has organized the dictionary with two types of users in mind: the experienced individual who desires the precise and exact meaning of a term and the newcomer who is looking for general definitions. Words are in alphabetical order with the most popular term functioning as the main entry and other terms cross-referenced to it or to related words in the forms of "see," "see also," and "compare." An appendix consisting of an alphabetical list of countries and their currency codes follows the main text.

HF1416.5.F72 1999
(International Trade—United States; Exports—United States)

Slater, Courtenay. Foreign Trade of the United States:
Including State and Metro Area Export Data
(Washington, DC: Bernan Press)

This work is the first edition of a compilation of data on U.S. imports and exports nationally, statewide as well as in major metropolitan areas. It also includes data showing U.S. Foreign trade as a percent of gross domestic product.

HF1416.5 .W45 1996 (Export Marketing—United States—Handbooks, Manuals, etc.)

Wells, L. Fargo. Exporting: From Start to Finance (New York: McGraw-Hill) 1996.

This work provides information on basic tools of exporting. It provides guidelines on how to evaluate a company's export potential in terms of opportunities, skills, and type of products, as well as addresses other factors involved in establishing or expanding an export business. It includes bibliographical references and index.

HF 1429 .I62 (Foreign Licensing Agreements; Investments, American; Foreign Trade Regulations)

Business International Corp. Investing, Licensing, and
Trade Conditions Abroad (New York, NY: Business
International Corp.)

Known as the ILT, this publication provides information for international business enterprises, and it is organized into sections by the world regions of Europe, Africa/Middle East, Asia, North America, and Latin America. The sections begin with a discussion of issues impacting each region as a whole. Individual nations are then profiled in terms of a general introduction, the state's role in industry, organizing, rules of competition, price controls, licensing, remittability of funds, corporate taxes, personal taxes, incentives, capital sources, labor, and foreign trade. There are many specific topics covered in the 13 fields above including additional sources of business information, attitudes toward free enterprise, currency outlook, profitability of foreign investments, nationalism and privatization policy, acquisition of real estate, establishing local companies or branches, mergers, patent and trade mark protection, royalty and fee patterns, exchange controls, transfer of interest, repatriation of capital, corporate income tax rates, excess profits taxes, personal tax rates, qualifying for incentives, tariff incentives, short-term credit, medium- to long-term credit, unions and work stoppage, nontariff barriers and export insurance. Supplements provide yearly updating.

HF 1455 .A2 (Export Controls—United States; Foreign Trade Regulation—United States)

United States Office of Export Administration. Export
Administration Regulations (Washington, DC: U.S.
Government Printing Office)

This government manual provides information on export controls and licensing procedures mandated by Congress. The regulations' policy guidelines are geared toward preventing significant contributions to the military power of nations that would be detrimental to national security, furthering U.S. foreign policy goals and commitments and protecting America's domestic economy. The introduction provides information on using the manual and a summary of each part of the regulations. Following sections provide the addresses of Department of Commerce offices and a copy of the empowering legislation. The individual parts of the manual deal with U.S. import certificate and delivery verification procedures, restrictive trade practices or boycotts, export licensing general policy and related information, general licenses, individual validated licenses and amendments, special licensing procedures, reexports, documentation requirements, special commodity policies and provisions, short supply controls and monitoring, special nuclear controls, technical data, special entry policies and provisions, export clearance, enforcement, administrative proceedings, appeals, denial orders, general orders, foreign availability procedures and criteria, commodity control lists, and commodity interpretations. Sections on forms and Office of Export Administration bulletins that serve as supplements to the regulations are also included. An alphabetical subject index directs users to the relevant paragraph and section needed.

HF1455 .E97 1988 (Foreign Trade Promotion—Directories; Small Business—United States—Information Services; Export Marketing—United States—Information Services; Administrative Agencies—United States—Information Services)

Exporter's Guide to Federal Resources for Small Business.
(Washington, DC: Interagency Task Force on Trade,
For sale by the Supt. of Docs., U.S. GPO) 1988.

This guide lists federal support programs available for small-business entrepreneurs who are interested in broadening their market areas to include international trade. The document summarizes federal programs, provides U.S. contacts for international trade both at home (state-by-state) and abroad, identifies each agency's focus concerning foreign trade that can assist small business people in understanding each exporting program's mission, and names key agency people who can provide technical assistance and support for small business personnel. The guide has an agency cross-reference and a classified annotated bibliography of governmental international trade publications.

HF1532.92.C73 1998 (European Economic Community Countries—Commercial Policy—Periodicals; Trade Regulation—European Economic Community Countries—Periodicals; Industrial Policy—European Economic Community Countries—Periodicals; Consumer Protection—European Economic Community Countries—Periodicals)

Commission of the European Communities, Report on Competition Policy/Commission of the European Communities (Brussels: The Commission)

This work highlights the competitive policies of the European communities to provide a guide for businesses that plan to enter the global market.

HF 1557 .L5611 1989 (Industrial Laws and Legislation—Soviet Union; Foreign Trade Regulation—Soviet Union; Commercial Law—Soviet Union)

Lindsay, Marjorie. International Business in Gorbachev's Soviet Union (London, UK: Printer Publishers) 1989.

This source has individual chapters that cover law and legislation under Gorbachev, the State Enterprise Law, and the Joint Enterprise Law with explanations of the laws and English translations of the summaries of the actual texts. Also included are chapters on banking and credit reform, prices and wages reform, and the law on Cooperatives. Appendices contain biographies of leading personalities of the Gorbachev regime, useful names and addresses, and background materials and sources.

HF1746.H24 1999 (Canada. Treaties, etc. 1992 Oct. 7; Industries—North America—Handbooks, Manuals, etc.; Free Trade—North America—Handbooks, Manuals, etc.)

Cremeans, John E. Handbook of North American Industry: 2nd Edition (Washington, DC: Bernan Press) 1999.

This work provides information on the economies of the United States, Canada, and Mexico, using tables and data for people selling in or buying from the North American market.

HF3000.D61 2000 (Commercial Statistics—Periodicals)

International Monetary Fund, Direction of Trade
Statistics, Yearbook (Washington, DC: International
Monetary Fund)

This work provides information on flows of trade among major parts of
the world as well as statistics on export and import values of merchandise by
trade partners.

HF3000.U575 1996 (Exports—United States—Statistics—Periodicals; United States—Commerce—Statistics—Periodicals)

United States, International Trade Administration, U.S. Foreign
Trade Highlights (Washington, DC: U.S. Dept. of Commerce,
International Trade Administration)

This work provides data on international trade with an emphasis on aggregate
exports and imports, as well as country/regional trade balances.

HF 3003 .A35 1990 (Commercial Products—Classification; United States—Commerce)

United States, Bureau of the Census, Schedule B: Statistical
Classification of Domestic and Foreign Commodities Exported
from the United States (Washington, DC: U.S. Government
Printing Office)

The U.S. government uses the two-volume Schedule B as a classification for
commodities, domestic or foreign, exported from this country. In addition, it
is utilized in publications on U.S. trade statistics. Schedule B can also be used
to access U.S. import statistics, which is of special importance because
Schedule A, specific to imports, has no guide. Although based on the United
Nation's Standard International Trade Classification (SITC), Schedule B's
breakdown of products is more thorough. Volume one provides conversion
tables as well as the breakdown of commodities. Volume two contains
*Schedule C: Classification of Country and Territory Designations for U.S.
Foreign Trade Statistics, Schedule D: Classification of U.S. Customs Districts
and Ports for Foreign Trade Statistics*, and an alphabetic index.

HF3003.F71
(Exports—United States—Statistics—Periodicals;
United States—Commerce—Statistics—Periodicals)

Slater, Courtenay M. Foreign Trade of the United States:
Including State and Metro Area Export Data (Washington, DC:
Bernan Press)

This work includes statistical information relating to U.S. foreign trade. Recognizing the importance of international economic relations in the global economy, this book includes a compilation of data on import and export of goods and services in the United States pertaining to balance of payments from 1960 to 1998, the annual data of exchange rates for different currencies, and data on trade from the Bureau of Census.

HF3010 .A56 1981 (United States—Commerce—
Directories)

American Export Register (New York: Thomas International
Pub. Co.)

The *American Export Register* is an annual two-volume directory that lists exporting companies through the products and services they offer. The first section contains a product index—written in French, German, Italian, Portuguese, Spanish, Arabic, Chinese, Japanese, and Russian—that refers the user to the English table which allows the individual access to the company name located in the product and services section. Entries here include the company name, address, city, state, ZIP code, telephone number, and a description of its goods and services. In the profile section, there is more company information under the specific alphabetical listing such as the cable address, TWX, telex, and FAX numbers, personnel in export sales, and the market areas the business enterprise serves. The second volume provides information and assistance for those who want to contact American exporters and importers. Listed are embassies, consulates, trade missions, international chambers of commerce, world trade center clubs, freight forwarders, customhouse brokers, banks, port authorities, air cargo carriers/couriers, and railroad and steamship lines. Each entry contains the address, telephone, telex, and FAX numbers, and key company officers. Included also are metric conversion tables, a map of the United States, and a guide to addressing U.S. mail.

HF3010.B97 2001 (Business Information Services; Industries—United States—Directories; Business Information Services—United States; United States—Commerce—Directories)

Business Organizations, Agencies, and Publications Directory (Detroit: Gale)

This directory provides information on publications of business, as well as organizations and agencies that serve business and industry.

HF3010 .C44 1981 (United States—Commerce—Periodicals)

Foreign Commerce Handbook (Washington, DC: International Division, Chamber of Commerce of the United States)

Foreign Commerce Handbook is a guide to import and export services and current information on important aspects of international trade and investment. The work covers public and private national and worldwide agencies and organizations in the United States that deal in international business and trade services, supply information and analyze issues, create international policy, and perform regulatory roles (domestic functions are left out.) The handbook also has an alphabetical listing of important topics and commonly used terms in foreign trade, a classified bibliography consisting of indexes to books, reference works, periodicals, and pamphlets, and an appendix that provides specific information concerning American chambers of commerce abroad, foreign embassies, and delegations in the United States, port authorities, small business administration field offices, and U.S. foreign trade zones. The volume has a master index.

HF 3010 .D58 (Corporations, Japanese—United States—Directories; Corporations, Japanese–Canada—Directories; Subsidiary Corporations—United States—Directories; Subsidiary Corporations—Canada—Directories)

Directory of Japanese-Affiliated Companies in USA and Canada, Japan External Trade Organization

This provides a list of Japanese-affiliated companies operating in the United States and Canada. It lists Japanese-related entities, Japanese-affiliated firms, subsidiaries, and professional service organizations (law and accounting firms). These companies are listed by American states, Puerto Rico, and Canada. They are indexed by products and services.

HF 3010 .H78 1996 (Business enterprises—United States—Directories; Corporations—United States—Directories)

Hoover's Handbook of American Business (Austin, Tex.: Reference Press)

Hoover's Handbook Of American Business profiles the largest and most influential companies in the United States. More than 600 of the 755 companies are public. There are two volumes. Volume One contains company profiles A through L. Volume Two, M through Z. Two pages are dedicated to each company profile. Profiles contain information on Who, What, When, Where, How Much, Key Competitors, and an Overview of the company. The Overview contains basic information on the company. Who lists the major officers. Their salaries are listed when available. What lists their type of business: their products and sales. When is an historical look at the company. Where gives the headquarters location and contact numbers. How Much is a table of the company financials: sales; stock prices; and dividends. Key Competitors list those companies in the same type of business. Volume two contains all three indexes. The first is an index of company profiles by their industry, the second is an index of company profiles by the location of their headquarters, and the third is an index of all the people, brands, and company names. Abbreviations used are listed in the front of volume one. There is also a section at the front of the book for "List-Lover's." Some of the lists are the 300 Most Profitable Companies, the 20 Largest Law firms in the United States, and the 20 Most Advertised Brands.

HF 3010 .H782 1995/96 (Business Enterprises—Directories; Corporations—Directories)

Hoover's Handbook of World Business (Austin, Tex.: Reference Press)

The only difference between *Hoover's Handbook Of World Business* and *Hoover's Handbook Of American Business* is the country focus. Hoover's Handbook of World Business focuses on companies located in Asia, Canada, Europe, and Latin America. There is also only one volume, instead of two. Abbreviations and major currency symbols are listed at the front. Two pages are dedicated to each company profile. Company profiles contain information on Who, What, When, Where, How Much, Key Competitors, and an Overview of the company. The Overview contains basic information on the company. Who lists the major officers. Their salaries are listed when available. What lists their type of business: their products and sales. When is an historical look at the company. Where gives the headquarters location and contact numbers. U.S. contact addresses and numbers are provided when available. How Much is a table of the company financials: sales; stock prices; and dividends. Key Competitors list those companies in the same type of business. There is also a section at the front of the book for "List-Lover's." Some of the lists are the Top 100 Companies ranked by sales, the Largest non public non-U.S. companies, and Asia's Top 100 Electronic Companies.

HF3011.D62 (United States—Commerce—Directories; Commercial Products—United States—Directories; Exports—United States—Directories)

Journal of Commerce, Directory of United States Exporters
(New York, NY: Journal of Commerce)

This annual directory provides geographical listing of U.S. exporters and alphabetical listing of exported products and company in addition to information on customs regulations.

HF3011.E9 (United States—Commerce—Handbooks, Manuals, etc.; Export Marketing—United States—Handbooks, Manuals, etc.; Commerce—Marketing—Handbooks, Manuals, etc.; Export Marketing—Handbooks, Manuals, etc.; Exports—United States—Handbooks, Manuals, etc.)

Dun's Marketing Services, Exporters' Encyclopedia
(New York: Dun and Bradstreet)

This annual encyclopedia includes information on trade regulations, documentation requirements, and import/export procedures.

HF3012.D62 (United States—Commerce—Directories; Commercial Products—United States—Directories; Imports—United States—Directories)

Journal of Commerce. Directory of United States Importers
(New York: Journal of Commerce)

This annual directory provides geographical listing of importers and an alphabetical listing of imported products in addition to information on customs regulations.

HF3023.A2 W64

Who's Who in Finance and Industry (Chicago:
Marquis-Who's Who)

This biennial work provides biographies of business people worldwide.

**HF3035.B29 1995 (Imports—United States—Handbooks,
Manuals, etc.; Foreign Trade Regulations—United
States—Handbooks, Manuals, etc.)**

U.S. Customs Service, A Basic Guide to Importing (Lincolnwood,
IL: NTC Business Books) 1995.

This work includes information on importing requirements according to
Customs laws and regulations.

**HF3035.I45 (United States—Commerce—Handbooks,
Manuals, etc.; Imports—United States—Handbooks,
Manuals, etc.)**

Importers Manual USA (San Rafael, CA: World Trade Press)

This annually published encyclopedia provides information on the process of
importing into the United States. It includes a Commodity Index that
contains articles on importing commodity groups.

**HF3035.M64 (United States—Commerce—Handbooks,
Manuals, etc.; United States—Commercial
Policy—Handbooks, Manuals, etc.; Foreign Trade
Regulation—United States—Handbooks, Manuals, etc.;
United States—Commerce—Bibliography)**

Willard, Miller. America's International Trade: A Reference
Handbook (Santa Barbara, CA: ABC-CLIO) 1995.

This work provides a review of the evolution of trade policies in the United
States as well as information on current national and international laws and
regulations. It also includes a chapter of references based on topics and a
glossary.

HF3065.5.I62 (Latin America—Commerce; Latin America—
Commerce—United States; United States—Commerce—
Latin America; Investments, American—Latin America)

Evans, Judith. Investing and Selling in Latin America
(Shawnee Mission, KS: Hemisphere Business) 1995.

This work provides country-by-country overviews of market trends and
resources available for businesses looking to enter the Latin American
market.

HF3099.U58 1999 (United States—Commerce—Germany
(West)—Periodicals; Germany (West)—Commerce—
Germany (West)—Periodicals; United States—Foreign
Economic Relations—Germany (West)—Periodicals;
Germany (West)—Foreign Economic Relations—United
States—Periodicals)

United States–German Economic Yearbook = Deutsch–
Amerikanisches Wirtschaftsjahrbuch (New York, NY:
German American Chamber of Commerce)

This yearbook includes articles that trace the evolution of U.S.–German
business and economic relationships, as well as the changes that have taken
place in German economy since 1988.

HF3230.5.A48 L36 (Latin America—
Commerce—Information Services—Directories;
Latin America—Industries—Information
Services—Directories; Commerce—Information
Services—Directories; Export Marketing—Directories)

Latin American Markets: A Guide to Company and Industry
Information Sources (Washington, DC: Washington
Researchers Ltd.) 1997.

This guide provides information sources on how to identify markets, monitor
companies, uncover industries, and locate trade partners in the Latin American market. It includes bibliographical references and an index.

**HF3500.7.A48.E13 (Europe, Eastern—Commerce—
Directories; Europe, Eastern—Economic Conditions—
Statistics—Periodicals; Europe, Eastern—Information
Services—Directories)**

Eastern Europe: A Directory and Sourcebook (London:
Euromonitor PLC)

This work provides not only a directory of companies in Eastern Europe but
also a market overview, which includes macroeconomic and consumer trends
in the region.

**HF 3800.67 .A48 K66 (Corporations, European—Singapore—
Directories; Industries—Singapore—Directories;
Singapore—Commerce—European—Directories;
Europe—Commerce—Singapore—Directories)**

Directory of European Business (Bowker-Saur) 1992.

The directory is a source of information about the important economic and
business organizations in each of the European countries. The information is
composed of a brief business report, which includes the political system,
economic policy, accounting rules and standards, and the tax system. The
directory data provides the address, telephone numbers, contact person's
name, and other details for major commercial, business, and industrial
enterprises. In addition, the directory includes information on major government agencies, regulatory bodies, newspapers, business periodicals for every
country, and pan-European organizations. Exchange rates for each currency
compared to the U.S. dollar, the German mark, and the British sterling are
given. Finally the directory lists all the abbreviations used and an index of the
companies and organizations.

**HF 3800.67 .A48 K66 (Corporations, European—Singapore—
Directories; Singapore—Commerce—Europe—Directories;
Europe—Commerce—Singapore—Directories;
Singapore—Industries—Directories)**

Kompass Directory of European Business In Singapore
(Singapore: Kompass South East Asia Ltd.)

The *Kompass Directory Of European Business In Singapore* is a list of European multinational companies with offices in Singapore. There are three

sections to the directory. Section One is an alphabetical list of companies, by country, with addresses and contact information located in Singapore. Section Two lists the European Principles and Agents, and Agents and Distributors. Section Three is a list of the European products and services in Singapore, including an index. The *Kompass Directory Of European Business In Singapore* was compiled by the Economic Development Board, based in Singapore. It is dedicated to bringing multinational companies to Singapore.

HF3821 .F68 (Japan—Commerce—Statistics)

White Paper on International Trade: Japan,
Ministry of International Trade and Industry

This is an English version of this Japanese white paper. Part I analyzes the world economy and Japan's changing trade structure. Part II provides statistics of export and imports, and trade by country and region.

HF 3823 .J36 (Corporations—Japan—Directories; Manufacturing Industries—Japan—Directories; Industries—Japan—Directories; Japan—Commerce—Directories)

OECD Economic Surveys—Japan, Organization for Economic
Cooperation and Development

This is an annual report on Japan's economy by OECD. It provides analyses and statistics of recent trends and short-term prospects, macroeconomic policies, trade policies, and issues in public finance. The appendix includes a chronology of a economic events and statistics.

HF 3823 .S78 (Japan—Commerce—Directories; Japan—Manufacturers—Directories; Japan—Industries—Directories

Standard Trade Index of Japan, Chamber of Commerce
and Industry of Japan

This is an index of products and commodities that Japanese companies and manufactures buy and sell. The data include company logos, contact addresses, main banks, as well as export and import products.

It also lists addresses for chambers of commerce, economic associations, industrial associations, trade international economic associations, convention and trade fair bureaus, major exhibition centers, and foreign trade organizations.

HF 5030 .H782 1992 (Business Enterprises—Directories; Corporations—Directories)

Hoover, Gary, Alta Campbell, Alan Chai, and Patrick J. Spain. Hoover's Handbook of World Business 1992 (Emeryville, CA: The Reference Press, Inc.)

Worldwide businesses such as in Asia, Europe, and other continents are discussed in this book. Business people can use this book to look for information on corporations. Major stocks are also available for the person who invests in companies. The work is composed of four groups. The first section analyzes international business, giving accurate and up-to-date information about them. Business is also rated on the basis of future outcomes in a country. The following section, "A List-Lover's Compendium," is made up of lists that include the largest companies in the text, key industries' largest companies, and indexes composed of major stocks. The third component has two main sections of precise one-page profiles of important economic entities. The first section of this component has information on nations and 66 significant regions, and the United Nations. The second section includes 165 globally important corporations. All of the corporations are sited outside the United States, most of them being public companies. The last component of the book has three indexes. The first one contains profiles by headquarters location. The second one includes industrial companies. Finally, the third index consists of profile names of people, brands, companies, and places.

HF 5256.J47 (Business Information Services—Japan; Business—Bibliography; Japan—Commerce—Bibliography)

Jeffries, Francis M. The English-Language Japanese Business Reference Guide (London: Jeffries & Associates) 1988.

This bibliography provides in English sources of Japanese business information, covering industries, taxation, laws and regulations, living conditions, associations and organizations, on-line services, and transportation equipment. The appendix includes useful lists of contacts, such as U.S. insurance companies, as well as U.S. State, regional and port representatives in Japan for doing business in Japan.

HF 5341 .E531 1988 (Business Information Services—Directories; Reference Books—Business—Bibliography; Business—Periodicals—Bibliography)

Mossman, Jennifer, Ed. Encyclopedia of Geographic Information Sources: International Volume (Detroit, MI: Gale Research) 1988.

This bibliographic guide to information sources on 160 foreign countries, cities, and regions provides over 13,000 citations. Types of sources covered include directories; on-line databases; guides to doing business; newspapers and periodicals; almanacs and yearbooks; and abstracting and indexing services. Most sources are in the English language. Multinational regions are listed first and then individual countries. Arrangement is alphabetic. Within each region and country section, arrangement is by type of source and then alphabetically by title. Separate citations for individual cities are also provided. Complete bibliographic citations are given and they may include a brief annotation. The section on the Soviet Union and Moscow covers nine pages and provides over 200 citations to sources of information. A city, country, and region index is included.

HF 5343 .D88 (Business Enterprises—United States)

Dun's Census of American Business (Parsippany, NJ: Dun's Marketing Services)

This source features coverage of businesses in the United States. National, state, and county business establishments are arranged by Standard Industrial Classification (SIC) and are grouped by sales volume and number of employees. A statistics section surveying the top U.S. businesses is included and alphabetic and numeric SIC indexes are included. *Dun's Census* is published annually.

HF 5353 .E62 (Business—Information Services; Information Services)

Wasserman, Paul, Ed. Encyclopedia of Business Information Sources (Detroit, MI: Gale Research)

Appearing approximately every 2 years, this directory serves as a guide to sources of information on business, financial, and industrial subjects. A wide

range of sources is listed including print, electronic, and organizational information sources. Sources include abstracting and indexing services, on-line
databases, statistical sources, directories, bibliographies, and price sources, as
well as research centers and institutes, trade associations, and professional
societies.

A variety of business and industrial subject headings appear including health insurance, solar energy, copyrights, trade shows, office management, civil rights, new products, and wages and salaries. Approximately 1100
subjects are listed. Entries are arranged in alphabetical order by subject
and then further divided by type of information source and publication title
or organization name. Data provided for each information source listed
include the title of the publication or database, author or editor name, publisher name, address and telephone number, and year of publication or frequency of issues and price. Brief descriptions are added sometimes for
clarification.

Materials are collected from the publishers, publishers' catalogs or
brochures, and business library material. There is no index. There is a subject
heading list of contents that lists cross-references to aid in searching. Addresses and telephone numbers of six major on-line database vendors are
given because the access to many of the listed databases are through these
vendors.

HF 5381 .E56 (Vocational Guidance—Handbooks, Manuals, etc.; Occupations—Handbooks, Manuals, etc.)

The Encyclopedia of Careers and Vocational Guidance
(Chicago, IL: J.G. Ferguson Pub. Co.) 1993.

The *Encyclopedia of Careers and Vocational Guidance* contains four volumes
dedicated to give accurate information on various occupations and careers.
Volume I profiles 74 major industries. For each profile, there are five chapters: general, structure, careers, education, and forecast. Volumes II, III, and
IV profile individual occupations. Specific information is given like training
and educational requirements. Volume IV has two appendixes at the end.
The first contains resources and associations for individuals with disabilities and the second lists internships, apprenticeships, and training programs.
There is also a Dictionary of Occupational Titles (DOT) Index. Included at
the end of the occupational profiles in Volumes II, III, and IV are relevant
Standard Occupational Classification (SOC) numbers issued by the Department of Labor, Standard Industrial Classification (SIC) codes, and the

Guide for Occupational Exploration (GOE) numbers used by the U.S. Employment Service.

HF 5382.5 .U5 D93

The Career Guide (Parsippany, NJ: Dun's)

This guide provides information about jobs in many of the leading career fields. Information on companies is arranged in three ways: alphabetically, geographically, and industrially. Contact information for each company is included. An index of SIC codes and a discussion of various job-search-related topics are also included.

HF 5382.5 .U5 N27

The National Job Bank (Holbrook, MA: Adams Medical Corporation)

This guide provides information on over 19,000 companies in the United States. Contact information, commonly filled positions, and job search advice are included. Companies are arranged alphabetically by state.

HF 5415 .C62 (Marketing—Handbooks, Manuals, etc.)

Clemente, Mark N. The Marketing Glossary (New York: American Management Association) 1992.

This reference source covers key terms and concepts and their application in many areas of business such as marketing management, advertising, sales promotion, public relations, direct marketing, market research, and sales. There are over 1400 terms included. The book has three main purposes: to be used as a dictionary, as an encyclopedia, and as a working reference guide.

There are in-depth explanations, real-life examples and formulae with most of the terms that help to clarify the meanings. The most popular meanings are listed and any existing secondary interpretations are included after that. The book has numerous cross-references in bold type and new terms such as "green marketing."

The book also has three appendices. The first is a marketing and media trade, commercial, and business organizations list. The second is a marketing and advertising trade publications list, and the third is a selected bibliography of books on how to do marketing.

HF 5415.12.J3 D43 (Marketing—Japan—Periodicals; Advertising—Japan—Periodicals; Japan—Industries— Periodicals; Industrial Management—Japan—Periodicals)

Japan Marketing and Advertising Yearbook (Tokyo: Dentsu Inc.)

This directory is prepared by Dentsu Inc., a marketing and advertising company in Japan. It provides a directory of advertisement organizations, agencies, public relations firms, market research organizations, magazines, broadcast media, and includes commercial rates. It contains product information about laws and trends for corporate advertising and marketing activities.

It also surveys topics in new advertisement areas such as multimedia and on-line newspaper and magazines.

HF 5415.124 .M34 1995 (Marketing—Information Services—United States; Marketing Research—United States—Directories; Marketing—Bibliography)

Barksdale, Hiram C. and Jac Goldstucker, Editors, Jennifer W. Delaune, Compiler. Marketing Information: A Professional Reference Guide. 3rd ed. (Atlanta, GA: Georgia State University Business Press) 1995.

This is a usefully organized directory and bibliography of resources necessary for intelligent market decision making. It can be used to develop marketing strategies and as a guide for developing marketing skills. Part I is a ready-reference directory with specific information on associations, agencies, businesses, and organizations serving the marketing field. Among the organizing elements that facilitate the use of this section are alphabetical listings: subject, geographic, and computer program indexes. Part II is a rich source of annotated bibliographic information for 27 subject areas in marketing. Generally, each medium is broken down into types. The media include books, periodicals, audiovisual materials, and on-line databases. At the end is a title and publisher index.

HF 5415.3 .E56 (Brand Choice—United States; Brand Name Products—United States; Consumers' Preferences—United States)

Encyclopedia of Consumer Brands (Detroit: St. James Press) 1994.

The *Encyclopedia of Consumer Brands* gives detailed information on products that have made a strong impact on the United States' popular culture and/or business. The brand names have become familiar in American households and have even gained international recognition. There are three volumes. Volume One is dedicated to Consumable Products like Bass Ale, and Wheaties. Volume Two contains Personal Products like Hush Puppies, Levis, and Nike. Volume Three profiles Durable Goods like BMW, Goodyear, and Whirlpool. The entries focus on brand names, trademarks, or individual products, depending on their marketing success. For example, Hostess makes Twinkies, but because of the marketing success of Twinkies, they are profiled individually. Each entry includes several Subheadings. These include Brand Origins, International Market, Trends, and Advertising. The entries also include an historical overview, an informative essay, logos of the brand and any photographs, and a bibliography for further reading. Cumulative indexes included are Brand Names, Brand Categories, Companies and Persons, and Advertising Agencies.

HF 5415.33 .U6 L73 1995 (Consumer Behavior—United States—Statistics—Periodicals; Market Surveys—United States—Periodicals; Life Style—United States—Statistics—Periodicals)

The Lifestyle Market Analyst (Wilmette, IL: Standard Rate and Data Service)

This resource brings together demographic, geographic, and lifestyle information from 9.1 million households in the United States for convenient and efficient preliminary market analyses on a local, regional, national level. Section 1 divides the United States into 211 RMA markets and profiles, each containing demographic analyses along with data on lifestyles. Section 2 is broken down according to lifestyle interests with rankings. Section 3 coordinates the geographic information of the first section with the lifestyle information of the second part for market analysis. Section 4 is a guide to consumer magazines and mailing lists organized according to lifestyle profiles. This resource is regularly updated.

HF5415.2 .I58 (Marketing Research—Handbooks, Manuals, etc.; Demographic Surveys—Handbooks, Manuals. etc.; Consumers—Information Services—United States—Handbooks, Manuals, etc.)

The Insider's Guide to Demographic Know-How: Everything You Need to Find, Analyze, and Use Information About Your Customers (Chicago: Probus) 1993.

This handbook provides the sources of demographic data. The book is divided into eight chapters. The first chapter serves as an overview of the data different sources can provide. Chapter 2 is an in-depth discussion on how to locate the right source to obtain the data needed. Chapter 3 specifies on the usage and implications of the 1990 Census data. Chapters 4 to 6 provide listings of sources according to their types—federal government, private source, state and local sources, academic, industry, and nonprofit sources. Chapter 8 provides a list of international data sources.

HF5437 .A2 S96 (Consumers—United States—Statistics— Periodicals; Purchasing Power—United States— Statistics—Periodicals; Retail Trade—United States—Statistics—Periodicals)

Demographics USA, Zip Edition (New York: Market Statistics)

This annual guide consists of more than 500 pages of marketing statistics divided into six sections. Section 1 is on geographical correspondence where the areas to which the zips belonged are listed. Sections 2 and 3 provide the overview of the information in Sections 4 to 6, in which more detailed data are listed. Section 2 is a sectional summary while Section 3 is organized at state and regional level. Section 4 provides basic demographic, for example, the population, buying income, retail sales project, on every ZIP code in the States. Section 6 is organized by business characteristics, such as employment in different sectors of industries, and economic activities are listed.

HF5353 .E56 1995–96 (Business Information Services; Information Services)

Encyclopedia of Business Information Sources (Detroit: Gale)

This reference work is a bibliographic guide to materials for executives in business, researchers, students, and librarians. Each entry gives the topic, type of source, publication title, or name of the organization, publisher's name and address, regular and toll-free telephone numbers, fax numbers, frequency of publication, year of publication, price, and a brief annotation. The work includes data on abstracting and indexing services, almanacs and yearbooks, bibliographies, biographies, databases, directories, encyclopedias, dictionaries, financial ratios, handbooks, periodicals and newsletters, sources for prices, research centers and institutes, statistical sources, as well as trade associations and professional societies. It also has subjects that deal with automobile repair, convenience stores, business mathematics, corporate images, special event planning, computers in business, as well as composite materials, machine vision, and quality management.

HF 5548.2 .O32 (Office Practice—Automation—Dictionary)

Edwards, Nancy MacLellan. Office Automation: A Glossary and Guide (White Plains, NY: Knowledge Industry Publications) 1982.

The glossary contains definitions and descriptions of data processing hardware components, software packages, peripherals, interfaces, and general processing methodology. The entries are alphabetically arranged. The relationships between terms associated with compatible systems, such as similar terms found in data processing and word processing, are explained. The definitions are preceded by a terminology code to identify the category or categories that the term is associated with. These categories include data processing, word processing, telecommunications, record management systems, reprographics and micrographics. The source is indexed by the categories to which the terms pertain.

HF 5548.2 .V68 1983 (Business—Data Processing—Dictionaries; Management—Information Systems—Dictionaries; Systems Analysis—Dictionaries; Office Management—Dictionaries)

Vichas, Robert P. New Encyclopedic Dictionary of Systems and Procedures (Englewood Cliffs, NJ: Prentice-Hill) 1983.

This source is arranged alphabetically by terms and related terms and concepts are cross-referenced. The management language covered in the text includes accounting, administration, policy making, cost control and analysis, decision making, finance and analysis, marketing, organization, public policy, quality control, research, training, traffic, and warehouse management. Terms are defined and described in the context of their usage. The coverage includes basic terms and more complex terms. Diagrams and other descriptors are given to illustrate concepts.

HF5549 .A23 T76 (Personnel Management—Dictionaries)

The Human Resource Glossary (New York: American Management Association) 1991.

This glossary contains more than 300 definitions on terms concerning personnel management. The terms and abbreviations are arranged alphabetically. In addition, basic information of nearly 100 associations and societies of interest to the practitioners are listed in the book.

HF5549 .H25
(Personnel Management—Handbooks, Manuals, etc.)

Handbook of Modern Personnel Administration (New York: McGraw-Hill) 1972.

An authoritative and comprehensive handbook on modern personnel administration, the book is designed for the usage of personnel administrators, top management supervisors inclusive, and students of personnel administration. The articles are sorted into 15 sections from some broad topics to detailed principles of personnel administration.

HF5549.Z.J3 N55 (Personnel Management—Japan—
Dictionaries—Japanese; Industrial Sociology—
Japan—Dictionaries—Japanese; Japanese
Language—Dictionaries—English)

Selling in Japan (Tokyo: Japan External Trade Organization) 1985.

This is an introductory guide for those interested in doing business in Japan. It provides an overview of the Japanese market and consumer, distribution channels for various products, and industrial materials. It also contains instructions for labeling and marketing, lists of major trade fairs, principal import law, and explains the tax system.

HF 5549.5 .E45 D58 (Americans—Employment—Foreign
Countries—Handbooks, Manuals, etc.; International
Business Enterprises—Personnel Management—
Handbooks, Manuals, etc.; Travel—Handbooks,
Manuals, etc.)

Craighead's International Business, Travel, and Relocation Guide to ... Countries (Detroit, MI: Gale Research, Inc.)

Craighead's provides an objective in-depth country report to people relocating, traveling, or conducting business in various countries. Each country report was edited by individuals who either lived in or traveled in the specified country. The country reports include the section: Orientation to the Country; Economic and Political Overview; Doing Business in the Country; Money, Banking, and Taxes; Communications and Media; Living In the Country; Health and Safety; Preparing for Your Trip; Arriving In and Getting Around; Lodging, Dining, Nightlife; Leisure Activities; and Bibliography and Suggested Reading. Each section includes subsections for more specificity. Countries not included in the latest edition are because of political and social upheaval making current information unreliable.

HF 5549.5 .P4 F18
(Business Practices—Personnel Administration)

Famularo, Joseph J. Handbook of Personnel Forms, Records, and Reports (New York: McGraw-Hill) 1982.

This source is a volume of forms and records for the recording, organization, updating, and transmission of information. The book is designed as a companion to *The Handbook of Modern Personnel Administration*. The chapters are arranged in the order of recruitment, employment, training, career development, safety, benefits, communication, and termination. Each section of forms is introduced with a general statement of the purpose and nature of the forms. There are sections that discuss an employee's right-to-know policies and the formulation, maintenance and protection of personnel files. The use and roles of personnel data systems and computers in personnel administration are discussed in another section. The forms follow the general EEO regulations due to the variances in state law regulating the type of information employers can gather.

HF5601 .I584 1993 (Accounting—Standards—Periodicals)

International Accounting Summaries. Prepared by Coopers & Lybrand (International) (New York: Wiley)

This source summarizes accounting standards in 37 countries plus International Accounting Standards and European Community Directives. Each country contains a profile of accounting principles that are applicable to most of its business organizations. Specialized accounting practices found in entities such as banks, insurance companies, and governments are not included. Financial information concerning each country is in a separate chapter set out in the following standardized topic format: General Information including source of generally accepted accounting principles, and audit and public company requirements; General Accounting that embraces financial statements, business combinations, joint ventures, foreign currency translation, changing prices/inflation accounting, accounting changes, prior period adjustments, post balance sheet events, related party transactions, and segmental information; Accounting Principles for Specific Items—Balancing Sheet comprising property, plant and equipment, intangible assets, leases, investments, accountings receivable, inventories and work in progress, current liabilities, long-term debt, contingencies, and capital and reserves; and Accounting Principles for Specific Items—Income Statement consisting of revenue recognition, government grants and assistance, research and development, capitalized interest costs, imputed interest, extraordinary or unusual items, income taxes, postretirement benefits, discontinued operations, and earnings per share. Czech and Slovak Republics, Hungary, Poland, and Russia are together in a separate chapter on Central and Eastern Europe that summarizes economic and accounting reforms as well as each of the four country's accounting and financial reporting practices.

Every chapter except Central and Eastern Europe has an appendix that gives a macrolevel comparison of a particular country's standards with International Accounting Standards (IAS). Quick-reference matrices prepared by accounting topic enable comparisons to be made between the accounting standards of difference countries. New features in this edition include a checklist covering IASs and illustrative financial statements based on an imaginary company made in accordance with the IASs. A glossary of accounting terms is included at the end of the work.

HF5616 .S9 D66 1991 (Commercial Law—Switzerland; Business Enterprises—Switzerland; Taxation—Law and Legislation—Switzerland; Investments, Foreign—Law and Legislation—Switzerland)

Doing Business in Switzerland (New York: Price Waterhouse Center for Transnational Taxation)

This work is a business guide for developing export trade in Switzerland. It profiles the country itself and discusses its business environment, foreign investment and trade opportunities, investment incentives, restrictions on foreign investment and investors, regulatory environment, banking and finance, exporting, business entities, labor relations and social security, audit requirements and practices, accounting principles and practices, tax system, tax administration, taxation of corporations, taxation of foreign corporations, taxation of shareholders, partnerships and joint ventures, taxation of individuals, taxation of trust and estates, indirect taxes, and tax treaties. Twenty-six appendices supplement the main text with more specific technical information along with a reading list. There is also an introduction to Price Waterhouse worldwide organization and a description of the services it offers in Switzerland.

HF 5616 .U5 E53 1988
(Accounting Firms—United States—Directories)

Emerson's Directory of Leading U.S. Accounting Firms
(Redmond, WA: The Big Eight Review)

This volume contains information on 2500 accounting firms. The information
in the text was provided by the firms listed. The book is divided into four
parts. The first part is a listing of the key national offices of the 15 largest
accounting firms. The firms are alphabetically arranged. The data provided
include the names and positions of leading officers and estimates of both
American and foreign revenues. The second section is arranged by state. This
is an alphabetically arranged listing of CPA societies and accounting boards.
The information includes the name, address, and telephone number of the
organizations. The third part is an alphabetically arranged listing of firms by
state. The information includes the name, address, telephone number, the
names of the primary personnel, the size of the professional staff, and a
general statement of the location of other offices. The fourth section is an
alphabetical index of the firms listed in the directory. The source is indexed.

HF 5616 .U5 W63 (Auditors—United States—Directories;
Auditing—Directories)

Phels, Spence, Ed. Who Audits America, Corporations
and Accountants: A Directory of Publicly Traded Companies
& the Accounting Firms Who Audit Them (Menlo Park, CA:
The Financial Press)

This directory is divided into three sections that are then subdivided. The first
section contains information on companies. Part 1 is a master list of the
companies in alphabetical order. The information provided includes address,
telephone number, assets, profits, trading status, common stock symbol,
prices, and the number of employees. Part 2 consists of lists added to the 21st
edition of the source and companies removed due to acquisitions or mergers.
The listing of removed companies contains information on the acquiring
parent company and the year and month of the transaction. The second
section pertains to auditors. There is a summary of the auditors' clients and a
national list of the "Big 8" accounting firms. The information in this section
includes a listing of auditors by state. The offices of national accounting firms
are listed by street address and by cities in the United States. The third section
is comprised of appendices. These contain industry codes, both three digit and
four digit, and state abbreviations arranged alphabetically.

HF5621 .A16 1991 (Accounting)

Carmichael, D.R., Steven B. Lilien, and Martin Mellman, Eds.
Accountant's Handbook (New York: Wiley) 1991.

This source answers questions on accounting and financial reporting that would be of interest to accountants, auditors, executives, bankers, lawyers, and financial analysts. The work is divided into seven parts. Part I, Structure of Accounting Standards and Authoritative Rule-Making Organizations, contains articles on financial accounting concepts and standards; financial accounting regulation and organization; and Securities and Exchange Commission reporting requirements. Part II, Financial Statements—Presentation and Analysis, covers income statement presentation and earnings per share; business combinations accounting; consolidation, translation, and the equity method; cash flow statements; interim financial statements; and financial statement analysis. Part III, Financial Statement Areas, looks at cash and investments; revenues and receivables; inventory; property, plant, and equipment, and depreciation; intangible assets; leases; accounting for income taxes; liabilities; and shareholders' equity. Part IV, Specialized Industries, discusses oil, gas, and other natural resources; real estate and construction; financial institutions; regulated utilities; state and local government accounting; and nonprofit organizations. Part V, Compensation and Benefits, examines pension plans and other postemployment benefits, as well as employee stock compensation and other capital accumulation awards. Part VI, Special Areas of Accounting, deals with prospective financial statements; personal financial statements; partnerships; estates and trusts; valuation of nonpublic companies; bankruptcy; and forensic accounting and litigation consulting services. Part VII, Topics in Auditing and Management Information Systems, analyzes auditing standards and reports, as well as data processing and management information systems.

HF5621 .K79 1983 (Accounting—Dictionaries)

Kohler, Eric Louis. Kohler's Dictionary for Accountants. Edited by W. W. Cooper, Yuji Ijiri (Englewood Cliffs, NJ: Prentice-Hall) 1983.

Kohler's Dictionary for Accountants, 6th edition, contains 4538 entries; 1878 are newly defined to reflect current trends and 2660 were carried over from Eric Kohler's classic fifth edition of *A Dictionary for Accountants* and drastically revised. Terms follow the letter-by-letter alphabetizing principle and are cross-referenced either by italicizing or by the placement of "See . . ."

or "q.v." beneath the word. A new feature is the index, which alphabetically arranges terms and includes page numbers where they are located along with zero, one, two, or three dots that indicate the detail of the definition (the more dots, the lengthier the meaning). The user can scan this index and find a concept or its analogous form (that may be the only one in the dictionary) and judge its complexity more quickly than by thumbing through the main dictionary.

HF 5621 .S57 (Accounting—Dictionaries)

Siegel, Joel S. and Jay K. Shim. Dictionary of Accounting Terms (New York: Barrons) 1987.

This source is a dictionary for professional and academic use. The book contains approximately 2500 current definitions used in accounting and related business practices. The text is illustrated with charts, graphs, and tables. The terms are alphabetically arranged by letter. Multiple word terms are treated as a single word. The terms are cross-referenced to related and/or contrasting terms. A separate list of abbreviations and acronyms is provided. Major organizations and associations that are active in the accounting field, including journal publications, are listed with a brief mission statement.

HF 5621 .S79 1983 (Accounting—Dictionaries)

Cooper, W.W. and Yuji Ijiri, Eds. Kohler's Dictionary for Accountants (Englewood Cliffs, NJ: Prentice-Hall) 1983.

This source is a dictionary of the systematized terminology and definitions of the profession and practices of accounting. Words are alphabetically arranged. Definitions are brief essays with elaborations for synoptic insight into the issues, problems, and practices of accounting. Terms and concepts from related disciplines are presented and adapted for accounting purposes. The dictionary contains 4538 terms and is indexed.

HF5635 .E56 1994
(Accounting; Accounting—Data processing)

Encyclopedia of Accounting Systems. Edited by Tom M. Plank and Lois R. Plank (Englewood Cliffs, NJ: Prentice Hall) 1994.

This reference work is for public, industrial, and institutional accountants, managerial and legal personnel, and students. The first four chapters cover the general design and application of accounting information systems and the next 67 specifically analyze varied enterprises. Topics discussed are a summary of the particular industry; mechanization of the accounting function; account classifications and books of account; data processing applications; cost systems; time and payroll applications; purchasing and receiving applications; inventory control applications; production control applications; distribution and selling records; receivables and payables applications; depreciation of plant and equipment records; flow charts; time-saving techniques; and the reporting system. This updated edition adds growth industries and a variety of businesses, professions, farming enterprises, and nonprofit organizations. Each article was prepared by public accountants, company controllers and financial officers, and professors. Indexed.

HF5667 .C32 1986 (Auditing—Handbooks, Manuals, etc.)

Cashin's Handbook for Auditors. Edited by James A. Cashin, Paul D. Neuwirth, and John F. Levy (New York: McGraw-Hill) 1986.

This handbook is a reference source for public accountants, internal auditors, and government auditors and its purpose is to enable them to better serve their clients. It contains 50 articles that survey current branches of auditing practice. Each chapter was prepared by practitioners and specialists and falls under one of seven headings: (1) Principles, standards, and responsibilities; (2) Principal types of auditing; (3) Planning, evaluation, and administration; (4) Audit program, objectives, and procedures; (5) Analytical methods; (6) Conclusion, review, and reporting; and (7) Professional development. Subject index.

HF 5667 .M64 1990
(Auditing Practices; Accounting Practices)

Miller, Martin A. and Larry P. Bailey. Miller's Comprehensive GAAS Guide: A Comprehensive Restatement of Generally Accepted Auditing Standards (New York: Miller Accounting Publications/Harcourt Brace Jovanovich)

This source is a guide to the accepted auditing standards, practices, and procedures currently in use. The information contained in this volume includes GAAS, SAS and interpretations, SSARS and interpretations, SEC Auditing Releases, Special Industry audit guides, and statements on quality control standards and the code of conduct. The text is divided into 13 classified parts.

The title of the parts serve as a guide to the various auditing and/or accounting engagements an independent auditor and/or account may perform for a client.

HF 5668.25. R35 (Auditing, Internal; Auditing)

Reider, Harry. Operational Review: Maximum Results at Efficient Costs (New York: J. Wiley) 2002.

This work provides information regarding the basic elements of planning and conducting operational reviews. It introduces and explains the use of operational reviews for maximizing operating results while minimizing cost. The main objective is to provide basic tools for those with no previous experience and additional learning for readers with previous operational review experience.

HF 5681 .B2 A22 1989 (Accounting; Fiscal Reports)

Shohet, Jack and Richard Rikert. Accounting Trends & Techniques (New York: American Institute of Certified Public Accountants)

This volume contains a cumulative survey of accounting data from 600 annual stockholder reports. The companies surveyed are listed on the American and the New York Stock Exchanges and are registered with the Securities and Exchange Commission. The surveys are conducted to determine and analyze the accounting trends, techniques, and practices of the companies. The information found in the editions include comparative financial statements, disclosure of accounting practices, balance sheets data, income statements, stockholder equity, statements of cash flow, and independent auditor reports. The data are gathered on the basis of the fiscal year.

The appendix contains an alphabetically arranged list of the company names and reference numbers. An index is included too.

HF 5681 .B2 K66 1987 (Accounting; Financial Reports)

Solomon, Merton B., Kenneth J. Dirkes and John R. Deming. KMG Main Hurdman Guide to Preparing Financial Reports (New York: John Wiley & Sons) 1987.

This source is concerned with the form and content of financial reports for industrial and commercial companies. The book identifies the SEC compliance notes and requirements for the annual reports of publicly held companies. The test refers to the applicable authoritative literature for additional reference. References are made to the paragraph of the source.

The information contained in the text includes: Report cover and Title Page, Requirements for Auditor Reports, Basic Financial Statements, Notations on Financial Statements, Financial Statement formats, Information accompanying the Financial Statement, Terminology, and an illustrated report. The book is indexed.

HF 5681 .B2 T77 1989 (Financial Statements)

Tracy, John A. How to Read a Financial Report: Wringing Cash Flow and other Vital Signs Out of Numbers (New York: John Wiley & Sons)

This source serves both as an introduction and a reference source to fundamental accounting rules. The text explains how the figures contained in financial reports are arrived at and the meaning behind those figures. The book has been updated to include current practices in financial reporting and changes in the tax laws.

The topics covered include cash flow, balance sheets, income statements, sales revenue, accounts receivable, operating expenses, depreciation, income tax expenses, financing, and investing activities.

HF 5681 .R25 172 1990 (Financial Ratios; Ratio Analysis)

IRS Corporate Financial Ratios (Lincolnshire, IL: Schonfelf & Associates) 1998.

This source is a study of income statements and balance sheet data gathered by the Internal Revenue Service. The text is based on statistical information derived from the tax returns of 100,000 corporations. The information is compiled into a group of standard financial ratios used by business for planning, analysis, and credit evaluations. The ratios are based on the business activities of domestic and foreign corporations. The study is organized along the following classification of total assets: major and minor industry and division and subdivided by total assets.

This reference also contains the definitions of the underlying variables and ratio definitions and interpretations.

HF 5681 .R25 T98
(Ratio Analysis; Financial Planning and Reporting)

Tyran, Michael R. Handbook of Business and Financial Ratios
(Englewood Cliffs, NJ: Prentice Hall) 1986.

This source is a guide to the use of ratios for the evaluation, clarification, and planning of financial data for administrative purposes. The author places stress on the application of ratios for the recognition, separation, and emphasis of operating performance and financial position events. Additional attention is given to the interpretation of internal and external data that influence financial reports. The book contains models illustrating the use of ratios in the analysis and comparison by period data element account description and item variance. It also contains formulas and examples for the calculations of the various types of ratios.

The subjects covered in connection with ratios include financial analysis and planning operations, measurement of operational effectiveness and control of resource utilization, direct cost and G & A expenditures, overhead cost, cash flow planning, and analysis for industry comparison.

HF 5681 .R25 T875

Troy, Leo. Almanac of Business and Industrial Financial Ratios
(Englewood Cliffs, NJ: Prentice Hall)

Profiling corporate performance, tables, and charts comprise this publication. Each annual edition covers fiscal year data for the year three years before the publication. Industries are divided into major industry groups that include manufacturing, mining, construction, transportation, real estate, and banking. The industry groups are then broken down into subdivisions such as printing and publishing, textile mill products, and machinery under manufacturing. In addition to the industry group subdivisions, each industry is subdivided by assets.

The corporate performance profiles are reported in two analytical tables for each industry. The first table reports operating and financial information for the corporations with and without net income. The second table provides the same information as the first, but only for those corporations operating at a profit. Operating factors include the cost of operations, repairs, officer compensation, property, taxes, advertising, and bad debts. The financial ratios record current ratio, quick ratio, net sales to net working capital, coverage ratio (times interest earned), asset turnover, and total liabilities to net worth.

Other data provided include debt ratio, return of assets, return on equity, and return on net worth.

The charts include ratios of the number of enterprises, total receipts, operation costs, repairs, rent on business property, and net profit before tax. All the major industry groups are covered on the charts except finance, insurance, and real estate. Each industry is subdivided to show all business, that is, those with and without net income, as well as charts depicting only those with net income.

An appendix provides cross-references for each industry and Standard Industrial Classification codes for each industry. An additional index provides a listing of industry groups.

HF 5686 .C7 B35 (Finance; Auditing and Accounting)

Bavishi, Vinod B. International Accounting and Auditing Trends
(Princeton, NJ: Center for International Financial Analysis
and Research)

This source is a research study and analysis of financial data generated by international companies. The study is divided into two general parts. The first section is contained in Chapters 1 through 7 and examines international accounting trends. The second section is an examination of international auditing trends and is found in Chapters 8 through 14. The author's analysis is focused on establishing the similarities of practices as they exist within these fields in the different economic environments of the international community. His objective is to establish a set of those principles and practices that are standard in the analysis of the performance of businesses.

The analysis is based on data gathered from Australia, Austria, Belgium, Canada, Denmark, Finland, France, West Germany, Hong Kong, Italy, Japan, South Korea, Malaysia, Mexico, Netherlands, New Zealand, Norway, Singapore, South Africa, Spain, Sweden, Switzerland, United Kingdom, and the United States.

The volume contains an analysis of standards for the financial disclosure practices of banks and insurance and industrial companies. The coverage includes financial statements, reports, trade analysis, and regional analysis for trading partners.

Tables and charts are included as well as an accounting lexicon for eight languages. The data encompass a summary profile of 16 international accounting firms, a listing of audit fees, sales, and assets alphabetically arrange by country, a listing of client companies by country alphabetically arranged with listings of sales and assets and the number of audits.

HF 5686 .P93 H15 (Public Utilities Accounting)

Hahne, Robert L., Gregory E. Aliff, Deloitte Haskins,
et al. Accounting for Public Utilities (New York:
Matthew Bender) 1989.

This source is an examination of the fundamentals of accounting for public utilities. The focus is on those practices that make public utility accounting distinct from other accounting practices.

The book is divided into six sections. The first section contains a summary of the development of the utility industry in the United States and the parallel development of utility regulations. The characteristics of the services are presented. The second part addresses the basic concepts of pricing-utility-related services. The methods and steps for determining rate-making decisions are reviewed and analyzed. The third section examines the regulatory environment and its affect on the rate-making process, public utility accounting, and reporting. The difference between investor and publicly owned systems is presented along with the regulatory differences for accounting practices. The fourth part is a description of the accounting system. Section five examines the issue of the utility tax and its effect on the rate-making process. The sixth part of the book is an overview of recent events that affect utility accounting and rate-making decisions. These include significant political and economic events. This last section is updated annually. An index is included.

HF 5686 .R3 W68 1986
(Real Estate Investment—Finance; Accounting)

Wiley, Robert J. Real Estate Accounting and Mathematics
Handbook (New York: John Wiley & Sons) 1986.

This source is concerned with the provisions and methods of real estate investment properties. The text is divided into two sections. The first section, Chapters 1 through 7, deals with real estate accounting. The topics covered include financial statements, real estate partnership accounting, internal income and cash flow, return and risk ratios, income and expense analysis, cost accounting, and information for property management and property development.

The second section, Chapters 8 through 16, deals with the fundamental and traditional mathematical skills used in real estate finance. The subjects covered include compound interest calculations, mortgage calculations, computation of annual depreciation, finance calculation with Lotus 1-2-3, and real estate investment. Chapter 16 examines computer software for professional application. The individual chapters contain select bibliographies. The book contains an index.

HF 5699 .L76 1988 (Business Mathematics; Accounting)

Lipkin, Laurence, Irwin L. Feinstein and Lucile Derrick.
Accountants Handbook of Formulas and Tables
(Englewood Cliffs, NJ: Prentice Hall) 1988.

This is a reference book containing formulas and tables used by professional accountants. The author assumes the user has adequate knowledge of mathematics, accounting theory, and statistics to use the text.

The chapters and formulas are arranged by the operational problems addressed. The areas covered include simple interest, compound interest, annuities, basic computing, statistics: universe and sampler, statistical correlation, statistics index numbers and time series, depreciation, capitalized values marketing, cost and production, ratio analysis, pension plans, and other applications.

The chapters contain individual formulas, examples and solutions. There is a chapter on math tables for reference and an index.

HF 5712 .E25411 1992 (Weights and Measures—Tables; Metric System; Mensuration—Conversion Tables)

The Economist Desk Companion: How to Measure, Convert,
Calculate, and Define Practically Anything (New York: Henry
Holt and Company)

This reference source contains the units of measurement currently employed in the world today for quantifying everything from coffee and coal to radio waves and optics. The information presented in the book is updated, revised, and extended to reflect the latest changes in contemporary systems of measurement.

The book was developed from the *World Measurement Guide* and is divided into four different sections. Part I introduces the metric, British, and American systems of measurement. Part II provides an alphabetical subject-by-subject listing of various subjects areas. Part III contains conversion tables. Part IV consists of information on common abbreviations, rough conversions, units of measure in countries other than the United States and Great Britain, and a brief historical account of the unites of measurement employed in the United Kingdom. The book contains a detailed index in addition to an itemized table of contents.

HF 5728 .F8 G35 (French Language—Business French—Dictionaries—English)

Geoghegan C. and J. Gonthier Geoghegan. Handbook of Commercial French (London, UK: Routledge) 1988.

This is a reference of phrases and model correspondence in French and English. The text is designed for those whose primary language is English but need to use French for business. The text places emphasis on the functional use of French rather than the literal translation. The text is to be used in conjunction with French grammars and other relevant texts.

The book contains 2000 commonly employed English terms and 1000 of French phrases found in commercial correspondence. There are 32 models of business letters that follow the current usage of the terms and phrases.

HF 5801 .A13
(Marketing—United States; Advertising—United States)

AD & Summary: Leading National Advertisers Abritron Multi-Media Service (New York: Leading National Advertisers)

This is a report on the advertising expenditures of consumer magazines, Sunday magazines, outdoor, network television, spot television, syndicated television, cable television, and radio. The information contained here pertains to those company brands that involve marketing expenditures of $25,000 or more. The brands are alphabetically arranged and the data of the total expenditures in the nine media areas is provided in relationship to the brands. The parent company and PIB classification information is also profiled for the company brands. The data cover more than 1000 companies.

HF 5801 .E32 1990 (Market Analysis—United States; Market Analysis—Canada; Market Analysis—Puerto Rico)

Editors and Publishers Market Guide (New York, NY: The Editors & Publishers Company)

This volume is a survey guide to markets in the United States, Canada, and Puerto Rico. The surveys include market information on such subjects as town and/or city location, population, households, banks: commercial and savings and loan institutions, deposits, transportation, gas and electric meters, climate, retailing centers: principal stores with locations and hours, newspapers, and major businesses.

The guide is divided into four sections. The first sections contains market-ranking tables. This includes data on the population, disposable income, income per household, total retail sales, and major businesses in both the services and industrial sectors. The data in this section covers 250 cities in the United States. The second section contains information on daily newspapers. The newspapers are listed alphabetically by city and state in the United States and Puerto Rico. The information includes the name, address, and telephone number for the paper. Additional information is provided on the circulation statistics and the name of the market/advertising manager. The third section is identical to the second, but covers Canada and the provinces. The fourth section contains sales, population, and income tables for the United States and Canada. The data includes population, retail sales estimates, census estimates, and farm products.

The information in the text is based on national, state, provincial, and county surveys.

HF 5801 .I62 (International Advertising)

World Advertising Expenditures: A Survey of World
Advertising Expenditures (Mamaroneck, NY: Starch,
Inra, Hooper)

This is a survey of the advertising expenditures of 58 countries. The information included here covers a comparison of the previous year figures for total advertising; population figures and per capita advertising; advertising and gross national product; advertising expenditures for print, radio, television, and cinema, and the percentage of distribution through these media.

HF 5803 .D55 1986 (Advertising—Dictionaries—English)

Urdang, Laurence. The Dictionary of Advertising (Lincolnwood,
IL: NTC Business Book) 1988.

This dictionary covers advertising terms. There are over 4000 terms listed in the book. The text serves as a supplement to standard English dictionaries. The entries located here refer to the business usage of advertising terms for the broadcast media, industrial organizations, corporations, and research firms.

HF 5803 .K86
(Advertising—Dictionaries—English, German;
Mass Media—Dictionaries—English, German;
Marketing—Dictionaries—English, German)

Koschnick, Wolfgang J. Standard Dictionary of Advertising, Mass Media and Marketing: English–German (New York, NY: Walter de Gruyter) 1983.

This is a dictionary of advertising, mass media, and marketing terms in English and German. The dictionary contains 15,000 entries. The pages are arranged in columns. The left column contains the English term, definition, and appropriate abbreviations when applicable. The right column contains the same information for the German equivalent. The terms are arranged in alphabetical order.

HF 5803 .P13 (Advertising—German—Dictionaries;
Advertising—English—Dictionaries; Advertising—French—
Dictionaries; Marketing—German—Dictionaries;
Marketing—English—Dictionaries; Marketing—French—
Dictionaries; Communication—German—Dictionaries;
Communication—English—Dictionaries; Communication—
French—Dictionaries)

Paetze, Hans W. Complete Multilingual Dictionary of Advertising, Marketing and Communication: English, French, German (Lincolnwood, IL: Passport Books) 1984.

This is a multilingual dictionary containing 8000 entries of general and technical terms. The terms covered in the text are relevant to advertising, marketing, and communications. The book is divided into three sections: German, English, and French. The words are arranged alphabetically.

HF 5804 .A24
(Advertising Agencies—United States—Directories)

Adweek Agency Directory: National Directory (New York, NY: Adweek)

This is a reference-and-research guide containing the listings of 8000 agencies, public relations firms, and media buying services. The National Directory provides coverage to the entire United States. The directory is divided by national regions: New England, East, Southeast, Midwest, Southwest, and West. The listings are alphabetically arranged and the coverage provided includes agency name, address, telephone number, a listing of the agency billings by medium, primary accounts, service specialties, functional capabilities, and the number of employees. The data contained in the directory is provided by the agencies in response to questionnaires and telephone research follow-ups.

HF 5805 .S78
(Advertising Agencies—Directories;
Advertising—United States—Directories)

Standard Directory of Advertising Agencies (Skokie, IL:
National Register Publications)

U.S. advertising agencies and their branches that spend $75,000 or more on media are profiled here. The brief descriptions are alphabetically arranged. The information included in each description is title of the agency, address, telephone number, year founded, number of employees, approximate annual billing, list of important personnel, and specialization of the firm. The directory appears annually and has a monthly supplement known as *Agency News*. The *Agency News* introduces agencies recently added to the directory and provides the same information in its briefs as appears in the annual.

The directory has a subject and a name index located both at the front and the back. The indexes at the front mostly include different ways in which one may look for an agency. For instance, the mergers, acquisitions, and name changes index and the geographical index are two ways to look up an agency. In the back are indexes that are categories of agencies, including lists of sales promotions agencies, house agencies, media services organizations, and public relations agencies.

HF 5905 .S79 (Advertising, Newspaper—United
States—Rates—Periodicals; Advertising—United
States—Directories)

Newspaper Rates and Data (Wilmette, IL: Standard
Rate & Data Service, A Maxwell Macmillan Group)

Advertising rates for approximately 1500 newspapers published in the United States are presented here. The source details black/white and color rates, deadlines, circulation, zone editions, representatives or branch offices, classified rates, special editions, and magazine and comic sections. It includes sections on college and university newspapers, international newspapers, and ethnic and minority newspapers.

Using information from the U.S. Census Bureau and the U.S. Department of Commerce, the book lists consumer market data from 220 market areas, ranked according to population. The entries include the number of households, gross household income, total expenditures, and expenditures by store types. It also contains a section of state maps and market data, arranged alphabetically by state, city, and county. Also included are a media/market state map, population summaries, and newspaper markets.

HF 5905 .S792
(Radio Advertising—United States—Directories)

Spot Radio Rates and Data (Wilmette, IL: Standard
Rate & Data Service, A Maxwell Macmillan Group)

This source is a summary containing information on radio contract regulations, representatives, locations and rankings according to target population, radio terms, television market area rankings, explanations of consumer market data, summaries of areas of dominant influence and designated market areas, metro demographic explanations, radio station rates, and data listings arranged alphabetically by state, city, and call letters, rates and data for independent and/or syndicated comic sections, agri-radio station representatives and listings. Indexes are provided for call letter, stations in metropolitan statistical areas, national, regional, and state networks and groups, agri-radio networks, and groups and service ads. The format descriptions are voluntarily submitted by stations and reflect the current activity without promotional language. Acceptable classifications include music, sports, talk air personalities, news, farm, religious, entertainment, and commercial policy.

The information for the excerpts in this multivolume, triennial set is a current description of the Standard Rate Data Service listing organization of data voluntarily supplied by the station or strictly controlled, voluntary surveys. Numbered titled segments and various subjects within each listing are identified. Radio rates and data information are alphabetically arranged by state, city, target population, program format, and call letters. Radio representatives information include name, address, telephone number of headquarters and branch offices. Puerto Rico and the United States possessions are included.

HF 6146 .R3 I62 V. 1–2 (Business Enterprises—Statistics—Periodicals; Radio Advertising—Periodicals; Marketing Research—Periodicals)

Costa, Kenneth J., Ed. Instant Background (New York, NY: Radio Advertising Bureau)

This work, in a series, is part of modern radio marketing literature. Each volume offers 50 business categories with detailed industry profiles. It is mainly geared for marketers selling radio advertising space. It includes information on industries and products that allow analysis of businesses and marketing.

Business categories documented cover a full range including air conditioning, liquor stores, politics, supermarkets, and "no smoking" industries. Each profile outlines the industry's general characteristics such as size, revenues, leading businesses, types of customers, and sales. Also included are consumer behavior and purchasing data. Some profiles offer buyer demographics such as age, sex, income, and household size.

The data cited reflect the latest available information and statistics from the U.S., state or local governments, trade associations, trade publications, industry groups, and independent sources. No index is provided, but there is a table of contents. All volumes of Instant Information are also available on-line through RAB ON-LINE EXPRESS and are updated regularly.

HG—FINANCE

HG 11.A62 (Financial Times (London, England)—Indexes)

Financial Times Business Information Limited, Official Index to the Financial Times (London, England: Financial Times Business Information Ltd.)

The purpose of this index is to aid in locating material in the "Financial Times" through references to content. This index features publication codes, date references, page references, column references, alphabetical order, numeric headings, abbreviations, and cross-references. Companies, foreign countries, proper names, foreign names, organizations, societies, and institutions, with the exceptions of political parties and organizations, major public offices, educational establishments, and government departments, which are located under their respective countries, are indexed as main headings.

HG 30.17 .H66 (Industrial Management—Terminology; Business—Dictionaries)

Field Guide to Business Terms: A Glossary of Essential Tools and Concepts for Today's Manager (Boston: Harvard Business School Press) 1993.

The *Field Guide to Business Terms* is a small, compact dictionary that provides definitions for terms used in modern, corporate settings. The purpose of the guide is to aid persons involved with business, particularly with managerial duties, in understanding business terminology. The guide also provides some informative articles about management in the 1990s, including topics such as issues and trends, human resources, inflation, profit motives, and global corporate relations. These articles attempt to give an overview of future issues important to corporate managers and to offer some opinions about future trends in business.

The guide is presented in two major sections, with the management articles appearing first to provide some background information followed by the glossary. The management articles are organized by broad subject concepts which appear in the Table of Contents. The glossary includes not only traditional corporate terms but also modern and slang corporate terms. Some foreign words are defined also because of their common usage in business settings. The *Field Guide to Business Terms* defines terms and gives examples of their proper usages. Broad concept terms are broken into narrower terms, which are further defined. "See also" references allow users to find other relevant terms. The glossary is also interspersed with quotations and some management hints and tools.

HG 61 .H24
(Finance—United States—Directories; Capital; Business—Directories)

Rao, Dileep, Ed. Handbook of Business Finance and Capital Sources (Minneapolis, MN: Inter Finance)

This source is designed as a comprehensive source of information for businessmen and other entrepreneurs who are raising funds for their enterprises. The handbook is divided into four sections. The first section provides descriptive information on business finance. Chapters in this sections briefly cover fundamental points such as business financial requirements, cost of money, and private placements and public offering of securities; information on financial instruments including equities, debt instruments, equipment liens, real estate mortgages, and time sales financing; capital sources including commercial banks, factoring companies, foundations, investment bankers, and pension funds; and topics of special interest including legal considerations, startup and acquisitions financing, import and export financing, and Eurodollars. An index to the topics covered in these introductory chapters appears at the end of the work.

The second section provides this information for nongovernmental, private financial institutions: name, address, telephone, type of institution, contact officers, assets, types of financing provided, preferred types of industries, geographic limits to investments, and range of loan per business. Many entries also include address and contact information for branch offices of the institution. The institutions are listed by the type of institution, by state, and then alphabetically by cities in a state.

The third section of the book includes information regarding financial programs offered by state governments. An initial table summarizes the specific programs each state offers. Listings in this section include the name of the state organization, address, phone number, contact officer, description of program, range of investment per borrower, types of collateral accepted and terms of financing. Program information is in alphabetical order by state.

The fourth section provides information regarding federal programs that offer financial assistance for businessmen and farmers. An initial table list the programs by an index number and according to the type of beneficiary. Additional information is provided in the main entries of the section, including administering agency, type of assistance, restrictions and conditions, and the name of the contact office. Programs are arranged by ascending order of the assigned index numbers. A list of all the summary tables in the work appears in the table of contents.

HG65 .G95 1995
(Financial Institutions—United States—Directories;
Financial Institutions—Canada—Directories; Small Business
Investment Companies—United States—Directories)

Pratt's Guide to Venture Capital Sources (Wellesley Hills, MA:
Capital Pub.)

This work is a guide to venture capital investments and individual venture capital firms, and is a tool to help entrepreneurs and small-business managers understand the process of raising capital and locating compatible venture capital investors. The introductory text consists of four parts: 1) Background of Venture Capital, which helps budding businessmen and women comprehend the venture investment process; 2) How to Raise Venture Capital, which is a collection of essays prepared by industry professionals whose purpose is to precipitate the investing process for the investor and the business entrepreneur by discussing realistic expectations and standard procedures for approaching a venture capitalist; 3) Sources of Business Development Financing, which describes private- and public-sector money-making opportunities; 4) and Perspectives section, which analyzes the characteristics venture capitalists look for in their clients and gives the entrepreneur's interpretation of the venture process. The main body of the work, the Directories, lists 950 venture capital companies in America, Canada, Europe, and the Far East, and presents data that include name, address, telephone and fax numbers, company officers, contact people, type of firm, affiliation, project preferences, geographical preferences, and additional information such as year founded and method of compensation. Company, name, industry preferences, and stage preferences indexes.

HG 136. E85 H42 (Financial Institutions—Europe— Directories; Banks and Banking—Europe— Directories; Insurance—Europe—Directories; Securities—Europe—Directories)

Hay, Tony. A Guide to European Financial Centres (Chicago, London: St. James Press) 1990.

This work is designed to provide business professionals with information about the background, trends, and directions of financial centers in Western Europe. Each of the volume's 17 chapters covers one country and includes a narrative description and a directory. The narrative contains information about the type of government, population, gross national product, and discount rate. It describes the relationship of the country's laws and regulations to banking, insurance, and stock markets. The directory section lists financial resources by names, addresses, phone, and fax numbers. The contact information is followed by a list of officers and/or a brief description of each center's history and purpose. The front of the book contains a list of abbreviations. The appendices at the end of the work include a list of the translated titles of entries in the directories and an index to topics.

HG 151 .A96 (Finance—Dictionaries)

Avneyon, Eitan A. Dictionary of Finance (New York, NY: Macmillan) 1988.

This dictionary contains definitions of a wide range of terms used in finance and investment. Areas covered include economics, accounting, commodities and securities market trading procedures, public and private financing, banking, and tax and consumer legislation. Also covered are marketing, management, statistics, insurance and other related fields. No biographical entries for individuals are included. However, organizations such as the New York Stock Exchange, the Chicago Board of Trade, and various international entities do have entries. Some Latin terms dealing with finance are included. A number of entries refer the reader to additional information via cross-references. Entries having several meanings in different contexts are provided with numbered definitions given by order of importance. Acronyms are defined in full. Pronunciation of terms is not given. Terms considered to be of key importance are italicized in the text. The letter-by-letter system of alphabetizing is used so terms consisting of several words are treated as one word. A number of diagrams and illustration by individual economists are used to illustrate concepts. This dictionary is intended for use by businessmen, students, and professionals.

HG 151 .B21 (Finance—Dictionaries)

Bannock, Graham, and Manser, William. International Dictionary of Finance (New York: J Wiley) 2000.

This dictionary provides an alphabetical listing of thousands of terms with definitions and suggested pronunciations.

HG 151 .E49 (Finance)

Phillips, Diana/Bignaud, Marie-Claude. Elsevier's Dictionary of Financial Terms (Netherlands: Elsevier Science B.V.) 1997.

The Elsevier's Dictionary helps translate words used in the financial market from English to Dutch, Italian, and German. This is the second edition, and it has more than 400 new words compared to the first edition. The dictionary is in the form of a thesaurus, listing synonyms of different languages under one heading.

HG 151 .M68 (Finance—Terminology; Business Enterprises—Finance—Terminology)

Moffat, Donald W. Concise Desk Book of Business Finance (Englewood Cliffs, NJ: Prentice-Hall) 1984.

This work is intended to provide quick access to basic information on business finance. It is designed for a wide range of users, including business professionals, students, and casual information seekers. The work is arranged in dictionary format. Definitions are given for government agencies, accounting terms, economic "laws," stock market terms, government laws and regulations, and a wide variety of other business-related terms. Tests to measure financial soundness, such as operating ratio and current ratio, are included. Explanations of legal implications of such statutes as the Truth-in-Lending Act are given. Specialized terms are defined with a general audience in mind. References for further reading are given at the end of some of the lengthier entries. Mathematical equations are provided for many economic concepts. The tax implications of the latest federal statutes are explained. Examples utilizing actual business situations are used to demonstrate the meanings of many entries. Cross-references are extensively used to direct the reader to related and preferred terms. Acronyms are defined in full. Figures and diagrams are provided to elucidate many concepts. Separate computer and calculator programs have been made available for items such as compound interest tables, in order to reduce the bulkiness of the printed work.

HG 151 .M966
(Banks and Banking—Dictionaries; Finance—Dictionaries;
Banks and Banking—United States—Dictionaries)

Munn, Glenn Gaywaine. Encyclopedia of Banking and Finance (Boston, MA: Bankers Publishing) 1983.

This work provides a wide range of information on business, banking, and financial concepts. Its intended audience include bank officers, corporate treasurers, and institutional investors as well as the general public. The source contains nearly 4000 entries. In addition to basic definitions of terms, in-depth entries contain information concerning historical background, statistical data, analysis of present trends, illustrative examples, and citation of relevant regulations and laws. Specific information available includes interest rate tables, definitions of archaic and slang terms, the texts of major articles of the Uniform Commercial Code, entries defining specific public and private financial organizations, mathematical equations for economic concepts, and sample forms for business agreements. Bibliographies and across references are included at the end of many definitions. Lists of abbreviations are provided for foreign currencies, U.S. government entities, and general business terms. Numerous diagrams and illustrations are used to explain concepts. A "quick index" at the end of the volume includes all entry terms and their page numbers.

HG151 .N53 (Finance—Dictionaries)

The New Palgrave Dictionary of Money & Finance. Edited by
Peter Newman, Murray Milgate, John Eatwell (London:
Macmillan; NY: Stockton Press) 1992.

This dictionary consists of 1008 signed essays prepared by 800 contributors
on the theoretical aspects of monetary economics and their applications in
business, finance, and banking. Many entries are current and explanatory
such as "American banking legislation, recent" and "European monetary
system," while others define standard technical terms and describe well-
known institutions. The work covers 30 countries emphasizing France,
Germany, and Japan, although the main focus is on North America and
Britain with two-thirds of the writers dealing with the former, and 20% with
the latter areas. Modern concepts of economic analysis such as "the Nash
equilibrium in noncooperative game theory" and biographies of economic
theorists such as Hume, Thornton, Friedman, and Keynes are excluded, and
can be found in the less-specialized and more inclusive *The New Palgrave: A
Dictionary of Economics*. This work contains full bibliographic citations in a
variety of formats that include books, periodical articles, dissertations,
working papers, discussion documents, and unpublished pieces. The systematic cross-referencing procedure, acronym list, and subject classification
table integrate the wide range of material without the need for an general
index.

HG 151 .N481 1992 (Finance—Dictionaries)

Newman, Peter, Murray Milgate, and John Eatwell, Eds. New
Palgrave Dictionary of Money and Finance (New York, NY:
Stockton Press) 1992.

This source is a companion work to the Dictionary of Political Economy and
the New Palgrave Dictionary of Economics. It contains essays written by
numerous Nobel laureates and contemporary financial experts. Information
contains up-to-date events and their significance to the economy.

Subjects are arranged in alphabetical order and are written in an
encyclopedic style. It is geared to an educated audience, but the language is
easy to understand and numerous cross-references are provided. British
spelling and punctuation are used. A list of entries and acronyms are at the
beginning of each volume followed by the dictionary entries. Subject classification, a list of contributors and their affiliations at the time of publication
are included at the end of volume three. Entries that were originally included
in the *Dictionary of Political Economy* are indicated by brackets. Most essays

are author-signed and are followed by "see also" references and a bibliography for further study. About 420 cross-references are included that lead to other relevant essays and, when followed in succession, lead to an overall treatment of an entire subject.

Great Britain and North America receive about 80% of the focus of the book. The remaining 20% is devoted to other countries including those with non-Western economies. Illustrations are limited to graphs, formulas, and tables.

HG 151 .R82
(Finance—Dictionaries; Banks and Banking—Dictionaries)

Rosenberg, Jerry M. Dictionary of Banking and Financial Services. (New York, NY: John Wiley & Sons) 1985.

This source aims to provide definitions of banking and financial services terms for both the business professional and the layperson or student seeking general explanations. The dictionary is arranged alphabetically. Compound terms are entered under their main component, usually the nouns. The most widely used terms is usually listed as the main entry, with less well-known related terms cross-referenced via see-also references. Some historical terms are included even if they are no longer commonly used. Words that are utilized differently in various disciplines are listed with their full range of definitions. The most widely applicable definition is given first, with succeeding definitions given by area of specialization. Areas of specialization are identified by boldface italic type. Words and phrases defined include both Latin and English legal terms, accounting terms, the names of Congressional and state legislative acts, acronyms, and slang terms used in finance. No illustrations are used in the work. All appendices have been removed from this edition because of the difficulty of keeping them up-to-date. Sources of definitions for some terms are listed in numbered references at the end of the work.

HG 151 .R661 1993 (Banks and Banking—Dictionaries)

Rosenberg, Jerry M. Dictionary of Banking (New York: John Wiley & Sons, Inc.) 1993.

Jerry M. Rosenberg includes in this dictionary current terminology dealing with today's banking industry because of the many changes and new regulations added to the industry. This work helps the reader to handle banking and financial problems. The dictionary's main purpose is to clarify and establish a clearer communication process among banking and financial fields. This reference source has been modified for both the person who needs precise information and for students unfamiliar with the text. The terms are taken from accounting, banking, brokerage, capital structure, capitalization, collections, commercial banking, commodities markets, computer systems, credit, credit unions, financial institutions, financial law, financial management, financial planning, financial reports, foreign trade, funding, government regulations and agencies, import–export, insurance, investments, lending, methods of financing, manpower and human savings and loan associations, saving banks, securities markets, services, sources of bank and financial information, systems, transfers, and trusts. Terms are organized for the educated, specialized person and for the student. The dictionary was organized for the main purpose of finding entries easily and rapidly. Words can be found in alphabetical order, under compound terms, synonyms, variant spellings, headings, and cross-references. Terms have multiple definitions, based on the usage of various fields of activities. The first definition contains the wide application, while the remainder are given by the area of specialty. To obtain the exact definition for a certain area, all the definitions should be read.

HG 151 .T48 (Insurance—Dictionaries; Insurance—Abbreviations—Dictionaries)

Thomsett, Michael C. Insurance Dictionary (Jefferson, NC: McFarland) 1989.

This work is intended to be a comprehensive summary of words and phrases, and their meanings are used in the insurance industry. The wide range of actuarial, legal, investment, and marketing terms are defined to be comprehensible to the layperson as well as to professionals in the field. The dictionary is divided into four sections. The main section provides a fully cross-referenced glossary of terms for insurance practices, agencies, and theories. Diagrams and graphs are used to facilitate explanations of some concepts. The next section provides a current listing of state insurance commissioner addresses in the United States. Contact officials are listed, including phone numbers. A similar list of contact addresses for Canadian provincial insurance agencies comprises the third section. The last section of the work is an alphabetical list of definitions of abbreviations, including terms, phrases, associations, and agencies.

HG 151.7 .B24 (Finance)

Barbuto, Domenica M. The International Financial Statistics
Locator (New York: Garland Publishing) 1995.

The statistics are mainly beneficial to investors trying to understand the market. Information is also provided on 175 countries, and they are listed in a manner that aids the user in finding the country that interests the individual. A list of securities on 125 markets is available in the Appendix, and also included are their addresses and telephone numbers.

HG 173 .D74 1998 (Finance)

Downes, John and Goodman, Jordan E. Finance Investment
Handbook (New York: Barron's Educational Series) 1998.

The Finance and Investment Handbook is divided into five sections, each one touches upon a lesson in understanding about finance and investment. Some of the topics covered in the sections are tax issues, the importance of knowing what to look for in financial reports, and the language on Wall Street.

HG 173 .D75 (Finance—Handbooks, Manuals, etc.; Investments—Handbooks, Manuals, etc.; Finance—Dictionaries; Investments—Dictionaries)

Downes, John and Jordan Elliot Goodman. Barron's Finance
and Investment Handbook (Hanppauge, NY: Barron's) 1998.

The objective of this source is to cover in a single volume the different elements that comprise today's world of investment and finance. Part one provides information on 30 important personal investment opportunities. Among the topics covered are annuities, corporate bonds, closed-end funds, and common stocks: futures contracts on commodities, interest rates, and stock indexes: government agency securities, life insurance, money market funds, and mutual funds; option contracts, precious metals, real estate, and treasury securities. Part two gives detailed information on how to read an annual report. Part three provides similar instruction for reading the financial pages. Part four, the main section of the handbook, is a dictionary of finance and investment. More than 2500 key terms are comprehensively defined, using examples and illustrations. Part five is a "ready reference" section con-

taining addresses of sources of information such as federal regulatory agencies in the United States and Canada; U.S. state attorney generals' offices;
U.S. state banking, insurance, and securities regulators; and computerized
databases for investors. Also included are lists of major financial institutions
and mutual funds; historical data on the various stock market averages and
indexes; and lists of publicly traded companies on the various stock exchanges. The appendix of the work includes an annotated bibliography for
chosen works on investment and finance, and a listing of foreign currencies.
The index at the end of the handbook facilitates access to all the information
on a particular topic.

**HG 173 .F52 (Finance—Information Services—Directories;
Market Surveys—Information Services—Directories;
Business—Information Services—Directories;
Finance—Bibliography; Market Surveys—Bibliography;
Business—Bibliography)**

Financial Sourcebooks' Sources: The Directory of Financial
Research, Marketing Surveys and Services (Naperville, IL:
Financial Sourcebooks) 1987.

This work is designed to provide marketing professionals in all types of
businesses with the information they need to develop effective marketing
plans. It directs business professionals to sources of information to assist in
effective targeting of people, programs, and products. The volume is divided
into eight chapters. Each chapter lists names, addresses, contact personnel,
and phone numbers of organizations that have produced reports, surveys,
and services of interest to marketing professionals. Chapter topics include
general background information on consumers, such as treads, values, demographics, and attitudes; consumer finances and financial attitudes; consumer
segments including Asians, baby boomers, blacks, college students, Hispanics, and women; and consumer financial products such as credit cards, IRAs,
and mutual funds. Also covered are businesses and institutional services, and
institutions such as banks, brokerage firms, and credit unions; U.S. geographical information, Census Bureau regional information services, and
state data center agencies; and international sources of marketing information for various regions of the world. Appendices at the end of the work include a directory of research publishers, lists of free reports, and government
reports, and a detailed listing of assistance available from the Bureau of
the Census.

HG173 .H23 1987 (Finance—Handbooks, Manuals, etc.; Finance—United States—Handbooks, Manuals, etc.; Corporations—Finance—Handbooks, Manuals, etc.; International Finance—Handbooks, Manuals, etc.)

Handbook of Financial Markets and Institutions. Edited by Edward I. Altman (New York: Wiley) 1987.

This is a work prepared for students of finance and professionals who need a reference source to understand essential concepts and practices of three major designated areas related to monetary affairs: markets, institutions, and investments. (The fourth, corporate finance, is a separate volume, *The Handbook of Corporate Finance*.) Business executives, academic financial economists, business financial economists, government authorities, former government authorities now working in the private sector, financial consultants, and other subject specialists authored the 27 sections. Some of the writers who worked on the previous *Financial Handbook, Fifth Edition* have returned to discuss their fields in essentially the same way, while others have substantially updated their information on such topics as estate financing, mortgage back securities, options and future markets, commercial banking, and debt and equity markets. New sections appear on investment banking, microcomputer and investments, the bond rating process, option, and insurance strategies for fixed income portfolios, high-yield bonds, asset-pricing models, and small business financing. Appendices on the mathematics of finance and sources of financial and investment information have been expanded. Indexed.

HG173 .H24 1990 (Finance—Handbooks, Manuals, etc.)

Handbook of Modern Finance. Edited by Dennis E. Logue (Boston: Warren, Gorham & Lamont)

This handbook is a reference source for corporate financial and business executives, strategic planners, public and private accountants, lawyers, security analysts, and bankers for answering everyday financial questions.

The work contains seven parts. Part I, The Financial System and Markets, discusses the financial system, the banking system, nonbank financial institutions, investment banking, money markets, mathematics of finance, the long-term bond market, municipal securities, corporate equities, trading and option markets, and financial futures markets. Part II, Security Analysis, Pricing, and Portfolio Management, looks at the determinants of interest rates, modern portfolio analysis, financial statement analysis, security analysis, managing security portfolios, and historical returns on investment instruments. Part III, Short-Term Financial Management, examines credit analysis, cost accounting, cash-budgeting—The Annual Plan, financial forecasting and planning, short-run financial management, and dynamics of cash management.

Part IV, Long-Term Financial Management, discusses capital budgeting, managing the capital structure, evaluating a lease, project financing, and venture capital. Part V, Financial Policy, analyzes mergers and acquisitions, the effects of mergers and acquisitions on the governance of the modern corporation, dividend policy, pension plans, bank risk management, real estate finance, financial strategy, and bankruptcy liquidation and reorganization. Part VI, Financial Policy, deals with such issues as executive pay, incentives, and performance, and executive financial planning, and Part VII, International Dimensions of Finance, treats such topics as the evolution of the international monetary system, foreign exchange markets and currency risk, international financial markets, international portfolio diversification, international banking, international accounting, and investment and financing decisions for multinational corporations.

The work explains institutional arrangements and discusses important economic and financial theory and practice. Much of the quantitative analyses are given real-world application and are illustrated by many charts and tables. Each essay has been written by a subject specialist who appends to his or her article a bibliography to direct the reader to additional technical literature in the field. The handbook is updated annually to reflect current economic trends, new business practices, and changes in laws, and contains cumulative indexes.

HG 174 .O58 (Finance—Databases—Directories; Securities— Databases—Directories; Business—Databases—Directories)

Online Databases in the Securities and Financial Markets (New York, NY: Cuadra-Elsevier) 1987.

This directory is a subset of the larger *Directory of Online Databases* produced by the same publisher. It has been designed to provide securities and financial professionals with a resource for identifying databases that can be useful in their work. Alphabetically arranged entries for over 1600 databases are included. Information on the more than 300 on-line services that furnish access to these databases are also provided. This work focuses on databases covering corporations, industries and countries. Databases on corporations include basic address and personnel information, financial data both current and historical and securities information. Databases covering specific industries provide data on production and consumption, imports and exports, orders and shipments, and data on commodities. Databases covering countries and groups of countries include general financial and economic data. Commentaries, analyses, and forecasts are included in many databases to provide contexts for the "raw" data and the directory listings indicate the existence of these expert assessments. A typical directory entry include information on database type, subject, producer, on-line service, conditions of availability, content, language, geographic coverage, time span of coverage, and frequency of updating. Three indexes provide access to the directory listings: a subject index grouping databases by area of coverage; an on-line service-gateway index grouping databases by vendors; and an alphabetical master index including both databases and vendors.

HG 175 .C76 (Finance; Financial Institutions; Capital Market; International Finance)

Havrilesky, Thomas M. and Robert Schweitzer, Eds.
Contemporary Developments in Financial Institutions (Arlington
Heights, VA: Harlan Davidson) 1983.

The growth, integration, and evolution of financial markets and services are examined by this textbook for business students. The editors have made a special effort to incorporate current articles by executives and scholars to insure the information is timely. The four sections of the book examine each area of finance separately, thus reducing confusion for students. The first section explores interest rates, yield curves, and capital flow. The past, present, and future impact of financial institutions is the subject of the second section. The third section examines the relationship of supply and demand, and the fourth presents borrowing and lending in the international market.

HG 175. F47 (Finance; Economic Policy; International Economic Relations)

Calverly, John and Richard O'Brien, Eds. Finance and the
International Economy (London, UK: Oxford University Press)

The essays presented in this source analyze current issues in the study of international economics. The function of exchange controls and the need for greater equilibrium in exchange rates are evaluated in the first two essays. The next four essays discuss the value of information as related to wealth, the way to allow debtor countries to decrease debt by targeting export growth, the need for more information about equity markets, and the salutary effects on society of modern methods in the financial market. The final essays concentrate on the results of the trade imbalance between the United States and Japan.

HG 175 .F52
(Financial Institutions—Management; Finance—Industry)

Friars, Eileen M. and Robert N. Gogel, Eds. The Financial
Services Handbooks: Executive Insights and Solutions
(New York, NY: John Wiley & Sons) 1987.

The growing integration of the financial industry is analyzed from the
perspectives of several leading authorities in different financial fields. The
editors asked bankers, brokers, insurance executives, and others to contribute
their viewpoints of common problems and creative solutions that have led
to success. Each avenue to success, however, is unique. A right way for all
does not exist. The editors stress that total integration will not occur soon or
easily, given the inherent differences that characterize each industry. This
handbook for managers in financial industries allows managers an overview
of the industry.

HG 177 .C82
(Fund Raising—United States—Directories; Corporations—
Charitable Contributions—United States—Directories)

The Corporate Fund Raising Directory (Washington, DC:
Public Service Materials Center)

This directory lists American corporations committed to funding grants
alphabetically by name. Entries include application information, primary
areas of funding interest, amount of available funding, and geographic
preferences. In most cases, guidelines for proposals must be requested directly
from the corporation: query addresses and telephone numbers are provided.
    Five indexes help to limit and define the search for corporation within
the directory. The indexes divide materials into corporations by state,
corporations by geographic preference, corporations by area of interest,
corporations issuing guidelines, and an alphabetical list of contact persons.

HG 177.5 .U6 C4381 (Financing, Government—United
States—Directories; Research Support—United States—
Directories; Training Support—United States—Directories;
Writing)

The Action Guide to Government Grants, Loans, and Giveaways
(Putnam) 1993.

This guidebook was written to assist students, entrepreneurs, artists, researchers, and other individuals work through the federal and state government
bureaucracies to obtain funding. The author's step-by-step approach gives

the reader suggestions on how to improve his or her chances of obtaining government money, details of the terms of the loans, samples of actual applications, and a comprehensive list of current federal and state programs. The agencies' addresses are alphabetically arranged by state. The text of this book is supplemented by an extensive bibliography and a glossary. However, the book does not contain an index. The U.S. government has agencies which have funds to help a group or individual that shows the initiative by applying for a grant or loan. The government's money is allocated according to the value and thoughtfulness of the group or individual's proposal. More of the book's emphasis is placed on financial assistance as opposed to financial giveaways. The author, George Chelekis, uses a straightforward approach to prepare the reader for what is in store and makes the book available at a price the consumer can afford.

HG 179 .R52 (Finances, Personal—Dictionaries)

Richards, Robert William. The Dow Jones–Irwin Dictionary of Financial Planning (Homewood, IL: Dow Jones–Irwin) 1986.

The broad heading, "Financial Planning," encompasses many professions, each with its own specialized language. Compiled with both the professional and the layperson in mind, this dictionary of terms aims to mitigate confusion by providing concise definitions for unfamiliar jargon. One chart and many equations appear in entries that have graphics to aid the explanation. Located at the end of the dictionary is a subject index where terms peculiar to specific professions, such as real estate or business law, are grouped together and may be viewed at a glance.

HG 181 .A1 A26 (International Finance; Balance of Payments—United States)

National Advisory Council on International Monetary and Financial Policies, Annual Report to the President and to the Congress (Washington, DC: U.S. Government Printing Office)

Reporting on multilateral development banks and activity of the United States in the International Monetary Fund, this yearly account provides information on world economic trends, international monetary relations, multilateral development assistance, trade policy, and foreign indebtedness to the government of the United States, in the form of brief updates with textual tables interspersed. Five appendices discuss special topics, the longest of which deals with loans made by multilateral development banks. The final section consists of statistical tables that included explanatory notes.

HG 181 .B98
(Finance—Vocational Guidance—United States—
Periodicals; Banks and Accounting—Vocational
Guidance—United States—Periodicals; Accounting—
Vocational Guidance—United States—Periodicals;
Insurance—Vocational Guidance—United States—
Periodicals)

Business and Finance Career Directory. Career Directory Series
(Hawthorne, NJ: Career Press)

This source is a guidebook for anyone contemplating a career in business and
finance. Articles by professionals introduce various opportunities and explain
why they may be of interest. The second section offers suggestions for
evaluating personal and career objectives, as well as for the preparation of
résumés, interview techniques, and other job search strategies. A small
directory of prospective employers for jobs at entry level comprises the third
section of the book. Some entries list the size of the company and employment
opportunities, while others only give an address. Appendix A provides an
alphabetical listing of trade organizations with a summary of their activities
and contact addresses. Appendix B is a bibliography of trade and consumer
publications organized by subject areas and includes addresses.

HG181 .F48 1995 (Financial Services Industry—United
States—Statistics—Periodicals; Insurance
Companies—United States—Statistics—Periodicals)

Finance, Insurance, Real Estate USA (Detroit MI:
Gale Research)

This source is a guide to statistics on finance, insurance, and real estate
industries, and covers 36 major sectors and their activities in 50 states and
2500 counties. The work contains two parts. Part I consists of national and
state industry profiles that are arranged by Standard Industrial Classification
(SIC) number and provides information on the establishments, employment,
and payroll from 1986 through 1991; 24 four-digit and 12 three-digit SIC
classifications; industrial activity at this level of detail covering the span of
Finance, Insurance, and Real Estate industries; financial performance and
history and geography on some industries until 1992; over 2900 company
listings that are arranged by sales, revenues, or assets; 100 leading companies
listed by 4-digit SIC industry that gives company name, address, telephone,

CEO, sales, revenues, assets, and employment; occupations for industrial groups in 1992, showing the most important occupations in the group and the projected trends in employment up to 2005; and input and output tables for the 1982 benchmark year. Part II presents state rankings and state industry data for 1989 and 1991 along with state tables included for each industry and maps, and information for counties for the years 1989 and 1991 arranged by state, county, and SIC number. Included are keyword, company, SIC, and occupation indexes.

HG 181 .M74 (Finance—United States—Dictionaries; Financial Institutions—United States—Dictionaries; Money—United States—Dictionaries)

Rachlin, Harvey. The Money Encyclopedia (New York, NY: Harper & Row) 1984.

The entries included in this dictionary of terms, some concise definitions and other long articles, attempt to build a basic understanding of money, its applications, and institutions. Brief sketches of the experience and education of the contributors are provided and many entries are signed. Numerous tables appear throughout the volume and a list of acronyms and abbreviations is included at the end.

HG186 .E85 H42 (Financial Institutions—Europe; Banks and Banking—Europe; Insurance—Europe; Securities—Europe)

Hay, Tony. A Guide to European Financial Centres (Chicago: St. James Press) 1990.

This guide for bankers, investment advisers, fund managers, stock brokers, corporate treasurers, and other financial professionals aims to give information about the background, current trends, and future developments of European financial centers. The work consists of 17 chapters, each of which deals with a particular country that belongs to the Western European economic community. Each entry contains a discussion of the country's political structure and general economic climate, banking regulations and statistics, insurance, stock market, information sources such as publications, relevant libraries, and the nation's main statistics bureau, and concludes with a directory that lists government departments, regulatory authorities, trade associations, and important financial markets. A table of contents, abbreviation list, translated titles, and translation, officers, and general indexes provide multiple access points to the main work for the English-speaking user.

HG 219 .P59 (Money—Periodicals; Banks and Banking, Central—Directories—Periodicals)

World Currency Yearbook (Brooklyn, NY: International Currency Analysis)

This source details 147 world currencies in alphabetical order within geographic sections. The world is divided into geographic sections including Africa; Americas: Central, North, South, and the Caribbean; Asia and Oceania; and Europe and the Middle East. An area map precedes each section, while black-and-white photographs of a bank note introduce each entry. Entries examine currency history, transferability, development, varieties, and administration. Increased circulation of $100 bills as a result of drug-money laundering, for example, is discussed in the development section under United States dollar. A monetary glossary as well as charts detailing currency control are provided at the beginning of the volume and articles with tables explaining the eurocurrency market, currency circulation, money supply, and the destruction of paper money appear in the appendix. Additionally, the volume includes a directory of central banks and an index for the volume.

HG 1501 .A48 (Banks and Banking—United States—Periodicals; Banks and Banking—United States—Statistics—Periodicals)

American Banker Yearbook (New York, NY: American Banker)

Prepared by the staff of the financial newspaper the *American Banker*, this reference work provides statistics, key trends, special reports, and company addresses of interest to those in the banking profession. The editorial sections adopt a newspaper format, complete with boldface paragraph breakers, at-a-glance summary graphics, and by-lines. The chapter titled "Dates and Events" summarizes key developments for each month of the past year and goes on to forecast potentially important date for the upcoming year, as well as to list the place and date of major meetings. The lengthiest section presents tables of statistics for commercial banks, nonbanks, international banks and thrifts. For each heading, a detailed table of contents is provided. In keeping with the editors' wish that this book enable executives to "put their hands on information" the volume ends with a directory of names, addresses, and phone numbers divided under various subject headings such as "Washington's Most Influential People" and "Top Banks." An index of selected articles from the previous year of American Banker follows, arranged by subject and in chronological order. An index to the volume is included as well.

HG1536 .B22 1995 (Banks and Banking—Directories; Banks and Banking, International—Directories)

The Bankers' Almanac (West Sussex, England: Reed Information Services)

Volumes 1 and 2 contain information on 4000 major international banks arranged in an alphabetical sequence. Each entry gives the registered address of the bank's head office; the bank's full registered title; comparable balance sheets; balance sheet figures and profit and loss statements that are derived from audited accounts; two year abridged balance sheets; balance sheet total figures given in U.S. dollars for the most recent year; performance ratios that cover Net Profit/Total Assets and Equity Capital/Total Assets; Equity Capital that includes the paid-up capital and reserves; world and country rankings for banks; and the latest long- and short-term credit ratings provided by IBCA, Moody's, Standard Poor's, Thomson Bank Watch, and BREE. Volume 3 presents a geographical listing of the banks and their 179,000 branches, agencies, or representative offices in over 78,000 cities and towns. Volume 4 gives 23,000 authorized banks, bank owners that are listed in the first two volumes, changes in bank names and liquidations, international law firms that are involved in banking law, and a general information section that provides data such as telegraphic addresses, banking associations, and coins and notes of the world. Thoroughly indexed.

HG 1536. W64 1993 (Banks and Banking—Directories; Bank Holding Companies—Directories)

Who Owns What in World Banking (London: Banker Research Unit, Financial Times Limited)

This book is a guide to the subsidiary and affiliated banking interests of scores of banks, including multinational and of consortia. The parent banks are listed in the first section. Financial summaries are included to give a clear picture of the development of the bank during the past 5 years. For each bank, domestic and international subsidiaries and affiliates are listed showing the percentage holding of the parent bank. Data about the banks of consortia are in the second section with financial summaries for the past 5 years.

HG 1626 .T481 (Interest—Tables—Periodicals; Interest Rates—Tables—Periodicals; Banks and Banking—Tables—Periodicals)

Thorndike, David. Thorndike Encyclopedia of Banking and Financial Tables (Arlington, VA: A.S. Pratt and Sons)

This reference work, divided into 17 parts, has information about the investing and banking industries. Parts 1–3 give information on the growth rates and returns on investments. Parts 4–9 provide data on interest rates and inflations. Parts 10–14 have data on the benefits and drawbacks of Individual Retirement Accounts. Parts 15–17 present information on the growth of markets, and the effects that such have on the finances of individuals.

HG 2150. U58 (Savings and Loan Associations—United States—Directories; Savings Banks—United States—Directories)

Thomson Savings Directory (Skokie, IL: Thomson)

This directory includes institutions chartered as savings and loans and savings banks in the United States. The institutions have an individual listing for its head office and its branches which are recorded in alphabetical sequence by state, city, and the institution's legal title.

HG 2401 .B18 (Banks and Banking—United States—Statistics; Banks and Banking—United States—Finance—Statistics; Savings and Loan Associations—United States—Finance—Statistics; Savings and Loan Associations—United States—Statistics)

Sheshunoff Information Services. Bank and S&L Quarterly (Austin: Sheshunoff)

This reference work, divided into eight sections, provides data on financial institutions and their performances. Section one shows current highlights and trends in banking. Section two gives the reader information on how to use this manual. Section three state and national overviews of banks. Section four provides ratings and analyses for Federal Deposit Insurance Corporation insured banks. Sections five through eight give identical data for savings and loan institutions in the United States.

HG 2431. P76
(Financial Institutions—North America—Directories;
Banks and Banking—North America—Directories)

Polk Financial Institutions Directory, North American Edition
(Skokie, IL: Thomson)

This work provides information on banks and their branches in the United States, Canada, the Caribbean, Central America, and Mexico. A detailed subject index is included in the first few pages. The volume includes lists of abbreviations, associations, and bank transit numbers. It provides lists of the ranking of large commercial banks, savings and loan institutions, and credit unions. Thumb tab indexes exist for financial sections, states, and some countries. Information on Federal Reserve Banks, Federal Insurance Deposit Corporation districts, the Federal Bureau of investigation, the U.S. Secret Service, and other government agencies and associations is included.

The financial institutions directory for each state includes a city/county map, demographic and legislative information, state bank holidays, state officials names, and names of bank examiners. Entries for some financial institutions include the hours of operation, date of establishment, names of officers, and directors. Larger institutional entries include asset balance sheet information.

HG 2431 .P77 1993 (Banks and Banking—Directories)

Polk World Bank Directory (Nashville, Tenn.: R. L. Polk Co.)

This directory contains information on banks and their branches in the United States and other countries. Information in this book can be easily acquired by the use of tab indexing, 42 maps located throughout the book, the from section of the book, and an alphabetical index to banks. Countries are arranged in alphabetical order. After this section, there are the largest 1000 banks in the United States. Within these, countries, cities, and towns are listed in alphabetical order with population, province, or territory indicated on the same line. Lists of advertisements are located throughout the directory referred to by a bank's reference line. To obtain information about certain banks, the reader must look under the country in which it is located. Banks are listed in alphabetical order with their address, telephone, cable address, etc. The directory now includes an expanded financial statement data.

HG 2441 .R18

Thomson/Polk Bank Directory (Skokie: Thomson Financial
Publishing)

This reference work begins with a short explanation of the information
provided, a list of currency evaluations, and a map showing time zones and
locations of the countries included in the remainder of the book. The main
section of this work is the Principal Correspondents Directory, in which
industrialized nations are chronicled with major banks listed. Also provided is
a guide for monitoring interbank liability.

HG2493 .S78 1993 (Financial Institutions—United States—Statistics; Banks and Banking—United States—Statistics)

Statistical Information on the Financial Services Industry
(Washington, DC: American Bankers Association)

This compilation consists of statistics and information collected from government bureaus, banking and financial organizations, insurance companies,
and other trade groups and sources. Data tables are arranged in 12 sections
and depict economic trends; demographics; trends in assets, liabilities, and
financial flows of nonfinancial sectors; consumer attitudes; sources of funds;
uses of funds; capital; earnings; structure; payment systems; international
banking; and government credit operations. Each entry consists of a heading,
comments, numbered figures, and numbered tables. Selected bibliography
and subject index.

HG 2974 .D58 (Banks and Banking—Europe)

Dorscheid, Peter. Elsevier's Dictionary of Export Financing
and Credit Insurance (New York: Elsevier) 1989.

This source is a trilingual dictionary (English, French, and German) of export
financing and credit insurance terms. The author does not attempt to define
the terms, merely to provide the proper equivalent. Phrases appear under the
first word of the phrase unless the phrase begins with an article or a
preposition. Acronyms are generally not spelled out and are listed as
themselves. Abbreviations of a term are explained in the section with the
term in its respective language. The source contains three sections, the first
alphabetically in English, the second in German, and the third in French.
There are no illustrations, indexes, or appendices.

HG 3753 .T92 (Export Credit—Information Services—Handbooks, Manuals, etc.; Investments, Foreign—Information Services—Handbooks, Manuals, etc.; International Finance—Information Services—Handbooks, Manuals, etc.; International Trade—Information Services—Handbooks, Manuals, etc.)

Tuller, Lawrence W. The McGraw-Hill Handbook of Global Trade and Investment Financing (New York: McGraw-Hill, Inc.) 1992.

This source aims to provide an overview of global trade and direct investment financing. It discusses the banking situation each country, giving the general background and an explanation of the different types of banking performed. In addition to discussing the banking situation in each country, this source also gives an overview of global banking, development banks, countertrade, private export trade financing, and government supported trade financing. This source contains appendices, tables, and an index.

HG 3834 .I61 (Foreign Exchange—Law and Legislation— Periodicals; Foreign Exchange—Control—Periodicals)

Annual Report on Exchange Arrangements and Exchange Restrictions (Washington, DC: International Monetary Fund)

Previously titled the *Annual Report on Exchange Restrictions* (1950–1978), this publication utilizes a variety of sources, including national governments, to provide information on exchanges and trade systems around the world. The first part of each issue provides an introduction to the topic, as well as sections detailing developments in exchange arrangements and rates, main developments in restrictive exchange and trade practices, and main developments in regional arrangements. Some of the specific topics covered are global environment, developments effecting the classification of exchange agreements, quantitative restrictions on trade, exports and exports proceeds, and gold. An appendix of summary measures effecting member exchange and trade systems rounds out this section. The second part of the source covers individual nations in terms of exchange arrangements, administration of control, prescription of currency, nonresident accounts, imports and import payments, exports and export proceeds, payments for invisibles, proceeds from invisibles and capital, and changes in the year covered. Completing the second part are a section on summary features of exchange and trade systems in member countries and a list of abbreviations.

HG 3851 .H21 (Foreign—Exchange Brokers—Directories; Banks and Banking, International—Directories; Financial Institutions, International—Directories)

Norton, Guy, Ed. The Cedel Euromoney Directory (London: Euromoney Publications PLC)

This source gives information on over 12,000 banks throughout the world. The major banks of each country are listed by name (former names given in parenthesis) followed by its address, telephone number, facsimile number, and telex number. Some of the entries also have their cable address, Reuters identification code, and Swift identification code listed. Occasionally, the bank's logo will be displayed. The names of bank officers in Senior Executive positions are given, as well as a list of the departments and their heads. There is an index at the front of the source listing all the banks by country, followed by a second index listing the banks by name. An addendum at the back of the book lists several additional banks.

HG 3851 .T76 (Foreign—Exchange Brokers—Directories; Commodity Exchanges—Directories)

Inglis-Taylor, Andrew, Ed. The Traders Dictionary '86: Foreign Exchange, Futures, and Options Dealers (London: Euromoney Publications, Ltd.) 1986.

This source aims to provide an overview of banks, futures dealers, and options dealers. There are two indexes at the beginning: one listing all the banks, the second all the options and futures dealers (by country). There is also a list of abbreviations used for currencies. The companies are listed alphabetically with companies beginning with "the" listed under the first noun and companies whose names begin with initials being listed under the first complete word. All companies are listed with some or all of the following: address, telephone number, telex, Swift name, cable, Reuters name, directors, managers, exchange dealers, and specializations.

HG 3863 .W93 (Dollar, American—Periodicals; Foreign Exchange—Periodicals; Money—Tables—Periodicals)

Bank of America World Information Services, World Currency Monitor Annual 1976–1989: US Dollar, The Value of the US Dollar in Foreign Terms (Westport, CT: Meckler Corp.) 1990.

This source contains the weekly exchange rate data for the U.S. Dollar (in terms of 99 foreign currencies) for the period January 5, 1976–December 25, 1989. Most of the book is a chart listing the date and the dollar's foreign equivalent, alphabetically arranged by country. All the information comes from the Bank of America World Information Service. New currencies introduced during this period are noted and a list of currency exchange rate arrangements is provided.

HG 3879 .G95 (Capital Market—Statistics—Periodicals; Euro-bond Market—Statistics—Periodicals; Euro-dollar Market—Statistics—Periodicals; International Finance—Statistics—Periodicals)

Cossan, Ruth and Mark Johnson, Eds. The Guide to International Capital Markets (London: Euromoney Publications)

This source is written by a team of 25 bank officers, journalists, and economists and attempts to give an explanation of the trends in international markets since the late 1980s. Twenty-one major currencies are discussed in depth. Other sections discuss swaps, commercial paper, medium term notes, corporate bond defaults, default rates, offshore securities, Australian dollar Eurobonds, and domestic securities. Many charts are included.

HG 3881 .E34 1999 (Finance)

Eichengreen, Barry. Toward a New International Financial Architecture (Washington DC: Institute for International Economics) 1999.

Over the years, there has been lot of debate about reforming the international financial architecture. Eichengreen's book advances this debate. Reasons for the crisis in Asia and Mexico were traced back to the international monetary and financial system. The book also proposes reasonable solutions to reform this system.

HG 3881 .E84 (International Finance—Periodicals; International Finance—Statistics—Periodicals; Banks and Banking, International—Periodicals)

Hornbrook, Adrian. Euromoney International Finance Yearbook (London: Euromoney Publications PLC)

This source discusses international banking reviews in 12 countries, and is designed to be a complete reference source on international finance. A variety of topics are addressed although the book is divided into three major sections: sector reviews written by managers of 12 principal banking centers analyzing the current state of business; financial data in statistically supported reviews; and statistics covering foreign exchange rates, financial futures rates and currency-adjusted equity, and bond and money market returns. A brief biography of the author follows each article. Many advertisements are interspersed throughout the text.

HG3881 .F84 (International Finance—History—20th Century)

Fraser, Robert. The World Financial System (Harlow, Essex: Longman) 1987.

The purpose of this reference source is first to describe how the world financial system has evolved, and second to deal with the aims, structures, methods, and operations of international and regional organizations having responsibilities in this field. The work is divided into three parts. The first, International Monetary Relations, 1944–1986, discusses the wartime background to the postwar international economic cooperation-operation period, and describes the assistance given by America and Canada to European allies. This part includes such chapters as Political Background; U.S. and Canadian Wartime and Immediate Postwar Assistance; Postwar U.S. Assistance to Europe, and Development of European Payment Arrangements; Establishment of the IMF; The Spread of Convertibility and the Growing Problems of the U.S. Dollar; Growth of International Collaboration to Correct Disruptive Capital Flows; 1967 Devaluation of Sterling; International Monetary Disturbance, 1968–1969; The Question of International Liquidity and the Creation of Special Drawing Rights; Renewed International Monetary Disturbance, 1970–1971; The 1971–1972 Smithsonian Currency Realignment; European Community Margin Arrangement and Floating of Sterling; Further Devaluation of U.S. Dollar and Other Exchange Rate Changes in 1973; The October–December 1973 Oil Price Increases; Gold and Further Exchange Rate Decisions; Initiation of IMF Reform; IMF Outline of Reform; Implementation of Reform; IMF Oil Facility, "Safety Net" Arrangements and World Bank "Third Window"; Second Amendment to IMF Articles of Agreement; External Monetary Difficulties of France, Italy, the UK and the United States; The "Witteveen" Facility; Paris Meetings of Conference on International Economic Cooperation; Oil Price Increases, 1979–1981; SDR Allocations and Prescriptions; Increases in IMF Facilities and Quotas; Cancun Conference on International Cooperation and Development; Growing Debt Problems of Developing Countries; Consideration of Functioning and Improvement of International Monetary System; Moves to Coordinate–ordinate Exchange Rate and

Interest Rate Policies; and Summit Meetings of Leaders and Major Market-economy Industrialized Countries.

The second part, International Economic Organizations, gives comprehensive and objective data on over 50 separate major international or regional bodies in the monetary and financial sphere. These are grouped by chapter under the headings of General Organizations, Monetary Organizations, Developmental Organizations, Trade Organizations, and OPEC and OAPEC. The final section, United Nations Development Declarations, covers in its chapters, the Third UN Development Decade and The New International Economic Order. Three appendices record the growth of UN and IMF membership, give country nomenclature, and describe currency fluctuation trends between 1970 and 1986. Selected bibliography and general index.

HG 3881 .I62 (Finance—Statistics)

International Financial Statistics (Washington, DC: International Monetary Fund)

This periodical is a statistical publication of the International Monetary Fund and provides a variety of world financial data. The work is organized in three parts. All issues begin with the exchange rate tables and an exchange rate agreement table. The exchange rate tables provide special drawing rates (SDR) via time series, daily exchange rates per U.S. dollar or SDR, and market rates by industrial country and developing countries-world area by SDR. The exchange rate data is followed by special tables, varying by issue, on such topics as fund accounts, reserves, and commodity prices. Data for the special tables comes from the country tables that comprise the bulk of the work. Each country table provides information on exchange rates, again utilizing U.S. dollars and SDR; fund position; international liquidity; monetary survey; monetary authorities; deposit money banks; nonbank or other finance institutions; interest rates; prices, production, employment; international transactions; government finance; national accounts; and population. Source information is provided for selected nations.

HG 3881 .I6 (International Monetary Fund—Periodicals; Foreign Exchange—Periodicals)

Annual Report of the Executive Board (Washington DC: International Monetary Fund)

This reference work seeks to determine how to make the global economy work for all. The eight sections of the book provide a read through of the recommendations of the executive board with charts and tables provided throughout to increase the understanding of the text. Included is an appendix giving key financial data from many economies of the world. Also provided is a list of abbreviations vital to the understanding of the rest of the work.

HG 3881 .I584 (International Finance Corporation)

International Finance Corporation, Annual Report
(Washington: IFC)

This source contains the annual report of the International Finance Corporation (IFC). Included is a report on operations, financial review, portfolio, climate for private investment, regional reports, capital market development, IFC and the environment, management and organization, financial statements, investment portfolio, cumulative commitments. Additional articles are offset from the main text in green boxes. The appendix contains a list of the management employees, addresses, and definitions of acronyms, abbreviations, notes, and definitions. The source as a whole is printed on glossy paper and contains color photographs.

HG 3881 .I586 (International Finance—Handbooks, Manuals, etc.; International Business Enterprises—Finance— Handbooks, Manuals, etc.)

George, Abraham M. and Ian H. Giddy, Eds. International
Finance Handbook (New York, NY: John Wiley & Sons)
1983.

This source is intended to be a ready reference source for dealing with the practical problems and difficulties of international finance, banking, and investment for the nonspecialist. It is applicable to the professional as well. The eight sections are composed of chapters introducing the field of world finance in general and dealing with the specific topics of exchange markets; Euromarkets; national banking, money and bond markets; the international bond market; international equity markets; special financing techniques; and the management of international finance. Also included in the second volume are a glossary and a cross-referenced, alphabetically arranged subject index. The chapters in each sections are written by individual authors and several include bibliographies.

HG3881 .I637 1982 (International Monetary Fund—Dictionaries; International Finance—Dictionaries; Dictionaries, Polyglot; International Monetary Fund; Associations, Institutions, etc.—Abbreviations; Money—Tables)

IMF Glossary: English–French–Spanish, International Monetary Fund, Bureau of Language Services (Washington DC: International Monetary Fund) 1982.

This glossary contains English words, phrases, and institutional titles—including French and Spanish equivalents—that are commonly found in International Monetary Fund documents. English terms that are synonymous and are in general use are listed under the main entry, whereas composite phrases containing the key English term are rendered only according to their frequency of use in IMF translations. Many main entries followed by codes that indicate source, subject, or country refer the user to an equivalency table at the beginning of the work. French and Spanish indices provide access to main English terms. Appendices describe the IMF organizational structure, list abbreviations and acronyms of international organizations and institutions, and give currency units of various countries and areas.

HG 3881 .I5866 (International Finance Management; International Business Enterprises—Finance)

Dickinson, Gerard, et al. International Financial Management: A Working Handbook (London: Kluwer Pub.) 1983.

This source intends to provide information to aid financial directors, treasurers, and financial managers in making decisions on international finance. It is comprised of two loose-leaf binders in nine major sections divided by tabbed indexes. The nine sections cover the following: international expansion policies; international mergers and takeovers; international sources of external funds; financing of international trade; financing long-term projects and acquiring major assets; profit cash and financial control in international groups; foreign exchange, interest rates, and commodity risks; factors influencing the investment decision; and, an index. There are some charts and bibliographies provided for every section. Country-specific information is discussed. The index is arranged by major topics with subheadings of related topics. Names are listed by the first noun and acronyms are listed as they appear.

HG 3881 .M72 (Finance)

Moles, Peter/Terry, Nicholas. The Handbook of International
Financial Terms (New York: Oxford University Press) 1997.

The *Handbook of International Financial Terms* contains expressions used in
financial markets. It is intended for practitioners, while students can use it to
learn the terminology used in the financial world.

HG 3881 .I5868

International Financial Statistics (New York: World Bank)

International Financial Statistics is a source of reference for international
statistics and is available as a monthly publication and a yearbook. Subjects
covered include international payments, inflation, exchange rates, international transactions, commodity production and prices, individual country
finance, and interest rates.

HG 3881 .O75 (International Finance; International Trade)

Orr, Bill. The Global Economy in the 90s: A User's Guide
(New York: New York University Press) 1992.

This source is aimed toward the average person and discusses macro trends in
economics, output, products, merchandise trade, trade geography, trade in
services, foreign exchange, balance of payments, capital markets, bond
markets, stock markets, banking, external debts, development aid, prices
and wages, saving and investment, fiscal management, energy, and human
capital. Each section consists mainly of charts and graphs with text in the
margins. The sources for the author's information come from a wide variety
of sources including (but not limited to) the General Agreement on Tariff and
Trades, the International Monetary Fund, the United Nations, and the
Central Intelligence Agency.

HG 3881.5 .I58 H92 (International Monetary Fund—History— Dictionaries; International Finance—Dictionaries; International Monetary Fund—History)

Humphreys, Norman K. Historical Dictionary of the International
Monetary Fund (Metuchen, NJ: Scarecrow Press) 1993.

This source intends to provide the history of the International Money Fund
(IMF). It details the history of the IMF from the events that led to its founding,

the founding itself, to its present operations. This source also contains a selective bibliography of many of the publications of the IMF and cites material dealing with the IMF's work and related matters. There is a statistical appendix, as well as an index. Within the index acronyms are spelled out, phrases are entered by the first noun in the phrase, and "see" references are utilized. All acronyms and abbreviations used by the authors are also defined.

HG 4001 .C57
(Corporations—Finance; International Business Enterprises—Finance; Corporations—Rankings—Directories; Business Enterprises—Rankings—Directories)

Cifar, Inc. Global Company Handbook, 2d. Ed. (Princeton, NJ: Center for International Financial Analysis and Research)

The *Global Company Handbook* provides information about major companies around the world in capital markets. These companies were selected based on total assets and market value within their respective countries.

Volume 1 contains an analysis of capital markets and lists averages on industries and countries. Volumes 2, 3, and 4 provide specific data about companies.

This source also provides information on a) the top performing companies worldwide; b) data on financial averages; c) rankings according to industry, region, and country; d) changes in the corporations within the past 7 years and; e) an index of company names by country and industry.

HG 4008 .G25
(Risk Management—Terminology—Dictionaries; Banks and Banking—Terminology—Dictionaries)

Gastineau, Gary L. Dictionary of Financial Risk Management (Chicago, IL: Probus Publishing Company) 1992.

The *Dictionary of Financial Risk Management* is intended for financial professionals. Terminology from market centers including equity, bond and currency cash markets, and derivative markets is given. Entries are arranged alphabetically on a word-by-word basis.

This source also covers statistical concepts that play a role in the analysis of risk management. Terminology used by professionals such as lawyers, regulators, accountants, and other professionals from the field of risk management is included.

Items not included in this book are (a) basic terms that pertain to cash markets, (b) exchange-listed products and the exchanges due to frequent updates appearing in trade publications, and (c) index of acronyms.

HG 4009 .W92 1992 (Corporations—Directories)

World Trade Centers Association World Business Directory
(Detroit, MI: Gale Research)

This four-volume annual reference source provides international trade information and coverage of world business. It lists more than 100,000 trade-
oriented companies and businesses involved in international trade from 190
countries.

Coverage is approximately in proportion to the country's level of participation in world trade. The selection criterion is a company's importance to
or interest in international trade. The World Trade Center provided information on their members and additional information was obtained from
chambers of commerce, trade officials, questionnaires sent to individual companies, annual reports, and telephone interviews. The financial data presented
are in the currency that was provided.

The individual company profiles include company name, address, tele-
phone/telex/fax numbers, executive officers, financial data, employee figures,
and extensive product and industry activity information. Product information is provided using the internationally recognized Harmonized System.
Designed to standardize commodity classification, it assigns two- or four-
digit codes to products and a description of the term. Additionally, the World
Trade Center (WTC) company's affiliates are specially marked and WTC
membership and NETWORK (WTC's electronic communication system)
codes are designated. The main entries are alphabetical by company name
within specific geographic regions. Indexes are included and are arranged by
product, industry, and company name. In addition, each volume contains lists
of abbreviations and acronyms.

HG 4026 .C68 (Corporations—Finance)

Cohen, Jerome B. et al. The Financial Manager (Columbus, OH:
Publishing Horizons Inc.) 1986.

In this book the author facilitates readers' understanding of problems encountered by financial managers and shows how these problems are addressed. Suggested readings are given at the end of each section.

Part one covers the relationship between theory and practice and gives
an overview of the organization and functions of financial management. A
discussion on the evolution of financial theories and how they support the
managerial functions is also covered.

Part two covers techniques used in financial analysis; part three covers
management of working capital; and part four discusses management of

different sources of funds. Controlling the use of raised funds is covered in part five.

Part six covers several issues: mergers and acquisitions, repurchases and other capital structure rearrangements and reorganizations, leasing, financial aspects of multinational operations, corporate tax planning and management, and the financial aspects of employee pension programs and other forms of extra compensation are discussed.

HG 4027 .5 .I58 (Corporations—Directories)

International Corporate Yellow Book: Who's Who at the Leading Non-U.S. Companies (New York, NY: Monitor Leadership Directories Inc.)

This source provides information about non-U.S. corporations as well as the individuals who make the decisions and manage the company operations. The data contained in the book cover corporations, subsidiaries, senior executives, and board members. Companies were selected on various factors: revenues, assets, and the company influence in national and world markets.

Information about the companies consists of company name, acronyms, headquarters addresses, phone and fax numbers, names and titles of top executives, and the names of board members and their affiliations. This edition also contains a list of U.S. representatives with the names of contacts in the United States and other locations. Other company information includes principal subsidiaries in the United States, the affiliates, as well as the divisions.

The companies are listed in alphabetical order within their respective region of the world. The six regions covered in this book are Europe, Canada, Asia, Australasia, The Middle East and Africa, and Latin America.

This book also has five indices that provide a cross-reference about the names of companies and the names of people: Company Index, U.S. Subsidiary and Representative Office Index, Geographical Index, Industry Index, and Individuals' Name Index.

HG4027.7 .B65

Blum, Laurie. Free Money for Small Businesses and Entrepreneurs (New York, NY: Wiley) 1995.

The purpose of the book, *Free Money*, is to provide a source for small businesses and nonprofit corporations in obtaining loans, endowments, and federal aid to communities. It lists sources of money that are available and the requirements that must be meet to receive them.

The book is divided into three sections. Section one is a list of program-related investments arranged by states and type of business. These program-related investments are funds and investments that foundations make available to further the objectives of the foundation, such as funding low-cost housing development. Section two lists sources of flow through funding. Flow through fundings are cash awards for such things as consulting services and technical assistance, given directly to the business for work preformed. This type of funding is directed at charitable organizations. Section three is a list of grants available from various government agencies listed by types of business. Examples are shipping, ranching, agriculture, and technology.

HG 4028 .B8 R15 (Research, Industrial—United States—Finance—Statistics—Periodicals; Research, Industrial—United States—Costs—Statistics—Periodicals)

R&D Ratios & Budgets (Evanston, IL: Schonfeld & Associates)

The information contained in this source is designed to help individuals wanting to learn about the research and budgeting practices of corporations. Data compiled for this book come from various sources: statistical services, government reports, newspapers, registration statements, and company documents.

This book lists companies by industry class and SIC number. Top companies are listed by the size of the budget as well as the growth rate of the companies' budget. In a separate section companies are listed alphabetically.

R&D Ratios & Budgets also provides information on industries by the industry class, the size of the budget as well as the growth rate of the budget. The information is also listed by industry name in alphabetical order.

HG 4028 .C6 B58 (Corporations—United States—Charitable Contributions—Periodicals)

Corporate Contributions (New York, NY: Conference Board)

The information in this source is compiled from surveys mailed to companies. Companies participating in the surveys come from the Fortune 500 U.S. manufacturers as well as the Fortune 500 U.S. service companies. Additionally, some companies below the Fortune 1000 and companies participating in previous years also provide input to *Corporate Contributions*.

Companies are asked to give financial information about the following: foundation assets, company direct giving and foundation programs, cash and noncash giving, overseas giving, and corporate assistance expenditures. Other information requested about companies relates to these four categories of beneficiaries: Health and Human Services, Education, Culture and Arts,

Civic and Community. The response rate of companies providing information for this issue of *Corporate Contributions* is approximately 18%.

This source also contains charts and tables of corporate contributions measured against different variables: per employee, cash and noncash, and other categories. Additionally, information by industry is also provided as well as statistics on contributions by program size.

Other information provided consists of top donors in several categories and profiles on participants that responded.

HG 4028 .M4 S57 (Leveraged Buyouts; Consolidation and Merger of Corporations—Finance; Business Enterprises—Purchasing)

Silver, David A. The Middle-Market Business Acquisition Directory and Sourcebook. New York, NY: Harper Business, 1990

This book covers the process of the leveraged buyout in detail. Terms specific to the leveraged buyout and how to find companies that are seeking a buyer are discussed. The first chapter consists solely of the introduction. Chapter two focuses on the structured process of the leveraged buyout and also includes a discussion on the myths pertaining to leveraged buyouts.

Chapter three shows readers how to build a team required to accomplish a leveraged buyout. Chapter four covers the process of marketing and how to attract companies that are searching for buyers. Chapter five discusses the analysis of companies that may be suitable for takeover.

Four common methods of acquisition, purchase of stock, purchase of assets, purchase of stock with a Section 338 election, and reorganization, are covered in chapter six; the legal aspects of acquisition are covered in chapter seven.

This book also contains two directories. The first directory is a Directory of Corporate Divestiture Officers and the second one is a Directory of Merger and Acquisition Intermediaries. The information provided in these directories consists of: company names, the names of contact individuals, addresses, as well as phone and fax numbers.

HG 4028 .M4 S58 (Leveraged Buyouts—United States; Leveraged Buyouts—United States—Finance—Directories)

Silver, David A. The Middle-Market Leveraged Financing Directory and Sourcebook (New York, NY: Harper Business) 1990.

In the first part of this source a detailed discussion of the leverage buyout process is given. The second part contains directories for sources of funding.

The first chapter contains the introduction. An explanation on how to analyze candidates for a leverage buyout is given in the second chapter. Key terms are also explained to help readers' understand the amount of money as well as type of money that is required in the leveraged buyout.

In the third chapter, three types of leveraged buyouts are introduced; these are the divisional, the private company, and the boneyard buyout. Each type is discussed in detail in individual chapters.

Two directories are provided in this book. The first directory contains a list of sources that provide asset-based loans for leveraged buyouts. The information given consists of names, addresses, phone numbers, fax numbers, and branch offices. The latter includes the names of key personnel. The directory also contains the minimum and maximum loan amounts, the type of assets that are preferred as collateral, the willingness of lenders to over-advance on collateral, the industries that are preferred, and the names and addresses of borrowers.

The second directory, Sources of Mezzanine Capital, contains similar information. Additionally, this directory lists the following information about each source of capital: maximum and minimum amounts on subordinated loans or investments, industry preferences, and the names and addresses of investors.

HG 4028 .V3 D46 (Small Business—Valuation—United States)

Desmond, Glenn M. Handbook of Small Business Valuation
Formulas and Rules of Thumb. 3d. Ed. (Camden, ME:
Valuation Press) 1993.

This book is written for individuals involved in the appraisal of small businesses. The first chapter covers background information, terms, definitions, as well as benefits and cautions in the use of valuation formulas and rule-of-thumb methods. Additionally, factors that can affect the value of a business are discussed. The second chapter shows how to calculate net revenue and the annual owners' cash flow.

Chapter three covers the profiles of small businesses with descriptions of valuation formulas and applicable rules of thumb. Valuation considerations for some industries and how to apply valuation methods for these industries are also covered. The fourth chapter covers additional businesses with rule-of-thumb multipliers not covered in chapter three.

In chapter five, formula methods for valuing specifically the intangibles and goodwill of small businesses are discussed. These methods are not industry specific but can be applied to many small businesses.

Chapter six contains a list of sources that provide more information on the valuation of small businesses and the final section of the book contains a glossary.

Features of the book include prefaces in English, French, and German and an outline of the contents of the book that provides a list of the subject headings used in the book.

HG 4050.G62
(Corporations—United States—Finance—Periodicals)

Going Public: The IPO Reporter (Philadelphia: Howard & Co.)

Each week *Going Public: The IPO Reporter* profiles businesses which are beginning to offer public stock and provides statistical stock market information and articles relating to the Initial Public Offering (IPO) market. It includes descriptions of the businesses, addresses, and financial data. The *Reporter* also publishes a weekly tabular review of the IPO Aftermarket, including the prices of shares, closing dates, and percentage of change in the stock of companies. The Aftermarket year-end report published by the *Reporter* provides financial information and statistics on companies that went pubic during the year. It is indexed by performance and alphabetically by names of companies.

HG 4050 .M82 (Corporations—United States—Finance; Dividends—United States)

Armbruster, Brad A. Handbook of Dividend Achievers
(New York: Mergent FIS) 2000.

This reference handbook, divided into 15 sections, ranks hundreds of companies by many different factors. The first four sections rank corporations in order of their assets, return on assets, return on equity, and yield. The remainder of the book rates companies in terms of their long- and short-term growth rates, price-to-earnings ratios, growth, and cash dividends. Also included in this handbook is an alphabetical listing of company reports including financial data for each company profiled.

HG 4050 .R64

Annual Statement Studies (Philadelphia, PA: Robert Morris Associates)

Collecting fiscal year data (July 1–June 30), this publication provides financial data on manufacturing, wholesale, retail, service, and contracting lines of business. The series of tables includes comparative historical data and other sources of composite financial data. The book is divided by industry and the table of contents includes brief descriptions of each industry division with its Standard Industrial Classification (SIC) code.

At the top of each industry table are the SIC code, the breakdown of size categories by types of financial statements reported, the number of statements in each category, the dates of statements used, and the size categories. The sum of sales/revenues and total assets can be found at the bottom of each table. The tables provide information on assets, liabilities, and income data. Assets include cash and equivalents, inventory, joint ventures and investments, and trade receivables. Liability financial figures include notes payable, trade payable, debt, net worth, and income taxes payable, while the income data cover net sales, gross profit, operating expenses, operating profit, profit before taxes, and contract revenues. The broad industries (e.g., manufacturing or retail) are subdivided and further subdivided into like sections.

HG 4057 .A2 A54 (Corporations—United States—Directories; Holding Companies—United States—Directories; Subsidiary Corporations—United States—Directories)

America's Corporate Families (Parsippany, NJ: Dun's Marketing Services)

This publication is a directory of corporate linkages in America compiled by Dun & Bradstreet. It covers 11,000 American parent corporations and their 40,000 subsidiaries and indigenous divisions. The listings are alphabetically arranged in five sections that include parent companies, geographic location, industrial classification, product/service classification, and subsidiaries. The data given for the parent companies include the nature and the line of the business, state of incorporation, SIC codes, principle personnel, bank, accountants, attorneys, stock exchange, and annual sales. The data provided for the subsidiaries include addresses, telephone numbers, principal personnel, SIC codes, and the nature and the line of the business. There is a cross-referenced index of the divisions, subsidiaries, and the parent companies.

HG 4057 .A2 B98 (Corporations—United States—Directories; Risk Managers—United States—Directories; Personnel Directors—United States—Directories; Insurance, Business—United States—Directories)

Directory of Corporate Buyers of Insurance, Benefit Plans and Risk Management Services (Chicago, Ill.: Business Insurance)

The *Business Insurance Directory* is a compilation of statistical information about thousands of companies in the United States. The purpose of the directory is to provide basic company statistical information for direct and quick access for users. Entries provide the company's title, address, telephone and fax numbers, sales or assets, and number of employees from the past year. Personnel information on the companies include the names of the chief financial officer and executives in charge of major divisions of the company. The *Business Insurance Directory* provides a brief description of the type of business dealings of the company, and the Standard Industrial Classification (SIC) codes are given also if available.

Interspersed with occasional advertisements, the directory provides user accessibility by arranging the main company entries alphabetically and by providing additional indexes. One index arranges companies geographically by state and alphabetically within each state. Another index arranges companies in descending order by number of employees. Other indexes arrange companies in descending order by sales and by assets. The *Business Insurance Directory* also includes a brief table of contents and a preface which gives a small summary on its research methods for obtaining company statistics.

HG 4057 .A2 C78 (Corporations—United States—Directories; Executives—United States—Directories; Directors of Corporations—United States—Directories)

Flinsch-Rodriguez, Patricia A. et al. America's Corporate Finance Directory (New Providence: Reed Elsevier)

This reference work, divided into four sections, provides information on thousands of companies. Section one, the financial responsibilities index, shows who is in which position at each company profile. Section two, company listings, gives a short breakdown of each company, along with financial data, pension information, and a business description. Section three, the SIC index, starts with an alphabetical listing of SIC codes and is followed by a listing of each company by its SIC category. Section four, the geographical index, shows each company in terms of where its corporate headquarters are stationed. Also included is an index of a list of companies.

HG 4057 .A2 C78 (Corporations—United States—Directories; Executives—United States—Directories; Directors of Corporations—United States—Directories)

Flinsch-Rodriguez, Patricia A. et al. America's Corporate Finance Directory (New Providence: Reed Elsevier)

This reference work, divided into four sections, provides information on thousands of companies. Section one, the financial responsibilities index, shows who is in which position at each company profile. Section two, company listings, gives a short breakdown of each company, along with financial data, pension information, and a business description. Section three, the SIC index, starts with an alphabetical listing of SIC codes and is followed by a listing of each company by its SIC category. Section four, the geographical index, shows each company in terms of where its corporate headquarters are stationed. Also included is an index of a list of companies.

HG 4057 .A2 C82 (Corporations—United States—Finance— Directories; Finance—United States—Directories)

Stewart, Joseph A. et al. The Corporate Finance Sourcebook
(New Providence: Reed Elsevier)

This reference work seeks to provide the reader with a comprehensive guide to investment resources and financial services. Containing over 3500 different companies, this sourcebook categorizes companies by the services they offer. Also included is an in-depth profile of each of the companies previously listed. Also provided is a personnel index.

HG 4057 .A2 D58 (Corporations—United States—Directories; Corporations—Directories; Holding Companies—United States—Directories; Holding Companies—Directories)

Mysel, Randy H. Directory of Corporate Affiliations
(New Providence: Reed Elsevier)

This reference work, divided into four sections, provides a hierarchical list of major companies in the world. Section one is a master list of company names, their subsidiaries, and parent companies. Section two provides a list of thousands of brand names associated with different products, and who the true owner of those names is. Sections three and four provide geographical indices to U.S.- and non-U.S.-located companies, respectively. Also included is a list of mergers, acquisitions, and name changes in the past 20 years.

HG 4057 .A2 D93 (Corporations—United States—Directories; Business Enterprises—United States—Directories)

Dun's Business Rankings (Parsippany: Dun's Marketing Services)

It ranks over 25,000 of the nation's leading private and public businesses. It ranks these businesses by annual sales volume and number of employees, in five separate sections: alphabetically by company name; by state; by industry; category (SIC codes); public businesses; private businesses. Information is obtained from Dun & Bradstreet information base. For easy use, it is divided into 10 sections and an alphabetic cross-reference. It provided definitions of business terms and an understanding of the Standard Industrial Codes (SIC codes) along with list of chief executives and other officers by function.

HG 4057 .A2 H78 (Corporations—United States—Directories; Business Enterprises—United States—Directories)

Regent, Nancy. Hoover's Handbook of Emerging Companies (Austin: Hoover's Business Press)

This handbook, divided into two sections, gives information on the emerging companies of today. Section one provides full profiles of over 100 companies, with each profile including a corporate overview, a list of corporate officers, different locations, products produced, competitors, and historical financial and employee data. Section two goes into the future of each company and the share that each company can hope to achieve in their respective markets. Each company's future is discussed from an editorial standpoint in a less-traditional format than many other works in its genre. Also included are indices by both industry and location of headquarters.

HG 4057 .A2 J37 1993 (Corporations—United States—Directories; United States—Industries—Directories)

Jarrel, Howard R. Directory of Corporate Name Changes (Metuchen: Scarecrow Press, Inc.) 1993.

The emphasis is on English-speaking nations. It provides names of companies as they change and some of the companies listed have either merged with other companies thereby changing their name(s) once again or have completely changed their name(s) since the publication of this book. It focused on U.S. companies and some Canadian ones with a few foreign-owned once with U.S. subsidiaries. A cross-reference of the original name with the new one is provided.

HG 4057 .A2 M17 1992 (Private Companies—United States—Directories; Corporations—United States—Directories; United States—Industries—Directories)

Directory of Leading Private Companies Including Corporate Affiliations (Wilmette, IL: National Register Publication) 1992.

This reference work includes approximately 10,000 U.S. private companies and wholly owned subsidiaries. The sole standard of admission is that the company's sales must exceed $10,000,000 annually. It consists of one main bound volume, updated five times a year by Corporate Action, which reports on mergers, acquisitions, name changes, and major officer changes that occur after the publication of the volume, keeping the user up-to-date.

The information on the listed companies is compiled and updated continually by the research and editorial staff of the publisher. They take information from various business publications and annual reports. This information is further verified by the company when possible and companies are sent questionnaires annually as well. The individual sketches include company name, address, telephone/telex numbers, SIC code, company production line, state of incorporation, various financial data, number of employees, name and title of key officers, executive and management personnel, and names and addresses of the firm's outside legal counsel and their accounting firm. Arrangement of the main entries is alphabetical by company name, but also included are five indexes: Alphabetical Cross-Reference Index, SIC Index, Geographical Index, Parent Company Index, and Personnel Responsibilities Index.

HG 4057.A2 N27
(Corporations—United States—Rankings—Directories; Business Enterprises—United States—Directories)

The National Book of Lists 1992 (San Ramon, CA: Local Knowledge) 1992.

The National Book of Lists is a collection of lists of the top 40 companies or institutions in America in 50 industries. The lists provide brief information on industry leaders by industries and by geographical locations. The data provided include the names of the companies or institutions, street or mailing addresses, cities, states, zip codes, telephone numbers, fax numbers. The table of contents explains the format of the lists, which are divided by types of industry. Along with names, addresses, and phone numbers, each list provides other business information, such as the names of company presidents or chief executive officers, numbers of employees, and revenues. The companies included also are indexed geographically by states and then by cities.

HG 4057 .A2 P82
(Directors of Corporations—United States—Directories; Directors of Corporations—Directories; Corporations— United States—Directories; Corporations—Directories)

Standard and Poor's Register (Charlottesville: McGraw-Hill)

This reference work, divided into three volumes, produced annually, provides information on over 100,000 corporations in America. Volume one profiles each corporation, including contact information, executive officers, the firm in charge of their accounting, their primary bank, their sales, their number of employees, products they produce, their Standard Industry Classification (SIC) codes, the stock exchange in which their shares are traded, and their ticker symbol. Also provided is a list of abbreviations used. Volume two focuses on the executives and directors that run and manage the corporations listed in volume one. For each executive is a short biography, including the age of each, the university they attended, contact information, and the company for which they work. Volume three has alphabetical listings for the companies profiled in the first volume, divided into three different indices, the Standard and Poor's 500, the Standard and Poor's mid cap 400, and the Standard and Poor's small cap 600. Also included in this volume are sections of both new individuals and new corporations included in this volume.

HG 4057 .A2 W265 (Corporations—United States—Directories; Private Companies—United States—Directories; Industries—United States—Directories; Corporations—United States—Rankings—Directories)

Ward's Business Directory (Detroit: Gale Group)

This business directory, divided into eight volumes, gives information on thousands of businesses across the United States. Volumes one through three provide alphabetical listings of the companies profiled. For each company, important data are provided, including the company's address, contact information, revenues, number of employees, website address, officers, Standard Industrial Classifications (SIC), and North American Industry Classification System (NAICS) coding. Volume four provides special features of each company and another listing of the companies arranged by geography. Volumes five through seven rank the companies by sales and categorize them by their four-digit SIC code. Volume eight includes state rankings, with businesses classified by their six-digit NAICS code. Also included are a list of abbreviations, codes, and symbols, a classification of industries, an SIC to NAICS conversion guide, and an NAICS to SIC conversion guide.

HG 4061 .T86 1989 (Partnership—United States—Finance—Statistics)

Troy, Leo. The Partnership Almanac: A Source Book of Financial Data, Trends, and Performance Ratios (Englewood Cliffs: Prentice Hall Press) 1989.

It provides, among others, tables, graphs, Standard Industrial Codes (in the appendix), and highlights of the past 2 years of the financial market. This is a very good source for financial data, trends, and ratios as they occur and change in the market. Partnerships reported here include both general and limited partnerships. It provides the user with a comprehensive financial data and ratios on partnerships covering all industries, from agriculture to services for most recent years (especially 1984/1985). Also provided are key financial data showing trends from 1976 through 1985.

HG 4095 .M79 (Stocks—Corporations—Stock Exchanges)

Moody's Handbook of Commonstock (New York:
Moody's Investors Service)

The *Moody's Handbook of Commonstock* is a collection of financial and business information on companies. It has price charts and statistics for each stock listed and is revised quarterly. It also has a special section to help the investor on the use of the handbook.

It has a special feature section that provides the investor with an analysis of stock price movements by companies and classifications of companies by industries. It also gives the investor an addenda of the latest such as the names of companies added and the ones dropped from the handbook. It also provides recent and pending stock dividends and splits, dividend changes, corporate earnings, changes in a company's quality grade, recent and pending name changes, and developments in the company. The main section of the handbook is company reports arranged alphabetically.

HG 4132 .E91 (Corporations—Europe—Directories; Business Enterprises—Europe—Directories)

Newman, Oksana and Allan Foster. European Business
Rankings: Lists of Companies, Products, Services and Activities
Compiled from a Variety of Published Sources. Manchester
Business School Library and Information Service (Detroit, MI:
Gale Research)

This source contains 2260 numbered lists relating to business in Europe. The lists cover a range of topics including "Leading European banking centers" and the "U.K.'s favorite drinks." The lists are relatively brief, containing 4 to 10 items each. The purpose of the book is to answer a variety of questions on European business, including such questions as "Who are the top ten French chemical companies?" and "Who are the most successful firms of accountants throughout Europe?" A variety of sources were used for this book, including newspapers, directories, statistical series, and over 800 periodicals. Most of the sources are 1991 publications. The lists include 1990 and 1991 data.

The lists are arranged alphabetically by subject on a word-by-word basis. The subjects used in this book are based on the Library of Congress subject headings. Some very broad topics are subdivided, usually geographically. "See" and "see also" cross-references are used. Each list includes a brief description of the topic, the criteria used to establish the rankings, the number of items in the list, and the source for the list. A comprehensive index includes names of companies, products, and people. The bibliography gives addresses, telephone numbers, and fax numbers of publishers for the sources. Prices are listed in British pounds. Sources in foreign languages are included, but most of the sources are British publications.

The book covers both Western and Eastern Europe, but it has a British focus in the sources and the data. British spellings are also used throughout the source. Special.

HG 4501 .D58
(Corporations—United States—Finance—Directories; Investment Banking—United States—Directories)

Corporate Finance: The IDD Review of Investment Banking
(New York, NY: Investment Dealers' Digest)

This book provides information to individuals that make decisions about finances. The methods used to raise capital by competitors as well as the terms arranged are included in this book.

The first half of *Corporate Finance* contains information organized by type of industry. The data show information about public offerings completed in the United States during the first half of the year; the data are broken down by the type of security and underwriter. Additionally, composite data for each quarter for the first six months are included.

The second half of this book shows information about the terms of all deals done in the U.S. market during the second part of the year. This information is organized in alphabetical order by issuer.

The charts, graphs, and league tables used in this book are provided by Securities Data Company and information about issue listings is given by Investment Dealers' Digest. The data only include U.S. issuers in the domestic market. Information that is not included pertains to debt-for-equity swaps, best efforts deals, private placements, and over-allotments.

HG 4501 .F57 (Bonds—Handbook, Manuals, etc.—Periodicals; Fixed Income Securities—Handbook, Manuals, etc.—Periodicals)

Douglas, Livingston G, Ed. The Fixed Income Almanac
(Chicago, IL: Probus Publishing Company) 1993.

This book provides information to individuals investing in fixed-income. A variety of information is contained in this book and a review of 1992 is included.

The first chapter provides information about statistics on the economy, stock price actions, foreign currency levels, commodity prices; in many cases, the data cover the past 20–30 years. The second chapter covers information on federal policy. Bond markets as well as bond mutual funds are covered in chapter three.

Historical yield levels including prime rate, mortgage rates, junk bond, and international bond yields are discussed in chapter four. Chapter five provides information about bond yield spreads for the Treasury yield curve, bank and finance company bonds, industrial and utility bonds, international bonds, etc.

Chapter six covers historical information about returns on a variety of bond indices; the data are broken down by annual, quarterly, and monthly statistics. The volatility of the bond market is covered in chapter seven. Chapter eight includes information about new issues; a history (1977–1992) of U.S. Treasury notes and bond auctions as well as a compilation of every asset-backed security (ABS) that came in 1992 are also included.

Chapter nine shows information about mortgage prepayment speeds and gives a historical perspective on prepayments. Chapter ten provides historical information about bond upgrades, downgrades, and defaults. Chapter eleven contains several tables of information including price/yield, present and future value, and duration, and taxable equivalent yields.

HG 4501.M82 (Over-The-Counter Markets—United States; Corporations—United States—Finance)

Moody's OTC Unlisted Manual (New York. NY:
Moody's Investor's Service)

This source is a guide to over-the-counter corporations within the United States that are not listed on regional or national stock exchanges. Each entry contains a brief description and history of the company, provides the address and telephone number of the main office, identifies company officials, and covers general information relating to company management and production.

Financial activity of the business is thoroughly examined. Previous years' income figures, including assets, liabilities, revenues, and expenditures, are reported. Long-term debt statistics and capital stock information are also included.

Companies are categorized into two sections within the manual: *Corporate Visibility and Standard Coverage.* Entries for companies with *Corporate Visibility include a Capital Structure Table* that outlines stocks and bonds.

Organizations represented in the manual are indexed alphabetically at the beginning of the volume. A definition section describing terms used in the manual precedes the index. Keys to bond and stock ratings are also provided.

Special features include a list of companies previously covered arranged alphabetically with pertinent information regarding mergers, acquisitions, name changes, and special notations for companies with preferred stock as rated by *Moody's Investor's Service.*

An insert at the center of the volume indexes companies according to geographic location, classifies companies by industry and product, and covers stock splits for previous years. The manual is updated weekly by *Moody's OTC Unlisted News Reports.*

HG 4501 .S74 (Stocks—United States—Periodicals; Stock Ownership—United States—Periodicals; Stockholders—United States—Periodicals)

CDA/Investnet Insider Holdings (Ft. Lauderdale, FL: CDA/Investment Technologies Inc.)

Data for this source are compiled from company reports, financial reporting services, and other sources. Company officers, directors, and principal stockholders (holders of 10% or more) of companies having securities registered with the Securities and Exchange Commission are required to file reports showing information about the initial equity ownership and all the subsequent transactions.

CDA/Investment Insider Holdings provides information of all insiders that own 1000 shares or more ($25,000 principal amount).

The information is organized in alphabetical order by the name of the security. Data provided consist of the name of the individual or entity that is filing the report and the relationship between the filer and the corporate issuer. Several codes for relationships are listed.

Additional information contained in this book shows whether the filer has direct or indirect ownership, the month of the latest trade if available, and the amount of the current holdings.

The title for this book was formerly *Spectrum 6.*

HG 4501 .S76
(Stocks—United States; Corporations—United States)

Standard & Poor's O.T.C. Stock Reports (New York, NY:
Standard & Poor's)

This source is a four-volume work providing comprehensive coverage of all
companies on over-the-counter and regional stock exchanges. In each volume, companies are divided alphabetically and are numbered sequentially.
An index contained at the front of the manual provides the company name,
report number, and volume that the information can be found in. A glossary
preceding the reports defines terms used in different categories within the
manuals.

Each entry contains a description of the company and its functions and
provides a current review of the stock status, including price, range, dividend,
yield, and ranking. Earnings and sales for the upcoming year are predicted,
yearly developments are outlined and trading volume is recorded. Various
tables show stock value per share, investment and dividend data, and yearly
financial activity.

Contact information, including the location and telephone number of
the main office and the names of company officials, is listed at the end of each
report. *O.T.C. Profiles*, published three times a year, supplements *Standard &
Poor's O.T.C. Stock Reports* and examines smaller corporations not listed
with a major or regional stock exchange.

HG 4501 .S78
(Securities—United States; Corporations—United States)

Standard & Poor's Corporation Records (New York, NY:
Standard & Poor's)

This source is a semiweekly publication describing companies within the
United States, including those on the New York, American, and regional
stock exchanges. For each corporation indexed. *Corporation Records* provides a brief description and history that includes place and date of incorporation, company functions, names of chief officers, and the address and
telephone number of the main offices.

Financial activity is examined in detail. Previous years' earning and
finances are reported as well as stock statistics and bond descriptions. An
annual report section provides current income figures, investments, operational expenses, assets, and liabilities.

Corporations are indexed alphabetically at the front of the volume. A
cross-reference section follows the index, providing pertinent information on
mergers, acquisitions, and name changes.

An index in the final volume organizes companies using the Standard Industrial Classification (SIC) Code. An explanation of SIC codes and an alphabetical listing of major groups are included.

A special section in volume T–Z outlines new stock and bond offerings, providing the name of the issue, amount, price per share, and rating. The Standard & Poor's rating system is defined on the last page of the section. The *Daily News* supplements the *Standard & Poor's Corporation Records* and provides current information including Hourly Stock Prices, Weekly Bond Yields, and New Registrations.

HG 4501 .S776 Dec. 2000 (Finance)

Standard & Poor's Stock Report (New York: Standard & Poor's)

This report contains date on companies that are listed on the New York Stock Exchange, NASDAQ, and American Stock Exchange. Alphabetized, each company has a two-page report that contains key information such as their income statement and earnings. Combined, the two volumes cover more than 3500 companies.

HG 4501 .S784 (Stocks—United States—Periodicals; Bonds—United States—Periodicals)

Standard & Poor's Stock and Bond Guide, Standard & Poor's Corporation (New York, NY: McGraw-Hill)

This source is designed to help readers select appropriate securities for their portfolios; data about common and convertible preferred stocks are covered in the first section.

The information that is provided about stocks includes ticker symbols, the names of the exchanges where the stock is traded, call prices are shown for preferred stocks, the number of financial institutions that hold the stock as well as the number of shares held, and the stock's latest price–earnings ratio. Additionally, historical information about stock dividends and stock splits is listed.

Data relating to the companies' dividend policy, information about the balance sheet and long-term debts, as well as earnings per share for the last 5 years are included in this book.

Data about nonconvertible preferred issues include ticker symbols, exchanges, call features as well as yield and stock ratings. *Standard & Poor's Stock and Bond Guide* also provides information about mutual funds. The information about mutual funds shows the name of the fund, the principal objective of the fund, and the total net assets at market value less current liabilities.

Information provided about annuities includes the name of the contract and the issuing company, the name of the manager or submanager, as well as the objective of the investment.

This book also contains information on domestic corporate bonds as well as foreign bonds. Additionally, ratings on several municipal bonds and statistical data on convertible bonds are provided.

HG 4509 .D58 (Pension Trusts—United States—Directories; Mutual Funds—United States—Directories; Money Market—United States—Directories)

Directory of Pension Funds and their Investment Managers
(Charlottesville: Money Market Directories, Inc.)

It provides information on over 39,000 employee benefit plans with combined assets of $2.504 trillion and also a description of 1790 asset managers controlling over $5,088 trillion. In fact, it provides a complete coverage of the pension fund industry, especially its comprehensive detailed information on tax-exempt pension and endowment funds, profiling the individuals and organizations that manage and provide services for these assets. It is arranged in terms of tables which are statistically derived with some rankings of both the tax-exempt assets and the investment managers' assets. There are global information provided and a concise review of each industry by research analysts. There is some information on real estate that is very valuable and helps people in understanding the relationship between real estate and tax-exemption. Also provided at the front is a directory of advertisers in the publication. Information was obtained from questionnaires sent to the different firms reviewed.

HG 4509 .G94 (Investment Advisers—Directories)

Scott-Roberts, Fiona. Guide to International Asset Managers
(New York, NY: Stockton Exchange Press) 1989.

This book provides investors with detailed information about managers of international assets. Data for this source come from questionnaires mailed to asset managers that claim to have international expertise. (The author points out that many respondents only answered some of the questions.)

Profiles of companies in this source consist of a brief history of the company and information about the current ownership. A section called Fund Management History contains details about portfolios and the type of clients handled by each manager.

Other information listed in this book shows the amount of education and experience of each investment professional as well as the method used to conduct research by the organization.

The investment strategy of each firm is also provided. Additionally, information about the process used by each firm in making decisions in the selection of stock portfolios is also given.

The last section on the company profiles lists information about administration and fees such as the type of information that clients receive as well as the types of record keeping and administrative services that are provided.

HG 4513 .H64 (Investments—Dictionaries)

Hildreth, Sandra S. The A to Z of Wall Street (Chicago, IL: Longman Financial Services Pub.) 1988.

The objective of this source is to provide a guidebook to the financial world. Part one of the book provides definitions to the thousands of terms and acronyms used in the economic market. This alphabetic listing includes words such as fixed-income securities, roll down, and risk and reward. The second section of the book contains information about common abbreviations. It also offers a guide to reading financial reports like the *Wall Street Journal*, mutual fund quotations, futures prices, and stock market data bank.

HG 4513 .I23 1990
(Investments—Directories; Securities—Directories)

IFR Financial Glossary, 2nd Ed. (London, England: IFR Publishing Ltd.) 1990.

This a compilation of definitions of terminologies, abbreviations, and so on used in the financial world. It provides the meaning of words used in the international securities markets. It has an encyclopedic-style of arrangement of its contents. At the beginning of each section of the book, acronyms are grouped together for easier referencing. It is just a plain "dictionary" of the financial market and good for a novice to understand the terms used in that "world."

HG4513 .P46 (Securities—Dictionaries;
Investments—Dictionaries; Stock Exchanges—Dictionaries)

Pessin, Allan H. The Illustrated Encyclopedia of the Securities Industry (New York, NY: New York Institute of Finance) 1988.

This work is essentially a dictionary of finance and investment. Entries vary from brief definitions to extended discussions that are complemented with charts, graphs, security tables, mathematical formulas, and facsimile illustrations taken from company financial records. The "see" and "see also" notes for the all citations make the work an invaluable one-volume reference source.

HG 4513 .R82 1993 (Investments—Dictionaries)

Rosenberg, Jerry M. Dictionary of Investing (New York, NY: John Wiley & Sons) 1993.

This source is designed to introduce the newcomer and update the experienced investor with international investing terms. Originally published as *The Investor's Dictionary*, the 1993 edition incorporates the previously listed traditional terms with new terminology to reflect global changes in financing. Such terms as cats and dogs (highly speculative stocks), bed and breakfast deals (short selling abuses), hacking the pie (dividing profits), and daisy chain (manipulative dealings) are defined. Common symbols, acronyms, and abbreviations are listed. Foreign words or phrases are included only if they have become part of the English vocabulary. Terms are presented alphabetically with no pronunciation guide and cross-references are done from the general to the specific. Some 7500 entries cover areas of investing in antiques, art, bank depositories and securities, bonds, collectibles, commodity markets, currency trading, debentures, diamonds, exchanges, futures, government issues, insurance, investment trusts, legislation, metals, mortgage-backed bonds, mutual funds, oil investments, pass-through securities, pension plans, real estate/property ownership, stocks, tax-exempt bonds, tax shelters, and venture capital.

HG 4513 .R681 1992 (Investments—Acronyms; Securities—Acronyms; Stock—Exchange—Acronyms)

Rosenberg, Jerry M. McGraw-Hill Dictionary of Wall Street Acronyms, Initials and Abbreviations (New York, NY: McGraw-Hill) 1992.

This dictionary contains over 10,000 abbreviations and acronyms commonly used in the stock market and gives brief definitions for each. This resource was put together by Jerry Rosenberg, a professor of business administration at Rutgers. The entries were gathered from a variety of information sources used to prepare the author's previous five dictionaries as well as from trade associations and U.S. and foreign agencies.

The arrangement of the entries is alphabetical by letter. In cases where the proper form of an abbreviation is unclear, the most common form was used. Where the acronyms are trade symbols of public corporations, the definition is followed by a notation about which stock exchange the company's stock is traded on. Most of the entries seem to be of this type.

HG4513 .S43 (Investments—Dictionaries; Securities—Dictionaries; Stock Exchanges—Dictionaries)

Scott, David L. Wall Street Words (Boston: Houghton Mifflin Co.) 1988.

Wall Street Words is a reference source containing over 3600 investment terms and 87 tips prepared by 32 specialists. It is directed to professionals such as brokers, dealers, traders, analysts, planners, consultants, and bankers as well as to the novice investor who may not understand the language of the changing market to make intelligent and informed decisions. Drawing its terminology from the language found in the financial broadcasts such as *Wall Street Week with Louis Rukeyser*, newspapers and periodicals such as *The Wall Street Journal, Business Week, Forbes, Barron's, Fortune, Investor's Daily*, and financial newsletters, this work traces the words of stock and bond trading, options and futures trading, brokerage, financial planning, technical analysis, banking and investment banking, accounting and finance, economics and business law, taxation, insurance, and corporate structure/operations. Many terms are presented here that are not found in similar type sources. The "tips" located near the selected entries were written by experts and are intended to answer questions that are most often asked by investors. The words in this dictionary are alphabetically arranged and include brief definitions that are often elaborated into paragraphs. Some entries are supplemented with case study dialog boxes that illustrate the entry's meaning with real-life accounts of strategies, maneuvers, procedures, laws, concepts, or actions and that give the investor access to colloquial language that is heard on the floor of the marketplace, a unique feature of a reference source whose focus is on the explication of formal terminology. Included are 24 typical examples of technical analysis chart patterns and a selected bibliography.

HG 4513 .S45 (Securities—Dictionaries)

The Securities Industry Glossary (New York, NY: New York Institute of Finance) 1988.

This book provides definitions for thousands of terms commonly used in the securities industry. These expressions are used by most experts and professionals in the financial world. The source includes words such as futures, mortgage-backed securities, compliance, and municipal bonds. This reference is alphabetically organized.

HG 4513. T48
(Investments—Dictionaries; Securities—Dictionaries)

Thomsett, Michael C. Investment and Securities Dictionary
(Jefferson, NC: McFarland) 1986.

This dictionary is an extensive summary of terms used in the stock exchange markets, syndications, broker–dealers, investment managers, sponsors, and financial planners. It covers technical words and phrases, industry agencies and associations, and regulatory bodies. Four main sections are included: (1) glossary of terms, (2) abbreviations list, (3) guide to prospectus and offering documents, and (4) bond classification list.

HG 4513 .V15 (Investments—Dictionaries—Polyglot; Securities—Dictionaries—Polyglot; Stock Exchanges—Dictionaries—Polyglot; English Language—Dictionaries—Polyglot; Dictionaries, Polyglot)

Valentine, Stuart P. International Dictionary of the Securities Industries (Homewood, IL: Dow Jones-Irwin) 1989.

This book provides information to individuals interested in the investment market. The readers' are guided through the jargon of the market and explanations on some of the words and institutions of the overseas markets are included.

Dictionary entries are listed in alphabetical order by phrase order and the entries have a cross-reference to English as well as foreign words. Some entries list sources that can provide additional information and further clarify the term.

A table of World Stock Exchange Indices is also included in this book. Information provided in the table consists of the name of the index, the number of companies in the index, the base date, the base value, and the frequency of the calculation.

HG 4515 .I38 1996 (Finance)

The Individual Investor's Guide to Computerized Investing
(Chicago: American Association of Individual Investors)

Software containing financial data on companies has now become easily accessible to individual investors. This guide informs investors as to what they should look for before buying any software. It analyzes software for personal finance, stock screening, portfolio management, and various other tasks.

HG 4515.9 .M14 (Finance)

McGowan, Spencer. The Investor's Information Sourcebook
(New York: Spencer McGowan) 1995.

Numerous sources, categorized by the type of source, are listed. Types of sources include newsletter and chart services, as well as magazines, which are each put in a separate chapter. Chapters contain sources listed alphabetically, their content, and instructions to order.

HG 4519 S77 (Stocks—United States—Periodicals)

Standard & Poor Analysts Handbook (New York, NY:
Standard & Poor's Corp.)

This annual guide provides a detailed timeline of the performance of various categories of stocks. The stock categories are divided further into four sections—Industrials, Transportation, Utilities, and Financial. The Industrial section includes chemical, telecommunication, and hospital management companies. The Transportation section contains information about railroads, trucks, and airlines. The Utilities section details telephone, electric, and natural gas companies, while the Financial section deals with insurance brokers and major regional banks. Each category gives data such as total sales, dividends per share, price of stock, working capital, and return percentage of the book value of the stock, over a period of 30 years.

HG 4521 .C68 (Stock Exchanges; Investments; Stocks)

Colby, Robert W. and Meyers, Thomas A. The Encyclopedia
of Technical Market Indicators (New York: McGraw-Hill) 2003.

This book provides a detailed analysis of the numerous technical indicators that analysts use to predict the behavior of the stock market. Part one examines the methods and information that experts use to calculate these indicators. It includes chapters on short-term trading with daily data and buy-and-hold strategy. Part two presents an explanation of what the indicator is supposed to forecast and its formula. This guide contains information about hundreds of indicators such as the margin requirement, put/call ratio, and absolute breadth index.

HG 4521. F48 1988 (Investment Analysis)

Sumner N. Levine. The Financial Analyst's Handbook
(Homewood, IL: Dow Jones-Irwin) 1988.

This handbook serves as a guide to the principles and procedures necessary for successful investment management. The nine main sections are examined:

1) background information, 2) economic analysis, 3) company and industry analysis, 4) equity investment analysis, 5) fixed-income investing, 6) portfolio theory and practice, 7) quantitative aids, 8) information sources, and 9) legal and ethical standards.

HG 4521. W22 (Securities; Financial Futures)

Walmsley, Julian. The New Financial Instruments: An Investor's Guide (New York: Wiley) 1988.

This book presents a wide range of new instruments in financial markets in a systematic way to allow comparison of their different features. Part 1 gives the background environment in which the new instruments were born. Part 2 includes an outline of the basic building blocks of securities markets. Part 3 examines futures, options, and swaps. Part 4 includes a detailed description of the new instruments individually.

HG 4527 .B95 (Investments—Handbooks, Manuals, etc.)

Burgauer, James. The Do-it-Yourself Investor (Chicago, IL: Probus Publishing) 1987.

This reference guide provides detailed information about learning to invest in the stock market. It is divided into two main sections entitled "Analytical Techniques" and "Doing-it Yourself." The first section is further divided into three subsections, which are "Life Cycle Analysis," "Fundamental Analysis," and "Technical Analysis." The first of these subsections explores how a company matures and changes over the life of the business. The next topic explains fundamental analysis and provides a set of equations used in formulas, such as the price–earnings ratio or total asset turnover. The last subsection examines analyzing trends, charts, gaps, and patterns found in the market. The second main section begins with a discussion of "Discount Brokerage." It reviews how the brokerage industry formed and the main brokerage firms in the nation. The second subsection, "Databases," provides information about consulting on-line databases to invest and surveys some services. The third subsection, "Investment Publications," overviews various publications that are available in the market. The last subsection, "Reference Books," lists numerous sources of books recently released. Finally, there are three appendices that have data about common stock market anagrams, office locations for two major brokerage firms, and a glossary of terms.

HG4527 .H24 1986 (Investments—Handbooks, Manuals, etc.; Securities—Handbooks, Manuals, etc.; Options (Finance)—Handbooks, Manuals, etc.; Commodity Exchanges—Handbooks, Manuals, etc.)

Handbook of Financial Markets: Securities, Options, and Futures, Edited by Frank J. Fabozzi and Frank G. Zarb (Homewood, IL: Dow Jones-Irwin) 1986.

This handbook is intended for novice and experienced investors who need to know more about securities, options, and futures markets. The work contains three books in which the instruments and trading mechanics for each market and the basic provisions of the tax code applicable to instruments traded in the three markets are discussed. The first, SECURITIES MARKETS, consists of four parts: Environment; The Structure of the Securities Markets; The Instruments of the Securities Markets; and Private Financial Intermediaries and the Securities Markets. Each part contains from five to seven essays. The second book, THE OPTIONS MARKETS, has six essays: The Different Types of Options; The Risk/Reward Characteristics of Options and Options Portfolios; Mechanics and Regulation of Options Trading; Market Participants: Individuals and Market Professionals; Market Participants: Institutions; Tax Planning and Options Trading. The third book, FUTURES MARKETS, consists of 12 articles: Introduction to Futures Contracts; Mechanics of Futures Trading; Commodity Futures Markets: General Information; The Futures Markets for Precious Metals; Foreign Currency Futures Markets; Financial Instruments Futures Markets; Participants in the Futures Markets; Speculative Markets: Valuable Institutions or Dens of Inequity?; Regulation of Futures Trading; Income Tax Considerations of Commodity Futures Transactions for the Individual Investor; New Frontiers: Market Index Futures Contracts; and New Frontiers: Living with Inflation—A Proposal for New Futures and Options Markets. A subject specialist has written each essay. Bibliographic references, name, and subject indexes.

HG 4529 .H91 (Investment Analysis—Periodicals—Evaluation; Investments—Periodicals—Evaluation)

Hulbert, Mark. The Hulbert Guide to Financial Newsletters (Chicago, IL: Dearborn Financial Publishing Co.) 1993.

This guide provides information about evaluating the numerous financial advisory companies that are available in the market. These industries offer advice and pointers to investing in the stock market, and are found in financial newsletters, television, newspapers, and magazines. The book first answers various questions about the risks of consulting advisory agencies, then analyzes hundreds of newsletters, such as *Investment Horizons* and *Mutual Fund Forecaster*. The entries contain information about the price, address and telephone number, and analysis of the newsletters. The publication also has four appendices that comment on the performance of newsletters, market timing, and a newsletter directory.

HG 4530 I58 (Mutual Funds—United States—Statistics; Investments—Statistics—Periodicals; Investment Trusts—United States—Periodicals)

Investment Companies Yearbook (Rockville, MD: CDA Investment Technologies)

This annual publication provides a broad overview about investment companies, mutual funds, and variable annuities and closed-end funds. Part one, General Information about Investment Companies, contains information about how investment companies developed, how to select investment companies, and determining cost basis. Part two, How Investment Companies are Used, details how one can reduce risks through systematic investing, chart an investment course, and the benefits of money market funds. The third part, Mutual Fund Listings, contains an index of mutual fund management companies. It also has a directory of mutual funds as well as profile and performance reports for each fund. The fourth part provides a directory and performance records for variable annuities and closed-end funds. The final section has a glossary of technical terms.

HG 4530 M86 (Mutual Funds—Statistics—Periodicals; Investments—Statistics—Periodicals)

Morningstar Mutual Fund 500 (Chicago, IL: Morningstar, Inc.)

The purpose of this annual book is to provide a directory of the growing amount of mutual funds on the market. The book starts with a detailed user's guide which outlines how to read the entries. Next there is a section of tables and charts that summarize the performance of various classes of mutual funds. There are also two tables of the highest/lowest potential capital gain exposure and foreign percentage. The next section details thousands of mutual funds. This section is divided into categories such as hybrid funds, stock funds—core, and bonds fund—municipal. Each of the entries in this section contains information such as the sector weightings, tax analysis, composition of fund, and the performance or risk. The final section is one alphabetical index of funds and a fund manger index.

HG 4530 .M98 (Mutual Funds—United States—Directories)

Mutual Fund Directory (New York: Investment Dealers' Digest)

This directory provides information on over 3000 mutual funds and is arranged into 22 different investment objectives. Each entry includes the name, address, phone number, the date the fund was established, the fund's advisor, the fund's assets, investment amounts, the fees it charges, and the fund's method of share distribution. The text also provides background information on mutual funds in general, how to read a prospectus, specialty funds, and a glossary.

HG 4530 .P46 1994/95 (Mutual Funds—United States)

Perritt, Gerald W. The Mutual Fund Encyclopedia (Chicago, IL: Dearborn Financial Pub.)

This reference book provides information on over 3100 load and no-load mutual funds. Each entry includes the name of the portfolio manager, address, phone number, the investment portfolio, the percentage of total return over 5 years, an objective statement, the date the fund began, information on the minimum investment, distribution, front-end load, redemption fee, management company, and the ticker symbol. Background information also is provided on mutual fund history, recent industry trends, the future of mutual funds, how the funds are managed and regulated, the different types of funds that are available, discount brokers, taxation, understanding the prospectus, and market timing.

HG 4534 .H34 1996 (Finance)

Krish, Vijay/LaGorga, Linda. Career Guide: Finance (Harvard Business School)

The *Career Guide* contains information on various sectors of finance for those people who have just begun their job search. It provides contacts of the investment banks, commercial banks, and Fortune 500 companies that are listed in the book. Each firm's recruiting process and the experiences of alumni from the Harvard Business School help job seekers anticipate what to expect.

HG 4538 .A1 D59 (Corporations. American—Directories)

Directory of American Firms Operating in Foreign Countries
(New York: Simon & Schuster)

This three volume reference guide provides information on American business affiliates and subsidiaries abroad. Volume 1 contains a list of American companies with operations outside of the United States. Each entry includes a U.S. address, phone number, primary product/service, the names of the chief executives of the company, the number of employees, and the locations of the company's subsidiaries or affiliates. Volumes 2 and 3 are arranged alphabetically by the countries that are the homes of U.S. company's operations. Each entry includes the name of the U.S. company, the address, phone number, primary product/service, and the address of the affiliate or subsidiary in that country.

HG 4538 .E61 (Investments, Foreign; Environmental Law; Industry—Environmental Aspects; Comparative Law)

Environmental Regulation: Its Impact on Foreign Investment
(Boston: Martinus Nijhoff) 1992.

This reference book is intended for anyone interested in the various environmental regulations involved in foreign investment. The text deals with the business and legal aspects of environmental regulations for 21 countries and the European Community.

HG 4538 .F48 (Investments—American; International Financing; Foreign Trade Regulations; Foreign Exchange; International Business Enterprises—Finance)

Business International Corp. Financing Foreign Operations
(New York, NY: Business International Corp.)

Comprising two volumes, this collection of loose-leaf files provides an analysis of factors concerning sources of capital for both national and international marketing enterprises. Covered in the first volume are interest rates and updated foreign exchange rates: international financial techniques such as global financial management, swap financing, export financing and global cash management; and information on cross-boarder sources of financing from regional development banks. North American governments, European governments, Euromarkets, and the World Bank. The second section deals with individual countries organized by the world regions of Europe, Africa–Middle East, Asia, Latin America, and North America. The domestic financ ing in each nation is dealt with through an introduction detailing political developments, economic environments, financial conditions, discrimination against foreigners, and corporate financial strategies; prevailing currency conditions; foreign exchange regulations; the monetary system; sources of capital; short-term financing techniques; medium- and long-term financing; equity financing; capital incentives; cash management; short-term investment instruments; and trade financing and insurance. Important financial events are highlighted for each country and international economic organizations are also covered. Updating with supplements takes place throughout the year.

HG 4538 .G68 (Investments, Foreign—Handbooks, Manuals, etc.; Business Enterprises, Foreign—Handbooks, Manuals, etc.)

Gottschalk, Jack A. The Global Trade and Investment Handbook (Chicago, IL: Probus Publishing Co.) 1993.

This directory provides trade and foreign investment information for 155 countries. The text is arranged alphabetically by country and each entry includes information on the country's political climate, foreign investment policy, environmental regulations, dealings with foreign investors, labor, accounting requirements, currency controls, taxation, legal system, customs and duties, intellectual property protection, immigration, and foreign investment assistance. The text is supplemented by an index and a bibliography.

HG 4538 .I56 (Investments, Foreign—Statistics—Periodicals; Investments, Foreign—Developing Countries—Statistics—Periodicals)

International Direct Investment Statistics Yearbook (Paris: Organisation for Economic Co-Operation and Development)

This reference guide provides direct investment statistics for OECD countries. The text is arranged into three parts. Part 1 provides flow and stock data in summary tables for each OECD country. Part 2 contains country data focusing on outflows and inflows as part of each GDP and stock tables. Part 3 provides the technical notes on statistical sources, FDI definitions, and the methods used for collecting data.

HG 4538 .N74 (Investments, Foreign; International Finance; Risk Management; Securities)

Nix, William E. The Dow Jones-Irwin Guide to International Securities, Futures, and Options Markets (Homewood, IL: Dow Jones-Irwin) 1988.

This reference guide provides information for investors looking to invest in international markets. The text includes an introduction to securities, futures, and options markets and information on international mutual and closed-end funds, portfolio and risk management strategies for international equities markets and international debt securities, exchange rate risks of foreign currency, developing a computer model for evaluating foreign equity and debt securities, corporate and public finance in international markets, computer database information sources, and a series of financial market summaries for various countries.

HG 4538 .U55315 (Investments, American—Statistics)

U.S. Direct Investment Abroad (Washington DC: U.S. Department of Commerce)

This reference guide provides financial data on American companies and their affiliates abroad. The data are presented in tables including all affiliates of all U.S. parents, nonbank affiliates of nonbank U.S. parents, majority-owned nonbank affiliates of nonbank U.S. parents, nonbank affiliates of U.S. parents in banking, and bank affiliates of all U.S. parents. The text is supplemented by a section on methodology and a benchmark survey of U.S. direct investment abroad.

HG4551 .D58 (Stock Exchanges—Directories; Stock Exchanges—History)

Directory of World Stock Exchanges, Compiled by the Economist Publications (Baltimore: Johns Hopkins University Press) 1988.

This source is for the professional practitioner who needs to know specific information on various stock exchanges throughout the world. The compilers sent questionnaires to each of the national exchanges which provided the necessary data. The entry format therefore is standardized and somewhat uneven in terms of amount of information available. For each exchange there are dialog boxes that include the exchange's position in world time, currency the exchange's securities are quoted in, exchange name, address, telephone, telex, cable, facsimile, and trading hours. The body of the citation is organized into the following major categories: organization of exchange; background information; types of market; systems of quotation for securities; ordering and settlement procedure; price publication procedure; new issues procedure; takeovers and mergers procedure; special rules for foreign investors; taxation of income from securities; transaction charges, commissions and fees; affiliated broking firms; technical publications and information sources; and history. Categories are broken down into topical sections that give more specific data. The directory is arranged by country and then city. No indexes.

HG 4551 .G12
(Stocks—Periodicals; Investments, Foreign—Periodicals; Stock Exchanges—Periodicals; Securities—Periodicals)

The GT Guide to World Equity Markets (London: Euromoney Publications Ltd.)

This reference guide provides profiles of international equity markets for 39 countries plus a section on emerging markets and Eastern European markets. Each country listing contains an introduction and information on market performance, the stock market, market size, types of shares, other markets, investors, operations, taxation and regulations, reporting, and research. The text is supplemented by the Morgan Stanley World Capital Indices and the Financial Times–Actuaries World Indices.

HG 4551 .G12 2000 (Finance)

The Salomon Smith Barney Guide to World Equity Markets (East Rutherford: Euromoney Books)

Each chapter is dedicated to covering one country. The chapter includes several key statistics such as growth in the market value over 5 years, and budget deficit. It provides extensive information on the country's stock market, the type of shares traded, the brokerage rates, taxes on foreign investors, and many such details. The Appendix has charts of countries' markets in U.S. dollars.

HG 4551 .N24 (NASDAQ Market System)

NASDAQ/CQS Symbol Directory (Washington DC: National Association of Securities Dealers)

This directory provides background information on NASDAQ and CQS, and lists the NASDAQ securities alphabetically by name and by symbol, the market makers alphabetically by member name and by MMID, and the CQS securities and CQS securities tables.

HG 4551 .W92 (Markets—World—Advice)

Park, Keith, K.H. The World's Emerging Stock Markets
(Chicago, Ill: Probus Publishing Company) 1994.

This book consists of three major sections. First, the book discusses the opportunities and risks of investing in the emerging markets with a presentation of portfolio management and research techniques. In the second section, individual markets are examined with brief portfolio of their major listed companies. The last section of the book compiles articles which discuss the important issues in deciding how to distribute a portfolio across the markets.

HG 4572 .N534 (Markets—Constitutions—United States)

New York Stock Exchange Commission, New York Stock
Exchange Constitution and Rules (New York, NY: Commerce
Clearing House) 1989.

This is the full text of the Exchange's Constitution with references.

HG 4636 .B52 (Markets—United States—References)

Berlin, Howard M. The Handbook of Financial Market Indexes,
Averages, and Indicators (Homewood, Ill: Dow Jones-Irwin) 1990.

The nine chapters of this reference cover subjects as varied as the mathematics of how averages and indexes are determined to the measure of U.S. stocks, commodities, money mutual funds, and bonds. This book describes nearly all of the major financial market barometers, market averages, indexes, and indicators.

HG4636 .J37 (Stock Quotations—United States—Handbooks, Manuals, etc.; Stock Exchanges—United States—Abbreviations)

Jarrell, Howard R. Common Stock Newspaper Abbreviations and
Trading Symbols (Metuchen, NJ: Scarecrow Press) 1989.

Common Stock Newspaper Abbreviations and Trading Symbols is a ready reference source that provides specific information on 6300 companies holding common stock on the American Stock Exchange, the New York Stock Exchange, and the National Association of Security Dealers Automated Quotations (NASDAQ) over-the-counter lists. Pertinent facts include the company name, the Associated Press abbreviation for the company name as it appears in newspaper stock quotations, the major U.S. stock exchange where the company stock is traded, and the company's ticker or trading symbol. These data are presented in alphabetical order in three separate sections and they allow the user, knowing any one component, to gain access to all the information.

HG 4661 .d74 (Stocks—Corporations—Stock Exchange)

The Dow Jones Guide to the Global Stock Market (Englewood Cliffs, NJ: Prentice Hall)

The Dow Jones Guide to the Global Stock Market is a collection of information about corporate stocks from the world's major stock markets. It contains data on the largest stocks from key markets around the globe. The index is grouped into three geographic areas, the Asia/Pacific, Europe, and the American regions. It also has indexes comparing markets and industries.

It lists the country's name with a market overview for each company. The index can be used to locate the company by name if the home country's name is not known. The guide provides a brief portrait of each corporation by giving a description of the companies' main lines of business, sometimes a brief history and major news events effecting the companies. It also includes 2 years of sales of data about such matters as revenues, earnings, and dividends. Included in the data is the name of the companies with their addresses and phone numbers.

HG 4726 .A1 B71 (Municipal Bonds—United States—Directories; Brokers—United States—Directories)

Bond Buyer's Municipal Marketplace (New York: American Banker, Bond Buyer)

The *Bond Buyer's Municipal Marketplace*, which is published twice a year, is a directory of municipal bond dealers of the United States. Its purpose is to provide bond buyers with a list of dealers and underwriters in municipal bonds, municipal bond attorneys, and officials in the industry. It also contains advertisements of dealers, underwriters, and municipal bond attorneys.

It includes information of the top 100 underwriters in long- and short-term issues as well as other leading municipal bond industry rankings for the past year. The index provides information on dealers and underwriters from various regions in the United States by providing the names and addresses of firms as well as the amount of their capital. Hence the bond buyer is able to determine the size and relative strength of the firm. It also includes listings of financial and investment advisers, derivative specialists, attorneys, and rating agencies. The index provides a listing of officials by municipal bond issuers, regulators and depository, and associations. It, moreover, has a master index.

HG 4751 .M82 (Corporations—Finance—Directories; Securities—Directories; Investments)

Moody's International Manual (New York, NY: Moody's
Investor's Service)

This source profiles over 106 countries and 5000 international corporations in a two-volume set. Each entry in the manual is divided into two sections: country and corporate. The first portion provides facts on the country's population, geography, economy, industry, and government and includes figures on banking, currency, exchange, and international transactions.

The corporate section contains a brief description and history of the company, lists the address and telephone number of the main office, identifies corporate officials, and covers general information relating to company management and production. Data contained in the corporate section are gathered from stockholders' reports and registrations and reports of the Securities and Exchange Commission.

Financial activity of the business is thoroughly examined. Previous years' income figures, including assets, liabilities, and mergers and acquisitions data, are reported.

Moody's rates each company from "aaa" to "c" in regards to stocks and bonds. This rating system is explained in the front of the volume with a key for the user's reference.

Information in the work is indexed alphabetically at the beginning of each volume. A definition section describing terms used throughout the manual precedes the index. An insert in both volumes indexes corporations according to geographic locations and classifies companies by industry and product. Money market and exchange rates are provided and tables on imports, exports, and gold reserves are included.

Material in the manual has been edited and revised by Moody's where necessary. Stock and bond descriptions are abridged and financial and statistical data have been condensed. The volumes are updated semiweekly by *Moody's*.

HG 4905 .M795 (References—Markets)

Wittebort, Suzanne. Moody's Handbook of NASDAQ Stocks
(New York, NY: Moody's Investor Services)

This is a reference of basic financial and business information on 624 companies of high investor interest. The information includes price charts, statistics, business descriptions, and discussion of recent developments. The reference is updated four times a year and contains a detailed section of how to most effectively use the reference.

HG 4905. N252 (Securities—United States—Periodicals; Over-The-Counter Markets—United States—Periodicals)

National Association of Securities Dealers, Inc. NASDAQ Fact
Book and Company Directory (Washington, DC: NASD)

This book provides data on the performance of National Association of Securities Dealers Automated Quotations (NASDAQ) securities, statistics on the NASDAQ Stock Market and directory information for each NASDAQ company.

HG 4907 .N43 (Investment Advisors—Directories; Brokers—Directories; Corporations—Directories; Securities—Research—Directories)

Nelson's Directory of Investment Research (Port Chester, NY:
Nelson)

This directory is a reference source detailing up-to-date information on investment. It is updated yearly and 10 supplements are sent to subscribers throughout the year. The information in each volume is divided into seven sections. These include investment research sources, company profiles and analysis coverage, company index (geographic), company index by industry group, analysts by industry specialty, analyst register and master index of companies and research sources. Volume one covers U.S. companies and volume two covers international companies.

Entries within each section are arranged alphabetically by words and include listings from research firms, over 9000 publicly owned companies internationally, sell-side security analysts, and investment research professionals.

Special features include an explanation of the data layout at the front of each volume, cross-references in sections three and four to the main entries and a Master Index at the end of each volume with cross-references to volume and page number.

HG 4907 .S74 (Stocks—United States—Directories; Bank Investments—United States—Directories)

CDA/Spectrum 13 (f) Institutional Stock Holdings (Rockville, MD: CDA Investment Technologies, Inc.)

This text provides data for institutions with portfolio holdings containing assets over $1,000,000. The body of the text is composed of a survey of institutional stock holdings and is updated quarterly. Each entry contains the name of the institution followed by an alphabetical listing of the stocks in its portfolio, any changes in the number of held shares, and the number of shares held at the end of the quarter. The text is supplemented by an alphabetical list of institutions, a holdings summary grouped by industry, and a list of the top 100 holdings, sales, and purchases.

HG 4907 .S78 (Brokers—Directories)

Standard & Poor's Security Dealers of North America (New York: Standard & Poor's)

This reference book provides information on security dealers and is updated twice a year to keep up with changes in the investment industry. The body of the text contains entries for investment firms in North America and their representatives abroad. The firms are separated according to their geographic location and then listed alphabetically by state, city, and firm name. Each one provides the name of the firm, the address and phone number, a list of other states where the firm is registered, the number of employees, the officers of the firm, and a list of the exchanges and associations that the firm belongs to. The publishers have included explanations of the symbols, a list of the North American exchanges and associations, an alphabetical list by state of North American securities administrators, a list of the major stock exchanges abroad, and three indexes regarding the firm listings.

HG 4910.O83 (Finance)

O'Shaughnessy, James P. What Works on Wall Street (New York: McGraw-Hill) 1997.

This book contains performances of some popular stocks over the past 43 years. Investment strategies are included, and these strategies have been obtained from the Standard and Poor's Compustat database.

HG 4915 .I12 (Stocks—Prices—United States—Periodicals; American Stock Exchange—Periodicals)

Daily Stock Price Record: American Stock Exchange
(New York: Standard & Poor's Corp.)

This reference book provides information on stocks traded on the American Stock Exchange. The text is divided into two parts. Part one describes market indicators which are used as guides to each of the three stock markets including the American Stock Exchange, the New York Stock Exchange, and NASDAQ. Part two provides a record of the daily and weekly movements of the stocks on the American Stock Exchange. The specific information includes the company name, security number, ticker symbol, volume of shares traded, a 30-week average of the stock's change, the relative strength of the stock, the stock's earnings, and the dividend rate over 12 months.

HG 4915 .I13 (Stocks—Prices—United States—Periodicals; New York Stock Exchange)

Daily Stock Price Record: New York Stock Exchange
(New York: Standard & Poor's)

This reference book provides information on the stocks traded on the New York Stock Exchange. The text is divided into two parts. Part one describes the market indicators which are used as guides to each of the three stock markets including the New York Stock Exchange, the American Stock Exchange, and NASDAQ. Part two provides a record of the daily and weekly movements of the stocks on the New York Stock Exchange. The specific information includes the company name, security number, ticker symbol, volume of shares traded, a 30-week average of the stock's change, the relative strength of the stock, the stock's earnings, and the dividend rate over 12 months.

HG 4915 .I14 (Stocks—Prices—United States—Periodicals; Stock Price Indexes—United States—Periodicals; Over-the-Counter Markets—United States—Periodicals)

Daily Stock Price Record: NASDAQ (New York: Standard & Poor's Corp.)

This reference book provides information on the stocks traded on NASDAQ. The text is divided into two parts. Part one describes the market indicators which are used as guides to each of the three stock markets including the New York Stock Exchange, the American Stock Exchange, and NASDAQ. Part two provides a record of the daily and weekly movements of the stocks on NASDAQ. The specific information includes the company name, security number, ticker symbol, volume of shares traded, a 30-week average of the stock's change, the relative strength of the stock, the stock's earnings, and the dividend rate over 12 months.

HG 4915 .N28 (Stocks—United States—Directories; Corporations—United States—Finance—Directories; Stocks—Prices—United States—Periodicals; Stocks—United States—Tables—Periodicals)

The National Stock Summary (New York: National Quotation Bureau)

This reference book lists securities from the Pink Sheets, NASDAQ, the New York Stock Exchange, the American Stock Exchange, and the OTC Bulletin, and is published biannually. The entries are arranged alphabetically by the issuer's name and contain the address of the issuer, date of merger, information regarding a change of name, date and terms of reorganization, bankruptcy information, par value, name of exchange on which the security is traded, dividend type and amount, change in capital, new issues, closing price, trading range, transfer agent, shares outstanding, exchange offer, purchase offer, and distribution upon liquidation.

HG 4915 .S85 (Stocks—Tables; Stocks—Prices—United States)

Stock Values and Dividends for Tax Purposes (New York: Commerce Clearing House)

This reference guide of stock values and dividends provides assistance for those preparing income tax and personal property tax returns. The text is arranged alphabetically by the name of the stock and is separated into three sections. The first section lists stocks and closed-end funds with their corresponding dividends and market values at the end of the year. Section two lists mutual funds and their year-end values. Section three lists mutual funds and investment firms with their net asset and taxable values.

HG 4915 .S86 1999 (Finance)

Stocks Bonds Bills and Inflation (Chicago: Ibbatson Associates)

Data on capital markets in the United States from the year 1926 as well as a guide on how to use this historical data can be found in this book. It is useful for a wide variety of people, historians, students, teachers, investors, and even CEOs of companies.

HG 4921 .B98 (Investments, Foreign—United States—Handbooks, Manuals, etc.; Investments, Foreign—Law and Legislation—United States—Handbooks, Manuals, etc.)

Business Opportunities in the United States: The Complete
Reference Guide to Practices and Procedures
(Homewood, IL: Business One Irwin) 1992.

This reference guide outlines key information and provides guidance for those interested in investing in the United States. The text's contents include sections on planning, communications, acquisition candidates, special planning for Japanese and German investors, insurance, finance, banking, legal issues, taxation, employee relations, and real estate development. A bibliography and an index are supplied as well.

HG 4921 .D74 (Stocks—United States—Handbooks, Manuals, etc.; Bonds—United States—Handbooks, Manuals, etc.)

The Irwin Investor's Handbook (Burr Ridge, IL: Irwin
Professional Publishing)

This reference guide provides a past, present, and future look at the happenings in the investment industry. The text is divided into sections including the Dow Jones averages, Barron's confidence index, the Wall Street journal prime rate, the New York Stock Exchange, major indexes, stock and bond trading for the year, the Dow Jones world stock index, foreign markets, and the Asia-Pacific indexes.

HG 4921 .V38 (Capital Markets—United States—Mathematics—Handbooks, Manuals, etc.; Investment Analysis—United States—Mathematics—Handbooks, Manuals, etc.; Portfolio Management—United States—Mathematics—Handbooks, Manuals, etc.)

Veale, Stuart R. The Handbook of U. S. Capital Markets
(New York: Harper Business) 1991.

This reference book provides general background information, as well as technical information dealing with fixed income markets. The text includes a general guide to the money market, working with a fixed income, a section on fixed income securities, managing a fixed income portfolio, and analysis of derivative instruments.

HG 4930 .M98 (Mutual Funds—United States—Periodicals)

Mutual Fund Fact Book (New York: Investment Co. Institute)

This reference book provides a yearly wrap-up of the data and trends related to the mutual fund industry. The text outlines what a mutual fund is including background, development, growth, services, how investor acquires shares, professional management, taxation, regulations, recent trends, institutional markets, a global perspective, retirement, and risk. This is followed by information on the yearly economic environment in the United States and the contributions made by mutual funds to the American economy. The text is supplemented by data tables, a glossary, an index, and a list of other publications dealing with mutual funds.

HG 4930 .M983 (Mutual Funds—United States—Periodicals)

Morningstar Mutual Funds (Chicago: Morningstar)

Morningstar Mutual Fund reports provide data and analysis on a large number of mutual funds to aid prospective investors. Each report is sent out weekly, where a certain sector of mutual funds is reviewed. Each page contains a different mutual fund and a large number of statistics about the fund, including name, investment style, performance history on a graph, quarterly returns, and an evaluation of the mutual fund's performance and risk.

HG 4930 .M985 (Mutual Funds—United States—Statistics)

Mutual Funds Panorama (Boston: Warren, Gorkom, and Lamont)

Mutual Funds Panorama is a comprehensive directory on 3800 mutual funds. Part one contains general information on mutual funds, such as how to chart your investment course, how to select investment companies, and appraisal of management. Part two contains mutual fund data. It gives a directory for all of the funds that it contains, shows performance data, investment objective descriptions, name changes, and stock splits.

HG 4930 .M986 (Mutual Funds—United States—Periodicals)

Mutual Funds Update (Rockville, MD: CDA/Wiesenberger)

Mutual Funds Update gives monthly information about mutual funds. It starts with a general overview of the market in the past month, and then follows with information on performance by investment objective. There is also an alphabetical list for cross-referencing mutual funds by portfolio, risk, and dividend data.

HG 4930. S78 (Mutual Funds—United States—Periodicals)

Standard and Poor's/Lipper Mutual Fund Profiles (New York, NY: Standard and Poor's Corporation, Lipper Analytical Services)

This book lists hundreds of funds including general equity, specialized equity, and balanced and long-term taxable fixed income mutual funds. Taxable funds and municipal bond funds are listed in the back of the book.

HG 4930 .U223 (Investments—Periodicals)

Value Line Mutual Fund Advisor (New York, NY: Value Line Publishing)

The *Value Line Mutual Fund Advisor* is published monthly and is an eight-page newsletter covering investment trends and ideas. Each issue includes a featured fund highlight, articles on current investment topics, fund news and developments, and a perspective on the current economic outlook and specific investment advice.

HG 4931 .M82
(Bonds—United States; Municipal Bonds—United States)

Moody's Municipal and Government Manual (New York, NY: Moody's Investor's Service)

This source is a comprehensive guide to the financial functions of the individual governments and municipalities of the United States. An examination of the Federal government's revenues and expenditures is contained at the beginning of the three-volume work. This section includes data on U.S. securities, internal and external finance, debt bearing interest, and loan trusts.

States are indexed alphabetically following the section on the Federal government. Financial and statistical facts on industry, agriculture, government debt, and taxes are reviewed.

Financial responsibilities of state educational institutions and specially funded programs are described in the section on state agencies. Municipalities are assessed by population, bonded debt, tax allocations, revenues, and expenditures.

Revenue bonds are examined in detail in volume three. Date of issue, amount, interest rate, and underwriter information are provided for municipal bonds relating to industrial development and pollution control.

Bond ratings and short-term loan ratings are supplied in each entry. An explanation and key to Moody's rating system can be found at the front of each volume.

A special features section included in volume one covers the following information: *Moody's Municipal Bond Yield Averages*, *State Bonds Compared with U.S. Treasuries*, *State Highway Fund Analysis*, *State Income Statistics*, *Comparative Yields on Municipals*, *Treasury Bonds*, *Corporate Bonds*, and *State and Municipal News Issue Activity*. The manual is updated semiweekly by *Moody's Municipal and Government News Reports*.

HG 4936 .C71 (Treasury Bills—United States—Statistics)

Coleman, Thomas S. Historical United States Treasury Yield Curves (Chicago, Ill: Moody's Investors Service) 1994.

This work is primarily a book of tables. The tables and graphs reveal estimates of the yield curves and forward rates at each month-end over the period. This book is intended to serve as a reference source on risk-free interest rates over various horizons. The book also reviews definitions of "the interest rate" and reviews various methodologies for estimating yield curves.

HG 4951 .P93
(Municipal Bonds—United States—Periodicals)

Barbato, Kelly. KIS Prerefunded Bond Service (New York, NY: Kenny Information Systems)

The *KIS Prerefunded Bond Service* book contains 350 pages of issues that are escrowed to maturity or prerefunded by bond number. There is an appendix. The reference is published in two volumes. Each volume contains an index by description and by state. The pages are in numerical order from one volume to the next. Information includes the CUSIP or KIS issuer number, coupon, maturity, dated date, Moody's and Standard and Poor's ratings, insurance status, and escrowed or prerefunded information.

HG 4961 .M83 (Finance—United States; Securities— United States; Corporations—United States)

Moody's Bank and Finance Manual (New York, NY: Moody's Investor's Service)

This reference source is a four-volume work on finance within investment companies, banks, insurance companies, unit investment trusts, real estate investments, and trusts. Information contained in the manual is gathered from stockholder's reports, registrations and reports of the Securities and Exchange Commission, and from the companies themselves.

Material has been edited and revised by Moody's where necessary. Stock and bond descriptions are abridged, and financial and statistical data have been condensed. The manual is updated semiweekly by *Moody's Bank and Finance News Reports*.

Volume one contains information on banks, trust companies, savings and loan associations, and federal credit agencies. The bank section profiles approximately 3000 institutions and includes facts on bank history, bank officials, stocks, and dividends. Up to 2400 smaller institutions are also represented. Government credit agencies are examined in the Federal Agency section. The Federal National Mortgage Association, Student Loan Marketing Association, and the Federal Reserve System are examples of the contents of this section. Savings and loan associations whose shares are traded publicly are also covered.

Volume two covers insurance, investment companies, and real estate. Primarily, the insurance portion is concerned with investments, underwriting, assets, liabilities, and annual financial activities.

Financial business related to mutual funds and investment companies comprises the Investment Company section. Volume two also devotes a section to all aspects of investment and real estate. Monetary dealings such as installments, mortgages, loans, and titles are contained in the Finance section.

Volumes three and four outline unit investment trusts. Trust history and policy are the central points of focus.

All information contained in the manual is indexed alphabetically at the beginning of each volume. A definition section describing terms used in the manual follows the index. Keys to bond and stock ratings are also provided.

Special features include a list of companies previously covered by Moody's, arranged alphabetically with pertinent information regarding mergers, acquisitions, name changes, and a special notation for companies with preferred stock as rated by Moody's Investor's Service. A listing of the largest banks according to deposits and the largest insurance companies according to assets is included in volumes one and two as a special feature.

HG 4961 .M84 (Corporations—United States; Securities—United States; United States—Industries)

Moody's Industrial Manual (New York, NY: Moody's Investor's Service)

This source is a two-volume work reviewing all corporations on the American and New York Stock Exchanges. Information contained in the manual is gathered from stockholders's reports and registrations and reports of the Securities and Exchange Commission.

Material has been edited and revised by Moody's where necessary. Stock and bond descriptions are abridged and financial and statistical data have been condensed. The manual is updated semiweekly by *Moody's Industrial News Reports.*

Each entry contains a brief description and history of the corporation, provides the address and telephone number of the main office, identifies company officials, and covers general information relating to company management and production. Financial activity of the business is thoroughly examined. Previous years's income figures, including assets, liabilities, and merger and acquisitions data, are reported.

Moody's rates each company from "aaa" to "c" in regards to stocks and bonds. This rating system is explained in the front of the volume with a key for the user's reference.

Information contained in the work is indexed alphabetically at the beginning of each volume. A definition section describing terms used throughout the manual precedes the index.

Special features include a list of companies previously covered by Moody's arranged alphabetically with pertinent information regarding mergers, acquisitions, name changes, and a special notation for companies with preferred stock as rated by Moody's Investor's Service. An insert in volumes one and two indexes corporations according to geographic location, classifies companies by industry and product, and covers securities and statistics on preferred stock and commodities.

HG 4961 .M844 (Corporations—United States; Stocks—United States)

Moody's Industry Review (New York, NY: Moody's Investor's Service)

This industry review is updated biannually. It is a statistical reference guide comprised of pertinent financial information, operating data, and ratios. Arranged by industry, a table of comparative statistics is entered for each industry group. The tables of statistics include the locations where common stocks are traded, ticker symbols, recent 12-month price ranges, current prices, share earnings, books values per share for the last year and the 3 years prior, and estimated annual income.

In addition to general industry reviews, this work lists specific company rankings within the industry groups according to net income, market evaluation of stock, the stocks price behavior and profitability, as well as special ranking pertaining only to certain industries. By comparison to composite stock price movements with the New York Stock Exchange Composite Index over a 10-year period, a chart outlining market trends for each industry group completes each industry review.

HG 4961 .M847 (United States—Industries; Corporations—United States; Securities—United States; Over-The-Counter Markets—United States)

Moody's O.T.C. Industrial Manual (New York, NY: Moody's Investor's Service)

This source indexes over 1800 over-the-counter corporations of the United States that are not on the regional or national stock exchanges. Companies are categorized into areas of coverage within the manual: Corporate Visibility Plus, Corporate Visibility Select, Corporate Visibility, and Standard Coverage. Corporations subscribing to Corporate Visibility Plus receive the greatest coverage, while companies choosing Standard Coverage receive the least.

Each entry contains a brief description and history of the corporation, provides the address and telephone number of the main office, identifies company officials, and covers general information relating to company management and production. Financial activity of the business is thoroughly examined. Previous years's income figures, including assets, liabilities, and merger and acquisition data, are reported.

Moody's rates each company from "aaa" to "c" in regards to stocks and bonds. This rating system is explained in the front of the volume with a key for the user's reference.

Information contained in the manual is indexed alphabetically at the beginning of each volume. A definition section describing terms used throughout the manual precedes the index.

Special feature includes a list of companies previously covered by Moody's arranged alphabetically with pertinent information regarding mergers, acquisition, name changes, and a special notation for companies with preferred stock as rated by Moody's Investor's Service. An insert in volume one indexes corporations according to geographic location, classifies companies by industry and product, and covers stock splits for previous years.

HG 4971 .C7 (Railroads—United States—Finance)

Commercial and Financial Chronicle (New York:
William B. Dana)

This source deals with investments opportunities. For NYSE issues, it offers daily high and low prices, closing prices and bids, and asked quotations for each stock listed. It also gives yearly ranges, daily sales, weekly volumes of trading, yields, and indicated annual dividends.

It gives the consolidated trading for all AMEX issues; for NASDAQ, it gives the National and Supplemental Securities and the NASDAQ Bond Record. The source also lists information for the American Stock Exchange Bond Record. Information on mutual funds, money markets, U.S. government securities and agencies, the Federal National Mortgage Association, and the Federal Home Bank loans also can be found here.

The data are listed weekly. The paper also prides itself on extensive stock market quotes.

HG 4971 .M83 (Transportation—United States—Finance; Corporations—United States—Finance; Securities—United States—Finance)

Moody's Transportation Manual (New York, NY: Moody's
Investor's Service)

This source analyzes over 1000 companies in the transportation industry. Financial and statistical data are provided for railroad, trucking and busing industries, airlines, steamships, and vehicle rental agencies.

Each entry contains a brief history and description of the company, identifies corporate officials, and covers general information relating to company management, including mileage and operational statistics. Financial activity of the business is thoroughly examined. An expense analysis covers employee and payroll costs, income and efficiency factors, seasonal trends, and income accounts for the past 10 years. Long-term debt statistics and capital stock information are also included.

Companies are categorized into areas of coverage with the manual: Corporate Visibility Plus, Corporate Visibility Select, and Standard Coverage. Corporations subscribing to Corporate Visibility Plus receive the greatest coverage, while companies choosing Standard Coverage receive the least.

Moody's rates each company from "aaa" to "c" in regards to stocks and bonds. This rating system is explained in the front of the volume with a key for the user's reference.

Information contained in the manual is indexed alphabetically at the beginning of each volume. A definition section describing terms used throughout the manual precedes the index. Transportation maps are scattered throughout the material and are listed in the front of the volume. Facts contained in the manual are gathered from stockholders's reports, reports and registrations of the Interstate Commerce Commission and the Securities and Exchange Commission, and directly from the corporations.

A special features section is included in the center of the volume.

HG 5095 .D62
(Real Estate Investment Trusts—United States—Periodicals)

Directory of Obsolete Securities (Jersey City, NJ: Financial Information Inc.)

The *Directory of Obsolete Securities* contains a brief profile of banks and companies whose original identities have been lost as a result of a change in name, a merger, an acquisition, or a reorganization. The listing for each company indicates the manner in which the company's identity or securities became obsolete, the new name of the company, and the year in which the action occurred.

HG 5095 .N27
(Real Estate Investment Trusts—United States—Periodicals)

REIT Handbook (Washington, DC: NAREIT Inc.)

The *REIT Handbook* is divided into three main sections: NAREIT, REIT/ Member Profiles, and Industry Stats. NAREIT covers the National Association of Real Estate Investment Trusts, Inc. It includes information on the purpose, composition, and goals of the REIT industry's only association. REIT/Member Profiles are presented in alphabetical order. Part three focuses on the REIT industry. The last section is a compilation of the statistical information that is maintained by NAREIT's research department on a continual basis.

HG 5151 .C18 (Investments—Canada; Canada—Commerce; Canada—Industries)

The Canadian Trade and Investment Guide (Toronto, ON: Financial Post) 1989.

This guide provides a general overview and specific information on the Canadian business environment. The work is arranged in 14 sections and discusses the Canadian market in national and regional terms. It covers such topics as corporate performance, industry sectors, infrastructure, and sources of capital. Information on consumer markets, trade, investment, and taxation is useful to anyone with an interest in business activities in Canada. Legal and regulatory aspects of business are also included. Current impacting factors, such as the Canada–U.S. Free Trade Agreement and deregulation in transportation, are discussed. Graphs, figures, cross-references, and contact information are provided throughout the work.

HG 5432 .V13 (Finance)

Vaitinlingam, Romesh. Guide to Using the Financial Pages
(London: Pitman Publishing) 1996.

The Financial Times is a source for information on the stock market and the economy as a whole. This guide will help stock market investors interpret information in the Financial Times better. Over the last decade, the reporting methods have changed, which is why this is the third edition.

HG 5772 .S48
(Investment, Foreign—Japan; Corporations,
Foreign—Taxation—Law and Legislation—
Japan; Foreign Trade Regulations—Japan)

Setting Up Enterprises in Japan (Tokyo: Compiled by TMI
Associates Shimazaki International Law Office Chuo Coopers &
Lybrund International Tax Office)

This is a guidebook on how to set up a business in Japan, with practical information, such as data on incorporating a company, initiating capital transactions, and taxation system.

HG 5782 .D58 (Investments, Foreign—China; Joint
Ventures—China; Technology Transfer—China)

Shapiro, James E. et al. Direct Investment and Joint Ventures in
China: A Handbook for Corporate Negotiations (New York, NY:
Quorum Books) 1991.

This handbook combines an appreciation of the nuances faced in negotiations of joint venture with an examination of the investment environment in China. It assesses past traditions, current policies, and emerging problems.

The important issues regarding investment ventures in China, such as the investment environment, cultural environment, legal environment, etc., are dealt with in this work. Furthermore, the strategies involved in business negotiations with Chinese companies, including psychological preparation, procedures and issues, and relations with Chinese partners, are also discussed in detail.

One of the major objectives of this handbook is to help transnational enterprises to explain their contributions to Chinese officials more completely throughout all stages of negotiating a joint venture. Appendices concerning joint venture law of China and provisions of the State Council of China for the encouragement of foreign investment are attached. A selected bibliography and index are included in the handbook to facilitate readers in further research and expansion to related topics.

HG 5851.A2 S86 (Securities—South Africa—Periodicals)

Stock Exchange Handbook (Johannesburg: Flesch)

This handbook provides information on company ranking and lists the larger ones. It also provides data on overseas companies by country of origin, date of listing, and their equities.

HG 5993 .E53
(Stock Exchange—Developing Countries—Periodicals; Investments, Developing Countries—Periodicals)

Emerging Stock Markets Factbook (Washington, DC: Capital Markets Department, International Finance Corporation)

Leading stock markets from 19 developing Third-World nations are analyzed in this book from the International Finance Corporation (IFC). This single volume compiles data from various sources and compares it to other markets in the developed world. The factbook covers both the best and worst markets from emerging nations, principally in Latin America and South Asia.

The factbook is divided into five parts. First is a short introduction including subscription information to the IFC's emerging market database. Part two is an overview of emerging markets that contains commentaries, stock market indexes, and performance indexes. It also provides comparisons by country. The third part is the stock market indexes describing methodology used in the factbook. Analyses of the stock market performance using local market indexes are in this section as well. The fourth section, Equity Market profiles, takes a statistical look at the emerging markets. It includes trading values, market capitalization, and exchange rates. The final section is a directory of the stock exchange operations listing address, hours of operation, and holidays of the nations' stock exchanges.

HG 6024 .A3 S82 (Financial Futures—Dictionaries; Commodity Exchanges—Dictionaries)

Steinbeck, George and Rosemary Erickson. The Futures Markets Dictionary (New York, NY: New York Institute of Finance) 1988.

Formerly titled *The Language of Commodities*, this dictionary contains abbreviations, words, and phrases that are related to the commodity industry. Terms that are frequently used in peripheral industries, such as banking and shipping, are also included. The entries are alphabetically arranged and contain definitions, synonyms, examples, and cross-references as appropriate. The appendix provides information on reading commodity financial quotes, performing basic calculations, and finding commodity factors.

HG 6024.3 .C74 (Commodity Exchanges—United States—Charts, Diagrams, etc.)

Encyclopedia of Historical Charts: Financial Products (New York, NY: Knight-Ridder Financial Publishing) 1994.

The *Encyclopedia of Historical Charts* consists of two sections: I) Metals, Financial Instruments, and Currencies and II) Energy. There are various types of charts presented for each specific commodity within each division.

HG 6024.5 .H24 (Interest Rate Futures—Handbooks, Manuals, etc.; Hedging (Finance)—Handbooks, Manuals, etc.; Speculation—Handbooks, Manuals, etc.)

Rothstein, Nancy H. and James M. Little, Eds. The Handbook of Financial Futures: A Guide for Investors and Professional Financial Managers (New York, NY: McGraw-Hill) 1984.

This source discusses the growing field of financial futures markets in terms of risk management. The focus is on interest rate futures markets, although stock indexes, currencies, and interest rate options are also covered. The expansion of these markets on the exchanges and the implications are discussed. The work is arranged into five sections. The first section deals with the mechanical aspects of financial futures market, including the role of clearing houses, trading procedures, and market participants. Section two covers speculation and hedging, strategy design and application to financial institutions, broker–dealers, and corporations. Section three is on market analysis and includes technical aspects, the yield curve, and the implied repo rate. Section four covers trading rules, regulatory considerations, accounting concepts, control techniques, and income tax considerations. Section five contains references including a list of financial futures exchanges and contract specifications. A glossary, bibliography, and an index are provided.

HG 6046 .G95 (Commodity Exchanges)

Buckley, John, Ed. Guide to World Commodity Markets: Physical, Futures, and Options Trading (Chicago, IL: Probus Publishing Co.)

This reference source is divided into four sections, including: brief essays on international commodity agreements; information on history, production, price, and use of metals and softs; descriptions of the international commodity exchanges and associations with address, hours of trading, trading currency and unit, minimum lot size, trading limits, delivery points, currency dealt in, membership, date of establishment of the market, branches and affiliates; and commodity market trading members.

Appendices provide a glossary of commodity market terms, world time zones, weight conversion tables, and a table of average monthly dollar/sterling rates. Indexes are included.

HG 6046 .H24
(Commodity Exchanges—Handbooks, Manuals, etc.)

Kaufman, Perry J. Handbook of Futures Markets (New York, NY: John Wiley & Sons) 1984.

This handbook of commodity futures markets provides an overview of the futures markets and covers techniques and methods of analysis for commodity trading. General as well as in-depth information on the markets and the commodities is included. The work contains 49 chapters that are arranged into six parts. Part one deals with the operation of commodity markets, including information on the clearinghouse, regulation, and taxation. Part two covers market influences, including those resulting from macroeconomic factors and the U.S. Department of Agriculture. Part three, on the use of markets, details market development, interest-rate risk management, hedging, and commodity options. Part four covers forecasting tools and methods, such as bar charting and point-and-figure charting. Part five deals with money management and risk, including chapters on the effects of capitalization and the measurement of trading performance. Part six deals with the commodities themselves and is divided into chapters such as grains, livestock, foods, energy, and metals. A glossary, bibliography, and an index are provided.

HG 6046 .I15 (Commodity Exchanges—Periodicals)

ICCH Commodities and Financial Futures Yearbook (London, UK: Landell Mills Commodities Studies in Association with International Commodities Clearing House)

This annual reference work describes and analyzes the commodity and the financial futures markets with an emphasis on London trading. The work is arranged into six parts. Part one contains several articles relating to commodity markets. Part two profiles agricultural commodities. Part three deals with energy, specifically coal and gasoil. Part four covers financial instruments, including interest rate futures, foreign exchange futures, and stock market futures. Part five describes metals, including strategic and minor metals. Part six provides a directory of ICCH members and to the major futures markets, with members listed by geographic region. Graphs, charts, and tables are used throughout the work to supplement the text.

HG 6049 .C73 1985 (Commodity Exchanges—United States—Handbooks, Manuals, etc.)

Besant. Lloyd, Ed. Commodity Trading Manual (Chicago, IL: Chicago Board of Trade) 1998.

This work begins with a brief history of the marketplace and an overview of futures trading. Information on commodity exchanges is provided, including memberships, governing bodies, committees, and staff. Chapters are devoted to the many aspects of trading, including clearing operations, price reporting, hedging, price forecasting, speculating, and federal, industry, and exchange regulation. The commodities are arranged according to type (e.g., grains, livestock, and textiles) with a chapter on each that details information on supply, production, and demand. The work also covers financial instruments, foreign currencies, stock indices, and options. A glossary and an index are provided.

HG 6049 .S78 (Commodity Exchanges—United States—Statistics—Periodicals)

Chicago Mercantile Exchange, Statistical Yearbook (Chicago, IL: The Exchange)

This annual reference book contains statistical data relating to activity on the Chicago Mercantile Exchange. The work includes daily volumes and daily open interest for agricultural, currency, equity, and interest rate products. Data are available for deliveries/exercises and the agricultural and financial cash markets. In addition, daily and monthly price ranges in volume and open interest according to contract are provided.

HG 8019 .B56 (Insurance—Property; Insurance—Casualty; Insurance Companies)

Best's Insurance Reports—Property—Casualty (Oldwick, NJ: A.M. Best Company)

Over 2450 property/casualty insurers actively operating in the United States are profiled here. Rated on financial performance, information is compiled from annual financial statements, questionnaires provided by A.M. Best, quarterly National Association of Insurance Commissioners statement filings, state insurance department examination reports, audit reports, loss reserve reports, annual reports to stock and policy holders, and reports filed with the Securities and Exchange Commission.

Profiles of the companies include the full name of the company, address, phone, fax, a rating (letter grade), assets, history, directors and officers, and operations. Other listings included in the volume are companies by states, the 200 largest companies, name changes, and retired companies.

HG 8019 .I5 (Insurance—Yearbooks)

The Insurance Almanac: Who, What, When and Where in Insurance: An Annual of Insurance Facts (Englewood, NJ: Underwriter Press and Publishing)

Directory information on U.S. insurance companies and national, state, and local groups, as well as local organizations and associations such as agents, brokers, adjusters, etc. is located here. Lloyds companies in the United States are also included.

Entries contain name, address, phone, and often main personnel and short descriptions of services provided. Information on insurance companies or groups may also include branch offices, affiliated companies, and territory of operation. Organization and association entries often provide information on date first organized, date of annual meeting, and the purpose of the organization or association. Within each category of insurance, entries are arranged alphabetically by state and subdivided alphabetically by city, locality, and name of company or organization.

This one-volume annual includes an index that is arranged alphabetically by name of the insurance company or organization.

HG 8025 .D25 1990 (Insurance—Dictionaries)

Davids, Lewis E. Dictionary of Insurance (Savage, MD: Littlefield Adams Quality Paperbacks) 1990.

This dictionary, currently in its seventh edition, provides brief definitions of insurance terms. The work is intended for general use by laypersons as well as by professionals in the insurance industry. Entries are arranged in alphabetical order and include abbreviations. Lists of insurance-related organization and of state commissioners of insurance are also provided.

HG 8025 .R88 1991 (Insurance—Dictionaries)

Rubin, Harvey W. Dictionary of Insurance Terms (New York, NY: Barron's) 1991.

This pocket-size dictionary provides concise definitions to abbreviations, words, and phrases that are associated with the insurance industry. The work is appropriate for personal and business activities and is arranged alphabetically and contains new and traditional terms. Examples and cross-references are provided. A separate list of abbreviations and acronyms is appended.

HG 8077 .G17
(Insurance—Accounting—Handbooks, Manuals, etc.)

Galloway, Clair J. and Joseph M. Galloway. Handbook of Accounting for Insurance Companies (New York, NY: McGraw-Hill) 1986.

This comprehensive handbook serves as a reference source for financial reporting and accounting for all areas of the insurance industry. The focus is on the theory and rules of accounting rather than on the mechanics. The information is useful for fulfilling company and public reporting requirements and is intended for professionals, educators, and students. The work contains 23 chapters, most of which deal with a single topic in accounting, such as mortgage loans and life insurance companies reserves. Chapters are subdivided by type of company when different accounting methods are used. The appendix contains sample annual statement forms and an index is provided.

HG 8525 .B56 (Insurance—United States—Directories)

Best's Trend Report, Property–Casualty Edition
(Oldwick, NJ: A.M. Best Co.)

This report presents a 5-year tabulation of the Best's Ratings and results of selected Best's profitability, leverage, and liquidity tests for over 2300 U.S. property/casualty insurance companies. Other information, such as annual statement data and financial size category of each insurer, the states in which the companies are licensed or approved to do business, and listings of the various members of company groups and/or fleets, are also shown. To aid in the analysis of the data in this report, the introduction contains an explanation of Best's Rating system and procedures.

Arrangement is by alphabetical order by individual company. This book provides a dimension of analysis for identifying the current condition of carrier solvency and stability. Users can also consult Best's Insurance Reports Property/Casualty Edition or International Edition to get more detailed information on this topic.

HG 8759 .I62 (Insurance, Life—United States—Dictionaries; Insurance, Health—United States—Dictionaries)

The Insurance Dictionary: Life and Health Edition
(Chicago, IL: Newkirk Longman) 1990.

A compilation of life and health insurance terms and definitions is presented here. Related subjects are defined as well, including agent training and agency building concepts, retirement and estate planning, investments and securities, government benefit programs, and taxation. Names and descriptions of organizations and government agencies related to the life and health insurance field are also provided.

The definitions included in this dictionary are not intended to be legal or contract definitions. Terms are arranged alphabetically, and a list of abbreviations is provided at the back of the book.

HG 8943 .B56
(Insurance, Life—United States; Insurance, Life—Canada)

Best's Insurance Reports—Life–Health
(Oldwick, NJ: A.M. Best)

This report provides information on the financial stability of life and health insurance companies in the U.S. and Canadian companies that operate in the United States. Best's gives insurance companies a rating that indicates their opinion of a particular company's financial strength, operating performance, and ability to meet its obligation to policyholders. The 1993 edition discusses over 1700 companies. Reports are included on major stock and mutual fund companies as well as fraternal societies. Smaller companies are covered, but may be rated differently than the large insurers.

The information included in the book comes primarily from the National Association of Insurance Commissioners (NAIC) annual financial statement that insurance companies are required to file with the state insurance commissioner. Best's gets further financial information from sources such as company annual reports, audit reports, state insurance department examination reports, and through talking directly with company management. Insurance companies are listed alphabetically, and there is an index at the front of the book.

In addition, there are directories of fraternal societies and life/health HMO companies that are not included in the main body of the work. There are listings of group affiliations of life/health and property/casualty insurance carriers and of legal reserve life insurance companies by state. Finally, there is a list of company name changes, retired companies, and reinsurance companies since 1981.

HG 8943 .L72 (Insurance, Life—Yearbooks; Insurance, Life—United States—Periodicals)

Life Insurance Fact Book (Washington, DC: American Council of Life Insurance)

This work is an overview of the U.S. life insurance industry and covers many aspects of it through the use of text, historical tables, and graphics. One of the efforts of this industry is to provide the public with current data on its performance and this work is published for this purpose. A full-text edition is published during even-numbered years, and an abbreviated, tables-only update edition is published during odd-numbered years.

The source for each table is given and there is text that goes with the tables and graphs as well. Tables consist of information about the United States, but there is a specific section on life insurance information for various other countries. There is a very thorough table of contents along with a glossary and an index.

Examples of information included are purchases, ownership, annuities, pension and retirement programs, income, reserves and obligations, companies, causes of death, life expectancy, types of life insurance, state officials, lapses and surrenders, mortality tables, employment in life insurance, organizations, and historic dates.

In the update edition of the odd-numbered years, there is a key to help locate data in the update that corresponds to tables in the full-text edition of the year before.

HG 9226 .C73 (Insurance, Fraternal—United States—Statistics—Periodicals; Insurance, Life—United States—Statistics—Periodicals; Insurance, Fraternal—Canada—Statistics—Periodicals; Insurance, Life—Canada—Statistics—Periodicals)

Statistics of Fraternal Benefit Societies (Chicago: National Fraternal Congress of America)

This reference book provides information and statistics relating to the fraternal benefit system in the United States and Canada. The topics covered include fraternal certificates, insurance in force, premiums, assets, social members, lodges, benefits, and state fraternal insurance laws. The text is supplemented by data tables and indexes of fraternal societies, National Fraternal Congress of America members, Canadian Fraternal Association members, and nonmember societies.

HG 9228 .B56 (Insurance, Life—United States—Directories; Insurance, Health—United States—Directories)

Best's Trend Report, Life–Health Insurance Companies (Oldwick, NJ: A.M. Best)

This report contains 5-year compilations of Best's Ratings and results of selected tests for profitability, leverage, and liquidity of life and health insurance companies in the United States. These data are in tabular form. The report for each company includes numeric information from annual statements, results of 17 quantitative formulas applied to financial data, and an annual Best's Rating (ranging from A+ to C−) or an explanatory "not assigned" code for those companies not eligible for a rating.

The ratings reflect Best's opinion of each company's relative financial strength and ability to meet its contractual obligations. Best's review is based on information derived from the company's sworn financial statements, as prescribed by the National Association of Insurance Commissioners. That may be supplemented by information obtained from questionnaires, state insurance department reports, audits, and annual reports to stockholders. A qualitative evaluation of factors including the company's spread of risk, diversification of investments, and experience of the management is part of the rating procedure, but it is not depicted in the tables.

Arrangement of the tables is alphabetical by company name.

HG 9395.S72
(Insurance, Health—United States—Periodicals)

Sourcebook of Health Insurance Data (New York: Health
Insurance Institute)

This book provides statistics on the major forms of health insurance coverage,
medical care costs, utilization of the nation's medical facilities, and national
morbidity trends.

HG 9396 .H46
(Insurance, Health—United States—Periodicals)

Source Book of Health Insurance Data (Washington, DC:
Health Insurance Association of America)

This volume presents a collection of statistical data on the health insurance
industry in the United States. Numerous charts and tables, compiled by the
Health Insurance Association of America's Department of Policy and Research, provide the latest available data on major forms of health insurance
coverage, medical care expenses, utilization of the country's medical facilities,
managed-care programs, and national morbidity and mortality trends. Special features of the 1992 volume include tables on preventable medical conditions, emergency room fees, dental fees, and health insurance coverage by
age and race.

Data are arranged into six major sections: the history of health insurance, private health insurance industry, public health coverage, medical care
costs, health services and utilization, and disability, morbidity, and mortality.
Also included are appendices on health-care acronyms and historical insurance facts, as well as a glossary of health insurance terms and an alphabetical
subject index. This volume is intended to serve as a reference for writers,
researchers, educators, government officials, medical professionals, and all
others interested in health care.

HG 9658 .N29 v.1–3
(Insurance—Fire; Insurance—Casualty)

Fire, Casualty Surety Bulletins (Cincinnati, OH: National
Underwriter)

This set of bulletins is intended to provide concise, accurate, and up-to-date
information on the various forms of property and casualty insurance,

personal and commercial, and fidelity and surety bonds. It is for commercial underwriters in the United States and the format allows for easy access and frequent updates. Organization of the source is by subject with three primary divisions. The divisions are Fire and Marine, Casualty and Surety, and Personal Lines. A series of monthly updates are provided. The updates allow the copyright date to vary by subject.

Each volume is in loose-leaf format and has an annotated table of contents with corresponding tabbed entries in the text. Each volume also has an individual index. There is a master index for the entire set. Finally, there is a checklist to assure completeness and monthly instructions for organization and filing.

HG 9765 .B55 (Insurance, Property—United States—Statistics—Periodicals; Insurance, Casualty—United States—Statistics—Periodicals; Insurance, Fire—United States—Statistics—Periodicals)

Best's Aggregates & Averages: Property–Casualty
(Oldwick, NJ: A. M. Best)

This reference book provides aggregates and averages for the property–casualty section of the insurance industry. The major headings include balance sheets and summary of operations, annual statements and insurance expense exhibits, time series, lines of business, and leading companies and groups. The text is supplemented by an index of exhibits.

HG 9765 .B56 (Insurance, Property—United States—Directories; Insurance, Casualty—United States—Directories)

Best's Key Rating Guide: Property–Casualty
(Oldwick, NJ: A. M. Best)

This reference book provides statistics and ratings for property–casualty insurers. The text begins with an explanation of the ratings system and the ratings monitor. The major headings include financial and operating exhibits with key ratings, directory of other U.S. property–casualty insurers, company groups or fleets, retired companies, states and territories in which licensed, underwriting organizations and combinations policies, the largest 200 American stock companies, and property–casualty guaranty funds. The text is supplemented by an index of licensed insurance carriers and a glossary.

HJ—PUBLIC FINANCE

HJ 9 .U561 (Budget—United States—Statistics—Periodicals; Budget—United States—History—Periodicals)

United States, Office of Management and Budget, Historical Tables, Budget of the United States Government (Washington, DC: U.S. Government Printing Office)

This source is a companion to the *Budget of the United States Government* and contains budget information, not only for the current year, but summarizes former years and predicts future budgets in table form. The book is divided into 16 sections, each covering a single topic, thus allowing historical as well as present and speculative data to be presented together. Each section is prefaced by a short introduction to the topic and, if a new budget category is created, definitions appear in nontechnical terms. Descriptive information has been included where necessary as well as cross-references. If more than one table is presented in a particular topic, the table showing the most general information is presented first.

Due to changes in types of data, historical comparisons are presented in relation to the present budgetary topic. The budget is a unified one, including all topics presented in the *Report of the President's Commission on Budget Concepts.*

Percentages have been calculated from the most detailed information possible and not rounded. Percentages presented for the Gross National Product or for budget totals are listed in current, not constant, dollars.

HJ 10 .H261 (Taxation—United States—Law; Law Reports, Digests—United States)

United States Tax Court Reports (Washington, DC: U.S. Government Printing Office)

This book summarizes all of the cases held in the United States Tax Court in chronological order, according to the date the case was filed. Each summary lists the names of all parties involved, docket numbers, and the judge's opening words. These are followed by a finding of facts summary and opinions or rulings by the judge. The appendix contains tables of memorandum opinions and an index digest. The index digest gives a one-paragraph summary of the subject and rulings, citing the names of the case and the page number.

HJ 10 .H271
(Income Tax—United States—Case Studies;
Taxation—United States—Case Studies)

2000 Tax Court Memorandum Decisions
(New York: RIA) 2000.

This reference work provides full texts of the major Tax Court memo decisions in the first half of 2000. Included with each case is all the critical information to show the importance of the case and any precedents which may have been set by it. Also included is an index of the cases which are reported on and the opinion which the court ruled.

HJ 10 .H272
(Law Reports, Digests, etc.—United States;
Taxation—Law and Legislation—United States; Income
Tax—Law and Legislation—United States)

Tax Court Reported Decisions (Englewood Cliffs, NJ:
Prentice-Hall)

This reference book is updated annually and provides texts from all of the United States tax-court-reported decisions. The text includes a table of cases, a topic index, and a section of tax-court decisions. Each case entry contains the defendant's name, the case background, the monetary values involved, the judge's name, the section numbers, the rules violated, and the opinion.

HJ 101 .G72 (Finance, Public—Statistics)

International Monetary Fund, Government Finance Statistics
Yearbook (Washington, DC: IMF)

This reference work, divided into three sections, provides data on the financial well being of over 75 countries. Section one deals with the economy of the world, giving financial tables relating to trade and expenditures. Section two shows tables for numerous countries with various financial figures for each. Section three gives information on the institutional aspects of each of these same countries showing the hierarchy of each country's government.

HJ 236 .B65
(Fiscal Policy—States, Small—Economic Conditions)

Blöndal, Gisáli. Fiscal Policy in the Smaller Industrial Countries, 1972–1982 (Washington, DC: International Monetary Fund) 1986.

Part one of this study is a comparative analysis of fiscal policies of industrial countries with gaps in fiscal policy literature. The countries chosen were those with accessible statistical information. Part two is a summary of expenditures, revenues, balancing and financing, and fiscal policies. Countries surveyed were Australia, Austria, Belgium, Denmark, Finland, Iceland, Ireland, Luxembourg, Netherlands, New Zealand, Norway, Spain, and Sweden. Tables of selected economic indicators and consolidated central government finances are included for each country. A bibliography of appropriate reference materials is included.

HJ 257 .T23 (World War, 1939–1945—Finance—United States; Finance, Public—United States—1933–)

Moody, Scott. Facts and Figures on Government Finance (Washington, DC: Tax Foundation)

This reference work, divided into six sections, presents data on local, state, federal, and international taxes. Section one provides an overview of all governments with key economic figures for each aspect of the economy. Section two gives selected economic statistics for the United States. Section three has information on the federal government, and a summary of its spending and outlays. Section four gives information on local governments, and their revenues, expenditures, and debts. Section five presents the same types of information for state governments. The sixth section provides data on international governments with population figures, and tax revenues. Also included is a glossary and an index of tax foundation advisors.

HJ 257.2 P41
(Fiscal Policy—United States; Taxation—United States)

Pechman. Joseph A. Federal Tax Policy (Washington, DC: The Brookings Institution) 1987.

Aimed at the public taxpayer, this handbook provides explanations of the 1986 federal tax reforms in lay persons' terms. An emphasis is placed on such subjects as comprehensive income taxation, the relationship between taxation and economic incentives and inflation adjustments, graduated taxes, and expenditure taxes. The book is arranged systematically with chapters on taxes and economic policy, the legislative tax process, individual income tax, corporate income tax, consumption taxes, payroll taxes, estate and gift taxes, and state and local taxes. A summary is included at the end of each chapter. Appendices include an historical summary of major federal taxes, tax bases of the major federal taxes, tax expenditure, and statistical tables and bibliographic notes.

HJ 2050 .E19 (Budget—United States—Periodicals; Government Spending Policy—United States—Periodicals; United States—Appropriations and Expenditures— Periodicals; Tax Revenue Estimating—United States—Periodicals)

Congressional Budget Office, The Budget and Economic Outlook: Fiscal Years 2001–2010 (Washington, DC: CBO)

The reference work produced by the United States Congress, divided into five sections, looks to predict the future of the economy of America. Sections one through four provide outlooks on the budget, the economy, the revenue, and the spending of the United States respectively. Section five deals with the uncertainties of any budget projections made, and provides statistical data to show the range of error which must be assumed. Also included are six appendices that seek to answer commonly asked questions about these types of projections.

HJ 2052 .G56 1981 (Budget—United States—Dictionaries; Finance, Public—United States—Dictionaries)

A Glossary of Terms Used in the Federal Budget Process (Washington, DC: U.S. General Accounting Office) 1982.

Under the direction of Congress, the Comptroller General of the United States published a book in 1974 standardizing the terminology, definitions, classifications, and codes used in the Federal budget and its conjunctive data and information. This source, in its third edition, was compiled under the premise of improving communication between the government and the public.

Most of the terms contained in this document are used in the budget, but related terms referring to taxation, economics, and accounting are also included. Terms were included based on the frequency of their appearance in the budget. The book also contains an overview of the Federal budget process. The main body of work is cross-referenced and an index to those cross-references is included. Entries include examples of usage taken from specific parts of the budget. Budgetary terms, tax terms, economic terms, and accounting terms each have their own glossary.

Four appendices list the documents that the Federal budget is published in, functional classifications within the budget, a listing of budget account identification codes, and program and finance schedule. A bibliography is listed at the end.

HJ 2279 .O68 (Revenue—Statistics—Periodicals; Taxation—Statistics—Periodicals)

Revenue Statistics of OECD Member Countries (Paris: Organisation de Cooperation et de Development Economiques)

This reference book provides tax statistics and analysis for OECD member countries. The major headings include comparative graphs relating to taxes and GDP, OECD classification of taxes, comparative statistical tables and country tables, estimates of tax revenues, historical statistics on tax revenues, nontax revenue, capital revenue, and grants. The text is supplemented by a list of tables and background on the OECD.

HJ 2976 .O94 (Taxation—Japan)

An Outline of Japanese Taxes (Tokyo: Tax Bureau Ministry of Finance)

This book briefly overviews the historical background of Japan's tax system. It provides an explanation of types of taxes, including their calculation methods.

HJ 3251 .A39 C695 (Taxation—Law and Legislation—United States; Income Tax—Law and Legislation—United States)

CCH Editorial Staff, U.S. Master Tax Guide (Chicago: Commerce Clearing House)

This tax handbook, divided into 29 chapters, seeks to help all tax filers simplify the process of filing their taxes. The first five sections are an overview of the different tax tables and the respective filers that should use each.

Sections 6 through 29 are explanatory texts that give information on the process behind filing taxes for many different complicated situations. Included are sections for individuals and businesses with explanations of relevant tax credits, exemptions, exclusions, deductions, and securities transactions. Updated yearly, this work lists the most recent changes made to Federal Tax law from the previous year.

HJ 3251 .A39 C69 (Taxation—Law and Legislation—United States; Income Tax—Law and Legislation—United States; Excess Profits Tax—Law and Legislation—United States)

Standard Federal Tax Reporter. Chicago: Commerce Clearing House

This reference set is composed of several volumes relating to the internal revenue code, tax statutes, and U.S. tax cases. The major headings include tax planning, tax credits, income, deductions, corporate distributions, employee benefits, tax accounting, exempt organizations, trust funds, foreign income, gain/loss, returns, excise taxes, interest, penalties, crimes, and tax court rules. The text is supplemented by a list of new matters, topical and cumulative indexes, finding lists, case tables, and the Supreme Court docket.

HJ 3251 .A39 C695 (Taxation—Law and Legislation—United States; Taxation—Law and Legislation—United States; Income Tax—Law and Legislation—United States)

U.S. Master Tax Guide (Chicago: Commerce Clearing House) 1994.

This source provides information on all changes made to income tax law that affects 1994 tax returns and includes legislative amendments made by Social Security Domestic Employment Reform Act of 1994, and the "Nanny Tax" legislation (made law 1994). There are separate sections for significant tax provisions and important nonlegislative changes. This source gives tax rate schedules for 1994 and 1995, a 1995 tax calendar, and a checklist to help determine if an item is taxable, nontaxable, or deductible. This source is intended to aid in the preparation of returns and also to serve as a reference tool for the 1995 Commerce Clearing House (CCH) Standard Federal Tax Reports. There is a topical index that refers back to paragraphs, acronyms are spelled out, and "see" references are used. This source is designed to be authoritative.

HJ 3251 .A39 C7 1994 (Income Tax—United States—Case Studies; Income Tax—United States—Case Studies; Taxation—United States—Case Studies)

U.S. Tax Cases (Chicago: Commerce
Clearing House) 1994.

This two-volume source contains all the full text decisions rendered by Federal Courts throughout the United States on federal tax problems. (Exempted from this source are decisions of the U.S. Tax Court.) All cases are listed alphabetically by both the plaintiff and the defendant, and if neither was available at the time of printing, by reporter citation. All references are given in the form of a Commerce Clearing House (CCH) citation with both the volume number and paragraph where a full text citation can be found. The cases listed are reprints of decisions reported in the Standard Federal Tax Reports, Federal Estate and Gift Tax Reports, and Federal Excise Tax Reports. The decisions appear in chronological order of publication and are designated by paragraph number. (These numbers are the same as in the original publication.) This source is authoritative.

HJ 4635 .G55 (International Business Enterprises—Taxation; International Business Enterprises—Taxation—Law and Legislation)

Glautier, Michel and Frederick Bassinger. A Reference Guide to International Taxation (Lexington, MA: D.C. Heath and Co.) 1987.

International taxation arises from international businesses paying taxes in more than one country. The purpose of this source is to provide general information about the guidelines for international business taxation to business laypersons. Since there are no standard laws, the law of several countries may be introduced in particular subject areas. Examples of problems that have occurred are used to illustrate each topic.

This source is arranged into four categories: tax systems, double taxation, tax havens, and international tax planning. The section on tax systems contains a general overview of tax systems in different countries. Topics covered in this section are taxes applicable to business operations, taxable entities, taxation bases, direct taxation, taxation of business profits, taxation of capital gains, taxation of wealth, taxation of transfers by gifts and on death and on indirect taxation.

The section on double taxation explains how it occurs and what measures may be taken to alleviate the problem. Topics covered include the nature of double taxation, the relief of double taxation on income and capital, double taxation relief for business income, double taxation relief for personal income, and rules for allowing double taxation relief.

Tax haven countries are used to avoid double taxation and high-level direct taxation on large profits. The tax haven section reviews the kind of protection tax haven countries offer, as well as the allowed tax savings and problems resulting from their use. Topics under examination include identification of tax havens, facilities offered by tax havens, selecting a tax haven, and tax avoidance and its users in tax havens.

In the last section on tax planning, an exploration of elements of international tax planning, tax planning for personal wealth, tax planning for the management of corporate assets, and constraints arising from anti-avoidance legislation is used to provide an overview of international tax planning.

The book contains a bibliography, tables, and an appendix that the authors use to present their model for double taxation conventions.

HJ 4652 .P7 (Income Tax—Law and Legislation—United States; Taxation—Law and Legislation—United States)

Federal Tax Handbook (New York: Research Institute of America)

This work attempts to assist individuals and businesses in the preparation of their taxes. Starting each volume is a section highlighting changes made from the edition of the previous year. Following is a breakdown of relevant tax information giving advice, and the laws pertaining to many unique situations. Also included are tables of standard deductions, along with many other deductions that can arise in more complicated tax filings.

HJ 4653 .C7 1982 (Income Tax—United States)

Internal Revenue Service Statistics of Income: Sole Proprietorship Returns, 1979–1980 (Washington, DC: United States Government Printing Office) 1982.

This source reports statistical data on adjusted gross income, selected tax credits, and total income tax paid from tax returns filed by sole proprietors for the income years 1979 and 1980. The information reported concerns cost of sales and operations, deductions, and net income or deficit. Data is classified according to industry, businesses with or without net income, size of adjusted gross income, and gender of the proprietors. Filers of sole proprietary businesses must be unincorporated, one-owner businesses or farmers or professional practices. The report is divided into five sections: introduction and discussion of changes in laws that effect comparability of data from year to year; description of the sample of data taken and its limitations; tables of data; explanation of terms; and forms and instructions.

HJ 4653 .C7 S78 (Income Tax—United States)

Internal Revenue Statistics of Income: Partnership Returns
(Washington, DC: United States Government Printing
Office) 1982.

Because of the rise in the number of partnership filings between 1978 and 1982, this source of statistics was published. Information of this type had been previously included in a series of articles published in the Statistics of Information Bulletin. In this source, statistical information on receipts, costs of sales and operations, deductions, net income and deficit, capital gains and losses, and the number of limited partnerships is reported. The information contained in the tables is arranged according to industry, size of total assets, states, and numbers of partners. One section describes the terms used and another lists the criteria for classification. Forms and instructions are also included.

HJ 4653 .S3 C24 (Taxation of Bonds, Securities, etc.—United States; Corporate Reorganizations—Taxation—United States; Dividends—Taxation—United States; Stockholders' Preemptive Rights—United States)

Capital Adjustments; Stock Dividends, Stock Rights,
Reorganizations (Englewood Cliffs, NJ: Prentice-Hall)

This source describes capital changes in corporations from 1980 to 1989 resulting from stock dividends, split-ups, subscription rights, exchanges of stocks and securities effected in recapitalizations, reorganizations, and mergers. This source is aimed towards the stock or shareholder and gives information on changes in corporations that affects the tax rates on stock or securities. The latest information is available in loose-leaf volumes as are the instructions on how to use the source. Everything is arranged alphabetically.

HJ 7539 .I38 (United States—Appropriation and Expenditures—Effect of Inflation on)

Indexation of Federal Programs (Washington, DC: United States
Government Printing Office) 1981.

This source lists federal aid programs whose provisions are subject to change in relation to economic factors as indicated by some index, such as the Consumer Price Index, or the minimum-wage scale. Part one gives descriptions of each program and the history behind the indexing formulas used. Also listed are the number of recipients in 1979 and yearly revisions made to each program according to the Inventory of Federally Indexed Programs.

Part two discusses issues about indexing in major programs that provide monetary benefits, social security, Federal pensions, state and local pensions, medical benefits, cash and food assistance, veterans' and workman's compensation for Federal employees, unemployment insurance, and educational grants.

HJ 4653 .T38
(Tax shelters—United States—Periodicals;
Investments—Taxation—United States—Periodicals)

Allaire, Keith, et al. The Stranger Report (Shrewsbury, NJ: Robert A. Stranger and Co.)

This pamphlet, published quarterly, provides information on thousands of different companies that lie for the most part in the real estate sector. For each company, the ticker symbol, recent price, 52-week high and low, yield, market cap, and 12-month total return are all given.

HJ 8011 .W9
(Debts—External—Developing Countries—Statistics)

World Debt Tables: External Developing Countries, 1988–1989 (Washington, DC: The World Bank) 1988.

This source contains three volumes and the first is concerned with international lending to developing countries. Information is arranged by geographical area and according to high or low debt for each country. Volumes two and three contain statistical tables compiled from 111 countries that reported public external debt under the Debtor Reporting System of the World Bank that shows data for the last 10 years. Figures are rounded to the nearest $1,000,000. The tables also contain data on long-term debts and macroeconomic information. This edition include the balance owed to the World Bank and the shift in outstanding debts caused by currency and historical value changes.

HJ 8011 .W93
(Debts, External—Developing Countries—Statistics;
Finance—Developing Countries; International Finance)

Global Development Finance (Washington, DC: The World Bank)

This work, divided into two volumes, examines the past, present, and future of developing countries. Volume one, subtitled "Country Tables," provides financial figures for 137 countries. Some of the data provided include outstanding debt, principal repayments, interest payments, and debt service. Also given with Volume one is a list of acronyms and abbreviations, a section indicating the sources of data, and a table of countries. Volume two, subtitled "Analysis and Summary Tables," gives more actual reading than Volume one as it describes the plight that many developing countries find themselves in, along with economic recommendations on how such countries can get themselves out of debt. Also provided are sections chronicling the risks associated with the many different strategies that the countries can use to try to accomplish their goals.

HJ 8899 .E96 1987 (Debts—External—Developing Countries; International Finance)

Financing and External Debt of Developing Countries, 1987
Survey (Paris, France: Organisation for Economic Co-Operation
and Development)

This annual publication surveys the flow of financial resources to developing countries and lists their individual indebtedness. It also defines related terminology within the context. Statistical tables of aggregate resource flows are arranged geographically and by income group. Information from 140 countries is drawn from reports by the Organisation for Economic Co-operation and Development.

HJ 8899 .S78
(Debts, External—Developing Countries—Statistics)

Statistics on External Indebtedness: The Debt and other External
Liabilities of Developing CMEA and Certain other Countries and
Territories at End-December 1983 and End-December 1985
(Paris, France: Organisation for Economic Co-Operation
and Development)

This source presents data on debt and liabilities of developing countries according to totals borrowed. Data was compiled by both the Bank for International Settlement and the OECD. Debts include money borrowed by governments or government organizations, guaranteed or insured buyers' and suppliers' credits. Each table presents the following data: official development assistance, that is, money appropriated by federal, state and local governments; nonbank trade claims, including export credits, long- and short-term credits, except those by banks; bank claims, defined as guaranteed or insurers' buyers' credits; private bonds and nonguaranteed credits (intercompany loans); loans given by non-OECD creditors; and multilateral concessional loans that are below market rates and combined with IMF trust funds.

HJ 9777 .A1 C67
(Finance, Public—Accounting—Standards—United States—Periodicals; Local Finance—Accounting—Standards—United States—Periodicals)

Codification of Governmental Accounting and Financial Reporting Standards (Stamford, CT: Governmental Accounting Standards Board)

This source outlines and explains the basic guidelines to governmental accounting principles as they differ from commercial accounting principles. The guidelines accord with the standards set by the National Council on Governmental Accounting and the Governmental Accounting Standards Board. These standards are set by the acceptance of practices by accountants, administrators, public finance operators, and tax auditors.

HJ 9801 .H24 (Finance, Public—United States—Accounting—Handbooks, Manuals, etc.)

Apostolou, Nicholas G. and D. Larry Crumbley, Eds. Handbook of Governmental Accounting and Finance, 2nd Ed. (New York: Wiley) 1992.

This source provides information and new ideas to improve governmental accounting and financial management practices. This source is divided into five sections: governmental environment and general principles observed by federal, state, and local governments; governmental accounting processes and various fund and account groups; standard management practices (budgeting, cash management, internal controls) and repurchase agreements, infrastructure financing and cost evaluation, enhancing local government revenue and controlling local government expenditures; how internal and external auditing can be used to improve financial management of cities; and the effective methods of computing tax revenue sources for federal, state, and local governments, evaluation of government performance, and the future course of governmental accounting. This source contains many charts and some sample forms. A list of sources and suggested references is provided at the end of every chapter. There is an index that lists phrases by the first noun in the phrase, acronyms are spelled out, and some "see" references are used.

HJ 9801 .S34 (Finance, Public—Accounting; Intergovernmental Fiscal Relations)

Schermann, Kenneth R. Governmental Financial Reporting Model
(Norwalk, CT: Government Accounting Standards
Board of the Financial Accounting Foundation) 1994.

This source is the proposal of the Government Accounting Standards Board for comments on proposed financial reporting models. The source is intended to give and individuals knowledge of the project so that they may make suggestions at any of the public hearings or through the form provided in the book. This source is most useful to those with a knowledge of financial reporting models and users of financial reports. This source provides a history of the financial reporting model project, gives an overview of the project, and discusses the key features of both proposed models. Many charts are used throughout the text.

HJ 9816 .I62
(Finance, Public—United States—States—Accounting)

Inventory of Current State Government Accounting and Reporting
Practices (Lexington, KY: The Council of State Governments)
1980.

This source presents the results of a 226-page survey of the accounting methods used by each state. It is intended for use by government officials, those issuing credits, and constituents. Topics covered include fund accounting and fund structure, basis of accounting, accounting for assets, accounting for liabilities, accounting for equities, budgetary–accounting relationships, and financial reporting.

HM—SOCIOLOGY (GENERAL)

HM 263 .O27 (Public Relations Consultants—United States—Directories; Public Relations Consultants—Directories)

O'Dwyer's Directory of Public Relations Firms (New York:
J. R. O'Dwyer Co.)

This directory lists over 2100 public relations firms across the United States and abroad. The first index of public relations firms is arranged alphabetically by the name of the firm, the second is arranged by country, and the third index provides the clients of the listed firms. The text is supplemented by statistical tables, dealing with firm rankings and areas of specialization, and a list of new firms added to the directory.

HQ—THE FAMILY, MARRIAGE, AND WOMEN

HQ 536 .S82 (Family—United States—Statistics; United States—Statistics, Vital)

Chadwick, Bruce A. and Tim B. Heaton, eds. Statistical Handbook on the American Family (Phoenix, AZ: Oryx Press) 1992.

This source gives statistical information on marriage, quality of marriage and family life, divorce, children, sexual attitudes and behavior and contraceptive use, living arrangements and kinship ties, working women, wives and mothers, family violence, and elderly families for American families. The book is divided into sections with each section having a one- to two-page introduction and the rest of the section consisting of charts. Each chart is labeled with the question asked, the group responding, the total number responding, and a source citation. The index lists phrases by the first noun in the phrase and "see"/"see also" references are used.

HQ 1064 .U5 S78 (Aged—United States—Statistics; Aging—United States—Handbooks, Manuals, etc.)

Schick, Frank L. and Renee Schick, Eds. Statistical Handbook on Aging Americans (Phoenix, AZ: Oryx Press) 1994.

This source provides access to statistical information on demographics, social characteristics, health status, employment, economic conditions, and expenditures of the elderly. Also provided is a guide to relevant statistical information resources, both public and private. Addresses or phone numbers are provided for all. This source also contains a glossary of terms used within the book and an index that spells out acronyms, cross-references, and provides "see" references. The bulk of the source is divided into sections, each with a one- to two-page introduction and the rest charts. All charts are labeled and the source of the information is cited.

HQ 1154 .W93 (Women—Statistics)

The World's Women, 1970–1990: Trends and Statistics (New York: United Nations) 1991.

This source provides an overview of all the world's women from the developed regions, Africa, Latin America and the Caribbean, and Asia and the Pacific. It shows the status of women in families and households, public life and leadership, education and training, health and childbearing, human settlements and the environment, and women's work and the economy through charts and graphs. This source aims to inform people of the contributions of women and their status through the past 20 years. This source was compiled by the Statistical Office, Department of International Economic and Social Affairs of the United Nations Secretariat.

HQ 1420 .T12 (Women—United States—Statistics)

Taeuber, Cynthia Murray. Statistical Handbook on Women in America (Phoenix, AZ: Oryx Press) 1991.

This source provides access to statistical information on demographic characteristics, employment and economic status, health aspects, and social characteristics of women in America. Also provided is a guide to relevant statistical resources, a list of sources used, and an index. All acronyms are spelled out and "see"/"see also" references are used. The majority of the sources are divided into sections, each with a several page description of the section, with the rest being charts and graphs, each one labeled with the source cited.

HT—COMMUNITIES, CLASSES, AND RACES

HT 123 .A51 (Cities and Towns—United States—Ratings; Cities and Towns—United States—Statistics; Social Indicators—United States; Quality of Life—United States—Statistics; United States—Social Conditions—1980–)

Garoogian, Rhoda. America's Top Rated Cities: A Statistical Handbook (Boca Raton: Universal Reference Publications)

This work, divided into five geographical regions, looks to determine the cities that are the best place to live in the United States. Each region is divided into two sections with each city rated by both living and business conditions. Within each living conditions section, there are ratings for housing, climate, population, healthcare, education, recreation, and air and water quality. Within each business section, each city is rated in terms of its taxes, state and municipal finances, employment, and local businesses.

HT 167 .B12 (City planning—United States; Community Development, Urban—United States)

Bacow, Adele Fleet. Designing the City: A Guide for Advocates and Public Officials (Washington, DC: Island Press) 1995.

The objective of this work is to provide guidelines for citizens, activists, and policy makers who want to improve their community or the public environment. This manual helps people find successful strategies for working with developers and designers to change the way communities are designed and built.

HT 325. W26 (City promotion—History; Municipal Government—Public Relations—History)

Ward, Stephen Victor. Selling Places: The Marketing and Promotion of Towns and Cities 1850–2000 (London: E&FN Spon; New York, NY: Routledge) 1998.

This book explains the notions of place marketing and promotion and presents important differences in place selling traditions between nations and between individual towns and cities. The structure of the book identifies various stages in place selling: agricultural colonization, urban functional diversity, residential suburb, industrial town, and postindustrial city.

HT 334 U5 U93

Barlow, Diane and Steve Wasserman. Moving and Relocating Sourcebook (Detroit, MI: Omnigraphics, Inc.) 2001.

Moving and Relocating Sourcebook is designed for those who plan to move or to help others in planning a move. This book presents information on 100 major metropolitan areas in the United States. The work presents information figure and descriptions for those metropolitan areas. It was compiled from reports of federal, state, and local agencies. The methods used in compilation of the work includes searches in libraries as well as mail and telephone inquiries to organizations and institutions.

HT 395. E8 G56 (Regional Planning—Europe; Europe—Economic Policy)

Amin, Ash and N. J. Thrift, Globalization, Institutions and Regional Development in Europe (Oxford; New York: Oxford University Press) 1994.

This book is concerned with two distinct concepts. One deals with the possibility that the nation-state is losing its organizational importance because of the development of local, sociopolitical movements, and self-contained regional economies and because of the reinforcement of local identities fighting globalization. The other concept is that local and national identities are drawn into the pool of global forces.

HT 2721 .I631 1988 v.3 (Big business—History; Business Enterprises—History; Corporations—History)

Hast, Adele, ed. International Directory of Company Histories, Volume 3 (Chicago, IL: St. James Press)

This third volume in a five-volume reference series surveys both large international companies with at least $2,000,000,000 in sales and smaller companies who are leaders in their industries. Abstracts cover the subjects of health and personal care products, health care services, hotels, information technology, insurance, and manufacturing and materials. Companies are arranged alphabetically by these broad subject headings and alphabetically within each subject area. The articles, introduced with a picture of the company's logo, contain referential information as well as internal statistics as of fiscal year 1989–1990. The 740 to 1500 word entries, based on a combination of publicly accessible sources and data provided by the companies, offer clearly written accounts of the development of each industry from its origins to the present.

　　A table of contents precedes each subject area, and a short bibliography, containing recent and older sources in English and other languages, follows each signed article. Articles written in a foreign language list both the author and the translator. Additionally, each volume contains both a cumulative index of companies and persons as well as information about the contributors and advisors to the volume. The original five-volume series has recently been updated in a sixth and seventh volume issued in 1992 and 1993.

HV—SOCIAL PATHOLOGY, SOCIAL AND PUBLIC WELFARE, AND CRIMINOLOGY

HV 91.S16 (Charities—United States; Nonprofit Organizations—United States; Human Services—United States; Public Welfare—United States)

Salamon, Lester M. America's Nonprofit Sector: A Primer (New York, NY: Foundation Center) 1999.

This work examines the scope, scale, and structure of America's nonprofit sector, aiming to explain its role in America's life. The book is constructed in such a manner as to progressively answer questions about the nature of the nonprofit organizations, their funding, government's involvement with them and the role they play in the fields such as health care and education.

HV97.A3T12 (Endowments—United States—Directories; Corporations—Charitable Contributions—United States—Directories)

Taft Corporate Giving Directory: Comprehensive Profiles of America's Corporate Foundations and Corporate Charitable Giving Programs (Washington, DC: The Taft Group, An International Thomson Publishing Co.)

The *Corporate Giving Directory* assists development officers and others seeking charitable support for nonprofits by providing corporation-reported information about corporate foundations and corporate giving programs. The directory is arranged alphabetically by sponsoring company and whether the contributions are given by a foundation or directly by the corporation.

Included in each entry on the corporation/foundation are eighteen categories of information including: name of corporation and foundation, sales profits, contact people, types of grants, other types of support, granting priorities, typical recipients, location of the company operations and where the company gives money, the philosophy of the company/foundation, how to approach the foundation for funding, how granting decisions are made, restrictions on grantees, as well as recent giving profiles and recent grants.

Twelve indexes assist in identifying grantors. They include indexes by company headquarters locations(by state), operating locations, locations of grant recipients, grant types, nonmonetary support types, and recipient types. In addition, biographical information is provided for officers and directors of the companies including indexes by names, places of birth, alma maters, corporate affiliations, and nonprofit affiliations.

J—POLITICAL SCIENCE

J 2000 .B8

Monthly Bibliography of Selected Articles, United Nations Library

This source is published in two parts. Part one is the United Nations Library acquisitions list that contains books, official documents, and serials. It also serves as a current awareness list of materials relevant to the programs of the UN office. The bibliography section provides full citations. Citations are followed by three indexes: personal and corporate author index, subject index that includes geographical terms, and a title index.

Part two includes a selective list of articles from 700 periodicals indexed at the United Nations Library in Geneva and New York. It also has current information on periodical literature and contributors to collective works of interest to the United Nations and the international community. Two call numbers are supplied for each entry, one for the Geneva location and one for the New York location. Entries are followed by three indexes; personal and corporate author index, subject index and title index. The January issue provides a list of periodicals analyzed during the previous year.

JA—POLITICAL SCIENCE (GENERAL)

JA 51 .S8 (Political Science—Periodicals)

The Statesman's Year-Book (New York: St. Martin's Press)

This reference guide reports on the major historical events and statistics of the world's countries on a yearly basis. Part one focuses on international organizations including, the United Nations, various European organizations, and many other global councils. Part two provides an alphabetical list of the countries of the world. Each entry includes information on the history, boundaries, population, climate, government, constitution, the capital, defense, international relations, the economy, energy, natural resources, industry, overseas economic relations, communications, the social system, diplomatic representatives, a bibliography, and a human development index ranking that rates the country's overall standard of living. The text is supplemented by a chronology of the years major events, statistical tables comparing the production of different crops and oil of various countries, an addenda, a list of weights and measures, conversion units, a product index, a person index, and a index of international organizations and places.

JA 73 .G95 (Political Sciences—Research—Handbooks, Manuals, etc.; Social Sciences—Research—Handbooks, Manuals, etc.; Social Sciences—Research—Bibliography; Social Sciences—Research—Information Services)

Guide to Resources and Services (Ann Arbor, MI: Inter-University Consortium for Political and Social Research)

This reference book provides an introduction to the publications and services provided by the Inter-university Consortium for Political and Social Research

(ICPSR). ICPSR provides social science data bases available on the computer, training techniques in quantitative analysis, and other resources for social scientists to be able to work more easily with advanced technology. The text is composed of three indexes of data and reference collections. The first index lists each data collection arranged numerically by its catalog number, the second index lists each data collection alphabetically by title, and the third index is arranged by the name(s) of the researcher(s). Each collection entry includes a brief summary of its contents, the subject being studied, the sampling, the extent of the collection, data format, processing steps, file structure, number of cases and variables, length of the record, and a list of related publications. The data included in these collections come from more than 130 countries and is obtained through attitudinal surveys, census records, election results, international exchanges, and legislative reports.

JK—POLITICAL INSTITUTIONS AND PUBLIC ADMINISTRATION

JK 6 .G61 (State Government—United States—Directories; Local Government—United States—Directories; State Government—United States—Telephone Directories; Local Government—United States—Telephone Directories; United States—Politics and Government—Directories; United States—Politics and Government—Telephone Directories)

The Government Directory of Addresses and Telephone Numbers (Detroit, MI: Omnigraphics) 1992.

This one-volume comprehensive directory compiles the addresses and telephone numbers of federal, state, county, and local government offices in the United States. Most recently published as a 1994 edition, the directory is divided into four sections. The first section covers federal office listings in detail, including the executive branch, cabinet departments, and administrative agencies. Congress is also covered in this section, including listings for the Senate, House of Representatives, and joint committees, among others.

The second section covers federal regional offices. Addresses and telephone numbers are given for regional offices of cabinet departments, administrative agencies, Congress, and the court system. Regional maps are included, displaying which areas of the country are covered by particular regional offices.

The third section lists state government offices while the fourth covers all city and county offices. The main office address is given for the smallest cities and the directory also lists several departments and agencies for larger cities.

Addresses in this directory are easy to locate because each of the four directory sections offers a quick reference guide at the beginning and a keyword index at the end. This source does not provide the office holder's name though.

JK421.A3 (United States—Executive Departments; United States—Politics and Government—Handbooks, Manuals, etc.)

United States Government Manual (Washington, DC: Office of the Federal Register)

The United States Government Manual is the official handbook of the government with information on agencies of the legislative, executive, and judicial branches of government as well as many international organizations in which the United States participates, quasi-official agencies, government corporations and boards, commissions, and committees. Each entry usually provides a brief description of the agency's purpose, programs, activities and history, a list of the principal officials, and its legislative or executive authority. Entries on departments in the executive branch provide an organizational chart as well.

In addition to the descriptions, the Manual has an organizational chart of the United States government, an appendix identifying the Standard Federal Regions used by government departments, a list of common government abbreviations and acronyms, and list of terminated and transferred agencies.

The Manual has an index that includes names of officials and officers of agencies. Lists of senators and representatives are in the body of the Legislative Branch description. Judges are listed in the judicial Section. A Subject/Agency index and an index of agencies in the Code of Federal Regulations are also provided.

JK 1011 (United States Congress—Registers; United States Congress—Biography; United States Congress—Directories)

Official Congressional Directory (Washington: G. P. O.)

This annual publication contains information on the past year's congressional proceedings. The directory includes brief biographies of the senators and representatives along with their addresses and phone numbers, a list of committee assignments, legislative commissions, and government departments and agencies, an overview of the executive office and its affairs, information on the press galleries, and a brief history of the District of Columbia along with a list of its current elected officials. The text is supplemented by a name index, maps of the congressional districts, and a list of foreign embassies.

JK 2403 .B72 (State Governments—Yearbooks)

The Book of the States (Chicago, IL: The Council of State Governments and the American Legislators' Association)

This reference book provides an overview of current information relating to state constitutions, state executive, judicial, and legislative branches, state campaigns and elections, state finances, state regulation and management, state programs, intergovernmental affairs, and state pages that contain a wide range of statistical information. Each section includes several essays and numerous data tables relating to the subject heading.

JN 94 .A792 P7 D57 1991 (Pressure Groups—European Economic Community Countries—Directories)

Philip, Alan B., ed. Directory of Pressure Groups in the European Community (Essex, UK: Longman Group UK) 1991.

Organizations that influence the work of the European Community are detailed in this source. This includes lobbying groups and other organizations that have at least some influence on or interest in the European Community. In total, there are more than 800 groups and over 200 consultancies listed. The information is supplemented by a variety of other sources and research.

In this single-volume book, the organizations are arranged by sector (agriculture, food and drink, industry type, etc.) as well as into two main sections. The first main section is EC-wide pressure groups, such as trade and professional associations and other nongovernmental associations. European organizations involved in EC policy making, such as research institutes, government agencies, think tanks, etc., make up the second main section.

Entries include the acronym, name, address and telephone number, status, date of foundation, officers, aims, organization and structure, resources, scope of membership, history and achievements, links with EC institutions, affiliations, committees, activities, statistics, member organizations, contact person and as assessment.

JS—LOCAL GOVERNMENT AND MUNICIPAL GOVERNMENT

JS 48 .C34 (Local Government—Dictionaries—Polyglot; Business—Dictionaries—Polyglot; Dictionaries, Polyglot)

Cassell Multilingual Dictionary of Local Government and Business (London; New York: Cassell) 1993.

This dictionary provides translations for almost 3500 government and business terms in English, French, and German. The French and German nouns are followed by "m" or "f" to indicate their gender. The text is intended for government officials and businesspeople who work within the European Community. Included is a list of local government departments translated into the three languages and a bibliography.

JS 141 .M861 (Municipal Government—United States—Directories; County Government—United States—Directories; Local Government—United States—Directories)

Mayberry, et al., Eds. Municipal Yellow Book (New York, NY: Monitor Publishing)

Intended as a who's who of selected leading local governments at the county and city level, this reference source identifies and gives addresses and telephone numbers for over 15,000 elected and administrative officials. Published semiannually, the summer 1993 issue contains entries for 130 cities, 115 counties, and 21 operating authorities selected on the basis of the 1990 Census Bureau data. At the beginning of each issue, the editor makes note of important changes that have occurred since the previous edition.

The text is arranged in three sections: cities, counties, and authorities (e.g., Washington Metropolitan area transit authority, Nebraska Public Power District), and each section is ordered alphabetically by city, county, or authority name. A typical entry lists elected officials first and then departments in alphabetical order and would contain, for example, the name, address, and telephone numbers of the mayor, city manager, city attorney, police chief, fire chief, and many more. Fax numbers are also given when available.

The publication also has three indexes. The geographic index lists contents according to state. The population index lists the top 100 cities and counties according to 1990 Census Bureau data. Finally, the staff index lists individual officials alphabetically by name and gives the exact title and department for each.

There are no illustrations or maps.

JX—INTERNATIONAL LAW

JX 1977 .A1 U6 (International Relations—Periodicals; United Nations—Periodicals)

UN Chronicle (New York, NY: United Nations Office of Public Information)

This periodical source, formerly called the *UN Monthly Catalog*, is published quarterly in Arabic, Chinese, English, French, Russian, and Spanish. It reports on the activities of the United Nations and the problems they deal with, ranging from food and health to the world economy. The journal is indexed in the following serials: Reader's Guide to Periodical Literature, Social Science Index, Magazine Index (1977–), Magazine Article Summaries CD-ROM (Jan 1989–), Middle East Abstract Index, and Peace Research Abstract Journal (1975–1981).

K—LAW

K 54 .W47 1985 (Law—Dictionaries; English Language—Dictionaries—Polyglot)

West's Law and Commercial Dictionary in Five Languages, 2 Volumes (St. Paul, MN: West Publishing Company) 1985.

This dictionary is the first of its kind and is intended to serve the needs of attorneys and business executives. With companies doing increasing transnational business, this lexicon is useful in alleviating the misunderstandings that can follow from working with foreign parties, documents and transactions. It includes the qualities of a law dictionary and combines them with a multitude of commercial terms to provide access to the legal and commercial systems of not only the United States but also Germany, Spain, France, and Italy. The work translates English terms into foreign ones and also contains hundreds of foreign entries, defined in English. In addition to defining legal and commercial terms, it can be used as a starting point for further research, as quick reference for understanding foreign legal documents or technical literature, and as a guide to drafting legal documents for foreign clients. The two volumes are alphabetized according to the English entries. Each entry provides an understandable definition of the term. The equivalent terms in German, Spanish, French, and Italian follow the definition of each English entry. The publisher also offers four separate bilingual dictionaries, covering German, Spanish, French, and Italian, to accompany the dictionary. Appendices provide tables of legal abbreviations commonly used in these languages and other useful information such as a list of countries and capitals of the world, an international telephone code directory, a chart showing air distances between some major world cities and a table of weights and measures for metric conversion.

K 1005.4 .I61 (International Business Enterprises; Commercial Law; Foreign Trade Regulation)

Sealy, Leonard S. International Corporate Procedures
(Bristol, UK: Jordan & Sons, Ltd.)

This three-volume source provides information relating to the business scene in other countries with different legal environments. The main focus is on companies. The material within was prepared by area experts and was then edited in the United Kingdom to ensure consistency within the sections. This source aims to provide, in detail, day-to-day information needed in business and to give insight into the legal and institutional environments of other jurisdictions. This source covers formation procedures, accounting requirements, taxation system, and disclosure obligations. It does not aim to be academic or theoretical. Special terms are printed in the original language and followed by a literal translation. Two indexes are provided, one by subject and the other a listing of headings in numerical order. Comparative tables are also included.

K 1322 .A12 W18 (International Business Enterprises—Law and Legislation—Bibliography; Investments, Foreign—Law and Legislation—Bibliography; Investments, Foreign—Bibliography)

Wallace, Cynthia Day, Ed. Foreign Direct Investment and the Multinational Enterprise: A Bibliography (Kluwer Academic Publishers) 1988.

This source intends to provide access to the large amount of information now available on foreign direct investment and multinational enterprise. The idea for this source grew out of another book the editor was writing and therefore focuses on legal, operational, and policy aspects of multinational enterprise. The source is broken down into subjects and the citations are arranged alphabetically within each section. Citations are entered under every relevant category to provide better access. This book contains no index or table of contents.

K 1530 .E33 (Foreign Licensing Agreements)

Ehrbar, Thomas J. Business International's Guide to International
Licensing: Building a Licensing Strategy for 14 Key Markets
Around the World (New York: McGraw-Hill) 1993.

This source provides licensing information on 14 developing markets (Argentina, Brazil, Mexico, Venezuela, Japan, South Korea, Taiwan, Thailand, China, India, Czechoslovakia, Hungary, Poland, and Russia). Each country has its own section in which background on the area is given along with experiences other companies have had in those countries. Charts are included. There are three appendices: what to include in a foreign licensing agreement, typical licensing agreements for Argentina and Brazil, and questions to ask when fixing a price on patents abroad. The index gives phrases by the first noun in the phrase and larger topics have subheadings.

K 3823 .O68 (International Economic Integration; International Economic Integration; International Economic Relations; Invisible Items of Trade)

Organisation for Economic Co-Operation and Development. Code
of Liberalisation of Current Invisible Operations (Paris, France:
Organisation for Economic Co-Operation and Development) 1993.

This source provides the text of the OECD *Code of Liberalisation of Current Invisible Operations* divided into the following subsections: undertakings with regard to current invisible operations, procedure, terms of reference, and miscellaneous applicable information. There are four annexes listing current invisible operations (and notes), reservations to the code, and the decision of the council for the code taken by states of the United States and provinces of Canada. A list of council acts (with dates) are included.

K 4440 .A13 A62
(Foreign Exchange—Law and Legislation—Periodicals)

Exchange Arrangements and Exchange Restrictions
(Washington, DC: International Monetary Fund)

This source provides a description of exchange and trade systems of individual member countries of the International Monetary Fund (IMF). For each country the following information is provided: exchange agreements, administration of control, prescription of currency, resident and nonresident accounts, imports and import payments, payments for invisibles, exports and export procedures, proceeds from invisibles, capital, gold, and changes during the previous year (1993). There is an appendix of selected trade measure introduced (and eliminated) on a Euro Union-wide basis during 1993. There is also a chart of summary features of exchange and trade systems in member countries. A list of abbreviations is provided.

K 4473.2 .U58
(Taxation, Double—United States—Treaties;
Tax Evasion (International Law))

Doernberg, Richard L. and Kees van Raad, Eds. US Tax Treaties (Deventer, Netherlands: Kluwer Law and Taxation Publishers) 1991.

This source provides the text of 20 U.S. tax treaties with other nations intended to prevent double taxation and the protocol provisions attached to those treaties. It is intended to be useful to lawyers and those in business as well as students. Four model treaties are included as is commentary on those models. Also included are two treaties addressing the exchange of information between nations that is necessary for the enforcement of domestic law. There are many charts and tables. The countries whose treaties are included are Australia, Belgium, Canada, China, Egypt, France, Germany, India, Ireland, Italy, Japan, Korea, Luxembourg, the Netherlands, the Philippines, Spain, Sweden, Switzerland, the USSR, and the United Kingdom.

K 4505.4 .I38 (Income Tax—Rates and Tables;
(Social Security—Handbooks, Manuals, etc.)

Individual Taxes, A Worldwide Summary (New York: Price Waterhouse Center for Transnational Taxation)

This source is intended for expatriate employees and the multinational employers. Tax information on 116 countries and territories is provided along with a sample tax calculation. This source is intended to be a general guide, not to provide detailed rules. For every geographical region a Price Waterhouse tax manager contact is given. Each section covers territoriality and residence, gross income, deductions, tax credits, other taxes, tax administration, and tax rates. This source has no appendix or index.

KF 190 .C67 1993 (Law Firms—United States—Directories)

West's Legal Directory Corporate Guide to U.S. Law Firms (St. Paul, MN: West Publishing Company)

Serving as a print version of *West's Legal Directory on WESTLAW*, and containing additional information not available in the electronic format, this directory is produced to assist chief legal officers of the world's leading corporations in selecting legal counsel for virtually any short- or long-term need. The information contained is submitted by the top 500 law firms in the United States as identified by various independent sources. The *Directory* is organized into sections based on geographic location, practice area, and alphabetical listing. The areas of practice section is divided into 24 broad categories of law. The geographic section is arranged alphabetically by state. A lawyer can be located by consulting the appropriate geographic or practice area section. Specific information about the lawyer or firm is given in the alphabetical index, a comprehensive list of every firm in the *Directory* alphabetically arranged by firm name. A basic listing consists of law firm name, address of main office and any branches, telephone number and electronic mail numbers. A professional profile, offered for some firms, contains names of contact person, number of attorneys, honors and awards, representative clients and types of cases, areas of practice and descriptive text describing the firm's history, mission or specialized activities. A brief listing of specific state restrictions on lawyer advertising with respect to specialties appears at the end of the volume. Also included is a section containing straightforward instructions for retrieving additional information on *West's Legal Directory on WESTLAW.*

KF480 .A955 1992 (Handicapped—Legal Status, Laws, etc.—United States; Handicapped—Employment—Law & Legislation—United States)

Accommodating Disabilities: Business Management Guide
(Chicago, IL: Commerce Clearing House)

Intended as a guide for business, this two-volume loose-leaf service, prepared by the CCH Business Editors, gives detailed coverage of all the information necessary to understand the complicated federal requirements for providing access for people with disabilities to employment opportunities, public accommodations, commercial facilities, and transportation services. The *Guide* is referred to by the publisher as a service, is updated at least every other month, and includes a monthly publication, *Accommodating Disabilities Newsletter*, which highlights current changes in the law and focuses on "hot topics." Volume 1 contains explanatory text and related laws, regulations, and guidelines. Volume 2 reprints agency manuals, forms, policies, job descriptions, access guidelines, and surveys. Footnotes contain citations to relevant cases, statutes, and regulations. Arrangement of the material follows the standard CCH procedure of Divisions instead of Chapters, and paragraph numbers instead of pages. Tab guides provide quick access. The suggested method of locating desired information is to consult the Topical Index leading to the appropriate Explanation and possibly law or regulation, then consult the Cumulative Index to New Developments and then New Developments. Other methods of access include the Volume Table of Contents, Division Table of Contents, and Questions and Answers at the front of each Division providing quick review of high points of the law, regulations, decisions, rulings, and comments. Special features of the work include Checklists for Compliance, Accommodations Associations—a list of organizations and agencies with addresses, Employment Issues—with examples, sample compliance surveys, Agency manuals and handbooks, State Law Correlator—overviews state legislation, New Developments, and Abbreviations and Citations.

KF641.5 .B87 1991 (Corporations—Taxation-Law and Legislation—United States; Tax Planning—United States)

Business Transactions: Tax Analysis (New York, NY: Research Institute of America)

This three-volume loose-leaf set is a complete and authoritative analysis of the tax rules governing major business transactions such as forming, acquiring, recapitalizing, selling, and liquidating a business. Material is arranged by subject with chapters divided by guide cards with identifying tabs. Each chapter contains a detailed analysis of the tax rules relating to a particular area. Both current and prior law is analyzed with footnotes making reference in the text to IRS Code and Regulation sections. To locate information on a desired topic a subject approach can be employed utilizing the tabs on the chapter divisions; volume spines show general contents. Each chapter begins with a broad and then detailed Reference Table of Chapter Discussion pointing to the information sought and possible related information. A Topic Index can also be used to find information; a Current Topic Index is used to find new material. Finally, the Finding Tables list citations to IRS Code and Regulation sections, and cases and rulings with appropriate paragraphs in the work. A Current Matter section in Volume 1 holds new material which is issued biweekly.

KF801 .S58 1993 (Contracts—United States)

Siviglia, Peter. Commercial Agreements: A Lawyer's Guide to Drafting and Negotiating (Rochester, NY: Lawyer's Cooperative Publishing Co.) 1993.

Although written for attorneys, the author's straightforward approach and plain language make this work useable by the average person seeking some practical help in connection with drafting legal documents. Separated into Part 1, Drafting, and Part 2, Negotiating, each chapter contains understandable explanations and helpful hints on drafting legal documents. The work begins with a discussion of the basic elements of drafting legal documents and moves to separate chapters on the creation of special documents, e.g., promissory notes, security agreements, employment contracts, license agreements, and corporate authorizations. Part 2 is a brief exposition of the finer points of negotiating notes, contracts, and agreements. An index and table of authorities can be used to locate specific information. The publisher intends the volume to be supplemented by pocket parts to slip into the rear of the book.

KF 879 .A2 1978
(Commercial Law—United States; Commercial Law—States)

American Law Institute, National Conference on Commissions on Uniform State Laws, Uniform Commercial Code: Official Text, 1978 with Comments and Appendices Showing 1972 and 1977 Changes (Philadelphia, PA: The Institute)

This single-volume American business reference source is a comprehensive modernization of statutes relating to commercial transactions including sales, commercial paper, bank deposits and collections, letters of credit, bank transfers, warehouse receipts and other documents of title, investment securities, and secured transactions. In 1952 it replaced the former Uniform Laws relating to sales, conditional sales, negotiable instruments, warehouse receipts, bills of lading, stock transfers, and trust receipts. It has been revised in 1958, 1962, 1966, 1972, and 1977. The UCC, between 1958 and 1967, was enacted in all states, but Louisiana and the District of Columbia. Louisiana later enacted Articles 1–5, 7, and 8 out of the 11 articles.

Arrangement is by numbered Article. Each article deals with a different commercial transaction topic such as sales or commercial paper. Within each article are numbered parts and within those are numbered sections. Each section covers a single rule about the commercial transaction. In each section, there is the official comment, prior uniform statutory provision, changes, purpose of changes and new matter, cross references, and definitional cross references. Special features include a preliminary part that lists the permanent Editorial Board, reports from current and prior Editorial Boards, forewords to prior official texts, and tables of jurisdictions that have adopted the UCC and prior Uniform acts displaced by the UCC. Appendices list the 1977 and 1972 amendments to the UCC.

KF879.527 .H38 1982
(Commercial Law—United States—States)

Hawkland, William. Uniform Commercial Code Series (Deerfield, IL: Clark Boardman Callaghan)

This nine-volume set has grown to 13 separate loose-leaf binders as new material, issued periodically, has accumulated concerning this substantial body of codified law applicable to commercial transactions. The author notes that while there is a great quantity of material published each year in books and law reviews on the Uniform Commercial Code, nothing has provided the practitioner with a systematic section-by-section analysis of the Code. This treatise, written with the assistance of seven additional contributors, provides such an analysis. The work is arranged in numeric sections corresponding to the nine Articles of the UCC. Within each section the text of the Code section is quoted in full. Next, the Official Comments are included followed by State variations of the Code. Then, the specific Code section, and its meaning and relationship to the entire body of the Code, is discussed in full. The numbering system of the work follows that of the Code. The Articles are divided in each volume by guide cards with identifying tabs. Access to the material is obtained by use of a complete table of contents located at the beginning of Volume 1. Each volume contains a table of contents for the material contained therein. An index is found at the end of each Article. A master treatise index covering the entire set is located in the last volume. The spines of each binder give information on that volume's contents. Special features of this set include a comprehensive Concordance, functioning as an extremely detailed index, and Commentaries of the Permanent Editorial Board of the National Conference of Commissioners on Uniform State Laws and the American Law Institute.

KF 887 .R67 1981
(Commercial Law—United States—Dictionaries)

Ross, Martin J. & Ross, Jeffrey S. New Encyclopedic Dictionary of Business Law (Englewood Cliffs, NJ: Prentice-Hall, Inc.) 1981.

Intended by the authors to edify a general audience, this dictionary gives simplified and understandable definitions of legal words and phrases from Abandoned Property to Zoning Ordinances. In addition to being a lexicon, the work doubles as an encyclopedia, presenting sometimes lengthy explanations of legal principles in a quick-find, alphabetical arrangement. Entries might also include cross references, illustrations or sample specimen forms.

KF889 .S67 (Commercial Law—United States; Trade Regulation—United States; Corporation Law—United States; Investments, Foreign—Law and Legislation—United States)

Spires, Jeremiah J. Doing Business in the United States
(New York, NY)

This comprehensive statement of the business law of the United States is intended to serve as a kind of guidebook to foreign participants in the American economy, whether factory or business owners, securities investors or exporters to the United States. Mr. Spires, of the New York Bar, has been assisted by over two dozen other contributors in the production of the work. New developments are covered by twice annual supplements inserted into the front of the loose-leaf binders. Use of the Table of Contents or Index will allow the reader to locate information in chapters which either broadly discuss certain legal areas or provide more detailed discussion. Volume 1 deals with government and the legal system, including general business law. Volume 2 discusses some specific areas, e.g., business taxation and the Uniform Commercial Code. Volume 3 covers the regulation of business in general, while Volumes 4 and 5 explain business organizations. Volume 6 covers certain regulated businesses, e.g., banks. A synopsis of each chapter appears at its beginning. A helpful Glossary is located in the last volume, just prior to the detailed index.

KF889.3 .L384 1985 (Commercial Law—United States—Miscellanea; Business Enterprises—United States—Miscellanea; Industrial Law and Legislation—United States—Miscellanea)

Hughes, Robert B. Legal Compliance Checkups: Business Clients (Deerfield, IL: Callaghan & Co.)

The author, with several other contributors, devised this set to be the basis of a legal checkup with an emphasis on helping a practitioner to assist a client in preventing problems. Attorneys as general counsel for a business client, attorneys who specialize in the business area, new attorneys and attorneys who want to keep their own business affairs in order are considered the audience. Material is arranged by subject, chosen by the writers to represent those areas where business clients are likely to experience problems. Through an "active," off-the-shelf use of the work the practitioner can help a client to identify problems, then recommend measures for solution and prevention. Where more depth is required the reader is referred to more complete texts. A systems approach is advocated; each chapter begins with both client and attorney ques-

9.33333

tionnaires to produce facts and promote legal analysis. Explanatory text follows. The volumes, which are updated annually, contain chapters on such topics as labor relations, professional incorporation, government contracts, securities, patents, product liability, and computer software agreements. Tab guides separate chapters. A comprehensive index is contained in the last volume.

KF974 .B37 (Banking Law—United States)

Schlichting, William. Banking Law (New York, NY: Mathew Bender & Co., Inc.)

Banking Law, an 11-volume set, grown with added material to 14 loose-leaf binders, presents the confusing array of statutes, agency regulations and financial institutions which forms the law of banking in the United States. The work covers the organization, operation, examination, regulation, powers, and liquidation of commercial banks; it discusses the legal requirements governing structural changes including branching, mergers and consolidations, and bank holding company formation, expansion and divestiture; and it examines the operations of commercial banks including transfers and negotiation of checks and notes, use of credit cards and electronic banking, and permissible loans and investments. Bank regulation, and the impact of federal securities and tax laws, is surveyed. The set is designed to enable attorneys and professionals representing or dealing with commercial banks to gain in-depth knowledge of banking law and keep abreast of frequent changes through periodic updates. The spines of the volumes reveal their basic contents which are arranged by subject and presented in chapters in a textual format with footnotes citing cases, statutes, and other authorities. A Complete Table of Contents appears in Volume 1; each volume contains its own Table of Contents. At the end of each chapter is a useful bibliography. Selected regulations are reprinted in appendices. The last volume contains the main methods of access: Table of Cases, Statutes and Rules, and a detailed index.

KF 1074 .A4 A52 (Stock Exchanges—Law and Legislation—United States; Securities—Listing—United States)

Company Guide: Rules and Policies Applicable to Companies with Securities Listed on the American Stock Exchange (New York, NY: American Stock Exchange) 1988.

This source is in a loose-leaf binder with tabbed dividers and provides access to the rules and policies applicable to companies with securities listed in the

American Stock Exchange (AMEX). It is divided into 11 sections: original listing requirements, additional listings requirements and procedures, disclosure policies, dividends and stock splits, accounting (annual and quarterly reports), shareholders meeting (approval and voting of proxies), transfer facilities (certificate requirements), treasury shares, suspension and delisting, and a guide to filing requirements. Also provided is an appendix of listing forms and emerging companies marketplace. The index utilizes "see" references and lists acronyms as themselves. The corner of each page bears the date it was last amended. The names and phone numbers of AMEX executives are provided. This source is directed at those who wish to apply to be listed in the AMEX and details the steps that must be taken to do so.

KF 1078 .A6 C73 (Mutual Funds—United States; Mutual Funds—Law and Legislation—United States)

CCH Mutual Funds Guide: Continuing Guidance on Federal and State Controls Governing the Operation of Mutual Funds and Investment Companies (Chicago: Commerce Clearing House, Inc.)

The *Commerce Clearing House Mutual Funds Guide* is a loose-leaf service in two basic volumes, plus a series of binders for new developments by chronological period. Its purpose is to provide a convenient resource to keep subscribers abreast of matters affecting the mutual fund industry. Updates in the form of new Guide Report loose-leaf pages are received by subscribers every other week. Each Guide Report is arranged so that new pages either replace existing pages or are added to the contents of the volumes. When warranted by the significance of particular developments, Special Reports of the Guide are issued. The Guide is designed to blend federal and state regulatory requirements with practical explanatory guidance.

Volume One begins with a section entitled "How to use this Guide." A Topical Index, Finding Lists, and Case Table follow. The remainder of Volume One presents information, arranged by topics, intended to provide answers on problems ranging from initial planning, formation, and organizing of mutual funds to day-to-day operating details. Volume Two contains texts of federal statutes, regulations, forms, and interpretative releases on mutual funds. Applicable state requirements are outlined in helpful charts. Volume Two also contains a cumulative index to new developments.

Subsequent binders, each spanning a range of two or more years, cover new developments. Each contains an alphabetical Case Table, No-Action and Interpretative Letters, and finally Rulings and Decisions—including Facts of the case, Statutes of Limitation, Damages, and Opinions in full text.

KF1335 B87 1963 (Corporation Law—United States; Partnership—United States)

Cavitch, Solman. Business Organizations with Tax Planning
(New York, NY: Mathew Bender & Co., Inc.)

This multivolume set has grown over the years, with the addition of periodical updates creating parts and subparts, to nearly a hundred loose-leaf binders. Each of the 19 volumes was prepared by a separate author, assisted by over 20 additional contributors. The set is written for the business practitioner to provide a pragmatic tool covering Federal taxes, finance, and other pertinent matters of the broad field of business organizations; the approach has been to meet the day-to-day problems of the attorney advising business clients. The advantages and disadvantages of various forms of business organization are considered with anticipation of the problems which may arise under each and possible solutions to those problems. A Table of Contents appears at the front of each volume and a general table covering all volumes is contained in Volume 1. Each volume's general contents is listed on the spine. An index appears at the end of a series of volumes which cover a topic, e.g., Trade Secrets. Appendices include the text of relevant state statutes and commentaries on the topic. Sample forms appear throughout the work. A special feature of this set, contained in a separate binder, is a regular monthly update, the *Antitrust Report*, giving current developments in this area of law.

KF1384 .F55 (Corporation Law—United States)

Fletcher, William Meade. Fletcher Cyclopedia of the Law of
Private Corporations (Deerfield, IL: Callaghan & Company)

Because of its length of publication and definitive and scholarly coverage of the field of private corporations, this work is considered a classic in the field and is often cited for its authority. Its original 20 casebound volumes have swelled to 36. The set is kept up to date by annual supplements of pocket parts and occasional replacement volumes. A Table of Chapters for the complete set appears in Volume 1. Detailed and exhaustive coverage of all aspects of corporations, from the commonplace to the arcane, is contained in 67 separate chapters. The explanatory text is heavily footnoted with references to case citations. Volume 19, the *Corporate Practice Deskbook*, gives nuts-and-bolts information about organizing and operating a corporation, and its books and records. An Appendix, containing forms, and a Glossary, are included. Volume 20 is a comprehensive index.

KF1414 .R52 1992 (Private Companies—United States)

Ribstein, Larry. Ribstein and Keating on Limited Liability
Companies (Colorado Springs, CO: Shepard's/McGraw-Hill)

While the Limited Liability Company form of business organization is only a couple decades old, it has accounted for one of the fastest growing areas of business law. This treatise gives full coverage to all aspects of this area. The work is updated with supplements semiannually; the authors acknowledge they expect to replace much of what they have written because of frequent changes in this very dynamic field. Volume 1 contains the explanatory text, grouped into heavily footnoted chapters covering an overview of business law aspects, formation of the Limited Liability Company, capital structure and contributions, distributions, ownership and transfer, management and control, fiduciary duties, litigation, dissolution, members' liability, foreign Limited Liability Companies, the effect of securities and bankruptcy laws, use of this form in particular transactions, and aspects of taxation. Volume 2 contains the Appendices with forms, an operation agreement, the Uniform Limited Liability Company Act and various state statutes. A Table of Contents, Summary and Detailed, appears at the beginning of Volume 1; a Table of Cases and Index are located at the end.

KF 1423 .Z9 B65

Block, Dennis J., Barton, Nancy E., and Radin, Stephen A. The
Business Judgement Rule: Fiduciary Duties of Corporate Directors
and Officers (Clifton, New Jersey: Prentice-Hall Law & Business)

This text includes discussions of recent decisions regarding duties of care and loyalty, prelitigation demand requirements in derivative litigation, termination of derivative litigation in cases in which the demands were refused and in cases in which the demands were excused as well as directors' indemnification and officers' liability insurance.

KF 1428.A6 C24 CCH 1993
(Corporation—Finance—Law and Legislation—United
States; Corporation—Taxation—Law
and Legislation—United States)

Capital Change Reporter (Illinois: Commerce Clearing House)

The weekly *Capital Changes Reporters* gives detailed information on the effects of federal taxes on security holders and debt structure. It also provides summaries of corporate war casualty recoveries, liquidating distributions, interest on bonds acquired "flat," and nontaxable/capital gain cash dividends. In general, the Reports give figures and facts to compute the gain or loss to the security holder because of capital changes and show the difference in the new basis of securities received and the basis of securities held. It then uses these data to calculate the gain or loss on the subsequent sale of these securities. Because all information is cumulated from the date of incorporation of the specific corporation.

KF 1439.F93 1993
(Securities, Privately Placed—United States;
Securities, Privately Placed—United States—Forms)

Brown, J. Robert. Raising Capital: Private Placement Forms
& Techniques (Englewood Cliffs, NJ: Prentice-Hall Law &
Business)

Raising Capital gives an overview of how the federal securities laws affect private placements. The book also provides forms of agreements and other types of documents as a guide to investment transactions. The book is divided into seven sections. The first discusses the formation of the entity. The second gives examples of investment agreements. The third contains types of instruments used to gain capital. The focuses of this section are on warrants, equity instruments, options, ranging from common stock and preferred stock. This section also has forms used to assist with corporate formalities in giving the instruments. The fourth discusses debt instruments. Besides the debt instruments, the section also discusses common instruments that have to do with debtor–creditor relationships. The fifth provides agreements among shareholders. The sixth discusses the effects of the Federal Securities Laws. This section includes exemptions, resales, and clauses that explain the registration rights of investors. Finally, the seventh section contains forms used in relation to the investment process.

KF1439 .S45 1995 (Securities—United States—Periodicals;
Investments—Law and Legislation—United States—
Periodicals; Corporation Law—United States—Periodicals)

Bloomenthal, Harold S. and Holme Roberts & Owen. Securities
Law Handbook (New York: C. Boardman)

The *Securities Law Handbook* presents an overview of American securities law and practice. The intent of this guide is to outline current securities law. It divides securities law into topical chapters, each of which examines a subsection of law or practice by citing laws, regulations, and court cases. The *Securities Law Handbook* is footnoted and has a general index and an alphabetical index to court cases cited in the text. Each subsection is numbered and listed in a detailed table of contents. The handbook is updated annually.

KF 1449. C76 (Disclosure of Information (Securities Law)—United States; Business Communication—United States—Handbooks, Manual, etc.; Corporation Law—United States; Stockholders—United States—Handbooks, Manuals, etc.)

Walton, S. Wesley and Brissman, P. Charles. Corporate Communications Handbook (New York: Clark Boardman Co.)

The *Handbook* focuses on "soft information" and predictive disclosures. The information on disclosure is complemented by additional Security Exchange Commissions pronouncements with respect to management discussion and analysis. The *Handbook* is divided into five sections. The first gives an overview of informal disclosure. The second deals with the legal issues of informal disclosures. The third discusses considerations in making a corporation's informal disclosure program. The fourth gives examples of different situations to demonstrate the principles of informal disclosure. Finally, the fifth section is the Appendices that provides forms and source materials.

The Handbook is a reference for persons responsible for dealing with informal disclosure. It is also designed as a resource for setting up a framework for the preparation and dissemination of informal disclosure.

KF1466 .K45 1990
(Family Corporations—United States; Family Corporations—Taxation—United States)

Kelley, Donald & Ludtke, David. Family Business Organization (Colorado Springs, CO: Shepard's/McGraw-Hill, Inc.)

This two-volume set, loose-leaf and updated annually, is intended to provide, for lawyers who have a business practice, a "how to" manual for the organization and maintenance of the family-oriented small business. While the subject matter applies to any group carrying on a business, the emphasis is on the family in business, and the structure of business ownership among members of a family. Coverage is given to the tax, state law, and practical aspects of the organization of the business, comparative legal entities, ongoing tax problems, practical maintenance of the ongoing business entity, future control, including sale to family members, and estate planning and administration of family business entities. Access to information is through the Tables of Contents, both Summary and Detailed, and a lengthy subject index at the end of Volume 2. An Appendix in each volume provides forms and tables. The chapters follow the familiar format of legal treatises, presenting a textual discussion of the law with footnotes making reference to statutes, cases, and other sections and authorities; each chapter ends with a list of sources for recommended reading directing the reader for further research in specialized legal problems of family business entities.

KF 1477 .A7 G48 1995 (Finance)

Gibson, Ronald J. and Black, Bernard S. The Law and Finance of Corporate Acquisitions (New York: The Foundation Press)

The second edition of this book related to corporate acquisitions is divided into four parts. Part I deals with financial theory, Part II with motives for acquisitions, Part III has discussions on friendly and hostile acquisitions, and Part IV covers noncorporate law planning. Legal concepts have been explained in more detail to make it more useful for business students.

KF1609 .C33 1981 (Competition, Unfair—United States; Trademarks—United States)

Callman, Rudolf. The Law of Unfair Competition, Trademarks and Monopolies (Wilmette, IL: Callaghan & Co.)

Mr. Callman wrote this six-volume treatise in 1945 to integrate the antitrust laws into the area of unfair competition and provide a fundamental theory of unfair competition law. And, although there are numerous case references for the practitioner, the approach of the work is primarily theoretical. In 1981 the set was thoroughly revised into the form in which it now exists. Divided into eight parts, the work covers basic concepts in Part 1, then moves to unfair advertising and pricing, unfair interference with a competitor's business, misappropriation of a competitor's values, unlawful conduct of a business, the law of trademarks and product simulation, parties, remedies and procedure, and international protection. An Appendix contains relevant Federal statutes, guidelines and regulations, treaties and international agreements, and sample pleadings. Volume 1 contains a Table of Contents for the complete set; a separate Table appears at the front of each volume. The quickest access to various sections is by use of the detailed Index in the last volume. Supplements, issued annually in yellow pages, are inserted into the front of each volume using the corresponding numbers of the sections they update.

KF1659 .A94 1989
(Small Business—Law and Legislation—United States)

Alberty, Steven C. Advising Small Businesses (Deerfield, IL: Clark Boardman Callaghan) 1988.

This three-volume set and its companion set, *Advising Small Businesses Forms*, are written for the practitioner who represents small businesses. Excluded from coverage are the aspects and problems of large, publicly held businesses. The work provides a pragmatic guide to the organization, operation, and termination of small businesses. Treated in detail is the selection of a form and the creation of an entity for the operation of a business, corporate formalities and operations, employee relations and compensation, and termination of interests in business. There is also an overview of such topics as insurance, antitrust, franchising, and intellectual property. References to other sources of information for further research are included. The companion volumes provide practice forms and checklists. The main set is organized into Volume 1, covering business entities and financing, Volume 2, covering corporate operations and business transactions, and Volume 3, dealing with employees and business terminations. Information on a topic can be found by using the Table of Contents or the Index, in Volume 3, which uses the format of major and minor headings.

KF1659 .F75 1993
(Small Business—Law and Legislation—United States)

Friedman, Robert. The Complete Small Business Legal Guide (Chicago, IL: Dearborn Publishing Group) 1993.

Avoiding "legalese," this guide, written by an attorney of the New York Bar, is targeted at and written for the average reader seeking understandable and helpful information about starting a small business. The emphasis is on keeping the information extremely practical. A subject arrangement is used to cover the basic aspects and issues of a small business, including buying and selling, recordkeeping, taxes, insurance, and credit and collections. In addition to the text, the book contains ready-to-use forms, checklists, worksheets, tips, resource lists, warnings about pitfalls, and specific advice about when to contact an attorney. A table of contents and index direct the reader to desired material.

KF 1976 .F28 (Foreign Trade Regulation—United States)

Malawer, S. Stuart. Federal Regulation of International Business (Washington, DC: National Foundation)

This book contains information on federal regulation of international business. The codes are explained by using examples from different contexts. It covers many issues, such as dumping, taxation, corrupt practices, antitrust, assets control, securities, energy, and international litigation.

KF 1987 .A329 (Export Controls—United States—Periodicals; Foreign Trade Regulation—United States—Periodicals)

Export Administration Regulation/United States, Bureau of Export Administration (Washington, DC: U.S. Department of Commerce, Bureau of Export Administration)

The Export Administration Regulations are published by the Department of Commerce and the Bureau of Export Administration and are divided into 20 parts. Part 768 discusses the two procedures to enforce the control of international trade. Part 769 covers different aspects of restrictive trade practices. Part 770 states why controls are imposed and define the terms used in the Regulations. Part 771 defines the purpose of general license, restrictions, and other requirements. Part 772 deals with the prerequisites of the Office of Export Licensing concerning licensee's responsibilities. Part 773 describes six unique licensing procedures. Part 774 covers the regulations on reexports. Part 775 contains the documentation needed for export transactions. Part 776 deals with special requirements on specific commodities. Part 777 covers specific commodities that require special documentation and other special procedures. Part 778 identifies which commodities would be restricted because of the harmful potential of the commodities. Part 779 covers the special documentation needed for technical data. Part 785 deals with different treatment to different countries. Part 786 discusses the proper procedure of going through custom. Part 787 discusses the rules of the Export Administration Regulations. Part 788 explains the proper procedures to prosecute violators of the Export Administration Regulations. Part 789 deals with individual's right to appeal to any of the regulations. Part 790 describes a number of administrative actions carried out by the Export

Administration Regulations. Part 791 covers the special treatment of commodities related to national securities. Finally, part 799 is the Commerce Control List, which lists the control level of different items.

KF2023 .A6 C65 (Franchises (Retail Trade)—Law and Legislation—United States)

Business Franchise Guide (Chicago, IL: Commerce Clearing House, Inc.)

This loose-leaf service describes the laws and rules regulating presale disclosures and the franchise relationship at both the state and federal levels. Coverage includes legislation, court decisions, and agency advisory and adjudicative determinations. The material is presented in a format of explanatory text, compiled annotations, and summaries. The arrangement is by subject matter and jurisdiction within divisions, separated by guide cards with tabs identifying the contents of each division. A table of contents appears at the beginning of each division. Each month subscribers are sent a *Report* containing supplementary material and a *Report Letter* which highlights and summarizes reported developments. Volume 1 deals with an explanation of franchises and dealerships and state and federal legislation including laws and regulations. Volume 2 contains the material focusing on new developments. A separate binder holds the current year's new developments. Separate chapters extend the coverage of the topic to Canada, Mexico, and the global economy. Access to the information begins by use of the Topical Index in Volume 1; the Current Topical Index in Volume 2 locates current material. Special features of the *Guide* include a Cumulative Index to New Developments and a Finding List of Cases, State and Federal laws, and Congressional and Agency Reports and Decisions.

KF 2120.A15 .B84 1994 (Environmental Law—United States—Periodicals; Energy Policy—United States—Periodicals)

Briefing Book on Environmental and Energy Legislation (Washington, DC: The Environmental and Energy Study Institute)

The annual *Briefing Book* is prepared by the Environmental and Energy Study Conference (EESC) for members of Congress and their staffs. The EESC is a bipartisan legislative organization funded by the Environmental and Energy Study Institute (EESI).

The *Briefing Book* is divided into five main sections. The first is the Issue Papers of more than 30 environmental, energy, and natural resources issues. The Issue Papers gives the background, federal legislative status, and recent actions concerning the issues. The second is the Summary of Law. It contains more than 60 federal environmental, energy, and natural resources laws. The third is the Committee Jurisdictions and Memberships; this describes the responsibilities of key committees and subcommittees and their memberships concerning environmental, energy, and natural resources. The fourth is the Budget Primer, consisting of a timetable for events in the Budget Act of 1974 and a summary of the Congressional budget process. Finally, the fifth is the glossary of key acronyms and phrases. The *Briefing Book* also contains a Reference Guide to help one locate information on the different topics covered.

KF2976.4 .M38 1991 (Intellectual Property—United States—Encyclopedias; Intellectual Property—Encyclopedias)

McCarthy, Thomas J. McCarthy's Desk Encyclopedia of Intellectual Property (Washington, DC: Bureau of National Affairs) 1991.

Intellectual property, the author notes, is now an all-encompassing term widely used to designate a number of field of law, including patent, trade-mark, unfair competition, copyright, trade secret, moral rights, and the right of publicity. "Intellectual" distinguishes creations of the human mind from real estate and personal property. This work is intended as a ready-reference tool with the material organized into a dictionary arrangement. Each entry is immediately followed by an indication in brackets as to the field of intellectual property into which the concept falls. Words are then plainly defined and explained followed by references to those sections of the leading treatises providing more exploration. Most entries also contain references to and quotations from important cases, legislation, rules, and other useful sources. Helpful usage examples are marked by bullets. Cross references to other entries often follow definitions. The length and complexity of the entries varies with the difficulty and intricacy of the concept being explained. Intended for attorneys who practice in this field, the author suggests the work is useful to a wider audience, e.g., business clients. Appendices provide tabular presentation of some historical information such as former Superintendents of Patents and Trademarks, applications filed during certain years, Registers of Copyrights, etc.

KF 2989.5 1993 (Copyright—United States)

Library of Congress, Copyright Office, Copyright Law of the United States of America: Contained in Title 17 of the United States Code. Rev. to February 1, 1993. Circular 92 (Washington, DC: U.S. Government Printing Office) 1992.

Copyright Law of the United States of America, Rev. to February 1, 1993 includes the Act for General Revision of the Copyright Law, Chapters 1 through 8 of Title 17 of the United States Code, the Transitional and Supplementary Provisions of October 19, 1976, and amendments in chronological order of enactment. Amendments are listed in chronological order in the preface. All amendments to Title 17 through 1992, except the addition of Chapter 9, are incorporated. This amendment is considered a separate act ("Semiconductor Chip Protection Act of 1984") rather than part of the Copyright Law. The contents include a detailed definition of copyright, as well as guidelines for ownership, duration, notice, and information about the copyright office. Title 17 and the Supplementary Provisions of 1976 outline intellectual property rights for print, pictorial, graphic, sculptural, architectural, and audio works as well as performances and ephemera.

Copyright Law is divided into sections: Subject Matter and Scope of Copyright, Copyright Ownership and Transfer, Duration of Copyright, Copyright, Notice, Deposit, and Registration, Copyright Infringement and Remedies, Manufacturing Requirement and Importation, Copyright Office, Copyright Royalty Tribunal, Digital Audio Recording Devices and Media, and Transitional and Supplementary Provisions to the Copyright Act of 1976. Each section is then divided into numbered subsections to address specifically different types of works and their uses. The appendix includes the Bern Convention Implementation Act of 1968, which covers international copyright convention. The work is not indexed, so chapter subheadings may be used as a guide to the contents.

KF3180 .G54 1976 (Trademarks—United States; Competition, Unfair—United States)

Gilson, Jerome. Trademark Protection and Practice (New York, NY: Mathew Bender and Company, Inc.) 1977.

This seven-volume set published in 1977 provides a broad and exhaustive survey of the law of trademarks and trade names in the United States. Not precisely an encyclopedia or book of rules, Mr. Gilson, of the Illinois Bar, intended the work as a distillation of legal principles and a working tool adapted to an extremely dynamic field by the use of annual supplementation. The supplements are inserted into the front of the set's loose-leaf binders. Footnotes, containing references to legal cases, support and illustrate each principle. Analysis of the dual system of state and federal trademark law results in thorough coverage. Volumes 1 and 1A provide the detailed textual treatment. Volume 2 contains appendices of rules, statutes, forms, and other related materials. Volume 2A offers various items useful to the practitioner, e.g., the Patent and Trademark Office Application Guides for Examining Attorneys. Volumes 3, 4, and 5 contain legislative history and text of the main federal legislation together with a section-by-section analysis. The general topic of each volume is noted on the spine and each contains a Table of Contents. Volume 1 also contains a current bibliography. The set includes a detailed index.

KF3305. 99. U58 1991

US Department of Labor, US Labor and Employment Laws
(Washington, DC: Government Printing Office)

The statutes listed in this volume were intended to provide and maintain fair labor and employment relations. The parts include Constitutional Provisions, Anti-Trust Laws, Labor–Management Relations Laws, and Federal Sector Labor Relations. Following each law is the date of its initiation and its amendments' dates, as well as the dates of approval. Under each regulation, the acts are divided by section numbers, with each division describing the details of that decree. Following the table of contents, a findings list, with the ordinance titles, sections, names of the statutes, and pages, is provided.

KF 3369 .D48 1992

Developing Labor Law: The Board, the Courts, and the National
Labor Relations Act, 3d Ed. (Washington, DC: Bureau
of National Affairs) 1992.

This work has three main purposes: to report on developments in labor law relations, to assist the professional growth and development of practitioners in the field of employment and labor relations law, and to promote justice, human welfare, industrial peace, and the recognition of the supremacy of law in labor–management relations. This work is divided into parts, consisting of the history of the national Labor Relations Act, protected employee activities, representation processes and union recognition, collective bargaining processes, arbitration and the Act, economic actions, relations between employees and unions, as well as the administration of the Act. A table of cases and a cumulative index are also provided.

KF3455 .E47 1989 (Labor Laws and Legislation—United States; Discrimination in Employment—Law and Legislation—United States)

Harrison, Bruce. Employment Law Deskbook (New York, NY: Mathew Bender & Co., Inc.)

Bruce Harrison, of the Washington D.C. Bar, with contributors from his law firm of Shawe and Rosenthal, has created this work to serve the needs of the employment law practitioner. Offered is an understanding of labor and employment law and theory and clear and concrete guidelines for management's compliance with its legal obligations to employees. Preventive labor relations practices are emphasized. While large portions of the text address substantive employment decisions, practices, and policies, some chapters provide overviews of specific statutes and the legal principles that have evolved in the process of their interpretation. A textual treatment of the law is organized into a subject arrangement with chapters on several topics, such as recruiting, hiring, training, promotions, wages and compensation, labor relations, and drug and alcohol testing policies. Footnotes contain references to cases, statutes, and regulations. A Detailed Table of Contents serves as one method of access to the material; the beginning of each chapter contains a boxed synopsis and scope notes. The Index and Table of Cases can also be used to lead the user to desired information on a topic. The work is contained within a loose-leaf binder allowing for periodic updating. A special feature is the State Labor and Employment Law Summary appearing near the end. Sample forms are included in various chapters.

KF 3464.Z9 C73 (Discrimination in Employment—Law and Legislation—United States)

Fair Employment Practices (Chicago: Commerce Clearing House)

This guide aims to provide a general understanding of employment regulations. It outlines the federal system of employment practices and illustrates how such practices are considered fair. It provides brief descriptions of federal laws and regulations and indicates how they apply to employers, labor unions, and employment agencies. The text includes summaries of fair employment regulations and explains the legal and regulatory bases for nondiscrimination. Case studies and examples of the application of fair employment rules for recruitment, screening, hiring, and assignment are used to demonstrate application of laws and regulations. It is organized topically by employment issues. The manual includes a detailed table of contents and a topical index of material contained within the handbook.

It summarizes fair employment practices as they apply to public employers, educational institutions, employment agencies and labor unions, private industry, and government agencies. It includes a summary of affirmative action and its effect on employers. It also describes the legal ramifications of employment discrimination, court procedures, and possible remedies for discrimination. The text refers readers to the Commerce Clearing House's *Employment Practice Guide* for more specific information.

KF 3509 .E55 (Employee Fringe Benefits—Law and Legislation—United States; Employee Fringe Benefits—Taxation—Law and Legislation—United States; Employee Fringe Benefits—United States)

Mamorsky, Jeffrey D. Employee Benefits Handbook (Boston, MA: Warren, Gorham, and Lamont)

This work is divided into six parts: benefit objectives and administration; replacement income for retirement; legal requirements; replacement income for disability, unemployment, and death; protection against extraordinary or catastrophic costs; and specialized plans. It is intended for employers, plan sponsors, benefits and human resources managers, lawyers, certified public accountants, actuaries, and consultants. Charts, tables, and sample forms are included. The source is kept current through annual supplements with cumulative indexes.

KF3568.4 .E4 (Industrial Safety—Law and Legislation—United States; Industrial Hygiene—Law and Legislation—United States)

Employment Safety and Health Guide (Chicago, IL: Commerce Clearing House)

The *Employment Safety and Health Guide* offers encyclopedic coverage of the Occupational Safety and Health Act of 1970 and the Federal Mine Safety and Health Act of 1977 and exhaustive, in-depth coverage of all legal aspects of job safety and health. Authored by the CCH Business Law Editors and contained in five loose-leaf binders, the work is intended to be useful to attorneys engaged in employment safety and health counseling and litigation, the corporate official responsible for complying with the myriad safety and health regulations, and other persons in need of up-to-date and detailed coverage of the subject. The text of all relevant regulations and safety and health standards is included and kept current through regular weekly Reports. The current year Reports are coordinated into the volumes while prior year's Reports are bound separately. Each Report comes with a Summary that provides a quick insight into the contents and the week's developments. The Summary is designed so that it could be circulated to interested individuals. In addition to reporting decisions of the Occupational Safety and Health Review Commission and the Federal Mine Safety and Health Review Commission, the *Guide* provides coverage of all administrative actions and directives of the Occupational Safety and Health Administration and Mine Safety and Health Administration. A Topical Index, Current Topical Index, and Latest Additions to Current Topical Index assist in locating information. Guide cards with tabs listing general contents provide quick access to various sections. Other finding aids include an Index to OHSA Standards, Case Table, Current Case Table and Latest Additions to Current Case Table, and Issues Pending Before the Review Commissions. The Calendar of Meetings and Hearings, located in Volume 4, gives a chronological listing of meetings, conferences and hearings, related to occupational health and safety, to be held over the next few months.

KF 3632 .I53 Z953 1993 (Workers' Compensation—Law and Legislation—United States—States; Independent Contractors—Legal Status, Laws, etc.—United States—States; Insurance, Unemployment—Law and Legislation—United States—States)

Wood, Robert W., Editor. Independent Contractor Status State by State Legal Guide (New York, NY: John Wiley & Sons, Inc.) 1993.

In addition to Mr. Wood, of the California Bar, the work is coauthored by over 50 contributors representing all of the states and the District of Columbia. The publisher offers this volume as a companion to its *Legal Guide to Independent Contractor Status*. The focus is on the specific rules of each state governing the effect of the independent contractor/employee distinction for purposes of workers' compensation and unemployment compensation. Offering simplification of what can be a difficult area of the law, the publisher has designed the book for use by lawyers and businesspersons alike. Access to the material is by an Index, at the end, or through the Summary of Contents and Detailed Summary of Contents. The information is arranged alphabetically by state, with each state constituting a chapter. A chapter is divided into sections for workers' compensation and unemployment compensation. Footnotes contain citations to statutes and cases. The publisher is planning on issuing periodic updates.

KF3775.A6 E61 (Environmental Law—United States; Environmental Law—Cases)

Environmental Law Reporter (Washington, DC: The Environmental Law Institute)

The *Environmental Law Reporter* is a loose-leaf tool. It has eight components:

1. "Update Newsletters" are published three times a month and are not included in binders. Its articles are reprinted in the monthly journal which is compiled in the binders.
2. The "News and Analysis" binder contains the "News and Analysis Journal," which includes articles, dialogues, and comments written by lawyers, summaries of recent legal actions, and a list of articles, symposia, and surveys.
3. The "Litigation" binder, which is supplemented monthly, contains full-text decisions of court cases, each of which is preceded by a summary prepared by an Environmental Law Institute staff attorney. This binder also provides an alphabetically organized table of cases with cross references to West Reporters and to pages previously provided in the "Pending Litigation" binder.
4. The "Pending Litigation" binder, which is updated monthly, includes digests of pleadings from a sampling of cases. This binder also includes a table of cases which is organized alphabetically.
5. The "Statutes and Treaties" binder, which is updated monthly, includes frequently used federal environmental statutes and many treaties in full-text. Also included are outlines of less-used statutes. The sections are organized alphabetically.
6. The "Administrative Materials" binder, which appears monthly, provides the full text of a selection of important regulatory documents issued by the federal government and the President. It is subdivided into broad listings, such as Policies and Executive Orders. The documents are organized by dates.
7. The "Indexes, Tables, and Bibliographies" binder, which is updated quarterly, includes five sections. The cumulative "Table of

Cases" lists cases decided since 1971, excluding the current year, which is located in the "Pending Litigation" binder. The "Subject Matter Indexes," in three parts (1971–1982; 1983–1991; 1992–), provide listings with references to ELR volumes and pages. The "Environmental Law Reporter Cite Conversion Table" is a subject index key. "Annual Bibliographies" is a compilation of the journal literature listings found in the "News and Analysis Journal," organized by subjects. "Briefs and Pleadings Index to Pending Litigation" is organized by subjects and referenced to the current Environmental Law Reporter.

8. The Document Service component is a source from which the user can order almost any document that has been summarized in the Environmental Law Reporter.

KF3775 .M377 1992 (Environmental Law—United States; Liability of Environmental Damages—United States; Vendors and Purchasers—United States)

Mays, Richard A. Environmental Laws: Impact on Business Transactions, A Practice Guide (Washington, DC: Bureau of National Affairs) 1992.

Believing environmental liabilities have created a special area of environmental law focused on business transactions, the author combines his expertise as an environmental practitioner and former Environmental Protection Agency official to produce a work which examines environmental requirements and liabilities with practical suggestions to avoid or minimize the liabilities. In addition to identifying and explaining the basic federal and state environmental laws, addressing the environmental aspects of a broad range of business transactions, and discussing methods by which potential environmental liabilities may be avoided, the work presents forms for guidance in drafting environmental provisions in documents and provides texts of major policies of the EPA and other agencies. The book is written in an informal style to be useful to private and corporate attorneys engaged in environmental, real estate, banking, and other areas of law, as well as to consulting firms, real estate professionals, bankers, and corporate environmental directors. Information is accessed through the Table of Contents or Index. An Appendix contains forms for contracts, attorney opinions, and government agency policies. Arrangement of the material is by subject with footnotes referring to statutory provisions and leading cases. Special features include a Table of Acronyms and Table of Important Cases. For ongoing developments covering the impact of environmental law on business transactions the publisher recommends the user consult its *Environmental Due Diligence Guide*, a monthly loose-leaf information service.

KF4829 .A6 K53 1987 (Alien Labor—United States; Alien Labor Certification—United States)

Klasko, Ronald. Employers' Immigration Compliance Guide
(New York, NY: Mathew Bender & Co., Inc.)

As a result of the passage of the Immigration Reform and Control Act of 1986, any employer who hires anyone, regardless of the employers' size and the nationality of who is hired, must comply with expansive requirements in hiring and employment practices. The *Employers' Immigration Compliance Guide* is specifically developed to aid employers in complying with the legal requirements and to assist in avoiding the substantial penalties for failure to do so. The author and contributors have avoided "legalese" where possible in favor of a plain style understood quickly and easily. The emphasis is on the pragmatic. Material in the two loose-leaf volumes is presented in a subject arrangement: Part 1 contains the Newsletter, a monthly discussion of recent developments; Parts 2–7 provide a practical discussion of complying with statutory requirements; Parts 8–10 reprint all necessary primary source materials, including the Act, regulations of the Immigration and Naturalization Service and the Special Counsel of the Department of Labor, and proposed statutes and regulations; Part 11 contains all relevant forms with commentary on their use; and Part 12 is the Topical Index. After review of the Table of Contents, guide cards with tabs provide easy access to the Parts. Boxes with special designations such as "N.B.," "WARNING," "ILLUS-TRATION," and "PLANNING NOTE" are used to call attention to particular problems, highlight certain risks, illustrate situations, or summarize and simplify information.

KF5753 .H85 (Government Information—United States; Freedom of Information—United States)

How to Use the Freedom of Information Act, 2d Ed. (Washington, DC: Washington Researchers Publishing) 1988.

Information about the Freedom of Information Act is made available in this guide. It provides the text of the Act as well as brief descriptions of it, its history, and its exemptions. Data covering procedural requirements and fees, as well as sample request and appeal letters, are included. Approximately half the volume is devoted to a directory of Information Act offices divided into two subsections. The first, "White House and Cabinet Level Departments," begins with the Executive Office of the President and proceeds alphabetically by department. Under the department headings, individual offices are listed alphabetically. The second section, "Regulatory and Other Agency Listings," is organized in the same way. Listings include the names of the offices, the names and titles of the contact persons, addresses, phone numbers, and a short description of the office and its functions as they pertain to the Freedom of Information Act.

KF6272.5 .c59 (Taxation—Law and Legislation—United States—Periodicals; Income Tax—Law and Legislation—United States—Periodicals)

U.S. Master Tax Guide (Chicago, IL: Commerce Clearing House)

This helpful guide, in its 78th edition (1995 Guide), is released at the beginning of each year to cover the changes affecting the prior tax year. Authored by the CCH Tax Law Editors, its brief but useful explanations of all aspects of Federal taxation make it an effective quick reference source. The *Guide* begins with an overview of highlights of the past year noting legislative changes affecting returns. A lengthy, detailed topical index allows the user to zero in on terse and understandable explanations of complicated IRS Code and Regulation sections; citations to those sections appear in the text in parenthesis. A Table of Contents can also be used to locate information. For more detailed tax research, footnotes refer the user to sections of the more comprehensive CCH tax publication, the *Standard Federal Tax Reporter*. An important feature of the *Guide*, which is extremely useful to the preparer of income tax forms, is the inclusion of Checklists for determining income, deductions, and medical expenses. References to relevant sections of the *Guide* follow in parenthesis.

KF 6287 .M66 (Taxation—Law and Legislation—United States—Dictionaries)

Minars, David, and Westin, Richard A. Shepard's/McGraw-Hill Tax Dictionary for Business (New York: McGraw-Hill) 1994.

Shepard's/McGraw-Hill Tax Dictionary for Business is an abridged version of Richard A. Westin's *Shepard's 1992–1993 Tax Dictionary*. It provides definitions of over 6000 tax terms for the tax professional, small business owner, and corporate manager. Tax terms included are an analysis of all regulations, procedures, revenue rulings, and all applicable sections of the Internal Revenue Code. Also included are any related tax terms.

KF 6335 .A65 F28 (Taxation—United States—Forms)

Federal Tax Forms (Chicago, IL: Commerce
Clearing House)

This reference book is a collection of income, gift, excise, employment, and estate tax forms. The forms are arranged numerically, but they can also be located by subject in the index. Section one is composed of rules and procedures. Section two provides all of the federal forms.

KF 6365 .M548 (Internal Revenue Law—United States; Taxation—Law and Legislation)

Mertens Law of Federal Income Taxation, Rulings
(Chicago, IL: Callaghan)

This reference book contains the IRS revenue rulings and procedures that require interpretation of the income tax of the Internal Revenue Code. The text is divided into six sections including code-rulings tables, rulings status tables, cumulative bulletin citation tables, revenue rulings, revenue procedures, and miscellaneous rulings.

KF 6365 .M583 (Internal Revenue Law—United States; Taxation—Law and Legislation—United States)

Mertens Law of Federal Income Taxation, Regulations
(Mundelein, IL: Callaghan)

This reference book is composed of the current regulations related to the income tax and provisions of the Internal Revenue Code. The text is divided into six sections including proposed regulations, regulations status tables, final regulations, miscellaneous regulations, the semiannual regulations agenda, and the IRS proposed procedural rules, amendments and preambles.

KF 6369.6 .E72 (Income Tax—Law and Legislation—United States—Popular Works; Tax Returns—United States—Handbooks, Manuals, etc.; Income Tax—United States—Handbooks, Manuals, etc.)

The Ernst and Young Tax Guide (New York: John Wiley and Sons)

This reference guide is helpful for those who are preparing their federal or state tax return. The text is divided into six sections including the income tax return, various forms of income, standard deduction and itemized deduction, figuring out taxes and credits, special situations and tax planning, and sample returns with usable federal tax forms. The text is supplemented by a list of common errors and easily overlooked deductions, the filing dates for each state, a yearly tax calendar, a personal tax organizer worksheet, a guide on which records you should keep, changes in the tax laws, and a special table of contents arranged by subject area.

KF 6450 .A59 F28 (Business Enterprises—Valuation—United States—Digests; Corporations—Valuation—Law and Legislation—United States—Digests)

Federal Tax Valuation Digest (Boston: Warren, Gorham & Lamont)

This reference book deals with federal tax valuation cases relating to various areas of tax proceedings. The subject areas include case analysis, business interests by class, types of businesses, valuation factors, market capitalization ratios, discounts and premiums, case studies, judicial and administrative history, cases to watch, and nontaxable federal business valuation cases. Each case entry provides the case name and number, judge's name, a synopsis, the nature of the business, pertinent information, a list of factors considered by the court, and excerpts from the opinion. The text is supplemented by tables of cross citations, courts, judges, and cases, and a words and phrases index.

KF 6452 .A59 .D74 (Partnership—Taxation—United States— Digests; Subchapter S Corporations—Taxation—Digests; Private Companies—Taxation—United States)

Furst, Bruce A. Pass-through Entity Tax Digest (Boston: Warren, Gorham & Lamont) 2000.

This reference book provides the Internal Revenue Service and federal court rulings and decisions dealing with federal taxes that apply to partnerships, limited liability companies, and S corporations. The text is divided into two major sections. Section one handles partnerships and limited liability companies. The subject areas include a definition, partner status of family members and donees, partnership interests received in exchange for property or services, tax concerns upon formation, basis for partnership interests, property, and optional adjustments, tax treatment of liabilities, partnership operations, distributive shares and allocation of tax items, limitations of losses, partnership distributions and transactions, transfers of partnership interests, termination of partnerships, and tax procedures. Section two handles S corporations. The subject areas include eligibility for and the mechanics of S corporation elections, tax treatment of S corporation shareholders and of the S corporation, and procedural matters. Each case entry provides the case name, the facts in evidence, the ruling, the page number in the report where the decision can be found, the court, and the date of the decision. The text is supplemented by tables of IRC sections, treasury regulations, revenue rulings and procedures, other IRS releases, and cases, and an index.

KF 6461.3 .F98 (Corporations—Taxation—Law and Legislation—United States—Digests)

Furst, Bruce A. Corporate Tax Digest (Boston: Warren, Gorham & Lamont) 1992.

This reference book provides the Internal Revenue Service and federal court rulings and decisions dealing with federal corporate tax cases since 1954. The subject areas include the definition of a corporation, organization and capitalization of corporations, special taxes on corporations, dividends and non-liquidating distributions, redemptions and partial liquidations, complete liquidations, collapsible corporations, related-party transactions, reorganizations, affiliated corporations and special purpose subsidiaries, carryover and survival of corporate tax attributes, special considerations in stock and securities transactions, and international tax considerations. Each case entry provides the case name, the facts in evidence, the ruling, the page number in the report where the decision can be found, the court, and the date of the decision. The text is supplemented by tables of IRC sections, treasury regulations, revenue rulings and procedures, other IRS releases, and cases, and an index.

KF 6464 .B62 (Corporations—Taxation—Law and Legislation—United States; Income Tax—Law and Legislation—United States)

Bittker, Borris I. Federal Income Taxation of Corporations and Shareholders (Boston: Warren, Gorham & Lamont)

This reference book deals with the contents of and the changes in revenue acts and the tax code as they apply to corporations and shareholders. The subject areas include definition and organization of a corporation, corporation's capital structure, corporate income tax, corporate elections under subchapter S, penalty taxes on undistributed corporate income, dividends and non-liquidating distributions, stock redemptions, complete liquidations and taxable dispositions of corporate stocks and assets in bulk, corporate divisions and reorganizations, affiliated corporations, corporate tax attributes, and foreign corporations and foreign-source income. The text is supplemented by a table of IRC sections and an index.

KF 6482 .O38
(Petroleum—Taxation—Law and Legislation—United States; Natural Gas—Taxation—Law and Legislation—United States; Income Tax—Law and Legislation—United States)

Oil and Gas Federal Income Taxation (New York: Commerce Clearing House)

This reference book deals with the taxation of oil and gas related income under the U.S. federal income tax system. The text explains theories of natural resource taxation and defines technical terms relating to the oil and gas industry. The subject areas include obtaining mineral rights, exploration of property, equipment and land development, production, dispositions, royalties, geological expenses, depletion, sharing arrangements, unitizations, taxable income, nontaxable exchanges, abandonment and losses, partnerships and associations, corporate issues, depreciation, accounting methods, and international provisions. The text is supplemented by a case table, a rulings finding list, and a topical index.

KF 6535 .A59 D73
(Real Property and Taxation—United States—Digests)

Douglas, James A. Real Estate Tax Digest (Boston: Warren, Gorham & Lamont) 1984.

This reference book provides the Internal Revenue Service and federal court rulings and decisions related to the field of real estate taxation. The subject areas include purchase and ownership of a residence, sale of a residence, leases and rents, operating expenses, taxes, depreciation and losses, mortgage and equity financing, settlement and foreclosure, real estate tax credits, sales and exchanges, charitable contributions, abandonment, partnerships and joint ventures, corporations, special entities for holding real estate, natural resources, farming, family and estate planning for real estate, and procedures. Each case entry provides the case name, the facts in evidence, the ruling, the page number in the report where the decision can be found, the court, and the date of the decision. The text is supplemented by tables of IRC sections, treasury regulations, revenue rulings and procedures, other IRS releases, and cases, and an index.

KF 6654.5 U62 (Tariff—United States—Periodicals;
Tariff—Law and Legislation—United States—Periodicals)

U.S. International Trade Commission, Harmonized Tariff Schedule of the United States (Washington, DC: United States Government Printing Office)

This government publication provides statistical information for importers, customs brokers, customs officials, and others involved with foreign trade. The schedule will enable individuals to determine appropriate classification, duty rates, and data reporting requirements for imported materials. Unless prohibited in the notice to exporters, the schedule may be used in lieu of Schedule B for reporting purposes. Each of the schedule's 22 main sections covers a wide variety of related importable items, such as live animals, vegetable products, edible fats, prepared food stuffs, mineral products, chemical or allied products, plastic and rubber articles, travel goods, wood and articles of wood, pulp of wood or other cellulosic material, textiles and textile articles, artificial flowers, ceramic products, precious or semiprecious stones, imitation jewelry, base metals and articles of base metals, machinery and mechanical appliances, aircraft, clocks and watches, arms and ammunition, miscellaneous items such as toys, and legal issues involving foreign trade.

General notes, rules of interpretation, and general statistical information proceed the main sections, many of which have special notes of their own. A chemical appendix follows the main sections. There are also three appendixes covering, respectively, classification of country and territory designations for U.S. import statistics, international standard country codes (ISO), and customs district and port codes. An alphabetic subject index and change record end the publication.

KF 6750 .A6 S782
(Taxation, State—Law and Legislation—Cases)

State Tax Cases (New York: Commerce Clearing House)

This reference book is published annually and reports on state tax cases. Case topics cover various areas of tax law including airlines, alcoholic beverages, banks, cigarettes, deductions, federal contractors, federal retirement benefits, franchise, gambling, gasoline, income taxes, Indian territory, insurance companies, interstate commerce, motor vehicles, partnerships, property, railroads, refunds, sales, utilities, and voter initiatives. Each case entry provides the case name, the court's location, plaintiff and defendant, the court's opinion, and figures used in the decision.

KF 9084 .A15 M37
(Dispute Resolution (Law)—United States—Directories)

Martindale–Hubbell Dispute Resolution Directory
(New Providence, NJ: M.H. Reed Reference Company)
1995.

Published in cooperation with the American Arbitration Association, this directory is a comprehensive reference guide to dispute resolution practitioners, organizations, areas of practice and rules, and is designed to be helpful and understandable to anyone with an interest in this field, whether they are a law firm, business, or government agency. The work is arranged into five basic sections. Part 1 is a general overview of the field of dispute resolution with special emphasis on its phenomenal growth in the last two decades. Part 2 contains the organizational profiles providing detailed information for dispute resolution organizations including addresses and phone numbers. Part 3 offers clear, in-depth, lengthy explanations of 15 different dispute resolution methods focusing on such issues as who should use the method, how to best prepare for the process, and what is involved in each step. Part 4 provides overviews of how different industries are currently using out-of-court dispute resolution. Part 5 contains the directory listings of dispute resolution service providers, organized alphabetically by state, and providing names, addresses, phone numbers, fax numbers, services provided, and practice areas. Access to the directory is accomplished through use of three indexes: a locator index, arranged alphabetically by last name of dispute resolution practitioner, an index of practice areas, e.g., consumer, labor/employment, or health care, and an index of service roles, e.g., negotiation, research, mediation. A final section, Dispute Resolution Reference, includes relevant statutes and acts, rules and codes, professional standards, forms and clauses for dispute resolution agreements, model programs and procedures, policy statements, and a glossary.

KF9350 .B87 (White Collar Crime—United States; Commercial Crime—United States; Actions and Defenses—United States)

Arkin, Stanley S. Business Crime: Criminal Liability of the Business Community (New York, NY: Mathew Bender & Co., Inc.)

Variously termed "white collar crime," or "economic crime," the authors use the phrase "business crime" and broadly define it as nonviolent crime with an underpinning of deceit or concealment, or nonviolent crime committed by those in privileged economic, social, or political positions. Included in the coverage of this area are violations of the tens of thousands of regulations not grounded on fraud but more on theories of social responsibility such as to the government, environment, and employees, resulting in criminal prosecution even in the absence of any specific intent. The set is intended for practitioners and advisors both for prosecution and defense as well as for in-house counsel and for those who advise business clientele on a more general basis. Part 1 deals with questions of procedure, strategy and technique covering preindictment to appeal. Part 2 surveys the substantive law as it most usually arises in the business crime context. A full Table of Contents is contained in Volume 1. Chapters begin with a boxed "Scope" note followed by a synopsis in outline form. Each chapter contains an Appendix with practice forms, handy checklists, a glossary, reprints of relevant statutes, regulations and court rules, and an extensive bibliography. An Index appears in the last volume. Housed in a separate volume, *Business Crime Commentary* is issued every other month offering brief articles on current topics and extensive commentary on recent cases of interest.

KJE947 .M48 (Law—European Economic Community Countries; European Communities)

Medhurst, David. A Brief and Practical Guide to EC Law
(Oxford; Boston: Blackwell Law) 1990.

This guide contains tables ranging from European Community (EC) Cases
to EC Court Rules. Treaties, interpretation and research, company law, as
well as social policy are explained.

KJE2598 .E88 (Economic Interest Groupings—European Economic Community Countries)

Gerven, Dirk van and Carel A.V. Aalders, Eds. European
Economic Interest Groupings: The EEC Regulation and
Its Application in the Member States of the European
Community (Deventer; Boston: Kluwer Law and
Taxation Publishers) 1990.

Entrepreneurs and lawyers use this guide to learn about the European Economic Interest Groupings (EEIG) and how the various nationalities within
it function in the European Community (EC). This work contains two parts.
Part I has the European Economic Community (EEC) Regulation in three
sections. The first explains the mission of EEIG as a European legal instru-
ment for collaboration between the EC member states. The second contains
the joint venture opportunities in the EEIG and test of the EEC Competition Law. The third section has the EEIG's description of the International
Tax. Part II is each member state's application of the EEC Regulation. The
EEC member states contributing their policy in Part II are Belgium, Denmark, France, the Federal Republic of Germany, Greece, the Republic of
Ireland, Italy, Luxembourg, the Netherlands, Portugal, Spain, and the United
Kingdom.

KM 505 .A68 1990

V.F. Novikov, V.F; Rutgaizaer, V.M. and Rysina, T.V. Arenda
Predpriiatii [Leasing of Soviet Companies] (Moskva: Ekonomika)
1990.

The authors discuss the value of leasing state companies in the Soviet Union.
The main issues discussed in the book are the financial regulations governing
companies and the state, the rates of leasing, and the mode of payment.

KM 505 .B7611 1990

BraginskiiM I. Khoziistvennyi Dogovor; Kakim emu Byt?
[Economic Agreements: How Should They Be Formulated?]
(Moskva: Ekonomika) 1990.

The author discusses the economic regulations affecting trade and business in the Soviet Union. Some of the areas covered are economic links between business and state. The author also points at the sanctions applied to businesses that break the economic rules.

KM 2405 .P911 (Law—Soviet Union; Foreign Trade Regulation—Soviet Union)

Posniakov, V.S. Ed. Pravo i Vneshniaia Torgovlia
[Law and International Trade] (Moskva, Russia:
Mezhdunar Otnosheniia) 1987.

This source casts light on general aspects of legal regulations governing export and import operations as they pertain to the Soviet Union. It explains existing agreements on international trade, agreements on specialization and cooperation, legal aspects of agreements dealing with international commissions, licensing, renting, and also legal procedures for solving arguments between Soviet and international companies. This source is intended for specialists involved in international trade.

KM 2800 .S7311 1988

Soymestnye Predpriiatiia Mezzhdunradnye Obedineniia I
Organizatsii na Territorii SSSR: Normativnye Akty I
Kommentarii. Edited by Golubov, G. D. Moskva, Lurid;
(English Translation: Joint Ventures, International
Conglomerates and Organizations on the Territory
of the USSR; Legal Statutes and Commentaries)

The book discusses legal topics about the establishment and operation of international joint ventures, international cooperative conglomerates, and organizations in Soviet Union. Some of the issues described in the book are laws on the establishment of companies, business partnership, relationship between the companies, the state, and economic authorities, and laws that protect foreign partnerships and investors.

KM 2802 .S7411 1990 (Joint Ventures—Soviet Union)

Butkevich, V.G., A.S. Filipenko and V.I. Kisil, Eds. Sovmestnye
Predpriiatiia: Sozdanie i Deiatelnost. Kiev, Russia: Lybid,
1990. (Translation—Joint Ventures: Their Creation
and Activities)

This source describes legal and economic aspects of creation and managing
international joint ventures on the territory of the USSR. Special attention is
dedicated to the issues dealing with the creation of joint ventures involving
former Soviet satellite countries and to legal and other practical issues of their
cooperation with Western companies. The book is addressed to scholars,
students, researchers, and business people.

KM 9999 .P92
(Labor Laws and Regulations—Soviet Union;
Industrial Relations—Soviet Union)

Pravovoe Regulirovanie Individualnoi Trudovoi i Kooperativnoi
Deiatelnosti. Sverdlovsk, Sverdlovskii Iuridecheskii in-t., 1989.
(Translation—Legal Regulation of Individual Labor and
Cooperative Enterprises)

This work presents basic legal regulations governing activities of cooperative
enterprises and individual labor in the territory of the USSR. These materials
are based on a pre-April 1989 law.

KNX1072 .C77
(Corporations—Accounting—Law and Legislation—Japan;
Corporation Reports—Law and Legislation—Japan)

Cooke, T.E. and M. Kikuya. Financial Reporting
in Japan: Regulation, Practice and Environment
(Oxford: Blackwell; Cambridge, MA: Three
Cambridge Center) 1992.

This book is about Japan's forms of business organization as well as the
history of Japan's way of doing business. The work also includes lists of
readings and references concerning Japan's accounting and reporting practices. The publication also has comparisons of Japan's practices and standards with those in the United Kingdom and the United States.

L—EDUCATION

L901 .H53 1995 (Education, Higher—Universities and Colleges—United States—Directories)

The HEP... Higher Education Directory (Washington, DC: Higher Education Publications, Inc.)

This volume has listings of accredited, degree-granting universities, colleges, and other postsecondary educational institutions.

Three indexes, "Index of Key Administrators," "Accreditation Index of Institutions by Regional, National, Professional, and Specialized Agencies," and "Index of Universities, Colleges, and Schools," are cross-referenced to the main "Universities, Colleges, and Schools" listing. There is also an index of Internet electronic access numbers of these institutions. Each entry in the "Universities, Colleges, and Schools" listing contains the address, Congressional District, county, telephone number, fax number, school calendar system, date enrollment number, affiliation or control, programs, accreditation, and list of the institutions' administrators.

The HEP directory also contains administrative officer descriptions and codes, statewide agencies of higher education, and higher education associations.

LB—THEOLOGY AND PRACTICE OF EDUCATION

LB2337.4 .A85 (Student Aid—United States; Student Loan Funds—United States; Master of Business Administration Degree—United States; Business Schools—Scholarships, Fellowships, etc.—United States)

Astor, Bart. The Official Guide to Financing your MBA, 1992–1994 (Princeton, NJ: Graduate Management Admission Council) 1992.

This guide was prepared to assist the Master in Business Administration (MBA) student with his/her budget during graduate school years. The guide contains a list of financial aid programs, financial planning and budgeting techniques, debt management and loan repayment information, realities facing international students in graduate management schools, descriptions of graduate schools of management, and scholarship opportunities. The appendices contain a sample promissory note, data on borrower rights and responsibilities, and a checklist for admission and financial aid applications.

LB 2369 .T93 (Dissertations—Academic)

Turabian, Kate L., A Manual for Writers of Term Papers, Theses, and Dissertations; 5th Edition (Chicago: University of Chicago Press) 1987.

The *Manual for Writers* is a short volume guiding the user in the writing of formal papers. In the manual, the author discusses the usage and structure of abbreviations and numbers; spelling and punctuation; capitalization, underlining, and other matters of style; quotations; footnotes; bibliographies; public documents; tables; illustrations; scientific papers; and the typing of the paper itself. Each major division of the *Manual* is numbered sequentially and within each section, points are further numbered. Examples are given for most points. The index directs the user to pertinent part of the *Manual*.

LC—SPECIAL ASPECTS OF EDUCATION

LC1059 .N28 (Interns—United States—Directories; Occupational Training—United States—Directories)

The National Directory of Internships (Raleigh, NC: National Society for Internships and Experiential Education) 1994.

Internship opportunities are listed in business and industry, communications, education, environmental affairs and outdoors, international affairs, museums, creative and performing arts, the public sector, social services, science and technology, as well as women's issues. The directory also includes a section for international internship resources. Each entry contains the name of the organization, address, contact person, description of the organization and internship, eligibility, and an explanation of the application process. The directory is updated annually and contains an alphabetical, geographical, and field-of-interest indexes.

LC1072.I58 G56 (Internship Programs—United States—Directories; American Students—Foreign Countries)

Charles A. Gliozzo, et al., Eds. Directory of International Internships. 3rd Ed. (East Lansing, MI: Career Development and Placement Services, Michigan State University)

Each entry contains the organization's name, address, contact information, description and the objectives, type of program, number of accepted interns, location, internship duration, prerequirements, deadline for applying, financial data, and academic credit information.

LC1072.I58 P95 1994 (Internship Programs—United States—Directories; Interns (Education)—United States—Directories)

The Princeton Review Student Access Guide to America's Top 100 Internships (New York, NY: Villard Books)

The exceptional internship programs in this guide are selected according to the sense of reward the past interns felt, the programs' accessibility to persons from a broad variety of environments, challenging projects, prestigious organizations, and an impressive background for future job offers. This publication is updated yearly and the location of the internships is limited to the United States.

Each internship entry has a scale to measure the programs' qualities. Some of these qualities are selectivity, compensation, quality of life, and busywork. Selectivity is the approximate number of applicants accepted. Compensation includes payment and any housing, transportation, and food included in the program. The quality of life encompasses a past intern's satisfaction with the program as well as the intern's evaluation of seminars, social activities, company culture, workspaces, and cafeterias. Lastly, busywork is defined as the amount of menial or meaningful work the intern performs in the program. Also, included with each internship entry are the location of the program, its field/occupational interest, duration of the program, application deadlines, contact information, prerequirements, and an overview of the program. The appendix contains short lists such as "America's Top 10 Internships," "Highest Compensation," and "Most Selective."

NA—ARCHITECTURE

NA53 .A52 1993/94 (Architectural Firms—American Institute of Architects; Architectural Practice—United States—Directories)

American Institute of Architects, ProFile: The Official Directory of the American Institute of Architects (Topeka, KS: Archimedia)

This source lists architectural design firms in alphabetical order by city and state. The information provided for each entry include the firm's name, address and phone number, location of its offices, the year established, key staff members, number of personnel by discipline, geographic distribution of the work, and title of award-winning projects. ProFile has indexes of firms; of principals, partners, and other staff; and lists of minority and women business firms.

P—LANGUAGE AND LITERATURE

P87.C72 (Communication—Abstracts—Periodicals)

Temple University, School of Communications and Theater, Communication Abstracts an International Information Source (Beverly Hills, CA: Sage Publications)

This is a source of worldwide communication-related publications, published four times annually. The range of material covered goes from the media to public relations and from public opinion to reports and books. Film-related topics are excluded, except those that are research items or experimental, because of the abstracting and bibliographic services available in that area.

PN—LITERATURE (GENERAL)

PN 4888 .E6 C671 1992 (Employees' Magazines, Handbooks, etc.—United States; Employees' Magazines, Handbooks, etc.—United States—Bibliography; House Organs—United States; House Organs—United States—Bibliography)

Riley, Sam G., Ed. Corporate Magazines of the United States (New York: Greenwood) 1992.

This very readable book provides short essays on 51 magazines published by corporations. The magazines profiled are of the type known as "house organs." The earliest of them, *Protection*, began publication in 1865 as a general circulation magazine and later switched to an internal focus. In addition to the specific information about subject matter, audience, and focus for specific publications, this book provides a fascinating and informative picture of how corporations represent their mission and activities to employees, customers, and the general public in general. Thus it possesses some value for social historians and as well as those interested in business journalism and corporate culture. The three appendices give a chronology of magazines profiled, location of magazines profiled by state, and a list of 273 magazines not profiled with date of origin when known, company, and place of publication. There is an index and list of contributors at the end.

PN6084.B87 E96 (Business—Quotations, Maxims, etc.)

The Executive's Book of Quotations, Compiled by Julia
Vitullo-Martin, J. Robert Moskin (New York: Oxford University
Press) 1994.

This work contains more than 5000 business-oriented quotations, organized
by topics. Also, this publication contains a list of sources from which the
quotations were taken. In addition, an Index of Names and an Index of Cross-
Topics are provided.

Q—SCIENCE

Q180.U5 R42 1993 (Research—United States—Directories; Research and Development Contracts—United States—Directories)

Unique 3-in-1 Research Development Directory (Washington:
Government Data Publications)

This volume has directories of companies, agencies, and the nature of work.
Companies with government research and development contracts are listed in
alphabetical order. Also listed are these companies in other geographical
areas; the companies are listed alphabetically by their state location and then
their city locations. The agencies awarding the contracts are listed in geographic order. Each entry includes the agency code and the mailing address of
the awarding organizations. Within each agency, the awarded companies are
listed alphabetically.

QA—MATHEMATICS

QA75.15 F7351 (Computers—Electronic Data Processing—Dictionaries)

Freedman, Alan. The Computer Glossary: The Complete Illustrated
Desk Reference, 6th Ed. (United States: Prentice Hall) 1993.

The Computer Glossary is an excellent reference book for the computer. It
provides meaningful definitions of every important computer term whether it
be a hardware or software product, a concept, or program for any type of
computer system.

 The Computer Glossary is arranged in alphabetical order like a dictionary. Many entries include a photograph. The reference also includes
history about the major hardware vendors.

While *The Computer Glossary* is an excellent reference for an in-depth explanation of an item, it is intended for every type of computer user. Entries that a novice might look up are explained for the layperson. More complicated technical terms are explained with other technical terms. However, all of the terms used in the definitions are defined in the book.

The first six pages contain overviews for the student, the business manager, and the personal computer buyer that form a helpful outline with which one can work their way through *The Computer Glossary*.

QA 75.5 .D16
(Computer industry—United States—Directories; Computer Industry—United States—Catalogs)

Data Sources (New York, NY: Ziff-Davis Publishing)

This source is a comprehensive guide to available data processing and data communications products. It provides information about equipment, software, and companies. Contained in the work are listings for 75,000 software, hardware, and communications products with specifications and prices. Also included are 14,000 company profiles with addresses, phone numbers, and key personnel.

Volume one contains information on hardware and data, communications products, and services. Volume two contains information about systems, applications, and data/telecommunications software. Appearance or absence of a product or company does not mean endorsement or nonendorsement. The information published is provided by vendors from returned surveys or technical manuals and is indexed to lead users to the product, service, or company they are seeking. Extensive cross-indexing, an alphabetical master index, and sectional directions provide easy access to find and compare products. This work is designed to provide current information for buying computer products by being continuously updated and issued every 6 months.

QA 75.5 .D63 (Information Storage and Retrieval Systems—Directories; Electronic Data Processing—Directories)

Directory of Online Databases (Santa Monica: CA: Cuadra Associates)

Published every 2 years, this directory provides current information on on-line databases. Almost 5000 databases are listed. With both reference and source databases recorded, database formats include numeric, text, numeric text, and image. Requirements for inclusion in the directory are availability to the public and accessibility through an on-line vendor that is connected to at least one network. Access is gained through subscription, membership, or other stated qualifications.

The directory is divided into three sections: database descriptions, address list of producers, on-line services, and gateways, and indexes. Arranged alphabetically by database name, the first section, database descriptions, provides in each entry the name of the database and its producer, subject, contents and coverage, time span, update frequency, access requirements, and language of the database. Information on the database types: reference (i.e., bibliographic and referral), source (original data), and full text or electronic distribution, is given. On-line service information and information on the availability of the database in other formats (CD-ROM, diskette, and/or magnetic tape) are also noted.

The listings of producers, on-line services, and gateways provide addresses, telephone, and fax numbers. The last section of the directory has the indexes that are divided into six sections. Included are subject, vendor geographically, producer, on-line service/gateway, telecommunications, and master (databases and organizations) index.

QA76 .C73 1994
(Electronic Data Processing—Indexes—Periodicals; Electronic Digital Computers—Indexes—Periodicals)

Computer Literature Index (Phoenix, AZ: Applied Computer Research)

The literature in the index leans toward the practical uses of the computer, such as computer-related trade publications, general business and management periodicals, and publications of computer and management-oriented professional societies and organizations. The author and publisher indexes refer to the subject index for full citations of titles.

The author index contains a listing of the authors, the title of their works, and a "See" pointer-assigned classification headings in the Subject Index. The publisher index has publishers' addresses.

QA76 .D638 1993–1995 (Computer Software—Catalogs; Computer Software Industry—Directories)

Directory of U. S. Government Software for Mainframes and Microcomputers (Springfield, VA: National Technical Information Service)

This annually produced directory provides information on approximately mainframe and microcomputer programs from federal agencies. Included in each entry is the National Technical Information Service (NTIS) order number used in the software order form, which is also provided. In addition, each entry has the software program's title, price code, a summary of the program's function, computer specifications for implementation of the program, and subject index keywords.

The programs are divided into areas such as Administrative Management; Biological and medical sciences; Business and economics; Cartography; Chemistry; Civil and structural engineering; Communications; Computer Science; Energy; Environmental pollution and control; Health care; Industrial and mechanical engineering; Library and information sciences; Mathematics and statistics; Natural resources and hydrology; Nuclear science and technology; Physics; Transportation; Urban Regional Development; and Miscellaneous. This book contains indexes of subject and agencies.

QA76.5 .A94 (Information Resources Management—Management Information Systems—Electronic Digital Computers—Periodicals)

Auerbach Information Management: Strategy, Systems, and Technologies (Boston, MA: Auerbach Publishers)

This work is a two-volume set of individually bound articles, the contents of which are divided into five divisions of information management. These five divisions are the issues, staffing, directions in technology, delivering of information systems, and operations. The articles are written by scholars and businesspersons in the field of information management.

Each article contains guidelines for analyzing and solving problems on a subject. Also, sample worksheets, forms, checklists, tables, charts, and diagrams are included to aid in understanding the concepts presented in the article.

QA76.6 .S68 1994 (Computer Programs—Directories; Microcomputers—Programming—Directories; Computer Industry—United States—Directories)

The Software Encyclopedia (New York: R.R. Bowker Co.)

This set is a guide to computer systems, their applications, and their publishers. Volume one consists of title listings and an index of publishers. The title index is an alphabetical listing of software applications. Information for each title includes the version number, publication date, compatible hardware, operating system requirements, memory required, price, description of the customer support available, package extras, International Standard Book Number (ISBN), publisher, and a brief description of the product. The publisher/title index has for each publisher the address, telephone number, listing of the publisher's titles, subsidiary information, and ordering information.

Volume two has a guide to systems along with software applications listed under each respective system. The guide to applications is organized under rubrics; then, the software applications are listed under the appropriate major headings. This volume also has a system compatibility/applications index. The Software Encyclopedia omits educational computer programs aimed at the scholastic market, but educational programs for home use are included.

QA 276.A1 C98
(Mathematical Statistics—Periodicals—Indexes)

American Statistical Association Institute of Mathematical Statistics, Current Index to Statistics: Applications, Methods and Theory (Washington, DC: American Statistical Association)

This index is a compilation of thousands of statistical analysis articles from 1975. Articles ranging from the basics like determining a method to increase the amount of responses for mail surveys to the abstract probability theory are the extent to which the index covers statistics.

QA276.14 .K461 1990 (Statistics—Dictionaries)

Marriott, F.H. A Dictionary of Statistical Terms, 5th Ed. Prepared for the International Statistical Institute (New York: Wiley) 1990.

This book contains equations and definitions of terms important in empirical and theoretical statistics. In this edition are two features used to help link the reader to further information about a term. First, a definition may cite the author and date of the publication from which the term was first used. Second, definitions may contain bolded words as well as "See" or "See also" references; these cues are pointers to related terms in the dictionary.

RK—DENTISTRY

RK1 .B97 (Commerce—United States—Directories; Telephones—United States—Directories)

The National Directory of Addresses and Telephone Numbers: The Business-to-Business Book that Covers the Entire USA. Edited by Steven A. Miles (Detroit, MI: Omnigraphics) 1992.

This directory contains addresses and telephone numbers of associations, companies, banks, embassies and consulates, and hotels. It also includes information on important federal agencies such as State Departments in the whole of the United States.

S—AGRICULTURE

S21 .A492 1994
(Agriculture—United States—Statistics—Periodicals)

Agricultural Statistics (Washington, D.C.: United States Department of Agriculture)

This work is statistical data compiled by the United States Department of Agriculture and other government agencies for which phone numbers and addresses are given.

Tables with historical data have been limited to data gathered from 1984 or later. Foreign agricultural trade statistics are included. These figures cover shipments of merchandise from the U.S. territories to foreign countries. Tables may contain extensive use of footnotes to inform the readers of the data's accuracy and origin.

T—TECHNOLOGY

T 12 .H37

Harris Manufacturers Directory. Edited by Richard M. Fein and Frances L. Carlsen. (Twinsburg, Ohio: Harris Publishing Company) 1993.

Harris Manufacturers Directory provides information on public and private manufacturing companies with 100 or more employees. In addition, companies involved in value-added services are covered by the directory as well. Information provided for each company includes address, telephone and fax numbers, number of employees, plant size, primary and secondary SIC, parent company, estimated annual sales, product description, principal officers, and ranking.

T12.T454 (United States—Manufacturers—Directories)

Thomas' Register of American Manufacturers and Thomas' Register Catalog (New York, Thomas Publishing Company)

In this multivolume collection, one can find information on products, services, and the companies that provide them. Part one, Products Services, contains detailed information for thousands of products and services. In addition to the heading for a product or service, a list of the known manufacturers is listed alphabetically by locations. The consumer can also make comparisons of vendors using the supplemental advertisements. Part two, Company Profiles, lists data about companies. The capabilities of hundreds of thousands of companies, listed alphabetically with contact information, can be accessed easily. Part three, the Catalog File, is full of detailed product information for approximately 2000 companies and contains catalogs for many of them. Each of the three parts includes a supplemental section. Part one has the "Product Index." Part two contains the "Trademarks and Brand Names Index." Part three contains the "Inbound Traffic Guide."

T12.3.M5 R33 1995 (Michigan—Manufactures—Directories)

Regional Industrial Buying Guide, Greater Michigan (New York, NY: Thomas Regional Directory Co.)

The *Regional Buying Guide* contains information about industrial manufacturers and suppliers within its region. Each publication has three sections: the Products and Services Index, the Products and Services Section, and the A–Z Company Index. The Products and Services Index is a cross-referenced guide to the headings in the Products and Services Section. The Products and Services Section is organized by headings; under each heading, the companies are listed by state, by city, and, alphabetically, by company name within each city. The following information is provided for each company: its address, area code, telephone number, zip code, description of the business, and the brand(s) the company carries. The A–Z Company Index lists manufacturers, distributors, manufacturers' representatives, and service companies.

This volume also provides "Sources of Industrial Information" to aid the reader in locating an office, department, or organization within the directory's specified region. In addition, this volume has the Metric Conversion Guide and a Calendar of Industrial Events, which includes regional and national conventions.

T58.6 .L82 (Management Information Systems)

Loehlein, Patricia. Management Information Systems: An Information Sourcebook (Phoenix: Oryx Press) 1988.

This book contains references and annotations of literature. The literature includes dictionaries, handbooks, annuals, encyclopedias, guides, indexes, journal, and journal articles. The references listed include classic MIS materials from the 1980s. Also, the sourcebook lists computer-related databases, societies, and associations. The chapters of this literature are divided into subtopics of the MIS industry, such as database management of an aspect of information systems (IS), computer graphics, and books with lists of computer-related products and companies.

T176 .I42 1994 (Research, Industrial—United States—Directories; Laboratories—United States—Directories)

Directory of American Research and Technology
(New York: Bowker)

The main section of this directory contains an alphabetical listing of organizations associated with research activity. Entries have information about the parent organization, such as its address, phone number, and fax number; other contact information; names of executives; subsidiaries; the fields of research and development with which a facility is involved; and the types and number of professional staff. This work also has the names of companies and their subsidiaries, indexes, and a subject guide to research and development activities.

T223.V4 A2 T78 1992 (Trademarks—United States; Business Names—United States; Corporations—United States—Directories)

Companies and their Brands (Detroit, MI: Gale
Research Inc.)

This two-volume set contains the names of manufacturers, their addresses, phone numbers, and the consumer products they create. Volume one has the company names starting with A–K and the Numerical Companies, an alphabetical listing of companies with a numeral in its title. Volume two has the company names starting with the letters L–Z. Both volumes contain a "List of Sources Used," a list of directories, and their publishers' addresses.

T325. R78 (Trademarks; Business Names)

Room, Adrian. NTC's Dictionary of Trade Name Origins (London; Boston: Routledge and Kegan Paul) 1982.

This dictionary describes how trade names developed, who devised them, and the thinking that lays behind the choice of particular names. Most trade names that have obvious origins are excluded, while many personal trade names are included.

T394 .T76 (Exhibitions—Directories)

Trade Shows Worldwide (Detroit, MI: Gale Research Inc.)

This international directory of events, facilities, and suppliers has three parts.

Part 1: Trade Shows and Exhibitions: Each entry contains prices for exhibition space, types of products displayed, registration fees and admission charges, types of programs featured, social events, number and sizes of meeting rooms needed, and number of hotel rooms needed.

Part 2: Directory of Trade Show Sponsors and Organizers: This section contains phone numbers and addresses for contacting trade show professionals, exhibition management companies, sponsors, cosponsors, and U.S. contacts for shows held abroad.

Part 3: Facilities, Services, and Information Sources: This section provides descriptions of conference and conventions, listings of industry services and suppliers, information about hotels and visitors centers, as well as sources for more trade show information, such as professional associations and consultants.

TD—ENVIRONMENTAL TECHNOLOGIES

TD180 .D22, 1994 (Pollution—United States—Statistics; Sanitation—United States—Statistics; Pollution Control Industry—United States—Statistics; Pollution—Law and Legislation—United States—Statistics; Environmental Policy—United States—Statistics)

Darnay, Arsen J., Ed. Statistical Record of the Environment, 2nd Ed. (Detroit: Gale Research) 1994.

This edition contains statistical data in tabular format provided by national and state government agencies as well as private sources. Each of its chapters contains tables that focus on the environmental topic of that chapter. The first appendix contains sources of information listed by agency, by publication, or by author. The second appendix lists abbreviations and acronyms. The third appendix is a keyword index, which displays subjects, companies, institutions, agencies, and geographical entities.

TH—BUILDING AND CONSTRUCTION

TH435 .M48 1993 (Building—Estimates)

Waier, Phillip R., Ed. Means Unit Price Estimating Methods:
Standards & Procedures for Using Unit Price Cost Data.
2nd Ed. (Kingston, MA: R. S. Means Co.) 1993.

Architects, engineers, contractors, and facilities managers use this book when
they need unit price estimates; this edition contains chronological steps to
acquiring them. The book also includes chapters on "Computerized Estimating Methods" and "Pre-Bid Scheduling." Tables and charts are provided to
further exemplify the use of cost data in the estimation process.

 Appendix A contains "SPEC-AID," which is used to assist construction planners with detailed checklists for various phases of a project.
Appendix B includes tables to assist them in estimating people hours,
technical data, and construction material allowances within various phases
of a project.

TJ—MECHANICAL ENGINEERING AND MACHINERY

TJ153 .A1 U56, 1992 (Power Resources—Energy Industries—Statistics—Periodicals)

Energy Statistics Yearbook. Department of International
Economic and Social Affairs, Statistical Office (New York:
United Nations)

This book contains tables with international energy statistical data for commercial energy, solid fuels, liquid fuels, gaseous fuels, electricity and heat,
nuclear fuels, fossil fuels, as well as hydraulic resources. The notes for each
table have been placed in a separate section. The work also contains information on country nomenclatures, abbreviations and symbols, definitions,
and conversion factor tables.

TK—ELECTRICAL ENGINEERING, ELECTRONICS, AND NUCLEAR ENGINEERING

TK 5105 875 .I57

New Riders' Official Internet Yellow Pages

The *New Riders' Official Internet Yellow Pages* provides access to a great deal
of relevant materials found on the Internet. The book is primarily intended

for people who want to find information on a specific subject via the Internet. Nontechnical definitions of pertinent terms such as telnet and file transfer protocol (FTP) are given, so that previous Internet experience is not necessary to utilize this resource.

The format of the book is similar to the telephone version of the *Yellow Pages*, albeit on an international basis. Entries are listed under main headings or keywords. An alphabetical listing of entries is included in the main directory as well.

Listings in the Internet *Yellow Pages* provide information such as a brief description of the resource, the audience, how to participate, and the Internet address. The book uses a three-tier rating system and provides more detailed information for entries that are highly ranked.

An appendix is included as well. Among other things, it lists the keywords utilized in the main section of the book and provides a glossary of words and acronyms related to the Internet.

TK 5105 .875 .I57 G35

Gale Guide to Internet Databases

Published by the International Thomson Publishing Corporation, the *Gale Guide to Internet Databases* has descriptive abstracts to currently available databases. Its design, using nontechnical language that is easy to understand, is for both the experienced user and the beginning Internet user.

All of the 2000 domestic and international databases within this sourcebook offer unrestricted access. The compilers chose these databases especially for their broad audience and authoritative information. Each of these databases must have one of the following features: full text, image, numerical, software, bulletin board, bibliographical, dictionary, directory, properties, statistical, time series, or transactional.

A sample entry identifies the parts of the entry to guide the user in understanding the format. Also included is a glossary of Internet terms and a bibliography of the latest Internet reference books. Five indexes allow for a variety of access points: providers, organizations, names, and a subject index, which is cross-referenced and has "see also" notes. A master index has more than 8000 references from the descriptive listings.

Each entry provides access and retrieval information, required log-in and password prompts, and other special instructions unique to the database. Bibliographical information is listed, as well as the host name, data provider, and updating frequency. Searching routines and searching elements accompany each entry as they apply. The description covers the scope and contents of the database, and embedded file names for quicker access.

TK 5105.875 .I57 L371, 1992

LaQuey, Tracy. The Internet Companion: A Beginner's Guide to Global Networking, 1993.

This is a wonderful book for anyone needing an introduction and "road map" to the Internet. The book is written in a language that everyone can understand. It is not insulting, yet the author does not assume that the reader has a solid grasp of "computer lingo." The book starts out by explaining the unexpected shift that the Internet took. It began as a tool for researchers to access expensive hardware, but now it has reached out to many types of people for many different reasons. The book is broken up into six parts, or chapters. The first chapter, entitled "Why Everyone Should Know About Internet," gives reasons how everyone can benefit from the Internet. Business people who used to commute many miles every week can now stay at home with their families and still accomplish as much, if not more. At the other end of the spectrum exists people who are simply on the Internet for companionship. Lastly, this chapter discusses the diversity of people on the Internet. What began as a group of researchers has now opened up to children, librarians, farmers, politicians, activists, etc. The next chapter, "The Lowdown," explains what the basic principles of the Internet are. Great definitions are offered for words such as "remote log-in," "gateways," "protocols," "domain name," etc. You do not have to fully understand the Internet to use it, but every little bit counts. Chapter 3 deals with "Communicating with People." Basically, this chapter deals with the ins and outs of electronic mail (e-mail). LaQuey explains how to send mail and how to reply to mail. But more importantly, this chapter addresses the issue of showing emotion over e-mail. The author offers interesting and valuable advice on how to communicate emotion. The next section, "Finding Information," teaches the readers how to access information. Graphics, software, bulletin boards, journals, newsletters, magazines, to name a few, are some of the resources mentioned. The chapter also gives the readers addresses in which they can access resources. Chapter 5, "Internet In-The-Know Guide," is a more advanced chapter. This chapter deals with security issues, UNIX, viruses, suggestions as to where to go for help, and many other issues. Lastly, Chapter 6, "Getting Connected," explains how to do just that. This book has an appendix for resources and a valuable index. It is very helpful for anyone interested in learning how to be proficient on the Internet. You need a general understanding of computers, but from there, LaQuey expands your knowledge to bring you up to speed in the ever-changing, ever-exciting world of the Internet.

TK6540 .W927
(Radio Broadcasting; Television Broadcasting)

World Radio TV Handbook (Amsterdam: Billboard Books;
New York: BPI Communications [Distributors])

World Radio TV Handbook is a reference tool directed toward the audience for overseas broadcasting. Published annually, it is mainly devoted to radio; slightly less than 10% of the 1994 edition's contents deals with television. The largest sections of the volume consist of worldwide directories of broadcasters who can be received overseas. Long-wave, medium-wave, and short-wave stations, as well as satellite transmissions are covered. The radio portions include both a directory by country, subarranged by frequency, and an overall directory by frequency. These sections provide call numbers or names of stations, addresses, daily duration, and sometimes hours of transmission, and, in many cases, the names of the managing staff and the types of programming. There is also a list of broadcasts in English, by frequency, and brief directories of broadcasters' and listeners' associations worldwide. Discursive sections include a forecast of short-wave reception conditions for the current year (with a table of the most suitable frequency bands for reception), and an article on solar cycles with a forecast of the current year's solar activity. Also included in the 1994 edition are two monographic articles on special topics in broadcasting, a review of the previous year's events in broadcasting, and critical reviews of radio reception equipment and radio-related software marketed in the past year. The volume has a user's guide in English, French, German, and Spanish.

TN—MINING ENGINEERING AND METALLURGY

TN 23 .U582 (Mineral Industries—United States—Periodicals;
Mines and Mineral Resources—United States—Periodicals)

Minerals Yearbook (Washington, DC: U.S. Department
of the Interior, Bureau of Mines)

Minerals Yearbook is a world survey of annual developments in the metal and mineral industries, prepared by the Bureau of Mines.

Volume I, *Metals and Minerals*, is comprised of detailed chapters by bureau scientists. For the most part, each chapter is devoted to a commercially important metal or mineral. The arrangement is alphabetical by chapter title, usually the name of a mineral. Most chapters contain background data on the mineral; a review of the past year's events, including sections on legislation and government programs, production, consumption and uses, prices, foreign trade, a world review by country, and current research; and a section on the current outlook for production and consumption. Most chapters also include numerical data tables on U.S. consumption of specific ores, prices, U.S. exports and imports, and world production by country.

Volume II, *Area Reports: Domestic*, contains chapters on the mineral industry of each state, with sections on the past year's production, employment, environmental issues, exploration activity, legislation and government programs, and a review by mineral, including specific companies' activities. Also included for each state are numerical tables of the quantity and value of production; maps showing deposits and operations; and lists of principal producers, including their addresses.

Volume III, *International Review*, is published in six physically separate reports: five area reports on world regions and Part 6 is *Minerals in the World Economy*. The area reports are subdivided by country into chapters written by bureau scientists, economists, or engineers. Most chapters include government policies and programs, production, trade, industry structure, a review by mineral, infrastructure, and outlook. Also provided for each country are addresses of other sources of information; tables of production data; and information on the structure of the industry, including major companies and their major ownership, and location and annual capacity of facilities. Part 6 consists of an article on the past year's developments in the global minerals economy and numerous data tables, including ones showing the leading producing countries for each mineral.

TS—MANUFACTURERS

TS155 .G26 (Production Management; Production Control; Materials Management)

Gardner, James Allen. Common Sense Manufacturing: Becoming A Top Value Competitor (Homewood, IL: Business One Irwin) 1992.

According to the author, *Common Sense Manufacturing: Becoming A Top Value Competitor* deals with the competitive manufacturing environment by being customer-focused, maintaining an integrated system, creating a "living" people-dependent system, utilizing technologies appropriate for the company, and building flexible strategic plans. The author explains how an organization should plan, control, and manage in the age of information. Also, the author defines the just-in-time philosophy for productivity and efficiency, based on successful business practices in Japan.

The book includes a bibliography and extensive use of tables and flowcharts. The three appendixes are reports entitled "The Japanese Connection," "Inventory Accuracy and the Annual Aberration," and "System Assessment and Performance Measurements."

TS203 .D91 1994/95 (Metalwork—United States—Directories)

Dun's Industrial Guide, The Metalworking Directory
(Parsippany, NJ: Dun and Bradstreet)

Dun's Industrial Guide, The Metalworking Directory is a three-volume work listing manufacturing plants, distributors, and machinery distributors. Manufacturing data include Standard Industrial Classification (SIC) codes, principal manufacturing processes, products purchased, and names of key contacts. Entries are compiled from questionnaires distributed by Dun and Bradstreet.

Volumes 1 and 2 list corporation names in alphabetical order by states and towns. Volume 3 indexes manufacturing plants alphabetically by name and industry. Each volume contains an alphabetical and numerical index of SIC codes and a user's guide.

Z—BIBLIOGRAPHY, LIBRARY SCIENCE, AND INFORMATION RESOURCES (GENERAL)

Z 674.5 .U5 I571 1987
(Information Services—United States—Directories)

Makower, Joel. Instant Information (New York, NY: Prentice Hall Press) 1987.

This source is a guide to information sources. It lists some 9000 organizations, groups, agencies, and university programs. Citations are listed alphabetically by state. Also included in this list are Canada, Puerto Rico, and the Virgin Islands. Entries describe each organization's interests, goals, and the type of information offered. Costs and information use restrictions, if any, are also noted. State agencies are generally excluded. An organization index and subject index are included in an appendix.

Z675 .B8 B97 (Business Libraries; Business—Research—Methodology; Reference Books—Business—Bibliography)

The Business Library and How to Use it (Detroit, MI: Omnigraphics) 1996.

This is a complete guide to the business library as a source of information and service for research. The book is divided into four sections. The first three sections familiarize the readers with the environment of a business library. They focus on how to locate materials, such as books, journals, databases, and indexes in the library. They also help the readers to understand the library as a tool and strategy for research. The last section is devoted to the writing of a business report for research. There indexes are provided in the book: subject index, author/title index, and organization and association index for convenience.

Z 675 .E75 A16 (United States Environmental Protection Agency—Information Services—Directories; Environmental Libraries—Directories; Environmental Policy–United States—Information Services—Directories; Environmental Protection—United States—Information Services—Directories)

ACCESS EPA (Washington, DC: U.S. Environmental Protection Agency, Office of Information Resources Management, Information and Management and Services Division, Information Access Branch)

ACCESS EPA, its introduction states, "is a directory of U.S. Environmental Protection Agency (EPA) and other public sector environmental resources." Published annually, it mainly covers avenues of access to environmental documents and publications. Its purpose is to help the public gain access to the EPA and to environmental information to foster environmental awareness.

Chapter 1 of the 1993 edition includes an organizational overview of the EPA, with contact information for various offices nationwide, and directories of other agencies that provide access to EPA information, including federal depository libraries for each state. It also includes information on documents, publications, and other information resources produced or managed by the EPA. Chapter 2, "Major EPA Dockets," is an overview of the document collections used for EPA rulemaking actions, with descriptions of access services and contact information for each. Chapter 3 provides information on clearinghouses, hotlines, and electronic bulletin boards, most of which are maintained by the EPA, that facilitate the dissemination of environmental information. Chapter 4 is a directory of records management contacts for each office or facility of the EPA. Chapter 5 is a directory of automated databases on environmental topics, most of which are maintained by the EPA, arranged by subjects. Chapter 6 provides information on EPA's libraries and information services. Chapter 7 is a directory of state-maintained environmental libraries, and state environmental contacts in states without environmental libraries. Chapter 8, "EPA Scientific Models," describes a sampling of computational models being implemented in various EPA research facilities. Appendices include an acronym list, and a list by state of all environmental libraries listed elsewhere in the volume, with page references.

The index includes topics, organizational names, and publication titles, interfiled. There are both overall and chapter tables of contents. In addition to its printed form, *ACCESS EPA* is available online through the EPA Online Library System [epaibm.rtpnc.epa.gov, or dial (919) 549-0720], and through the Government Printing Office Federal Bulletin Board [(202) 512-1387; also searchable in dialog file 166].

Z 678.9 .T421 (Libraries—Automation)

Tedd, Lucy. An Introduction to Computer-Based Library Systems (Chichester, NY: J. Wiley) 1993.

The preface explains the format and organization of the book and informs the reader of numerous developments that have occurred in computer-based library systems. These changes, according to the author, have brought about the need for another edition. This is followed by a brief summary of the contents of each chapter. The author outlines not only the changes in the chapters in the first edition, but adds that new chapters on the new computer technology that has enabled different library systems to merge almost into one unified system have been included. The author notes that even by the time that this book is released, further developments will arise, which will differ from the information in the book.

The author then says that traveling around the world and teaching international students has enabled her to gain a greater knowledge of the different computer-based systems of the world. A list and a brief explanation of the figures and tables included throughout the book follow.

Z 699.22 .C66
(Machines—Readable Bibliographical Data—Directories)

Marcaccio, Kathleen Young, Ed. Computer-Readable Databases
(Washington, DC: American Society for Information Science)

This reference guide covers more than 4200 databases produced worldwide
and available publicly. The databases described are those that are available on
the following formats: online, CD-ROM, diskette, magnetical tape, and/or
batch access. The book itself is divided into three sections. The sections are
database profiles, producers, and vendors.

The first section provides information about the database itself. Information includes database name and acronym, producer name and address,
subjects, contents and coverage, type of database, time span covered,
frequency of updates, and print and microform products. Also included is
information on availability, including the database format, access requirements, vendor names, and rates. Availability of print and/or microform
products is also noted, as well as the contact name, address, telephone, and
fax numbers if they are different from the address information listed in the
beginning of the entry.

The producers section lists more than 1700 database producers and
provides the name of the producer and a contact with a list of databases produced. The last section gives approximately 170 vendors' names and addresses, including contact name with a list of databases available. The indexes
are divided into CD-ROM product index, subject index, and master index.

Z 699.22 .D23 (Information Storage and Retrieval
Systems—Directories; Online Data Processing—Directories)

Database Directory (White Plains, NY: Knowledge
Industry Publications)

This source offers an alphabetical listing of databases accessible online. It
provides information on more than 2650 databases. Those covered include
full text, textual and numerical, property, bibliographical, and referral online
databases in all subject areas. The coverage of databases is worldwide, the
only requirement being that the databases must be accessible in North
America. Information on the databases is obtained through questionnaires
that are sent to the producers. The directory consists of main database entries
and vendor, producer, and subject indexes.

The main entries are alphabetical by database name. To assist in
locating database entries, a list of alternate names can be used to check for
former names, acronyms, or alternate names. Each entry provides a general

description of the content and scope of the database, along with the number of
records, the frequency of updates, time coverage, and document types (i.e.,
articles, news releases, wire services, and government documents). Also
included are corresponding print sources, producers, addresses, telephone
and fax numbers, and names of contact persons. Price and availability data
are included here. Up to six subject categories are provided. The language of
the database and search aids are also noted. If a database is available
from more than one vendor in similar formats, it is listed only under the
name of the producer.

The three indexes follow the main entries. The vendor index is an
alphabetical listing of vendor names with contact information, address and
telephone number, and a list of available databases. The producer index lists
more than 1000 producers. Along with the producer name, address, and
telephone number is a list of the databases created by the producer. Those
producers who serve as their own online vendors are listed in both the
producer and vendor indexes. The subject index classifies databases by
subjects. Databases are placed in several categories when appropriate.

A few databases that are not available in the United States are added to
the directory's main entries and are accompanied by notes on restrictions and
conditions. Such a database is usually added if it is likely to become available
in the United States or Canada in the near future. In addition, there are brief
entries for those databases taken offline since the last publication.

Z 881 .N523 S632 (Europe, Eastern—Imprints—Periodicals)

Bibliographic Guide to Soviet and East European Studies
(Boston, MA: G. K. Hall)

This source is a comprehensive record of all materials dealing with Eastern
Europe and Russia that were acquired by the Library of Congress and the
New York Public Library throughout the past year. Books and nonbook
media in English, Slavic, and Eastern European languages are featured. It is
published annually.

Z1035.1 .S431 (Reference Books—Bibliography)

Balay, Robert, Ed., Guide to Reference Books, 11th Ed.
(Chicago: American Library Association) 1996.

The *Guide to Reference Books* is a volume that describes 16,000 reference
works in print and electronic formats. The entries cover not only reference

materials focused on the United States but also works that are international. Information in each entry includes: title, author/editor, publisher, publication date, size, pagination, special features, bibliography, and Library of Congress classification numbers when available.

Historically, the *Guide to Reference Books* began as a 104-page manual by Alice Bertha Kroeger. Subsequent editors included Gilbert Mudge, Constance M. Winchell, and Eugene Sheehy.

Z 1223 .A18 (United Nations Library, Geneva, Switzerland—Catalogs; World Politics—Bibliography–Periodicals)

United Nations Library, Monthly Bibliography (New York, NY: United Nations Bibliographic Information Service)

This source is a bibliography published in two sections by the United Nations Bibliographic Information Service (UNBIS). It serves as the acquisitions list for the United Nations Library in Geneva and the Dag Hammarskjold Library in New York. It is international in scope and indexes publications dealing with worldwide economic, political, industrial, social, and demographic issues.

Part 1 lists books, official documents, and serials. Part 2 indexes selected articles from over 700 periodicals held by libraries. Each entry contains full bibliographical data and notes the library that holds it.

Z 1223 .A18 (United States—Government Publications—Bibliographies)

United States Superintendent of Documents, Monthly Catalog of United States Government Publications (Washington, DC: United States Government Printing Office)

This source is a current bibliography of publications issued by all branches of the U.S. Government that are available through the Government Printing Office, including congressional, department, and bureau publications. Each issue contains general instructions on how to order documents. The source has a cumulative index semiannually, annually, and quinquennially, and includes a classification number index. Descriptive catalog entries follow the Anglo-American Cataloging rules and use the Library of Congress subject headings.

Bibliographical entries are arranged in Superintendent of Documents classification number order. Bibliographical information supplied are monthly catalog entry number, main entry, title phrase and statement of responsibility, imprint, collation, subject headings, Library of Congress classification number, Dewey classification number, Superintendent of Documents number, edition, series statement, notes, item number, stock number, price from the Government Printing Office, added entry, OCLC number, and Library of Congress card number.

Each volume also contains an author index, subject index, series report index by number, title index, contract number index, stock number index, and a title keyword index that is an alphabetical list of truncated titles.

Z 1223 .Z7 C73 (Bills, Legislative—United States—Indexes; United States—Registers)

Congressional Index, 75th Congress (Chicago, IL: Commerce Clearing House)

This source was designed to aid research on the status and history of legislation and other matters in Congress. It provides current reporting and a historical reference on the activities of each Congress. It is contained in two columns for each congressional year beginning with the 75th Congress on 1937/1938. Volume 1 covers activities common to both houses of Congress and specific to the U.S. Senate, including presidential action. Volume 2 reports on activities of the U.S. House of Representatives and actions taken by the Senate on house measures. Public bills and resolutions are listed, summarized, and indexed by subject, and their progress through Congress is covered from introduction to final disposition. The author index lists public bills and resolutions under the name of the author or principal sponsor. Sections on enactment/vetoes, congressional members, committees/hearings, bills and resolutions (listed by date of introduction), status of bills and resolutions, and voting records are included also.

Z 1764 .C81 M42 (Business—Periodicals—Indexes— Periodicals; International Business Enterprises— Periodicals—Indexes—Periodicals)

Publications Index, Business International Index (New York, NY: Business International Corp.)

Publications Index is a guide to the information system of Business International and its subsidiary, Economic Intelligence Unit. The work includes global, regional, and country business monitors as well as industry outlooks, business forecasting services, currency advisories, international banking reports, and tourism analysis. Business International's reports and publications are directed primarily toward entrepreneurs or investors, rather than researchers or government analysts. Publications outline potential areas of growth, guide investment and incorporation, analyze market activities and trends, and advise on licensing, contracts, and tariffs. The abstracts of Business International's publications, given at the beginning of the index, emphasize their brevity and graphics.

The index is cumulative for 1 year and arranged alphabetically by country. Articles that address global issues are indexed as "Worldwide." Within the country headings, publications are indexed by subjects. Cross-referencing is minimal. Under each subheading, the index lists titles, dates, publications, and pages. Publications codes are given in the front. Business International's publications, numbering in the hundreds, are then described in greater detail in the pages immediately following the publication codes.

Z 2483 .E89
(Slavic Countries—Study and Teaching; Europe, Eastern—Bibliography; Soviet Union—Bibliography)

European Bibliography of Soviet, East European, and
Slavonic Studies (Birmingham, UK: University
of Birmingham)

This annual bibliography features European periodical and newspaper articles, books, and essays covering Russia and Eastern Europe. It is arranged by subject and geographical locations. Social sciences and the humanities are largely represented in this source.

Z 2491 .E98 (Russian Literature—Bibliography—Catalogs)

Ezhegodnik Knigi SSSR: Sistematicheskii Ukazatel [Annual of
Book Publishing in the USSR: A Systematic Index] (Moskva,
SSSR: Izd-vo Vsesoiuz'noi Knizhnoi Palaty)

This annual publication contains bibliographical descriptions of books, booklets, and pamphlets published in Russia in all languages of the country. The bibliography is divided into categories of scientific literature, popular science, trade, educational, reference works, and belles letters. Each volume is indexed by name and title in the languages of Russia (excluding Russian), and it is supplied by the subject index of translations into foreign languages.

Z 2491 .K71 (Russian Literature—Bibliography)

Knizhnaia Letopis: Osnovnoivypusa [Chronicle of Book
Publishing, Main Edition] (Moskva, SSSR: Vsesoiuznaia
Knizhnaia Palata)

This primary source of Soviet bibliography, written in Russian, contains the
titles of all pamphlets and books published in Russia. Publications in all
languages are included. The book is divided into 31 classes and includes
geographical, subject, and name indexes. It is published weekly, supplemented monthly, and cumulated annually in Ezhegodnik Knigi SSSR.

Z 2491 .K711 (Russian Literature—Bibliography)

Knizhnaia Letopis, Dopolnitelnyi Vypusk, Kniyii Broshiury
[Chronicle of Book Publishing, Supplementary Edition, Books and
Pamphlets] (Moskva, SSSR: Vsesoiuznaia Knizhnaia Palata)

This source is a supplementary edition to *Knizhnaia Letopis Osnounoi Vypusk*.
It includes an annual index of serial publication with name and geographical
indexes.

Z 2491 .K7122 (Russian Literature—Bibliography)

Knizhnaia Letopis, Dopolnitelnyi Vypusk, Avtoreferaty Disssertatsii
[Chronicle of Book Publishing, Supplementary Edition,
Dissertation Abstracts] (Moskva, SSSR: Vsesoiuznaia
Knizhnaia Palata)

This periodical source indexes all dissertation abstracts in Russia. It is a vital
reference source for scholars and analysts in current and ongoing Soviet
research. It is indexed by subject and includes a name and geographical index
in each issue.

Z 2495 .L65 (Russian Literature—Bibliography—Periodical; Books—Reviews–Indexes)

Letopis Retsenzii [Chronicle of Reviews] (Moskva, SSSR:
Vsesoiuznaia Knizhnaia Palata)

This source is the most comprehensive general index to book reviews, both
Soviet and foreign, found in the central and republic level Soviet press. It
includes an annual index.

Z 2503.5 .E42 A32 (Russian Periodicals—Foreign Countries; Slavic Periodicals—Abstracts)

Abstracts of Soviet and East European Emigre Periodical Literature (Pacific Grove, CA)

This quarterly publication contains abstracts of articles from Russian and East European language periodicals and newspapers published in Western Europe, Israel, and the United States. Abstracts are arranged by subject with author and subject indexes.

Z 5640 .H62 (Computer Science Literature—Bibliography—Periodicals)

Hildebrandt, Darlene Myers. Computing Information Directory (Federal Way, WA: Pedaro) 1994.

This publication consolidates available computing literature into a highly structured directory. The catalog is divided into specific subject headings: computing journals, featuring titles despite their recognition or publication status; university newsletters; breakthrough technologies; software; hardware; Institute of Electronical and Electronics Engineering (IEEE) publications; and marketing research information. Each chapter is highlighted by an introduction, which outlines and explains provided information. Also included are an alphabetized subject index and a table of contents.

Z5814 .T4 C93 (Employees—Training Of—Bibliography)

Staff Training (New York: Garland Pub.) 1990.

This handbook provides a comprehensive guide to literature in the field of training in human services. There are five sections, namely, the instructional systems, assessment, design, implementation, and follow-up, covering different aspects of the field. An introduction is presented in the beginning of each chapter.

Z 6458 .R9 B97 (Law–Soviet Union–Bibliography; Soviet Union–Foreign Relations–Bibliography)

Butler, William Elliott. Russian and Soviet Law: An Annotated Catalogue of Reference Works, Legislation, Court Reports, Serials and Monographs on Russian and Soviet Law (Including International Law) (Zug, Switzerland: InterDocumentation) 1976.

This source is a catalog of those kinds of works mentioned in the subtitle. The entries are arranged by form and, where possible, by subject. It covers

Russian law prior to the 1917 Revolution, and then the law of the Soviet Union from 1917 to 1976. Works dealing with the civil law of Russia, where commercial and trade laws are involved, are covered. All titles are provided in English.

Z 6482 .U5531

UNDOC: Current Index; United Nations Documents Index
(New York, NY: United Nations)

This publication indexes current United Nations publications of international interest pertaining to economic development, international relations, demographic statistics, and human rights. UNDOC is published in four volumes. Volume 1 is "Documents and Publications." It has full bibliographical information and indicates what language the publication is available in. Volume 2 contains the subject index arranged alphabetically with references to full citations. Volume 3 is the personal and corporate name index. Volume 4 contains both the title index and a list of the United Nation's current periodicals. Materials indexed are available in English, French, Russian, Chinese, and Arabic.

Z 6941 .P461 (Periodicals—Directories)

Ulrich's International Periodicals Directory (New Providence, NJ:
R. R. Bowker)

Printed annually in three volumes, this directory indexes more than 118,500 serials. The listed serials include CD-ROMs and serials available through online services. Information is acquired through questionnaires that are sent to serial publishers. Volumes 1 and 2 contain bibliographical information for currently published serials. In addition to the indexes, the third volume is comprised of listings of such information as vendor information and refereed serials.

The bibliographical entries in the first and second volumes are arranged alphabetically by subject; there are approximately 696 subject headings. Citations for the serials are arranged alphabetically by title under the subject headings. If a serial covers several subjects, title cross-references appear under related headings; only under one heading is the full citation recorded. Each entry reports the serial title, publication frequency, name of the editor, and circulation, along with the publisher address, telephone, and fax number. In addition, the first year of publication, price, language, and former titles are given. The format of the serial is reported if it is other than the standard magazine format (i.e., microform, loose-leaf, or newspaper). A brief description provides information on the contents and editorial focus.

Two indexes provide access to the main bibliographical entries: a title index and an International Standard Serial Number (ISSN) index. The third volume also has several lists of specific serials; these lists also refer readers to Volumes 1 and 2 for the main bibliographical entries. The refereed serials directory lists serials that are peer-reviewed, whereas the controlled circulation serials list records those serials that are sent to specific qualified audiences. Controlled circulation serials are intended for target groups such as members of a profession and are not available publicly. Also found in this volume are listings for serials available on CD-ROM and online. Finally, in the third volume, there are alphabetical listings of vendors and producers. All lists in this volume are alphabetical.

Z 6956 .R9 V96 (Russian Periodicals—Bibliography; Russian Newspapers—Bibliography)

Letopis Periodicheskikh i Prodolzhaiushchikhsia Izdanii Builleteni [Chronicle of Periodical and Serial Publications, Bulletins] (Moskva, SSSR: Kniga)

This source is a biennial record of Russian newspapers and other periodical literature.

Z 6956 .R9 V98 (Russian Periodicals—Bibliography)

Letopis Periodicheskikh Izdanii SSSR (Moskva, SSSR: Izd-vo Vsesoiuzhoi Palaty)

This source is a comprehensive listing of Soviet periodicals featuring bulletins and journals in Section 1 and a geographical arrangement of Soviet newspapers in Section 2. Alphabetical and subject indexes are included.

Z 7162 .C81 B54 (Business—Bibliography—Periodicals; Economics—Bibliography—Periodicals)

Bibliographic Guide to Business and Economics (Boston, MA: G. K. Hall)

This source is an annual subject bibliography consisting of publications catalogued in the previous year by the New York Public Library and the Library of Congress. Books included are taken from Library of Congress

Marc tapes HA–HJ (those in the business subject area) and from the New York Public Library if the record contains two or more subject headings that correspond to Library of Congress subject headings. The following are some of the major subject areas included: economic theory, population, demography, economic history, land and agriculture, industry, labor, transportation and communication, commerce, business administration, finance, foreign exchange, insurance, revenue, taxation, public finance, and statistics. The bibliography is not restrictive in language or format. Each citation contains complete Library of Congress cataloging information, International Standard Book Number (ISBN), and identification of New York Public Library holding. Access is by main entry, added entry, title, series title, and subject headings, with entries organized in a single alphabetical listing. Full bibliographical information, including tracings, is given in the main entry, with condensed citations for secondary entries.

Z 7164 .C4 F13
(Europe—Industries—Periodicals—Indexes; Corporations—Europe—Periodicals—Indexes; Commercial Products—Europe—Periodicals—Indexes; Securities—Europe—Periodicals)

Predicasts F&S Index Europe (Cleveland, OH: Predicasts)

This source is a Predicasts index that covers more than 750 business, trade, and finance publication pertaining to the activities and challenges of European, Japanese, and U.S. companies operating in Europe.

Periodicals covered include financial publications, trade magazines, business-oriented newspapers, and special reports. Coverage includes the European Community or Common Market, non-European Community Western Europe, Eastern Europe, Scandinavia, and the Soviet Union. The topics dealt with are economic information, agriculture, mining, construction, manufacturing, transport and utilities, trade and services, government and international groups, and business. Information can be found on corporate acquisitions and mergers, new products, technological developments, and social and political factors.

The first section covers industries and products, with a major industry group arrangement utilizing the SIC coding system. The second section deals with individual countries, arranging information by region with SIC subdivisions. The third section provides information on companies and is organized alphabetically by company name. Individual entries in each section provide titles, brief citations, and a short synopsis of article contents. Yearly cumulations contain a source list and an alphabetical guide to SIC codes.

Z7164 .C81A23 (Accounting—Indexes—Periodicals; Taxation—Indexes–Periodicals)

The Accounting & Tax Index (Ann Arbor, MI: UMI)

This index offers citations to articles in essentially every aspect of taxation and accounting. Related subjects covered are financial compensation, financial consulting, the financial services industry, and financial management. Each entry has a bibliographical citation and occurs under multiple headings. The alphabetized headings available for scanning are authors, government agencies, names of corporations, and organizations.

Z 7164 .C81 B48 (Accounting—Bibliography; Bookkeeping—Bibliography; Copyright–United States)

Bentley, Harry C. Bibliography of Works on Accounting by American Authors (Boston, MA: H. C. Bentley)

This source is a historical bibliography of accounting works copyrighted by American authors from the late 18th to the early 20th centuries. The first volume consists of four parts: (1) a chronological listing of accounting studies published between 1796 and 1901; (2) a classification of these sources excluding those that deal with the general principles of bookkeeping theory and practice; (3) a bibliography of copyrighted materials published before 1901 for restricted use in schools or correspondence courses; and (4) a chronological listing of pre-1901 accounting imprints that lack complete bibliographical information. The second volume is directed to accountants, teachers, students, and librarians interested in 20th century accounting literature and spans the period from January 1, 1901 to January 1, 1935. Part 1 is a chronological bibliography of accounting works by American authors that were published for general distribution during the 20th century. Part 2 is a classification of sources listed in Part 1 and covers the following topics: bookkeeping texts for high schools and private business schools; elementary and advanced accounting books for college students or for general reference; accounting materials that look at the preparation and interpretation of financial statements; cost accounting and system building studies that deal with general principles and practice and that are applicable to specific business and professions; auditing works that embrace general principles and procedures and treatises applicable to specific businesses and professions; certified public accountant examination questions and answers; and encyclopedias, handbooks, guides, and other sources. The supplement describes efforts put forth by trade associations, professional and industrial organizations, government bureaus, and federal and state government regulatory bodies to make accounting practice and procedure uniform. The appendix lists accounting sources published during the last 10 years (i.e., 1924–1934), national associations of accountants and the periodicals they sponsor, histories and bibliographies of accounting, and other relevant information. Both volumes have author indexes.

Z 7164 .C81 B72 (Business—Periodicals—Databases—Directories; Business—Bibliography—Periodicals; Law—Periodicals—Databases—Directories; Law—Bibliography–Periodicals)

Nobari, Nuchine, Ed. Books and Periodicals Online: A Guide to Publication Contents of Business and Legal Databases. (New York, NY: Books and Periodicals) 1990.

This source is a reference guide to over 17,658 publications in approximately 480 databases. Areas of information included are business, marketing, taxation, accounting, bibliographical, law, and general news. The guide begins with a table of contents, followed by an introduction detailing what is new in this edition. It then provides a sample entry with descriptors, format information, and an explanation section, identifying and detailing the scope and usefulness of the publication.

The main body of the guide is arranged in four alphabetized section. The first section is a listing by publication titles, the second is a listing of publishers' names and addresses, the third is a listing of producers' and vendors' names and addresses, and the fourth section is a listing of books and periodicals grouped by databases available. Coverage includes periodicals and serials from throughout the world and databases published in the United States, the UK, and *Canada. Information is based primarily on Ulrich's International Periodicals Directory*, the *Standard Periodical Directory*, *Ebsco's Serials Directory*, and OCLC.

This directory is intended as a guide to determining, if and where a publication is available online, how many years of backfiles are available and current addresses of publishers for ordering articles or other information. A new feature added to this edition is an inverted pyramid symbol at the beginning of an entry to indicate that the title is available on CD-ROM.

The directory does not provide full bibliographical information or sources, or give complete subject access to the publications listed.

Z 7164 .C81 B88 (Accounting—Bibliography)

Brown, Lawrence D., Gardner, John C., and Miklos A. Vasarhelyi. Accounting Research Directory: The Database of Accounting Literature (Princeton, NJ: M. Wiener; London: Paul Chapman) 1994.

This publication describes and analyzes journal articles published between the years 1963 and 1992 from seven prominent accounting journals. Its purpose is to guide the research of accounting professors and practitioners rapidly and efficiently. It serves as an outline for professors in choosing relevant articles for lectures and assignments and as an aid for practitioners, with its specific and accurate categorizations of articles. The first part of the publication contains an alphabetized list by author and co-author(s), meaning articles will appear as many times as there are authors listed. The second part of the publication divides the listings into four major subheadings, including mode of reasoning, research method, school of thought, and subject area. A table of contents, which also classifies the articles into the four taxonomies, is provided. A citation index also is provided.

Z 7164 .C81 B984 (Business—Periodicals—Indexes; Industry—Periodicals—Indexes)

Business Periodicals Index (New York, NY: H. W. Wilson Co.)

Published monthly with annual cumulations, this source is an index to English language periodicals. The selection of indexed periodicals is done by sub-scriber vote. Subscribers are asked to place emphasis on the reference value of the periodicals considered. The main body of the index is subject entries to business periodical articles. A separate listing of citations to book reviews follows this main body of the index.

Under a variety of alphabetically listed subject headings are the article citations. Topics include accounting, industrial relations, occupational health and safety, regulation of industry, communications and other specific business, and industry and trade subjects. Articles concerning a company or person are indexed under the specific name. Entries provide basic citation information: article and periodical title, author, periodical volume and date, and page numbers. If an article includes illustrations, that is noted also. Clarification of the meaning of article titles is done by editors at times. Book review citations provide the same type of information.

Z 7164 .C81 C57 (Corporation Reports—United States—Indexes—Periodicals; Corporation—United States—Directories)

CIRR/Corporate & Industry Research Reports
(Eastchester, NY: JA Micropublishing)

This reference source brings together research reports and other publications generated by major worldwide securities and investment firms. Coverage focuses largely on North American and Western European companies. However, other areas, especially the Pacific Rim, are also represented. The reports, forecasts, periodicals and newsletters are prepared by leading economists and corporate analysts for over one hundred major investment firms. Coverage is regularly expanded to include new investment companies. The style of the reports is technical and oriented towards readers with a background in securities and investments.

The CIRR is available on microfiche, with printed indexes issued bimonthly and superseded annually. Microfiche indexes run two years behind the current year. In addition, the CIRR can be accessed by CD-Rom and online through BRS and DIALOG. Online reports are kept current on a quarterly basis.

The research reports, composed largely of charts and graphs, are signed and dated and include report objectives and a stock rating for the subject company. General headings provide topical divisions within each report; however, bibliographies and indexes are not provided.

Subject access is provided for the online and CD-Rom versions of CIRR by the name of the company that the report is about. Annual printed indexes provide more complicated access to the microfiche version by company name, general industry and name of the firm preparing the report. Economic trends and forecasts, periodicals and newsletters are indexed by the name of the firm that prepared them. Fiche and control numbers in the index citation direct the user to the microfiche themselves and these are organized by control number within a broader alphabetical arrangement by the name of the securities and investment firm that prepared the report.

Z 7164 .C81 P48

Personnel Literature (Washington, DC: GPO)

This guide, published monthly, collects journal articles, scholarly documents, and book reviews that deal with issues in personnel management. A variety of topics, including absenteeism, hiring ethics, removal, and training, is covered.

Z 7164 .C81 S77 (Accounting—Periodicals—Bibliography; Accounting Literature—Publishing—Directories)

Spiceland, J. David and Surendra P. Agrawal. International Guide to Accounting Journals (Princeton, NJ: Markus Wiener) 1992.

This edition contains an alphabetized listing of journals that publish articles on topics in accounting. It is designed to aid the researcher in finding pertinent journals for her/his publication. Each entry contains information concerning the intended audience, frequency of publication, and acceptance rate. A separate listing of the journals by the country in which they are published also is provided. A table of contents is included as well.

Z 7164 .C81 S927 1988 (Reference Books—Business—Bibliography—Handbooks, Manuals, etc.; Business—Information Services—United States—Handbooks, Manuals, etc.; Government Publications—United States—Handbooks, Manuals, etc.; Business—Databases—Handbooks, Manuals, etc.)

Strauss, Diane Wheeler. Handbook of Business Information: A Guide for Librarians, Students, and Researchers (Englewood, CO: Libraries Unlimited) 1988.

The purpose of this source is to give the reader knowledge of the basics in business and to identify and describe the use of important sources of business information. The book is not inclusive and limits sources to topics covering business in the United States.

Each chapter begins with an introduction of the fundamentals of business, as well as basic concepts and vocabulary, enabling the reader to understand the sources of information available. Important business information sources are described and some illustrations from the texts are given. Information is given on how to use these sources.

The book is divided into two parts. The first part consists of eight chapters and gives information on business sources according to formats available, including bibliographies, quick reference sources, directories, loose-leaf services, government documents, vertical file material and databases. The second part, chapters nine through eighteen, focuses on specific fields of business. Topics include marketing, investment, insurance and real estate.

An index that combines author, title and subject is located at the back of the book. There are a variety of appendices. Some of the topics covered are business acronyms and abbreviations, selected government agencies and their publications and a list of free materials for a business oriented vertical file.

Z 7164 .C81 T66 (Business—Periodicals—Bibliography; Commerce—Periodicals—Bibliography; American Periodicals—Bibliography)

Trade, Industrial, and Professional Periodicals of the United States (Westport, Conn.: Greenwood Press) 1994.

The periodicals listed in the Trade, Industrial, and Professional Periodicals of the United States have played an important roll to the industry, trade, or profession in all aspects of American economic life. Publications are from a wide variety of industries, and is not meant to include all business periodicals, only the most important. The editors have made sure that all periodicals have available back issues. Included is a list of periodicals, a chronological list, a bibliography, and an index.

Z 7164 .C81 W72 (Advertising—United States—Bibliography)

Williams, Emelda L. and Donald W. Hendon. American Advertising: A Reference Guide (New York: Garland) 1988.

This publication contains summaries of articles in journals and books in American advertising. The annotated bibliography is comprised of four chapters: Advertising Overview, Institutions in Advertising, Creating the Advertising, and Special Types of Advertising. The data are further separated into twenty-four subheadings that fall within these divisions. Entries are listed alphabetically within each chapter and selections are cross-referenced if they fit more than one category. A table of contents and an author index are provided.

Z 7164 .E2 A52 (Economics—Periodicals—Indexes)

Index of Economic Articles in Journals and Collective Volumes (Homewood, IL: T.D. Irwin)

This annual publication indexes English language articles, conference proceedings and committee reports originating from approximately 200 international economic journals. Full bibliographic information is provided for each entry. The index is available online through Economic Literature Index.

Z 7164 .E2 E19 Subject:
(Economics—Bibliography—Periodicals)

Fletcher, John (Editor, University of Warwick), Economics
Working Papers Bibliography (Dobbs Ferry, NY: Trans-Media)

Draft papers that have not reached the final state needed for publication, which are available for critiquing by interested people before they are published, are known as "Working Papers." A majority of working papers are mimeographed typescript, in which publication is never achieved. The few that are published were most likely available as working papers several years before publication.

Within the Bibliography papers are chosen by subject. The coverage of the Bibliography and microfilm service has returned to its subject of the past, economics. Economics is defined as broadly as possible to include all areas of interest to economists. It includes the economics aspects of most fields of interest excluding management.

The Working papers are dated upon receipt to the University of Warwick library. The papers received by the library within one year of their writing, which were not previously published will be included in the bibliography.

The Microfilm Service contains all of the papers the bibliography has except those that are of too poor quality to film or are incomplete. All of the papers in the microfilm service have copyright permission.

There are Three indexes within the bibliography. They are: the Author Index, the Series Index, and the Subject Index. In each index papers ore arranged.

For the Author Index the papers are arranged by the first authors name. If more than exists the words "and others" follow the first.

The Series Index contains papers that were issued a numbered series for the sponsoring institution of the author. The numbered series is followed by the author of each paper in the bibliography and the EWP number (the microfilm copy number). Few papers have do not receive a series. They are entered as "Miscellaneous Series", which are located at the end of the series list. If papers have not been numbered the University of Warwick issues one. The papers are usually issued in numerical order, but when they aren't the list of papers under the series title may be incomplete.

In the Subject Index specific subject headings were used as long as possible. See reference offered from never before used terms to preferred terms.

The bi-annually issued Bibliographies are not cumulative from January 1980 on.

Z 7164 .E2 H96 (Economic History—1945—Bibliography)

Huq, A. M. Abdul. The Global Economy: An Information Sourcebook (Phoenix, AZ: Oryx Press) 1988.

This annotated bibliography incorporates world economic literature dating primarily after 1980. It is designed to educate the American reader on foreign economic issues. The sources contained within this publication include book and book-like selections, although some periodicals, annuals, and yearbooks are included as well. A table of contents, a title index, and a subject index also are provided.

Z 7164 .E2 I62 (Economics—Bibliography)

International Bibliography of Economics (Chicago, IL: Bibliographie Internationale de Science E'conomique)

This source is an international bibliography listing journal articles, pamphlets, books and other government publications in several different languages. It contains author and subject indexes and is printed in both English and French.

Z7164 .F5 A52 (Banks and Banking—Periodicals—Indexes; Bank Management—Periodicals—Indexes)

American Bankers Association, Banking Literature Index (Washington DC: The Association)

The focus of this index is bank management. It includes current periodical articles dealing with banking issues, trends, operations, and topics. The articles are chosen for their statistical or substantive contribution to the knowledge of the industry. This index, published monthly, compiles the annual cumulation.

Z 7164 .F5 B67 (Investments—Japan—Bibliography)

Boger, Karl. Japanese Direct Foreign Investments: An Annotated Bibliography (New York: Greenwood Press) 1989.

This annotated bibliography is comprised of books, short monographs, U.S. government documents, Japanese government reports, and articles from journals focusing on overseas Japanese investments after the second world war. The publication is heavily weighted with book selections, for they cover theoretical and statistical information in greater depth. Media articles have been omitted. The chapters are divided into geographical distributions of Japan's investments with the greatest attention on the United States and Southeast Asia. An author and editor index, a title index, a subject index, and a table of contents also are provided.

Z 7164 .F5 B82 (Finance—Bibliography)

Brealey, Richard A. and Helen Edwards. A Bibliography
of Finance (Cambridge, MA: MIT Press) 1991.

This publication is comprised of analytic articles from journals written primarily by financial economists. Relevant books, such as Keyne's General Theory, and assorted papers which are frequently referenced when researching topics on finance, are included as well. The majority of the articles are recent, published between 1980 and 1989. The selections are divided into chapters of general subject heading and listed more specifically in the table of contents. An author index, where entries are cross-referenced according to second and third authors, and a subject index are provided. All subjects are listed alphabetically. An index of key words and a listing of journal abbreviations are also included.

Z 7164. F5 D48
(Banks and Banking—United States—Bibliography)

Deuss, Jean. Banking in the U.S. (Metuchen, NJ: Scarecrow
Press) 1990.

This bibliography lists books on the history, organization, regulation and management of banks and banking in the United States. The focus is on commercial banking, savings institutions and investment banking.

Z 7164 .F5 F48 (Finance—Bibliography—Periodicals;
Finance—Periodicals—Indexes—Periodicals)

Finance Literature Index (New York: McGraw-Hill, Inc.)

Finance Literature Index provides bibliographic references for articles published in leading finance journals. First published in 1988, in the fourth edition a total of fifty-five journals are indexed. Since the first edition, coverage of banking, investments, and finance literature has been broadened to include journals from the insurance and real estate areas.

The index is divided into two parts. Part One contains a chronological listing of articles, by journal, from first issue published through 1992. To limit size, this will likely be the last edition that contains the history of every journal's table of contents in Part One, which now contains more than 20,000 references. All journal issues are numbered. Appendix A, beginning on page 561, contains a cross reference, by journal, that notes any monthly, quarterly, or seasonal names corresponding to particular issues. Part Two, beginning on page 221, lists articles in alphabetical order by author. For multiple author articles, the citation is repeated in its entirety for each co-author. Because of space considerations, Part Two does not include many of the pre-1960 articles. Article titles and authors' names are directly from the journal tables of contents.

Z 7164. F5F54 (Finance—Periodicals—Bibliography; Finance—Periodicals—Indexes)

Fisher, William. Financial Journals and Serials: An Analytical Guide to Accounting, Banking, Finance, Insurance and Investment Periodicals (New York: Greenwood Press)

This volume attempts to establish some kind of bibliographic control over the serial literature in the areas of accounting, banking, finance, insurance and investments. A whole range of types of publications, such as scholarly journals, periodicals and newsletters, is included.

Z 7164 .F5 F95 (Industry—Periodicals—Indexes; Commercial Products—Periodicals—Indexes; Business Enterprises—Periodicals—Indexes)

Predicasts F & S Index, International (Cleveland, OH: Predicasts)

This source is another index in the Predicasts line and it covers Canada, Africa, Japan, Oceania, Latin America, the Middle East and other Asian countries. It is cumulated quarterly and annually. Information on U.S. companies located in these areas of the world are found in this index, rather than in the United States Index.

More than 750 publications, including financial publications, trade magazines, business oriented newspapers and special reports, are indexed. This index provides information on products, companies and industries. Data can be found on corporate acquisitions and mergers, new products, technological developments and social and political factors. Entries provide brief descriptions of article contents, date and page number of the article and the journal that it appeared in. In addition, entries indicate the region or country that the article concerns.

The index is divided into three sections. The first section is arranged by Standard Industrial Classification (SIC) codes; an alphabetical listing of the SIC codes is included. Information is given on new products, plant capacities, market data, technology, equipment expenditures and general economic factors, such as wages, business investments, consumer spending and government regulation and spending. Country and regional entries are provided for general economic factors.

Arranged alphabetically by region and country, the second section provides industry, product and general economic data for each country, as well as government entries for each country. The third section is arranged alphabetically by company name. This section reports merger and acquisition data, joint venture information, sales and profits, analyses of companies by securities firms and other corporate and financial information. Parent and subsidiary company cross references are given.

Z 7164 .F5 F97 (Finance—Periodicals—Indexes; Investments—Periodicals—Indexes; Securities—United States—Periodicals)

Predicasts F & S Index, United States (Cleveland, OH: Predicasts)

This index is published weekly, with quarterly and annual cumulations. Information is provided only on those companies within the United States. Data on foreign companies located in the United States is found in this index, while information on U.S. companies located abroad can be found in Predicasts F & S Index, International and Predicasts F & S Index, Europe.

More than 750 publications, including financial publications, trade magazines, business oriented newspapers and special reports, are indexed. This two volume publication provides information on products, companies and industries. Information can be found on corporate acquisitions and mergers, new products, technological developments and social and political factors. Entries provide brief descriptions of article contents, date and page number of the article and the journal that it appeared in.

The first volume provides information on industries and products. It is arranged by Standard Industrial Classification (SIC) codes; an alphabetical list of the SIC codes is given. Information is given on new products, plant capacities, market data, technology, equipment expenditures and general economic factors, such as wages, business investments, consumer spending and government regulation and spending.

The second volume is arranged alphabetically by company name. This section reports merger and acquisition data, joint venture information, sales and profits, analyses of companies by securities firms and other corporate and financial information. Parent and subsidiary company cross references are given.

Z 7164 .F5 H45 (New York Stock Exchange—Bibliography)

Heckman, Lucy. The New York Stock Exchange: A Guide
to Information Sources (New York, NY: Garland) 1992.

This source is a selected bibliography on the New York Stock Exchange (NYSE) and contains 484 English language sources. Entries are annotated and are indexed by author, title and subject. The opening chapter discusses the organization and history of the NYSE.

The bibliography is divided into chapters based on the source type, such as general guides and dictionaries, bibliographies, biographies of men and women who influenced the NYSE, general histories and histories covering specific time periods, including 1792–1816, 1817–1860, 1861–1870, 1871–1914, 1915–1929, the Crash of 1929, 1930–1934, 1935–1949, 1950–1987, October 1987 Crash and 1988–1991.

Also included are chapters on statistics sources concerning the NYSE and directories of international exchanges and brokerage firms. Appendices cover the chronology of the NYSE, presidents and chairmen of the NYSE, online databases and CD-Rom products and a directory of selected serial publications.

Z7164 .F5 S72 (Finance—Bibliography; Banks and Banking—Bibliography; Finance—Information Services—Directories; Banks and Banking—Information Services—Directories)

Sources of World Financial and Banking Information. Edited by
G. R. Dicks (Westport, CT: Greenwood Press) 1981.

This directory consists of three parts. The first lists 5,000 publications which include the following information for each citation: the full title in the language in which it was published; the publisher; publication language; date and frequency of publication; pages; country or countries covered; subscription price; and summary of the contents. The source publications are in alphabetical order by country except when more than one is covered. Then they can be found in the international section which is subdivided into the six continents: Asia, Africa, Europe, Australia, and North and South America. The second part lists the publishing bodies (in the same classified order as in part one) and gives their name, address, and telephone and telex numbers.

Part three is a classification of the material according to a seven part indexing system that consists of 1) general economic and financial information, 2) national income accounts and public finance, 3) money and banking, 4) companies and stocks and shares, 5) household and persons, 6) the balance of payments and energy, and 7) prices. Part three allows the user to find a subject of interest in any country. Reference to part one will provide information on the each publication which, if desired, the user can follow up in part two by getting the name, address, and necessary numbers.

Z 7164 .G7 G23 (Government Publications—Bibliography—Methodology; Bibliographical Citations)

Garner, Diane L. and Diane H. Smith. The Complete Guide to Citing Government Information Resources: A Manual for Writers and Librarians (Bethesda, MD: Congressional Information Service) 1993.

This work is divided into five sections: United States federal, state-local-regional, international, foreign, and electronic documents. It is intended for writers, reference librarians, and government document specialists. Two appendices provide a list of style manuals and a list of standard reference sources for government information. A glossary and an index are included.

Z 7164 .L1 E55
(Labor Movement—Bibliography—Periodicals; Industrial Relations—Bibliography—Periodicals)

Work Related Abstracts (Warren, MI: Harmonie Park Press)

This source is a monthly loose-leaf abstracting/indexing service of over 250 management, labor, government, professional and academic periodicals from around the world. Abstracts are arranged chronologically within twenty broad subject categories, including Behavior at Work, Labor-Management Relations, Human Resource Management, Compensation and Fringe Benefits, Safety and Health, Education and Training, Industrial Engineering, Government Policies and Actions, Litigation and Management Science. A selected list of United States based labor unions and employee organizations is included in each volume.

An alphabetical index to subjects, organizations and individuals is cumulated continuously for the current year. Cross references for subject

headings can be found in the final cumulated January–December index and in
the biennial Work Related Abstracts Subject Heading List. Work Related
Abstracts continues Employment Relations Abstracts (1950–1972).

Z7164 .L1 V77
(Industrial Relations—Periodicals—Bibliography)

Vocino, Michael and Cameron, Lucille W. Labor and
Industrial Relations Journals and Serials (Westport, CT)
1989.

This book is a guide to serials, labor and industrial relations and draws from
the examination of other fields such as economics, history, law, and political
science. Some indexes are of newsletters, newspapers and bulletins. The
subject, publisher's or geographic indexes can be used to find bibliographic
information and an annotation which outlines the type and tone of the articles
contained in the serial.

Z 7164 .M18 D55 (Marketing Research—Bibliography)

The Bibliography of Marketing Research Methods (Lexington,
Mass.: Lexington Books) 1990.

The Bibliography of Marketing Research Methods is a one volume collection
of more than 14,000 references on the methods of marketing research. The
purpose of this bibliography is to provide a directory of publications for
studying how to do research in marketing. The references made are from
national and international periodicals, conference proceedings, and other similar forms of literature. Some citations are drawn from non-marketing
literature such as social-science and technical science sources. The Bibliography of Marketing Research Methods provides full bibliographic citations
for research methods, and it gives some references on the applications of
these techniques.

   The references made in The Bibliography of Marketing Research
Methods are indexed extensively. An overview of the detailed table of
contents shows how the citations are organized into major sections. These
sections are divided into numbered headings and subheadings so the nature
and content of the listed reference is immediately known. Entries are arranged
alphabetically and in reverse chronological order. The Bibliography of
Marketing Research Methods also provides subject and author indexes and
cross references. Entries include the chief person responsible for the material

cited, title, publisher, publication date, issue or volume number, and related page numbers.

Z 7164 .M18 H56
(Marketing—United States—Management—Bibliography; Sales Management—United States—Bibliography; Marketing Information Services—United States—Directories; Selling—Information Services—United States—Directories)

Herold, Jean. Marketing and Sales Management: An Information Sourcebook (Phoenix, AZ: Oryx Press) 1988.

This annotated bibliography contains books dating primarily after 1980 which focus on techniques of management and topics in sales and marketing. It is designed to aid the business person, educator, researcher, and student in the United States. Most of the selections are available on a commercial basis in public and college libraries. This publication is divided into topical chapters which are cataloged in the table of contents. Each chapter also contains a list of related journals. An abbreviation index, an author index, a subject index, and a title index are included as well.

Z7164 .P9555 M37 (Finance, Public—Bibliography; Finance, Public—United States—Bibliography)

Marshall, Marion B. Public Finance: An Information Sourcebook (Phoenix, AZ: Oryx Press) 1987.

This source is a selective bibliography on public finance and is directed to the student, professional, or interested individual who does not understand the interdisciplinary nature or the concepts of the field. The work is arranged by subject into four parts. The first, public finance theory and practice, surveys public goods and services, distributive justice, fiscal policy, history, statistical sources on public finance, and resources providing continuing reporting on public finance theory; the second, financial management, looks at budgeting, accounting and auditing, and lists relevant periodicals; the third, federal government finances, discusses federal government receipts and expenditures, budget processes, expenditure controls, proposals to reduce the federal government role and spending, and federal credit programs, trust funds, and financial management systems; and the fourth chapter lists reference works and explains the history of the federal tax system, federal taxation, taxation and politics, public opinion on taxes, other kinds of taxation, and taxation and pollution control. The systematic inclusion of sources for this bibliography extends to publications that were issued through mid-1986, though a few more important ones that came out before 1987 are also included. Author, title, and subject indexes.

Z 7164 .S37 G731 (United States. Securities and Exchange Commission—Bibliography)

Graham, John W. The U.S. Securities and Exchange
Commission: A Research and Information Guide
(New York: Garland) 1993.

This is a well-annotated bibliography of materials by and about the Securities and Exchange Commission as well as a guide to information concerning the structure and functions of the organizations. Four appendices serve to introduce the S.E.C. to the reader. Among topics covered are accounting, corporate governance, disclosure policy, S.E.C. history, and regulation. Bibliographic items represent the period 1933–1990 with a scattering of pre-1933 items. The emphasis is on long, significant or illustrative works. Items take the form of books, journal and law review articles, U.S. government documents, S.E.C. published items, dissertations, special issues of periodicals, loose-leaf services, and online sources. There are three indexes: author, title, and subject.

Z7164 .S68 S87 (Leadership—Bibliography)

Leadership Abstracts and Bibliography (Columbus: College
of Administrative Science, Ohio State University) 1977.

This book gives an analysis of the literature published from 1874 onwards on leadership. Abstracts on the significant findings on leadership in each publication is included and organized in alphabetical order by author.

Z 7164 .T87 N26 (Corporations—United States—History—Bibliography)

Nasrallah, Wahib. United States Corporation Histories:
A Bibliography, 1965–1990 (New York: Garland) 1991.

This publication is an index to the histories of various corporations, ranging from large companies to more private businesses. Histories include the heritage, the corporate traditions, and the progress through the years. Covering the span of 1965 to 1990, this bibliography utilizes articles from newspapers, books, articles from periodicals, theses, dissertations, pamphlets, and collected works of specific companies for documentation. The journal alphabetizes the list of corporations. Related citations and cross-references are cited as well. An index to United States corporations' histories by industry also is provided, in addition to an executive officer index and an author index.

Z 7164 .U5 A6641 1988 (Government Publications—United States—Bibliography; United States—Economic Conditions—Periodicals—Bibliography)

Geahigan, Priscilla C. and Robert F. Rose, Editors. Business Serials of the U.S. Government, 2nd Edition (Chicago: ALA) 1988.

The U.S. government provides a wealth of business information from which the editors have selected some of the most relevant, mostly leaving aside the ephemeral, agency reports, and court cases and decisions (except Internal Revenue publications). The material is divided into 14 business-related topics. Brief and clear instruction in deciphering government documents citations may be found in the introduction. Annotations (signed) are descriptive, evaluative, and/or comparative, indicate relationships to other titles, and known indexing sources. Such sources, along with their abbreviations are listed at the beginning. There are separate title and subject indexes at the end. Authority control based on the Business Periodicals Index forms the basis for the subject index.

Z 7164.07 B22 (Decision-Making—Bibliography)

Balachandran, Sarojini; Decision Making: An Information Sourcebook (Phoenix. AZ: Oryx Press) 1987.

The many disciplines encompassed by the subject of decision making from accounting to psychology necessitate a selective approach. This book makes such a selection in the form of an annotated bibliography of materials in English that deal exclusively with managerial decision making, its methodology and application.The items include books, reports, databases, dissertations, and journal articles. Separate chapters cover methodology, applications, decision aids, quantitative techniques, a useful core library collection, and other sources of information. There indexes by author, title, and subject.

Z 7165 .E2 H96 (Economic History—1945—Bibliography)

Huq, A. M. Abdul. The Global Economy: An Information Sourcebook (Phoenix, AZ: Oryx Press) 1988.

This annotated bibliography incorporates world economic literature dating primarily after 1980. It is designed to educate the American reader on foreign economic issues. The sources contained within this publication include book and book-like selections, although some periodicals, annuals, and yearbooks are included as well. A table of contents, a title index, and a subject index also are provided.

Z 7165 .J3 B67 (Industrial Policy—Japan—Bibliography)

Boger, Karl. Postwar Industrial Policy in Japan: An Annotated Bibliography (Metuchen, New Jersey: The Scarecrow Press) 1988.

This reference is a bibliography of materials dealing with the issue of Japanese industrial policy in the postwar period. There are eight chapters covering various economic and social aspects of Japanese industrial policy. In addition, there are several indexes to facilitate the use of this reference, including an Authors and Editors Index, a Title Index, and a Subject Index.

Z 7165 .R9 E37 1960 (Marxian Economics—Bibliography; Economic History—Bibliography; Economics—Bibliography; Soviet Union—Economic Conditions—Bibliography)

Ekonomicheskaia Istoriia: Ukazatel' Sovetskoi Literatury (Moskva, SSSR: INIBOM AN SSSR)

This source is an irregular publication tied to the International Congress of Economic History. It is a bibliography dealing with basic trends in the development of Soviet Economic History and covering works of Soviet scholars on world economic history from antiquity to the present time. This bibliography is divided into two basic categories: "History of economic thought" and "History of world economics." It covers textbooks, books and articles written by Soviet scholars and published in scholarly journals and serial publications. It is indexed by geographical names, names of figures of importance, by author/edition and title.

Z 7165 .R93 B (Soviet Union—Economic Conditions—1918—Bibliography—Periodicals)

Novaia Sovetskaia Literatura po Obshchestvennym Naukam, Ekonomika [New Soviet Literature on Social Sciences, Economics] (Moskva, SSSR: AnN SSSR, INION)

This source is monthly bibliographic index published by the Institute of Scientific Information on Social Sciences (INION) of the Soviet Academy of Sciences. This index informs users about new publication in the field of economics published in the USSR in Russian and other Soviet languages. The index covers scholarly and popular works on economics, including monographs, serials, textbooks, pamphlets, dissertations, articles and essays from numerous serials and periodicals. It is a must for people working on the issues of Soviet economics.

Z 7551 .S84 (Statistics—Bibliography)

Wasserman, Paul and Joanne Paskar, Eds. Statistics Sources
(Detroit, MI: Gale Research)

A subject guide to current statistical sources, this directory covers more than 20,000 subject areas. Sources are given for industrial, business and financial interests and many other topics also. Sources named are available in both print and non-print forms and are both published and unpublished works. The listings are alphabetical by subject with the sources then listed by organization. Within the subject groupings are geographic headings for states and individual countries. Topics range from transportation to Brazil to federal aid, with many subdivisions.

Entries provide names and addresses of organization and titles of their publications and/or databases. National and international organizations, governmental agencies and trade and professional groups are listed as sources in addition to print and machine-readable published sources, despite the fact that statistics compiled by the organizations, agencies, etc. are not always published. The statistics are available nonetheless.

In addition to the main directory of sources, there are three sections providing additional information. The first is a selected bibliography with annotations of major, general statistical publications. These include dictionaries, almanacs, census publications, periodicals and guides to machine-readable and online data sources. Both governmental and non-governmental sources are named. Another section gives names and telephone numbers of individuals and U.S. government agencies that can aid in identifying current statistical sources. The third section is a guide to federal statistical databases and identifies significant government files available on magnetic tape diskette and CD-Rom. Appendices provide information on source publications and organizations used for this publication. Names and addresses of organizations and complete bibliographies for publications are recorded.

Z 7552 .I38 (Statistics—Indexes—Periodicals;
Vital Statistics—Indexes—Periodicals)

Index to International Statistics: A Guide to the Statistical
Publications of International Intergovernmental Organizations
(Bethesda, MD: Congressional Information Service)

Covering approximately 1,800 titles from more than 130 periodicals and 500 annuals, this reference work is published in two volumes. The first volume is an index and the second volume contains abstracts. Both volumes are published monthly, with quarterly and annual cumulations. The work provides a guide and index to current English language statistical publications from approximately ninety-five intergovernmental organizations. The intergovernmental organizations include the UN system, Organization for Economic Cooperation and Development, the European Community, the Organization of Americn States, commodity organizations and development banks. A wide range of publication types are covered: periodicals, annuals, biennials, series and monographs or special one-time studies. All listed publications must be available publicly through an intergovernmental organization.

The statistical publications that are indexed focus on basic economic, demographic, industrial and social statistics. These include statistics on business and finance, economic development, foreign trade, energy, government and employment. The statistics result from primary data, research data, secondary data for comparative purposes and bibliographical and methodological works. Program and budget statistics are reported also.

The first volume is divided into six indexes that are subject, name, geographic areas, categories, issuing sources, titles and publication numbers. The subject, name and geographic index entries provide brief notations on publication content and time coverage along with the publication's reference number that points to the correlating abstract in the second volume. The issuing source index is alphabetical by the name of the intergovernmental organization and gives report title, microfiche availability and frequency of the publication. The title index is alphabetical by title.

The second volume has the abstracts that provide fuller information on the listed publications. Information included is bibliographic data, giving title, frequency, publication date, language and availability (print or microfiche). A description of the main topics covered by the publication or article follows. The abstracts also identify the sources of the data and give information on the format and presentation of the data (i.e., narrative discussion, charts, tables, etc.). Finally, the abstracts name the reviewed issues.

Z 7553 .C3 U482
(United States—Census—Bibliography—Catalogs)

Krismann, Carol. Quality Control: An Annotated Bibliography
(White Plains, NY: Quality Resources) 1990.

This bibliography lists books, magazine articles, dissertations, and audiovisual materials about quality and the quality function in business and industry. The book contains ten sections arranged according to the ASQC Literature Classification Code System. Section A lists books, journal articles, and dissertations about quality, the quality function, and quality control. Section B covers statistical process control and statistical quality control, while Section C lists items about sampling. Section D focuses on the management of quality assurance and lists works about the implementation of quality programs, training and education for quality improvement and control and employee involvement. Sections E, F, and G lists general statistical works relating to quality control, while H and I focuses on measurement and control.

Z 7553 .C3 U482
(United States—Census—Bibliography—Catalogs)

United States Census Catalog and Guide (Washington DC: United States Government Press)

The Census Catalog and Guide is a comprehensive catalog and guide to the programs and services of the Census Bureau. The Census Guide also includes a number of guide features, such as a chart on product series. Chapters have introductions that provide information about the censuses, surveys, and other programs that are the sources of data products described in the chapters.

Z 7554 .A34 H34 (Africa—Statistics—Bibliographies;
Africa—Statistical Sources—Directories)

Harvey, Joan M. Statistics Africa: Sources for Social, Economic and Market Research (Beckenham, UK: CBD Research Ltd.) 1970.

The agencies and publications supplying statistical information on Africa are identified for researchers by this source. The arrangement is alphabetical by nation, with a section on Africa in general preceding those on individual countries. Each national section begins with information on the central statistical office, principle depository libraries within the country, libraries outside the country with holdings and major bibliographies of statistics.

The statistical publication entries that follow cover general topics such as production, external trade, internal distribution and service trades, population, social topics, finance, transportation and communication. Individual entries provide the title, with an English translation if needed; name of the originating organization if not the publisher; name and address of the publisher; other agency or sales offices; first publication date; date of the latest issue; publication frequency; price; number of pages or volumes; time lapse between publication and collection if applicable; description of contents; and an indication of the language of the text. The opening section on Africa is similarly constructed, but has an international focus. Alphabetical title, subject and organization indexes are provided.

Z 7554 .A5 H34 (America—Statistics—Bibliographies; America—Statistical Sources—Directories)

Harvey, Joan M. Statistics America: Sources for Social, Economic and Market Research (North, Central & South America) (Detroit, MI: Gale Research) 1980.

The agencies and publications supplying statistical information on North, South and Central America are identified for researchers by this source. The arrangement is alphabetical by nation, with a section on the Americas in general preceding those on individual countries. Each national section begins with information on the central statistical office, principle depository libraries within the country, libraries outside the country with holdings and major bibliographies of statistics.

The statistical publication entries that follow cover general topics such as production, external trade, internal distribution and service trades, population, social topics, finance, transportation and communication. Individual entries provide the title, with an English translation if needed; name of the originating organization if not the publisher; name and address of the publisher; other agency or sales offices; first publication date; date of the latest issue; publication frequency; price; number of pages or volumes; time lapse between publication and collection if applicable; description of contents; and an indication of the language of the text. The opening section on the Americas is similarly constructed, but has an international focus. Alphabetical title, subject and organization indexes are provided.

Z 7554 .A775 H34 (Asia—Statistics—Bibliographies; Australia—Statistics—Bibliographies; Asia—Statistics—Bibliographies; Australsia—Statistical Sources—Directories; Australia—Statistical Sources—Directories; Australasia—Statistical Sources—Directories)

Harvey, Joan M. Statistics Asia & Australasia: Sources for Social, Economic and Market Research (Beckenham, UK: CBD Research) 1983.

The agencies and publications supplying statistical information on Asia, Australia and the surrounding area are identified for researchers by this source. The arrangement is alphabetical by nation, with a section on Asia and Australasia in general preceding those on individual countries. Each national section begins with information on the central statistical office, principle depository libraries within the country, libraries outside the country with holdings and major bibliographies of statistics.

The statistical publication entries that follow cover general topics such as production, external trade, internal distribution and service trades, population, social topics, finance, transportation and communication. Individual entries provide the title, with an English translation if needed; name of the originating organization if not the publisher; name and address of the publisher; other agency or sales offices; first publication date; date of the latest issue; publication frequency; price; number of pages or volumes; time lapse between publication and collection if applicable; description of contents; available International Standard Serial Numbers (ISSN); and an indication of the language of the text. The opening section on Asia and Australasia is similarly constructed, but has an international focus. Alphabetical title, subject and organization indexes are provided.

Z 7554 .E8 H34 (Europe—Statistics—Bibliographies; Europe—Statistical Sources—Directories)

Harvey, Joan M. Statistics Europe: Sources for Social, Economic and Market Research (Beckenham, UK: CBD Research) 1987.

The agencies and publications supplying statistical information on Europe are identified for researchers by this source. The arrangement is alphabetical by United Nations international traffic code letters, with a section on Europe in general preceding those on individual countries. Each national section begins with information on the central statistical office, principle depository libraries within the country, libraries outside the country with holdings and major bibliographies of statistics.

The statistical publication entries that follow cover general topics such as production, external trade, internal distribution and service trades, population, social topics, finance, transportation and communication. Individual entries provide the title, with an English translation if needed; name of the originating organization if not the publisher; name and address of the publisher; other agency or sales offices; first publication date; date of the latest issue; publication frequency; price; number of pages or volumes; time lapse between publication and collection if applicable; description of contents; available International Standard Serial Numbers (ISSN); and an indication of the language of the text. The opening section on Europe is similarly con-

structed, but has an international focus. Alphabetical title, subject and organization indexes are provided.

Z 7554 .U5 A46 (United States—Statistics—Bibliography; United States—Statistics—Abstracts)

American Statistics Index (Washington, DC: Congressional Information Service)

This publication is a two part guide and index to all statistical publications of the U.S. government. Its purpose is to identify all statistical publications of the federal government, catalog and describe fully the publications, announce new publications and index all this information. A wide range of subjects is covered and data comes from hundreds of central and regional government agencies. All federal publications with primary data are listed. Continuing series, annual reports and one time reports, as well as other statistical material, are included. In addition to printed materials, the American Statistics Index (ASI) covers CD-Rom releases, microfiche, charts and maps that present current statistics. Most of the data comes from six major federal agencies. These are the Department of Agriculture, the Census Bureau, the Bureau of Labor Statistics, the Energy Information Administration, the National Center for Educational Statistics and the National Center for Health Statistics. Many other departments and agencies also supply data.

The index section is divided into five parts in order to facilitate searching. The first is the subject and name index that covers places, government agencies, individuals and major surveys or programs. The category index is divided into geographic, economic and demographic topics. The remaining three indexes are title, agency report numbers and Superintendent of Documents numbers.

Abstracts are arranged first by issuing agency and then subdivided by publication type and individual publication. Entries provide issuing agency names, publication titles, frequency of publication, publication descriptions and summaries of individual reports. Any tables and charts included in individual reports are listed. In addition, references to previous reports and related publications are included, as well as the reporting time span and the geographic coverage of publications.

There are some exclusions to this reference guide. Classified and confidential data are not listed. Contract studies are limited to those issued by an agency as its own publication, while Congressional publications are listed only if they have considerable statistical information. Selected coverage of scientific and technical data is done when the data are of broad social or economic interest or of specific current interest.

Z 7554 .U5 S79
(United States—Statistics—Indexes—Periodicals; United States—Statistics—Abstracts—Periodicals)

Statistical Reference Index, Annual Abstracts/Cumulative Index
(Washington, DC: Congressional Information Service)

The Statistical Reference Index (SRI) is a large collection of various financial, social, and economical data. The purpose of the index is to provide a method by which statistical data can be researched and found. This data includes numerical information published by business organizations, universities, commercial publishers, state government agencies, and independent research organizations. The index provides national data (economic trends, earnings of industries, corporate rankings, and demographics), statewide data (vital statistics—crime, health—government finances, and elections), foreign country data (world economic trends, international investment), and any local unmentioned data.

The user's guide explains the format of the index volumes, which are divided by the subject and/or name of the data, geographic, economic, or demographic categories, issuing sources, or title of the information. The abstract volumes are classified by an accession number (numbers assigned by the SRI). They provide the title, periodicity, publication date, collation, report number, and the ISSN for periodicals. These abstract volumes give a brief summary, overview, and explanation of the data. The index also includes information about where to obtain the source publication of the data.

Z 7962. W87 (Women—Abstracts)

Women Studies Abstracts (Rush, NY: Rush Publishing Co.)

Women Studies Abstracts summarizes articles related to women's studies, feminism and gender issue. The intended audience includes social scientists and scholars as well as students in college. The serial provides summaries of articles from scholarly, political, and popular journals concentrating on women. The series also abstracts conference proceedings and pamphlets. By abstracting the content of journal articles, the editors facilitate differentiation between types of sources and data. Each brief summary, usually three to six sentences, outlines the basic theme and the context of the article. The source of each abstract, whether taken from the article's introduction or the journal's synopsis or written by a contributing editor, is designated. The publication lists sources for other articles, media reviews, women studies resources, and book reviews at the end of each volume.

Abstracts is published quarterly. Each issue is indexed to the abstract number. The final issue of each year contains a cumulative index. Journals from which articles were selected for review are named at the front of each issue by title, volume, issue, and year. Article sources for abstracts vary slightly in every issue and include international sources. Abstracts are divided by subject areas such as education and socialization, psychology, employment, sexuality, family, society, politics and government, science and technology, and violence against women. At the beginning of each subject heading, related articles are listed by title and abstract number in a "see also" section. Article citations follow, listing author, title, journal, volume, issue, pages.

Index